Poets on poets

Poets on poets

EDITED BY NICK RENNISON & MICHAEL SCHMIDT

CARCANET

IN ASSOCIATION WITH WATERSTONE'S

Published in Great Britain in 1997 by
Carcanet Press Limited
4th Floor, Conavon Court
12–16 Blackfriars Street
Manchester M3 5BQ

in association with Waterstone's

A CIP catalogue record for this book is available
from the British Library.
ISBN 1 85754 339 4

The publisher acknowledges financial assistance
from the Arts Council of England

Designed by Rob Andrews, Newell and Sorrell
Set in Trinité by Ensystems, Saffron Walden
Printed and bound in England by SRP Ltd, Exeter

CONTENTS

INTRODUCTION

How can we best discover where English poetry is today? Would an anthology of contemporaries tell us much? It would certainly tell us something – but mainly, perhaps, about an editor's individual bias which gives a distinct inflection to the age: readers and critics invariably take exception, according to their own biases. The critical reception of any recent anthology will prove the point. Such books are vivid distortions at best, caricatures at worst.

As editors we decided to make an anthology by our contemporaries, not of our contemporaries: to see what poetry we were reading and, as important, how we were reading it. We wanted to cast light, by historical defraction, as it were, on the places our poetry has reached. How could we characterise the continuities between our poetry and that of the past? How could we produce a two-way mirror? We had some dazzling stars to steer by.

Dr Johnson's *Lives of the Poets* were introductions for his collections from the works of his predecessors and contemporaries. They tell us as much about him and his age as they do about the poets he evokes. We learn a great deal about Samuel Taylor Coleridge from his singling out of George Herbert, and the way he describes him in the *Biographia*; when we hear Sir Philip Sidney's cadences and paradoxes sounding in George Herbert's poems, both poets assume a different valency; we see a different Blake and a different Hardy when we consider their (very distinct) early enthusiasms for Spenser, and what Dryden did to and for Chaucer underlines the virtues of both writers. Swinburne was brought alive by Herrick, Dickinson by Waller. Milton was affronted by Skelton, Crabbe (looking the other way) was fascinated by Wordsworth. These creative perspectives and tensions are part of the weave of a continuing tradition. Poets are never free of debt or creative connection. They are never alone.

As editors we considered how best to draw out, in a 'post-modern' age, these connections, persuaded that whatever the changes in modern culture, they persist and must persist as long as poetry is written. We remembered the Penguin Poet to Poet series,

and earlier series by other houses, in which important rediscoveries and revaluations were made by poet-editors: Thom Gunn's Ben Jonson, with an introduction that contains Gunn's most stimulating suggestions about the 'occasions' of poetry, Ted Hughes's Emily Dickinson, and his Shakespeare which explores the 'humours' and illuminates *Crow*, Robert Graves's *Ballads*, W. H. Auden's Herbert, Elizabeth Jennings's Christina Rossetti, Peter Levi's Pope, Kathleen Raine's timely Shelley, William Empson's splendidly controversial Coleridge, and others.

These books differed in kind from standard critical selections. A critic makes a critical case for a poet, displaying the representative virtues of the work. A poet will be less interested in doing 'objective' justice, more interested in advocacy and in indicating or repaying creative debts. The difference between an essay by T. S. Eliot or C. H. Sisson on Andrew Marvell and an essay by Dame Helen Gardner on the same subject makes this point: Eliot places the poet in a field of imaginative comprehension, Sisson in an historical and political field which realises many of the nuances in the Horatian Ode. Dame Helen interprets, contextualises, explicates. Each essay has its value: for the poets the project is continuous with their own creative project. Their essays remain a durable part of their *oeuvre*.

We invited English-language poets from around the world to visit in the past poets who we, or they, regarded as abiding presences or resources, to knock on specific doors and bring back the work they thought best characterised the *originality* of the poet they were visiting, with a brief prose account of their journey. We decided to begin with the great Middle English writers and to come up to the beginning of our century. By asking poets to select, and to describe (in no more than 300 words) the grounds on which they did so, we were not so much abdicating our editorial responsibilities as proving theirs, and the anthology that results is, we believe, unprecedented and unique. *Poets on Poets* is proof, if proof were needed, that achieved English poems from various periods and places are unconfined; that in a post-Modern age the pre-Modern speaks and sings with unabated energy.

We have placed the selected poets in alphabetical rather than chronological order. Because the selectors are numerous and the approaches diverse, no 'chronological narrative' emerges, but some of the alphabetical juxtapositions are eloquent, both in terms of selectors and in terms of the work selected. The run from Chatterton to Chaucer, Clare and Clough, is more telling, perhaps in a book of this kind, than to have Chatterton marooned in his thankless century, or Clare in his. Another arresting run is Hopkins, Housman, Hymns. The Middle English poets seem much more accessible, in a standardised presentation, cheek by jowl with poets whose Modern English complexities are of a different order. Readers who find the look of the older poems rebarbative should try reading them aloud: many difficulties disappear on the tongue.

There are some fervent and witty advocacies in this anthology. John Ashbery makes a staunch case for the neglected Thomas Lovell Beddoes, for example; Bernard O'Donoghue pricks more than a passing curiosity about Hoccleve and Lydgate, who are nowhere near as boring as we were told at school. Is the fifteenth century less of a black hole in England's poetry (Scotland we always except) than we thought? And is the Cowper we find here, or the Kipling, or the Dryden, quite the one we expect? Some of the selections and introductions succinctly redefine a poet, others remind us of why certain writers will always be well loved. Our editors are significant practitioners of the art of poetry and what they have to say is worth attending to.

This is one of the rare anthologies that insists that English poetry is poetry in the English language. If the riches of the tradition through to the end of the nineteenth century were largely confined to the British Isles and North America, this is no reason to neglect the earliest evidences of new English poetries in other lands.

There are omissions. We have not included poetry originating in the other languages of the British Isles – Scots Gaelic, Irish or Welsh. In breaking the geographical boundaries, we had to confine ourselves to a language boundary: otherwise we would have had to find space for the pre- or un-English literatures of other lands where English has become the dominant language. Some of our omissions result from writers accepting with alacrity the opportunity of contributing to *Poets on Poets*, but finding in the end that they had nothing to say. A number of such omissions were remedied, others were beyond remedy when we went to press. We have no doubt overlooked or deliberately excluded a hundred poets with some claim to be here. Our aim was to assemble a compendious and rewarding book for the general reader who, like Janus, and like most poets, likes to stand at the crossroads and look both ways, to see what has been and what is coming into being on the same broad highway.

There is a compelling end-of-our century logic to our approach as well. It has to do with the great shifts that technology have effected within our culture, the ways that – as Lampedusa puts it in *The Leopard* – we must change to stay the same. Forty years ago Donald Davie wrote two essays: 'The Poet in the Imaginary Museum'. He took his title from André Malraux's book published ten years earlier, *Le Musée imaginaire*, and he summarises Malraux's argument in this way:

> it is no accident that what we recognise as 'the modern movement' in the arts appears on the historical scene at roughly the same time as certain techniques of reproduction, like gramophone recording in the case of music and colour-photography in the cases of painting, sculpture, and architecture.

The modern artist differs from those who came before in a crucial respect, and the consequences of that difference are momentous, for he (in 1957 critics did not say 'he or she') 'has immediately at his disposal, in a way his predecessors had not, the whole achievement of worldwide artistic endeavour over the centuries'.

Since Malraux's time, and since Davie wrote his two-part essay, technology has not stood still. The potential 'universality' already implicit in the inventions of Gutenberg half a millennium ago and evolved and perfected down the centuries has, in the last two decades, led to the incalculable riches of the electronic library. Any surviving piece of English literature and much that is not literature from outside the seventy years of copyright, as well as much copyrighted work, can be accessed by millions of readers throughout the world on computer screens. We once enjoyed the imaginary museum, where we could go during opening hours and take down dusty tomes to pore over: Mohammed went to the mountain. But with electronic magic the mountain comes to us. Without getting our fingers dirty or risking the ladders to neglected top shelves, we can access whatever we wish from the past. We take our bearings by choice or by chance rather than by pressure of precedent. The imaginary museum is now also a virtual museum: we are free to enter at any time of the day or night, to download texts, to perform searches and electronic analyses on a canon which has become so capacious that it is virtually chaotic, unless we know what we are looking for before we set out, or have a trusty guide. This book offers a number of guides.

Malraux's and Davie's essays suggest that modern technology and modernism go hand in hand. An anthology of this kind accepts the reality of the new order; it accepts on its own terms, too, the Modern and post-Modern, assembling a collaborative (one is almost tempted to risk the word 'democratic') canon. But it places its trust in the author, who evidently is not dead, and in poems from seven centuries which survive despite neglect on the one hand and the harshest attentions of the theorists on the other.

The poets represented in this book are those whose work emerged before the First World War. This is not an entirely arbitrary break-point, though some omissions will inevitably *appear* arbitrary to some readers. We and our selectors have included poets whose poems seem 'to add to the resources of poetry, to be likely to influence the future development of poetry and language, and to please [us] for reasons neither personal nor idiosyncratic' – the terms Michael Roberts used in introducing that notable volume the *Faber Book of Modern Verse* (1936). But instead of his 'and please [us]' we would prefer 'and/or'. Taste is one function, judgement another, and they do not always run in synch. It is possible (if taste is to develop) for it to be led by judgement; there are poets in this book whose work puzzles us and our selectors in ways that will turn to pleasure in due course,.

What is the purpose of *Poets on Poets*? To celebrate English-language poetry past and present, to insist that there is continuity between radical experimental writers and those usually presented as 'main stream'; to select poets who engage readers because of what they do with language, regardless of subject matter and formal propensity. The over-riding perspectives are those of particularists, not theorists of literature.

This book is not a representative anthology. It does not set out to achieve gender, ethnic, or any other sorts of parity – an impossibility given the printed record; or to exhibit every kind of activity in the field of poetry. It indicates – collaboratively – a significant and enabling constellation of poets, and in so doing is of use to readers of poetry and to poets for whom the hollow triumph of journalism and the politics of 'the poetry business' and the 'poetry community' (few artistic tribes have less sense of community than poets) cannot displace the hard choices, the hard definitions that trace what makes a tradition, as against the weary repetitions of convention.

NICK RENNISON AND MICHAEL SCHMIDT

Since, to me, a poem is an organism, rather than the 'machine' Paul Valéry called it – and even a machine is not likely to function without all its parts – I have confined my selection to complete poems, resisting the temptation to extract passages from the best-known longer poems, meditative, narrative or dramatic.

Some of my choices among the shorter poems are the inevitable ones, including 'Dover Beach'; but, as Beerbohm's famous caricature implied, despite Arnold's pervasive awareness that all was far from well with his world and age, that things were falling apart and what are now called 'Victorian values' no more secure in his century than in ours, Matthew Arnold (1822–88) was 'not always wholly serious'. His last poems were elegies not for poets or other cultural heroes, but for pets, dogs and a canary. That is why I chose the less grandiloquent sonnet 'West London' and the less than solemn lyric 'New Rome', which has some of the mundane irony more usually associated with the work of his older friend Arthur Hugh Clough.

The one longer poem I was able to include, 'Rugby Chapel', was chosen because it is metrically innovative, breaking away from the iambic beat that persisted even in the seeming 'free verse' of Arnold's 'Philomela'. It goes without saying that I chose the poems that appeal to me and convince me for one reason or another; and this has to do with diction and dynamic as much as with stance and gist. As an intellectual and man of letters, Arnold was a representative figure, like Samuel Johnson and Coleridge before him or T. S. Eliot after him. As a poet he had to grapple with the multifarious and uncomfortable knowledge that pressed upon him as an intellectual and critic – not only of literature but of life. In various ways all the poems I have chosen came out of this discomfort, more than out of Arnold's attempts to escape from it into modes and paradigms owed to cultures more homogeneous than his own.

WEST LONDON

Crouch'd on the pavement, close by Belgrave Square,
A tramp I saw, ill, moody, and tongue-tied.
A babe was in her arms, and at her side
A girl; their clothes were rags, their feet were bare.

Some labouring men, whose work lay somewhere
    there,
Pass'd opposite; she touch'd her girl, who hied
Across, and begg'd, and came back satisfied.
The rich she had let pass with frozen stare.

Thought I: 'Above her state this spirit towers;
She will not ask of aliens, but of friends,
Of sharers in a common human fate.

'She turns from that cold succour, which attends
The unknown little from the unknowing great,
And points us to a better time than ours.'

DESPONDENCY

The thoughts that rain their steady glow
Like stars on life's cold sea,
Which others know, or say they know –
They never shone for me.

Thoughts light, like gleams, my spirit's sky,
But they will not remain.
They light me once, they hurry by;
And never come again.

SELF-DECEPTION

Say, what blinds us, that we claim the glory
Of possessing powers not our share?
– Since man woke on earth, he knows his story,
But, before we woke on earth, we were.

Long, long since, undower'd yet, our spirit
Roam'd, ere birth, the treasuries of God;
Saw the gifts, the powers it might inherit,
Ask'd an outfit for its earthly road.

Then, as now, this tremulous, eager being
Strain'd and long'd and grasp'd each gift it saw;
Then, as now, a Power beyond our seeing
Staved us back, and gave our choice the law.

Ah, whose hand that day through Heaven guided
Man's new spirit, since it was not we?
Ah, who sway'd our choice, and who decided
What our gifts, and what our wants should be?

For, alas! he left us each retaining
Shreds of gifts which he refused in full.
Still these waste us with their hopeless straining,
Still the attempt to use them proves them null.

And on earth we wander, groping, reeling;
Powers stir in us, stir and disappear.
Ah! and he, who placed our master-feeling,
Fail'd to place that master-feeling clear.

We but dream we have our wish'd-for powers,
Ends we seek we never shall attain.
Ah! *some* power exists there, which is ours?
Some end is there, we indeed may gain?

DOVER BEACH

The sea is calm to-night.
The tide is full, the moon lies fair
Upon the straits; – on the French coast the light
Gleams and is gone; the cliffs of England stand,
Glimmering and vast, out in the tranquil bay.
Come to the window, sweet is the night-air!
Only, from the long line of spray
Where the sea meets the moon-blanch'd land,
Listen! you hear the grating roar
Of pebbles which the waves draw back, and fling
At their return, up the high strand,
Begin, and cease, and then again begin,
With tremulous cadence slow, and bring
The eternal note of sadness in.

Sophocles long ago
Heard it on the Ægæan, and it brought
Into his mind the turbid ebb and flow
Of human misery; we
Find also in the sound a thought,
Hearing it by this distant northern sea.

The Sea of Faith
Was once, too, at the full, and round earth's shore
Lay like the folds of a bright girdle furl'd.
But now I only hear
Its melancholy, long, withdrawing roar,
Retreating, to the breath
Of the night-wind, down the vast edges drear
And naked shingles of the world.

Ah, love, let us be true
To one another! for the world, which seems
To lie before us like a land of dreams,
So various, so beautiful, so new,
Hath really neither joy, nor love, nor light,
Nor certitude, nor peace, nor help for pain;
And we are here as on a darkling plain
Swept with confused alarms of struggle and flight,
Where ignorant armies clash by night.

GROWING OLD

What is it to grow old?
Is it to lose the glory of the form,
The lustre of the eye?
Is it for beauty to forego her wreath?
– Yes but not this alone.

Is it to feel our strength –
Not our bloom only, but our strength – decay?
Is it to feel each limb
Grow stiffer, every function less exact,
Each nerve more loosely strung?

Yes, this, and more; but not
Ah, 'tis not what in youth we dream'd 'twould be!
'Tis not to have our life
Mellow'd and soften'd as with sunset-glow,
A golden day's decline.

'Tis not to see the world
As from a height, with rapt prophetic eyes,
And heart profoundly stirr'd;
And weep, and feel the fulness of the past,
The years that are no more.

It is to spend long days
And not once feel that we were ever young;
It is to add, immured

In the hot prison of the present, month
To month with weary pain.

It is to suffer this,
And feel but half, and feebly, what we feel.
Deep in our hidden heart
Festers the dull remembrance of a change,
But no emotion – none.

It is – last stage of all –
When we are frozen up within, and quite
The phantom of ourselves,
To hear the world applaud the hollow ghost
Which blamed the living man.

NEW ROME

‹Lines written for Miss Story's album›

The armless Vatican Cupid
   Hangs down his beautiful head;
For the priests have got him in prison,
   And Psyche long has been dead.

But see, his shaven oppressors
   Begin to quake and disband!
And *The Times*, that bright Apollo,
   Proclaims salvation at hand.

'And what,' cries Cupid, 'will save us?'
   Says Apollo: '*Modernise Rome!*
What inns! Your streets, too, how narrow!
   Too much of palace and dome!

'O learn of London, whose paupers
   Are not pushed out by the swells!
Wide streets with fine double trottoirs;
   And then – the London hotels!'

The armless Vatican Cupid
   Hangs down his head as before.
Through centuries past it has hung so,
   And will through centuries more.

A WISH

I ask not that my bed of death
From bands of greedy heirs be free;
For these besiege the latest breath
Of fortune's favour'd sons, not me.

I ask not each kind soul to keep
Tearless, when of my death he hears.
Let those who will, if any, weep!
There are worse plagues on earth than tears.

I ask but that my death may find
The freedom to my life denied;
Ask but the folly of mankind
Then, then at last, to quit my side.

Spare me the whispering, crowded room,
The friends who come, and gape, and go;
The ceremonious air of gloom –
All, which makes death a hideous show!

Nor bring, to see me cease to live,
Some doctor full of phrase and fame,
To shake his sapient head, and give
The ill he cannot cure a name.

Nor fetch, to take the accustom'd toll
Of the poor sinner bound for death,
His brother-doctor of the soul,
To canvass with official breath

The future and its viewless things –
That undiscover'd mystery
Which one who feels death's winnowing wings
Must needs read clearer, sure, than he!

Bring none of these; but let me be,
While all around in silence lies,
Moved to the window near, and see
Once more, before my dying eyes,

Bathed in the sacred dews of morn
The wide aerial landscape spread –
The world which was ere I was born
The world which lasts when I am dead;

Which never was the friend of *one*,
Nor promised love it could not give,
But lit for all its generous sun,
And lived itself, and made us live.

There let me gaze, till I become
In soul, with what I gaze on, wed!
To feel the universe my home;
To have before my mind – instead

Of the sick room, the mortal strife,
The turmoil for a little breath –
The pure eternal course of life,
Not human combatings with death!

Thus feeling, gazing, might I grow
Composed, refresh'd, ennobled, clear;
Then willing let my spirit go
To work or wait elsewhere or here!

THE FUTURE

A wanderer is man from his birth.
He was born in a ship
On the breast of the river of Time;
Brimming with wonder and joy
He spreads out his arms to the light,
Rivets his gaze on the banks of the stream.

As what he sees is, so have his thoughts been.
Whether he wakes,
Where the snowy mountainous pass,
Echoing the screams of the eagles,
Hems in its gorges the bed
Of the new-born clear-flowing stream;
Whether he first sees light
Where the river in gleaming rings
Sluggishly winds through the plain;
Whether in sound of the swallowing sea –
As is the world on the banks,
So is the mind of the man.

Vainly does each, as he glides,
Fable and dream
Of the lands which the river of Time
Had left ere he woke on its breast,
Or shall reach when his eyes have been closed.
Only the tract where he sails
He wots of; only the thoughts,
Raised by the objects he passes, are his.

Who can see the green earth any more
As she was by the sources of Time?

Who imagines her fields as they lay
In the sunshine, unworn by the plough?
Who thinks as they thought,
The tribes who then roam'd on her breast,
Her vigorous, primitive sons?

What girl
Now reads in her bosom as clear
As Rebekah read, when she sate
At eve by the palm-shaded well?
Who guards in her breast
As deep, as pellucid a spring
Of feeling, as tranquil, as sure?

What bard,
At the height of his vision, can deem
Of God, of the world, of the soul,
With a plainness as near,
As flashing as Moses felt
When he lay in the night by his flock
On the starlit Arabian waste?
Can rise and obey
The beck of the Spirit like him?

This tract which the river of Time
Now flows through with us, is the plain.
Gone is the calm of its earlier shore.
Border'd by cities and hoarse
With a thousand cries is its stream.
And we on its breast, our minds
Are confused as the cries which we hear,
Changing and shot as the sights which we see.

And we say that repose has fled
For ever the course of the river of Time.
That cities will crowd to its edge
In a blacker, incessanter line;
That the din will be more on its banks,
Denser the trade on its stream,
Flatter the plain where it flows,
Fiercer the sun overhead.
That never will those on its breast
See an ennobling sight,
Drink of the feeling of quiet again.

But what was before us we know not,
And we know not what shall succeed.

Haply, the river of Time –
As it grows, as the towns on its marge
Fling their wavering lights

On a wider, statelier stream –
May acquire, if not the calm
Of its early mountainous shore,
Yet a solemn peace of its own.

And the width of the waters, the hush
Of the grey expanse where he floats,
Freshening its current and spotted with foam
As it draws to the Ocean, may strike
Peace to the soul of the man on its breast –
As the pale waste widens around him,
As the banks fade dimmer away,
As the stars come out, and the night-wind
Brings up the stream
Murmurs and scents of the infinite sea.

RUGBY CHAPEL

‹ November 1857 ›

Coldly, sadly descends
The autumn-evening. The field
Strewn with its dank yellow drifts
Of wither'd leaves, and the elms,
Fade into dimness apace,
Silent; – hardly a shout
From a few boys late at their play!
The lights come out in the street,
In the school-room windows; – but cold,
Solemn, unlighted, austere,
Through the gathering darkness, arise
The chapel-walls, in whose bound
Thou, my father! art laid.

There thou dost lie, in the gloom
Of the autumn evening. But ah!
That word, *gloom*, to my mind
Brings thee back, in the light
Of thy radiant vigour, again;
In the gloom of November we pass'd
Days not dark at thy side;
Seasons impair'd not the ray
Of thy buoyant cheerfulness clear.
Such thou wast! and I stand
In the autumn evening, and think
Of bygone autumns with thee.

Fifteen years have gone round
Since thou arosest to tread,

In the summer-morning, the road
Of death, at a call unforeseen,
Sudden. For fifteen years,
We who till then in thy shade
Rested as under the boughs
Of a mighty oak, have endured
Sunshine and rain as we might,
Bare, unshaded, alone,
Lacking the shelter of thee.

O strong soul, by what shore
Tarriest thou now? For that force,
Surely, has not been left vain!
Somewhere, surely, afar,
In the sounding labour-house vast
Of being, is practised that strength,
Zealous, beneficent, firm!

Yes, in some far-shining sphere,
Conscious or not of the past,
Still thou performest the word
Of the Spirit in whom thou dost live –
Prompt, unwearied, as here!
Still thou upraisest with zeal
The humble good from the ground,
Sternly repressest the bad!
Still, like a trumpet, dost rouse
Those who with half-open eyes
Tread the border-land dim
'Twixt vice and virtue; reviv'st,
Succourest! – this was thy work,
This was thy life upon earth.

What is the course of the life
Of mortal men on the earth? –
Most men eddy about
Here and there – eat and drink,
Chatter and love and hate,
Gather and squander, are raised
Aloft, are hurl'd in the dust,
Striving blindly, achieving
Nothing; and then they die –
Perish; – and no one asks
Who or what they have been,
More than he asks what waves,
In the moonlit solitudes mild
Of the midmost Ocean, have swell'd,
Foam'd for a moment, and gone.

And there are some, whom a thirst
Ardent, unquenchable, fires,

Not with the crowd to be spent,
Not without aim to go round
In an eddy of purposeless dust,
Effort unmeaning and vain.
Ah yes! some of us strive
Not without action to die
Fruitless, but something to snatch
From dull oblivion, nor all
Glut the devouring grave!
We, we have chosen our path –
Path to a clear-purposed goal,
Path of advance! – but it leads
A long, steep journey, through sunk
Gorges, o'er mountains in snow.
Cheerful, with friends, we set forth –
Then, on the height, comes the storm.
Thunder crashes from rock
To rock, the cataracts reply,
Lightnings dazzle our eyes.
Roaring torrents have breach'd
The track, the stream-bed descends
In the place where the wayfarer once
Planted his footstep – the spray
Boils o'er its borders! aloft
The unseen snow-beds dislodge
Their hanging ruin; alas,
Havoc is made in our train!
Friends, who set forth at our side,
Falter, are lost in the storm.
We, we only are left!
With frowning foreheads, with lips
Sternly compress'd, we strain on,
On – and at nightfall at last
Come to the end of our way,
To the lonely inn 'mid the rocks;
Where the gaunt and taciturn host
Stands on the threshold, the wind
Shaking his thin white hairs –
Holds his lantern to scan
Our storm-beat figures and asks:
Whom in our party we bring?
Whom we have left in the snow?

Sadly we answer: We bring
Only ourselves! we lost
Sight of the rest in the storm.
Hardly ourselves we fought through,
Stripp'd, without friends, as we are.
Friends, companions, and train,
The avalanche swept from our side.

But thou would'st not *alone*
Be saved, my father! *alone*
Conquer and come to thy goal,
Leaving the rest in the wild.
We were weary, and we
Fearful, and we in our march
Fain to drop down and to die.
Still thou turnedst, and still
Beckonedst the trembler, and still
Gavest the weary thy hand.

If, in the paths of the world,
Stones might have wounded thy feet,
Toil or dejection have tried
Thy spirit, of that we saw
Nothing – to us thou wast still
Cheerful, and helpful, and firm!
Therefore to thee it was given
Many to save with thyself;
And, at the end of thy day,
O faithful shepherd! to come,
Bringing thy sheep in thy hand.

And through thee I believe
In the noble and great who are gone;
Pure souls honour'd and blest
By former ages, who else –
Such, so soulless, so poor,
Is the race of men whom I see –
Seem'd but a dream of the heart,
Seem'd but a cry of desire.
Yes! I believe that there lived
Others like thee in the past,
Not like the men of the crowd
Who all round me to-day
Bluster or cringe, and make life
Hideous, and arid, and vile;
But souls temper'd with fire,
Fervent, heroic, and good,
Helpers and friends of mankind.

Servants of God! – or sons
Shall I not call you? because
Not as servants ye knew
Your Father's innermost mind,
His, who unwillingly sees
One of his little ones lost –
Yours is the praise, if mankind
Hath not as yet in its march
Fainted, and fallen, and died!

See! In the rocks of the world
Marches the host of mankind,
A feeble, wavering line.
Where are they tending? – A God
Marshall'd them, gave them their goal.
Ah, but the way is so long!
Years they have been in the wild!
Sore thirst plagues them, the rocks,
Rising all round, overawe;
Factions divide them, their host
Threatens to break, to dissolve.
– Ah, keep, keep them combined!
Else, of the myriads who fill
That army, not one shall arrive;
Sole they shall stray; in the rocks
Stagger for ever in vain,
Die one by one in the waste.

Then, in such hour of need
Of your fainting, dispirited race,
Ye, like angels, appear,
Radiant with ardour divine!
Beacons of hope, ye appear!
Languor is not in your heart,
Weakness is not in your word,
Weariness not on your brow.
Ye alight in our van! at your voice,
Panic, despair, flee away.
Ye move through the ranks, recall
The stragglers, refresh the outworn,
Praise, re-inspire the brave!
Order, courage, return.
Eyes rekindling, and prayers,
Follow your steps as ye go.
Ye fill up the gaps in our files,
Strengthen the wavering line,
Stablish, continue our march,
On, to the bound of the waste,
On, to the City of God.

Most poets have a love-affair with language, but for William Barnes (1801–86) it was more. Not an affair, but a passion. Son of a Dorset tenant-farmer, he left school at thirteen and moved to Dorchester when he was seventeen. But Blackmore Vale, his birthplace (much of the scene of Hardy's *Tess*) stayed with him for ever in its ways of speaking and seeing. The post-Napoleonic depression and the enclosure movement, both resulting in ferocious rural poverty, account for the sadness and estrangement in much of his work.

He was strenuously self-educated, moving from lawyer's clerk to schoolmaster to clergyman; his *Philological Grammar* draws on seventy-two languages. A pioneer writer of textbooks and a wood-engraver, he wrote on political economy, folklore, Dorset dialect and the proper hanging of farm gates. As a poet, he wanted to celebrate the language, pronunciation and cadences of Blackmore Vale, seeing in them the legitimate historical heirs of Old English. Hence the almost complete absence of romance words in his work. Such poetry needs to be read aloud; the apostrophes, diaereses and glossaries may discourage nervous readers. Clare, who had much less learning, presents an altogether easier surface. But these intensely *heard* poems, with their obsessive rhymes and metrical sophistication, which Hopkins and Hardy were the first to spot, are also a sombre and comic rehearsal of the great themes of rural life: dispossession, labour, spring and fall, love.

Barnes never achieved national fame, and seems not to have wanted it, except insofar as he saw himself as a spokesman for a community undervalued, derided as 'Hodge', driven from home. To that community he gave the dignity of forms derived from Virgil's *Eclogues*, and an idiom that was, as Wordsworth thought it should be, 'language really used by men'.

WILLIAM BARNES

FALSE FRIENDS-LIKE

When I wer still a bwoy, an' mother's pride,
A bigger bwoy spoke up to me so kind-like,
'If you do like, I'll treat ye wi' a ride
In theäse wheel-barrow here.' Zoo I wer blind-like
To what he had a-workèn in his mind-like,
An' mounted vor a passenger inside;
An' comèn to a puddle, perty wide,
He tipp'd me in, a grinnèn back behind-like.
Zoo when a man do come to me so thick-like,
An' sheäke my hand, where woonce he pass'd me
    by,
An' tell me he would do me this or that,
I can't help thinken o' the big bwoy's trick-like.
An' then, vor all I can but wag my hat
An' thank en, I do veel a little shy.

THE LEÄNE
(lines 1–22; 45–55)

They do zay that a travellèn chap
    Have a-put in the newspeäper now,
That the bit o' green ground on the knap
    Should be all a-took in vor the plough.
He do fancy 'tis easy to show
    That we can be but stunpolls at best,
Vor to leäve a green spot where a flower can grow,
    Or a voot-weary walker mid rest.
'Tis hedge-grubbèn, Thomas, an' ledge-grubbèn,
        Never a-done
While a sov'ren mwore's to be won.

The road, he do zay, is so wide
    As 'tis wanted vor travellers' wheels,
As if all that did travel did ride,
    An' did never get galls on their heels.
He would leäve sich a thin strip o' groun',
    That, if a man's veet in his shoes
Wer a-burnèn an' zore, why he coulden zit down
    But the wheels would run over his tooes.
Vor 'tis meäke money, Thomas, an' teäke money,
        What's zwold an' bought
Is all that is worthy o' thought.

[. . .]

Vor to breed the young fox or the heäre,
    We can gi'e up whole eäcres o' ground,

But the greens be a-grudg'd, vor to rear
    Our young childern up healthy an' sound;
Why, there woon't be a-left the next age
    A green spot where their veet can goo free;
An' the gookoo wull soon be committed to cage
    Vor a trespass in zomebody's tree.
Vor 'tis lockèn up, Thomas, an' blockèn up,
        Stranger or brother,
Men mussen come nigh woone another.

LWONESOMENESS

As I do zew, wi' nimble hand,
    In here avore the window's light,
How still do all the housegear stand
    Around my lwonesome zight.
How still do all the housegear stand
Since Willie now 've a-left the land.

The rwose-tree's window-sheädèn bow
    Do hang in leaf, an' win'-blow'd flow'rs
Avore my lwonesome eyes do show
    Theäse bright November hours.
Avore my lwonesome eyes do show
Wi' nwone but I to zee em blow.

The sheädes o' leafy buds, avore
    The peänes, do sheäke upon the glass,
An' stir in light upon the vloor,
    Where now vew veet do pass.
An' stir in light upon the vloor,
Where there's a-stirrèn nothèn mwore.

This win' mid dreve upon the maïn,
    My brother's ship, a-plowèn foam,
But not bring mother cwold, nor raïn,
    At her now happy hwome.
But not bring mother cwold, nor raïn,
Where she is out o' païn.

Zoo now that I'm a-mwopèn dumb,
    A-keepèn father's house, do you
Come of'en wi' your work vrom hwome,
    Vor company. Now do.
Come of'en wi' your work vrom hwome,
Up here a-while. Do come.

THE GEÄTE A-VALLÈN TO

(lines 1–24)

In the zunsheen ov our zummers
   Wi' the häy time now a-come,
How busy wer we out a-vield
   Wi' vew a-left at hwome,
When waggons rumbled out ov yard
   Red wheeled, wi' body blue,
As back behind 'em loudly slamm'd
   The geäte a-vallèn to.

Drough däysheen ov how many years
   The geäte ha' now a-swung
Behind the veet o' vull-grown men
   An' vootsteps ov the young.
Drough years o' days it swung to us
   Behind each little shoe,
As we tripped lightly on avore
   The geäte a-vallèn to.

In evenèn time o' starry night
   How mother zot at hwome,
An' kept her bleäzèn vire bright
   Till father should ha' come,
An' how she quicken'd up an' smiled
   An' stirred her vire anew,
To hear the trampèn ho'ses' steps
   An' geäte a-vallèn to.

Thomas Lovell Beddoes was born in Clifton, Shropshire, in 1803, to a distinguished and eccentric family. His mother was a sister of the novelist Maria Edgeworth; his father, often referred to in his time as 'the celebrated Dr Beddoes', was a colleague of Sir Humphry Davy, who lived with the Beddoes family and taught at the Pneumatic Institution in Clifton, where Dr Beddoes administered laughing-gas to Coleridge. The doctor also tried his hand at poetry; his long poem 'Alexander's Expedition down the Hydaspes and the Indus to the Indian Ocean' has been called 'one of the strangest books in English'.

As a student at Charterhouse School, Beddoes wrote prose narratives of which only *Scaroni* survives, and probably began there his long poem 'in three fyttes', *The Improvisatore*, which he would publish with other juvenilia in 1821 as a pamphlet while still an undergraduate at Oxford. These early works promise little for the future except their ghoulish atmosphere, which was to remain a constant. His next volume, the only other one published during his lifetime, was *The Brides' Tragedy*, which appeared the following year and was a critical success. In 1825 Beddoes left England to study medicine in Göttingen where he eventually received his MD. He would spend most of the remainder of his life on the continent, frequently in trouble with the authorities for drunken and disorderly behaviour and for his involvement in radical political movements. He lived for a year with a Russian Jewish student named Bernhard Reich, who may be the 'loved, longlost boy' of 'Dream Pedlary'. During his last years his companion was a young baker named Konrad Degen, who later became an actor of note. A pleasant stay of seven years in Zurich ended with Beddoes' expulsion on political grounds. In June 1848 he left Degen behind in Frankfurt and returned to Switzerland, where he put up at the Cigogne Hotel in Basle; the next morning he cut open an artery in his leg with a razor, gangrene set in and the leg was amputated below the knee. Finally, on 26 January 1849, he succeeded in taking his life with poison, having written the same day to his executor, Revell Phillips: 'I am food for *what I am good for* – worms.'

Beddoes has often been called a 'poet of fragments', most of which are embedded in unfinished Jacobean-style tragedies. Their dramatic structure has the form of quicksand, in which dazzling shreds of poetry sink or swim. His magnum opus was to have been *Death's Jest Book*, a kind of bottomless pit that absorbed most of his creative energies during his final years. As in all his plays, the plot is murky to the point of incomprehensibility, and the characters exist mainly to mouth Beddoes' extraordinary lines, though they do collide messily with one another. One critic has observed that they have 'the essential unity of dream characters' who meet 'in the dreamer' and are merely 'emanations of the central idea'. All this does result in a bizarre kind of theatricality, and it might be interesting to try to sit through a staged version of *Death's Jest Book*. Unlikelier closet dreams have made it to the boards.

Death was Beddoes' main subject, both as a poet and as a medical man; he seems relaxed and happy only when writing about it. Pound (in the *Pisan Cantos*) mentions 'Mr Beddoes/(T.L.) prince of morticians ... centuries hoarded/to pull up a mass of algae/(and pearls).' Any anthologist is bound to include a bit of the former (the creepy 'Oviparous Tailor', for instance) as well as some of the latter, and none can avoid 'Dream Pedlary': his most anthologized poem, it is also one of the most seamlessly beautiful lyrics in the English language.

Pound evokes 'the odour of eucalyptus or sea wrack' in Beddoes; one could add those of rose, sulphur and sandalwood to this unlikely but addictive bouquet. Edmund Gosse, whose landmark edition of Beddoes' work appeared in 1890, got it almost right in his preface: 'At the feast of the muses he appears bearing little except one small savoury dish, some cold preparation, we may say, of olives and anchovies, the strangeness of which has to make up for its lack of importance. Not every palate enjoys this *hors d'oeuvre*, and when that is the case, Beddoes retires; he has nothing else to give. He appeals to a few literary epicures, who, however, would deplore the absence of this oddly flavoured dish as much as that of any more important piece de resistance.' One should qualify that by adding that in the century since it was written, the little band has swollen to something like a hungry horde, avid for what Pater called 'something that exists in this world in no satisfying measure, or not at all.'

Early Fragments

◄ I ►

One drop of Manna in a shower of brine.

◄ IV ►

Sailing together
Over that heaven painted in the sea
Which leans its curly head o'er Naples' shoulder,
We oft have marked two cities, one above
Climbing the coast, and underneath another,
Its watery twin even to the upper suburb.

◄ IX ►

A ship alone upon the sea
And at its prow a gray old man.

◄ XIV ►

Thy gloomy features, like a midnight dial,
Scowl the dark index of a fearful hour.

◄ X. Rosily Dying ►

I'll take that fainting rose
Out of his breast; perhaps some sigh of his
Lives in the gyre of its kiss-coloured leaves.
O pretty rose, hast thou thy flowery passions?
Then put thyself into a scented rage,
And breathe on me some poisonous revenge.
For it was I, thou languid, silken blush,
Who orphaned thy green family of thee,
In thy closed infancy: therefore receive
My life, and spread it on thy shrunken petals,
And give to me thy pink, reclining death.

◄ XI ►

The ghost of wasps shall haunt thee, naughty bud.

◄ XIII ►

Bury him deep. So damned a work should lie
Nearer the Devil than man. Make him a bed
Beneath some lock-jawed hell, that never yawns
With earthquake or eruption; and so deep
That he may hear the devil and his wife
In bed, talking secrets.

WEDNESDAY EVENING

Honoured Miss H.
On my visage
   You might see
Smiles of pleasure
Without measure,
   Fol de ree,
Since I'm writing
And inviting
   You to T.

If I'm not wrong,
Fine strong souchong
   From Miss Sally,
Extra Hyson,
Teacake, a nice one,
Will be smelling
At six right well in
   This here valley.

But here the muse
   Lays down her lyre –
Pray don't refuse,
   And bring the Squire.

THE BRIDES' TRAGEDY

‹Act I, Scene i›

Hesperus: Of all the posy
Give me the rose, though there's a tale of blood
Soiling its name. In elfin annals old
'Tis writ, how Zephyr, envious of his love,
(The love he bore to Summer, who since then
Has weeping visited the world;) once found
The baby Perfume cradled in a violet;
('Twas said the beauteous bantling was the child
Of a gay bee, that in his wantonness
Toyed with a peabud in a lady's garland;)
The felon winds, confederate with him,
Bound the sweet slumberer with golden chains,
Pulled from the wreathed laburnum, and together
Deep cast him in the bosom of a rose,
And fed the fettered wretch with dew and air.
At length his soul, that was a lover's sigh,
Waned from his body, and the guilty blossom
His heart's blood stained. The twilight-haunting
   gnat

His requiem whined, and harebells tolled his knell,
And still the bee in pied velvet dight
With melancholy song from flower to flower
Goes seeking his lost offspring.

LIFE'S UNCERTAINTY

‹(unknown play)›

   A. The king looks well, red in its proper place
The middle of the cheek, and his eye's round
Black as a bit of night.
   B.   Yet men die suddenly:
One sits upon a strong and rocky life,
Watching a street of many opulent years,
And Hope's his mason. Well! to-day do this,
And so to-morrow; twenty hollow years
Are stuffed with action: – lo! upon his head
Drops a pin's point of time; tick! quoth the clock,
And the grave snaps him.
   A.   Such things may have been;
The crevice 'twixt two after-dinner minutes,
The crack between a pair of syllables
May sometimes be a grave as deep as 'tis
From noon to midnight in the hoop of time.
But for this man, his life wears ever steel
From which disease drops blunted. If indeed
Death lay in the market-place, or were – but hush!
See you the tremble of that myrtle bough?
Doth no one listen?
   B.   Nothing with a tongue:
The grass is dumb since Midas, and no Æsop
Translates the crow or hog. Within the myrtle
Sits a hen-robin, trembling like a star,
Over her brittle eggs.
   A.   Is it no more?
   B. Nought: let her hatch.

DREAM-PEDLARY

‹I›

If there were dreams to sell,
   What would you buy?
Some cost a passing bell;
   Some a light sigh,
That shakes from Life's fresh crown

Only a roseleaf down.
If there were dreams to sell,
Merry and sad to tell,
And the crier rung the bell,
    What would you buy?

◄ II ►

A cottage lone and still,
    With bowers nigh,
Shadowy, my woes to still,
    Until I die.
Such pearl from Life's fresh crown
Fain would I shake me down.
Were dreams to have at will,
This would best heal my ill,
    This I would buy.

◄ III ►

But there were dreams to sell,
    Ill didst thou buy;
Life is a dream, they tell,
    Waking, to die.
Dreaming a dream to prize,
Is wishing ghosts to rise;
    And, if I had the spell
    To call the buried, well,
    Which one would I?

◄ IV ►

If there are ghosts to raise,
    What shall I call,
Out of hell's murky haze,
    Heaven's blue hall?
Raise my loved longlost boy
To lead me to his joy,
    There are no ghosts to raise;
    Out of death lead no ways;
    Vain is the call.

◄ V ►

Know'st thou not ghosts to sue?
    No love thou hast.
Else lie, as I will do,
    And breathe thy last.
So out of Life's fresh crown
Fall like a rose-leaf down.
    Thus are the ghosts to woo;
    Thus are all dreams made true,
    Ever to last!

LEONIGILD'S APPREHENSION

◄ (from *Love's Arrow Poisoned*) ►

What's going on in my heart and in my brain,
My blood, my life, all over me, all through me?
It cannot last! quickly I shall not be
What I am now. – Oh I am changing, changing,
Dreadfully changing. – Aye, even as I stand
A transformation will come over me,
I am unsouled, dishumanised, and now
My passions swell and grow like brutes conceived;
My feet will soon be fixed – and every limb
Be swollen, distorted, till I am become
A wild old mountain, forest over-grown,
And have a dreadful tempest for a voice;
Aye, the abhorred conscience of this murder,
It will grow up a Lion, all alone,
A mighty-maned, grave-mouthed prodigy,
And live within my caves; – the other passions,
Some will be snakes, and bears, and savage wolves –
And when I lie tremendous in the desart
Or abandoned sea, murderers and idiot men
Will come to live upon my ragged sides,
Die and be buried in me. – Now it comes,
I break and magnify. – Heaven pours down sleet
And snow and hail, and hell rains up its fire.

AN UNFINISHED DRAFT

◄ (from *The Ivory Gate*) ►

A thousand buds are breaking
    Their prisons silently;
A thousand birds are making
    Their nests in leafy tree;
A thousand babes are waking
    On woman's breast to-day;

[. . .]

    Is born to man, to-day
    Beneath the sun of May:
Whence come ye, babes of flowers, and, Children,
    whence come we?

The snow falls by thousands into the sea;
    A thousand blossoms covers
        The forsaken forest,
    And on its branches hovers
        The lark's song thousandfold;

And maidens hear from lovers
    A thousand secrets guessed
    In June's abundant breast
    Before and yet are blessed –
Whence, blossoms rich, birds bold, beloved
    maidens, whence come ye?

The snow falls by thousands into the sea;
    A thousand flowers are shedding
      Their leaves all dead and dry;
    A thousand birds are threading
      Their passage through the sky;
    A thousande mourners treading
      The tearful churchyard way
      In funeral array:
Birds, whither fly ye? – whither, dead, pass ye?
The snow falls by thousands into the sea.

THE CITY OF THE SEA

‹An abandoned fragment›

Flowed many a woodbird's voice, and insects
    played
On wings of diamond o'er the murmuring tide,
So on the billows of thy ocean's heaven,
Dark with the azure weight of midnight hours,
Thy marble shadow like a root of towers
Young city of the sea, –

THE SECOND BROTHER
‹Act I, Scene ii›

Orazio . . . Sweet, did you like the feast?
Armida   Methought, 'twas gay enough.
Orazio   Now, I did not.
'Twas dull: all men spoke slow and emptily.
Strange things were said by accident. Their tongues
Uttered wrong words: one fellow drank my death,
Meaning my health; another called for poison,
Instead of wine; and, as they spoke together,
Voices were heard, most loud, which no man owned:
There were more shadows too than there were men;
And all the air more dark and thick than night
Was heavy, as 'twere made of something more
Than living breaths.

Armida   Nay, you are ill, my lord:
'Tis mere melancholy.
Orazio   There were deep hollows
And pauses in their talk; and then, again,
On tale and song and jest and laughter rang,
Like a fiend's gallop. By my ghost, 'tis strange.

‹Act III, Scene ii›

Marcello
Thou dost me wrong. Lament! I'd have thee do't:
The heaviest raining is the briefest shower.
Death is the one condition of our life:
To murmur were unjust; our buried sires
Yielded their seats to us, and we shall give
Our elbow-room of sunshine to our sons.
From first to last the traffic must go on;
Still birth for death. Shall we remonstrate then?
Millions have died that we might breathe this
    day:
The first of all might murmur, but not we.
Grief is unmanly too.

TORRISMOND
‹Act I, Scene iv›

Torrismond   We talk like fighting boys:
Out on't! I repent of my mad tongue.
Come, sir; I cannot love you after this,
But we may meet and pass a nodding question –
    Duke.   Never! There lies no grain of sand
    between
My loved and my detested. Wing thee hence,
Or thou dost stand to-morrow on a cobweb
Spun o'er the well of clotted Acheron,
Whose hydrophobic entrails stream with fire;
And may this intervening earth be snow,
And my step burn like the mid coal of Ætna,
Plunging me, through it all, into the core
Where in their graves the dead are shut like seeds,
If I do not – O but he *is* my son!
If I do not forgive thee then – but hence!
Gaudentio, hence with him, for in my eyes
He does look demons. –
    Melchior (to TORRISMOND) Come out with me and
    leave him:
You will be cool, to-morrow.
    Torris.   That I shall;
Cool as an ice-drop in a dead man's eye,

For winter is the season of the tomb,
And that's my country now.

DEATH'S JEST BOOK
‹Act V, Scene iii›

   Wolfram: As I was newly dead, and sat beside
My corpse, looking on it, as one who muses
Gazing upon a house he was burnt out of,
There came some merry children's ghosts to play
At hide-and-seek in my old body's corners [. . .]

‹Act I, Scene iii›

   Wolfram: This is the oft-wished hour, when we
   together
May walk upon the sea-shore: let us seek
Some greensward overshadowed by the rocks.
Wilt thou come forth? Even now the sun is setting
In the triumphant splendour of the waves.
Hear you not how they leap?
   Sibylla: Nay; we will watch
The sun go down upon a better day:
Look not on him this evening.
   Wolfram: Then let's wander
Under the mountain's shade in the deep valley,
And mock the woody echoes with our songs.
   Sibylla: That wood is dark, and all the mountain
   caves
Dreadful and black, and full of howling winds:
Thither we will not wander.
   Wolfram: Shall we seek
The green and golden meadows, and there pluck
Flowers for thy couch, and shake the dew out of
   them?
   Sibylla: The snake that loves the twilight is come
   out,
Beautiful, still, and deadly; and the blossoms
Have shed their fairest petals in the storm
Last night; the meadow's full of fear and danger.
   Wolfram: Ah! you will to the rocky fount, and
   there
We'll see the fireflies dancing in the breeze,
And the stars trembling in the trembling water,
And listen to the daring nightingale
Defying the old night with harmony.
   Sibylla: Nor that: but we will rather here remain,
And earnestly converse.

‹Act III, Scene iii›

   Siegfried: How? do you rhyme too?
   Isbrand: Sometimes, in leizure moments
And a romantic humour; this I made
One night a-strewing poison for the rats
In the kitchen corner.
   Duke: And what's your tune?
   Isbrand: What is the night-bird's tune,
   wherewith she startles
The bee out of his dream and the true lover,
And both in the still moonshine turn and kiss
The flowery bosoms where they rest, and
   murmuring
Sleep smiling and more happily again?
What is the lobster's tune when he is boiled?
I hate your ballads that are made to come
Round like a squirrel's cage, and round again.
We nightingales sing boldly from our hearts:
So listen to us.

ISBRAND'S REVENGE
‹The Ballad›

He reads
'Harpagus, hast thou salt enough,
   Hast thou broth enough to thy kid?
And hath the cook put right good stuff
   Under the pasty lid?'

'I've salt enough, Astyages,
   And broth enough in sooth;
And the cook hath mixed the meat and grease
   Most tickling to my tooth.'

So spake no wild Red Indian swine,
   Eating a forest rattle-snake:
But Harpagus, that Mede of mine,
   And King Astyages so spake.

'Wilt have some fruit? Wilt have some wine?
   Here's what is soft to chew;
I plucked it from a tree divine,
   More precious never grew.'

Harpagus took the basket up,
   Harpagus brushed the leaves away;
But first he filled a brimming cup,
   For his heart was light and gay.

And then he looked, and saw a face,
   Chopped from the shoulders of some one;
And who alone could smile in grace
   So sweet? Why, Harpagus, thy son.

'Alas!' quoth the king, 'I've no fork,
   Alas! I've no spoon of relief,
Alas! I've no neck of a stork
   To push down this throttling grief.

'We've played at kid for child, lost both;
   I'd give you the limbs if I could;
Some lie in your platter of broth:
   Good-night, and digestion be good.'

Now Harpagus said not a word,
   Did no eye-water spill:
His heart replied, for that had heard;
   And hearts' replies are still.

‹ The Application ›

A cannibal of his own boy,
   He is a cannibal uncommon;
And Harpagus, he is my joy,
   Because he wept not like a woman.

From the old supper-giver's poll
   He tore the many-kingdomed mitre;
To him, who cost him his son's soul,
   He gave it; to the Persian fighter:
      And quoth,
'Old art thou, but a fool in blood:
   If thou has made me eat my son,
Cyrus hath ta'en his grandsire's food;
   There's kid for child, and who has won?

'All kingdomless is thy old head,
   In which began the tyrannous fun;
Thou'rt slave to him, who should be dead:
   There's kid for child, and who has won?'

❧

THE OVIPAROUS TAILOR

Wee, wee tailor,
   Nobody was paler
   Than wee, wee tailor;
And nobody was thinner.

Hast thou mutton-chops for dinner,
My small-beer sinner,
My starveling rat, – but haler, –
   Wee, wee tailor?

Below his starving garret
Lived an old witch and a parrot, –
   Wee, wee tailor, –
Cross, horrid, and uncivil,
For her grandson was the Devil,
Or a chimney-sweeper evil:
She was sooty, too, but paler, –
   Wee, wee tailor.

Her sooty hen laid stale eggs,
And then came with his splay legs
   Wee, wee tailor,
And stole them all for dinner;
Then would old witch begin her
Damnations on the sinner, –
'May the thief lay eggs, – but staler;'
   Wee, wee tailor.

Wee, wee tailor,
Witch watched him like a jailor.
   Wee, wee tailor
Did all his little luck spill.
Tho' he swallowed many a muck's pill,
Yet his mouth grew like a duck's bill,
Crowed like a hen, – but maler, –
   Wee, wee tailor.

Near him did cursed doom stick,
As he perched upon a broomstick, –
   Wee, wee tailor.
It lightened, rained, and thundered,
And all the doctors wondered
When he laid above a hundred
   Gallinaceous eggs, – but staler –
      Wee, wee tailor.

A hundred eggs laid daily;
No marvel he looked palely, –
   Wee, wee tailor.
Witch let folks in to see some
Poach'd tailor's eggs; to please 'em
He must cackle on his besom,
   Till Fowl-death did prevail o'er
      Wee, wee tailor.

William Blake (1747–1827) described himself as a 'prophet' and his major works as 'prophetic books'. For these he found no publisher and therefore produced them himself, their pages illuminated and illustrated with extraordinary beauty. He is no less honoured as a painter than as a poet. An engraver by profession, he produced some of the finest works of engraving in the illustrations to the Book of Job. His *Songs of Innocence* and *Songs of Experience* have long been treasured, but the mythological narratives of the Prophetic Books remained unknown until Geoffrey Keynes's edition, first published in 1927, made Blake's works generally available, and the revised 1957 edition remains the standard text.

Mystic and visionary as he was, Blake's 'prophecies' are concerned with the world of history, denouncing in the name of eternal values the evils of his time: war, and the cruelties of a loveless moral law. He proclaimed the supremacy of the Imagination, which he called 'the divine humanity' and 'the true man' as against the rationalist materialism already prevailing in his time, and the industrial revolution – with its devastating effects on human lives – which was its outcome. For Blake the world was not a mechanism but a place where 'every particle of dust breathes forth its joy' and 'everything that lives is holy'.

Blake is above all the poet of London, which for him was not its buildings but its people: 'For cities are men, fathers of multitudes'. For three years he lived at Felpham, in a cottage on the estate of his well-intentioned but uncomprehending patron, William Hayley, country squire and biographer of Cowper. During this time he wrote *Milton*; Milton was for Blake the type of 'the inspired man', and the poem's theme is Imagination. His last and weightiest poem, *Jerusalem*, was written after his return to London, which is the theme and setting of his mythological vision of the inner realities reflected in the lives of its inhabitants.

◂ from *Songs of Innocence* ▸

INTRODUCTION

Piping down the valleys wild,
Piping songs of pleasant glee,
On a cloud I saw a child,
And he laughing said to me:

'Pipe a song about a lamb!'
So I piped with merry chear.
'Piper, pipe that song again;'
So I piped: he wept to hear.

'Drop thy pipe, thy happy pipe;
'Sing thy songs of happy chear:'
So I sung the same again,
While he wept with joy to hear.

'Piper, sit thee down and write
'In a book that all may read.'
So he vanish'd from my sight
And I pluck'd a hollow reed,

And I made a rural pen,
And I stain'd the water clear,
And I wrote my happy songs
Every child may joy to hear.

THE ECCHOING GREEN

The Sun does arise,
And make happy the skies;
The merry bells ring
To welcome the Spring;
The skylark and thrush,
The birds of the bush,
Sing louder around
To the bells' chearful sound,
While our sports shall be seen
On the Ecchoing Green.

Old John, with white hair,
Does laugh away care,
Sitting under the oak,
Among the old folk.
They laugh at our play,
And soon they all say:
'Such, such were the joys

'When we all, girls & boys,
'In our youth time were seen
'On the Ecchoing Green.'

Till the little ones, weary,
No more can be merry;
The sun does descend,
And our sports have an end.
Round the laps of their mothers
Many sisters and brothers,
Like birds in their nest,
Are ready for rest,
And sport no more seen
On the darkening Green.

THE DIVINE IMAGE

To Mercy, Pity, Peace, and Love
All pray in their distress;
And to these virtues of delight
Return their thankfulness.

For Mercy, Pity, Peace, and Love
Is God, our father dear,
And Mercy, Pity, Peace, and Love
Is Man, his child and care.

For Mercy has a human heart,
Pity a human face,
And Love, the human form divine,
And Peace, the human dress.

Then every man, of every clime,
That prays in his distress,
Prays to the human form divine,
Love, Mercy, Pity, Peace.

And all must love the human form,
In heathen, turk, or jew;
Where Mercy, Love, & Pity dwell
There God is dwelling too.

THE LITTLE BLACK BOY

My mother bore me in the southern wild,
And I am black, but O! my soul is white;
White as an angel is the English child,
But I am black, as if bereav'd of light.

My mother taught me underneath a tree,
And sitting down before the heat of day,
She took me on her lap and kissed me,
And pointing to the east, began to say:

'Look on the rising sun: there God does live,
'And gives his light, and gives his heat away;
'And flowers and trees and beasts and men receive
'Comfort in morning, joy in the noonday.

'And we are put on earth a little space,
'That we may learn to bear the beams of love;
'And these black bodies and this sunburnt face
'Is but a cloud, and like a shady grove.

'For when our souls have learn'd the heat to bear,
'The cloud will vanish; we shall hear his voice,
'Saying: "Come out from the grove, my love & care,
'"And round my golden tent like lambs rejoice."'

Thus did my mother say, and kissed me;
And thus I say to little English boy.
When I from black and he from white cloud free,
And round the tent of God like lambs we joy,

I'll shade him from the heat, till he can bear
To lean in joy upon our father's knee;
And then I'll stand and stroke his silver hair,
And be like him, and he will then love me.

‹ from *Songs of Experience* ›

THE CLOD & THE PEBBLE

'Love seeketh not Itself to please,
'Nor for itself hath any care,
'But for another gives its ease,
'And builds a Heaven in Hell's despair.'

So sang a little Clod of Clay
Trodden with the cattle's feet,

But a Pebble of the brook
Warbled out these metres meet:

'Love seeketh only Self to please,
'To bind another to Its delight,
'Joys in another's loss of ease,
'And builds a Hell in Heaven's despite.'

THE CHIMNEY SWEEPER

A little black thing among the snow,
Crying "'weep! 'weep!' in notes of woe!
'Where are thy father & mother? say?'
'They are both gone up to the church to pray.

'Because I was happy upon the heath,
'And smil'd among the winter's snow,
'They clothed me in the clothes of death,
'And taught me to sing the notes of woe.

'And because I am happy & dance & sing,
'They think they have done me no injury,
'And are gone to praise God & his Priest & King,
'Who make up a heaven of our misery.'

THE FLY

Little Fly,
Thy summer's play
My thoughtless hand
Has brush'd away.

Am not I
A fly like thee?
Or art not thou
A man like me?

For I dance,
And drink, & sing,
Till some blind hand
Shall brush my wing.

If thought is life
And strength & breath,

And the want
Of thought is death;

Then am I
A happy fly,
If I live
Or if I die.

THE TYGER

Tyger! Tyger! burning bright
In the forests of the night,
What immortal hand or eye
Could frame thy fearful symmetry?

In what distant deeps or skies
Burnt the fire of thine eyes?
On what wings dare he aspire?
What the hand dare sieze the fire?

And what shoulder, & what art,
Could twist the sinews of thy heart?
And when thy heart began to beat,
What dread hand? & what dread feet?

What the hammer? what the chain?
In what furnace was thy brain?
What the anvil? what dread grasp
Dare its deadly terrors clasp?

When the stars threw down their spears,
And water'd heaven with their tears,
Did he smile his work to see?
Did he who made the Lamb make thee?

Tyger! Tyger! burning bright
In the forests of the night,
What immortal hand or eye
Dare frame thy fearful symmetry?

AH! SUN-FLOWER

Ah, Sun-flower, weary of time,
Who countest the steps of the Sun,
Seeking after that sweet golden clime
Where the traveller's journey is done:

Where the Youth pined away with desire,
And the pale Virgin shrouded in snow
Arise from their graves, and aspire
Where my Sun-flower wishes to go.

THE GARDEN OF LOVE

I went to the Garden of Love,
And saw what I never had seen:
A Chapel was built in the midst,
Where I used to play on the green.

And the gates of this Chapel were shut,
And 'Thou shalt not' writ over the door;
So I turned to the Garden of Love
That so many sweet flowers bore;

And I saw it was filled with graves,
And tomb-stones where flowers should be;
And Priests in black gowns were walking their
    rounds,
And binding with briars my joys & desires.

LONDON

I wander thro' each charter'd street,
Near where the charter'd Thames does flow,
And mark in every face I meet
Marks of weakness, marks of woe.

In every cry of every Man,
In every Infant's cry of fear,
In every voice, in every ban,
The mind-forg'd manacles I hear.

How the Chimney-sweeper's cry
Every black'ning Church appalls;

And the hapless Soldier's sigh
Runs in blood down Palace walls.

But most thro' midnight streets I hear
How the youthful Harlot's curse
Blasts the new born Infant's tear,
And blights with plagues the Marriage hearse.

A DIVINE IMAGE

Cruelty has a Human Heart,
And Jealousy a Human Face;
Terror the Human Form Divine,
And Secrecy the Human Dress.

The Human Dress is forged Iron,
The Human Form a fiery Forge,
The Human Face a Furnace seal'd,
The Human Heart its hungry Gorge.

AUGURIES OF INNOCENCE

To see a World in a Grain of Sand
And a Heaven in a Wild Flower,
Hold Infinity in the palm of your hand
And Eternity in an hour.

A Robin Red breast in a Cage
Puts all Heaven in a Rage.
A dove house fill'd with doves & Pigeons
Shudders Hell thro' all its regions.
A dog starv'd at his Master's Gate
Predicts the ruin of the State.
A Horse misus'd upon the Road
Calls to Heaven for Human blood.
Each outcry of the hunted Hare
A fibre from the Brain does tear.
A Skylark wounded in the wing,
A Cherubim does cease to sing.
The Game Cock clip'd & arm'd for fight
Does the Rising Sun affright.
Every Wolf's & Lion's howl
Raises from Hell a Human Soul.
The wild deer, wand'ring here & there,
Keeps the Human Soul from Care.

The Lamb misus'd breeds Public strife
And yet forgives the Butcher's Knife.
The Bat that flits at close of Eve
Has left the Brain that won't Believe.
The Owl that calls upon the Night
Speaks the Unbeliever's fright.
He who the Ox to wrath has mov'd
Shall never be by Woman lov'd.
The wanton Boy that kills the Fly
Shall feel the Spider's enmity.
He who torments the Chafer's sprite
Weaves a Bower in endless Night.
The Catterpiller on the Leaf
Repeats to thee they Mother's grief.
Kill not the Moth nor Butterfly,
For the Last Judgment draweth nigh.
He who shall train the Horse to War
Shall never pass the Polar Bar.
The Beggar's Dog & Widow's Cat,
Feed them & thou wilt grow fat.
The Gnat that sings his Summer's song
Poison gets from Slander's tongue.
The poison of the Snake & Newt
Is the sweat of Envy's Foot.
The Poison of the Honey Bee
Is the Artist's Jealousy.
The Prince's Robes & Beggar's Rags
Are Toadstools on the Miser's Bags.
A truth that's told with bad intent
Beats all the Lies you can invent.
It is right it should be so;
Man was made for Joy & Woe;
And when this we rightly know
Thro' the World we safely go.
Joy & Woe are woven fine,
A Clothing for the Soul divine;
Under every grief & pine
Runs a joy with silken twine.
The Babe is more than swadling Bands;
Throughout all these Human Lands
Tools were made, & Born were hands,
Every Farmer Understands.
Every Tear from Every Eye
Becomes a Babe in Eternity;
This is caught by Females bright
And return'd to its own delight.
The Bleat, the Bark, Bellow & Roar
Are Waves that Beat on Heaven's Shore.
The Babe that weeps the Rod beneath
Writes Revenge in realms of death.
The Beggar's Rags, fluttering in Air,

Does to Rags the Heavens tear.
The Soldier, arm'd with Sword & Gun,
Palsied strikes the Summer's Sun.
The poor Man's Farthing is worth more
Than all the Gold on Afric's Shore.
One Mite wrung from the Labrer's hands
Shall buy & sell the Miser's Lands:
Or, if protected from on high,
Does that whole Nation sell & buy.
He who mocks the Infant's Faith
Shall be mock'd in Age & Death.
He who shall teach the Child to doubt
The rotting Grave shall ne'er get out.
He who respects the Infant's faith
Triumphs over Hell & Death.
The Child's Toys & the Old Man's Reasons
Are the Fruits of the Two seasons.
The Questioner, who sits so sly,
Shall never know how to Reply.
He who replies to words of Doubt
Doth put the Light of Knowledge out.
The Strongest Poison ever known
Came from Caesar's Laurel Crown.
Nought can deform the Human Race
Like to the Armour's iron brace.
When Gold & Gems adorn the Plow
To peaceful Arts shall Envy Bow.
A Riddle or the Cricket's Cry
Is to Doubt a fit Reply.
The Emmet's Inch & Eagle's Mile
Make Lame Philosophy to smile.
He who Doubts from what he sees
Will ne'er Believe, do what you Please.
If the Sun & Moon should doubt,
They'd immediately Go out.
To be in a Passion you Good may do,
But no Good if a Passion is in you.
The Whore & Gambler, by the State
Licenc'd, build that Nation's Fate.
The Harlot's cry from Street to Street
Shall weave Old England's winding Sheet.
The Winner's Shout, the Loser's Curse,
Dance before dead England's Hearse.
Every Night & every Morn
Some to Misery are Born.
Every Morn & every Night
Some are Born to sweet delight.
Some are Born to sweet delight,
Some are Born to Endless Night.
We are led to Believe a Lie
When we see not Thro' the Eye

Which was Born in a Night to perish in a Night
When the Soul Slept in Beams of Light.
God Appears & God is Light
To those poor Souls who dwell in Night,
But does a Human Form Display
To those who Dwell in Realms of day.

VALA OR THE FOUR ZOAS

‹Night the Third›

(lines 388–418)

'I am made to sow the thistle for wheat, the nettle
    for a nourishing dainty.
'I have planted a false oath in the earth; it has
    brought forth a poison tree.
'I have chosen the serpent for a councellor, & the
    dog
'For a schoolmaster to my children.
'I have blotted out from light & living the dove &
    nightingale,
'And I have caused the earth worm to beg from door
    to door.

'I have taught the thief a secret path into the house
    of the just.
'I have taught pale artifice to spread his nets upon
    the morning.
'My heavens are brass, my earth is iron, my moon a
    clod of clay,
'My sun a pestilence burning at noon & a vapour of
    death in night.

'What is the price of Experience? do men buy it for
    a song?
'Or wisdom for a dance in the street? No, it is
    bought with the price
'Of all that a man hath, his house, his wife, his
    children.
'Wisdom is sold in the desolate market where none
    come to buy,
'And in the wither'd field where the farmer plows
    for bread in vain.

'It is an easy thing to triumph in the summer's sun
'And in the vintage & to sing on the waggon loaded
    with corn.
'It is an easy thing to talk of patience to the
    afflicted,

'To speak the laws of prudence to the houseless
    wanderer,
'To listen to the hungry raven's cry in wintry season
'When the red blood is fill'd with wine & with the
    marrow of lambs.

'It is an easy thing to laugh at wrathful elements,
'To hear the dog howl at the wintry door, the ox in
    the slaughter house moan;
'To see a god on every wind & a blessing on every
    blast;
'To hear sounds of love in the thunder storm that
    destroys our enemies' house;
'To rejoice in the blight that covers his field, & the
    sickness that cuts off his children,
'While our olive & vine sing & laugh round our
    door, & our children bring fruits & flowers.

'Then the groan & the dolor are quite forgotten, &
    the slave grinding at the mill,
'And the captive in chains, & the poor in the prison,
    & the soldier in the field
'When the shatter'd bone hath laid him groaning
    among the happier dead.

'It is an easy thing to rejoice in the tents of
    prosperity:
'Thus could I sing & thus rejoice: but it is not so
    with me.'

MILTON

‹Book the First: Plate 26›

(lines 1–12)

These are the Sons of Los, & these the Labourers of
    the Vintage.
Thou seest the gorgeous clothed Flies that dance &
    sport in summer
Upon the sunny brooks & meadows: every one the
    dance
Knows in its intricate mazes of delight artful to
    weave:
Each one to sound his instruments of music in the
    dance,
To touch each other & recede, to cross & change &
    return:
These are the Children of Los; thou seest the Trees
    on mountains,

The wind blows heavy, loud they thunder thro' the
    darksom sky,
Uttering prophecies & speaking instructive words to
    the sons
Of men: These are the Sons of Los: These the Visions
    of Eternity,
But we see only as it were the hem of their
    garments
When with our vegetable eyes we view these
    wondrous Visions.

◄ Book the First: Plate 27 ►

(lines 8–28)

This Wine-press is call'd War on Earth: it is the
    Printing-Press
Of Los, and here he lays his words in order above
    the mortal brain,
As cogs are form'd in a wheel to turn the cogs of the
    adverse wheel.

Timbrels & violins sport round the Wine-presses;
    the little Seed,
The sportive Root, the Earth-worm, the gold Beetle,
    the wise Emmet
Dance round the Wine-presses of Luvah: the
    Centipede is there,
The ground Spider with many eyes, the Mole
    clothed in velvet,
The ambitious Spider in his sullen web, the lucky
    golden Spinner,
The Earwig arm'd, the tender Maggot, emblem of
    immortality,
The Flea, Louse, Bug, the Tape-Worm, all the
    Armies of Disease,
Visible or invisible to the slothful vegetating Man.
The slow Slug, the Grasshopper that sings & laughs
    & drinks:
Winter comes, he folds his slender bones without a
    murmur.
The cruel Scorpion is there, the Gnat, Wasp, Hornet
    & the Honey Bee,
The Toad & venomous Newt, the Serpent cloth'd in
    gems & gold.
They throw off their gorgeous raiment: they rejoice
    with loud jubilee
Around the Wine-presses of Luvah, naked & drunk
    with wine.

There is the Nettle that stings with soft down, and
    there

The indignant Thistle whose bitterness is bred in
    his milk,
Who feeds on contempt of his neighbour: there all
    the idle Weeds
That creep around the obscure places shew their
    various limbs
Naked in all their beauty dancing round the Wine-
    presses.

◄ Book the First: Plate 28 ►

(lines 44–63)

But others of the Sons of Los build Moments &
    Minutes & Hours
And Days & Months & Years & Ages & Periods,
    wondrous buildings;
And every Moment has a Couch of gold for soft
    repose,
(A Moment equals a pulsation of the artery),
And between every two Moments stands a Daughter
    of Beulah
To feed the Sleepers on their Couches with maternal
    care.
And every Minute has an azure Tent with silken
    Veils:
And every Hour has a bright golden Gate carved
    with skill:
And every Day & Night has Walls of brass & Gates
    of adamant,
Shining like precious Stones & ornamented with
    appropriate signs:
And every Month a silver paved Terrace builded
    high:
And every Year invulnerable Barriers with high
    Towers:
And every Age is Moated deep with Bridges of silver
    & gold:
And every Seven Ages is Incircled with a Flaming
    Fire.
Now Seven Ages is amounting to Two Hundred
    Years.
Each has its Guard, each Moment, Minute, Hour,
    Day, Month & Year.
All are the work of Fairy hands of the Four
    Elements:
The Guard are Angels of Providence on duty
    evermore.
Every Time less than a pulsation of the artery
Is equal in its period & value to Six Thousand
    Years [. . .]

◄ Book the First: Plate 29 ►

(lines 1–24)

For in this Period the Poet's Work is Done, and all
the Great
Events of Time start forth & are conceiv'd in such a
Period,
Within a Moment, a Pulsation of the Artery.

The Sky is an immortal Tent built by the Sons of
Los:
And every Space that a Man views around his
dwelling-place
Standing on his own roof or in his garden on a
mount
Of twenty-five cubits in height, such space is his
Universe:
And on its verge the Sun rises & sets, the Clouds
bow
To meet the flat Earth & the Sea in such an order'd
Space:
The Starry heavens reach no further, but here bend
and set
On all sides, & the two Poles turn on their valves of
gold;
And if he move his dwelling-place, his heavens also
move
Where'er he goes, & all his neighbourhood bewail
his loss.
Such are the Spaces called Earth & such its
dimension.
As to that false appearance which appears to the
reasoner
As of a Globe rolling thro' Voidness, it is a delusion
of Ulro.
The Microscope knows not of this nor the
Telescope: they alter
The ratio of the Spectator's Organs, but leave
Objects untouch'd.
For every Space larger than a red Globule of Man's
blood
Is visionary, and is created by the Hammer of Los:
And every Space smaller than a Globule of Man's
blood opens
Into Eternity of which this vegetable Earth is but a
shadow.
The red Globule is the unwearied Sun by Los
created
To measure Time and Space to mortal Men every
morning.

◄ Book the Second: Plate 40 ►

(lines 32–7)

'There is a Negation, & there is a Contrary:
'The Negation must be destroy'd to redeem the
Contraries.
'The Negation is the Spectre, the Reasoning Power
in Man:
'This is a false Body, an Incrustation over my
Immortal
'Spirit, a Selfhood which must be put off &
annihilated alway.
'To cleanse the Face of my Spirit by Self-
examination,

◄ Book the Second: Plate 41 ►

(lines 1–28)

'To bathe in the Waters of Life, to wash off the Not
Human,
'I come in Self-annihilation & the grandeur of
Inspiration,
'To cast off Rational Demonstration by Faith in the
Saviour,
'To cast off the rotten rags of Memory by
Inspiration,
'To cast off Bacon, Locke & Newton from Albion's
covering,
'To take off his filthy garments & clothe him with
Imagination,
'To cast aside from Poetry all that is not Inspiration,
'That it no longer shall dare to mock with the
aspersion of Madness
'Cast on the Inspired by the tame high finisher of
paltry Blots
'Indefinite, or paltry Rhymes, or paltry Harmonies,
'Who creeps into State Government like a caterpiller
to destroy;
'To cast off the idiot Questioner who is always
questioning
'But never capable of answering, who sits with a sly
grin
'Silent plotting when to question, like a thief in a
cave,
'Who publishes doubt & calls it knowledge, whose
Science is Despair,
'Whose pretence to knowledge is envy, whose whole
Science is
'To destroy the wisdom of ages to gratify ravenous
Envy
'That rages round him like a Wolf day & night
without rest:

'He smiles with condescension, he talks of Benevolence & Virtue,
'And those who act with Benevolence & Virtue they murder time on time.
'These are the destroyers of Jerusalem, these are the murderers
'Of Jesus, who deny the Faith & mock at Eternal Life,
'Who pretend to Poetry that they may destroy Imagination
'By imitation of Nature's Images drawn from Remembrance.
'These are the Sexual Garments, the Abomination of Desolation,
'Hiding the Human Lineaments as with an Ark & Curtains
'Which Jesus rent & now shall wholly purge away with Fire
'Till Generation is swallow'd up in Regeneration.'

❧

JERUSALEM

‹Chapter 1: Plate 5›

(lines 16–24)

Trembling I sit day and night, my friends are astonish'd at me,
Yet they forgive my wanderings. I rest not from my great task!
To open the Eternal Worlds, to open the immortal Eyes
Of Man inwards into the Worlds of Thought, into Eternity
Ever expanding in the Bosom of God, the Human Imagination.
O Saviour pour upon me thy Spirit of meekness & love!
Annihilate the Selfhood in me: be thou all my life!
Guide thou my hand, which trembles exceedingly upon the rock of ages,
While I write of the building of Golgonooza [. . .]

‹Chapter 1: Plate 12›

(lines 25–44)

What are those golden builders doing? where was the burying-place
Of soft Ethinthus? near Tyburn's fatal Tree? is that

Mild Zion's hill's most ancient promontory, near mournful
Ever weeping Paddington? is that Calvary and Golgotha
Becoming a building of pity and compassion? Lo!
The stones are pity, and the bricks, well wrought affections
Enamel'd with love & kindness, & the tiles engraven gold,
Labour of merciful hands: the beams & rafters are forgiveness:
The mortar & cement of the work, tears of honesty: the nails
And the screws & iron braces are well wrought blandishments
And well contrived words, firm fixing, never forgotten,
Always comforting the remembrance: the floors, humility:
The ceilings, devotion: the hearths, thanksgiving,
Prepare the furniture, O Lambeth, in thy pitying looms,
The curtains, woven tears & sighs wrought into lovely forms
For comfort; there the secret furniture of Jerusalem's chamber
Is wrought. Lambeth! the Bride, the Lamb's Wife, loveth thee.
Thou art one with her & knowest not of self in thy supreme joy.
Go on, builders in hope, tho' Jerusalem wanders far away
Without the gate of Los, among the dark Satanic wheels.

‹Chapter 3: Plate 65›

(lines 16–28)

And all the Arts of Life they chang'd into the Arts of Death in Albion.
The hour-glass contemn'd because its simple workmanship
Was like the workmnanship of the plowman, & the water wheel
That raises water into cisterns, broken & burn'd with fire
Because its workmanship was like the workmanship of the shepherd;
And in their stead, intricate wheels invented, wheel without wheel,

To perplex youth in their outgoings & to bind to
    labours in Albion
Of day & night the myriads of eternity: that they
    may grind
And polish brass & iron hour after hour, laborious
    task,
Kept ignorant of its use: that they might spend the
    days of wisdom
In sorrowful drudgery to obtain a scanty pittance of
    bread,
In ignorance to view a small portion & think that
    All,
And call it Demonstration, blind to all the simple
    rules of life.

◄ Chapter 4: Plate 91 ►

(lines 5–31)

[. . .] Go to these Friends of Righteousness,
'Tell them to obey their Humanities & not pretend
    Holiness
'When they are murderers: as far as my Hammer &
    Anvil permit.
'Go, tell them that the Worship of God is
    honouring his gifts
'In other men: & loving the greatest men best, each
    according
'To his Genius: which is the Holy Ghost in Man;
    there is no other
'God than that God who is the intellectual fountain
    of Humanity.
'He who envies or calumniates, which is murder &
    cruelty,
'Murders the Holy-one. Go, tell them this, &
    overthrow their cup,
'Their bread, their altar-table, their incense & their
    oath,
'Their marriage & their baptism, their burial &
    consecration.
'I have tried to make friends by corporeal gifts but
    have only
'Made enemies. I never made friends but by
    spiritual gifts,
'By severe contentions of friendship & the burning
    fire of thought.
'He who would see the Divinity must see him in his
    Children,
'One first, in friendship & love, then a Divine
    Family, & in the midst
'Jesus will appear; so he who wishes to see a Vision,
    a perfect Whole,

'Must see it in its Minute Particulars, Organized, &
    not as thou,
'O Fiend of Righteousness, pretendest; thine is a
    Disorganized
'And snowy cloud, brooder of tempests &
    destructive War.
'You smile with pomp & rigor, you talk of
    benevolence & virtue;
'I act with benevolence & Virtue & get murder'd
    time after time.
'You accumulate Particulars & murder by analyzing,
    that you
'May take the aggregate, & you call the aggregate
    Moral Law,
'And you call that swell'd & bloated Form a Minute
    Particular;
'But General Forms have their vitality in Particulars,
    & every
'Particular is a Man, a Divine Member of the Divine
    Jesus.'

The recent emphasis on narrative in poetry might lead one to believe that this is an entirely new phenomonen – that poetry has abandoned the lyrical and philosophical areas it once inhabited and has moved into the territory of the novel and film. This would be an erroneous belief. There has always been a strand of poetry that was narrative, a strand that belongs strongly to the oral tradition, and nowhere is this more evident than in the anonymous works of the Balladeers.

I have chosen three of the Border Ballads: 'The Demon Lover', 'Lizie Wan' and 'The Twa Corbies'. What they share – apart from the repetitive, musical structure that gives them another life in song – is a grimness of subject matter, a spareness of narration, and beautifully judged endings. In other ways they are very different, though.

'The Demon Lover' is a wonderfully eerie and dramatic concretisation of the abstract idea that unfaithfulness leads to hell. No one beginning the poem can have any idea that it will end up where it does, or abandon so completely the realism it started with.

'Lizie Wan' is more direct and doesn't move so far. But its compactness, and what Swinburne called its 'brusque abruptness of style' contribute greatly to its kick and arguably make it especially suited to a reader of today.

'The Twa Corbies' is probably the best known of the three but that doesn't take away from its power that's based so much in the surprise of its angle, and the unsentimental matter of factness of its tone – never more obvious than in the detail of the crows' plan to use the dead knight's golden hair to line their nests with. Curiously contemporary, almost.

All in all, any writer of narrative poetry could learn from the way these and other traditional ballads keep the tension of their narrative going.

THE DEMON LOVER

'O where have you been, my long, long love,
This long seven years and more?
'O I've come to seek my former vows
You granted me before.' –

'O hold your tongue of your former vows,
For they will breed sad strife;
O hold your tongue of your former vows,
For I am become a wife.'

He turned him right and round about
And the tear blinded his ee;
'I wad never hae trodden on Irish ground,
'If it had not been for thee.

'I might have had a king's daughter,
Far, far beyond the sea;
I might have had a king's daughter
If it had not been for the love o' thee. –

'I despised the crown of gold,
The yellow silk also;
And I am come to my true love,
But wi' me she will not go.'

'If ye might have had a king's daughter,
Yoursell ye hae to blame;
Ye might have taken the king's daughter,
For ye kent that I was nane.'

'O false are the vows of womenkind,
But fair is their false body;
I wad never hae trodden on Irish ground,
If it had not been for the love o' thee.'

'O what hae you to keep me wi'
If I should with you go?
If I would leave my husband dear,
My little young babes also?' –

'I hae seven ships upon the sea
Laden wi' the finest gold;
And mariners to wait us upon;
All these you may behold.'

'And I hae shoes for my love's feet,
Beaten o' the purest gold,
And lined wi' the velvet soft,
To keep my love's feet frae the cold.'

She's tane up her little young babes,
Kissed them baith cheek and chin;
'O fare ye weel, my ain twa babes,
For I'll never see you again.'

She set her foot upon the ship,
Nae mariners could she behold,
But the sails were of the taffetie
And the masts o' the beaten gold.

'O how do you love the ship,' he said
'Or how do you love the sea?
Or how do you love the bold mariners
That wait upon thee and me?'

'O I do love the ship,' she said,
'And I do love the sea;
But woe be to the dim mariners
That nowhere I can see.'

They had not sailed a league, a league,
A league but barely three,
When dismal grew his countenance
And drumlie grew his ee.

They had not sailed a league, a league,
A league but barely three,
Until she espied his cloven foot
And wept right bitterly.

'O hold your tongue of your weeping,' he says,
'Of your weeping now let me be;
I will shew you how the lilies grow
On the banks of Italy.' –

'O what hills are yon, yon pleasant hills,
That the sun shines sweetly on?'
'O yon are the hills of heaven,' he said,
'Where you will never win.' –

'O whatten a mountain is yon,' she said,
'All so dreary wi' frost and snow?'
'O yon is the mountain of hell,' he said,
'Where you and I will go.'

And aye when she turned her round about,
Aye taller he seem'd for to be;
Until that the tops o' that gallant ship,
Nae taller were than he.

He strak the tapmast wi' his hand,
The foremast wi' his knee;
And he brake that gallant ship in twain,
And sank her in the sea.

LIZIE WAN

Lizie Wan sits at her father's bower door
Weeping and making a mane;
And by there came her father dear;
'What ails thee, Lizie Wan?'

'I ail, and I ail, dear father,' she said
'And I can shew you why;
There is a child between my twa sides
Between my dear billie and I.'

Now Lizie Wan sits at her father's bower door
Sighing and making a mane;
And by there comes her brother dear,
'What ails thee, Lizie Wan?'

'I ail, I ail, dear brother,' she said,
'And I can shew you why;
There is a child between my twa sides
Between you, dear billie and I.'

'And hast thou told father and mother o' that,
And hast thou told sae o' me?'
And he has drawn his good braid sword
That hung down by his knee.

And he has cutted off Lizie Wan's head
And her fair body in three;
And he's awa' to his mother's bower,
And sair aghast was he.

'What ails thee, what ails thee, Geordie Wan,
What ails thee so fast to run?
For I see by thy ill colour
Some fallow's deed thou's done.'

'Some fallow's deed I have done, mither,
And I pray you pardon me;
For I've cutted off my greyhound's head
He wadna rin for me.'

'Thy greyhound's blood was never sae red,
O my son, Geordie Wan;
For I see by thy ill colour
Some fallow's deed thou's done.'

'Some fallow's deed I hae done, mither,
And pray you pardon me;
For I hae cutted off Lizie Wan's head
And her fair body in three.'

'O, what will thou do when thy father comes hame,
O my son, Geordie Wan?'
'I'll set my foot in a bottomless boat
And swim to the sea ground.'

'And when will thou come hame again,
O my son Geordie Wan?'
'The sun and the moon shall dance on the green
That night when I come hame.'

THE TWA CORBIES

As I was walking all alane
I heard twa corbies making a mane;
The tane unto the t'other say,
'Where sall we gang and dine to-day?'

' – In behint yon auld fail dyke,
I wot there lies a new-slain Knight;
And naebody kens that he lies there,
But his hawk, his hound, and lady fair.

'His hound is to the hunting gane,
His hawk to fetch the wild-fowl hame,
His lady's ta'en another mate,
So we may make our dinner sweet.

'Ye'll sit on his white hause-bane,
And I'll pick out his bonny blue een:
Wi' ae lock o' his gowden hair
We'll theek our nest when it grows bare.

'Mony a one for him makes mane,
But nane sall ken where he is gane;
O'er his white banes, when they are bare,
The wind sall blaw for evermair.'

Anne Bradstreet (1612–72), mother of American poetry, has above all been celebrated for poems inserted posthumously in the second edition of *The Tenth Muse Lately Sprung Up in America* (1650), from which I select; I have added a poem from the 1897 edition.

'The Author to Her Book' says as much about mothering as about authoring. The idea of books as children is familiar, of writing as single-parenting less so, but of sending children out into the world as a form of publishing, rare.

Her love poems to her husband have the grace that a sense of divine union is privy to. In these, and in 'A Letter to her Husband' (not included), which has the line, 'If two be one, as surely thou and I, / How stayest thou there, whilst I at Ipswich lie?', I hear – along with Sidney, Donne, the Metaphysicals – the voice of Rumi: 'This is the greatest wonder, that thou and I, sitting here in the same nook, / Are at this moment both in Irak and Khurasan, thou and I.'

The simplicity of 'To My Dear and Loving Husband' was perhaps fresher to her contemporaries than the elaboration and wordplay of 'Another'. For me, the reverse is true – surprised by the mullet I last met in Catullus being thrust, along with radishes, through the flesh's open gate. But it was the sixteenth-century French poet Du Bartas, a much derided influence, who gave Bradstreet her mullet and mate.

Among her elegies this, for Simon, the third grandchild lost, I find the most moving, in its faltering faith, that equivocal 'Let's'.

'Verses upon the Burning of our House', transcending its Puritan aesthetic to strike that intimate note we sound so frequently today, I include to concur, with her, that 'there is nothing that can be sayd or done, but either that or something like it hath been done and sayd before'.

THE AUTHOR TO HER BOOK

Thou ill-formed offspring of my feeble brain,
Who after birth didst by my side remain,
Till snatched from thence by friends, less wise than
    true,
Who thee abroad, exposed to public view,
Made thee in rags, halting to th' press to trudge,
Where errors were not lessened (all may judge).
At thy return my blushing was not small,
My rambling brat (in print) should mother call,
I cast thee by as one unfit for light,
Thy visage was so irksome in my sight;
Yet being mine own, at length affection would
Thy blemishes amend, if so I could:
I washed thy face, but more defects I saw,
And rubbing off a spot still made a flaw.
I stretched thy joints to make thee even feet,
Yet still thou run'st more hobbling than is meet;
In better dress to trim thee was my mind,
But nought save homespun cloth i' th' house I find.
In this array 'mongst vulgars may'st thou roam.
In critic's hands beware thou dost not come,
And take thy way where yet thou art not known;
If for thy father asked, say thou hadst none;
And for thy mother, she alas is poor,
Which caused her thus to send thee out of door.

TO MY DEAR AND LOVING HUSBAND

If ever two were one, then surely we.
If ever man were loved by wife, then thee;
If ever wife was happy in a man,
Compare with me, ye women, if you can.
I prize thy love more than whole mines of gold
Or all the riches that the East doth hold.
My love is such that rivers cannot quench,
Nor ought but love from thee, give recompense.
Thy love is such I can no way repay,
The heavens reward thee manifold, I pray.
Then while we live, in love let's so persevere
That when we live no more, we may live ever.

ANOTHER
‹(Letter to her Husband,
Absent upon Public Employment)›

As loving hind that (hartless) wants her deer,
Scuds through the woods and fern with hark'ning
    ear,
Perplext, in every bush and nook doth pry,
Her dearest deer, might answer ear or eye;
So doth my anxious soul, which now doth miss
A dearer dear (far dearer heart) than this.
Still wait with doubts, and hopes, and failing eye,
His voice to hear or person to descry.
Or as the pensive dove doth all alone
(On withered bough) most uncouthly bemoan
The absence of her love and loving mate,
Whose loss hath made her so unfortunate,
Ev'n thus do I, with many a deep sad groan,
Bewail my turtle true, who now is gone,
His presence and his safe return still woos,
With thousand doleful sighs and mournful coos.
Or as the loving mullet, that true fish,
Her fellow lost, nor joy nor life do wish,
But launches on that shore, there for to die,
Where she her captive husband doth espy.
Mine being gone, I lead a joyless life,
I have a loving peer, yet seem no wife;
But worst of all, to him can't steer my course,
I here, he there, alas, both kept by force.
Return my dear, my joy, my only love,
Unto thy hind, thy mullet, and thy dove,
Who neither joys in pasture, house, nor streams,
The substance gone, O me, these are but dreams.
Together at one tree, oh let us browse,
And like two turtles roost within one house,
And like the mullets in one river glide,
Let's still remain but one, till death divide.
        Thy loving love and dearest dear,
        At home, abroad, and everywhere.

ON MY DEAR GRANDCHILD
SIMON BRADSTREET, WHO DIED ON
16 NOVEMBER, 1669, BEING BUT A
MONTH, AND ONE DAY OLD

No sooner came, but gone, and fall'n asleep,
Acquaintance short, yet parting caused us weep;
Three flowers, two scarcely blown, the last i' th' bud,

Cropt by th' Almighty's hand; yet is He good.
With dreadful awe before Him let's be mute,
Such was His will, but why, let's not dispute,
With humble hearts and mouths put in the dust,
Let's say He's merciful as well as just.
He will return and make up all our losses,
And smile again after our bitter crosses
Go pretty babe, go rest with sisters twain;
Among the blest in endless joys remain.

❧

HERE FOLLOWS SOME VERSES UPON THE BURNING OF OUR HOUSE JULY 10TH, 1666. COPIED OUT OF A LOOSE PAPER

In silent night when rest I took
For sorrow near I did not look
I wakened was with thund'ring noise
And piteous shrieks of dreadful voice.
That fearful sound of 'Fire!' and 'Fire!'
Let no man know is my desire.
I, starting up, the light did spy,
And to my God my heart did cry
To strengthen me in my distress
And not to leave me succorless.
Then, coming out, beheld a space
The flame consume my dwelling place.
And when I could no longer look,
I blest His name that gave and took,
That laid my goods now in the dust.
Yea, so it was, and so 'twas just.
It was His own, it was not mine,
Far be it that I should repine;
He might of all justly bereft
But yet sufficient for us left.
When by the ruins oft I past
My sorrowing eyes aside did cast,
And here and there the places spy
Where oft I sat and long did lie:
Here stood that trunk, and there that chest,
There lay that store I counted best.
My pleasant things in ashes lie,
And them behold no more shall I.
Under thy roof no guest shall sit,
Nor at thy table eat a bit.
No pleasant tale shall e'er be told,
Nor things recounted done of old.
No candle e'er shall shine in thee,
Nor bridegroom's voice e'er heard shall be.

In silence ever shall thou lie,
Adieu, Adieu, all's vanity.
Then straight I 'gin my heart to chide,
And did thy wealth on earth abide?
Didst fix thy hope on mold'ring dust?
The arm of flesh didst make thy trust?
Raise up thy thoughts above the sky
That dunghill mists away may fly.
Thou hast an house on high erect,
Framed by that mighty Architect,
With glory richly furnished,
Stands permanent though this be fled.
It's purchased and paid for too
By Him who hath enough to do.
A price so vast as is unknown
Yet by His gift is made thine own;
There's wealth enough, I need no more,
Farewell, my pelf, farewell my store.
The world no longer let me love,
My hope and treasure lies above.

When Charlotte Brontë (1816–55) sent her poems to Robert Southey, he told her to write for poetry's sake and 'not with a view to celebrity.' 'Literature', he said, 'cannot be the business of a woman's life, and it ought not to be.' No use now to rage at Southey. He was a man of his time. Today every television viewer knows the story of *Jane Eyre*, of *Wuthering Heights* by Emily Brontë (1818–48) and *The Tenant of Wildfell Hall* by Anne Brontë (1820–49), while Southey and his reputation have fallen from attention. The business of the three daughters of Haworth parsonage *was* literature. They wrote, read and discussed it obsessively. They made a private world out of language, filling little notebooks with their tiny handwriting. Their literary game of the imaginary Gondal gave them inner worlds as rich and real as the wild beauty of the Yorkshire moors surrounding them. In particular it is Emily whose poetry rings true and original, alive with the sky and the stars, the weather, the wind and the snow, with her favourite echoing words like 'midnight moonlight', her insights into the very sounds and silences of Haworth parsonage, 'The old clock in the gloomy hall/Ticks on from hour to hour', and her keen observation of nature, 'the blue ice curdling on the stream.' Few novels can have had a more powerful effect on so many young women's lives than *Wuthering Heights*. I read it at an age when dreams are wild and longing is boundless. All the restless energy of adolescence mixed with the unschooled creativity of the hopeful writer lay waiting to be reflected in the pages of Emily Brontë's passionate book. This reader found a sister there, and permission to be a poet. At that moment all literature opened itself to me, and the spell was cast.

'LOOK INTO THOUGHT'
◄ Charlotte Brontë ►

Look into thought and say what dost thou see,
    Dive, be not fearful, how dark the waves flow,
Sink through the surge, and bring pearls up to me,
    Deeper, ay, deeper; the fairest lie low.

I have dived, I have sought them, but none have I found,
    In the gloom that closed o'er me no form floated by,
As I sunk through the void depths so black and profound
    How dim died the sun and how far hung the sky!

What had I given to hear the soft sweep
    Of a breeze bearing life through that vast realm of death!
Thoughts were untroubled and dreams were asleep,
    The spirit lay dreadless and hopeless beneath.

SONG
◄ Anne Brontë ►

We know where deepest lies the snow,
And where the frost-winds keenest blow.
      O'er every mountain's brow,
We long have known and learnt to bear
The wandering outlaw's toil and care,
But where we late were hunted, there
      Our foes are hunted now.

We have their princely homes, and they
To our wild haunts are chased away,
      Dark woods, and desert caves.
And we can range from hill to hill,
And chase our vanquished victors still;
Small respite will they find until
      They slumber in their graves.

But I would rather be the hare,
That crouching in its sheltered lair
      Must start at every sound;
That forced from cornfields waving wide
Is driven to seek the bare hillside,
Or in the tangled copse to hide,
      Than be the hunter's hound.

'REDBREAST, EARLY IN THE MORNING'
‹Emily Brontë›

Redbreast, early in the morning
  Dark and cold and cloudy grey,
Wildly tender is thy music,
  Chasing angry thought away.

My heart is not enraptured now,
  My eyes are full of tears,
And constant sorrow on my brow
  Has done the work of years.

It was not hope that wrecked at once
  The spirit's calm in storm,
But a long life of solitude,
Hopes quenched, and rising thoughts subdued,
  A bleak November's calm.

What woke it then? A little child
  Strayed from its father's cottage door,
And in the hour of moonlight wild
  Lay lonely on the desert moor.

I heard it then, you heard it too,
And seraph sweet it sang to you;
But like the shriek of misery
That wild wild music wailed to me!

❧

'THE SUN HAS SET'
‹Emily Brontë›

The sun has set, and the long grass now
Waves dreamily in the evening wind;
And the wild bird has flown from that old grey
  stone,
In some warm nook a couch to find.

In all the lonely landscape round
I see no light and hear no sound,
Except the wind that far away
Comes sighing o'er the heathy sea.

❧

'THE NIGHT IS DARKENING'
‹Emily Brontë›

The night is darkening round me,
  The wild winds coldly blow;
But a tyrant spell has bound me,
  And I cannot, cannot go.

The giant trees are bending
  Their bare boughs weighed with snow,
The storm is fast descending,
  And yet I cannot go.

Clouds beyond clouds above me,
  Wastes beyond wastes below;
But nothing dread can move me –
  I will not, cannot go.

❧

A DAY DREAM
‹Emily Brontë›
(lines 1–4; 41–68)

On a sunny brae alone I lay
  One summer afternoon;
It was the marriage-time of May,
  With her young lover, June.

[. . .]

A thousand thousand gleaming fires
  Seemed kindling in the air;
A thousand thousand silvery lyres
  Resounded far and near:

Methought the very breath I breathed
  Was full of sparks divine,
And all my heather-couch was wreathed
  By that celestial shine!

And, while the wide earth echoing rung
  To that strange minstrelsy,
The little glittering spirits sung,
  Or seemed to sing, to me.

'O mortal! mortal! let them die;
  Let time and tears destroy,
That we may overflow the sky
  With universal joy!

Let grief distract the sufferer's breast,
   And night obscure his way;
They hasten him to endless rest,
   And everlasting day.

'To thee the world is like a tomb,
   A desert's naked shore;
To us, in unimagined bloom,
   It brightens more and more!

'And, could we lift the veil, and give
   One brief glimpse to shine eye,
Thou wouldst rejoice for those that live,
   Because they live to die.'

❧

'IT WAS NIGHT'
‹ Emily Brontë ›

It was night, and on the mountains
   Fathoms deep the snowdrifts lay;
Streams and waterfalls and fountains
   Down the darkness stole away.

Long ago the hopeless peasant
   Left his sheep all buried there,
Sheep that through the summer pleasant
   He had watched with tend'rest care.

Now no more a cheerful ranger,
   Following pathways known of yore,
Sad he stood, a wild-eyed stranger,
   On his own unbounded moor.

❧

THE SIGNAL LIGHT
‹ Emily Brontë ›

Silent is the house: all are laid asleep:
One alone looks out o'er the snow-wreaths deep,
Watching every cloud, dreading every breeze
That whirls the 'wildering drift, and bends the
   groaning trees.

Cheerful is the hearth, soft the matted floor;
Not one shivering gust creeps through pane or
   door;

The little lamp burns straight, its rays shoot strong
   and far:
I trim it well, to be the wanderer's guiding-star.

Frown, my haughty sire! chide, my angry dame;
Set your slaves to spy; threaten me with shame!
But neither sire nor dame, nor prying serf shall
   know
What angel nightly tracks that waste of frozen snow.

What I love shall come like visitant of air,
Safe in secret power from lurking human snare;
What loves me, no word of mine shall e'er betray,
Though for faith unstained my life must forfeit pay.

Burn, then, little lamp; glimmer straight and clear –
Hush! a rustling wing stirs, methinks, the air:
He for whom I wait, thus ever comes to me;
Strange Power! I trust thy might; trust thou my
   constancy!

❧

'FALL, LEAVES, FALL'
‹ Emily Brontë ›

Fall, leaves, fall; die, flowers, away;
Lengthen night and shorten day!
Every leaf speaks bliss to me,
Fluttering from the autumn tree.
I shall smile when wreaths of snow
Blossom where the rose should grow;
I shall sing when night's decay
Ushers in a drearier day.

❧

'ALL HUSHED AND STILL'
‹ Emily Brontë ›

All hushed and still within the house;
   Without, all wind and driving rain;
But something whispers to my mind,
Wrought up in rain and wailing wind:
Never again? Why not again? Never again!
   Memory has power as well as wind!

❧

REMEMBRANCE
◄ Emily Brontë ►

(lines 1–12; 29–32)

Cold in the earth – and the deep snow piled above
   thee,
Far, far removed, cold in the dreary grave!
Have I forgot, my only Love, to love thee,
Severed at last by Time's all-severing wave?

Now, when alone, do my thoughts no longer hover
Over the mountains, on that northern shore,
Resting their wings where heath and fern-leaves
   cover
Thy noble heart for ever, ever more?

Cold in the earth – and fifteen wild Decembers,
From those brown hills, have melted into spring:
Faithful, indeed, is the spirit that remembers
After such years of change and suffering!

[…]

And, even yet, I dare not let it languish,
Dare not indulge in memory's rapturous pain;
Once drinking deep of that divinest anguish,
How could I seek the empty world again?

❧

'IT WAS THE AUTUMN OF THE YEAR'
◄ Emily Brontë ►

(lines 30–end)

Wood-shadowed dales; a harvest moon
Unclouded in its glorious noon;
A solemn landscape, wide and still,
A red fire on a distant hill;
A line of fire, and deep below,
Another dusker, drearier glow;
Charred beams, and lime, and blackened stones
Self-piled in cairns o'er burning bones;
And lurid flames that licked the wood,
Then quenched their glare in pools of blood.

Whatever degree of faculty I have, lies in poetry – still more of my personal happiness lies in it – still more of my love. I cannot remember the time when I did not love it – with a lying-awake sort of passion at nine years old, and with a more powerful feeling since, which even all my griefs such as have shaken life, have failed to shake. At this moment I love it more than ever – and am more bent than ever, if possible, to work into light … not into popularity but into expression … whatever faculty I have (January 1842)

Elizabeth Barrett (1806–61) had strong feelings. She often suffered from the violence or conflict of her emotions – but she set about working into light her poetic longing, 'Oh, to shoot/My soul's full meaning into future years…' (Sonnets, no. 38) against many odds.

She was an intense woman, excited by ideas, who read widely. But at the time of writing, this 38-year-old life had been shaken by many griefs. A spinster and chronic invalid (spinal damage since age 14 and suspected TB), she was on morphine for the pain. All summer in black silk, and all winter in black velvet, she rested on a little sofa ('Winters shut me up as they do dormouse's eyes'), hyper-tense with 'fits of fearfulness', introspective yet dreaming of a wider world; grieving a dead brother; her best friend a dog. So, a clever but restricted and lonely person – with an Old Testament-style father whom she loved, but whose emotional dominance still oppressed all his adult children.

Soon she would meet her Nemesis, Robert Browning, and have her life turned around into wildest-dream happiness. They felt like each other's personal destiny, and recognized this. Such emotions sometimes felt comfortably ordinary to Elizabeth – 'I love thee to the level of everyday's/Most quiet need, by sun and candlelight' (Sonnets, no. 43), sometimes divinely transfiguring: 'Surely I have loved you, in the idea of you, my whole life long…. You have lifted my soul up into the light of your soul, & I am not ever likely to mistake it for the common daylight' (letter to Robert, 15 August 1846). They eloped to Italy – permanently.

Travel and marriage enlarged and illuminated her world. She was alert to change, especially social change, and would call it in, in her poetry. How relevant, still, sounds: 'The old world waits the time to be renewed' with 'New churches, new oeconomies. new laws/Admitting freedom, new societies'. And she published under her own name, at a time when many women writers hid their identities behind a male pseudonym.

I find certain of her ideas interesting but much of the work stylistically dated, ornate and busy, not travelling easily through time. More than her poems, I enjoy her correspondence (she wrote volumes of letters), because she writes letters with verve, instinctively a poet, observant, creative – more lively, responsive, direct than sometimes in her verse.

So the lines I've selected below are those that feel most direct and individual: awake to new emotional experience. They speak of honesty – a heart breaking open into love; taking in wide-open landscapes; the utter stuckness and bleakness of grief; feeling close to angels, to light and to the infinite.

With typical passion, she saw poets as having to deal in essential truth – and working in a direct way that leaves all who encounter this work changed for good. For her, poets are:

> The only truth-tellers now left to God,
> The only speakers of essential truth,
> Opposed to relative, comparative
> And temporal truths . . .

> [The poet] says the word so that it
>   burns you through
> With a special revelation, shakes the
>   heart
> Of all the men and women in the
>   world. . . .
> (Aurora Leigh, i, 859–62; 905–7)

Lady Geraldine's Courtship
(lines 22; 229–32)

In nympholeptic climbing, poets pass from mount
    to star . . .'

. . . The book lay open, and my thoughts flew from
    it, taking from it
A vibration and impulsion to an end beyond its
    own,
As the branch of a green osier, when a child would
    overcome it,

Springs up freely from his claspings and goes
    swinging in the sun.

Sonnets from the Portuguese: XIV

Say over again, and yet once over again.
That thou dost love me. Though the word repeated
Should seem a cuckoo-song, as thou dost treat it.
Remember never to the hill or plain.
Valley and wood, without her cuckoo-strain
Comes the fresh Spring in all her green completed!
Beloved, I, amid the darkness greeted
By a doubtful spirit-voice, in that doubt's pain
Cry . . . speak once more . . . thou lovest! Who can
    fear
Too many stars, though each in heaven shall roll –
Too many flowers, though each shall crown the
    year?
Say thou dost love me, love me, love me – toll
The silver iterance! – only minding, Dear.
To love me also in silence, with thy soul.

Aurora Leigh
(lines 437–44)

. . . You forget too much
That every creature, female as the male.
Stands single in responsible act and thought
As also in birth and death. Whoever says
To a loyal woman, 'Love and work with me.'
Will get fair answers if the work and love
Being good themselves, are good for her – the best
She was born for . . .

The Cry of the Children
(lines 141–2)

. . . the child a sob in the silence curses deeper
Than the strong man in his wrath'.

Sonnets from the Portuguese: X

Yet love, mere love, is beautiful indeed
And worthy of acceptation. Fire is bright,
Let temple burn, or flax. An equal light
Leaps in the flame from cedar-plank or weed.
And love is fire; and when I say at need
I love thee . . . mark! *I love thee . . .* in thy sight
I stand transfigured, glorified aright,
With conscience of the new rays that proceed
Out of my face toward thine. There's nothing low
In love, when love the lowest: meanest creatures
Who love God, God accepts while loving so.
And what I *feel*, across the inferior features
Of what I *am*, doth flash itself, and show
How that great work of Love enhances Nature's.

A Prospect of Florence

(lines 1–2; 10–20)

I found a house at Florence on the hill
Of Bellosguardo

[. . .]

No sun could die nor yet be born unseen
By dwellers at my villa: morn and eve
Were magnified before us in the pure
Illimitable space and pause of sky,
Intense as angels' garments blanched with God,
Less blue than radiant. From the outer wall
Of the garden, drops the mystic floating grey
Of olive trees (with interruptions green
From maise and vine), until 'tis caught and torn
Upon the abrupt black line of cypresses
Which signs the way to Florence . . .

Grief

I tell you, hopeless grief is passionless;
That only men incredulous of despair,
Half-taught in anguish, through the mid-night air
Beat upward to God's throne in loud access
Of shrieking and reproach. Full desertness
In souls as countries, lieth silent-bare
Under the blanching, vertical eye-glare

Of the absolute Heavens. Deep-hearted man, express
Grief for the Dead in silence like to death –
Most like a monumental statue set
In everlasting watch and moveless woe,
Till itself crumble to the dust beneath.
Touch it; the marble eyelids are not wet.
If it could weep, it could arise and go.

The Soul's Expression

With stammering lips and insufficient sound
I strive and struggle to deliver right
That music of my nature, day and night
With dream and thought and feeling interwound,
And inly answering all the senses round
With octaves of a mystic depth and height
Which step out grandly to the infinite
From the dark edges of the sensual ground.
This song of soul I struggle to outbear
Through portals of the sense, sublime and whole,
And utter all myself into the air;
But if I did it, – as the thunder-roll
Breaks its own cloud, my flesh would perish there
Before that dread apocalypse of soul.

Life

Each creature holds an insular point in space;
Yet what man stirs a finger, breathes a sound,
But all the multitudinous beings round
In all the countless worlds with time and place
For their conditions, down to the central base,
Thrill, haply, in vibration and rebound,
Life answering life across the vast profound,
In full antiphony, by a common grace?
I think this sudden joyaunce which illumes
A child's mouth sleeping, unaware may run
From some soul newly loosened from earth's tombs:
I think this passionate sigh, which half-begun
I stifle back, may reach and stir the plumes
Of God's calm angel standing in the sun.

The antique tapestries of Robert Browning (1812–89) figure a world of scoundrels, poisoners, ambitious painters, greedy bishops terrified of dying, jealous lovers devoured by longing. The fact that this universe is historical points to a chilly sense of mortality; the speakers of these tales, the hands that wove this luscious fabric lie, now, in darkness and silence. If 'A Toccata of Galuppi's' underlines the futility of art, indeed of all human endeavours and follies, then 'Fra Lippo Lippi' offers us another vision altogether of what art might accomplish. 'Make them forget there's such a thing as flesh. / Your business is to paint the souls of men...' say the learned religious to the painter, but Lippi – and Browning – know better: 'The world's no blot for us, / Nor blank; it means intensely, and means good...'

Painter and poet's credo is the revelation of world as it is, of soul-in-the-world; meaning resides in us, the craven and corruptible. Even the rats in 'The Pied Piper of Hamelin, A Child's Story', follow a tempting vision of fulfilled desire to their watery grave. Though one stout rodent author, who cherishes his manuscript, lives to sing the tale: a figure of the poet as one among his fellow rats, we who occupy the imperfect realm of intense meaning. 'The beauty and the wonder and the power,' Lippo tells us, 'God made it all! – For what?' To be 'dwelt upon' is the surprising and affirmative answer. The world's to be lived in, considered, and represented, by we who cannot reproduce such perfection, but are ourselves imperfect, consumed and consuming, inextricable from history, implicated in the human narrative of desire.

A TOCCATA OF GALUPPI'S

◄ I ►

Oh, Galuppi, Baldassaro, this is very sad to find!
I can hardly misconceive you; it would prove me
    deaf and blind;
But although I take your meaning, 'tis with such a
    heavy mind!

◄ II ►

Here you come with your old music, and here's all
    the good it brings.
What, they lived once thus at Venice where the
    merchants were the kings,
Where St. Mark's is, where the Doges used to wed
    the sea with rings?

◄ III ►

Ay, because the sea's the street there; and 'tis arched
    by ... what you call
... Shylock's bridge with houses on it, where they
    kept the carnival:
I was never out of England – it's as if I saw it all!

◄ IV ►

Did young people take their pleasure when the sea
    was warm in May?
Balls and masks begun at midnight, burning ever to
    mid-day
When they made up fresh adventures for the
    morrow, do you say?

◄ V ►

Was a lady such a lady, cheeks so round and lips so
    red, –
On her neck the small face buoyant, like a bell-
    flower on its bed,
O'er the breast's superb abundance where a man
    might base his head?

◄ VI ►

Well, (and it was graceful of them) they'd break talk
    off and afford
– She, to bite her mask's black velvet, he, to finger
    on his sword,
While you sat and played Toccatas, stately at the
    clavichord?

◄ VII ►

What? Those lesser thirds so plaintive, sixths
    diminished, sigh on sigh,

Told them something? Those suspensions, those
    solutions – 'Must we die?'
Those commiserating sevenths – 'Life might last! we
    can but try!'

◄ VIII ►

'Were you happy?' – 'Yes.' – 'And are you still as
    happy?' – 'Yes. And you?'
– 'Then, more kisses!' – 'Did I stop them, when a
    million seemed so few?'
Hark! the dominant's persistence, till it must be
    answered to!

◄ IX ►

So an octave struck the answer. Oh, they praised
    you, I dare say!
'Brave Galuppi! that was music! good alike at grave
    and gay!
I can always leave off talking, when I hear a master
    play.'

◄ X ►

Then they left you for their pleasure: till in due
    time, one by one,
Some with lives that came to nothing, some with
    deeds as well undone,
Death came tacitly and took them where they never
    see the sun.

◄ XI ►

But when I sit down to reason, think to take my
    stand nor swerve,
While I triumph o'er a secret wrung from nature's
    close reserve,
In you come with your cold music, till I creep thro'
    every nerve.

◄ XII ►

Yes, you, like a ghostly cricket, creaking where a
    house was burned –
'Dust and ashes, dead and done with, Venice spent
    what Venice earned!
The soul, doubtless, is immortal – where a soul can
    be discerned.

◄ XIII ►

'Yours for instance, you know physics, something of
    geology,
Mathematics are your pastime; souls shall rise in
    their degree;

Butterflies may dread extinction, – you'll not die, it
    cannot be!

◄ XIV ►

'As for Venice and its people merely born to bloom
    and drop,
Here on earth they bore their fruitage, mirth and
    folly were the crop:
What of soul was left I wonder, when the kissing
    had to stop?

◄ XV ►

'Dust and ashes!' So you creak it, and I want the
    heart to scold.
Dear dead women, with such hair, too – what's
    become of all the gold
Used to hang and brush their bosoms? I feel chilly
    and grown old.

FRA LIPPO LIPPI

I am poor brother Lippo, by your leave!
You need not clap your torches to my face.
Zooks, what's to blame? you think you see a monk!
What, it's past midnight, and you go the rounds,
And here you catch me at an alley's end
Where sportive ladies leave their doors ajar?
The Carmine's my cloister: hunt it up,
Do, – harry out, if you must show your zeal,
Whatever rat, there, haps on his wrong hole,
And nip each softling of a wee white mouse,
Weke, weke, that's crept to keep him company!
Aha, you know your betters? Then, you'll take
Your hand away that's fiddling on my throat,
And please to know me likewise. Who am I?
Why, one, sir, who is lodging with a friend
Three streets off – he's a certain . . . how d'ye call?
Master – a . . . Cosimo of the Medici,
In the house that caps the corner. Boh! you were
    best!
Remember and tell me, the day you're hanged,
How you affected such a gullet's-gripe!
But you, sir, it concerns you that your knaves
Pick up a manner nor discredit you.
Zooks, are we pilchards, that they sweep the streets
And count fair prize what comes into their net?
He's Judas to a tittle, that man is!
Just such a face! why, sir, you make amends.

Lord. I'm not angry! Bid your hangdogs go
Drink out this quarter-florin to the health
Of the munificent House that harbours me
(And many more beside, lads! more beside!)
And all's come square again. I'd like his face –
His elbowing on his comrade in the door
With the pike and lantern, – for the slave that holds
John Baptist's head a-dangle by the hair
With one hand ('look you, now,' as who should say)
And his weapon in the other, yet unwiped!
It's not your chance to have a bit of chalk,
A wood-coal or the like? or you should see!
Yes, I'm the painter, since you style me so.
What, brother Lippo's doings, up and down,
You know them and they take you? like enough!
I saw the proper twinkle in your eye –
'Tell you, I liked your looks at very first.
Let's sit and set things straight now, hip to haunch.
Here's spring come, and the nights one makes up
    bands
To roam the town and sing out carnival,
And I've been three weeks shut within my mew,
A-painting for the great man, saints and saints
And saints again. I could not paint all night –
Ouf! I leaned out of window for fresh air.
There came a hurry of feet and little feet,
A sweep of lute-strings, laughs, and whiffs of
    song, –
Flower o' the broom,
Take away love, and our earth is a tomb!
Flower o' the quince,
I let Lisa go, and what good's in life since?
Flower o' the thyme – and so on. Round they went.
Scarce had they turned the corner when a titter
Like the skipping of rabbits by moonlight, – three
    slim shapes –
And a face that looked up . . . zooks, sir, flesh and
    blood,
That's all I'm made of! Into shreds it went,
Curtain and counterpane and coverlet,
All the bed-furniture – a dozen knots.
There was a ladder! down I let myself,
Hands and feet, scrambling somehow. and so
    dropped,
And after them. I came up with the fun
Hard by Saint Laurence, hail fellow, well met, –
Flower o' the rose,
If I've been merry, what matter who knows?
And so as I was stealing back again
To get to bed and have a bit of sleep
Ere I rise up to-morrow and go work

On Jerome knocking at his poor old breast
With his great round stone to subdue the flesh,
You snap me of the sudden. Ah, I see!
Though your eye twinkles still you shake your
    head –
Mine's shaved, – a monk, you say – the sting's in
    that!
If Master Cosimo announced himself
Mum's the word naturally; but a monk!
Come, what am I a beast for? tell us, now!
I was a baby when my mother died
And father died and left me in the street.
I starved there, God knows how, a year or two
On fig skins, melon-parings, rinds and shucks,
Refuse and rubbish. One fine frosty day
My stomach being empty as your hat,
The wind doubled me up and down I went.
Old Aunt Lapaccia trussed me with one hand,
(Its fellow was a stinger as I knew)
And so along the wall, over the bridge,
By the straight cut to the convent. Six words, there,
While I stood munching my first bread that month:
'So, boy, you're minded,' quoth the good fat father
Wiping his own mouth, 'twas refection-time, –
'To quit this very miserable world?
Will you renounce' . . . The mouthful of bread?
    thought I;
By no means! Brief, they made a monk of me;
I did renounce the world, its pride and greed,
Palace, farm, villa, shop and banking-house,
Trash, such as these poor devils of Medici
Have given their hearts to – all at eight years old.
Well, sir, I found in time, you may be sure,
'Twas not for nothing – the good bellyful,
The warm serge and the rose that goes all round,
And day-long blessed idleness beside!
'Let's see what the urchin's fit for' – that came next.
Not overmuch their way, I must confess.
Such a to-do! they tried me with their books.
Lord, they'd have taught me Latin in pure waste!
Flower o' the clove
All the Latin I construe is, 'amo' I love!
But, mind you, when a boy starves in the streets
Eight years together, as my fortune was,
Watching folk's faces to know who will fling
The bit of half-stripped grape-bunch he desires,
And who will curse or kick him for his pains –
Which gentleman processional and fine,
Holding a candle to the Sacrament
Will wink and let him lift a plate and catch
The droppings of the wax to sell again,

Or holla for the Eight and have him whipped, –
How say I? – nay, which dog bites, which lets drop
His bone from the heap of offal in the street, –
Why, soul and sense of him grow sharp alike,
He learns the look of things, and none the less
For admonitions from the hunger-pinch.
I had a store of such remarks be sure,
Which, after I found leisure, turned to use:
I drew men's faces on my copy-books,
Scrawled them within the antiphonary's marge,
Joined legs and arms to the long music-notes,
Found nose and eyes and chin for A.s and B.s.
And made a string of pictures of the world
Betwixt the ins and outs of verb and noun,
On the wall, the bench, the door. The monks
    looked black
'Nay,' quoth the Prior, 'turn him out, d ye say?
In no wise. Lose a crow and catch a lark.
What if at last we get our man of parts.
We Carmelites, like those Camaldolese
And Preaching Friars, to do our church up fine
And put the front on it that ought to be!'
And hereupon they bade me daub away.
Thank you! my head being crammed, their walls a
    blank,
Never was such prompt disemburdening.
First, every sort of monk, the black and white,
I drew them, fat and lean: then, folks at church,
From good old gossips waiting to confess
Their cribs of barrel-droppings, candle-ends, –
To the breathless fellow at the altar-foot,
Fresh from his murder, safe and sitting there
With the little children round him in a row
Of admiration, half for his beard and half
For that white anger of his victim's son
Shaking a fist at him with one fierce arm,
Signing himself with the other because of Christ
(Whose sad face on the cross sees only this
After the passion of a thousand years)
Till some poor girl, her apron o'er her head
Which the intense eyes looked through, came at eve
On tip-toe, said a word, dropped in a loaf,
Her pair of earrings and a bunch of flowers
The brute took growling, prayed, and then was
    gone.
I painted all, then cried "tis ask and have –
Choose, for more's ready!' – laid the ladder flat,
And showed my covered bit of cloister-wall.
The monks closed in a circle and praised loud
Till checked, – taught what to see and not to see,
Being simple bodies, – 'that's the very man!

Look at the boy who stoops to pat the dog!
That woman's like the Prior's niece who comes
To care about his asthma: it's the life!'
But there my triumph's straw-fire flared and
    funked –
Their betters took their turn to see and say:
The Prior and the learned pulled a face
And stopped all that in no time. 'How? what's here?
Quite from the mark of painting, bless us all!
Faces, arms, legs and bodies like the true
As much as pea and pea! it's devil's-game!
Your business is not to catch men with show,
With homage to the perishable clay,
But lift them over it, ignore it all,
Make them forget there's such a thing as flesh.
Your business is to paint the souls of men –
Man's soul, and it's a fire, smoke . . . no it's not . . .
It's vapour done up like a new-born babe –
(In that shape when you die it leaves your mouth)
It's . . . well, what matters talking it's the soul!
Give us no more of body than shows soul!
Here's Giotto, with his Saint a-praising God,
That sets you praising, – why not stop with him?
Why put all thoughts of praise out of our heads
With wonder at lines, colours and what not?
Paint the soul, never mind the legs and arms!
Rub all out, try at it a second time.
Oh, that white smallish female with the breasts,
She's just my niece . . . Herodias I would say, –
Who went and danced and got men's heads cut off –
Have it all out!' Now, is this sense I ask?
A fine way to paint soul by painting body
So ill, the eye can't stop there, must go further
And can't fare worse! Thus, yellow does for white
When what you put for yellow's simply black,
And any sort of meaning looks intense
When all beside itself means and looks nought.
Why can't a painter lift each foot in turn,
Left foot and right foot, go a double step,
Make his flesh liker and his soul more like,
Both in their order? Take the prettiest face,
The Prior a niece . . . patron-saint – is it so pretty
You can't discover if it means hope, fear,
Sorrow or joy? won't beauty go with these?
Suppose I've made her eyes all right and blue,
Can't I take breath and try to add life's flash,
And then add soul and heighten them threefold?
Or say there's beauty with no soul at all –
(I never saw it – put the case the same –)
If you get simple beauty and nought else,
You get about the best thing God invents, –

That's somewhat. And you'll find the soul you have
    missed,
Within yourself when you return Him thanks,
'Rub all out!' Well, well, there's my life, in short.
And so the thing has gone on ever since.
I'm grown a man no doubt, I've broken bounds –
You should not take a fellow eight years old
And make him swear to never kiss the girls.
I'm my own master, paint now as I please –
Having a friend, you see, in the Corner-house!
Lord, it's fast holding by the rings in front –
Those great rings serve more purposes than just
To plant a flag in, or tie up a horse!
And yet the old schooling sticks, the old grave eyes
Are peeping o'er my shoulder as I work,
The heads shake still – 'It's Art's decline, my son!
You're not of the true painters, great and old;
Brother Angelico's the man, you'll find;
Brother Lorenzo stands his single peer:
Fag on at flesh, you'll never make the third!'
Flower o' the pine,
You keep your mistr . . . manners, and I'll stick to mine!
I'm not the third, then: bless us, they must know!
Don't you think they're the likeliest to know,
They with their Latin? so, I swallow my rage,
Clench my teeth, suck my lips in tight, and paint
To please them – sometimes do, and sometimes
    don't.
For, doing most, there's pretty sure to come
A turn, some warm eve finds me at my saints –
A laugh, a cry, the business of the world –
(*Flower o' the peach,*
Death for us all, and his own life for each!)
And my whole soul revolves, the cup runs over,
The world and life's too big to pass for a dream,
And I do these wild things in sheer despite,
And play the fooleries you catch me at,
In pure rage! the odd mill-horse, out at grass
After hard years, throws up his stiff heels so,
Although the miller does not preach to him
The only good of grass is to make chaff.
What would men have? Do they like grass or no –
Slay they or mayn't they? all I want's the thing
Settled for ever one way: as it is,
You tell too many lies and hurt yourself.
You don't like what you only like too much,
You do like what, if given you at your word,
You find abundantly detestable.
For me, I think I speak as I was taught –
I always see the Garden and God there
A-making man's wife – and, my lesson learned,

The value and significance of flesh,
I can't unlearn ten minutes afterwards.

    You understand me: I'm a beast, I know.
But see, now – why, I see as certainly
As that the morning-star's about to shine,
What will hap some day. We've a youngster here
Comes to our convent, studies what I do,
Slouches and stares and lets no atom drop –
His name is Guidi – he'll not mind the monks –
They call him Hulking Tom, he lets them talk –
He picks my practice up – he'll paint apace,
I hope so – though I never live so long,
I know what's sure to follow. You be judge!
You speak no Latin more than I, belike –
However, you're my man, you've seen the world
– The beauty and the wonder and the power,
The shapes of things, their colours, lights and
    shades,
Changes, surprises, – and God made it all!
For what? do you feel thankful, ay or no,
For this fair town's face, yonder river's line,
The mountain round it and the sky above,
Much more the figures of man, woman, child,
These are the frame to? What's it all about?
To be passed over, despised? or dwelt upon,
Wondered at? oh, this last of course! – you say.
But why not do as well as say, – paint these
Just as they are, careless what comes of it?
God's works – paint anyone, and count it crime
To let a truth slip. Don't object, 'His works
Are here already – nature is complete:
Suppose you reproduce her – (which you can't)
There's no advantage! you must beat her, then.'
For, don't you mark, we're made so that we love
First when we see them painted, things we have
    passed
Perhaps a hundred times nor cared to see;
And so they are better, painted – better to us,
Which is the same thing. Art was given for that –
God uses us to help each other so,
Lending our minds out. Have you noticed, now,
Your cullion's hanging face? A bit of chalk,
And trust me but you should, though! How much
    more
If I drew higher things with the same truth!
That were to take the Prior's pulpit-place,
Interpret God to all of you! oh, oh,
It makes me mad to see what men shall do
And we in our graves! This world's no blot for us,
Nor blank – it means intensely, and means good:

To find its meaning is my meat and drink.
'Ay, but you don't so instigate to prayer!'
Strikes in the Prior: 'when your meaning's plain
It does not say to folks – remember matins,
Or, mind you fast next Friday.' Why, for this
What need of art at all? A skull and bones,
Two bits of stick nailed cross-wise, or, what's best,
A bell to chime the hour with, does as well.
I painted a Saint Laurence six months since
At Prato, splashed the fresco in fine style:
'How looks my painting, now the scaffold's down?'
I ask a brother: 'Hugely,' he returns –
'Already not one phiz of your three slaves
That turn the Deacon off his toasted side,
But's scratched and prodded to our heart's content,
The pious people have so eased their own
When coming to say prayers there in a rage:
We get on fast to see the bricks beneath.
Expect another job this time next year,
For pity and religion grow i' the crowd –
Your painting serves its purpose!' Hang the fools!

   – That is – you'll not mistake an idle word
Spoke in a huff by a poor monk, God wot,
Tasting the air this spicy night which turns
The unaccustomed head like Chianti wine!
Oh, the church knows! don't misreport me, now!
It's natural a poor monk out of bounds
Should have his apt word to excuse himself:
And hearken how I plot to make amends.
I have bethought me: I shall paint a piece
. . . There's for you! Give me six months, then go,
   see
Something in Sant' Ambrogio's! Bless the nuns!
They want a cast of my office. I shall paint
God in the midst, Madonna and her babe,
Ringed by a bowery, flowery angel-brood,
Lilies and vestments and white faces, sweet
As puff on puff of grated orris-root
When ladies crowd to church at mid-summer.
And then in the front, of course a saint or two –
Saint John, because he saves the Florentines,
Saint Ambrose, who puts down in black and white
The convent's friends and gives them a long day,
And Job, I must have him there past mistake,
The man of Uz, (and Us without the z,
Painters who need his patience.) Well, all these
Secured at their devotions, up shall come
Out of a corner when you least expect,
As one by a dark stair into a great light,
Music and talking, who but Lippo! I! –

Mazed, motionless and moon-struck – I'm the man!
Back I shrink – what is this I see and hear?
I, caught up with my monk's things by mistake,
My old serge gown and rope that goes all round,
I, in this presence, this pure company!
Where's a hole, where's a corner for escape?
Then steps a sweet angelic slip of a thing
Forward, puts out a soft palm – 'Not so fast!'
– Addresses the celestial presence, 'nay –
He made you and devised you, after all,
Though he's none of you! Could Saint John there,
   draw –
His camel-hair make up a painting-brush?
We come to brother Lippo for all that,
Iste perfecit opus!' So, all smile –
I shuffle sideways with my blushing face
Under the cover of a hundred wings
Thrown like a spread of kirtles when you're gay
And play hot cockles, all the doors being shut,
Till, wholly unexpected, in there pops
The hothead husband! Thus I scuttle off
To some safe bench behind, not letting go
The palm of her, the little lily thing
That spoke the good word for me in the nick,
Like the Prior's niece . . . Saint Lucy, I would say.
And so all's saved for me, and for the church
A pretty picture gained. Go, six months hence!
Your hand, sir, and good-bye: no lights, no lights!
The street's hushed, and I know my own way back
Don't fear me! There's the grey beginning. Zooks!

THE PIED PIPER OF HAMELIN

‹ VII ›

Into the street the Piper stept,
   Smiling first a little smile,
As if he knew what magic slept
   In his quiet pipe the while;
Then, like a musical adept,
To blow the pipe his lips he wrinkled,
And green and blue his sharp eyes twinkled
Like a candle-flame where salt is sprinkled;
And ere three shrill notes the pipe uttered,
You heard as if an army muttered;
And the muttering grew to a grumbling;
And the grumbling grew to a mighty rumbling;
And out of the houses the rats came tumbling.
Great rats, small rats, lean rats, brawny rats,

Brown rats, black rats, grey rats, tawny rats,
Grave old plodders, gay young friskers,
   Fathers, mothers, uncles, cousins,
Cocking tails and pricking whiskers,
   Families by tens and dozens,
Brothers, sisters, husbands, wives –
Followed the Piper for their lives.
From street to street he piped advancing,
And step for step they followed dancing,
Until they came to the river Weser
Wherein all plunged and perished!
– Save one who, stout as Julius Cæsar,
Swam across and lived to carry
(As he, the manuscript he cherished)
To Rat-land home his commentary:
Which was, 'At the first shrill notes of the pipe,
I heard a sound as of scraping tripe,
And putting apples, wondrous ripe,
Into a cider-press's gripe:
And a moving away of pickle-tubboards,
And a leaving ajar of conserve-cupboards,
And a drawing the corks of train-oil-flasks,
And a breaking the hoops of butter-casks;
And it seemed as if a voice
(Sweeter far than by harp or by psaltery
Is breathed) called out, Oh rats, rejoice!
The world is grown to one vast dry-saltery!
So, munch on, crunch on, take your nuncheon,
Breakfast, supper, dinner, luncheon!
And just as a bulky sugar-puncheon,
All ready staved, like a great sun shone
Glorious scarce an inch before me,
Just as methought it said, Come, bore me!
– I found the Wester rolling o'er me.'

❧

MEMORABILIA

◄ I ►
Ah, did you once see Shelley plain,
   And did he stop and speak to you
And did you speak to him again?
   How strange it seems and new!

◄ II ►
But you were living before that,
   And also you are living after;
And the memory I started at –
   My starting moves your laughter.

◄ III ►
I crossed a moor, with a name of its own
   And a certain use in the world no doubt,
Yet a hand's-breadth of it shines alone
   'Mid the blank miles round about:

◄ IV ►
For there I picked up on the heather
   And there I put inside my breast
A moulted feather, an eagle-feather!
   Well, I forget the rest.

❧

MY STAR

     All that I know
     Of a certain star
     Is, it can throw
       (Like the angled spar)
     Now a dart of red,
       Now a dart of blue;
     Till my friends have said
       They would fain see, too,
My star that dartles the red and the blue!
Then it stops like a bird; like a flower, hangs furled:
   They must solace themselves with the Saturn
     above it.
What matter to me if their star is a world?
   Mine has opened its soul to me; therefore I love
     it.

Recently, a prominent Labour MP, column-ist and would-be littérateur declared that, among their other national delusions, the Scots still believed Robert Burns to be a poet. It's hard to imagine anyone saying the same of Keats and thinking they might get away with it, and a measure of just how far Burns's stock has fallen. The Scots, though, have managed his estate badly, over-prizing the songs and the narratives at the expense of the satirical and polemical work, and presenting even the best of *those* as tea-towel and shortie-tin kitsch.

RLS disparaged Burns's lyric-writing and collecting (the occupation that filled most of his later years) as 'whittling cherry-stones' – too dismissively, since some of the lyrics are among the finest in the language. They're still better sung, so of the pure lyrics only the peerless 'Ae fond Kiss' appears here. 'Now Westlin' Winds' ('Song Composed in August') is somewhere between: but it still stands up as a fine poem, even if you don't know the tune. If the lyrics suffer from not being sung, the long narrative poems would suffer far more from selective quotation, which is why *Tam O'Shanter* isn't here. So I've chosen from the satires – the hilarious 'Holy Willie's Prayer', and a quick epitaph; the letters – one of the brilliantly extemporised 'Epistles to J. Lapraik'; the great apostrophes – my own personal favourite, the grimly pessimistic 'To a Mountain Daisy'; and finally the superb 'Address to the Unco Guid,' the last verse of which is less well known than the penultimate, but whose immaculate music leaves you in no doubt as to the order of Burns's talent.

Robert Burns (1759–96) saw his political, moral and aesthetic responses to the world as perfectly coterminous, and often consub-stantial, in a way that seems alien to us today: but his is the attitude we must re-embrace if poetry is going to mean any-thing to anyone except its practitioners. And he was as good a poet as Keats, who would've told you the same.

AE FOND KISS

◄(Tune: Rory's Dall's Port)►

Ae fond kiss, and then we sever;
Ae farewell and then forever!
Deep in heart-wrung tears I'll pledge thee,
Warring sighs and groans I'll wage thee.

Who shall say that Fortune grieves him
While the star of hope she leaves him?
Me, nae cheerfu' twinkle lights me;
Dark despair around benights me.

I'll ne'er blame my partial fancy,
Naething could resist my Nancy!
But to see her, was to love her;
Love but her, and love for ever.

Had we never lov'd sae kindly,
Had we never lov'd sae blindly,
Never met – or never parted,
We had ne'er been broken-hearted.

Fare thee weel, thou first and fairest!
Fare thee weel, thou best and dearest!
Thine be ilka joy and treasure,
Peace, Enjoyment, Love and Pleasure!

Ae fond kiss, and then we sever;
Ae fareweel, Alas, for ever!
Deep in heart-wrung tears I'll pledge thee,
Warring sighs and groans I'll wage thee.

SECOND EPISTLE TO JOHN LAPRAIK

April 21st, 1785

While new-ca'd kye rowte at the stake,
An' pownies reek in pleugh or braik,
This hour on e'enin's edge I take,
        To own I'm debtor,
To honest-hearted, auld Lapraik,
        For his kind letter.

Forjesket sair, with weary legs,
Rattlin the corn out-owre the rigs,
Or dealing thro' amang the naigs
        Their ten-hours bite,
My awkart Muse sair pleads and begs,
        I would na write.

The tapetless, ramfeezl'd hizzie,
She's saft at best an' something lazy,
Quo' she, 'Ye ken we've been sae busy
This month an' mair,
That trowth, my head is grown right dizzie,
An' something sair.'

Her dowff excuses pat me mad;
'Conscience,' says I, 'ye thowless jad!
I'll write, an' that a hearty blaud,
This vera night;
So dinna ye affront your trade,
But rhyme it right.

'Shall bauld Lapraik, the king o' hearts,
Tho' mankind were a pack o' cartes,
Roose you see weel for your deserts,
In terms sae friendly,
Yet ye'll neglect to shaw your parts
An' thank him kindly?

Sae I get paper in a blink,
An, down gaed stumpie in the ink:
Quoth I, 'Before I sleep a wink,
I vow I'll close it;
An' if ye winna mak it clink,
By Jove, I'll prose it!'

Sae I've begun to scrawl, but whether
In rhyme, or prose, or bait thegither,
Or some hotch-potch that's rightly neither,
Let time mak proof;
But I shall scribble down some blether
Just clean aff-loof.

My worthy friend, ne'er grudge an' carp,
Tho' Fortune use you hard an' sharp;
Come, kittle up your moorlan harp
Wi' gleesome touch!
Ne'er mind how Fortune waft and warp;
She's but a bitch.

She's gien me monie a jirt an' fleg,
Sin' I could striddle owre a rig;
But by the Lord, tho' I should beg
Wi' lyart pow,
I'll laugh, an' sing, an' shake my leg,
As lang's I dow!

Now comes the sax an' twentieth simmer.
I've seen the bud upo' the timmer,

Still persecuted by the limmer
Frae year to year;
But yet, despite the kittle kimmer,
I, Rob, am here.

Do ye envy the city-gent,
Behint a kist to lie an' sklent,
Or, purse-proud, big wi' cent per cent,
An' muckle wame,
In some bit brugh to represent
A baillie's name?

Or is't the paughty, feudal thane,
Wi' ruffl'd sark an' glancin cane,
Wha thinks himsel nae sheep-shank bane
But lordly stalks;
While caps an' bonnets aff are taen,
As by he walks?

'O Thou wha gies us each guid gift!
Gie me o' wit an' sense a lift,
Then turn me, if Thou please, adrift,
Thro' Scotland wide;
Wi' *cits* nor *lairds* I wadna shift,
In a' their pride!'

Were this the charter o' our state,
'On pain o' hell be rich an' great,'
Damnation then would be our fate,
Beyond remead;
But, thanks to Heav'n, that's no the gate
We learn our creed.

For thus the royal Mandate ran,
When first the human race began,
'The social, friendly, honest man,
Whate'er he be,
'Tis he fulfils great Nature's plan,
And none but he.'

O Mandate, glorious and divine!
The followers o' the ragged Nine,
Poor, thoughtless devils! – yet may shine
In glorious light,
While sordid sons o' Mammon's line
Are dark as night!

Tho' here they scrape, an' squeeze, an' growl,
Their worthless nievefu' of a soul,
May in some future carcase howl,
The forest's fright;

Or in some day-detesting owl
      May shun the light.

Then may Lapraik and Burns arise,
To reach their native, kindred skies,
And sing their pleasures, hopes and joys,
      In some mild sphere,
Still closer knit in friendship's ties
      Each passing year!

TO A MOUNTAIN DAISY
ON TURNING ONE DOWN WITH THE
PLOUGH IN APRIL – 1786

Wee, modest, crimson-tippèd flow'r,
Thou's met me in an evil hour;
For I maun crush amang the stoure
      Thy slender stem:
To spare thee now is past my pow'r,
      Thou bonie gem.

Alas! it's no thy neebor sweet,
The bonie lark, companion meet!
Bending thee 'mang the dewy weet,
      Wi' speckl'd breast!
When upward-springing, blythe, to greet
      The purpling East.

Cauld blew the bitter-biting North
Upon thy early, humble birth;
Yet cheerfully thou glinted forth
      Amid the storm,
Scarce rear'd above the Parent-earth
      Thy tender form.

The flaunting flow'rs our gardens yield,
High-shelt'ring woods and wa's maun shield,
But thou, beneath the random bield
      O' clod or stane,
Adorns the histie stibble-field,
      Unseen, alane.

There, in thy scanty mantle clad,
Thy snawy bosom sun-ward spread,
Thou lifts thy unassuming head
      In humble guise;
But now the share uptears thy bed,
      And low thou lies!

Such is the fate of artless Maid,
Sweet flow'ret of the rural shade!
By love's simplicity betray'd,
      And guileless trust,
Till she, like thee, all soil'd, is laid
      Low i' the dust.

Such is the fate of simple Bard,
On life's rough ocean luckless starr'd!
Unskilful he to note the card
      Of prudent lore,
Till billows rage, and gales blow hard,
      And whelm him o'er!

Such fate to suff'ring worth is giv'n,
Who long with wants and woes has striv'n,
By human pride or cunning driv'n
      To mis'ry's brink,
Till wrench'd of every stay but Heav'n,
      He, ruin'd, sink!

Ev'n thou who mourn'st the Daisy's fate;
That fate is thine – no distant date;
Stern Ruin's plough-share drives, elate,
      Full on thy bloom,
Till crush'd beneath the furrow's weight,
      Shall be thy doom!

HOLY WILLIE'S PRAYER

'And send the Godly in a pet to pray – ' Pope

O Thou, wha in the heavens dost dwell,
Wha, as it pleases best thysel',
Sends ane to heaven and ten to hell,
      A' for thy glory,
And no for ony guid or ill
      They've done afore thee!

I bless and praise thy matchless might,
Whan thousands thou hast left in night,
That I am here afore thy sight,
      For gifts an' grace,
A burnin' an' a shinin' light,
      To a' this place.

What was I, or my generation,
That I should get such exaltation,

I wha deserve sic just damnation,
        For broken laws,
Five thousand years ere my creation,
        Thro' Adam's cause.

When frae my mither's womb I fell,
Thou might ha'e plunged me deep in hell,
To gnash my gums, to weep and wail,
        In burnin' lake,
Whar damnèd devils roar and yell,
        Chain'd to a stake.

Yet I am here a chosen sample,
To show thy grace is great an' ample;
I'm here a pillar in thy temple,
        Strong as a rock,
A guide, a buckler, an' example
        To a' thy flock.

But yet, O Lord! confess I must,
At times I'm fash'd wi' fleshly lust
An' sometimes too, wi' warldly trust,
        Vile self gets in;
But thou remembers we are dust,
        Defil'd in sin.

O Lord! yestreen, thou kens, wi' Meg –
Thy pardon I sincerely beg –
O may't ne'er be a living plague
        To my dishonor!
An' I'll ne'er lift a lawless leg
        Again upon her.

Besides, I farther maun avow –
Wi' Leezie's lass, three times, I trow –
But, Lord, that Friday I was fou,
        When I cam near her,
Or else, thou kens, thy servant true
        Wad never steer her.

Maybe thou lets this fleshly thorn
Buffet thy servant e'en and morn,
Lest he owre proud and high should turn
        That he's sae gifted:
If sae, thy han' maun e'en be borne
        Until thou lift it.

Lord, bless thy Chosen in this place,
For here thou has a chosen race!
But God confound their stubborn face
        An' blast their name,

Wha bring thy elders to disgrace
        An' open shame!

Lord mind Gau'n Hamilton's deserts:
He drinks, an' swears, an' plays at carts,
Yet has sae mony takin' arts,
        Wi' great an' sma',
Frae God's ain priest the people's hearts
        He steals awa'.

An' when we chasten'd him therefore,
Thou kens how he bred sic a splore,
As set the warld in a roar
        O laughin' at us;
Curse thou his basket and his store,
        Kail an' potatoes!

Lord hear my earnest cry an' pray'r
Against that presbyt'ry o'Ayr;
Thy strong right hand, Lord make it bare,
        Upo' their heads,
Lord weigh it down, and dinna spare,
        For their misdeeds.

O Lord my God, that glib-tongu'd Aiken,
My very heart an' soul are quakin',
To think how we stood, sweatin', shakin',
        An' pissed wi' dread,
While Auld wi' hingin lip gaed sneakin',
        And hid his head.

Lord in the day of vengeance try him,
Lord visit them wha did employ him,
And pass not in thy mercy by 'em,
        Nor hear their prayer;
But for thy people's sake destroy 'em,
        And dinna spare.

But Lord remember me and mine
Wi' mercies temp'ral and divine,
That I for gear and grace may shine,
        Excell'd by nane,
An' a' the glory shall be thine,
        Amen, Amen.

Address to the Unco Guid, or the Rigidly Righteous

My son, these maxims make a rule,
  And lump them ay thegither;
The Rigid Righteous is a fool,
  The Rigid Wise anither;
The cleanest corn that e'er was dight
  May hae some pyles o' caff in;
So ne'er a fellow-creature slight
  For random fits o' daffin.
        Solomon. – Eccles. 7:1–6

O ye wha are sae guid yoursel,
  Sae pious and sae holy,
Ye've nought to do but mark and tell
  Your neebours' fauts and folly!
Whase life is like a weel-gaun mill,
  Supply'd wi' store o' water,
The heaped happer's ebbing still,
  And still the clap plays clatter!

Hear me, ye venerable core,
  As counsel for poor mortals,
That frequent pass douce Wisdom's door
  For glaikit Folly's portals;
I, for their thoughtless, careless sakes
  Would here propone defences,
Their donsie tricks, their black mistakes,
  Their failings and mischances.

Ye see your state wi' theirs compar'd,
  And shudder at the niffer,
But cast a moment's fair regard
  What maks the mighty differ?
Discount what scant occasion gave,
  That purity ye pride in,
And (what's aft mair than a' the lave)
  Your better art o' hiding.

Think, when your castigated pulse
  Gies now and then a wallop,
What ragings must his veins convulse,
  That still eternal gallop!
Wi' wind and tide fair i' your tail,
  Right on ye scud your sea-way;
But in the teeth o' baith to sail,
  It maks an unco leeway.

See Social-life and Glee sit down,
  All joyous and unthinking,

Till, quite transmugrify'd, they're grown
  Debauchery and Drinking:
O would they stay to calculate
  Th' eternal consequences;
Or your more dreaded hell to state,
  Damnation of expences!

Ye high, exalted, virtuous Dames,
  Ty'd up in godly laces,
Before ye gie poor Frailty names,
  Suppose a change o' cases;
A dear-lov'd lad, convenience snug,
  A treacherous inclination –
But, let me whisper in your lug,
  Ye're aiblins nae temptation.

Then gently scan your brother Man,
  Still gentler sister Woman;
Tho' they may gang a kennin wrang,
  To step aside is human:
One point must still be greatly dark,
  The moving *why* they do it;
And just as lamely can ye mark,
  How far perhaps they rue it.

Who made the heart, 'tis He alone
  Decidedly can try us,
He knows each chord, its various tone,
  Each spring, its various bias:
Then at the balance let's be mute,
  We never can adjust it;
What's done we partly may compute,
  But know not what's resisted.

On a Suicide

Here lies in earth a root of Hell,
  Set by the Deil's ain dibble;
This worthless body damn'd himsel,
  To save the Lord the trouble.

SONG COMPOSED IN AUGUST

◄(Tunes: I had a Horse, I Had Nae Mair;
Port Gordon)►

Now westlin winds, and slaught'ring guns
  Bring Autumn's pleasant weather;
And the moorcock springs, on whirring wings,
  Amang the blooming heather:
Now waving grain, wide o'er the plain,
  Delights the weary farmer;
And the moon shines bright, when I rove at night,
  To muse upon my charmer.

The paitrick loves the fruitful fells;
  The plover loves the mountains;
The woodcock haunts the lonely dells;
  The soaring hern the fountains:
Thro' lofty groves, the cushat roves,
  The path of man to shun it;
The hazel bush o'erhangs the thrush,
  The spreading thorn the linnet.

Thus ev'ry kind their pleasure find,
  The savage and the tender;
Some social join, and leagues combine;
  Some solitary wander;
Avaunt, away! the cruel sway,
  Tyrannic man's dominion;
The sportsman's joy, the murd'ring cry,
  The flutt'ring, gory pinion!

But Peggy dear, the ev'ning's clear,
  Thick flies the skimming swallow;
The sky is blue, the fields in view,
  All fading-green and yellow:
Come let us stray our gladsome way,
  And view the charms of nature;
The rustling corn, the fruited thorn,
  And ilka happy creature.

We'll gently walk, and sweetly talk,
  Till the silent moon shine clearly;
I'll grasp thy waist, and fondly prest,
  Swear how I love thee dearly:
Not vernal show'rs to budding flow'rs,
  Not autumn to the farmer,
So dear can be, as thou to me,
  My fair, my lovely charmer!

Samuel Butler was born in 1612, son of a Worcestershire yeoman; he acquired erudition without benefit of university, and worked in a succession of posts as clerk or secretary to wealthy households. He was fifty when publication of the First Part of his satire upon Puritans *Hudibras* brought him fame, and entertained King Charles II, who however awarded the poet a small pension only three years before his death in 1680. It is known that he was married, but not to whom. While details of Butler's life are patchy, his trenchant values and attitudes proliferate in his poetry, his prose *Characters*, and observations in his commonplace books. He had a strongly empirical temper, was a rationalist scathing towards abuses of reason in the service of unverifiable dogma, and the delusive fancies of fanaticism. His pessimistic vision of human vice and folly has affinities with Ben Jonson before him, whom he admired, and Swift a generation later; but rather than the latter's savage indignation, Butler's characteristic mode is more purely comic: burlesque, parody and ridicule. Naturally his satire is rooted in the texture and details of the political and religious divisions that dominated the England he knew; but it is not confined by these, for his overriding target is the universal one of human hypocrisy; self-serving ideologues and canting pedants are always with us.

The farcical adventures and disputes of Butler's scholarly knight Hudibras and inwardly inspired squire Ralpho parody both epic and romance, the military and amorous ideals of which he thought fatuous; he precedes Dryden and Pope in making literary travesty a vehicle for moral satire. The gifts vivifying his contemptuous scepticism are agility of wit and diction, a command of deflating imagery drawn from life's commonplaces, and a rampant sense of the ludicrous. His vigour of invention allows epigram but lends itself best to cumulative effects. In the final excerpt from *Hudibras* I have chosen, the hero's philosophisings upon affliction are the more absurd because his specific 'durance' is to have been ignominiously drubbed and cast into the stock.

HUDIBRAS

‹First Part: Canto I›

(lines 187–234; 469–514)

For his religion it was fit
To match his learning and his wit:
'Twas Presbyterian true blue,
For he was of that stubborn crew
Of errant saints, whom all men grant
To be the true Church Militant:
Such as do build their faith upon
The holy text of pike and gun;
Decide all controversies by
Infallible artillery;
And prove their doctrine orthodox
By apostolic blows and knocks;
Call fire and sword and desolation,
A godly-thorough-reformation,
Which always must be carried on,
And still be doing, never done:
As if religion were intended
For nothing else but to be mended.
A sect, whose chief devotion lies
In odd perverse antipathies;
In falling out with that or this,
And finding somewhat still amiss:
More peevish, cross, and spleenatic,
Than dog distract, or monkey sick:
That with more care keep holy-day
The wrong, than others the right way:
Compound for sins, they are inclined to,
By damning those they have no mind to;
Still so perverse and opposite,
As if they worshipped God for spite.
The self-same thing they will abhor
One way, and long another for.
Free-will they one way disavow,
Another, nothing else allow.
All piety consists therein
In them, in other men all sin.
Rather than fail, they will defy
That which they love most tenderly,
Quarrel with minced pies, and disparage
Their best and dearest friend, plum-porridge;
Fat pig and goose itself oppose,
And blaspheme custard through the nose.
Th'apostles of this fierce religion,
Like Mahomet's, were Ass and Widgeon,
To whom our Knight by fast instinct
Of wit and temper was so linked,

As if hypocrisy and non-sense
Had got th'advowson of his Conscience.

[. . .]

This sturdy Squire had as well
As the bold Trojan knight, seen hell,
Not with a counterfeited pass
Of golden bough, but true gold-lace.
His knowledge was not far behind
The Knight's, but of another kind,
And he another way came by't:
Some call it gifts, and some new light;
A liberal art, that costs no pains
Of study, industry, or brains.
His wits were sent him for a token,
But in the carriage cracked and broken.
Like commendation nine-pence, crook'd
With to and from my love, it look'd.
He ne'er consider'd it, as loath
To look a gift-horse in the mouth;
And very wisely would lay forth
No more upon it than 'twas worth.
But as he got it freely, so
He spent it frank and freely too.
For saints themselves will sometimes be
Of gifts that cost them nothing, free.
By means of this, with hem and cough,
Prolongers to enlightned snuff,
He could deep mysteries unriddle,
As easily as thread a needle;
For as of vagabonds we say,
That they are ne'er beside their way:
Whate'er men speak by this new light,
Still they are sure to be i'th' right.
'Tis a dark-lanthorn of the spirit,
Which none see by but those that bear it:
A light that falls down from on high,
For spiritual trades to cozen by:
An *Ignis Fatuus*, that bewitches,
And leads men into pools and ditches,
To make them dip themselves, and sound
For Christendom in dirty pond;
To dive like wild-fowl for salvation,
And fish to catch regeneration.
This light inspires, and plays upon
The nose of saint, like bag-pipe drone,
And speaks through hollow empty soul,
As through a trunk, or whisp'ring hole,
Such language as no mortal ear
But spiritual eavesdroppers can hear.

‹ Second Part: Canto I ›

(lines 183–234; 255–66)

Quoth Hudibras, this thing call'd pain,
Is (as the learned Stoics maintain)
Not bad *simpliciter*, nor good,
But merely as 'tis understood.
Sense is deceitful, and may feign,
As well in counterfeiting pain
As other gross pháenomenas,
In which it oft mistakes the case.
But since th'immortal intellect
(That's free from error and defect,
(Whose objects still persist the same)
Is free from outward bruise or maim,
Which nought external can expose
To gross material bangs or blows:
It follows, we can ne'r be sure,
Whether we pain or not endure:
And just so far are sore and griev'd,
As by the Fancy is believ'd.
Some have been wounded with conceit,
And died of mere opinion straight;
Others, though wounded sore, in reason
Felt no contusion nor Discretion.

A Saxon duke did grow so fat,
That mice (as histories relate)
Eat grots and labyrinths to dwell in
His postique parts, without his feeling:
Then how is't possible a kick
Should e're reach that way to the quick?

Quoth she, I grant it is in vain,
For one that's basted, to feel pain;
Because the pangs his bones endure,
Contribute nothing to the Cure:
Yet honour hurt, is wont to rage
With pain no med'cine can assuage.

Quoth he, That honour's very squeemish
That takes a basting for a blemish:
For what's more honorable then scars,
Or skin to tatters rent in wars?
Some have been beaten, till they know
What wood a cudgel's of by th' blow;
Some kick'd, until they can feel whether
A shoe be Spanish or neats-leather:
And yet have met, after long running,
With some whom they have taught that cunning.
The furthest way about, t'orecome

In th'end does prove the nearest home;
By laws of learned duellists
They that are bruis'd with wood, or fists,
And think one beating may for once
Suffice, are cowards, and poltroons;
But if they dare engage t'a second,
They're stout and gallant fellows reckoned.

[…]

And though I'm now in durance fast,
By our own Party, basely cast,
Ransome, exchange, parole, refused,
And worse than by the enemy used;
In close catasta shut, past hope
Of wit, or valour, to elope.
As beards, the nearer that they tend
To th'earth, still grow more reverend:
And cannons shoot the higher pitches,
The lower we let down their breeches:
I'll make this low dejected fate
Advance me to a greater height.

'Mad, bad, and dangerous to know.' It might sound like a catchy slogan dreamed up by some modern advertising agency, but it was a phrase used to describe George Gordon, Lord Byron (1788–1824), and defines an image of him that still persists. Certainly Byron was no stranger to controversy and drama. Born to parents who separated two years later, he inherited his peerage after the death of his father, and enjoyed 'overnight success' with his book *Childe Harold's Pilgrimage*. After a scandalous affair, a failed marriage, financial chaos, and following the birth of his half-sister's daughter which was very probably Bryon's own child, he left England never to return. He died of a fever at the early age of 36, organizing military forces for Greek independence. The absence of a father figure and a physical deformity to one of his feet are often suggested as psychological motives behind his wild and erratic behaviour, as are accounts of unresolved sexual desires.

Byron's greatest poetic achievement is the unfinished epic *Don Juan*, a masterpiece of irony, comedy and passion, recalling the life and times of the infamous Spanish womanizer with his obvious resemblance to Byron himself. Written in the strict form of ottava rima, the tale spans almost 2,000 verses, with the rhymes ranging from the inspired to the hilarious. Amongst his contemporaries, only Byron could interrupt a delicate romantic scene with the arrival in a poem of fried eggs and coffee.

Some of Byron's longer work tends to be operatic, i.e. ordinary passages making the good bits seem better. A further criticism levelled at his writing in general is that it offers many different views but no sustained or developing vision. Nevertheless, his shorter lyrics are clear and memorable, and there is a confidence – almost a fearlessness – to his narrative poetry that confirms him as a great story-teller.

Many later poets, either naturally or with the encouragement of their publicity departments, have attempted to adopt the Byronic persona, although the standard set by the man himself was so high that the archetype has pretty much resisted impersonation.

'SHE WALKS IN BEAUTY'

◄ I ►

She walks in beauty, like the night
   Of cloudless climes and starry skies;
And all that's best of dark and bright
   Meet in her aspect and her eyes:
Thus mellow'd to that tender light
   Which heaven to gaudy day denies.

◄ II ►

One shade the more, one ray the less,
   Had half impair'd the nameless grace
Which waves in every raven tress,
   Or softly lightens o'er her face;
Where thoughts serenely sweet express
   How pure, how dear their dwelling-place.

◄ III ►

And on that cheek, and o'er that brow,
   So soft, so calm, yet eloquent,
The smiles that win, the tints that glow,
   But tell of days in goodness spent,
A mind at peace with all below,
   A heart whose love is innocent!

'SO, WE'LL GO NO MORE A ROVING'

◄ I ►

So, we'll go no more a roving
   So late into the night,
Though the heart be still as loving,
   And the moon be still as bright.

◄ II ►

For the sword outwears its sheath,
   And the soul wears out the breast,
And the heart must pause to breathe,
   And love itself have rest.

◄ III ►

Though the night was made for loving,
   And the day returns too soon,
Yet we'll go no more a roving
   By the light of the moon.

On Finding a Fan

In one who felt as once he felt,
    This might, perhaps, have fann'ed the flame;
But now his heart no more will melt,
    Because that heart is not the same.

As when the ebbing flames are low,
    The aid which once improved their light,
And bade them burn with fiercer glow,
    Now quenches all their blaze in night.

Thus has it been with passion's fires –
    As many a boy and girl remembers –
While every hope of love expires,
    Extinguish'd with the dying embers.

The *first*, though not a spark survive,
    Some careful hand may teach to burn;
The *last*, alas! can ne'er survive;
    No touch can bid its warmth return.

Or if it chance to wake again,
    Not always doom'd its heat to smother,
It sheds (so wayward fates ordain)
    Its former warmth around another.

❧

The Chain I Gave

‹From the Turkish›

The chain I gave was fair to view,
    The lute I added sweet in sound;
The heart that offer'd both was true,
    And ill deserved the fate it found.

These gifts were charm'd by secret spell,
    Thy truth in absence to divine;
And they have done their duty well, –
    Alas! they could not teach thee thine.

That chain was firm in every link,
    But not to bear a stranger's touch;
That lute was sweet – till thou could'st think
    In other hands its notes were such.

Let him who from thy neck unbound
    The chain which shiver'd in his grasp,

Who saw that lute refuse to sound,
    Restring the chords, renew the clasp.

When thou wert changed, they alter'd too;
    The chain is broke, the music mute.
'Tis past – to them and thee adieu –
    False heart, frail chain, and silent lute.

❧

Don Juan

‹Canto I›

‹54›

Young Juan now was sixteen years of age,
    Tall, handsome, slender, but well knit; he seemed
Active, though not so sprightly as a page,
    And everybody but his mother deemed
Him almost man, but she flew in a rage
    And bit her lips (for else she might have
        screamed),
If any said so, for to be precocious
Was in her eyes a thing the most atrocious.

‹55›

Amongst her numerous acquaintance, all
    Selected for discretion and devotion,
There was the Donna Julia, whom to call
    Pretty were but to give a feeble notion
Of many charms in her as natural
    As sweetness to the flower or salt to ocean,
Her zone to Venus or his bow to Cupid,
But this last simile is trite and stupid.

‹56›

The darkness of her oriental eye
    Accorded with her Moorish origin.
Her blood was not all Spanish, by the by;
    In Spain, you know, this is a sort of sin.
When proud Granada fell, and forced to fly,
    Boabdil wept, of Donna Julia's kin
Some went to Africa, some stayed in Spain.
Her great-great-grandmamma chose to remain.

‹57›

She married (I forget the pedigree)
    With an hidalgo, who transmitted down
His blood less noble than such blood should be.
    At such alliances his sires would frown,

In that point so precise in each degree
    That they bred in and in, as might be shown,
Marrying their cousins, nay, their aunts and nieces,
Which always spoils the breed, if it increases.

<58>
This heathenish cross restored the breed again,
    Ruined its blood, but much improved its flesh,
For from a root the ugliest in old Spain
    Sprung up a branch as beautiful as fresh.
The sons no more were short, the daughters plain.
    But there's rumour which I fain would hush;
'Tis said that Donna Julia's grandmamma
Produced her Don more heirs at love than law.

<59>
However this might be, the race went on
    Improving still through every generation,
Until it centered in an only son,
    Who left an only daughter. My narration
May have suggested that this single one
    Could be but Julia (whom on this occasion
I shall have much to speak about), and she
Was married, charming, chaste, and twenty-three.

<60>
Her eye (I'm very fond of handsome eyes)
    Was large and dark, suppressing half its fire
Until she spoke; then through its soft disguise
    Flashed an expression more of pride than ire,
And love than either. And there would arise
    A something in them which was not desire,
But would have been, perhaps, but for the soul
Which struggled through and chastened down the
        whole.

<61>
Her glossy hair was clustered o'er a brow
    Bright with intelligence and fair and smooth.
Her eyebrow's shape was like the aerial bow,
    Her cheek all purple with the beam of youth,
Mounting at times to a transparent glow,
    As if her veins ran lightning. She in sooth
Possessed an air and grace by no means common;
Her stature tall – I hate a dumpy woman.

<62>
Wedded she was some years and to a man
    Of fifty, and such husbands are in plenty;
And yet I think instead of such a one
    'Twere better to have two of five and twenty,

Especially in countries near the sun.
    And now I think on't, *mi vien in mente*,
Ladies even of the most uneasy virtue
Prefer a spouse whose age is short of thirty.

<63>
'Tis a sad thing, I cannot choose but say,
    And all the fault of that indecent sun,
Who cannot leave alone our helpless clay,
    But will keep baking, broiling, burning on,
That howsoever people fast and pray
    The flesh is frail, and so the soul undone.
What men call gallantry, and gods adultery,
Is much more common where the climate's sultry.

<64>
Happy the nations of the moral north,
    Where all is virtue, and the winter season
Sends sin without a rag on shivering forth
    ('Twas snow that brought St Anthony to reason)
Where juries cast up what a wife is worth
    By laying whate'er sum in mulct they please on
The lover, who must pay a handsome price,
Because it is a marketable vice.

<65>
Alfonso was the name of Julia's lord,
    A man well looking for his years, and who
Was neither much beloved, nor yet abhorred.
    They lived together as most people do,
Suffering each other's foibles by accord,
    And not exactly either one or two.
Yet he was jealous, though he did not show it,
For jealousy dislikes the world to know it.

<66>
Julia was – yet I never could see why –
    With Donna Inez quite a favourite friend;
Between their tastes there was small sympathy,
    For not a line had Julia ever penned.
Some people whisper (but no doubt they lie,
    For malice still imputes some private end)
That Inez had, ere Don Alfonso's marriage,
Forgot with him her very prudent carriage,

<67>
And that still keeping up the old connexion,
    Which time had lately rendered much more
        chaste,
She took his lady also in affection
    And certainly this course was much the best.

She flattered Julia with her sage protection
    And complimented Don Alfonso's taste;
And if she could not (who can?) silence scandal,
    At least she left it a more slender handle.

‹68›
I can't tell whether Julia saw the affair
    With other people's eyes, or if her own
Discoveries made, but none could be aware
    Of this; at least no symptom e'er was shown.
Perhaps she did not know or did not care,
    Indifferent from the first or callous grown.
I'm really puzzled what to think or say,
She kept her counsel in so close a way.

‹69›
Juan she saw and as a pretty child,
    Caressed him often. Such a thing might be
Quite innocently done and harmless styled
    When she had twenty years, and thirteen he;
But I am not so sure I should have smiled
    When he was sixteen, Julia twenty-three.
These few short years make wondrous alterations,
Particularly amongst sunburnt nations.

‹70›
Whate'er the cause might be, they had become
    Changed, for the dame grew distant, the youth
      shy,
Their looks cast down, their greetings almost dumb,
    And much embarrassment in either eye.
There surely will be little doubt with some
    That Donna Julia knew the reason why,
But as for Juan, he had no more notion
Than he who never saw the sea of ocean.

‹71›
Yet Julia's very coldness still was kind,
    And tremulously gentle her small hand
Withdrew itself from his, but left behind
    A little pressure, thrilling and so bland
And slight, so very slight that to the mind
    'Twas but a doubt; but ne'er magician's wand
Wrought change with all Armida's fairy art
Like what this light touch left on Juan's heart.

‹72›
And if she met him, though she smiled no more,
    She looked a sadness sweeter than her smile,
As if her heart had deeper thoughts in store
    She must not own, but cherished more the while,

For that compression in its burning core.
    Even innocence itself has many a wile
And will not dare to trust itself with truth,
And love is taught hypocrisy from youth.

‹73›
But passion most dissembles yet betrays
    Even by its darkness; as the blackest sky
Foretells the heaviest tempest, it displays
    Its workings through the vainly guarded eye,
And in whatever aspect it arrays
    Itself, 'tis still the same hypocrisy.
Coldness or anger, even disdain or hate
Are masks it often wears, and still too late.

‹74›
Then there were sighs, the deeper for suppression,
    And stolen glances, sweeter for the theft,
And burning blushes, though for no transgression,
    Tremblings when met and restlessness when left.
All these are little preludes to possession,
    Of which young passion cannot be bereft,
And merely tend to show how greatly love is
Embarrassed at first starting with a novice.

‹75›
Poor Julia's heart was in an awkward state;
    She felt it going and resolved to make
The noblest efforts for herself and mate,
    For honour's, pride's, religion's, virtue's sake.
Her resolutions were most truly great
    And almost might have made a Tarquin quake.
She prayed the Virgin Mary for her grace,
As being the best judge of a lady's case.

‹76›
She vowed she never would see Juan more
    And next day paid a visit to his mother
And looked extremely at the opening door,
    Which by the Virgin's grace, let in another.
Grateful she was and yet a little sore.
    Again it opens, it can be no other,
'Tis surely Juan now. No, I'm afraid
That night the Virgin was no further prayed.

‹77›
She now determined that a virtuous woman
    Should rather face and overcome temptation,
That flight was base and dastardly, and no man
    Should ever give her heart the least sensation,
That is to say, a thought beyond the common

Preference, that we must feel upon occasion
For people who are pleasanter than others,
But then they only seem so many brothers.

◄78►
And even if by chance – and who can tell,
  The devil's so very sly – she should discover
That all within was not so very well,
  And if still free, that such or such a lover
Might please perhaps, a virtuous wife can quell
  Such thoughts and be the better when they're
    over.
And if the man should ask, 'tis but denial.
I recommend young ladies to make trial.

◄79►
And then there are such things as love divine,
  Bright and immaculate, unmixed and pure,
Such as the angels think so very fine,
  And matrons who would be no less secure,
Platonic, perfect, 'just such love as mine'.
  Thus Julia said and thought so, to be sure.
And so I'd have her think, were I the man
On whom her reveries celestial ran.

◄80►
Such love is innocent and may exist
  Between young persons without any danger;
A hand may first, and then a lip be kist.
  For my part, to such doings, I'm a stranger,
But hear these freedoms form the utmost list
  Of all o'er which such love may be a ranger.
If people go beyond, 'tis quite a crime,
But not my fault – I tell them all in time.

◄81►
Love then, but love within its proper limits
  Was Julia's innocent determination
In young Don Juan's favour; and to him its
  Exertion might be useful on occasion,
And lighted at too pure a shrine to dim its
  Ethereal lustre. With what sweet persuasion
He might be taught by love and her together,
I really don't know what, nor Julia either.

◄82►
Fraught with this fine intention and well fenced
  In mail of proof, her purity of soul,
She for the future of her strength convinced,
  And that her honour was a rock or mole,
Exceeding sagely from that hour dispensed

With any kind of troublesome control.
But whether Julia to the task was equal
Is that which must be mentioned in the sequel.

◄83►
Her plan she deemed both innocent and feasible,
  And surely with a stripling of sixteen
Not scandal's fangs could fix on much that's
    sizeable,
  Or if they did so, satisfied to mean
Nothing but what was good. Her breast was
    peaceable;
  A quiet conscience makes one so serene.
Christians have burnt each other, quite persuaded
That all the apostles would have done as they did.

◄84►
And if in the meantime her husband died,
  But heaven forbid that such a thought should
    cross
Her brain, though in a dream, and then she sighed.
  Never could she survive that common loss.
But just suppose that moment should betide,
  I only say suppose it *inter nos*.
(This should be *entre nous*, for Julia thought
In French, but then the rhyme would go for
    nought.)

◄85►
I only say suppose this supposition:
  Juan being then grown up to man's estate
Would fully suit a widow of condition.
  Even seven years hence it would not be too late,
And in the interim (to pursue this vision)
  The mischief after all could not be great,
For he would learn the rudiments of love
(I mean the seraph way of those above).

◄86►
So much for Julia; now we'll turn to Juan.
  Poor little fellow, he had no idea
Of his own case and never hit the true one.
  In feelings quick as Ovid's Miss Medea,
He puzzled over what he found, a new one,
  But not as yet imagined it could be a
Thing quite in course and not at all alarming,
Which with a little patience might grow charming.

◄87►
Silent and pensive, idle, restless, slow,
  His home deserted for the lonely wood,

Tormented with a wound he could not know,
  His, like all deep grief, plunged in solitude.
I'm fond myself of solitude or so,
  But then I beg it may be understood;
By solitude I mean a sultan's, not
  A hermit's, with a harem for a grot.

<88>

'Oh Love! in such a wilderness as this,
  Where transport and security entwine,
Here is the empire of thy perfect bliss,
  And here thou art a god indeed divine.'
The bard I quote from does not sing amiss,
  With the exception of the second line,
For that same twining 'transport and security'
Are twisted to a phrase of some obscurity.

<89>

The poet meant, no doubt, and thus appeals
  To the good sense and senses of mankind,
The very thing which everybody feels,
  As all have found on trial, or may find,
That no one likes to be disturbed at meals
  Or love. I won't say more about 'entwined'
Or 'transport', as we knew all that before,
But bet 'security' will bolt the door.

<90>

Young Juan wandered by the glassy brooks
  Thinking unutterable things. He threw
Himself at length within the leafy nooks
  Where the wild branch of the cork forest grew.
There poets find materials for their books,
  And every now and then we read them through,
So that their plan and prosody are eligible,
Unless like Wordsworth they prove unintelligible.

<91>

He, Juan (and not Wordsworth), so pursued
  His self-communion with his own high soul
Until his mighty heart in its great mood
  Had mitigated part, though not the whole
Of its disease. He did the best he could
  With things not very subject to control
And turned, without perceiving his condition,
Like Coleridge into a metaphysician.

<92>

He thought about himself and the whole earth,
  Of man the wonderful and of the stars
And how the deuce they ever could have birth,

And then he thought of earthquakes and of wars,
  How many miles the moon might have in girth,
  Of air balloons and of the many bars
To perfect knowledge of the boundless skies.
And then he thought of Donna Julia's eyes.

<93>

In thoughts like these true wisdom may discern
  Longings sublime and aspirations high,
Which some are born with, but the most part learn
  To plague themselves withal, they know not why.
'Twas strange that one so young should thus
    concern
  His brain about the action of the sky.
If you think 'twas philosophy that this did,
I can't help thinking puberty assisted.

<94>

He pored upon the leaves and on the flowers
  And heard a voice in all the winds; and then
He thought of wood nymphs and immortal bowers,
  And how the goddesses came down to men.
He missed the pathway, he forgot the hours,
  And when he looked upon his watch again,
He found how much old Time had been a winner.
He also found that he had lost his dinner.

<95>

Sometimes he turned to gaze upon his book,
  Boscán or Garcilasso. By the wind
Even as the page is rustled while we look,
  So by the poesy of his own mind
Over the mystic leaf his soul was shook,
  As if 'twere one whereon magicians bind
Their spells and give them to the passing gale,
According to some good old woman's tale.

<96>

Thus would he while his lonely hours away
  Dissatisfied, nor knowing what he wanted,
Nor glowing reverie nor poet's lay
  Could yield his spirit that for which it panted,
A bosom whereon he his head might lay
  And hear the heart beat with the love it granted,
With several other things, which I forget
Or which at least I need not mention yet.

<97>

Those lonely walks and lengthening reveries
  Could not escape the gentle Julia's eyes;
She saw that Juan was not at his ease.

But that which chiefly may, and must surprise
Is that the Donna Inez did not tease
    Her only son with question or surmise;
Whether it was she did not see, or would not,
Or like all very clever people, could not.

◄ 98 ►

This may seem strange, but yet 'tis very common;
    For instance, gentlemen, whose ladies take
Leave to o'erstep the written rights of woman
    And break the – which commandment is't they
    break?
I have forgot the number and think no man
    Should rashly quote for fear of a mistake.
I say, when these same gentlemen are jealous,
They make some blunder, which their ladies tell us.

◄ 99 ►

A real husband always is suspicious,
    But still no less suspects in the wrong place,
Jealous of someone who had no such wishes,
    Or pandering blindly to his own disgrace
By harbouring some dear friend extremely vicious.
    The last indeed's infallibly the case,
And when the spouse and friend are gone off
    wholly,
He wonders at their vice, and not his folly.

◄ 100 ►

Thus parents also are times shortsighted.
    Though watchful as the lynx, they ne'er discover,
The while the wicked world beholds delighted,
    Young Hopeful's mistress or Miss Fanny's lover,
Till some confounded escapade has blighted
    The plan of twenty years, and all is over,
And then the mother cries, the father swears
And wonders why the devil he got heirs.

◄ 101 ►

But Inez was so anxious and so clear
    Of sight that I must think on this occasion
She had some other motive much more near
    For leaving Juan to this new temptation.
But what that motive was I shan't say here;
    Perhaps to finish Juan's education,
Perhaps to open Don Alfonso's eyes
In case he thought his wife too great a prize.

◄ 102 ►

It was upon a day, a summer's day –
    Summer's indeed a very dangerous season,
And so is spring about the end of May.
    The sun no doubt is the prevailing reason,
But whatso'er the cause is, one may say
    And stand convicted of more truth than treason
That there are months which Nature grows more
    merry in.
March has its hares, and May must have its heroine.

◄ 103 ►

'Twas on a summer's day, the sixth of June –
    I like to be particular in dates,
Not only of the age and year, but moon.
    They are a sort of post-house, where the Fates
Change horses, making history change its tune,
    Then spur away o'er empires and o'er states,
Leaving at last not much besides chronology,
Excepting the post-obits of theology.

◄ 104 ►

'Twas on the sixth of June about the hour
    Of half-past six, perhaps still nearer seven,
When Julia sate within as pretty a bower
    As e'er held houri in that heathenish heaven
Described by Mahomet and Anacreon Moore,
    To whom the lyre and laurels have been given
With all the trophies of triumphant song.
He won them well, and may he wear them long!

◄ 105 ►

She sate, but not alone, I know not well
    How this same interview had taken place,
And even if I knew, I should not tell.
    People should hold their tongues in any case,
No matter how or why the thing befell.
    But there were she and Juan face to face.
When two such faces are so, 'twould be wise,
But very difficult, to shut their eyes.

◄ 106 ►

How beautiful she looked! Her conscious heart
    Glowed in her cheek, and yet she felt no wrong.
Oh Love, how perfect is thy mystic art,
    Strengthening the weak and trampling on the
    strong.
Of mortals whom thy lure hath led along.
The precipice she stood on was immense,
So was her creed in her own innocence.

◄ 107 ►

She thought of her own strength and Juan's youth
    And of the folly of all prudish fears,

Victorious virtue and domestic truth,
    And then of Don Alfonso's fifty years.
I wish these last had not occurred in sooth,
    Because that number rarely much endears
And through all climes, the snowy and the sunny,
Sounds ill in love, whate'er it may in money.

◄ 108 ►

When people say, 'I've told you fifty times,'
    They mean to scold and very often do.
When poets say, 'I've written fifty rhymes,'
    They make you dread that they'll recite them too.
In gangs of fifty, thieves commit their crimes.
    At fifty love for love is rare, 'tis true;
But then no doubt it equally as true is,
A good deal may be bought for fifty louis.

◄ 109 ►

Julia had honour, virtue, truth, and love
    For Don Alfonso, and she inly swore
By all the vows below to powers above,
    She never would disgrace the ring she wore
Nor leave a wish which wisdom might reprove.
    And while she pondered this, besides much more,
One hand on Juan's carelessly was thrown,
Quite by mistake – she thought it was her own.

◄ 110 ►

Unconsciously she leaned upon the other,
    Which played within the tangles of her hair.
And to contend with thoughts she could not
        smother,
    She seemed by the distraction of her air.
'Twas surely very wrong in Juan's mother
    To leave together this imprudent pair,
She who for many years had watched her son so.
I'm very certain mine would not have done so.

◄ 111 ►

The hand which still held Juan's, by degrees
    Gently but palpably confirmed its grasp,
As if it said, 'Detain me, if you please.'
    Yet there's no doubt she only meant to clasp
His fingers with a pure Platonic squeeze.
    She would have shrunk as from a toad or asp,
Had she imagined such a thing could rouse
A feeling dangerous to a prudent spouse.

◄ 112 ►

I cannot know what Juan thought of this,
    But what he did is much what you would do.

His young lip thanked it with a grateful kiss
    And then abashed at its own joy, withdrew
In deep despair, lest he had done amiss.
    Love is so very timid when 'tis new.
She blushed and frowned not, but she strove to
        speak
And held her tongue, her voice was grown so weak.

◄ 113 ►

The sun set, and up rose the yellow moon.
    The devil's in the moon for mischief; they
Who called her chaste, methinks, began too soon
    Their nomenclature. There is not a day,
The longest, not the twenty-first of June,
    Sees half the business in a wicked way,
On which three single hours of moonshine smile,
And then she looks so modest all the while.

◄ 114 ►

There is a dangerous silence in that hour,
    A stillness, which leaves room for the full soul
To open all itself, without the power
    Of calling wholly back its self-control.
The silver light which, hallowing tree and tower,
    Sheds beauty and deep softness o'er the whole,
Breathes also to the heart and o'er it throws
A loving languor, which is not repose.

◄ 115 ►

And Julia sate with Juan, half embraced
    And half retiring from the glowing arm,
Which trembled like the bosom where 'twas placed.
    Yet still she must have thought there was no
        harm,
Or else 'twere easy to withdraw her waist.
    But then the situation had its charm,
And then – God knows what next – I can't go on;
I'm almost sorry that I e'er begun.

◄ 116 ►

Oh Plato, Plato, you have paved the way
    With your confounded fantasies to more
Immoral conduct by the fancied sway
    Your system feigns o'er the controlless core
Of human hearts than all the long array
    Or poets and romancers. You're a bore,
A charlatan, a coxcomb, and have been
At best no better than a go-between.

◄ 117 ►

And Julia's voice was lost, except in sighs,
    Until too late for useful conversation.
The tears were gushing from her gentle eyes;
    I wish indeed they had not had occasion,
But who, alas, can love and then be wise?
    Not that remorse did not oppose temptation;
A little still she strove and much repented,
And whispering, 'I will ne'er consent' – consented.

Thomas Campion (1567–1620) studied medicine and law; he was an expert musician and one of the most lucid and sure-footed of English poets. His settings of his own words have great naturalness and a freedom from clutter and the squeezing or stretching of syllables to fit. In making his songs Campion may well have exercised both crafts simultaneously. The words seem to progress by musical logic: the tunes speak. His curiosity about the possible uses of classical quantitative measures in English made him particularly alert to the effects of the crucial differences in duration between spoken and sung syllables. That interest led him into the poetry wars of the time, where he was a realistic and un-pedantic player in the exchange of polemics about the relative merits of Graeco-Roman forms and the vigorously developing native hybrids. 'Rose-cheeked Laura', from his *Observations in the Art of English Poesy*, is an illustration of his contention that a formal English lyric could hold itself together without the support either of heavy accents or bells and beeps of rhyme to emphasize the inner symmetry which should be there already. The four-line stanza, adapted from Greek, is light but instantly recognizable as a form, after which repetitions confirm and exploit it; each time with a different direction and task, so that the poem – a coherent treatise in aeshetics in sixty-odd words – quietly snakes its unpredictable way to its limpid conclusion. The falling rhythms, closer to conversation than were the powerful load-bearing iambics of the contemporary theatre, inevitably produce line-endings on unstressed syllables. Rhymed, such patterns tend to be brittle and showy: here they're confidently casual, part of the poem's light, inexorable movement, proposition by proposition, towards an exalted abstraction. Elsewhere he's sharply sensuous and capable of rhyming with neatness and audacity.

'Rose-cheeked Laura'

Rose-cheeked Laura, come,
Sing thou smoothly with thy beauty's
Silent music, either other
    Sweetly gracing.

Lovely forms do flow
From concent divinely framed;
Heaven is music, and thy beauty's
    Birth is heavenly.

These dull notes we sing
Discords need for helps to grace them;
Only beauty purely loving
    Knows no discord,

But still moves delight
Like clear springs renewed by flowing,
Ever perfect, ever in them-
    selves eternal.

'Follow thy fair sun, unhappy shadow'

Follow thy fair sun, unhappy shadow.
  Though thou be black as night,
  And she made all of light,
Yet follow thy fair sun, unhappy shadow.

Follow her whose light thy light depriveth.
  Though here thou liv'st disgraced
  And she in heaven is placed,
Yet follow her whose light the world reviveth..

Follow those pure beams whose beauty burneth,
  That so have scorchèd thee
  As thou still black must be
Till her kind beams thy black to brightness turneth.

Follow her while yet her glory shineth.
  There comes a luckless night,
  That will dim all her light;
And this the black unhappy shade divineth.

Follow still, since so thy fates ordainèd.
  The sun must have his shade,
  Till both at once do fade,
The sun still proud, the shadow still disdainèd.

'When thou must home to shades of under ground'

When thou must home to shades of under ground,
And there arriv'd, a new admirèd guest,
The beauteous spirits do ingirt thee round,
White Iope, blithe Helen, and the rest,
To hear the stories of thy finished love,
From that smooth tongue whose music hell can
    move;

Then wilt thou speak of banqueting delights,
Of masques and revels which sweet youth did make,
Of tourneys and great challenges of knights,
And all these triumphs for thy beauty's sake:
When thou hast told these honours done to thee,
Then Tell, O tell, how thou didst murder me.

'Kind are her answers'

Kind are her answers,
  But her performance keeps no day,
Breaks time, as dancers
  From their own music when they stray:
  All her free favours
And smooth words wing my hopes in vain.
O did ever voice so sweet but only feign?
  Can true love yield such delay,
  Converting joy to pain?

Lost is our freedom,
  When we submit to women so:
Why do we need them,
  When in their best they work our woe?
  There is no wisdom
Can alter ends by Fate prefixed;
O why is the good of man with evil mixed?
  Never were days yet call'd two,
  But one night went betwixt.

'Thrice toss these oaken ashes in the air'

Thrice toss these oaken ashes in the air;
Thrice sit thou mute in this enchanted chair:
Then thrice three times tie up this true love's knot,
And murmur soft she will, or she will not.

Go burn these pois'nous weeds in yon blue fire,
These screech-owl's feathers, and this prickling
   briar,
This cypress gathered at a dead man's grave;
That all thy fears and cares an end may have.

Then come you, you Fairies, dance with me a round,
Melt her hard heart with your melodious sound.
In vain are all the charms I can devise:
She hath an art to break them with her eyes.

Proserpina

Hark, all you ladies that do sleep,
   The fairy queen Proserpina
Bids you awake, and pity them that weep.
      You may do in the dark
        What the day doth forbid.
      Fear not the dogs that bark;
        Night will have all hid.

But if you let your lovers moan,
   The fairy queen Proserpina
Will send abroad her fairies every one,
      That shall pinch black and blue
        Your white hands and fair arms,
      That did not kindly rue
        Your paramours' harms.

In myrtle arbours on the downs,
   The fairy queen Proserpina,
This night by moonshine, leading merry rounds
      Holds a watch with sweet Love,
        Down the dale, up the hill;
      No plaints or groans may move
        Their holy vigil.

All you that will hold watch with Love,
   The fairy queen Proserpina
Will make you fairer than Dione's dove.

Roses red, lilies white,
   And the clear damask hue,
Shall on your cheeks alight.
   Love will adorn you.

All you that love or loved before,
   The fairy queen Proserpina
Bids you increase that loving humour more.
      They that have not yet fed
        On delight amorous,
      She vows that they shall lead
        Apes in Avernus.

He is one of the most awkward figures of genius in English poetry. Pope, Coleridge and Swinburne all praised his best-known work, the great volume of translations from Homer, while Keats famously looked into it with awe 'like some watcher of the skies / When a new planet swims into his ken'. Would Keats have read far enough to experience the same mixed feelings of respect and frustration as the others?

Chapman's long life (?1559–1634) was filled with unceasing, ill-rewarded creative activity. As playwright, he wrote several comedies and tragedies which were staged, and collaborated with important dramatist friends; but his plays are now rarely revived. Then there is the considerable body of original verse, from which the extracts here have been chosen. Work of ambitious construction and striking energy, it is flawed by hollow rhetoric and sheer syntactical complexity. It burdens the reader with what Swinburne called 'incongruous allusion' and 'preposterous symbolism'. And yet it remains remarkable, for its forceful moralising wit, bizarre description, and occasional appealing sensuousness.

The extract from *The Shadow of Night* shows Chapman sustaining a splendidly paradoxical preference for darkness over light. Ovid's reaction to Corinna's chaste kiss anticipates wilder metaphysical poets writing a generation later. Leander, in the lines from Chapman's completion of Marlowe's great unfinished poem, is the fulfilled lover still glowing after the event (Keats would surely have approved). Ben Jonson, Chapman's (envied?) friend receives fascinatingly tentative praise for his tragedy *Sejanus*, while passive idlers and time-wasters suffer eloquent moral censure in 'The Tears of Peace'.

Most extraordinary is the account of an approaching storm, from 'Eugenia'. Chapman's main fault was an inability to refine and direct his abundant, idiosyncratic talents. But when they run out of control so magnificently, who would complain?

THE SHADOW OF NIGHT
(lines 324–77)

Kneel then with me, fall worm-like on the
    ground,
And from th' infectious dunghill of this round,
From men's brass wits and golden foolery,
Weep, weep your souls into felicity:
Come to this house of mourning, serve the Night,
To whom pale Day (with whoredom soaked quite)
Is but a drudge, selling her beauty's use
To rapes, adulteries, and to all abuse.
Her labours feast imperial Night with sports,
Where loves are Christmass'd, with all pleasure's
    sorts;
And whom her fugitive and far-shot rays
Disjoin, and drive into ten thousand ways,
Night's glorious mantle wraps in safe abodes,
And frees their necks from servile labour's loads:
Her trusty shadows succour men dismay'd,
Whom Day's deceitful malice hath betray'd:
From the silk vapours of her ivory port,
Sweet Protean dreams she sends of every sort:
Some taking forms of princes, to persuade
Of men deject, we are their equals made,
Some clad in habit of deceased friends,
For whom we mourn'd, and now have wish'd
    amends;
And some (dear favour) lady-like attired,
With pride of beauty's full meridian fired:
Who pity our contempts, revive our hearts;
For wisest ladies love the inward parts.

If these be dreams, even so are all things else,
That walk this round by heavenly sentinels:
But from Night's port of horn she greets our eyes
With graver dreams inspired with prophecies,
Which oft presage to us succeeding chances,
We proving that awake, they show in trances.
If these seem likewise vain, or nothing are,
Vain things, or nothing come to virtue's share,
For nothing more than dreams with us she finds:
Then since all pleasures vanish with the winds,
And that most serious actions not respecting
The second light, are worth but the neglecting,
Since day, or light, in any quality,
For earthly uses do but serve the eye;
And since the eye's most quick and dangerous use,
Enflames the heart, and learns the soul abuse,
Since mournings are preferred to banquetings,
And they reach heaven, bred under sorrow's wings;

Since Night brings terrors to our frailties still,
And shameless Day, doth marble us in ill.

All you possess'd with indepressed spirits,
Endued with nimble and aspiring wits,
Come consecrate with me, to sacred Night
Your whole endeavours, and detest the light.
Sweet Peace's richest crown is made of stars,
Most certain guides of honour's mariners,
No pen can anything eternal write,
That is not steep'd in humour of the Night.

Ovid speaks of Corinna's kiss

‹ from *Ovid's Banquet of Sense* ›

(lines 883–909)

'And as a pebble cast into a spring,
We see a sort of trembling circles rise,
One forming other in their issuing,
Till over all the fount they circulize;
    So this perpetual-motion-making kiss
Is propagate through all my faculties,
    And makes my breast an endless fount of bliss,
Of which, if gods could drink, their matchless fare
Would make them much more blessed than they
        are.

'But as when sounds do hollow bodies beat,
Air gather'd there, compress'd and thickened,
The self-same way she came doth make retreat,
And so effects the sound re-echoed,
    Only in part because she weaker is
In that reddition than when first she fled;
    So I, alas! faint echo of this kiss,
Only reiterate a slender part
Of that high joy it worketh in my heart.

'And thus with feasting love is famish'd more,
Without my touch are all things turned to gold,
And till I touch I cannot joy my store;
To purchase others, I myself have sold;
    Love is a wanton famine, rich in food,
But with a richer appetite controll'd;
    An argument in figure and in mood,
Yet hates all arguments; disputing still
For sense 'gainst reason with a senseless will . . .'

Hero and Leander

(Sestiad 3, lines 83–104)

Love-blest Leander was with love so fill'd,
That love to all that touch'd him he instill'd.
And as the colours of all things we see,
To our sights' powers communicated be,
So to all objects that in compass came
Of any sense he had, his senses' flame
Flow'd from his parts with force so virtual,
It fired with sense things mere insensual.
    Now, with warm baths and odours comforted,
When he lay down, he kindly kiss'd his bed,
As consecrating it to Hero's right,
And vow'd thereafter, that whatever sight
Put him in mind of Hero or her bliss,
Should be her altar to prefer a kiss.
    Then laid he forth his late-enriched arms,
In whose white circle Love writ all his charms,
And made his characters sweet Hero's limbs,
When on his breast's warm sea she sideling swims
And as those arms, held up in circle, met,
He said, 'See, sister, Hero's carcanet!
Which she had rather wear about her neck
Than all the jewels that do Juno deck.'

'On Ben Jonson's *Sejanus*'

(lines 29–52)

For though thy hand was scarce address'd to draw
    The semi-circle of SEJANUS' life,
Thy muse yet makes it the whole sphere, and law,
    To all state lives; and bounds ambition's strife.
And as a little brook creeps from his spring,
    With shallow tremblings through the lowest
        vales,
As if he fear'd his stream abroad to bring,
    Lest profane feet should wrong it, and rude gales;
But finding happy channels, and supplies
    Of other fords mix with his modest course,
He grows a goodly river, and descries
    The strength that mann'd him since he left his
        source.
Then takes he in delightsome meads and groves,
    And with his two-edged waters, flourishes
Before great palaces, and all men's loves
    Build by his shores to greet his passages;
So thy chaste muse, by virtuous self-mistrust,

Which is a true mark of the truest merit,
In virgin fear of men's illiterate lust,
  Shut her soft wings, and durst not show her
    spirit;
Till, nobly cherish'd, now thou lett'st her fly,
  Singing the sable orgies of the Muses,
And in the highest pitch of Tragedy,
  Makest her command all things her ground
    produces.

❧

THE TEARS OF PEACE
(lines 427–46)

                Your Passive men –
So call'd of only passing time in vain –
Pass it in no good exercise, but are
In meats and cups laborious, and take care
To lose without all care their soul-spent time.
And since they have no means nor spirits to climb,
Like fowls of prey, in any high affair,
See how like kites they bangle in the air
To stoop at scraps and garbage, in respect
Of that which men of true peace should select,
And how they trot out in their lives the ring
With idly iterating oft one thing –
A new-fought combat, an affair at sea,
A marriage, or a progress, or a plea,
No news but fits them as if made for them,
Though it be forged, but of a woman's dream;
And stuff with such stolen ends their manless
    breasts –
Sticks, rags, and mud – they seem mere puttocks'
    nests:
Curious in all men's actions but their own,
All men and all things censure, though know none.

❧

EUGENIA
(lines 55–132)

They saw the sun look pale, and cast thro' air
Discolour'd beams, nor could he paint so fair
Heaven's bow in dewy vapours, but he left
The greater part unform'd, the circle cleft,
And like a bull's neck shorten'd, no hues seen
But only one, and that was waterish green:

His heat was choked up, as in ovens compress'd
Half stifling men; heaven's drooping face was
    dress'd
In gloomy thunderstocks: earth, seas array'd
In all presage of storm: the bittours play'd
And met in flocks; the herons set clamours gone
That ratteled up air's triple region.
The cormorants to dry land did address
And cried away all fowls that used the seas.
The wanton swallows jerk'd the standing springs
Met in dull lakes, and flew so close, their wings
Shaved the top waters: frogs croak'd; the swart crow
Measured the sea-sands, with pace passing slow,
And often soused her ominous heat of blood
Quite over head and shoulders in the flood,
Still scolding at the rain's so slow access;
The trumpet-throated, the Naupliades,
Their claugers threw about, and summon'd up
All clouds to crown imperious tempest's cup;
The erring dolphin puff'd the foamy main
Hither and thither, and did upwards rain;
The raven sat belching out his funeral din,
Venting his voice, with sucking of it in.
The patient of all labours, the poor ant,
Her eggs to caves brought; molehills proof did want
To keep such tears out, as heaven now would weep.
The hundred-footed cankerworms did creep
Thick on the wet walls. The slow crab did take
Pibbles into her mouth, and ballast make
Of gravel, for her stay, against the gales,
Close clinging to the shore. Sea-giant whales
The watery mountains darted at the sky.
And, no less ominous, the petulant fly
Bit bitterly for blood, as then most sweet.
The loving dog digg'd earth up with his feet;
The ass, as weather-wise, confirm'd these fears,
And never left shaking his flaggy ears.
Th' ingenious bee wrought ever near her hive.
The cloddy ashes kept coals long alive,
And dead coals quicken'd; both transparent clear;
The rivers crown'd with swimming feathers were.
The trees' green fleeces flew about the air,
And aged thistles lost their downy hair;
Cattle would run out from their sheds undriven
To th' ample pastures; lambs were sprightly given,
And all in jumps about the short leas borne:
Rams fiercely butted, locking horn in horn.
The storm now near, those cattle that abroad
Undriven ran from their shelter, undriven, trod
Homewards as fast: the large-boned oxen look'd
Oft on the broad heaven, and the soft air suck'd,

Smelling it in; their reeking nostrils still
Sucking the clear dew from the daffodil;
Bow'd to their sides their broad heads, and their
   hair
Lick' d smooth at all parts; loved their right-side
   lair;
And late in night, did bellow from the stall
As thence the tempest would his blasts exhale.
The swine her never-made bed now did ply
And with her snout strow'd every way her sty;
The wolf howl'd in her den; th' insatiate beast,
Now fearing no man, met him breast to breast,
And like a murtherous beggar, him allured;
Haunting the home-groves husbandmen manured.
Then Night her circle closed, and shut in day,
Her silver spangles shedding every way,
And earth's poor stars, the glow-worms, lay abroad
As thick as heaven's; that now no twinkle show'd,
Sudden'stly plucking in their guilty heads.
And forth the winds brake from their brazen beds,
That strook the mountains so, they cried quite out.
The thunder chid; the lightning leapt about;
And clouds so gush'd as Iris ne'er were shown,
But in fresh deluge, Heaven itself came down . . .

Thomas Chatterton (1752–70) was the first Romantic poet, and also the first *poète maudit*, as famous for his tragic death as for his poems. His father, a teacher and sub-chanter at the church of St Mary Redcliffe, Bristol, died before he was born, and Thomas, a brilliant, headstrong boy, grew up in poverty, fascinated by the architecture and documents of the great medieval church his father had served. He began writing poetry at the age of ten, and in 1768, whilst apprenticed to an attorney, he began to forge 'medieval' documents which he supplied to local historians. At first these were merely a clever hoax, but soon he was concocting the works of a fictitious fourteenth-century poet, 'Sir Thomas Rowley'. In the voice of this shadowy *alter ego* Chatterton wrote some of the most vivid and oddly memorable poems of the late eighteenth century. He went to London but plans to enter literary life there failed. The aesthete and novelist Horace Walpole rejected forged works which Chatterton sent him; the witty songs and satires he published in modern English under his own name earned too little to keep him. Ill and half-starved but too proud to return to Bristol a failure, he poisoned himself with arsenic on 24 August 1770, aged seventeen. His work inspired Coleridge, Wordsworth, Keats (who used to chant 'Comme, wyth acorne-coppe and thorne ...' as a kind of magical incantation) and Blake (whose print 'The Ghost of a Flea' shows the spectral bloodletter holding these delicate implements). His work combines boyish exuberance with a uniquely haunting poignancy. His fake-medieval English is largely a matter of 'antique' spelling, but in the following selection *cryne* = hair; *rode* = complexion; *cale* = cold; *celnesse* = coldness; *ouphante* = elphin; *faytours* = traveller's; *herehaughte* = herald; *mees* = meadows; *neders* = adders; *levyn* = lightning.

Thomas Chatterton ·

The Tournament

(lines 1–24)

The Matten Belle has sounded longe,
The Cocks han sang their morning songe;
When lo! the tuneful Clarions Sound,
Wherein all other Noise was drownd,
Did echo to the Rooms around,
And greet the Ears of Champyons stronge –
Arise Arise from downie Bedde,
For Sunne doth gin to shew his Hedde –

Then each did done in seemlie Gear,
What Armour eche beseemed to weare:
And on ech Sheelde devices shon,
Of wounded hearts, and Battels won,
All curious and nyce echon –
With manie a tassild Speare,
And mounted echone on a Steed,
Unwote made Ladies hartes to blede –

Heraulds eche Side the Clarions wound,
The Horses started at the sound:
The Knyghtes echone did poynt the Launce,
And to the Combattes did advaunce,
From Hyberne, Scotland, eke from Fraunce.
Thyre prancyng Horses tare the Ground,
Al strove to reche the Place of Fyghte;
The first to exercise theyre myghte –

Mynstrelles Song

O! synge untoe mie roundelaie,
O! droppe the brynie teare wythe mee,
Dance ne moe atte hailie daie,
Lycke a reyneynge ryver bee;
    Mie love ys dedde,
    Gon to hys dethe-bedde,
    Al under the wyllowe tree.

Blacke hys cryne as the wynter nyghte,
Whyte hys rode as the sommer snowe,
Rodde hys face as the morning lyghte,
Cale he lyes ynne the grave belowe;
    Mie love ys dedde,
    Gon to hys dethe-bedde,
    Al under the wyllowe tree.

Swote hys tyngue as the throstles note,
Quycke ynn daunce as thoughte canne bee,
Defte hys taboure, codgelle stote,
O! hee lyes by the wyllowe tree:
    Mie love ys dedde,
    Gon to hys dethe-bedde,
    Al under the wyllowe tree.

Harke! the ravenne flappes hys wynge,
In the briered dell below;
Harke! the dethe-owle loude dothe synge,
To the nyghte-mares as heie go;
    Mie love ys dedde,
    Gon to hys dethe-bedde,
    Al under the wyllowe tree.

See! the whyte moone sheenes onne hie;
Whyterre ys mie true loves shroude;
Whyterre yanne the mornynge skie,
Whyterre yanne the evenynge cloude;
    Mie love ys dedde,
    Gon to hys dethe-bedde,
    Al under the wyllowe tree.

Here, uponne mie true loves grave,
Schalle the baren fleurs be layde,
Nee one hallie Seyncte to save
All the celnesse of a mayde.
    Mie love ys dedde,
    Gon to hys dethe-bedde,
    Al under the wyllowe tree.

Wythe mie hondes I'le dente the brieres
Rounde hie hallie corse to gre,
Ouphante fairie, lyghte youre fyres,
Heere mie boddie stylle schalle bee.
    Mie love ys dedde,
    Gon to hys dethe-bedde,
    Al under the wyllowe tree.

Comme, wyth acorne-coppe and thorne,
Drayne mie hartys bludde awaie;
Lyfe and all yttes goode I scorne,
Daunce bie nete, or feaste bie daie.
    Mie love ys dedde,
    Gon to hys dethe-bedde,
    Al under the wyllowe tree.

Water wytches, crownede wythe reytes,
Bere mee to yer lethalle tyde.

I die; I comme; mie true love waytes.
Thos the damselle spake, and dyed.

NIGHT

When azure Skie ys veylde yn Robes of Nyghte;
    Whanne glemmrynge dewedrops stounde the
      Faytours Eyne;
    Whanne flying Cloudes betinged with roddie
      Lyghte
    Doth pon the brindlynge Wolfe and Wood bore
      shyne
    Whanne Even Star fayre Herehaughte of nyght
    Spreds the derke douskie Sheene alonge the Mees
    The wreethynge Neders sends a glumie Lyghte
    And houlets wynge from Levyn blasted Trees
    Arise mie Spryghte and seke the distant dele
And there to ecchoing Tonges thie raptured Joies
    ytele.

FAREWELL

... The Clock strikes Eight the Taper dully shines
Farewell, my Muse, nor think of further Lines
Nine Leaves and in two hours or something odd
Shut up the Book it is enough by God

The most monumental achievement of Geoffrey Chaucer (c. 1340–1400) is The Canterbury Tales. But none of the tales, or no part of them, can compare as a single poem with his great tragic romance Troilus and Criseyde, written when Chaucer was at the height of his powers, between 1385 and 1388. If it did not exist, there would be nothing to show that Chaucer possessed the Coleridgean shaping power of imagination to complete a large sustained canvas. Troilus is a loose translation of Boccaccio's lyrical and sentimental love-elegy Il Filostrato, but it entirely transcends its model, bringing to it a philosophical range, practicality and humanity which establish it as the first great long poem in English. It ranks with Paradise Lost and The Prelude; it outclasses in humane seriousness the Shakespeare plays which are indebted to it, Troilus and Cressida and Romeo and Juliet. It is more reminiscent of Antony and Cleopatra in its mixture of passion and folly and calculation.

From its opening lines the poem's outcome is never in doubt. We know that Troilus's double sorrow will take him from misery to happiness, 'and after out of joy' when Criseyde abandons him for Diomede. But Chaucer uses the tyranny of the received story to create a sense of the tragic inescapability of life: Criseyde knows she is fated to have for ever the name of love traitress, but what can she do, 'with women few among the Grekis stronge'? In the first three books Troilus and his crony Pandarus (Criseyde's uncle) bring about the passionate love affair that lasts for three years, before Criseyde joins her father Calcas in the Greek camp, exchanged for the real traitor Antenor. As she leaves, she vows that she will return to Troilus within ten days; but throughout this brilliantly dramatic excerpt from the Fifth and final book, as Troilus and Pandarus speculate desperately about her return, we know she won't return. The profundity of the passage is that all three characters know it too, whether or not they face the fact.

The second excerpt from Chaucer, a brief one, is the opening of the Prologue to his The Legend of Good Women. These legends were also broadly drawn from a work of Boccaccio, his Latin De Claris Mulieribus, though this time Chaucer makes much less of his narrative sources. However this Prologue, describing Chaucer's fealty to the daisy and – much more interesting to us – his veneration for 'olde bokes' without which we would have lost 'the key of remembrance, was in the late nineteenth century the most popular piece of Chaucer apart from the *General Prologue* to *The Canterbury Tales*. It was the next work written after *Troilus*, in the late 1380s, so it comes between Chaucer's two principal works. Apart from its intrinsic interest and charm, it represents a highly significant moment in the history of English metrics, as the first certain use of the European pentameter heroic line which was to be the staple of both rhyming poetry and blank verse for the next half-millennium.

Troilus and Criseyde

‹Book 5›

(lines 498–959)

Thus Pandarus, with alle peyne and wo,
Made hym to dwelle; and at the wikes ende,
Of Sarpedoun they toke hire leve tho,
And on hire wey they spedden hem to wende.
Quod Troilus, 'Now Lord me grace sende,
That I may fynden, at myn hom-comynge
Criseyde comen!' and therwith gan he synge.

'Ye, haselwode!' thoughte this Pandare,
And to hymself ful softeliche he seyde,
'God woot, refreyden may this hote fare,
Er Calkas sende Troilus Criseyde!'
But natheles, he japed thus, and pleyde,
And swor, ywys, his herte hym wel bihighte,
She wolde come as soone as evere she myghte.

Whan they unto the paleys were ycomen
Of Troilus, they doun of hors alighte,
And to the chambre hire wey than han they nomen.
And into tyme that it gan to nyghte,
They spaken of Criseÿde the brighte;
And after this, when that hem bothe leste,
They spedde hem fro the soper unto reste.

On morwe, as soone as day bygan to clere,
This Troilus gan of his slep t'abrayde,
And to Pandare, his owen brother deere,
'For love of God,' ful pitously he sayde,
'As go we sen the palais of Criseyde;
For syn we yet may have namore feste,
So lat us sen hire paleys atte leeste.'

And therwithal, his meyne for to blende,
A cause he fond in towne for to go,
And to Criseydes hous they gonnen wende.

But Lord! this sely Troilus was wo!
Hym thoughte his sorwful herte braste a-two.
For, whan he saugh hire dores spered alle,
Wel neigh for sorwe adoun he gan to falle.

Therwith, whan he was war and gan biholde
How shet was every wyndow of the place,
As frost, hym thoughte, his herte gan to colde;
For which with chaunged dedlich pale face,
Withouten word, he forthby gan to pace,
And, as God wolde, he gan so faste ride,
That no wight of his contenance espide.

Than seide he thus: 'O paleys desolat,
O hous of houses whilom best ihight,
O paleys empty and disconsolat,
O thow lanterne of which queynt is the light,
O paleys, whilom day, that now art nyght,
Wel oughtestow to falle, and I to dye,
Syn she is went that wont was us to gye!

'O paleis, whilom crowne of houses alle,
Enlumyned with sonne of alle blisse!
O ryng, fro which the ruby is out falle,
O cause of wo, that cause hast ben of lisse!
Yet, syn I may no bet, fayn wolde I kisse
Thy colde dores, dorste I for this route;
And farwel shryne, of which the seynt is oute!'

Therwith he caste on Pandarus his yë,
With chaunged face, and pitous to biholde;
And when he myghte his tyme aright aspie,
Ay as he rood, to Pandarus he tolde
His newe sorwe, and ek his joies olde,
So pitously and with so dead an hewe,
That every wight myghte on his sorwe rewe.

Fro thennesforth he rideth up and down,
And every thyng com hym to remembraunce
As he rood forby places of the town
In which he whilom hadde al his plesaunce.
'Lo, yonder saugh ich last my lady daunce;
And in that temple, with hire eyen cleere,
Me kaughte first my righte lady dere.

'And yonder have I herd ful lustyly
My dere herte laugh, and yonder pleye
Saugh ich hire ones ek ful blisfully.
And yonder ones to me gan she seye,
"Now goode swete, love me wel, I preye;"
And yond so goodly gan she me biholde,
That to the deth myn herte is to hire holde.

'And at that corner, in the yonder hous,
Herde I myn alderlevest lady deere
So wommanly, with vois melodious,
Syngen so wel, so goodly, and so clere,
That in my soule yet me thynketh ich here
The blisful sown; and in that yonder place
My lady first me took unto hire grace.'

Thanne thoughte he thus, 'O blisful lord Cupide,
Whan I the proces have in my memorie,
How thow me hast wereyed on every syde,
Men myght a book make of it, lik a storie.
What nede is the to seke on me victorie,
Syn I am thyn, and holly at thi wille?
What joie hastow thyn owen folk to spille?

'Wel hastow, lord, ywroke on me thyn ire,
Thow myghty god, and dredefull for to greve!
Now mercy, lord! thow woost wel I desire
Thi grace moost of alle lustes leeve,
And lyve and dye I wol in thy byleve;
For which I n'axe in guerdoun but o bone,
That thow Criseyde ayein me sende sone.

'Distreyne hire herte as faste to retorne,
As thow doost myn to longen hire to see,
Than woot I wel that she nyl naught sojorne.
Now blisful lord, so cruel thow ne be
Unto the blood of Troie, I preye the,
As Juno was unto the blood Thebane,
For which the folk of Thebes caughte hire bane.'

And after this he to the yates wente
Ther as Criseyde out rood a ful good paas,
And up and down ther made he many a wente,
And to hymself ful ofte he seyde, 'Allas!
Fro hennes rood my blisse and my solas!
As wolde blisful God now, for his joie,
I myghte hire sen ayein come into Troie!

'And to the yonder hille I gan hire gyde,
Allas, and ther I took of hire my leve!
And yond I saugh hire to hire fader ride,
For sorwe of which myn herte shal tocleve.
And hider hom I com when it was eve,
And here I dwelle out cast from alle joie,
And shal, til I may sen hire eft in Troie.'

And of hymself ymagened he ofte
To ben defet, and pale, and waxen lesse
Than he was wont, and that men seyden softe,

'What may it be? Who kan the sothe gesse
Whi Troilus hath al this hevynesse?'
And al this nas but his malencolie,
That he hadde of hymself swich fantasie.

Another tyme ymaginen he wolde
That every wight that wente by the weye
Hadde of hym routhe, and that they seyen sholde,
'I am right sory Troilus wol deye.'
And thus he drof a day yet forth or tweye,
As ye have herd; swich lif right gan he lede,
As he that stood bitwixen hoep and drede.

For which hym likede in his songes shewe
Th'enchesoun of his wo, as he best myghte,
And made a song of wordes but a fewe,
Somwhat his woful herte for to lighte.
And whan he was from every mannes syghte,
With softe vois he of his lady deere,
That absent was, gan synge as ye may heere.

◄ Canticus Troili ►

'O sterre, of which I lost have al the light,
With herte soor wel oughte I to biwaille,
That evere derk in torment, nyght by nyght,
Toward my deth with wynd in steere I saille;
For which the tenthe nyght, if that I faille
The gydyng of thi bemes bright an houre,
My ship and me Caribdis wol devoure.

This song whan he thus songen hadde, soone
He fil ayeyn into his sikes olde;
And every nyght, as was his wone to doone,
He stood the brighte moone to byholde,
And al his sorwe he to the moone tolde,
And seyde, 'Ywis, whan thow art horned newe,
I shal be glad, if al the world be trewe!

'I saugh thyn hornes olde ek by the morwe,
Whan hennes rood my righte lady dere,
That causes is of my torment and my sorwe;
For which, O brighte Latona the clere,
For love of God, ren faste aboute thy spere!
For whan thyne hornes newe gynnen sprynge,
Than shal she come that may my blisse brynge.'

The dayes moore, and lenger every nyght,
Than they ben wont to be, hym thoughte tho,
And that the sonne went his cours unright
By lenger weye than it was wont to do;

And seyde, 'Ywis, me dredeth evere mo,
The sonnes sone, Pheton, be on-lyve,
And that his fader carte amys he dryve.'

Upon the walles faste ek wolde he walke,
And on the Grekis oost he wolde se,
And to hymself right thus he wolde talke:
'Lo, yonder is myn owene lady free,
Or ellis yonder, ther the tentes be.
And thennes comth this eyr, that is so soote,
That in my soule I fele it doth me boote.

'And hardily this wynd, that more and moore
Thus stoundemele encresseth in my face,
Is of my ladys depe sikes soore.
I preve it thus, for in noon othere place
Of al this town, save onliche in this space,
Fele I no wynd that sowneth so lik peyne:
It seyth, 'Allas! whi twynned be we tweyne?'

This longe tyme he dryveth forth right thus,
Til fully passed was the nynthe nyght;
And ay bisyde hym was this Pandarus,
That bisily did al his fulle myght
Hym to conforte, and make his herte light,
Yevyng hym hope alwey, the tenthe morwe
That she shal come, and stynten al his sorwe.

Upon that other syde ek was Criseyde,
With wommen fewe, among the Grekis stronge;
For which ful ofte a day 'Allas!' she seyde,
'That I was born! Wel may myn herte longe
After my deth; for now lyve I to longe.
Allas! and I ne may it nat amende!
For now is wors than evere yet I wende.

'My fader nyl for nothyng do me grace
To gon ayeyn, for naught I kan hym queme;
And if so be that I my terme pace,
My Troilus shal in his herte deme
That I am fals, and so it may wel seme:
Thus shal ich have unthonk on every side.
That I was born, so weilaway the tide!

'And if that I me putte in jupartie,
To stele awey by nyght, and it bifalle
That I be kaught, I shal be holde a spie;
Or elles - lo, this drede I moost of alle -
If in the hondes of som wrecche I falle,
I nam but lost, al be myn herte trewe.
Now, myghty God, thow on my sorwe rewe!'

Ful pale ywoxen was hire brighte face,
Hire lymes lene, as she that al the day
Stood, whan she dorste, and loked on the place
Ther she was born, and ther she dwelt hadde ay;
And al the nyght wepyng, allas, she lay.
And thus despeired, out of alle cure,
She ladde hire lif, this woful creature.

Ful ofte a day she sighte ek for destresse,
And in hireself she wente ay purtrayinge
Of Troilus the grete worthynesse,
And al his goodly wordes recordynge
Syn first that day hire love bigan to springe.
And thus she sette hire woful herte afire
Thorugh remembraunce of that she gan desire.

In al this world ther nys so cruel herte
That hire hadde herd compleynen in hire sorwe
That nolde hen wepen for hire peynes smerte,
So tendrely she wepte, bothe eve and morwe.
Hire nedede no teris for to borwe!
And this was yet the werste of al hire peyne,
Ther was no wight to whom she dorste hire pleyne.

Ful rewfully she loked upon Troie,
Biheld the toures heigh and ek the halles:
'Allas!' quod she, 'the plesance and the joie,
The which that now al torned into galle is,
Have ich had ofte withinne tho yonder walles!
O Troilus, what dostow now?' she seyde.
'Lord! wheyther thow yet thenke upon Criseyde?

'Allas, I ne hadde trowed on youre loore,
And went with yow, as ye me redde er this!
Than hadde I now nat siked half so soore.
Who myghte have seyd that I hadde don amys
To stele awey with swich oon as he ys?
But al to late comth the letuarie,
Whan men the cors unto the grave carie.

'To late is now to speke of that matere.
Prudence, allas, oon of thyne eyen thre
Me lakked alwey, er that I come here!
On tyme ypassed wel remembred me,
And present tyme ek koud ich wel ise,
But future tyme, er I was in the snare,
Koude I nat sen; that causeth now my care.

'But natheles, bityde what bityde,
I shal to-morwe at nyght, by est or west,
Out of this oost stele on som manere syde,

And gon with Troilus where as hym lest.
This purpos wol ich holde, and this is best.
No fors of wikked tonges janglerie,
For evere on love han wrecches had envye.

'For whoso wol of every word take hede,
Or reulen hym by every wightes wit,
Ne shal he nevere thryven, out of drede;
For that that som men blamen evere yit,
Lo, other manere folk comenden it.
And as for me, for al swich variaunce,
Felicite clepe I my suffisaunce.

'For which, withouten any wordes mo,
To Troie I wole, as for conclusioun.'
But God it wot, er fully monthes two,
She was ful fer fro that entencioun!
For bothe Troilus and Troie town
Shal knotteles thorughout hire herte slide;
For she wol take a purpos for t'abyde.

This Diomede, of whom yow telle I gan,
Goth now withinne hymself ay arguynge
With al the sleghte, and al that evere he kan,
How he may best, with shortest taryinge,
Into his net Criseydes herte brynge.
To this entent he koude nevere fyne;
To fisshen hire, he leyde out hook and lyne.

But natheles, wel in his herte he thoughte,
That she nas nat withoute a love in Troie;
For nevere, sythen he hire thennes broughte,
Ne koude he sen hire laughe or maken joie.
He nyst how best hire herte for t'acoye.
'But for t'asay,' he seyde, 'it naught ne greveth;
For he that naught n'asaieth, naught n'acheveth.'

Yet seide he to hymself upon a nyght,
'Now am I nat a fool, that woot wel how
Hire wo for love is of another wight,
And hereupon to gon assaye hire now?
I may wel wite, it nyl nat ben my prow.
For wise folk in bookes it expresse,
"Men shal nat wowe a wight in hevynesse."

'But whoso myghte wynnen swich a flour
From hym for whom she morneth nyght and day,
He myghte seyn he were a conquerour.'
And right anon, as he that bold was ay,
Thoughte in his herte, 'Happe how happe may,

Al sholde I dye, I wol hire herte seche!
I shal namore lesen but my speche.'

This Diomede, as bokes us declare,
Was in his nedes prest and corageous,
With sterne vois and myghty lymes square,
Hardy, testif, strong, and chivalrous
Of dedes, lik his fader Tideus.
And som men seyn he was of tonge large;
And heir he was of Calydoigne and Arge.

Criseyde mene was of hire stature,
Therto of shap, of face, and ek of cheere,
Ther myghte ben no fairer creature.
And ofte tyme this was hire manere,
To gon ytressed with hire heres clere
Doun by hire coler at hire bak byhynde,
Which with a thred of gold she wolde bynde.

And, save hire browes joyneden yfere,
Ther was no lak, in aught I kan espien.
But for to speken of hire eyen cleere,
Lo, trewely, they writen that hire syen,
That Paradis stood formed in hire yën.
And with hire riche beaute evere more
Strof love in hire ay, which of hem was more.

She sobre was, ek symple, and wys withal,
The best ynorisshed ek that myghte be,
And goodly of hire speche in general,
Charitable, estatlich, lusty, and fre;
Ne nevere mo ne lakked hire pite;
Tendre-herted, slydynge of corage;
But trewely, I kan nat telle hire age.

And Troilus wel woxen was in highte,
And complet formed by proporcioun
So wel that kynde it nought amenden myghte;
Yong, fressh, strong, and hardy as lyoun;
Trewe as stiel in ech condicioun;
Oon of the beste entecched creature
That is, or shal, whil that the world may dure.

And certeynly in storye it is yfounde,
That Troilus was nevere unto no wight,
As in his tyme, in no degree secounde
In durryng don that longeth to a knyght.
Al myghte a geant passen hym of myght,
His herte ay with the first and with the beste
Stood paregal, to durre don that hym leste.

But for to tellen forth of Diomede:
It fel that after, on the tenthe day
Syn that Criseyde out of the citee yede,
This Diomede, as fressh as braunche in May,
Com to the tente, ther as Calkas lay,
And feyned hym with Calkas han to doone;
But what he mente, I shal yow tellen soone.

Criseyde, at shorte wordes for to telle,
Welcomed hym, and down hym by hire sette;
And he was ethe ynough to maken dwelle!
And after this, withouten longe lette,
The spices and the wyn men forth hem fette;
And forth they speke of this and that yfeere,
As frendes don, of which som shal ye heere.

He gan first fallen of the werre in speche
Bitwixe hem and the folk of Troie town;
And of th'assege he gan hire ek biseche
To telle hym what was hire opynyoun.
Fro that demaunde he so descendeth down
To axen hire, if that hire straunge thoughte
The Grekis gise, and werkes that they wroughte;

And whi hire fader tarieth so longe
To wedden hire unto som worthy wight.
Criseyde, that was in hire peynes stronge
For love of Troilus, hire owen knyght,
As ferforth as she konnyng hadde or myght,
Answerde hym tho; but, as of his entente,
It seemed nat she wiste what he mente.

But natheles, this ilke Diomede
Gan in hymself assure, and thus he seyde:
'If ich aright have taken of yow hede,
Me thynketh thus, O lady myn, Criseyde,
That syn I first hond on youre bridel leyde,
Whan ye out come of Troie by the morwe,
Ne koude I nevere sen yow but in sorwe.

'Kan I nat seyn what may the cause be,
But if for love of som Troian it were,
The which right sore wolde athynken me,
That ye for any wight that dwelleth there
Sholden spille a quarter of a tere,
Or pitously youreselven so bigile;
For dredeles, it is nought worth the while.

'The folk of Troie, as who seyth, alle and some
In prisoun ben, as ye youreselven se;
Nor thennes shal nat oon on-lyve come

For al the gold atwixen sonne and se.
Trusteth wel, and understondeth me,
Ther shal nat oon to mercy gon on-lyve,
Al were he lord of worldes twiës fyve!

'Swiche wreche on hem, for fecchynge of Eleyne,
Ther shal ben take er that we hennes wende,
That Manes, which that goddes ben of peyne,
Shal ben agast that Grekes wol hem shende.
And men shul drede, unto the worldes ende,
From hennesforth to ravysshen any queene,
So cruel shal oure wreche on hem be seene.

'And but if Calkas lede us with ambages,
That is to seyn, with double wordes slye,
Swiche as men clepen a word with two visages,
Ye shal wel knowen that I naught ne lye,
And al this thyng right sen it with youre yë,
And that anon, ye nyl net trowe how sone.
Now taketh hede for it is for to doone.

'What! wene ye youre wise fader wolde
Han yeven Antenor for yow anon,
If he ne wiste that the cite sholde
Destroied ben? Whi, nay, so mote I gon!
He knew ful wel ther shal nat scapen oon
That Troian is; and for the grete feere,
He dorste nat ye dwelte lenger there.

'What wol ye more, lufsom lady deere?
Lat Troie and Troian fro youre herte pace!
Drif out that bittre hope, and make good cheere,
And clepe ayeyn the beaute of youre face,
That ye with salte teris so deface.
For Troie is brought in swich a jupartie,
That it to save is now no remedie.

'And thenketh wel, ye shal in Grekis fynde
A moore parfit love, er it be nyght,
Than any Troian is, and more kynde,
And bet to serven yow wol don his myght.
And if ye vouchesauf, my lady bright,
I wol ben he to serven yow myselve,
Yee, revere than be lord of Greces twelve!'

And with that word he gan to waxen red,
And in his spectre a litel wight he quok,
And caste asyde a litle wight his hed,
And stynte a while, and afterward he wok,
And sobreliche on hire he threw his lok,

And seyde, 'I am, al be it yow no joie,
As gentil man as any wight in Troie.

'For if my fader Tideus,' he seyde,
'Ilyved hadde, ich hadde ben, er this,
Of Calydoyne and Arge a kyng, Criseyde!
And so hope I that I shal yet, iwis.
But he was slayn, allas! the more harm is,
Unhappily at Thebes al to rathe,
Polymytes and many a man to scathe.

'But herte myn, syn that I am youre man, –
And ben the first of whom I seche grace, –
To serve yow as hertely as I kan,
And evere shal, whil I to lyve have space,
So, er that I departe out of this place,
Ye wol me graunte that I may to-morwe,
At bettre leyser, tellen yow my sorwe.'

What sholde I telle his wordes that he seyde?
He spak inough, for o day at the meeste.
It preveth wel, he spak so that Criseyde
Graunted, on the morwe, at his requeste,
For to speken with hym at the leeste,
So that he nolde speke of swich matere.
And thus to hym she seyede, as ye may here,

As she that hadde hire herte on Troilus
So faste, that ther may it non arace;
And strangely she spak, and seyde thus:
'O Diomede, I love that ilke place
Ther I was born; and Joves, for his grace,
Delyvere it soone of al that doth it care!
God, for thy myght, so leve it wel to fare!'

THE LEGEND OF GOOD WOMEN

‹ Prologue ›

(lines 1–147)

A thousand tymes have I herd men telle
That ther ys joy in hevene and peyne in helle,
And I acorde wel that it ys so;
But, natheles, yet wot I wel also
That ther his noon dwellyng in this contree
That eyther hath in hevene or helle ybe,
Ne may of hit noon other weyes witen
But as he hath herd seyd or founde it writen;
For by assay ther may no man it preve.

But God forbede but men shulde leve
Wel more thing then men han seen with ye!
Men shal not wenen every thing a lye
But yf himself yt seeth or elles dooth;
For, God wot, thing is never the lasse sooth,
Thogh every wight ne may it nat ysee.
Bernard the monk ne saugh nat all, pardee!

    Than mote we to bokes that we fynde,
Thurgh whiche that olde thinges ben in mynde,
And to the doctrine of these olde wyse,
Yeve credence, in every skylful wise,
That tellen of these olde appreved stories
Of holynesse, of regnes, of victories,
Of love, of hate, of other sondry thynges,
Of whiche I may not maken rehersynges.
And yf that olde bokes were aweye,
Yloren were of remembraunce the keye.
Wel ought us thanne honouren and beleve
These bokes, there we han noon other preve.

    And as for me, though that I konne but lyte,
On bokes for to rede I me delyte,
And to hem yive I feyth and ful credence,
And in myn herte have hem in reverence
So hertely, that ther is game noon
That fro my bokes maketh me to goon,
But yt be seldom on the holyday,
Save, certeynly, whan that the month of May
Is comen, and that I here the foules synge,
And that the floures gynnen for to sprynge,
Farewel my bok and my devocioun!

    Now have I thanne eek this condicioun,
That, of al the floures in the mede,
Thanne love I most thise floures white and rede,
Swiche as men callen daysyes in our toun.
To hem have I so gret affeccioun,
As I seyde erst, whanne comen is the May,
That in my bed ther daweth me no day
That I nam up and walkyng in the mede
To seen this flour ayein the sonne sprede,
Whan it upryseth erly by the morwe.
That blisful sighte softneth al my sorwe,
So glad am I, whan that I have presence
Of it, to doon it alle reverence,
As she that is of alle floures flour,
Fulfilled of al vertu and honour,
And evere ilyke faire and fressh of hewe;
And I love it, and ever ylike newe,
And evere shal, til that myn herte dye.
Al swere I nat, of this I wol nat lye;
Ther loved no wight hotter in his lyve.
And whan that hit ye eve, I renne blyve,

As sone as evere the sonne gynneth weste,
To seen this flour, how it wol go to reste,
For fere of nyght, so hateth she derknesse.

Hire chere is pleynly sprad in the brightnesse
Of the sonne, for ther yt wol unclose.
Allas, that I ne had Englyssh, ryme or prose,
Suffisant this flour to preyse aryght!
But helpeth, ye that hen konnyng and myght,
Ye lovers that kan make of sentement;
In this cas oghte ye be diligent
To forthren me somwhat in my labour,
Whethir ye ben with the leef or with the flour.
For wel I wot that ye han her- biforn
Of makyng ropen, and lad awey the corn,
And I come after, glenyng here and there,
And am ful glad yf I may fynde an ere
Of any goodly word that ye han left.
And thogh it happen me rehercen eft
That ye han in your fresshe songes sayd.
Forbereth me, and beth nat evele apayd,
Syn that ye see I do yt in the honour
Of love, and eke in service of the flour
Whom that I serve as I have wit or myght.
She is the clernesse and the verray lyght
That in this derke world me wynt and ledeth.
The inert in-with my sorwfull brest yow dredeth
And loveth so sore that ye ben verrayly
The maistresse of my wit, and nothing I.
My word, my werk ys knyt so in youre bond
That, as an harpe obeieth to the hond
And maketh it soune after his fyngerynge,
Ryght so mowe ye oute of myn herte bringe
Swich vois, ryght as yow lyst, to laughe or pleyne.
Be ye my gide and lady sovereyne!
As to myn erthly god to yow I calle,
Bothe in this werk and in my sorwes alle.

    But wherfore that I spak, to yive credence
To olde stories and doon hem reverence,
And that men mosten more thyng beleve
Then men may seen at eye, or elles preve –
'That shal I seyn, whanne that I see my tyme;
I may not al at-ones speke in ryme.
My besy gost, that thursteth alwey newe
To seen this flour so yong, so fressh of hewe,
Constreyned me with so gledy desir
That in myn herte I feele yet the fir
That made me to ryse er yt were day –
And this was now the firste morwe of May –
With dredful hert and glad devocioun,
For to ben at the resureccioun

Of this flour, when that yt shulde unclose
Agayn the sonne, that roos as red as rose,
That in the brest was of the beste, that day,
That Agenores doghtre ladde away.
And doun on knes anoon-ryght I me sette,
And, as I koude, this fresshe flour I grette,
Knelyng alwey, til it unclosed was,
Upon the smale, softe, swote gras,
That was with floures swote enbrouded al,
Of swich swetnesse and swich odour overal,
That, for to speke of gomme, or herbe, or tree,
Comparisoun may noon ymaked bee;
For yt surmounteth pleynly alle odoures,
And of riche beaute alle floures.
Forgeten hadde the erthe his pore estat
Of wynter, that hym naked made and mat,
And with his swerd of cold so sore greved;
Now hath th'atempre sonne all that releved,
That naked was, and clad him new agayn.
The smale foules, of the sesoun fayn,
That from the panter and the net ben scaped,
Upon the foweler, that hem made awhaped
In wynter, and distroyed hadde hire brood,
In his dispit hem thoghte yt did hem good
To synge of hym, and in hir song despise
The foule cherl that, for his coveytise.
Had hem betrayed with his sophistrye.
This was hire song: 'The foweler we deffye,
And al his craft.' And somme songen clere
Layes of love, that joye it was to here,
In worship and in preysinge of hir make;
And for the newe blisful somers sake,
Upon the braunches ful of blosmes softe
In hire delyt they turned hem ful ofte,
And songen, 'Blessed be Seynt Valentyn,
For on his day I chees yow to be myn,
Withouten repentyng, myn herte swete!'

Glossary

ASSAY: experiment; BUT MEN: that men; WYSE: wise writers; APPREVED: proven true; YLOREN: lost; ILYKE: equally; WESTE: go westward; MAKE OF: write about; OF MAKING ROPEN: reaped (the fruit) of writing; GLENYNG: gleaning; ERE: ear (of grain); FORBERETH ME: bear with me; WYNT: turns, directs; BESY GOST: eager spirit; GLEDY: burning; IN THE BREST WAS OF THE BESTE: in the middle part of the zodiac sign Taurus (the Bull); ENBROUDED: adorned; GOMME: gum; PANTER: bird snare; AWHAPED: stunned

John Clare was born at Helpstone, Northamptonshire in 1793, his father a farm-labourer and his mother the daughter of a local shepherd. He was therefore deep-rooted in a place and in a class by his parents, and was also affected by their 'trash of Ballad Singing ... my first feelings and attempts at poetry were imitations of my father's songs ...' He worked as a labourer, continually composing poems and in 1820 a selection of these was published by John Taylor (Keats's publisher), which had a great and fashionable success.

Fashion changed, Clare continued to write, but further volumes failed. Disappointed, horrified by the cruel changes (enclosures) of the world he knew and loved, in 1837 he mentally broke down and was taken into a kindly private asylum in Epping Forest. Four years later he walked home from the place, eighty miles in three and a half days, subsisting on roadside grass. Later that year, 1841, he was certified insane and confined, again with much understanding, in the Northampton Asylum, where he remained, continuing to write, for twenty-three years until his death.

He composed ballads, long narratives in verse, philosophical poems, 'imitations' of other poets, and in this selection an attempt is made to suggest that variety: his genius lay in his quick observation of the people and places and creatures (especially birds) he saw around him. Edmund Blunden remarked on Clare's 'elemental terse-ness' and likened it to the nature-engravings of Bewick. Clare knew that accurate description is like turning down a page in a book to mark a favourite passage (which may be a bad habit but Coleridge used the butter-knife): 'How many pages of sweet nature's book/Has poetry doubled down as favourite things ...' and thereby fixed the transient. His genius was for detail. His milkmaid turns her buckets upside down so that she and Clare can sit, then she milks her 'breathing' cows – we see their steaming breath. His 'elemental terseness' can end a poem about a mouse's nest, suddenly, 'The water o'er the pebbles scarce could run/And broad old cesspools glittered in the sun.' After the close-up the long-shot, placing the mouse (and Clare) in their world and season.

from NORTHBOROUGH SONNETS

I often longed when wandering up & down
To hear the rustle of thy Sunday gown
& when we met I passed & let thee go
& felt I loved but dare not tell thee so
Snares are so thickly spread in womans way
The common ballad teaches men betray
I thought & felt it rudeness if I tried
& well meant kindness might be missapplied
I longed to walk with thee where waters play
& lined with water cresses all the way
I read the poets as I went along
& thought they knew thy name in every song
The mind on thee & beautys music dwells
& listens to the sound of Glinton bells

The weeds are dressing ready here
& spring is coming every where
The maid goes round in proud dislike
To shun the water in the dyke
She might stride oer but young & shy
She dare not lift her leg so high
Though beautiful & neat attired
Her very footmark is admired
The clown looks down with wondering eyes
& knows it womans by the size
They look upon the shape so rare
& know that beauty travelled there
The roads are padded far & near
& spring is coming every where

I found a ball of grass among the hay
& proged it as I passed & went away
& when I looked I fancied somthing stirred
& turned agen & hoped to catch the bird
When out an old mouse bolted in the wheat
With all her young ones hanging at her teats
She looked so odd & so grotesque to me
I ran & wondered what the thing could be
& pushed the knapweed bunches where I stood
When the mouse hurried from the crawling brood
The young ones squeaked & when I went away
She found her nest again among the hay
The water oer the pebbles scarce could run
& broad old cesspools glittered in the sun

YOUNG LAMBS

The spring is coming by a many signs
The trays are up the hedges broken down
That fenced the haystack & the remnant shines
Like some old antique fragment weathered brown
& where suns press in every sheltered place
The little early buttercups unfold
A glittering star or two – till many trace
The edges of the blackthorn clumps in gold
& then a little lamb bolts up behind
The hill & wags his tail to meet the yoe
& then another sheltered from the wind
Lies all his length as dead – & lets me go
Close bye & never stirs but beaking lies
With legs stretched out as though he could not rise

THE MILKING HOUR

The sun had grown on lessening day
A table large & round
& in the distant vapours grey
Seemed leaning on the ground
When Mary like a lingering flower
Did tenderly agree
To stay beyond her milking hour
& talk awhile with me

We wandered till the distant town
Had silenced nearly dumb
& lessened on the quiet ear
Small as a beetles hum
She turned her buckets upside & down
& made us each a seat
& there we talked the evening brown
Beneath the rustling wheat

& while she milked her breathing cows
I sat beside the streams
In musing oer our evening joys
Like one in pleasant dreams
The bats & owls to meet the night
From hollow trees had gone
& een the flowers had shut for sleep
& still she lingered on

We mused in rapture side by side
Our wishes seemed as one

We talked of times retreating tide
& sighed to find it gone
& we had sighed more deeply still
Oer all our pleasures past
If we had known what now we know
That we had met the last

THE OFFER A BALLAD

With my hair down my back & bibbed up to my
   chin
Friends had made me a child all the days of my life
Had'n't love a peeped through the disguise I was in
& whispered Bob Rattle to look for a wife
He made me supprised when I heard what he said
& I felt from that hour like a bird that is free
Childish thoughts all for ever went out of my head
& I 'greed Robin Rattles should come & court me

I grew mortal sick of my mothers old fashions
Tyed a bow 'gainst her will feth & shifted a pin
& little she guessed though she fell into passions
Twas done Robin Rattles the ploughman to win
& vain had she made me consciet I d been younger
She might as well said snow in harvest would be
As tye me a child at her woolen wheel longer
When Rob offered making a woman of me

MAYING OR LOVE AND FLOWERS
(lines 17–32; 49–56; 65–80; 89–130)

He gathered flowers a pleasing task
To crown her queen of may
But dare not give nor would she ask
So threw them all away
Then from her path she turned aside
& took a double pain
To gather others far & wide
& so he sighed again

The wind enamoured of the maid
Around her drapery swims
& moulds in luscious masquerade
Her lovely shape & limbs
Smiths 'Venus stealing Cupids bow'

In marble hides as fine
But hers was life & soul – whose glow
Makes meaner things divine

[. . .]

Her eyes like suns did seem to light
The beautys of her face
Streaming up her forhead white
& cheeks of rosey grace
Her bosom swelled to pillows large
Till her so taper waist
Scarce able seemed to bear the charge
Of each lawn-bursting breast

[. . .]

Then off she skips in bowers to hide
By Cupid led I ween
Putting her bosoms lawn aside
To place some thyme atween
The shepherd saw her skin so white
Two twin suns newly risen
Though love had chained him there till night
Who would have shunned the prison

Then off again she skipt & flew
With foot so light & little
That Cinderellas fairy shoe
Had fit her to a tittle
The shepherds heart like blazing coal
Beat as 'twould leave the socket
He sighed but thought it, silly fool,
The watch within his pocket

[. . .]

'Fair flower' said he 'Whose that' quoth she
& tied her flowers together
Then sought for more 'ah woe is me'
He said or sighed it rather
Then grasped her arm that soft & white
Like to a pillow dinted
& blushing red as at a bite
His fingers there were printed
& ah he sighed to mark the sight
That unmeant rudeness hinted . . .

But bold in love grow silly sheep
& so right bold grew he
He ran she fled & at bo-peep
She met him round a tree
A thorn enamoured like the swain
Caught at her lily arm

& then good faith to ease her pain
Love had a double charm

She sighed he wished it well I wis
The place was sadly swollen
And then he took a willing kiss
And made believe twas stolen
Then made another make believe
Till thefts grew past concealing
For when love once begins to thieve
Their grows no end to stealing

They played & toyed till down the skies
The sun had taken flight
And still a sun was in her eyes
To keep away the night
And there he talked of love so well
Or else he talked so ill
That soon the priest was sought to tell
The story better still

❧

SUDDEN SHOWER

Black grows the southern sky, betokening rain,
    And humming hive-bees homeward hurry by:
They feel the change; so let us shun the grain,
    And take the broad road while our feet are dry.
Ay, there some dropples moistened on my face,
    And pattered on my hat – 'tis coming nigh!
Let's look about, and find a sheltering place.
    The little things around, like you and I,
Are hurrying through the grass to shun the shower.
    Here stoops an ash-tree – hark! the wind gets
      high,
But never mind; this ivy, for an hour,
    Rain as it may, will keep us dryly here:
That little wren knows well his sheltering bower,
    Nor leaves his dry house though we come so
      near.

❧

Market Day

With arms and legs at work and gentle stroke
That urges switching tail nor mends his pace,
On an old ribbed and weather-beaten horse,
The farmer goes jogtrotting to the fair,
Both keep their pace that nothing can provoke,
Followed by brindled dog that snuffs the ground
With urging bark and hurries at his heels.
His hat slouched down, and greatcoat buttoned
   close
Bellied like hoopèd keg, and chuffy face
Red as the morning sun, he takes his round
And talks of stock: and when his jobs are done
And Dobbin's hay is eaten from the rack,
He drinks success to corn in language hoarse,
And claps old Dobbin's hide, and potters back.

Gipsies

The snow falls deep; the forest lies alone;
The boy goes hasty for his load of brakes,
Then thinks upon the fire and hurries back;
The gipsy knocks his hands and tucks them up
And seeks his squalid camp, half hid in snow,
Beneath the oak which breaks away the wind,
And bushes close in snow like hovel warm;
There tainted mutton wastes upon the coals,
And the half-wasted dog squats close and rubs,
Then feels the heat too strong, and goes aloof;
He watches well, but none a bit can spare,
And vainly waits the morsel thrown away.
'Tis thus they live – a picture to the place,
A quiet, pilfering, unprotected race.

The Flight of Birds

The crow goes flopping on from wood to wood,
The wild duck wherries to the distant flood,
The starnels hurry o'er in merry crowds,
And overhead whew by like hasty clouds;
The wild duck from the meadow-water plies
And dashes up the water as he flies;
The pigeon suthers by on rapid wing,
The lark mounts upward at the call of spring.

In easy flights above the hurricane
With doubled neck high sails the noisy crane.
Whizz goes the pewit o'er the ploughman's team,
With many a whew and whirl and sudden scream;
And lightly fluttering to the tree just by,
In chattering journeys whirls the noisy pie;
From bush to bush slow swees the screaming jay,
With one harsh note of pleasure all the day.

I Am

I am – yet what I am none cares or knows,
   My friends forsake me like a memory lost;
I am the self-consumer of my woes,
   They rise and vanish in oblivions host,
Like shadows in love – frenzied stifled throes
And yet I am, and live like vapours tost

Into the nothingness of scorn and noise,
   Into the living sea of waking dreams,
Where there is neither sense of life or joys,
   But the vast shipwreck of my life's esteems;
And e'en the dearest – that I love the best –
Are strange – nay, rather stranger than the rest.

I long for scenes where man has never trod,
   A place where woman never smiled or wept;
There to abide with my Creator, God,
   And sleep as I in childhood sweetly slept:
Untroubling and untroubled where I lie,
   The grass below – above the vaulted sky.

Mary Byfield

'Twas in the morning early,
The dew was on the barley,
   Each spear a string of beads;
Blue-caps intensely blue,
Corn poppies burnt me through,
   Seemed flowers among the weeds.

Her cheeks the rosy brere's bloom,
Her eyes like ripples, lately come
   From gravel-paven spring;
She looked across the red and blue,

Each colour wore a livelier hue,
  While larks popt up to sing.

How lovely hung the barley spears,
Beaded in morning's dewy tears
  Rich green and grey did seem;
The pea more rich than velvet glows,
Sweeter than double the dog-rose,
  A sweet midsummer dream.

The sun gleamed o'er that waving corn
Where her I kissed one dewy morn,
  A shining golden river.
I clasped her in a locked embrace,
And gazing on her bonny face,
  I loved her and for ever.

Glossary

PADDED: well-trodden; PROGED: poked; TRAYS: sheep-hurdles; YOE: ewe;
BEAKING: basking; FETH: faith! (interjection); BRAKES: braken;
STARNELS: starlings; SUTHERS: whirrs; PIE: magpie; SWEES: swings;
BLUE-CAPS: cornflowers; BRERE: briar.

Arthur Hugh Clough (Liverpool 1819 – Florence 1861, educated at Rugby and Balliol) wrote some neat short poems that have entered the anthologies, but his most original work was the not-very-poetic, indeed not-entirely-well-written long poems which aspire to the more inclusive reality of fiction. As if to emphasize their story-telling aim, the two best-known of these long poems were composed in an accentual version of Homer's hexameters (with a very liberal use of the double-spondaic ending rather than the more familiar dactyl-plus-spondee). These two, *The Bothie of Toper-na-Fuosich* (first published with this name in 1848 in England and in 1849 in America) and *Amours de Voyage* (*Atlantic Monthly*, 1858) were (characteristically) both revised by Clough after publication as if he could not accept that they were finished. The two other long poems, *Dipsychus and the Spirit* and *Mari Magno*, also much worked over, remained incomplete and unpublished on Clough's death at the age of forty-two.

Amours de Voyage, a short epistolary novel in verse set in Italy at the time of the brief Roman Republic (1849), binds together in its five cantos more Victorian themes than can easily be demonstrated in the space available, but perhaps this selection may arouse a desire to read the whole work. 'The American's Tale' is an extract from *Mari Magno*, a collection of stories about love and marriage told by friends met on a trip across the Atlantic to Boston.

AMOURS DE VOYAGE

‹Canto II: iv. Claude to Eustace›

Now supposing the French or the Neapolitan soldier
Should by some evil chance come exploring the
    Maison Serny
(Where the family English are all to assembly for
    safety),
Am I prepared to lay down my life for the British
    female?
Really, who knows? One has bowed and talked, till,
    little by little,
All the natural heat has escaped of the chivalrous
    spirit.
Oh, one conformed, of course; but one doesn't die
    for good manners,
Stab or shoot, or be shot, by way of graceful attention.
No, if it should be at all, it should be on the
    barricades there;
Should I incarnadine ever this inky pacifical finger,
Sooner far should it be for this vapour of Italy's
    freedom,
Sooner far by the side of the d—d and dirty plebeians.
Ah, for a child in the street I could strike; for the
    full-blown lady –
Somehow, Eustace, alas! I have not felt the vocation.
Yet these people of course will expect, as of course,
    my protection,
Vernon in radiant arms stand forth for the lovely
    Georgina,
And to appear, I suppose, were but common civility.
    Yes, and
Truly I do not desire they should either be killed or
    offended.
Oh, and of course you will say, 'When the time
    comes, you will be ready.'
Ah, but before it comes, am I to presume it will be so?
What I cannot feel now, am I to suppose that I shall
    feel?
Am I not free to attend for the ripe and indubious
    instinct?
Am I forbidden to wait for the clear and lawful
    perception?
Is it the calling of man to surrender his knowledge
    and insight,
For the mere venture of what may, perhaps, be the
    virtuous action?
Must we, walking our earth, discerning a little, and
    hoping
Some plain visible task shall yet for our hands be
    assigned us, –

Must we abandon the future for fear of omitting the
    present,
Quit our own fireside hopes at the alien call of a
    neighbour,
To the mere possible shadow of Deity offer the victim?
And is all this, my friend, but a weak and ignoble
    refining,
Wholly unworthy the head or the heart of Your
    Own Correspondent?

‹v. Claude to Eustace›

Yes, we are fighting at last, it appears. This morning
    as usual,
Murray, as usual, in hand, I enter the Caffè Nuovo;
Seating myself with a sense as it were of a change in
    the weather,
Not understanding, however, but thinking mostly
    of Murray,
And, for to-day is their day, of the Campidoglio
    Marbles,
Caffè-latte! I call to the waiter, – and *Non c' è latte,*
This is the answer he makes me, and this the sign of
    a battle.
So I sit; and truly they seem to think any one else
    more
Worthy than me of attention. I wait for my milkless
    nero,
Free to observe undistracted all sorts and sizes of
    persons,
Blending civilian and soldier in strangest costume,
    coming in, and
Gulping in hottest haste, still standing, their coffee,
    – withdrawing
Eagerly, jangling a sword on the steps, or jogging a
    musket
Slung to the shoulder behind. They are fewer,
    moreover, than usual,
Much, and silenter far; and so I begin to imagine
Something is really afloat. Ere I leave, the Caffè is
    empty,
Empty too the streets, in all its length the Corso
Empty, and empty I see to my right and left the
    Condotti.
    Twelve o'clock, on the Pincian Hill, with lots of
    English,
Germans, Americans, French, – the Frenchmen, too,
    are protected, –
So we stand in the sun, but afraid of a probable
    shower;
So we stand and stare, and see, to the left of St.
    Peter's,

Smoke, from the cannon, white, – but that is at
    intervals only, –
Black, from a burning house, we suppose, by the
    Cavalleggieri;
And we believe we discern some lines of men
    descending
Down through the vineyard-slopes, and catch a
    bayonet gleaming.
Every ten minutes, however, – in this there is no
    misconception, –
Comes a great white puff from behind Michel
    Angelo's dome, and
After a space the report of a real big gun, – not the
    Frenchman's? –
That must be doing some work. And so we watch
    and conjecture.
Shortly, an Englishman comes, who says he has been
    to St. Peter's,
Seen the Piazza and troops, but that is all he can tell us;
So we watch and sit, and, indeed, it begins to be
    tiresome. –
All this smoke is outside; when it has come to the
    inside,
It will be time, perhaps, to descend and retreat to
    our houses.
    Half past one, or two. The report of small arms
    frequent,
Sharp and savage indeed; that cannot all be for
    nothing:
So we watch and wonder; but guessing is tiresome,
    very.
Weary of wondering, watching, and guessing, and
    gossiping idly,
Down I go, and pass through the quiet streets with
    the knots of
National Guards patrolling, and flags hanging out
    at the windows,
English, American, Danish, – and, after offering to
    help an
Irish family moving *en masse* to the Maison Serny,
After endeavouring idly to minister balm to the
    trembling
Quinquagenarian fears of two lone British spinsters,
Go to make sure of my dinner before the enemy enter.
But by this there are signs of stragglers returning;
    and voices
Talk, though you don't believe it, of guns and
    prisoners taken;
And on the walls you read the first bulletin of the
    morning. –
This is all that I saw, and all I know of the battle.

‹ vii. Claude to Eustace ›

So, I have seen a man killed! An experience that,
    among others!
Yes, I suppose I have; although I can hardly be
    certain,
And in a court of justice could never declare I had
    seen it.
But a man was killed, I am told, in a place where I
    saw
Something; a man was killed, I am told, and I saw
    something.
    I was returning home from St. Peter's; Murray, as
    usual,
Under my arm, I remember; had crossed the St.
    Angelo bridge; and
Moving towards the Condotti, had got to the first
    barricade, when
Gradually, thinking still of St. Peter's, I became
    conscious
Of a sensation of movement opposing me, –
    tendency this way
(Such as one fancies may be in a stream when the
    wave of the tide is
Coming and not yet come, – a sort of poise and
    retention);
So I turned, and, before I turned, caught sight of
    stragglers
Heading a crowd, it is plain, that is coming behind
    that corner.
Looking up, I see windows filled with heads; the
    Piazza,
Into which you remember the Ponte St. Angelo
    enters,
Since I passed, has thickened with curious groups;
    and now the
Crowd is coming, has turned, has crossed that last
    barricade, is
Here at my side. In the middle they drag at
    something. What is it?
Ha! bare swords in the air, held up! There seem to
    be voices
Pleading and hands putting back; official, perhaps;
    but the swords are
Many, and bare in the air. In the air? They descend;
    they are smiting,
Hewing, chopping – At what? In the air once more
    upstretched! And
Is it blood that's on them? Yes, certainly blood! Of
    whom, then?
Over whom is the cry of this furor of exultation?

While they are skipping and screaming, and
    dancing their caps on the points of
Swords and bayonets, I to the outskirts back, and
    ask a
Mercantile-seeming by-stander, 'What is it?' and he,
    looking always
That way, makes me answer, 'A Priest, who was
    trying to fly to
The Neapolitan army,' – and thus explains the
    proceeding.
    You didn't see the dead man? No; – I began to be
    doubtful;
I was in black myself, and didn't know what
    mightn't happen; –
But a National Guard close by me, outside of the
    hubbub,
Broke his sword with slashing a broad hat covered
    with dust, – and
Passing away from the place with Murray under my
    arm, and
Stooping, I saw through the legs of the people the
    legs of a body.
    You are the first, do you know, to whom I have
    mentioned the matter.
Whom should I tell it to, else? – these girls? – the
    Heavens forbid it! –
Quidnuncs at Monaldini's? – idlers upon the
    Pincian?
    If I rightly remember, it happened on that
    afternoon when
Word of the nearer approach of a new Neapolitan
    army
First was spread. I began to bethink me of Paris
    Septembers,
Thought I could fancy the look of the old 'Ninety-
    two. On that evening
Three or four, or, it may be, five, of these people
    were slaughtered.
Some declare they had, one of them, fired on a
    sentinel; others
Say they were only escaping; a Priest, it is currently
    stated,
Stabbed a National Guard on the very Piazza
    Colonna:
History, Rumour of Rumours, I leave it to thee to
    determine!
    But I am thankful to say the government seems
    to have strength to
Put it down; it has vanished, at least; the place is
    most peaceful.

Through the Trastevere walking last night, at nine
    of the clock, I
Found no sort of disorder; I crossed by the Island-
    bridges,
So by the narrow streets to the Ponte Rotto, and
    onwards
Thence, by the Temple of Vesta, away to the great
    Coliseum,
Which at the full of the moon is an object worthy a
    visit.

‹viii. Georgina Trevellyn to Louisa – ›

Only think, dearest Louisa, what fearful scenes we
    have witnessed!

George has just seen Garibaldi, dressed up in a long
    white cloak, on
Horseback, riding by, with his mounted negro
    behind him:
This is a man, you know, who came from America
    with him,
Out of the woods, I suppose, and uses a *lasso* in
    fighting,
Which is, I don't quite know, but a sort of noose, I
    imagine;
This he throws on the heads of the enemy's men in
    a battle,
Pulls them into his reach, and then most cruelly
    kills them:
Mary does not believe, but we heard it from an
    Italian.
Mary allows she was wrong about Mr. Claude *being
    selfish*;
He was *most* useful and kind on the terrible thirtieth
    of April.
Do not write here any more; we are starting directly
    for Florence:
We should be off to-morrow, if only Papa could get
    horses;
All have been seized everywhere for the use of this
    dreadful Mazzini.

P.S.   Mary has seen thus far. – I am really so angry,
    Louisa, –
Quite out of patience, my dearest! What can the
    man be intending!
I am quite tired; and Mary, who might bring him to
    in a moment,
Lets him go on as he likes, and neither will help nor
    dismiss him.

◄ ix. Claude to Eustace ►

It is most curious to see what a power a few calm
    words (in
Merely a brief proclamation) appear to possess on
    the people.
Order is perfect, and peace; the city is utterly
    tranquil;
And one cannot conceive that this easy and
    nonchalant crowd, that
Flows like a quiet stream through street and
    market-place, entering
Shady recesses and bays of church, *osteria*, and *caffè*,
Could in a moment be changed to a flood as of
    molten lava,
Boil into deadly wrath and wild homicidal delusion.
    Ah, 'tis an excellent race, – and even in old
    degradation,
Under a rule that enforces to flattery, lying, and
    cheating,
E'en under Pope and Priest, a nice and natural
    people.
Oh, could they but be allowed this chance of
    redemption! – but clearly
That is not likely to be. Meantime, notwithstanding
    all journals,
Honour for once to the tongue and the pen of the
    eloquent writer!
Honour to speech! and all honour to thee, thou
    noble Mazzini!

◄ x. Claude to Eustace ►

I am in love, meantime, you think; no doubt you
    would think so.
I am in love, you say; with those letters, of course,
    you would say so.
I am in love, you declare. I think not so; yet I grant
    you
It is a pleasure, indeed, to converse with this girl.
    Oh, rare gift,
Rare felicity, this! she can talk in a rational way, can
Speak upon subjects that really are matters of mind
    and of thinking,
Yet in perfection retain her simplicity; never, one
    moment,
Never, however you urge it, however you tempt her,
    consents to
Step from ideas and fancies and loving sensations to
    those vain

Conscious understandings that vex the minds of
    man-kind.
No, though she talk, it is music; her fingers desert
    not the keys; 'tis
Song, though you hear in the song the articulate
    vocables sounded,
Syllabled singly and sweetly the words of melodious
    meaning.
    I am in love, you say; I do not think so exactly.

THE AMERICAN'S TALE
◄ or Juxtaposition ►

This incident, I have been told, befell
Once in a huge American hotel.
    Two sisters slept together in one bed.
The elder, suffering with an aching head,
Early retired: the younger, late who came,
Found her asleep; in haste to be the same,
Undressed, but ready into bed to go,
Her watch remembered in a room below.
Just-robed she slipped away; with silent pace
Returned, she thought, and took her usual place
And slept, nor woke the sleeper by her laid.
The sun was shining high, ere woke the maid;
At once she woke, and waking, wondering eyed
In bed upseated, gazing, at her side
A youth: – her error flashed upon her mind,
And from the stranger's bed her own to find
Just-robed, she fled, and left her watch behind.
    Easy in a row of twenty rooms or more
At night to be deceived about a door.
    One quarter of a morning hour had sped
While he the maiden slumbering in his bed
Silent had viewed: and he had nothing said
Or sought to say to appease her waking fright
Or to retard a moment of her flight.
The watch he took; it marked not noonday yet,
Its owner in the garden when he met,
Swift he went up and almost ere she knew
Swift in her hands he placed it, swift withdrew.
    I know not how it was, my tale affirms
That after this they met on happy terms,
And love, that lives by accident, they say,
And scorns occasion offering every day,
Love, from this accident, it seems, arose,
Love and a happy marriage were the close.
Who told me this, a lady, said she knew.

Coleridge is at his best when most unlike Wordsworth, as in 'The Ancient Mariner', 'Christabel' and 'Kubla Khan', poems which are admirably terse, fast-moving and uncluttered by 'the sublime'. Coleridge said of 'The Ancient Mariner' that its moral was too openly obtrusive for 'a work of such pure imagination'. Yet the moral is a sound one, and follows naturally from the 'epiphanic' incident of the water-snakes; since the poem is too long to print in its entirety, I have quoted the two relevant passages. That 'Christabel' was unfinished may owe as much to the nature of its subject as to Coleridge's nature: how could Christabel be saved, or Geraldine redeemed? I include one excerpt, the revelation of Geraldine as a species of lamia or vampire and her dominance over the seemingly defenceless heroine. As for 'Kubla Khan', Coleridge may have composed two or three hundred lines in his sleep, but the fifty-four he wrote down before the (possibly mythical) caller from Porlock broke the spell don't strike us as a mere fragment.

The other excerption is the final stanza of 'France: An Ode', which illustrates neatly the changing view of the French Revolution held by intellectuals on this side of the Channel. The previous stanzas describe the initial enthusiasm, the shame of Britain's intervention, then the growing revulsion caused by the Terror and the invasion of Switzerland in 1798. Finally Coleridge declares that the ideal of freedom and the associated feelings inspired by nature's grandeur cannot possibly be (as a note has it) 'either gratified or realized under any form of human government, but belong to the individual man'.

Other poems here indicate that what Coleridge most yearned for was human sympathy: 'To be beloved is all I need,/And whom I love, I love indeed' ('The Pains of Sleep'), rather than the healing influence of nature à la Wordsworth: 'O Lady! we receive but what we give,/And in our life alone does Nature live' ('Dejection'). 'Dejection' centres on the faltering of Coleridge's 'shaping spirit of Imagination' under the weight of various afflictions, estrangement from his wife, hopeless love for another woman, addiction to opium, or perhaps metaphysics. And 'Work Without Hope' mourns the loss of poetic power and – in lines that remind us of George Herbert and G. M. Hopkins – his sense of insufficiency and uselessness, of being (in the bleak words of 'Epitaph') one who 'found death in life'.

THIS LIME-TREE BOWER MY PRISON

◄ Addressed to Charles Lamb, of the India House, London ►

In the June of 1797 some long-expected friends paid a visit to the author's cottage, and on the morning of their arrival, he met with an accident, which disabled him from walking during the whole time of their stay. One evening, when they had left him for a few hours, he composed the following lines in the garden-bower.

Well, they are gone, and here must I remain,
This lime-tree bower my prison! I have lost
Beauties and feelings, such as would have been
Most sweet to my remembrance even when age
Had dimmed mine eyes to blindness! They,
    meanwhile,
Friends, whom I never more may meet again,
On springy heath, along the hill-top edge,
Wander in gladness, and wind down, perchance,
To that still roaring dell, of which I told;
The roaring dell, o'erwooded, narrow, deep,
And only speckled by the mid-day sun;
Where its slim trunk the ash from rock to rock
Flings arching like a bridge; – that branchless ash,
Unsunned and damp, whose few poor yellow leaves
Ne'er tremble in the gale, yet tremble still,
Fanned by the water-fall! and there my friends
Behold the dark green file of long lank weeds,
That all at once (a most fantastic sight!)
Still nod and drip beneath the dripping edge
Of the blue clay-stone.

            Now, my friends emerge
Beneath the wide wide Heaven – and view again
The many-steepled tract magnificent
Of hilly fields and meadows, and the sea,
With some fair bark, perhaps, whose sails light up
The slip of smooth clear blue betwixt two Isles
Of purple shadow! Yes! they wander on
In gladness all; but thou, methinks, most glad,
My gentle-hearted Charles! for thou hast pined
And hungered after Nature, many a year,
In the great City pent, winning thy way
With sad yet patient soul, through evil and pain
And strange calamity! Ah! slowly sink
Behind the western ridge, thou glorious sun!
Shine in the slant beams of the sinking orb,
Ye purple heath-flowers! richlier burn, ye clouds!
Live in the yellow light, ye distant groves!

And kindle, thou blue ocean! So my friend
Struck with deep joy may stand, as I have stood,
Silent with swimming sense; yea, gazing round
On the wide landscape, gaze till all doth seem
Less gross than bodily, and of such hues
As veil the Almighty Spirit, when yet he makes
Spirits perceive his presence.

> A delight
Comes sudden on my heart, and I am glad
As I myself were there! Nor in this bower,
This little lime-tree bower, have I not marked
Much that has soothed me. Pale beneath the blaze
Hung the transparent foliage; and I watched
Some broad and sunny leaf, and loved to see
The shadow of the leaf and stem above
Dappling its sunshine! And that walnut-tree
Was richly tinged, and a deep radiance lay
Full on the ancient ivy, which usurps
Those fronting elms, and now, with blackest mass
Makes their dark branches gleam a lighter hue
Through the late twilight: and though now the bat
Wheels silent by, and not a swallow twitters,
Yet still the solitary humble-bee
Sings in the bean-flower! Henceforth I shall know
That Nature ne'er deserts the wise and pure;
No plot so narrow, be but Nature there,
No waste so vacant, but may well employ
Each faculty of sense, and keep the heart
Awake to Love and Beauty! and sometimes
'Tis well to be bereft of promised good,
That we may lift the soul, and contemplate
With lively joy the joys we cannot share.
My gentle-hearted Charles! when the last rook
Beat its straight path along the dusky air
Homewards, I blest it! deeming its black wing
(Now a dim speck, now vanishing in light)
Had crossed the mighty orb's dilated glory,
While thou stood'st gazing; or, when all was still,
Flew creaking o'er thy head, and had a charm
For thee, my gentle-hearted Charles, to whom
No sound is dissonant which tells of Life.

THE RIME OF THE ANCIENT MARINER
(lines 308–23; 696–9)

Beyond the shadow of the ship,
I watched the water-snakes:
They moved in tracks of shining white,
And when they reared, the elfish light
Fell off in hoary flakes.

Within the shadow of the ship
I watched their rich attire:
Blue, glossy green, and velvet black,
They coiled and swam; and every track
Was a flash of golden fire.

O happy living things! no tongue
Their beauty might declare:
A spring of love gushed from my heart,
And I blessed them unaware:
Sure my kind saint took pity on me,
And I blessed them unaware.

[. . .]

He prayeth best, who loveth best
All things both great and small;
For the dear God who loveth us,
He made and loveth all.

CHRISTABEL
(lines 245–78)

Beneath the lamp the lady bowed,
And slowly rolled her eyes around;
Then drawing in her breath aloud,
Like one that shuddered, she unbound
The cincture from beneath her breast:
Her silken robe, and inner vest,
Dropt to her feet, and full in view,
Behold! her bosom and half her side –
A sight to dream of, not to tell!
O shield her! shield sweet Christabel!

Yet Geraldine nor speaks nor stirs;
Ah! what a stricken look was hers!
Deep from within she seems half-way
To lift some weight with sick assay,
And eyes the maid and seeks delay;
Then suddenly, as one defied,

Collects herself in scorn and pride,
And lay down by the maiden's side! –
And in her arms the maid she took,
     Ah well-a-day!
And with low voice and doleful look
These words did say:
'In the touch of this bosom there worketh a spell,
Which is lord of thy utterance, Christabel!
Thou knowest to-night, and wilt know to-morrow,
This mark of my shame, this seal of my sorrow;
    But vainly thou warrest,
      For this is alone in
    Thy power to declare,
      That in the dim forest
    Thou heard'st a low moaning,
And found'st a bright lady, surpassingly fair;
And didst bring her home with thee in love and in
   charity,
To shield her and shelter her from the damp air.'

❧

FROST AT MIDNIGHT

The frost performs its secret ministry,
Unhelped by any wind. The owlet's cry
Came loud – and hark, again! loud as before.
The inmates of my cottage, all at rest,
Have left me to that solitude, which suits
Abstruser musings: save that at my side
My cradled infant slumbers peacefully.
'Tis calm indeed! so calm, that it disturbs
And vexes meditation with its strange
And extreme silentness. Sea, hill, and wood,
This populous village! Sea, and hill, and wood,
With all the numberless goings-on of life,
Inaudible as dreams! the thin blue flame
Lies on my low-burnt fire, and quivers not;
Only that film, which fluttered on the grate,
Still flutters there, the sole unquiet thing.
Methinks, its motion in this hush of nature
Gives it dim sympathies with me who live,
Making it a companionable form,
Whose puny flaps and freaks the idling Spirit
By its own moods interprets, every where
Echo or mirror seeking of itself,
And makes a toy of Thought.

               But O! how oft,
How oft, at school, with most believing mind,

Presageful, have I gazed upon the bars,
To watch that fluttering stranger! and as oft
With unclosed lids, already had I dreamt
Of my sweet birth-place, and the old church-tower,
Whose bells, the poor man's only music, rang
From morn to evening, all the hot Fair-day,
So sweetly, that they stirred and haunted me
With a wild pleasure, falling on mine ear
Most like articulate sounds of things to come!
So gazed I, till the soothing things I dreamt
Lulled me to sleep, and sleep prolonged my dreams!
And so I brooded all the following morn,
Awed by the stern preceptor's face, mine eye
Fixed with mock study on my swimming book:
Save if the door half opened, and I snatched
A hasty glance, and still my heart leaped up,
For still I hoped to see the *stranger's* face,
Townsman, or aunt, or sister more beloved,
My play-mate when we both were clothed alike!

   Dear Babe, that sleepest cradled by my side,
Whose gentle breathings, heard in this deep calm,
Fill up the interspersèd vacancies
And momentary pauses of the thought!
My babe so beautiful! it thrills my heart
With tender gladness, thus to look at thee,
And think that thou shalt learn far other lore,
And in far other scenes! For I was reared
In the great city, pent 'mid cloisters dim,
And saw nought lovely but the sky and stars.
But thou, my babe! shalt wander like a breeze
By lakes and sandy shores, beneath the crags
Of ancient mountain, and beneath the clouds,
Which image in their bulk both lakes and shores
And mountain crags: so shalt thou see and hear
The lovely shapes and sounds intelligible
Of that eternal language, which thy God
Utters, who from eternity doth teach
Himself in all, and all things in himself.
Great universal Teacher! he shall mould
Thy spirit, and by giving make it ask.

   Therefore all seasons shall be sweet to thee,
Whether the summer clothe the general earth
With greenness, or the redbreast sit and sing
Betwixt the tufts of snow on the bare branch
Of mossy apple-tree, while the nigh thatch
Smokes in the sun-thaw; whether the eave-drops fall
Heard only in the trances of the blast,
Or if the secret ministry of frost

Shall hang them up in silent icicles,
Quietly shining to the quiet Moon.

❦

FRANCE: AN ODE

(lines 85–end)

The Sensual and the Dark rebel in vain,
Slaves by their own compulsion! In mad game
They burst their manacles and wear the name
    Of Freedom, graven on a heavier chain!
O Liberty! with profitless endeavour
Have I pursued thee, many a weary hour;
    But thou nor swell'st the victor's strain, nor ever
Didst breathe thy soul in forms of human power.
    Alike from all, howe'er they praise thee,
    (Nor prayer, nor boastful name delays thee)
    Alike from Priestcraft's harpy minions,
    And factious Blasphemy's obscener slaves,
    Thou speedest on thy subtle pinions,
The guide of homeless winds, and playmate of the
        waves!
And there I felt thee! – on that sea-cliff's verge,
    Whose pines, scarce travelled by the breeze above,
Had made one murmur with the distant surge!
Yes, while I stood and gazed, my temples bare,
And shot my being through earth, sea and air,
    Possessing all things with intensest love,
    O Liberty! my spirit felt thee there.

❦

KUBLA KHAN

In Xanadu did Kubla Khan
A stately pleasure-dome decree:
Where Alph, the sacred river, ran
Through caverns measureless to man
    Down to a sunless sea.
So twice five miles of fertile ground
With walls and towers were girdled round:
And there were gardens bright with sinuous rills
Where blossomed many an incense-bearing tree;
And here were forests ancient as the hills,
Enfolding sunny spots of greenery.

But oh! that deep romantic chasm which slanted
Down the green hill athwart a cedarn cover!

A savage place! as holy and enchanted
As e'er beneath a waning moon was haunted
By woman wailing for her demon-lover!
And from this chasm, with ceaseless turmoil
    seething,
As if this earth in fast thick pants were breathing,
A mighty fountain momently was forced:
Amid whose swift half-intermitted burst
Huge fragments vaulted like rebounding hail,
Or chaffy grain beneath the thresher's flail:
And 'mid these dancing rocks at once and ever
It flung up momently the sacred river.
Five miles meandering with a mazy motion
Through wood and dale the sacred river ran,
Then reached the caverns measureless to man,
And sank in tumult to a lifeless ocean:
And 'mid this tumult Kubla heard from far
Ancestral voices prophesying war!

    The shadow of the dome of pleasure
    Floated midway on the waves;
    Where was heard the mingled measure
    From the fountain and the caves.
It was a miracle of rare device,
A sunny pleasure-dome with caves of ice!

    A damsel with a dulcimer
    In a vision once I saw:
    It was an Abyssinian maid,
    And on her dulcimer she played,
    Singing of Mount Abora.
    Could I revive within me
    Her symphony and song,
    To such a deep delight 'twould win me,
That with music loud and long,
I would build that dome in air,
That sunny dome! those caves of ice!
And all who heard should see them there,
And all should cry, Beware! Beware!
His flashing eyes, his floating hair!
Weave a circle round him thrice,
And close your eyes with holy dread,
For he on honey-dew hath fed,
And drunk the milk of Paradise.

❦

LOVE

All thoughts, all passions, all delights,
Whatever stirs this mortal frame,
All are but ministers of Love,
    And feed his sacred flame.

Oft in my waking dreams do I
Live o'er again that happy hour,
When midway on the mount I lay,
    Beside the ruined tower.

The moonshine, stealing o'er the scene,
Had blended with the lights of eve;
And she was there, my hope, my joy,
    My own dear Genevieve!

She leant against the armèd man.
The statue of the armèd knight;
She stood and listened to my lay,
    Amid the lingering light.

Few sorrows hath she of her own,
My hope! my joy! my Genevieve!
She loves me best, whene'er I sing
    The songs that make her grieve.

I played a soft and doleful air,
I sang an old and moving story –
An old rude song, that suited well
    That ruin wild and hoary.

She listened with a flitting blush,
With downcast eyes and modest grace;
For well she knew, I could not choose
    But gaze upon her face.

I told her of the Knight that wore
Upon his shield a burning brand;
And that for ten long years he wooed
    The Lady of the Land.

I told her how he pined: and ah!
The deep, the low, the pleading tone
With which I sang another's love,
    Interpreted my own.

She listened with a flitting blush,
With downcast eyes, and modest grace;
And she forgave me, that I gazed
    Too fondly on her face!

But when I told the cruel scorn
That crazed that bold and lovely Knight,
And that he crossed the mountain-woods,
    Nor rested day nor night;

That sometimes from the savage den,
And sometimes from the darksome shade,
And sometimes starting up at once
    In green and sunny glade –

There came and looked him in the face
An angel beautiful and bright;
And that he knew it was a Fiend,
    This miserable Knight!

And that, unknowing what he did,
He leaped amid a murderous band,
And saved from outrage worse than death
    The Lady of the Land!

And how she wept, and clasped his knees;
And how she tended him in vain –
And ever strove to expiate
    The scorn that crazed his brain –

And that she nursed him in a cave;
And how his madness went away,
When on the yellow forest-leaves
    A dying man he lay –

His dying words – but when I reached
That tenderest strain of all the ditty,
My faltering voice and pausing harp
    Disturbed her soul with pity!

All impulses of soul and sense
Had thrilled my guileless Genevieve;
The music and the doleful tale,
    The rich and balmy eve;

And hopes, and fears that kindle hope,
An undistinguishable throng,
And gentle wishes long subdued,
    Subdued and cherished long!

She wept with pity and delight,
She blushed with love, and virgin-shame;
And like the murmur of a dream,
    I heard her breathe my name.

Her bosom heaved – she stepped aside,
As conscious of my look she stept –
Then suddenly, with timorous eye
    She fled to me and wept.

She half enclosed me with her arms,
She pressed me with a meek embrace;
And bending back her head, looked up
    And gazed upon my face.

'Twas partly love, and partly fear,
And partly 'twas a bashful art,
That I might rather feel, than see,
    The swelling of her heart.

I calmed her fears, and she was calm,
And told her love with virgin pride;
And so I won my Genevieve,
    My bright and beauteous Bride.

Dejection: An Ode

    Late, late yestreen I saw the new Moon,
    With the old Moon in her arms;
    And I fear, I fear, my Master dear!
    We shall have a deadly storm.
              Ballad of Sir Patrick Spence.

◄ I ►

Well! If the Bard was weather-wise, who made
  The grand old ballad of Sir Patrick Spence,
  This night, so tranquil now, will not go hence
Unroused by winds, that ply a busier trade
Than those which mould yon cloud in lazy flakes,
Or the dull sobbing draft, that moans and rakes
Upon the strings of this Aeolian lute,
    Which better far were mute.
  For lo! the New-moon winter-bright!
  And overspread with phantom light,
  (With swimming phantom light o'erspread
  But rimmed and circled by a silver thread)
I see the old Moon in her lap, foretelling
  The coming-on of rain and squally blast.
And oh! that even now the gust were swelling,
  And the slant night-shower driving loud and fast!
Those sounds which oft have raised me, whilst they awed,
    And sent my soul abroad,

Might now perhaps their wonted impulse give,
Might startle this dull pain, and make it move and
    live!

◄ II ►

A grief without a pang, void, dark, and drear,
  A stifled, drowsy, unimpassioned grief,
  Which finds no natural outlet, no relief,
    In word, or sigh, or tear –
O Lady! in this wan and heartless mood,
To other thoughts by yonder throstle wooed,
  All this long eve, so balmy and serene,
Have I been gazing on the western sky,
  And its peculiar hint of yellow green:
And still I gaze – and with how blank an eye!
And those thin clouds above, in flakes and bars,
That give away their motion to the stars;
Those stars, that glide behind them or between,
Now sparkling, now bedimmed, but always seen:
Yon crescent Moon, as fixed as if it grew
In its own cloudless, starless lake of blue;
I see them all so excellently fair,
I see, not feel, how beautiful they are!

◄ III ►

  My genial spirits fail;
  And what can these avail
To lift the smothering weight from off my breast?
  It were a vain endeavour,
  Though I should gaze for ever
On that green light that lingers in the west:
I may not hope from outward forms to win
The passion and the life, whose fountains are
    within.

◄ IV ►

O Lady! we receive but what we give,
And in our life alone does Nature live:
Ours is her wedding-garment, ours her shroud!
  And would we aught behold, of higher worth,
Than that inanimate cold world allowed
To the poor loveless ever-anxious crowd,
  Ah! from the soul itself must issue forth
A light, a glory, a fair luminous cloud
    Enveloping the Earth –
And from the soul itself must there be sent
  A sweet and potent voice, of its own birth,
Of all sweet sounds the life and element!

‹ V ›

O pure of heart! thou need'st not ask of me
What this strong music in the soul may be!
What, and wherein it doth exist,
This light, this glory, this fair luminous mist,
This beautiful and beauty-making power.
    Joy, virtuous Lady! Joy that ne'er was given,
Save to the pure, and in their purest hour,
Life, and Life's effluence, cloud at once and shower,
Joy, Lady! is the spirit and the power,
Which wedding Nature to us gives in dower,
    A new Earth and new Heaven,
Undreamt of by the sensual and the proud –
Joy is the sweet voice, Joy the luminous cloud –
    We in ourselves rejoice!
And thence flows all that charms or ear or sight,
    All melodies the echoes of that voice,
All colours a suffusion from that light.

‹ VI ›

There was a time when, though my path was rough,
    This joy within me dallied with distress,
And all misfortunes were but as the stuff
    Whence Fancy made me dreams of happiness:
For hope grew round me, like the twining vine,
And fruits, and foliage, not my own, seemed mine.
But now afflictions bow me down to earth:
Nor care I that they rob me of my mirth;
    But oh! each visitation
Suspends what nature gave me at my birth,
    My shaping spirit of Imagination.
For not to think of what I needs must feel,
    But to be still and patient, all I can;
And haply by abstruse research to steal
    From my own nature all the natural man –
    This was my sole resource, my only plan:
Till that which suits a part infects the whole,
And now is almost grown the habit of my soul.

‹ VII ›

Hence, viper thoughts, that coil around my mind,
    Reality's dark dream!
I turn from you, and listen to the wind,
    Which long has raved unnoticed. What a scream
Of agony by torture lengthened out
That lute sent forth! Thou Wind, that rav'st
        without,
    Bare crag, or mountain-tairn, or blasted tree,
Or pine-grove whither woodman never clomb,
Or lonely house, long held the witches' home,
    Methinks were fitter instruments for thee,

Mad Lutanist! who in this month of showers,
Of dark brown gardens, and of peeping flowers,
Mak'st Devils' yule, with worse than wintry song,
The blossoms, buds, and timorous leaves among.
    Thou Actor, perfect in all tragic sounds!
Thou mighty Poet, e'en to frenzy bold!
    What tell'st thou now about?
    'Tis of the rushing of an host in rout,
    With groans of trampled men, with smarting
        wounds –
At once they groan with pain, and shudder with the
        cold!
But hush! there is a pause of deepest silence!
    And all that noise, as of a rushing crowd,
With groans, and tremulous shudderings – all is
        over –
    It tells another tale, with sounds less deep and
        loud!
        A tale of less affright,
        And tempered with delight,
As Otway's self had framed the tender lay –
    'Tis of a little child
    Upon a lonesome wild,
Not far from home, but she hath lost her way:
And now moans low in bitter grief and fear,
And now screams loud and hopes to make her
        mother hear.

‹ VIII ›

'Tis midnight, but small thoughts have I of sleep:
Full seldom may my friend such vigils keep!
Visit her, gentle Sleep! with wings of healing,
    And may this storm be but a mountain-birth,
May all the stars hang bright above her dwelling,
    Silent as though they watched the sleeping Earth!
        With light heart may she rise,
        Gay fancy, cheerful eyes,
    Joy lift her spirit, joy attune her voice;
To her may all things live, from pole to pole,
Their life the eddying of her living soul!
    O simple spirit, guided from above,
Dear Lady! friend devoutest of my choice,
Thus mayst thou ever, evermore rejoice.

The Pains of Sleep

Ere on my bed my limbs I lay,
It hath not been my use to pray
With moving lips or bended knees;
But silently, by slow degrees,
My spirit I to Love compose,
In humble trust mine eye-lids close,
With reverential resignation,
No wish conceived, no thought exprest,
Only a sense of supplication;
A sense o'er all my soul imprest
That I am weak, yet not unblest,
Since in me, round me, every where
Eternal strength and wisdom are.

But yester-night I prayed aloud
In anguish and in agony,
Up-starting from the fiendish crowd
Of shapes and thoughts that tortured me:
A lurid light, a trampling throng,
Sense of intolerable wrong,
And whom I scorned, those only strong!
Thirst of revenge, the powerless will
Still baffled, and yet burning still!
Desire with loathing strangely mixed
On wild or hateful objects fixed.
Fantastic passions! maddening brawl!
And shame and terror over all!
Deeds to be hid which were not hid,
Which all confused I could not know
Whether I suffered, or I did:
For all seemed guilt, remorse or woe,
My own or others still the same
Life-stifling fear, soul-stifling shame.

So two nights passed: the night's dismay
Saddened and stunned the coming day.
Sleep, the wide blessing, seemed to me
Distemper's worst calamity.
The third night, when my own loud scream
Had waked me from the fiendish dream,
O'ercome with sufferings strange and wild,
I wept as I had been a child;
And having thus by tears subdued
My anguish to a milder mood,
Such punishments, I said, were due
To natures deepliest stained with sin –
For aye entempesting anew
The unfathomable hell within,
The horror of their deeds to view,

To know and loathe, yet wish and do!
Such griefs with such men well agree,
But wherefore, wherefore fall on me?
To be beloved is all I need,
And whom I love, I love indeed.

Work Without Hope

All Nature seems at work. Slugs leave their lair –
The bees are stirring – birds are on the wing –
And Winter, slumbering in the open air,
Wears on his smiling face a dream of Spring!
And I the while, the sole unbusy thing,
Nor honey make, nor pair, nor build, nor sing.

Yet well I ken the banks where amaranths blow,
Have traced the fount whence streams of nectar
    flow.
Bloom, O ye amaranths! bloom for whom ye may,
For me ye bloom not! Glide, rich streams, away!
With lips unbrightened, wreathless brow, I stroll:
And would you learn the spells that drowse my
    soul?
Work without Hope draws nectar in a sieve,
And Hope without an object cannot live.

Epitaph

Stop, Christian passer-by! – Stop, child of God,
And read with gentle breast. Beneath this sod
A poet lies, or that which once seemed he.
O, lift one thought in prayer for S. T. C.;
That he who many a year with toil of breath
Found death in life, may here find life in death!
Mercy for praise – to be forgiven for fame
He asked, and hoped, through Christ. Do thou the
    same!

'A Song from Shakespeare's Cymbeline' springs off from the well-known dirge for Fidele, alias Imogen, in Act 4 Scene 2 of the play. The poem by William Collins (1721–59) closely shadows Shakespeare: it, too, is half imprecation, half protective spell, ranging benign forces of every kind against the fiendish and the elemental. The poet's lightness of touch and the note of acceptance and consolation on which the poem ends give it something of the quality of a lullaby. The 'Ode Written in the Beginning of the Year 1746' locates consolation in the virtues of patriotism and courage. The battle of Falkirk (January 1746) and those of Fontenoy and Prestonpans in 1745 offered ready instances. Though 'fairy hands' and 'forms unseen' are in attendance here too, it is Honour and Freedom who come to salute the fallen, making for a distinctly Horatian echo. In 'Ode to Evening', Collins skilfully combines descriptions of the natural world with a direct address to the goddess. The poem begins with a conditional, and its 52 unrhymed lines might almost be read as a single sentence sustained by a succession of correlatives. The impression of seamlessness is heightened by assonance as well as by the thoroughly assimilated influence of Spenser and Milton. Brilliantly evoking the secretiveness of twilight and its 'gradual dusky veil', the poem rounds to expressions of gratitude and praise. The 'Ode Occasioned by the Death of Mr Thomson' envisages once more the decking of a grave: but this time it is the tomb of a fellow-poet, James Thomson, author of *The Seasons* and *The Castle of Indolence*. The setting is equally specific, the Thames close to Richmond Church, where Thomson was buried. Everything conspires with the elegiac mood, but the conclusion subtly subsumes grief. Here, remembrance acquires the same kind of permanence as the landscape in which the dead poet lies.

A SONG FROM SHAKESPEARE'S CYMBELINE

To fair Fidele's grassy tomb
   Soft maids and village hinds shall bring
Each op'ning sweet of earliest bloom,
   And rifle all the breathing spring.

No wailing ghost shall dare appear
   To vex with shrieks this quiet grove;
But shepherd lads assemble here,
   And melting virgins own their love.

No withered witch shall here be seen,
   No goblins lead their nightly crew;
The female fays shall haunt the green,
   And dress thy grave with pearly dew!

The red-breast oft at ev'ning hours
   Shall kindly lend his little aid:
With hoary moss and gathered flowers
   To deck the ground where thou art laid.

When howling winds and beating rain
   In tempests shake the sylvan cell,
Or midst the chase on ev'ry plain,
   The tender thought on thee shall dwell.

Each lonely scene shall thee restore,
   For thee the tear be duly shed:
Beloved, till life could charm no more,
   And mourned, till Pity's self be dead.

ODE TO EVENING

If aught of oaten stop, or pastoral song,
May hope, chaste Eve, to soothe thy modest ear,
   Like thy own solemn springs,
   Thy springs and dying gales,
O nymph reserved, while now the bright-haired sun
Sits in yon western tent, whose cloudy skirts,
   With brede ethereal wove,
   O'erhang his wavy bed;
Now air is hushed, save where the weak-eyed bat
With short shrill shriek flits by on leathern wing,
   Or where the beetle winds
   His small but sullen horn,
As oft he rises midst the twilight path,
Against the pilgrim borne in heedless hum:

Now teach me, maid composed,
To breathe some softened strain,
Whose numbers, stealing through thy dark'ning
vale,
May not unseemly with its stillness suit,
As, musing slow, I hail
Thy genial loved return!
For when thy folding-star arising shows
His paly circlet, at his warning lamp
The fragrant hours, and elves
Who slept in flowers the day,
And many a nymph who wreathes her brows with
sedge,
And sheds the fresh'ning dew, and, lovelier still,
The pensive Pleasures sweet,
Prepare thy shadowy car.
Then lead, calm vot'ress, where some sheety lake
Cheers the lone heath, or some time-hallowed pile,
Or upland fallows grey,
Reflect its last cool gleam.
But when chill blust'ring winds, or driving rain,
Forbid my willing feet, be mine the hut,
That from the mountain's side
Views wilds, and swelling floods,
And hamlets brown, and dim-discovered spires,
And hears their simple bell, and marks o'er all
Thy dewy fingers draw
The gradual dusky veil.
While Spring shall pour his show'rs, as oft he wont,
And bathe thy breathing tresses, meekest Eve!
While Summer loves to sport
Beneath thy ling'ring light;
While sallow Autumn fills thy lap with leaves,
Or Winter, yelling through the troublous air,
Affrights thy shrinking train,
And rudely rends thy robes;
So long, sure-found beneath the sylvan shed,
Shall Fancy, Friendship, Science, rose-lipped Health
Thy gentlest influence own,
And love thy fav'rite name!

ODE WRITTEN IN THE BEGINNING OF THE YEAR 1746

How sleep the brave, who sink to rest,
By all their country's wishes blest!
When Spring, with dewy fingers cold,
Returns to deck their hallowed mould,

She there shall dress a sweeter sod
Than Fancy's feet have ever trod.

By fairy hands their knell is rung,
By forms unseen their dirge is sung;
There Honour comes, a pilgrim grey,
To bless the turf that wraps their clay;
And Freedom shall a while repair,
To dwell a weeping hermit there!

ODE OCCASIONED BY THE DEATH OF MR THOMSON

In yonder grave a Druid lies,
Where slowly winds the stealing wave!
The year's best sweets shall duteous rise
To deck its poet's sylvan grave!

In yon deep bed of whisp'ring reeds
His airy harp shall now be laid,
That he, whose heart in sorrow bleeds,
May love through life the soothing shade.

Then maids and youths shall linger here,
And, while its sounds at distance swell,
Shall sadly seem in Pity's ear
To hear the woodland's pilgrim's knell.

Remembrance oft shall haunt the shore
When Thames in summer-wreaths is dressed,
And oft suspend the dashing oar
To bid his gentle spirit rest!

And oft as Ease and Health retire
To breezy lawn or forest deep,
The friend shall view yon whit'ning spire,
And mid the varied landscape weep.

But thou, who own'st that earthy bed,
Ah! what will ev'ry dirge avail?
Or tears, which Love and Pity shed
That mourn beneath the gliding sail!

Yet lives there one, whose heedless eye
Shall scorn thy pale shrine glimm'ring near?
With him, sweet bard, may Fancy die,
And Joy desert the blooming year.

But thou, lorn stream, whose sullen tide
   No sedge-crowned Sisters now attend,
Now waft me from the green hill's side,
   Whose cold turf hides the buried friend!

And see, the fairy valleys fade,
   Dun Night has veiled the solemn view!
– Yet once again, dear parted shade,
   Meek Nature's child, again adieu!

The genial meads, assigned to bless
   Thy life, shall mourn thy early doom,
Their hinds and shepherd-girls shall dress
   With simple hands thy rural tomb.

Long, long, thy stone and pointed clay
   Shall melt the musing Briton's eyes:
'O! vales and wild woods,' shall he say,
   'In yonder grave your Druid lies!'

'Yardley Oak' is an unfinished poem, written in 1791, which first appeared in Hayley's edition of 1809: Cowper had died in April 1800. In the manuscript, lines 144–166 were deleted. I have not found it in any anthology, though Cowper has 36 poems (against Pope's 42) on *The Oxford Book of Eighteenth Century Verse*. In my mental tree-catalogue the poem stands beside Delacroix's 'Antin oak' at Champrosay: 'Now that I see only the trunk (which I am almost touching) and the springing of the great limbs … I am astounded at the grandeur of its details. In short, I feel it to be great and even terrifying in its greatness' (*Journal*, 9 May, 1853).

Miltonic in its prosody and diction, the poem shows what a gift Cowper had for exact, animated description. No less vivid, sensuous, and detailed is the opening of Book V in *The Task* ('The Winter Morning Walk'). Even then, freighting every line with sublimity here need not deter a reader today or make us forget how impish Cowper's strange intelligence could also be (for example, 'The Colubriad', 41 lines about three kittens entranced by a snake, or 'To the Immortal Memory of the Halibut on Which I Dined This Day').

'Yardley Oak' breaks off before Cowper's usual passion for sermonizing took hold. His successive bouts of neurasthenia qualified him, no doubt, to discern in his tree a kindred figure. Yet he does not impose his anguish on the tree: he has transposed it into a dominant vocal tone. His insistently self-reflexive speech-act encircles the thing itself, presents it in the round, imagining the acorn dropped by the jay, the oak's slow organic emergence, its times, its space, and giving voice to its now ravaged and resistant mass. The 'egotistical sublime' monologue secretes from the start a dialogue, for the expressions of the oak have infiltrated sound and syntax. It was this *creole*, developing between the prodigious oak and the gnarled yet linear prosody, the rugged yet subtle texture, that first alerted me to gestural features of the poem. This might be, I thought, what they call *methexis*: A sensitive poetic sign, which circles, penetrates, and voices its referent with Orphic inwit, can irradiate the hardest objects in the world. Fragment though it is, the poem erupts at the close of the Enlightenment like a beacon for Coleridge, for Keats, who must have known it, and for Gerard Manley Hopkins, who might have done.

WILLIAM COWPER

YARDLEY OAK

Survivor sole, and hardly such, of all
That once liv'd here, – thy brethren, at my birth
(Since which I number three-score winters past)
A shatter'd veteran, hollow-trunk'd perhaps,
As now, and with excoriate forks deform,
Relics of ages! Could a mind, imbued
With truth from Heaven, created thing adore,
I might with rev'rence kneel, and worship thee.
    It seems idolatry with some excuse,
When our fore-father Druids in their oaks
Imagin'd sanctity. The conscience, yet
Unpurified by an authentic act
Of amnesty, the meed of blood divine,
Lov'd not the light, but gloomy, into gloom
Of thickest shades, like Adam after taste
Of fruit proscrib'd, as to a refuge, fled.
    Thou west a bauble once; a cup and ball,
Which babes might play with; and the thievish jay
Seeking her food, with ease might have purloin'd
The auburn nut that held thee, swallowing down
Thy yet close-folded latitude of boughs,
And all thine embryo vastness, at a gulp.
But Fate thy growth decreed: autumnal rains
Beneath thy parent tree mellow'd the soil
Design'd thy cradle, and a skipping deer,
With pointed hoof dibbling the glebe, prepar'd
The soft receptacle, in which, secure,
Thy rudiments should sleep the winter through.
    So fancy dreams – Disprove it, if ye can,
Ye reas'ners broad awake, whose busy search
Of argument, employ'd too oft amiss,
Sifts half the pleasures of short life away!
    Thou fell'st mature; and in the loamy clod
Swelling with vegetative force instinct
Didst burst thine egg, as theirs the fabled Twins,
Now stars; two lobes, protruding, pair'd exact;
A leaf succeeded, and another leaf,
And, all the elements thy puny growth
Fost'ring propitious, thou becam'st a twig.
    Who liv'd when thou wast such? Oh! couldst
        thou speak,
As in Dodona once thy kindred trees
Oracular, I would not curious ask
The future, best unknown, but at thy mouth
Inquisitive, the less ambiguous past.
    By thee I might correct, erroneous oft,
The clock of history, facts and events
Timing more punctual, unrecorded-facts
Recov'ring, and misstated setting right –

Desp'rate attempt, till trees shall speak again!
    Time made thee what thou wast – king of the
        woods;
And Time hath made thee what thou art – a cave
For owls to roost in. Once thy spreading boughs
O'erhung the champaign; and the numerous flock
That graz'd it stood beneath that ample cope
Uncrowded, yet safe shelter'd from the storm.
No flock frequents thee now. Thou hast outliv'd
Thy popularity and art become
(Unless verse rescue thee awhile) a thing
Forgotten, as the foliage of thy youth.
    While thus through all the stages thou hast
        push'd
Of treeship – first a seedling hid in grass;
Then twig; then sapling; and, as century roll'd
Slow after century, a giant bulk
Of girth enormous, with moss-cushion'd root
Upheav'd above the soil, and sides emboss'd
With prominent wens globose – till at the last
The rottenness, which time is charg'd t' inflict
On other mighty ones, found also thee.
    What exhibitions various hath the world
Witness'd of mutability in all
That we account most durable below!
Change is the diet, on which all subsist,
Created changeable, and change at last
Destroys them. – Skies uncertain now the heat
Transmitting cloudless, and the solar beam
Now quenching in a boundless sea of clouds, –
Calm and alternate storm, moisture and drought,
Invigorate by turns the springs of life
In all that live, plant, animal, and man,
And in conclusion mar them. Nature's threads,
Fine passing thought, e'en in her coarsest works,
Delight in agitation, yet sustain
The force, that agitates not unimpair'd;
But, worn by frequent impulse, to the cause
Of their best tone their dissolution owe.
    Thought cannot spend itself, comparing still
The great and little of thy lot, thy growth
From almost nullity into a state
Of matchless grandeur, and declension thence,
Slow, into such magnificent decay.
Time was, when, settling on thy leaf, a fly
Could shake thee to the root – and time has been
When tempests could not. At thy firmest age
Thou hadst within thy bole solid contents,
That might have ribb'd the sides and plank'd the
        deck
Of some flagg'd admiral; and tortuous arms,

The ship-wright's darling treasure, didst present
To the four-quarter'd winds, robust and bold,
Warp'd into tough knee-timber, many a load!
But the axe spar'd thee. In those thriftier days
Oaks fell not, hewn by thousands, to supply
The bottomless demands of contest wag'd
For senatorial honours. Thus to Time
The task was left to whittle thee away
With his sly scythe; whose ever-nibbling edge,
Noiseless, an atom and an atom more,
Disjoining from the rest, has, unobserv'd,
Achiev'd a labour, which had, far and wide,
(By man perform'd) made all the forest ring.
　　Embowell'd now and of thy ancient self
Possessing nought but the scoop'd rind, that seems
An huge throat calling to the clouds for drink,
Which it would give in rivulets to thy root,
Thou temptest none, but rather much forbid'st
The feller's toil, which thou couldst ill requite.
Yet is thy root sincere, sound as the rock,
A quarry of stout spurs, and knotted fangs,
Which, crook'd into a thousand whimsies, clasp
The stubborn soil, and hold thee still erect.
　　So stands a kingdom, whose foundation yet
Fails not, in virtue and in wisdom laid,
Though all the superstructure, by the tooth
Pulveriz'd of venality, a shell
Stands now, and semblance only of itself!
　　Thine arms have left thee. Winds have rent them
　　　　off
Long since, and rovers of the forest wild
With bow and shaft have burnt them. Some have
　　　　left
A splinter'd stump bleach'd to a snowy white;
And some memorial none where once they grew.
Yet life still lingers in thee, and puts forth
Proof not contemptible of what she can,
Even where death predominates. The spring
Finds thee not less alive to her sweet force
Than yonder upstarts of the neighb'ring wood,
So much thy juniors, who their birth receiv'd
Half a millennium since the date of thine.
　　But since, although well qualified by age
To teach, no spirit dwells in thee, nor voice
May be expected from thee, seated here
On thy distorted root, with hearers none,
Or prompter, save the scene, I will perform
Myself the oracle, and will discourse
In my own ear such matter as I may.
Thou, like myself, hast stage by stage attain'd
Life's wintry bourn; thou, after many years,

I after few; but few or many prove
A span in retrospect; for I can touch
With my least finger's end my own decease
And with extended thumb my natal hour,
And hadst thou also skill in measurement
As I, the past would seem as short to thee.
Evil and few – said Jacob – at an age
Thrice mine, and few and evil, I may think
The Prediluvian race, whose buxom youth
Endured two centuries, accounted theirs.
'Shortliv'd as foliage is the race of man.
The wind shakes down the leaves, the budding
　　grove
Soon teems with others, and in spring they grow.
So pass mankind. One generation meets
Its destin'd period, and a new succeeds.'
Such was the tender but undue complaint
Of the Mæonian in old time; for who
Would drawl out centuries in tedious strife
Severe with mental and corporeal ill
And would not rather choose a shorter race
To glory, a few decads here below?
　　One man alone, the father of us all,
Drew not his life from woman; never gaz'd,
With mute unconsciousness of what he saw,
On all around him; learn'd not by degrees,
Nor owed articulation to his ear;
But, moulded by his Maker into man
At once, upstood intelligent, survey'd
All creatures, with precision understood
Their purport, uses, properties, assign'd
To each his name significant, and, fill'd
With love and wisdom, render'd back to Heaven
In praise harmonious the first air he drew.
He was excus'd the penalties of dull
Minority. No tutor charg'd his hand
With the thought-tracing quill, or task'd his mind
With problems; history, not wanted yet,
Lean'd on her elbow, watching Time, whose course,
Eventful, should supply her with a theme,

When I gave a paper on the poetry of George Crabbe (1754–1832) at Loughborough University, I called it *The Couplet's Last Stand*, and this seems still a good sound-bite to describe his verse. No poet since Crabbe's heyday has used the heroic couplet for serious verse: it has been the exclusive resort of composers of Light Verse. Crabbe is thus the true inheritor and final adornment of the Augustan style which nourished Dryden and Pope. As *The Village*, which is represented in the selection by several passages, shows, Crabbe had a deliberately anti-romantic intention. After hundreds of years of European Pastoral, Crabbe wanted to work in strictly realistic vein. However, he managed to employ the couplet in the richest possible way. His poetry is virtuosic and his effects always spectacular. He is never drab however gloomy his view of the human condition. He also found the couplet an effective form for story-telling. His later poetry, in *The Borough* and *Tales*, comprises a set of brilliantly observed short stories. Benjamin Britten's finding inspiration for his opera *Peter Grimes* in Crabbe is only one example of the latent psychological power of his poetic fiction. The poems in *Tales* particularly make up as sharp a portrait of life in early Victorian England as any of the prose written by Dickens and Thackeray, while incoporating a kind of realistic wit reminiscent of Peacock. Byron ventured, in *Don Juan*, that 'With Crabbe it may be difficult to cope', but his assessment does not seem quite accurate today. In Crabbe's hands, the couplet does not creak, but swings open brilliantly, providing us with a window on the harshly crowded world of England at the beginning of the nation's most self-confident century.

THE VILLAGE

◂ Book I ▸

(lines 1–26; 39–54; 63–92; 131–55; 230–51; 276–97; 320–48)

The village life, and every care that reigns
O'er youthful peasants and declining swains;
What labour yields, and what, that labour past,
Age, in its hour of languor, finds at last;
What forms the real picture of the poor,
Demands a song – The Muse can give no more.

Fled are those times, if e'er such times were seen,
When rustic poets praised their native green;
No shepherds now in smooth alternate verse,
Their country's beauty or their nymphs' rehearse;
Yet still for these we frame the tender strain,
Still in our lays fond Corydons complain,
And shepherds' boys their amorous pains reveal,
The only pains, alas! they never feel.

On Mincio's banks, in Caesar's bounteous reign,
If *Tityrus* found the golden age again,
Must sleepy bards the flattering dream prolong,
Mechanic echoes of the Mantuan song?
From truth and nature shall we widely stray,
Where *Virgil*, not where fancy leads the way?

Yes, thus the Muses sing of happy swains,
Because the Muses never knew their pains:
They boast their peasants' pipes, but peasants now
Resign their pipes and plod behind the plough;
And few amid the rural tribe have time
To number syllables and play with rhyme;

[. . .]

I grant indeed that fields and flocks have charms
For him that grazes or for him that farms;
But, when amid such pleasing scenes I trace
The poor laborious natives of the place,
And see the mid-day sun, with fervid ray,
On their bare heads and dewy temples play;
While some, with feebler heads and fainter hearts,
Deplore their fortune, yet sustain their parts:
Then shall I dare these real ills to hide
In tinsel trappings of poetic pride?
No; cast by Fortune on a frowning coast,
Which neither groves nor happy valleys boast;
Where other cares than those the Muse relates,
And other shepherds dwell with other mates;

By such examples taught, I paint the Cot,
As Truth will paint it, and as Bards will not:

[. . .]

   Lo! where the heath, with withering brake grown
      o'er,
Lends the light turf that warms the neighbouring
      poor;
From thence a length of burning sand appears,
Where the thin harvest waves its wither'd ears;
Rank weeds, that every art and care defy,
Reign o'er the land, and rob the blighted rye:
There thistles stretch their prickly arms afar,
And to the ragged infant threaten war;
There poppies, nodding, mock the hope of toil;
There the blue bugloss paints the sterile soil;
Hardy and high, above the slender sheaf,
The slimy mallow waves her silky leaf;
O'er the young shoot the charlock throws a shade,
And clasping tares cling round the sickly blade;
With mingled tints the rocky coasts abound,
And a sad splendour vainly shines around.
So looks the nymph whom wretched arts adorn,
Betray'd by man, then left for man to scorn;
Whose cheek in vain assumes the mimic rose,
While her sad eyes the troubled breast disclose;
Whose outward splendour is but folly's dress,
Exposing most, when most it gilds distress.
   Here joyless roam a wild amphibious race,
With sullen wo display'd in every face;
Who far from civil arts and social fly,
And scowl at strangers with suspicious eye.
   Here too the lawless merchant of the main
Draws from his plough th' intoxicated swain;
Want only claim'd the labour of the day,
But vice now steals his nightly rest away.

[. . .]

But these are scenes where Nature's niggard hand
Gave a spare portion to the famished land;
Hers is the fault if here mankind complain
Of fruitless toil and labour spent in vain;
But yet in other scenes more fair in view,
Where Plenty smiles – alas! she smiles for few,
And those who taste not, yet behold her store,
Are as the slaves that dig the golden ore,
The wealth around them makes them doubly poor:
Or will you deem them amply paid in health,
Labour's fair child, that languishes with Wealth?
Go then! and see them rising with the sun,
Through a long course of daily toil to run;

Like him to make the plenteous harvest grow,
And yet not share the plenty they bestow;
See them beneath the dog-star's raging heat,
When the knees tremble and the temples beat;
Behold them leaning on their scythes, look o'er
The labour past, and toils to come explore;
See them alternate suns and showers engage,
And hoard up aches and anguish for their age;
Through fens and marshy moors their steps pursue,
When their warm pores imbibe the evening dew;
Then own that labour may as fatal be
To these thy slaves, as luxury to thee.

[. . .]

Theirs is yon house that holds the parish poor,
Whose walls of mud scarce bear the broken door;
There, where the putrid vapours flagging, play,
And the dull wheel hums doleful through the day;
There children dwell who know no parents' care,
Parents, who know no children's love, dwell there;
Heart-broken matrons on their joyless bed,
Forsaken wives and mothers never wed;
Dejected widows with unheeded tears,
And crippled age with more than childhood-tears;
The lame, the blind, and, far the happiest they!
The moping idiot and the madman gay.

Here too the sick their final doom receive,
Here brought amid the scenes of grief, to grieve;
Where the loud groans from some sad chamber flow,
Mixed with the clamours of the crowd below;
Here sorrowing, they each kindred sorrow scan,
And the cold charities of man to man.
Whose laws indeed for ruined age provide,
And strong compulsion plucks the scrap from pride;
But still that scrap is bought with many a sigh,
And pride embitters what it can't deny.

[. . .]

But soon a loud and hasty summons calls,
Shakes the thin roof, and echoes round the walls;
Anon, a figure enters, quaintly neat,
All pride and business, bustle and conceit;
With looks unaltered by these scenes of woe,
With speed that entering, speaks his haste to go;
He bids the gazing throng around him fly,
And carries fate and physic in his eye;
A potent quack, long versed in human ills,.
Who first insults the victim whom he kills;
Whose murderous hand a drowsy bench protect,
And whose most tender mercy is neglect.

Paid by the parish for attendance here,
He wears contempt upon his sapient sneer;
In haste he seeks the bed where misery lies,
Impatience marked in his averted eyes;
And, some habitual queries hurried o'er,
Without reply, he rushes on the door;
His drooping patient, long inured to pain,
And long unheeded, knows remonstrance vain;
He ceases now the feeble help to crave
Of man, and mutely hastens to the grave.

[. . .]

Now once again the gloomy scene explore,
Less gloomy now; the bitter hour is o'er,
The man of many sorrows sighs no more.
Up yonder hill, behold how sadly slow
The bier moves winding from the vale below;
There lie the happy dead, from trouble free,
And the glad parish pays the frugal fee.
No more, O Death! thy victim starts to hear
Churchwarden stern, or kingly overseer;
No more the farmer claims his humble bow,
Thou art his lord, the best of tyrants thou!
Now to the church behold the mourners come,
Sedately torpid and devoutly dumb;
The village children now their games suspend,
To see the bier that bears their ancient friend:
For he was one in all their idle sport,
And like a monarch ruled their little court;
The pliant bow he form'ed, the flying ball,
The bat, the wicket, were his labours all;
Him now they follow to his grave, and stand
Silent and sad, and gazing, hand in hand;
While bending low, their eager eyes explore
The mingled relics of the parish poor.
The bell tolls late, the moping owl flies round,
Fear marks the flight and magnifies the sound;
The busy priest, detain'd by weightier care,
Defers his duty till the day of prayer;
And, waiting long, the crowd retire distress'd,
To think a poor man's bones should lie unbless'd.

Alone he rowed his Boat, alone he cast
His Nets beside, or made his Anchor fast;
To hold a Rope or hear a Curse was none, –
He toiled and railed; he groaned and swore alone.

Thus by himself compelled to live each day,
To wait for certain hours the Tide's delay;
At the same times the same dull views to see,
The bounding March-bank and the blighted Tree;
The Water only, when the Tides were high,
When low, the Mud half-covered and half-dry;
The Sun-burnt Tar that blisters on the Planks,
And Bank-side Stakes in their uneven ranks;
Heaps of entangled Weeds that slowly float,
As the Tide rolls by the impeded Boat.

When Tides were neap, and, in the sultry day,
Through the tall-bounding Mud-banks made their
    way,
Which on each side rose swelling, and below
The dark warm Flood ran silently and slow;
There anchoring, Peter chose from Man to hide,
There hang his Head, and view the lazy Tide
In its hot slimy Channel slowly glide;
Where the small Eels that left the deeper way
For the warm Shore, within the Shallows play;
Where gaping Mussels, left upon the Mud,
Slope their slow passage to the fallen Flood; –
Here dull and hopeless he'll lie down and trace
How sidelong Crabs had scrawled their crooked race;
Or sadly listen to the tuneless cry
Of fishing Gull or clanging Golden-eye;
What time the Sea-birds to the March would come,
And the loud Bittern, from the Bull-rush home,
Gave the Salt-ditch side the bellowing Boom:
He nursed the Feelings these dull Scenes produce,
And loved to stop beside the opening Sluice;
Where the small Stream, confined in narrow bound,
Ran with a dull, unvaried, saddening sound;
Where all presented to the Eye or Ear,
Oppressed the Soul! with Misery, Grief, and Fear.

THE BOROUGH

‹ Peter Grimes ›

(lines 165–204)

Alas, for Peter not an helping Hand,
So was he hated, could he now command;

TALES

‹ The Dumb Orators ›

(lines 394–409)

'Is it not known, agreed, confirmed, confessed,
That of all people we are governed best?

We have the force of Monarchies; are free,
As the most proud Republicans can be;
And have those prudent counsels that arise
In grave and cautious Aristocracies:
And live there those, in such all-glorious state,
Traitors protected in the land they hate?
Rebels, still warring with the laws that give
To them subsistence? – Yes, such wretches live.

'Ours, is a Church reformed, and now no more
Is aught for man to mend or to restore;
'Tis pure in doctrines, 'tis correct in creeds,
Has nought redundant, and it nothing needs;
No evil in therein, – no wrinkle, spot,
Stain, blame, or blemish; – I affirm, there's not.

‹ Procrastination ›

(lines 158–89)

Within that fair apartment, guests might see
The comforts culled for wealth by vanity:
Around the room an Indian paper blazed,
With lively tint and figures boldly raised;
Silky and soft upon the floor below,
The elastic carpet rose with crimson glow;
All things around implied both cost and care,
What met the eye, was elegant or rare:
Some curious trifles round the room were laid,
By Hope presented to the wealthy Maid:
Within a costly case of varnished wood,
In level rows, her polished volumes stood;
Shown as a favour to a chosen few,
To prove what beauty for a book could do:
A silver urn with curious work was fraught;
A silver lamp from Grecian pattern wrought:
Above her head, all gorgeous to behold,
A time-piece stood on feet of burnished gold;
A stag's-head crest adorned the pictured case,
Through the pure crystal shone the enamelled face;
And, while on brilliants moved the hands of steel,
It clicked from prayer to prayer, from meal to meal.

Here as the Lady sate, a friendly pair
Stepped in to admire the view, and took their chair:
They then related how the young and gay
Were thoughtless wandering in the broad high-way;
How tender damsels sailed in tilted boats,
And laughed with wicked men in scarlet coats;
And how we live in such degenerate times,
The men conceal their wants, and show their
        crimes;

While vicious deeds are screened by fashion's name,
And what was once our pride is now our shame.

‹ Arabella ›

(lines 1–36)

Of a fair town where Doctor *Rack* was guide,
His only daughter was the boast and pride;
Wise *Arabella*, yet not wise alone,
She like a bright and polished brilliant shone;
Her father owned her for his prop and stay,
Able to guide yet willing to obey;
Pleased with her learning while discourse could
        please,
And with her love in languor and disease:
To every mother were her virtues known,
And to their daughters as a pattern shown;
Who in her youth had all that age requires,
And with her prudence, all that youth admires;
These odious praises made the damsels try
Not to obtain such merits, but deny;
For, whatsoever wise mammas might say,
To guide a daughter, this was not the way;
From such applause disdain and anger rise,
And envy lives where emulation dies:
In all his strength, contends the noble Horse,
With one who just precedes him on the course;
But when the rival flies too far before,
His spirit fails, and he attempts no more.

This reasoning Maid, above her sex's dread,
Had dared to read, and dared to say she read;
Not the last novel, not the new-born play;
Not the mere trash and scandal of the day;
But (though her young companions felt the shock)
She studied *Berkeley, Bacon, Hobbes*, and *Locke*;
Her mind within the maze of History dwelt,
And of the Moral Muse the beauty felt;
The merits of the Roman page she knew,
And could converse with *Moore* and *Montague*:
Thus she became the wonder of the town,
From that she reaped, to that she gave renown;
And strangers coming, all were taught to admire
The learned Lady, and the lofty Spire.

‹ The Lover's Journey ›

(lines 141–77)

Again, the country was enclosed, a wide
And sandy road has banks on either side;
Where, lo! a hollow on the left appeared,
And there a Gipsy-tribe their tent had reared;

'Twas open spread, to catch the morning sun,
And they had now their early meal begun,
When two brown Boys just left their grassy seat,
The early Traveller with their prayers to greet:
While yet *Orlando* held his pence in hand,
He saw their Sister on her duty stand;
Some twelve years old, demure, affected, sly,
Prepared the force of early powers to try;
Sudden a look of languor he descries,
And well-feigned apprehension in her eyes;
Trained but yet savage, in her speaking face,
He marked the features of her vagrant race;
When a light laugh and roguish leer expressed
The vice implanted in her youthful breast:
Forth from the tent her elder Brother came,
Who seemed offended, yet forbore to blame
The young designer, but could only trace
The looks of pity in the Traveller's face:
Within, the Father, who from fences nigh
Had brought the fuel for the fire's supply,
Watched now the feeble blaze, and stood dejected by:
On ragged rug, just borrowed from the bed,
And by the hand of coarse indulgence fed,
In dirty patchwork negligently dressed,
Reclined the Wife, an infant at her breast:
In her wild face some touch of grace remained,
Of vigour palsied and of beauty stained;
Her blood-shot eyes on her unheeding mate
Were wrathful turned, and seemed her wants to
      state,
Cursing his tardy aid – her Mother there
With Gipsy-state engrossed the only chair;
Solemn and dull her look; with such she stands,
And reads the Milk-maid's fortune in her hands.

‹The Struggles of Conscience›
(lines 461–95)

Soon as the morning came, there met his eyes
Accounts of wealth, that he might reading rise;
To profit then he gave some active hours,
Till food and wine again should renovate his powers:
Yet, spite of all defence, of every aid,
The watchful Foe her close attention paid;
In every thoughtful moment, on she pressed,
And gave at once her dagger to his breast:
He waked at midnight, and the fears of sin,
As waters, through a bursten dam, broke in;
Nay, in the banquet, with his friends around,
When all their cares and half their crimes were
      drowned,

Would some chance act awake the slumbering fear,
And care and crime in all their strength appear:
The news is read, a guilty Victim swings,
And troubled looks proclaim the bosom-stings;
Some Pair are wed; this brings the Wife in view,
And some divorced; this shows the parting too:
Nor can he hear of evil word or deed,
But they to thought, and thought to sufferings lead.

   Such was his life – no other changes came,
The hurrying day, the conscious night the same;
The night of horror – when he, starting, cried,
To the poor startled Sinner at his side:
'Is it in law? am I condemned to die?
Let me escape! – I'll give – oh! let me fly –
How! but a Dream – no Judges! Dungeon! Chain!
Or these grim Men! – I will not sleep again. –
Wilt thou, dread Being! thus thy promise keep?
Day is thy time – and wilt thou murder sleep?
Sorrow and Want repose, and wilt thou come,
Nor give one hour of pure untroubled gloom?

   Oh! Conscience! Conscience! Man's most faithful
      friend,
Him canst thou comfort, ease, relieve, defend:
But if he will thy friendly checks forgo,
Thou art, oh! woe for me, his deadliest foe!'

‹The Learned Boy›
(lines 309–27)

   The love of order – I the thing receive
From reverend men, and I in part believe –
Shows a clear mind and clean, and whoso needs
This love, but seldom in the world succeeds;
And yet with this some other love must be,
Ere I can fully to the fact agree:
Valour and study may by order gain,
By order sovereigns hold more steady reign;
Through all the tribes of nature order runs,
And rules around in systems and in suns:
Still has the love of order found a place,
With all that's low, degrading, mean, and base,
With all that merits scorn, and all that meets
      disgrace:
In the cold Miser, of all change afraid,
In pompous men in public seats obeyed;
In humble Placemen, Heralds, solemn drones,
Fanciers of Flowers, and Lads like *Stephen Jones*;
Order to these is armour and defence,
And love of method serves in lack of sense.

Samuel Daniel (1562/3–1619), brother of the composer and lutenist John Daniel, has been remembered largely as the author of *Delia* (1592), his first publication and one of the most successful of Elizabethan sonnet-sequences. Charming as these sonnets are (earning for their author the contemporary description 'sweet, honey-dripping Daniel'), they are not typical of his subsequent voluminous work in both verse and prose. His later poetry is passionately intellectual and ratiocinative; it is often cast in debate form (for example in 'Musophilus', arguably his greatest poem), and its typical subjects are the presence of the past (his unfinished, longest poem was the *Civil Wars*, on the Wars of the Roses), and the sufferings of the powerless (particularly women; he draws many sympathetic portraits of misused women).

'Honey-dripping Daniel' is here represented by three sonnets from *Delia*, as well as by the song 'Are they shadows that we see' from his masque *Hymen's Triumph*. The more cerebral side of his output can be seen in the two extracts from 'Musophilus' (the first, on the power of literature, is one of the most splendid apostrophes to letters in English; the second is an extraordinary passage on Stonehenge); the last extract is from his dramatic monologue 'A Letter from Octavia to Marcus Antonius', in which Daniel, through the mouthpiece of the abandoned Octavia, castigates 'undiscerning custom' which grants men sexual freedom while insisting on women's chastity ('we' in this passage means women, 'you' means men).

Daniel's sensibility is an extremely attractive one, and it is easy to see why Robert Southey wrote of him: 'there is no poet in our language of whom it may be affirmed with more certainty from his writings that he was an amiable and wise and good man'.

'CARE-CHARMER SLEEP, SON OF THE SABLE NIGHT'

Care-charmer Sleep, son of the sable Night,
Brother to Death, in silent darkness born,
Relieve my anguish, and restore the light:
With dark forgetting of my care return,
And let the day be time enough to mourn
The shipwreck of my ill-adventured youth:
Let waking eyes suffice to wail their scorn,
Without the torment of the night's untruth.
Cease, dreams, the images of day-desires,
To model forth the passions of the morrow;
Never let rising Sun approve you liars,
To add more grief to aggravate my sorrow:
    Still let me sleep, embracing clouds in vain,
    And never wake to feel the day's disdain.

'LET OTHERS SING OF KNIGHTS AND PALLADINES'

Let others sing of Knights and Palladines,
In agèd accents, and untimely words:
Paint shadows in imaginary lines,
Which well the reach of their high wits records;
But I must sing of thee and those fair eyes,
Authentic shall my verse in time to come,
When yet th' unborn shall say, lo where she lies,
Whose beauty made him speak that else was dumb.
These are the arks, the trophies I erect,
That fortify thy name against old age,
And these thy sacred virtues must protect,
Against the dark and time's consuming rage.
    Though th' error of my youth they shall discover,
    Suffice they show I lived and was thy lover.

'BEAUTY, SWEET LOVE, IS LIKE THE MORNING DEW'

Beauty, sweet love, is like the morning dew,
Whose short refresh upon the tender green,
Cheers for a time but till the Sun doth show,
And straight 'tis gone as it had never been.
Soon doth it fade that makes the fairest flourish,
Short is the glory of the blushing Rose,

The hue that thou so carefully dost nourish,
Yet which at length thou must be forced to lose.
When thou surcharged with burthen of thy years,
Shalt bend thy wrinkles homeward to the earth:
When time hath made a passport for thy fears,
Dated in age the Kalends of our death.
    But ah no more, this hath been often told,
    And women grieve to think they must be old.

'ARE THEY SHADOWS THAT WE SEE?'

Are they shadows that we see?
And can shadows pleasure give?
Pleasures only shadows be
Cast by bodies we conceive,
And are made the things we deem,
In those figures which they seem.
But these pleasures vanish fast,
Which by shadows are expressed:
Pleasures are not if they last,
In their passing is their best.
Glory is most bright and gay
In a flash and so away.
Feed apace then greedy eyes
On the wonder you behold,
Take it sudden as it flies,
Though you take it not to hold:
When your eyes have done their part,
Thought must length it in the heart.

MUSOPHILUS
(lines 189–240; 337–54)

O blessèd letters that combine in one
    All ages past, and make one live with all,
    By you we do confer with who are gone,
    And the dead living unto counsel call:
    By you th' unborn shall have communion
    Of what we feel, and what doth us befall.
Soul of the world, knowledge, without thee,
    What hath the earth that truly glorious is?
    Why should our pride make such a stir to be,
    To be forgot? What good is like to this,
    To do worthy the writing, and to write
    Worthy the reading, and the world's delight?

And let th'unnatural and wayward race
    Born of one womb with us, but to our shame,
    (That never read t'observe but to disgrace,)
    Raise all the tempest of their power to blame;
    That puff of folly never can deface,
    The work a happy Genius took to frame.
Yet why should civil learning seek to wound
    And mangle her own members with despite?
    Prodigious wits that study to confound
    The life of wit, to seem to know aright,
    As if themselves had fortunately found
    Some stand from of the earth beyond our sight,
    Whence overlooking all as from above,
    Their grace is not to work, but to reprove.
But how came they placed in so high degree
    Above the reach and compass of the rest?
    Who hath admitted them only to be
    Free denizens of skill, to judge the best?
    From whom the world as yet could never see
    The warrant of their wit soundly expressed.
T'acquaint our times with that perfection
    Of high conceit, which only they possess,
    That we might have things exquisitely done
    Measured with all their strict observances:
    Such would (I know) scorn a translation,
    Or bring but others' labours to the press;
    Yet oft these monster-breeding mountains will
    Bring forth small Mice of great expected skill.
Presumption ever fullest of defects,
    Fails in the doing to perform her part
    And I have known proud words and poor effects,
    Of such indeed as do condemn this Art:
    But let them rest, it ever hath been known,
    They others' virtues scorn, that doubt their own:
And for the diverse disagreeing chords,
    Of interjangling ignorance that fill
    The dainty ears, and leave no room for words,
    The worthier minds neglect, or pardon will;
    Knowing the best he hath, he frankly fords
    And scorns to be a niggard of his skill.

And whereto serves that wondrous trophy now,
    That on the goodly plain near Wilton stands?
    That huge dumb heap, that cannot tell us how,
    Nor what, nor whence it is, nor with whose
      hands,
    Nor for whose glory, it was set to show
    How much our pride mocks that of other lands?
Whereon when as the gazing passenger
    Hath greedy looked with admiration,

And fain would know his birth, and what he
    were,
How there erected, and how long agone:
Enquires and asks his fellow traveller
What he hath heard and his opinion:
And he knows nothing. Then he turns again
    And looks and sighs, and then admires afresh,
    And in himself with sorrow doth complain
    The misery of dark forgetfulness
    Angry with time that nothing should remain,
    Our greatest wonders' wonder to express.

From A LETTER FROM OCTAVIA TO MARCUS ANTONIUS

We in this prison of ourselves confined
Must here shut up with our own passions live,
Turned in upon us, and denied to find
The vent of outward means that might relieve:
That they alone must take up all our mind,
And no room left us but to think and grieve:
Yet oft our narrowed thoughts look more direct
Than your loose wisdoms born with wild
    neglect. [. . .]
What? are there bars for us, no bound for you?
Must levity stand sure, though firmness fall?
And are you privileged to be untrue
And we no grant to be dispensed withall?
Must we inviolable keep your due,
Both to your love and to your falsehood thrall?
Whilst you have stretched your lust upon your will
As if your strength were licensed to do ill.

Emily Dickinson was born in 1830 and died in 1886. She lived virtually all her life in her family's homes in Amherst, Massachusetts. She did not marry and her increasing withdrawal to her own household and garden created, in a friend's words, 'a lady whom the people call the Myth.' No collection of her poems was published while she lived.

Emily Dickinson is at home with the strangeness of things. She has the ruthlessness of absolute confidence. Her wit is accuracy. She is the spider, not the fly.

Her punctuation, at first so startling, comes to seem as natural as breath. So, too, does her familiarity with the universe and her lively interest in death.

Emily Dickinson's poems are often in that merciless form, the ballad. She is equal to its demands for clarity, brevity, and dramatic pace: 'And then a Plank in Reason broke/And I dropped down, and down – ' She is the quickest of poets. From her, a line of ten syllables appears as magnificent generosity. Most admirably, her ballads will tolerate a strange final openness of rhythm and meaning: 'And Finished knowing – then – '

Her best poems stand out like stones, and my choice does not disagree with previous anthologists'. If there are more spiders and leopards than usual, they are not sentimental. Her regard for all that lives is clear and fierce.

I have been startled to see again how short these poems are. Blake wrote of a world in a grain of sand. Emily Dickinson shows that half a line can glance at eternity as surely as an epic. If you have not read her memorable, isolated work, I hope there will be a start of recognition, from the first line of the first verse.

'THERE'S A CERTAIN SLANT OF LIGHT'

There's a certain Slant of light,
Winter Afternoons –
That oppresses, like the Heft
Of Cathedral Tunes –

Heavenly Hurt, it gives us –
We can find no scar,
But internal difference,
Where the Meanings, are –

None may teach it – Any –
'Tis the Seal Despair –
An imperial affliction
Sent us of the Air –

When it comes, the Landscape listens –
Shadows – hold their breath –
When it goes, 'tis like the Distance
On the look of Death –

'OUR LIVES ARE SWISS'

Our lives are Swiss –
So still – so Cool –
Till some odd afternoon
The Alps neglect their Curtains
And we look farther on!

Italy stands the other side!
While like a guard between –
The solemn Alps –
The siren Alps
Forever intervene!

'I FELT A FUNERAL, IN MY BRAIN'

I felt a Funeral, in my Brain,
And Mourners to and fro
Kept treading – treading – till it seemed
That Sense was breaking through –

And when they all were seated,
A Service, like a Drum –

Kept beating – beating – till I thought
My Mind was going numb –

And then I heard them lift a Box
And creak across my Soul
With those same Boots of Lead, again,
Then Space – began to toll,

As all the Heavens were a Bell,
And Being, but an Ear,
And I, and Silence, some strange Race
Wrecked, solitary, here –

And then a Plank in Reason, broke,
And I dropped down, and down –
And hit a World, at every plunge,
And Finished knowing – then –

'EXULTATION IS THE GOING'

Exultation is the going
Of an inland soul to sea,
Past the houses – past the headlands –
Into deep Eternity –

Bred as we, among the mountains,
Can the sailor understand
The divine intoxication
Of the first league out from land?

'THERE'S BEEN A DEATH, IN THE OPPOSITE HOUSE'

There's been a Death, in the Opposite House,
As lately as Today –
I know it, by the numb look
Such Houses have – alway –

The Neighbors rustle in and out –
The Doctor – drives away –
A Window opens like a Pod –
Abrupt – mechanically –

Somebody flings a Mattress out –
The Children hurry by –

They wonder if it died – on that –
I used to – when a Boy –

The Minister – goes stiffly in –
As if the House were His –
And He owned all the Mourners – now –
And little Boys – besides –

And then the Milliner – and the Man
Of the Appalling Trade –
To take the measure of the House –

There'll be that Dark Parade –

Of Tassels – and of Coaches – soon –
It's easy as a Sign –
The Intuition of the News –
In just a Country Town –

'I'VE KNOWN A HEAVEN, LIKE A TENT'

I've known a Heaven, like a Tent –
To wrap its shining Yards –
Pluck up its stakes, and disappear –
Without the sound of Boards
Or Rip of Nail – Or Carpenter –
But just the miles of Stare –
That signalize a Show's Retreat –
In North America –

No Trace – no Figment of the Thing
That dazzled, Yesterday,
No Ring – no Marvel –
Men, and Feats –
Dissolved as utterly –
As Bird's far Navigation
Discloses just a Hue –
A plash of Oars, a Gaiety –
Then swallowed up, of View.

'HOW NOTELESS MEN, AND PLEIADS, STAND'

How noteless Men, and Pleiads, stand,
Until a sudden sky
Reveals the fact that One is rapt
Forever from the Eye –

Members of the Invisible,
Existing, while we stare,
In Leagueless Opportunity.
O'ertakeless as the Air –

Why didn't we detain Them?
The Heavens with a smile,
Sweep by our disappointed Head!
Without a syllable –

'THE SOUL SELECTS HER OWN SOCIETY'

The Soul selects her own Society –
Then – shuts the Door –
To her divine Majority –
Present no more –

Unmoved – she notes the Chariots – pausing –
At her low Gate –
Unmoved – an Emperor be kneeling
Upon her Mat –

I've known her – from an ample nation –
Choose One –
Then – close the Valves of her attention –
Like Stone –

'AFTER GREAT PAIN, A FORMAL FEELING COMES'

After great pain, a formal feeling comes –
The Nerves sit ceremonious, like Tombs –
The stiff Heart questions was it He, that bore,
And Yesterday, or Centuries before?

The Feet, mechanical, go round –
Of Ground, or Air, or Ought –

A Wooden way
Regardless grown,
A Quartz contentment, like a stone –

This is the Hour of Lead –
Remembered, if outlived,
As Freezing persons, recollect the Snow –
First – Chill – then Stupor – then the letting go –

'I asked no other thing'

I asked no other thing –
No other – was denied –
I offered Being – for it –
The Mighty Merchant sneered –

Brazil? He twirled a Button –
Without a glance my way –
'But – Madam – is there nothing else –
That We can show – Today?'

'How many times these low feet staggered'

How many times these low feet staggered –
Only the soldered mouth can tell –
Try – can you stir the awful rivet –
Try – can you lift the hasps of steel!

Stroke the cool forehead – hot so often –
Lift – if you care – the listless hair –
Handle the adamantine fingers
Never a thimble – more – shall wear –

Buzz the dull flies – on the chamber window –
Brave – shines the sun through the freckled pane –
Fearless – the cobweb swings from the ceiling –
Indolent Housewife – in Daisies – lain!

'What Soft – Cherubic Creatures'

What Soft – Cherubic Creatures –
These Gentlewomen are –
One would as soon assault a Plush –
Or violate a Star –

Such Dimity Convictions –
A Horror so refined
Of freckled Human Nature –
Of Deity – ashamed –

It's such a common – Glory –
A Fisherman's – Degree –
Redemption – Brittle Lady –
Be so – ashamed of Thee –

'She rose to His Requirement – dropt'

She rose to His Requirement – dropt
The Playthings of Her Life
To take the honorable Work
Of Woman, and of Wife –

If ought She missed in Her new Day,
Of Amplitude, or Awe –
Or first Prospective – Or the Gold
In using, wear away,

It lay unmentioned – as the Sea
Develop Pearl, and Weed,
But only to Himself – be known
The Fathoms they abide –

'I dwell in Possibility'

I dwell in Possibility –
A fairer House than Prose –
More numerous of Windows –
Superior – for Doors –

Of Chambers as the Cedars –
Impregnable of Eye –
And for an Everlasting Roof
The Gambrels of the Sky –

Of Visitors – the fairest –
For Occupation – This –
The spreading wide my narrow Hands
To gather Paradise –

'IT MIGHT BE LONELIER'

It might be lonelier
Without the Loneliness –
I'm so accustomed to my Fate –
Perhaps the Other – Peace –

Would interrupt the Dark –
And crowd the little Room –
Too scant – by Cubits – to contain
The Sacrament – of Him –

I am not used to to hope –
It might intrude upon –
Its sweet parade – blaspheme the place –
Ordained to Suffering –

It might be easier
To fail – with Land in Sight –
Than gain – My Blue Peninsula –
To perish – of Delight –

'MY PERIOD HAD COME FOR PRAYER'

My period had come for Prayer –
No other Art – would do –
My Tactics missed a rudiment –
Creator – Was it you?

God grows above – so those who pray
Horizons – must ascend –
And so I stepped upon the North
To see this Curious Friend –

His House was not – no sign had He –
By Chimney – nor by Door
Could I infer his Residence –
Vast Prairies of Air

Unbroken by a Settler –
Were all that I could see –
Infinitude – Had'st Thou no Face
That I might look on Thee?

The Silence condescended –
Creation stopped – for Me –
But awed beyond my errand –
I worshipped – did not 'pray' –

'I TIE MY HAT – I CREASE MY SHAWL'

I tie my Hat – I crease my Shawl –
Life's little duties do – precisely –
As the very least
Were infinite – to me –

I put new Blossoms in the Glass –
And throw the old – away –
I push a petal from my Gown
That anchored there – I weigh
The time 'twill be till six o'clock
I have so much to do –
And yet – Existence – some way back –
Stopped – struck – my ticking – through –
We cannot put Ourself away
As a completed Man
Or Woman – When the Errand's done
We came to Flesh – upon –
There may be – Miles on Miles of Nought –
Of Action – sicker far –
To simulate – is stinging work –
To cover what we are
From Science – and from Surgery –
Too Telescopic Eyes
To bear on us unshaded –
For their – sake – not for Ours –
'Twould start them –
We – could tremble –
But since we got a Bomb –
And held it in our Bosom –
Nay – Hold it – it is calm –

Therefore – we do life's labor –
Though life's Reward – be done –
With scrupulous exactness –
To hold our Senses – on –

'It was not Death, for I stood up'

It was not Death, for I stood up,
And all the Dead, lie down –
It was not Night, for all the Bells
Put out their Tongues, for Noon.

It was not Frost, for on my Flesh
I felt Siroccos – crawl –
Nor Fire – for just my Marble feet
Could keep a Chancel, cool –

And yet, it tasted, like them all,
The Figures I have seen
Set orderly, for Burial,
Reminded me, of mine –

As if my life were shaven,
And fitted to a frame,
And could not breathe without a key,
And 'twas like Midnight, some –

When everything that ticked – has stopped –
And Space stares all around –
Or Grisly frosts – first Autumn morns,
Repeal the Beating Ground –

But, most, like Chaos – Stopless – cool –
Without a Chance, or Spar –
Or even a Report of Land –
To justify – Despair.

'A Bird came down the Walk'

A Bird came down the Walk –
He did not know I saw –
He bit an Angleworm in halves
And ate the fellow, raw,

And then he drank a Dew
From a convenient Grass –
And then hopped sidewise to the Wall
To let a Beetle pass –

He glanced with rapid eyes
That hurried all around –
They looked like frightened Beads, I thought –
He stirred his Velvet Head

Like one in danger, Cautious,
I offered him a Crumb
And he unrolled his feathers
And rowed him softer home –

Than Oars divide the Ocean,
Too silver for a seam –
Or Butterflies, off Banks of Noon
Leap, plashless as they swim.

'Civilization – spurns – the Leopard!'

Civilization – spurns – the Leopard!
Was the Leopard – bold?
Deserts – never rebuked her Satin –
Ethiop – her Gold –
Tawny – her Customs –
She was Conscious –
Spotted – her Dun Gown –
This was the Leopard's nature – Signor –
Need – a keeper – frown?

Pity – the Pard – that left her Asia –
Memories – of Palm –
Cannot be stifled – with Narcotic –
Nor suppressed – with Balm –

'The Spider holds a Silver Ball'

The Spider holds a Silver Ball
In unperceived Hands –
And dancing softly to Himself
His Yarn of Pearl – unwinds –

He plies from Nought to Nought –
In unsubstantial Trade –
Supplants our Tapestries with His –
In half the period –

An Hour to rear supreme
His Continents of Light –
Then dangle from the Housewife's Broom –
His Boundaries – forgot –

'He fumbles at your Soul'

He fumbles at your Soul
As Players at the Keys
Before they drop full Music on –
He stuns you by degrees –
Prepares your brittle Nature
For the Ethereal Blow
By fainter Hammers – further heard –
Then nearer – Then so slow
Your Breath has time to straighten –
Your Brain – to bubble Cool –
Deals – One – imperial – Thunderbolt –
That scalps your naked Soul –

When Winds take Forests in their Paws –
The Universe – is still –

'The Way I read a Letter's – this'

The Way I read a Letter's – this –
'Tis first – I lock the Door –
And push it with my fingers – next –
For transport it be sure –

And then I go the furthest off
To counteract a knock –
Then draw my little Letter forth
And slowly pick the lock –

Then – glancing narrow, at the Wall –
And narrow at the floor
For firm Conviction of a Mouse
Not exorcised before –

Peruse how infinite I am
To no one that You – know –
And sigh for lack of Heaven – but not
The Heaven God bestow –

'I cannot live with You'

I cannot live with You –
It would be Life –
And Life is over there –
Behind the Shelf

The Sexton keeps the Key to –
Putting up
Our Life – His Porcelain –
Like a Cup –

Discarded of the Housewife –
Quaint – or Broke –
A newer Sevres pleases –
Old Ones crack –

I could not die – with You –
For One must wait
To shut the Other's Gaze down –
You – could not –

And I – Could I stand by
And see You – freeze –
Without my Right of Frost –
Death's privilege?

Nor could I rise – with You –
Because Your Face
Would put out Jesus' –
That New Grace

Glow plain – and foreign
On my homesick Eye –
Except that You than He
Shone closer by –

They'd judge Us – How –
For You – served Heaven – You know,
Or sought to –
I could not –

Because You saturated Sight –
And I had no more Eyes
For sordid excellence
As Paradise

And were You lost, I would be –
Though My Name
Rang loudest
On the Heavenly fame –

And were You - saved -
And I - condemned to be
Where You were not -
That self - were Hell to Me -

So We must meet apart -
You there - I - here -
With just the Door ajar
That Oceans are - and Prayer -
And that White Sustenance -
Despair -

'My life closed twice before its close'

My life closed twice before its close -
It yet remains to see
If Immortality unveil
A third event to me

So huge, so hopeless to conceive
As these that twice befell.
Parting is all we know of heaven,
And all we need of hell.

'In falling Timbers buried'

In falling Timbers buried -
There breathed a Man -
Outside - the spades - were plying -
The Lungs - within -

Could He - know - they sought Him -
Could They - know - He breathed -
Horrid Sand Partition -
Neither - could be heard -

Never slacked the Diggers -
But when Spades had done -
Oh, Reward of Anguish,
It was dying - Then -

Many Things - are fruitless -
'Tis a Baffling Earth -

But there is no Gratitude
Like the Grace - of Death -

'He scanned it - staggered'

He scanned it - staggered -
Dropped the Loop
To Past or Period -
Caught helpless at a sense as if
His Mind were going blind -

Groped up, to see if God was there -
Groped backward at Himself
Caressed a Trigger absently
And wandered out of Life.

'I died for Beauty - but was scarce'

I died for Beauty - but was scarce
Adjusted in the Tomb
When One who died for Truth, was lain
In an adjoining Room -

He questioned softly 'Why I failed'?
'For Beauty', I replied -
'And I - for Truth - Themself are One -
We Brethren, are', He said -

And so, as Kinsmen, met a Night -
We talked between the Rooms -
Until the Moss had reached our lips -
And covered up - our names -

'We grow accustomed to the Dark'

We grow accustomed to the Dark -
When Light is put away -
As when the Neighbor holds the Lamp
To witness her Goodbye -

A Moment - We uncertain step
For newness of the night -

Then – fit our Vision to the Dark –
And meet the Road – erect –

And so of larger – Darknesses –
Those Evenings of the Brain –
When not a Moon disclose a sign –
Or Star – come out – within –

The Bravest – grope a little –
And sometimes hit a Tree
Directly in the Forehead –
But as they learn to see –

Either the Darkness alters –
Or something in the sight
Adjusts itself to Midnight –
And Life steps almost straight.

'I heard a Fly buzz – when I died'

I heard a Fly buzz – when I died –
The Stillness in the Room
Was like the Stillness in the Air –
Between the heaves of Storm –

The Eyes around – had wrung them dry –
And Breaths were gathering firm
For that last Onset – when the King
Be witnessed – in the Room –

I willed my Keepsakes – Signed away
What portion of me be
Assignable – and then it was
There interposed a Fly –

With Blue – uncertain stumbling Buzz –
Between the light – and me –
And then the Windows failed – and then
I could not see to see –

'I like to see it lap the Miles'

I like to see it lap the Miles –
And lick the Valleys up –
And stop to feed itself at Tanks –
And then – prodigious step –

Around a Pile of Mountains –
And supercilious peer
In Shanties – by the sides of Roads –
And then a Quarry pare

To fit its Ribs
And crawl between
Complaining all the while
In horrid – hooting stanza –
Then chase itself down Hill –

And neigh like Boanerges –
Then – punctual as a Star
Stop, docile and omnipotent
At its own stable door –

'I started Early – Took my Dog'

I started Early – Took my Dog –
And visited the Sea –
The Mermaids in the Basement
Came out to look at me –

And Frigates – in the Upper Floor
Extended Hempen Hands –
Presuming Me to be a Mouse –
Aground – upon the Sands –

But no Man moved Me – till the Tide
Went past my simple Shoe –
And past my Apron – and my Belt
And past my Bodice – too –

And made as He would eat me up –
As wholly as a Dew
Upon a Dandelion's Sleeve –
And then – I started – too –

And He – He followed – close behind –
I felt His Silver Heel

Upon my Ankle – Then my Shoes
Would overflow with Pearl –

Until We met the Solid Town –
No One He seemed to know –
And bowing with a Mighty look –
At me – The Sea withdrew –

'BECAUSE I COULD NOT STOP FOR DEATH

Because I could not stop for Death –
He kindly stopped for me –
The Carriage held but just Ourselves –
And Immortality.

We slowly drove – He knew no haste
And I had put away
My labor and my leisure too,
For His Civility –

We passed the School, where Children strove
At Recess – in the Ring –
We passed the Fields of Gazing Grain –
We passed the Setting Sun –

Or rather – He passed Us –
The Dews drew quivering and chill –
For only Gossamer, my Gown –
My Tippet – only Tulle –

We paused before a House that seemed
A Swelling of the Ground –
The Roof was scarcely visible –
The Cornice – in the Ground –

Since then – 'tis Centuries – and yet
Feels shorter than the Day
I first surmised the Horses' Heads
Were toward Eternity –

'A NARROW FELLOW IN THE GRASS'

A narrow Fellow in the Grass
Occasionally rides –
You may have met Him – did you not
His notice sudden is –

The Grass divides as with a Comb –
A spotted shaft is seen –
And then it closes at your feet
And opens further on –

He likes a Boggy Acre
A Floor too cool for Corn –
Yet when a Boy, and Barefoot –
I more than once at Noon
Have passed, I thought, a Whip lash
Unbraiding in the Sun
When stooping to secure it
It wrinkled, and was gone –

Several of Nature's People
I know, and they know me –
I feel for them a transport
Of cordiality –

But never met this Fellow
Attended, or alone
Without a tighter breathing
And Zero at the Bone –

'I GAVE MYSELF TO HIM'

I gave myself to Him –
And took Himself, for Pay,
The solemn contract of a Life
Was ratified, this way –

The Wealth might disappoint –
Myself a poorer prove
Than this great Purchaser suspect,
The Daily Own – of Love

Depreciate the Vision –
But till the Merchant buy –
Still Fable – in the Isles of Spice –
The subtle Cargoes – lie –

At least – 'tis Mutual – Risk –
Some – found it – Mutual Gain –
Sweet Debt of Life – Each Night to owe –
Insolvent – every Noon –

'DID OUR BEST MOMENT LAST'

Did Our Best Moment last –
'Twould supersede the Heaven –
A few – and they by Risk – procure –
So this Sort – are not given –

Except as stimulants – in
Cases of Despair –
Or Stupor – The Reserve –
These Heavenly Moments are –

A Grant of the Divine –
That Certain as it Comes –
Withdraws – and leaves the dazzled Soul
In her unfurnished Rooms.

Any selection from John Donne (c. 1572–1631) must be inadequate, and the object in making one can only be to tempt the reader to a more extensive exploration of his work. The selector can do no more than choose poems which speak out vividly one of the most forthright and at the same time most subtle minds of the seventeenth century in England. The man who became a famous preacher, as Dean of Saint Paul's, had been also an exponent of the pleasures of physical nakedness.

The reader will find here the poet addressing himself to several aspects of the relationships between men and women, by no means limited to the purely physical. In one poem, indeed, he speaks of what enables lovers to 'forget the He and She', and in 'The Autumnal' the Golden Age of youth is spoken of as having given way to 'gold oft tried, and ever new.' All is gathered together in the best of the religious poems: in 'A Hymn to Christ, at the Author's last going into Germany', he speaks of 'The amorousness of an harmonious soul'.

THE UNDERTAKING

I have done one braver thing
   Than all the Worthies did,
And yet a braver thence doth spring
   Which is, to keep that hid.

It were but madness now to impart
   The skill of specular stone,
When he which can have learned the art
   To cut it can find none.

So, if I now should utter this,
   Others (because no more
Such stuff to work upon there is)
   Would love but as before.

But he who loveliness within
   Hath found, all outward loathes,
For he who colour loves, and skin,
   Loves but their oldest clothes.

If, as I have, you also do
   Virtue attired in woman see
And dare love that, and say so too,
   And forget the He and She,

And if this love, though placed so,
   From profane men you hide,
Which will no faith on this bestow,
   Or, if they do, deride:

Then you have done a braver thing
   Than all the Worthies did.
And a braver thence will spring
   Which is, to keep that hid.

❧

THE ANNIVERSARY

   All kings, and all their favourites,
   All glory of honours, beauties, wits,
The sun itself, which makes times, as they pass.
Is elder by a year, now, than it was
When thou and I first one another saw:
All other things to their destruction draw,
   Only our love hath no decay;
This, no tomorrow hath, not yesterday;

Running it never runs from us away,
But truly keeps his first, last, everlasting day.

   Two graves must hide thine and my corse;
If one might, death were no divorce:
Alas, as well as other princes, we
(Who prince enough in one another be)
Must leave at last in death, these eyes, and ears,
Oft fed with true oaths, and with sweet salt tears;
   But souls where nothing dwells but love
(All other thoughts being inmates) then shall prove
This, or a love increased there above,
When bodies to their graves, souls from their graves
   remove.

   And then we shall be throughly blest,
   But we no more than all the rest;
Here upon earth, we're kings, and none but we
Can be such kings, nor of such subjects be;
Who is so safe as we, where none can do
Treason to us, except one of us two?
   True and false fears let us refrain,
Let us love nobly, and live, and add again
Years and years unto years, till we attain
To write threescore, this is the second of our reign.

❧

TWICKENHAM GARDEN

Blasted with sighs, and surrounded with tears,
   Hither I come to seek the spring,
   And at mine eyes, and at mine ears,
Receive such balms as else cure everything;
   But oh, self-traitor, I do bring
The spider love, which transubstantiates all,
   And can convert manna to gall;
And that this place may thoroughly be thought
   True Paradise, I have the serpent brought.

'Twere wholesomer for me, that winter did
   Benight the glory of this place,
   And that a grave frost did forbid
These trees to laugh, and mock me to my face;
   But that I may not this disgrace
Endure, nor leave this garden, Love, let me
   Some senseless piece of this place be;
Make me a mandrake, so I may groan here,
Or a stone fountain weeping out my year.

Hither with crystal vials, lovers, come,
    And take my tears, which are love's wine,
And try your mistress' tears at home,
For all are false, that taste not just like mine;
    Alas, hearts do not in eyes shine,
Nor can you more judge woman's thoughts by tear,
    Than by her shadow, what she wears.
O perverse sex, where none is true but she,
    Who's therefore true, because her truth kills me.

THE ECSTASY

Where, like a pillow on a bed,
    A pregnant bank swelled up, to rest
The violet's reclining head,
    Sat we two, one another's best.

Our hands were firmly cemented
    With a fast balm, which thence did spring;
Our eye-beams twisted, and did thread
    Our eyes upon one double string;

So to intergraft our hands, as yet
    Was all the means to make us one,
And pictures in our eyes to get
    Was all our propagation.

As, 'twixt two equal armies, Fate
    Suspends uncertain victory,
Our souls (which to advance their state
    Were gone out) hung 'twixt her and me.

And whilst our souls negotiate there,
    We like sepulchral statues lay;
All day, the same as our postures were,
    And we said nothing, all the day.

If any, so by love refined
    That he souls' language understood,
And by good love were grown all mind,
    Within convenient distance stood,

He (though he knew not which soul spake,
    Because both meant, both spake the same)
Might thence a new concoction take,
    And part far purer than he came.

This Ecstasy doth unperplex,
    We said, and tell us what we love;
We see by this it was not sex;
    We see, we saw not what did move:

But as all several souls contain
    Mixture of things, they know not what,
Love these mixed souls doth mix again,
    And makes both one each this and that.

A single violet transplant,
    The strength, the colour, and the size,
(All which before was poor, and scant)
    Redoubles still, and multiplies.

When love, with one another so
    Interinanimates two souls,
That abler soul, which thence doth flow,
    Defects of loneliness controls.

We then, who are this new soul, know
    Of what we are composed, and made,
For the atomies of which we grow
    Are souls, whom no change can invade.

But oh, alas, so long, so far
    Our bodies why do we forbear?
They're ours, though they're not we, we are
    The intelligences, they the sphere.

We owe them thanks because they thus
    Did us to us at first convey,
Yielded their forces, sense, to us,
    Nor are dross to us, but allay.

On man heaven's influence works not so,
    But that it first imprints the air;
So soul into the soul may flow,
    Though it to body first repair.

As our blood labours to beget
    Spirits as like souls as it can,
Because such fingers need to knit
    That subtle knot which makes us man:

So must pure lovers' souls descend
    To affections, and to faculties,
Which sense may reach and apprehend,
    Else a great Prince in prison lies.

To our bodies turn we then, that so
    Weak men on love revealed may look;

Love's mysteries in souls do grow,
    But yet the body is his book.

And if some lover, such as we,
    Have heard this dialogue of one,
Let him still mark us, he shall see
    Small change, when we're to bodies gone.

❧

THE RELIC

    When my grave is broke up again
    Some second guest to entertain,
    (For graves have learned that woman-head
    To be to more than one a bed)
        And he that digs it, spies
A bracelet of bright hair about the bone,
        Will he not let us alone,
And think that there a loving couple lies,
Who thought that this device might be some way
To make their souls, at the last busy day,
Meet at this grave and make a little stay?

    If this fall in a time, or land,
    Where mis-devotion doth command,
    Then he that digs us up will bring
    Us to the Bishop and the King
        To make us relics; then
Thou shalt be a Mary Magdalen, and I
        A something else thereby;
All women shall adore us, and some men;
And since at such time, miracles are sought,
I would have that age by this paper taught
What miracles we harmless lovers wrought.

    First, we loved well and faithfully,
    Yet knew not what we loved, nor why;
    Difference of sex no more we knew
    Than our guardian angels do;
        Coming and going, we
Perchance might kiss, but not between those meals;
        Our hands ne'er touched the seals
Which nature, injured by late law, sets free:
These miracles we did; but now alas,
All measure and all language I should pass,
Should I tell what a miracle she was.

❧

ELEGY IX: THE AUTUMNAL

No spring nor summer beauty hath such grace
    As I have seen in one autumnal face.
Young beauties force your love, and that's a rape;
    This doth but counsel, yet you cannot scape.
If 'twere a shame to love, here 'twere no shame:
    Affections here take reverence's name.
Were her first years the Golden Age? That's true;
    But now she's gold oft tried, and ever new.
That was her torrid and inflaming time,
    This is her tolerable tropic clime.

Fair eyes, who asks more heat than comes from
        hence,
    He in a fever wishes pestilence.
Call not these wrinkles, graves; if graves they were,
    They were Love's graves; or else he is no where.
Yet lies not Love dead here, but here doth sit
    Vowed to this trench like an anachorit.
And here, till hers, which must be his death, come,
    He doth not dig a grave, but build a tomb.
Here dwells he: though he sojourn everywhere,
    In progress, yet his standing house is here.
Here, where still evening is, not noon, nor night;
    Where no voluptuousness, yet all delight.
In all her words, unto all hearers fit:
    You may at revels, you at council, sit.
This is Love's timber, youth his underwood;
    There he, as wine in June, enrages blood,
Which then comes seasonabliest, when our taste
    And appetite to other things is past.
Xerxes' strange Lydian love, the platen tree,
    Was loved for age, none being so large as she,
Or else because, being young, nature did bless
    Her youth with age's glory, barrenness.
If we love things long sought, age is a thing
    Which we are fifty years in compassing.
If transitory things, which soon decay,
    Age must be loveliest at the latest day.
But name not winter-faces, whose skin's slack;
    Lank, as an unthrift's purse; but a soul's sack;
Whose eyes seek light within, for all here's shade;
    Whose mouths are holes, rather worn out than
        made.
Whose every tooth to a several place is gone,
    To vex their souls at Resurrection;
Name not these living death's-heads unto me,
    For these, not anciénts, but antiques be.
I hate extremes; yet I had rather stay
    With tombs than cradles, to wear out a day.

Since such love's natural ration is, may still
   My love descend, and journey down the hill;
Not panting after growing beauties, so,
   I shall ebb on with them, who homeward go.

ELEGY XIX. TO HIS MISTRESS GOING TO BED

Come, madam, come, all rest my powers defy,
Until I labour, I in labour lie.
The foe oft-times having the foe in sight,
Is tired with standing though he never fight.
Off with that girdle, like heaven's zone glistering,
But a far fairer world encompassing.
Unpin that spangled breastplate which you wear,
That the eyes of busy fools may be stopped there
Unlace yourself, for that harmonious chime
Tells me from you that now 'tis your bed time.
Off with that happy busk, which I envy,
That still can be, and still can stand so nigh.
Your gown, going off, such beauteous state reveals,
As when from flowry meads the hill's shadow steals.
Off with that wiry coronet and show
The hairy diadem which on you doth grow:
Now off with those shoes, and then safely tread
In this love's hallowed temple, this soft bed.
In such white robes, heaven's angels used to be
Received by men; thou, Angel, bring'st with thee
A heaven like Mahomet's Paradise; and though
Ill spirits walk in white, we easily know
By this these angels from an evil sprite:
Those set our hairs, but these our flesh upright.
   License my roving hands, and let them go
Before, behind, between, above, below.
O my America! my new-found-land,
My kingdom, safeliest when with one man manned,
My mine of precious stones, my empery
How blest am I in this discovering thee!
To enter in these bonds is to be free;
Then where my hand is set, my seal shall be.
   Full nakedness! All joys are due to thee,
As souls unbodied, bodies unclothed must be
To taste whole joys. Gems which you women use
Are like Atlanta's balls, cast in men's views,
That when a fool's eye lighteth on a gem,
His earthly soul may covet theirs, not them.
Like pictures, or like books' gay coverings made
For lay-men, are all women thus arrayed;

Themselves are mystic books, which only we
(Whom their imputed grace will dignify)
Must see revealed. Then, since that I may know.
As liberally as to a midwife, show
Thyself: cast all, yea, this white linen hence,
Here is no penance, much less innocence.
   To teach thee, I am naked first; why than,
What needst thou have more covering than a man.

SONNET XIV

Batter my heart, three-personed God; for you
As yet but knock, breathe, shine, and seek to mend;
That I may rise, and stand, o'erthrow me, and bend
Your force, to break, blow, burn, and make me new.
I, like an usurped town to another due,
Labour to admit you, but oh, to no end:
Reason your viceroy in me, me should defend,
But is captived, and proves weak or untrue;
Yet dearly'I love you, and would be loved fain,
But am betrothed unto your enemy:
Divorce me, untie, or break that knot again,
Take me to you, imprison me, for I
Except you enthral me, never shall be free,
Nor ever chaste, except you ravish me.

A HYMN TO CHRIST, AT THE AUTHOR'S LAST GOING INTO GERMANY

In what torn ship soever I embark
That ship shall be my emblem of thy ark;
What sea soever swallow me, that flood
Shall be to me an emblem of thy blood
Though thou with clouds of anger do disguise
Thy face, yet through that mask I know those eyes,
   Which, though they turn away sometimes,
     They never will despise.

I sacrifice this island unto thee,
And all whom I loved there, and who loved me;
When I have put our seas 'twixt them and me,
Put thou thy sea betwixt my sins and thee.
As the tree's sap doth seek the root below
In winter, in my wmter now I go,

Where none but thee, th' eternal root
　Of true love I may know.

Nor thou nor thy religion dost control
The amorousness of an harmonious soul;
But thou wouldst have that love thyself. As thou
Art jealous, Lord, so I am jealous now:
Thou lov'st not, till from loving more thou free
My soul; who ever gives, takes liberty:
　O, if thou car'st not whom I love
　　Alas, thou lov'st not me.

Seal then this bill of my divorce to all
On whom those fainter beams of love did fall;
Marry those loves, which in youth scattered be
On fame, wit, hopes (false mistresses), to thee.
Churches are best for prayer, that have least light:
To see God only, I go out of sight:
　And to scape stormy days, I choose
　　An everlasting night.

❧

HYMN TO GOD MY GOD, IN MY SICKNESS

Since I am coming to that holy room,
　Where, with thy choir of saints for evermore,
I shall be made thy music; as I come
　I tune the instrument here at the door,
　And what I must do then, think here before.

Whilst my physicians by their love are grown
　Cosmographers, and I their map, who lie
Flat on this bed, that by them may be shown
　That this is my south-west discovery
　Per fretum febris, by these straits to die.

I joy that in these straits I see my west;
　For though their currents yield return to none,
What shall my west hurt me? As west and east
　In all flat maps (and I am one) are one,
　So death doth touch the recurrection.

Is the Pacific Sea my home? Or are
　The eastern riches? Is Jerusalem?
Anyan, and Magellan, and Gibraltar,
　All straits, and none but straits, are ways to them,
　Whether where Japhet dwelt, or Cham, or Shem.

We think that paradise and Calvary,
　Christ's cross and Adam's tree, stood in one place:
Look, Lord, and find both Adams met in me;
　As the first Adam's sweat surrounds my face,
　May the last Adam's blood my soul embrace.

So, in his purple wrapped receive me Lord,
　By these his thorns give me his other crown;
And as to others' souls I preached thy word,
　Be this my text, my sermon to mine own,
　Therefore that he may raise the Lord throws
　　down.

❧

A HYMN TO GOD THE FATHER

Wilt thou forgive that sin where I begun,
　Which is my sin, though it were done before?
Wilt thou forgive that sin through which I run,
　And do run still, though still I do deplore?
　　When thou hast done, thou hast not done,
　　　For I have more.

Wilt thou forgive that sin which I have won
　Others to sin? and made my sin their door?
Wilt thou forgive that sin which I did shun
　A year or two, but wallowed in, a score?
　　When thou hast done, thou hast not done,
　　　For I have more.

I have a sin of fear, that when I have spun
　My last thread, I shall perish on the shore;
Swear by thyself, that at my death thy son
　Shall shine as he shines now and heretofore;
　　And, having done that, thou hast done,
　　　I fear no more.

Satirist, pedagogue, playright, proselyte, pornographer (mild), occasional plaigiary, songwriter, literary critic (our first), expert in three types of translation (including English to English), always, and above all, the master poet of his age, John Dryden (1631–1700), by today's standards, is worth at least three or four Nobel Prizes for Literature.

Quick, witty, sane, fertile, conversational, better able to argue in verse than any other English poet, for thirty years Dryden earned a good living from his plays only one of which, All for Love (1677), is still performed: it is their songs, Prologues and Epilogues we value.

This male/female duet from Marriage à-la-Mode (1673).

SONG

Why should a foolish marriage vow
  Which long ago was made,
Oblige us to each other now
  When passion is decayed?
We loved, and we loved, as long as we could,
  Till our love was loved out in us both:
But our marriage is dead when the pleasure is fled:
  'Twas pleasure first made it an oath.

If I have pleasures for a friend,
  And farther love in store,
What wrong has he whose joys did end,
  And who could give no more?
'Tis a madness that he should be jealous of me,
  Or that I should bar him of another;
For all we can gain is to give ourselves pain,
  When neither can hinder the other.

❧

This from An Evening's Love (pub. 1671) that Pepys found 'very smutty' (Diary 20.6.1668):

SONG

After the pangs of a desperate lover,
When day and night I have sighed all in vain,
Ah what a pleasure it is to discover
In her eyes pity, who causes my pain!

When with unkindness our love at a stand is,
And both have punished ourselves with the pain,
Ah what a pleasure the touch of her hand is,
Ah what a pleasure to press it again!

When the denial comes fainter and fainter,
And her eyes give what her tongue does deny,
Ah what a trembling I feel when I venture,
Ah what a trembling does usher my joy!

When with a sigh she accords me the blessing,
And her eyes twinkle 'twixt pleasure and pain,
Ah what a joy 'tis beyond all expressing,
Ah what a joy to hear, 'shall we again?'!

❧

Dryden's melodrama Tyrannic Love (produced, 1669) recounts the martyrdom of the (fictional) St Catherine of Alexandria, in which after an attempt to break her faith on a spiked wheel (hence Catherine-wheel) had failed, followed by the execution of the two hundred soldiers her constancy had converted, she is beheaded as the Prologue states. St Catherine was played by Nell Gwyn (Miss Ellen). After being the mistress of the actor, Charles Hart, and then of Charles Sackville, Earl of Dorset to be, Nell passed to Charles II – whom she nicknamed Charles the Third.

PROLOGUE TO TYRANNIC LOVE

Self-love (which never rightly understood)
Makes poets still conclude their plays are good;
And malice in all critics reigns so high,
That for small errors they whole plays decry;
So that to see this fondness, and that spite,
You'd think that none but madmen judge or write.
Therefore our poet, as he thinks not fit
T'impose upon you what he writes for wit,
So hopes that leaving you your censures* free,   *opinions*
You equal* judges of the whole will be: *impartial*
They judge but half who only faults will see.
Poets like lovers should be bold and dare,
They spoil their business with an over-care;
And he who servilely creeps after sense
Is safe, but ne'er will reach an excellence.
Hence 'tis our poet in his conjuring
Allowed his fancy the full scope and swing,

But when a tyrant for his theme he had,
He loosed the reins and bid his Muse run mad:
And though he stumbles in a full career,
Yet rashness is a better fault than fear.
He saw his way, but in so swift a pace
To choose the ground might be to lose the race.
They then who of each trip th' advantage take,
Find but those faults which they want wit to make.

≈

ITS EPILOGUE

‹Spoken by Mrs Ellen, when she was to be carried off dead by the bearers. ›

To the bearer:

    Hold, are you mad? you damned confounded
       dog,
    I am to rise, and speak the Epilogue.

To the audience:

    I come, kind gentlemen, strange news to tell ye,
    I am the ghost of poor departed Nelly,
    Sweet ladies, be not frighted, I'll be civil,
    I'm what I was, a little harmless devil.
    For after death we sprites have just such natures
    We had for all the world when human creatures;
    And therefore I that was an actress here,
    Play all my tricks in hell, a goblin there.
    Gallants, look to't, you say there are no sprites,
    But I'll come dance about your beds at nights.
    And faith, you'll be in a sweet kind of taking
    When I surprise you between sleep and waking.
    To tell you true, I walk because I die
    Out of my calling in a tragedy.
    O poet, damned dull poet, who could prove
    So senseless to make Nelly die for love!
    Nay, what's yet worse, to kill me in the prime
    Of Easter term, in tart and cheese-cake time!
    I'll fit the fop, for I'll not one word say
    T'excuse his godly out-of-fashion play:
    A play which if you dare but twice sit out,
    You'll all be slandered, and be thought devout.
    But farewell, gentlemen, make haste to me,
    I'm sure ere long to have your company.
    As for my epitaph when I am gone,
    I'll trust no poet, but will write my own:
    Here Nelly lies, who though she lived a slattern,
    Yet died a princess, acting in St Cathar'n.

≈

THE FIRST OF ITS SONGS

(set by Purcell, in which the aerial spirits Nakar and Damilcar are invoked to find out if Catherine will fall in love with the tyrant Maximim.)

Nakar and Damilcar descend in clouds, and sing:

Nak. Hark, my Damilcar, we are called below!
Dam. Let us go, let us go:
    Go to relieve the care
    Of longing lovers in despair!
Nak. Merry, merry, merry, we sail from the east,
    Half tippled* at a rainbow feast.   *drunk*
Dam. In the bright moonshine while winds whistle
    loud,
    Tivy,* tivy, tivy, we mount and we fly,   *tantivy*
    All racking* along in a downy white cloud: *driving*
    And lest our leap from the sky should prove
      too far,
    We slide on the back of a new-falling star.
Nak. And drop from above
    In a jelly of love!*   *supposedly the remains of a fallen star*
Dam. But now the sun's down, and the
    element's* red,   *sky*
    The spirits of fire against us make head!
Nak. They muster, they muster, like gnats in the air:
    Aas! I must leave thee, my fair,
    And to my light horsemen repair.
Dam. O stay, for you need not to fear 'em tonight;
    The wind is for us, and blows full in their sight,
    And o'er the wide ocean we fight!
    Like leaves in the autumn our foes will fall
      down,
    And hiss in the water –
Both. And hiss in the water and drown!
Nak. But their men lie securely entrenched in a
    cloud,
    And a trumpeter-hornet to battle sounds loud.
Dam. Now mortals that spy
    How we tilt in the sky
    With wonder will gaze,
    And fear such events as will ne'er come to pass!
Nak. Stay you to perform what the man will have
    done.
Dam. Then call me again when the battle is won.
Both. So ready and quick is spirit of air
    To pity the lover, and succour the fair,
    That silent and swift, the little soft god
    Is here with a wish, and is gone with a nod.

≈

ABSALOM AND ACHITOPEL

Dryden's most famous poem concerns the attempt made by Anthony Cooper, the 60-year-old Earl of Shrewsbury (Achitopel) to crown James Scott, Duke of Monmouth (Absalom) as King of England. The year was 1684. The ailing Charles II had sired fourteen children, none of them legitimate. The crown seemed certain to pass to Charles's brother, James, an unpopular, fundamentalist Catholic.

To prevent this, the Protestant politicians – united by Shrewsbury – determined that Charles should accept a Bill excluding his brother from the throne and then name Monmouth, the eldest of the male illegitimates – handsome, popular, vain – as his rightful heir. Dryden begins:

In pious times, ere priestcraft did begin,
Before polygamy was make a sin;
When man on many multiplied his kind,
Ere one to one was cursedly confined;
When nature prompted, and no law denied
Promiscuous use of concubine and bride;
Then Israel's monarch after Heaven's own heart,   *Charles II*
His vigorous warmth did variously impart
To wives and slaves; and wide as his command,
Scatter'd his maker's image through the land.
Michal, of royal blood, the crown did wear;   *Charles's queen*
A soil ungrateful to the tiller's care:
Not so the rest; for several mothers bore
To god-like David several sons before.   *Charles II*
But since like slaves his bed they did ascend,
No true succession could their seed attend.
Of all the numerous progeny was none
So beautiful, so brave, as Absalom:
Whether inspired by some diviner lust,
His father got him with a greater gust;
Or that his conscious destiny made way,
By manly beauty to imperial sway.
Early in foreign fields he won renown,
With kings and states allied to Israel's crown:
In peace the thoughts of war he could remove,
And seem'd as he were only born for love.
Whate'er he did, was done with so much ease,
In him alone 'twas natural to please:
His motions all accompanied with grace;
And paradise was open'd in his face.
With secret joy indulgent David view'd
His youthful image in his son renew'd:
What faults he had (for who from faults is free?)

His father could not, or he would not see.
Some warm excesses which the law forbore,
Were construed youth that purged by boiling o'er;
And Amnon's* murder by a specious   *Peter Vernell,*
  name,   *murdered in a brothel by among others, Monmouth.*
Was call'd a just revenge for injured fame.
Thus praised and loved, the noble youth remain'd,
While David indisturb'd in Sion reign'd.
The Jews*, a headstrong, moody, murmuring
  race,   *The English*
As ever tried the extent and stretch of grace;
God's pamper'd people, whom, debauch'd with ease,
No king could govern nor no god could please;
(Gods they had tried of every shape and size,
That god-smiths could produce, or priests devise):
These adam wits, too fortunately free,
Began to dream they wanted* liberty;   *lacked*
And when no rule, no precedent, was found
Of men by laws less circumscribed and bound
They led their wild desires to woods and caves,
And thought that all but savages were slaves.
They who, when Saul was dead, without   *Oliver Cromwell,*
  a blow,   *Lord Protector from 1653–58;*
Made foolish Ishbosheth the crown   *his son, Richard*
  forego;   *dismissed as Protector, 1659*
Who banish'd David did from Hebron* bring,   *Brussels*
And with a general shout proclaim'd him king:
Those very Jews, who, at their very best,
Their humour more than loyalty express'd,
Now wonder'd why so long they had obey'd
An idol monarch, which their hands had made;
Thought they might ruin him they could create,
Or melt him to that golden calf* – a state.   *an idol*
But these were random bolts*: no form'd design,   *shots*
Nor interest made the factious crowd to join:
The sober part of Israel, free from stain,
Well knew the value of a peaceful reign;
And, looking backward with a wise affright,
Saw seams of wounds dishonest* to the sight: *hideous*
In comtemplation of whose ugly scars,
They cursed the memory of civil wars.
The moderate sort of men thus qualified*,   *calmed*
Inclined the balance to the better side;
And David's mildness managed it so well,
The bad found no occasion to rebel.
But when to sin our biass'd nature leans,
The careful devil is still at hand with means;
Plots, true or false, are necessary things,
To raise up commonwealths, and ruin kings.

There were several plots; the Popish Plot, leading to the execution of 35 Catholics by 1681, being the most sensational. Shrewsbury used these executions to urge the exclusion of James and to promote Monmouth as heir. Dryden's portrait of Shaftesbury (MP for Wiltshire, Chancellor of the Exchequer, Lord Chancellor – when he was considered as a judge of integrity, created earl in 1672, arrested for high treason in 1681) is the most devastating of any English politician by any English poet; a superb example of satirical vigour.

This plot, which fail'd for want of common sense,   *The Popish*
Had yet a deep and dangerous consequence:
For as, when raging fevers boil the blood
The standing lake soon floats into a flood
And every hostile humour which before
Slept quiet in its channels, bubbles o'er,
So several factions from this first ferment
Work up to foam, and threat the government.
Some by their friends, more by themselves thought wise,
Opposed the power to which they could not rise.
Some had in courts been great, and thrown from thence,
Like fends were harden'd in impenitence.
Some, by their monarch's fatal mercy, grown
From pardon'd rebels, kinsmen to the throne,
Were raised in power and public office high –
Strong bands, if bands ungrateful men could tie.
  Of these, the false Achitophel was first;
A name to all succeeding ages cursed:
For close designs, and crooked counsels fit,
Sagacious, bold, and turbulent of wit;
Restless, unfix'd in principles and place,
In power unpleased, impatient of disgrace.
A fiery soul, which, working out its way,
Fretted* the pigmy body to decay,   *consumed / over-*
And o'er-inform'd the tenement of clay.*   *animated the body*
A daring pilot in extremity;
Pleased with the danger, when the waves went high,
He sought the storms; but for a calm unfit,
Would steer too nigh the sands, to boast his wit.
Great wits are sure to madness near allied,
And thin partitions do their bounds divide;
Else why should he, with wealth and honour blest,
Refuse his age the needful hours of rest?
Punish a body which he could not please;
Bankrupt of life, yet prodigal of ease?

And all to leave what with his toil he won,
To that unfeather'd two-legg'd thing, a son;
Got while his soul did huddled notions try
And born a shapeless lump, like   *Anthony Cooper, Shaftesbury's*
   anarchy.   *son, was sickly and politically insignificant.*
In friendship false, implacable in hate,
Resolved to ruin, or to rule the state.
How safe is treason, and how sacred ill,
Where none can sin against the people's will!
Where crowds can wink, and no offence be known,
Since in another's guilt they find their own!
Yet fame deserved no enemy can grudge;
The statesman we abhor, but praise the judge.
In Israel's courts ne'er sat an Abethdin
With more discerning eyes, or hands more clean,
Unbribed, unsought, the wretched to redress;
Swift of despatch, and easy of access.
O had he been content to serve the crown
With virtues only proper to the gown;
Or had the rankness of the soil been freed
From cockle, that oppress'd the noble seed,
David for him his tuneful harp had strung
And heaven had wanted one immortal song.
But wild ambition loves to slide, not stand,
And fortune's ice prefers to virtue's land.
Achitophel, grown weary to possess
A lawful fame, and lazy happiness,
Disdain'd the golden fruit to gather free,
And lent the crowd his arm to shake the tree.

Among Shaftesbury's supporters was George Villiers, the second Duke of Buckingham, said to be the richest man in England and part-author of *The Rehearsal*, a play in which Dryden is mocked. Dryden's revenge on this odd, generous, witty hedonist, was to make him the poem's second exceptional character, Zimri, an example of withering ridicule, considered by Dryden to be 'worth the whole poem', unfair as it is.

To further this, Achitophel unites
The malcontents of all the Israelites:
Whose differing parties he could wisely join,
For several ends to serve the same design.
The best – and of the princes some were such –
Who thought the power of monarchy too much,
Mistaken men, and patriots in their hearts,
Not wicked, but seduced by impious arts.
  Such were the tools: but a whole hydra more

Remains of sprouting heads too long to score.
Some of their chiefs were princes of the land:
In the first rank of these did Zimri stand;
A man so various, that he seem'd to be
Not one, but all mankind's epitome.
Stiff in opinions, always in the wrong,
Was everything by starts, and nothing long;
But in the course of one revolving moon
Was chemist, fiddler, statesman, and buffoon:
Then all for women, painting, rhyming, drinking,
Besides ten thousand freaks that died in thinking.
Blest madman, who could every hour employ
With something new to wish, or to enjoy!
Railing and praising were his usual themes,
And both, to show his judgment, in extremes:
So over violent, or over civil,
That every man with him was god or devil.
In squandering wealth was his peculiar art:
Nothing went unrewarded but desert.
Beggar'd by fools, whom still he found too late,
He had his jest, and they had his estate.

Seduced by Shaftesbury's words, Monmouth set out on a tour of the West Country to win support for himself as heir.

Surrounded thus with friends of every sort,
Deluded Absalom forsakes the court:
Impatient of high hopes, urged with renown,
And fired with near possession of a crown.
The admiring crowd are dazzled with surprise,
And on his goodly person feed their eyes.
His joy conceal'd he sets himself to show,
On each side bowing popularly low:
His looks, his gestures, and his words he frames,
And with familiar ease repeats their names.
Youth, beauty, graceful action seldom fail,
But common interest always will prevail:
And pity never ceases to be shown
To him who makes the people's wrongs his own.
The crowd (that still believe their kings oppress)
With lifted hands their young messiah bless:
Who now begins his progress to ordain
With chariots, horsemen, and a numerous train.
This moving court, that caught the people's eyes,
And seem'd but pomp, did other ends disguise:
Achitophel had form'd it, with intent
To sound the depths, and fathom where it went,
The people's hearts, distinguish friends from foes,
And try their strength, before they came to blows.

Yet all was colour'd with a smooth pretence
Of specious love, and duty to their prince.

The tour came to nothing. Charles banished Monmouth. Shaftesbury died in exile. In 1684 James became King James II against whom Monmouth, leading a rag-tag force from France, rebelled, was easily defeated, captured and executed.

John Oldham was a satirist and translator famed for the power of his invective. Some think that the race (line 10, below) Oldham won was for the publication of a satire on national themes, his Popish Plot poem, *Satires upon the Jesuits* – in which one of the Gunpowder Plotters rises from the dead to encourage those still living – coming out before *Abasalom and Achitophel*. He died of smallpox at the age of 30.

To the Memory of Mr Oldham

Farewell, too little and too lately known,
Whom I began to think and call my own;
For sure our souls were near allied, and thine
Cast in the same poetic mould with mine.
One common note on either lyre did strike,
And knaves and fools were both abhorred alike:
To the same goal did both our studies drive,
The last set out the soonest did arrive.
Thus Nisus fell upon the slippery place,   In the Aeneid
While his young friend performed and won the race.
O early ripe! to thy abundant store
What could advancing age have added more?
It might (what Nature never gives the young)
Have taught the numbers of thy native tongue;
But satire needs not those, and wit will shine
Through the harsh cadence of a rugged line:
A noble error, and but seldom made,
When poets are by too much force betrayed.
Thy generous* fruits, though gathered ere   abundant
    their prime
Still showed a quickness*; and maturing time   liveliness
But mellows what we write to the dull sweets of
    rhyme.
Once more, hail and farewell; farewell thou young,
But ah too short, Marcellus of our   The nephew of
    tongue;   Augustus, a youth of great promise.

Thy brows with ivy, and with laurels bound;
But fate and gloomy night encompass theee around.

Absalom and Achitophel brought Dryden many
attacks from Whig/Protestant writers,
among them the playrights, Richard Fleck-
noe, Elkanah Settle (who managed to ident-
ify Dryden's Absalom with James, Duke of
York) and Thomas Shadwell. Flecknoe's and
Shadwell's attacks were vicious and foul
mouthed. As John Cousin has said, Dry-
den's revenge brought them an immortal-
ity which, however unenviable, no efforts
of their own could have secured.

from MacFlecknoe *and* from THE SECOND PART OF ABSALOM AND ACHITOPHEL

All human things are subject to decay,
And, when Fate summons, monarchs must obey:
This Flecknoe found, who like Augustus   *1st Roman Emperor*
    young
Was called to empire, and had governed long;
In prose and verse was owned without dispute
Through all the realms of nonsense absolute.
This aged prince, now flourishing in peace,
And blessed with issue of a large increase,
Worn out with business*, did at length   *sexual intercourse*
    debate
To settle the succession of the state;
And pondering which of all his sons was fit
To reign, and wage immortal war with wit,
Cried, ''Tis resolved; for Nature pleads that he
Should only rule who most resembles me:
Shadwell alone my perfect image bears.
Mature in dullness from his tender years;
Shadwell alone, of all my sons, is he
Who stands confirmed in full stupidity.
The rest to some faint meaning make pretence,
But Shadwell never deviates into sense.
Some beams of wit on other souls may fall,
Strike through and make a lucid interval,
But Shadwell's genuine* night admits no ray,   *natural*
His rising fogs prevail upon the day.
Besides, his goodly fabric fills the eye.
And seems designed for thoughtless majesty:

When wine has given him courage to blaspheme
He curses God, but God before cursed him;
And if man could have reason, none has more
That made his paunch so rich, and him so poor.

With wealth he was not trusted, for heaven knew
What 'twas of old to pamper up a Jew;
To what would he on quail and pheasant swell,
That ev'n on tripe and carrion could rebel?
But though heaven made him poor (with rev'rence
    speaking)
He never was a poet of God's making.
The midwife laid her hand on his thick skull
With this prophetic blessing: 'Be thou dull.'

[...]

   Doeg, though without knowing how or why,
Made still a blundering kind of melody;
Spurred boldly on, and dashed through thick and
    thin,
Through sense and nonsense, never out nor in;
Free from all meaning, whether good or bad,
And in one word, heroically mad.
He was too warm on picking work to dwell,
But faggotted his notions as they fell,
And if they rhymed and rattled all was well.
Spiteful he is not, though he wrote a satire,
For still there goes some thinking to ill nature;
He needs no more than birds and beasts to think,
All his occasions are to eat and drink.
If he call 'rogue' and 'rascal' from a garret
He means you no more mischief than a parrot.
The words for friend and foe alike were made,
To fetter 'em in verse is all his trade.
For almonds he'll cry 'whore' to his own mother,
And call young Absalom King David's brother.
Let him be gallows-free by my consent,
And nothing suffer since he nothing meant.
Hanging supposes human soul and reason;
This animal's below committing treason.

Dryden translating from Greek, Theocritus'
Eighteenth Idyll, helped out by a Latin
paraphrase, 1685 (just under a quarter of
the lines are Dryden's own):

THE EPITHALAMIUM OF HELEN AND MENELAUS

Twelve Spartan virgins, noble, young and fair,
With violet wreaths adorned their flowing hair,

And to the pompous palace did resort,
Where Menelaus kept his royal court. *The King of Sparta*
There hand in hand a comely choir they led,
To sing a blessing to his nuptial bed,
With curious* needles wrought, and painted *skilful*
  flowers bespread.
Jove's beauteous daughter now his bride
  must be, *Helen, the daughter of Leda and Zeus*
And Jove himself was less a god than he.
For this their artful hands instruct the lute to
  sound,
Their feet assist their hands and justly beat the
  ground.
This was their song: 'Why, happy bridegroom, why
Ere yet the stars are kindled in the sky,
Ere twilight shades or evening dews are shed,
Why dost thou steal so soon away to bed?
Has Somnus brushed thy eyelids with his
  rod, *The god of sleep*
Or do thy legs refuse to bear their load,
With flowing bowls of a more generous god?* *Bacchus*
If gentle slumber on thy temples creep
(But, naughty man, thou does not mean to sleep),
Betake thee to thy bed, thou drowsy drone,
Sleep by thyself, and leave thy bride alone:
Go leave her with her maiden mates to play
At sports more harmless till the break of day;
Give us this evening: thou hast morn and night
And all the year before thee for delight.
O happy youth! to thee among the crowd
Of rival princes Cupid sneezed aloud,
And every lucky omen sent before
To meet thee landing on the Spartan shore.
Of all our heroes thou canst boast alone
That love, whene'er he thunders, calls thee son.
Betwixt two sheets thou shalt enjoy her bare,
With whom no Grecian virgin can compare:
So soft, so sweet, so balmy and so fair.
A boy like thee would make a kingly line,
But O, a girl like her must be divine.
Her equals we in years, but not in face,
Twelve score viragos of the Spartan race,
While naked to Eurotas'* banks we *The river of Sparta*
  bend,
And there in manly exercise contend,
When she appears are all eclipsed and lost,
And hide the beauties that we made our boast.
So when the night and winter disappear,
The purple morning rising with the year
Salutes the spring, as her celetial eyes
Adorn the world, and brighten all the skies:
So beauteous Helen shines among the rest,
Tall, slender, straight, with all the graces blessed.
As pines the mountains, or as fields the corn,
Or as Thessalian steeds* the race *The best horses of Greece*
  adorn,
So rosy-coloured Helen is the pride
Of Lacedaemon, and of Greece beside. *Sparta*
Like her no nymph can willing osiers bend
In basket-works which painted streaks commend;
With Pallas in the loom she may contend *Athene*
But none, ah none can animate the lyre,
And the mute strings with vocal souls inspire;
Whether the learned Minerva be her theme, *Latin for Athene*
Or chaste Diana bathing in the stream; *Latin for Artemis*
None can record their heavenly praise so well
As Helen, in whose eyes ten thousand Cupids dwell.
O fair, O graceful! yet with maids enrolled,
But whom tomorrow's sun a matron shall behold:
Yet ere tomorrow's sun shall show his head,
The dewy paths of meadows we will tread
For crowns and chaplets to adorn thy head:
Where all shall weep, and wish for thy return,
As bleating lambs their absent mother mourn.
Our noblest maids shall to thy name bequeath
The boughs of lotus, formed into a wreath;
This monument, thy maiden beauties' due,
High on a plane tree shall be hung to view:
On the smooth rind the passenger shall see *bark, passer-by*
Thy name engraved, and worship Helen's tree.
Balm from a silver box distilled around
Shall all bedew the roots and scent the sacred
  ground;
The balm, 'tis true, can agèd plants prolong,
But Helen's name will keep it ever young.
Hail bride, hail bridegroom, son-in-law to Jove!
With fruitful joys Latona bless your *Goddess of childbirth*
  love;
Let Venus furnish you with full desires,
Add vigour to your wills, and fuel to your fires.
Almighty Jove augment your wealthy store,
Give much to you, and to his grandsons more.
From generous loins a generous race will spring, *noble*
Each girl, like her, a queen; each boy, like you, a
  king.
Now sleep, if sleep you can; but while you rest
Sleep close, with folded arms, and breast to breast.
Rise in the morn, but O, before you rise
Forget not to perform your morning sacrifice.
We will be with you ere the crowing cock
Salutes the light, and struts before his feathered
  flock.

Hymen, O Hymen, to thy triumphs run,   *God of marriage*
And view the mighty spoils thou hast in battle
     won.'

Translation from English to English, two
masters at work on the same story. Dry-
den's opening of Chaucer's

THE TALE OF THE WIFE OF BATH

In days of old, when Arthur filled the throne,
Whose acts and fame to foreign lands were blown;
The king of elves and little fairy queen
Gamboll'd on heaths, and danced on every green;
And where the jolly troop had led the round,
The grass unbidden rose, and marked the ground:
Nor darkling did they dance, the silver light
Of Phœbe served to guide their steps aright,
And with their tripping pleased, prolong the night.
Her beams they followed, where at full she played,
Nor longer than she shed her horns they stayed;
From thence with airy flight to foreign lands
     conveyed
Above the rest our Britain held they dear,
More solmnly they kept their sabbaths here,
And made more spacious rings, and revelled half the
     year.
   I speak of ancient times, for now the swain
Returning late may pass the woods in vain,
And never hope to see the nightly train:
In vain the dairy now with mints is dressed,
The dairymaid expects no fairy guest,
To skim the bowls, and after pay the feast.
She sighs and shakes her empty shoes in vain,
No silver penny to reward her pain:
For priests, with prayers, and other godly gear,
Have made the merry goblins disappear;
And where they played their merry pranks before,
Have sprinkled holy water on the floor:
And friars, that through the wealthy regions run,
Thick as the motes that twinkle in the sun,
Resort to farmers rich, and bless their halls,
And exorcise the beds, and cross the walls:
This makes the fairy quires forsake the place,
When once 'tis hallowed with the rites of grace:

But in the walks where wicked elves have been,
The learning of the parish now is seen,
The midnight parson, posting o'er the green,
With gown tucked up, to wakes, for Sunday next,
With humming ale encouraging his text;
Nor wants the holy leer to country girl betwixt.
From fiends and imps he sets the village free,
There haunts not any incubus but he.
The maids and women need no danger fear
To walk by night, and sanctity so near:
For by some haycock, or some shady thorn,
He bids his beads both even-song and morn.

(1700; just under a third of the lines are Dryden's
own).

They would have disagreed about every-
thing except how to write fine verse.
Dryden knew when he was in the presence
of his betters.

UNDER MR MILTON'S PICTURE, BEFORE
HIS PARADISE LOST
[For Tonson's folio edition of 1688]

Three Poets, in three distant ages born,
Greece, Italy, and England, did adorn,
The first, in loftiness of thought surpass'ed;
The next, in majesty; in both the last.
The force of nature could no further go;
To make a third, she join'd the former two.

IAIN BAMFORTH ‹ on › WILLIAM DUNBAR

William Dunbar (c.1460–c.1520) is the best known figure in Scottish poetry after Burns and MacDiarmid, and a cult figure to its twentieth-century quickeners. He was a graduate of St Andrews University, and a Franciscan priest, later in life securing tenure as a poet to the ill-starred court of James IV. Influenced by Chaucer and the tradition of *amour courtois* – like the whole generation of craftsmen poets (*makars*) he mourns in his *Lament* – Dunbar's formal skills are fretted by a language which is as intimate with the Four Last Things as it is unembarrassed by vigorously alliterative popular invective. His beautiful, if conventional, religious poem on the Nativity (*Rorate Celi Desuper*) is a powerful (pre-Reformation) statement of his faith; like *Lament for the Makaris* it demonstrates his ability to incorporate stock Latin liturgy and make a solemn, sonorous music of it in vernacular settings; other poems exploit this interposing to raucously comic effect. *Lament for the Makaris* is stately and dignified, its melancholy lingered-over, symbol-laden and intense, the repetition of the refrain from the Office for the Dead a sober pedal-note on the inevitability of death. That contemplation of the same subject could lead him to produce a poem of utterly different tone is remarkable but characteristic: *The Dance of the Seven Deidly Sinnis* is a racy dream allegory in the Holbein mode which offers a very Scottish spasm of involuntary comic horror; the same eldritch, flamboyant wildness lowps out of Burns' *Tam o' Shanter*. The poem's zest and sense of occasion are attested to by the sizeable glossary of terms now unfamiliar to us but not, at some deeper level of language, entirely alien.

These versions of Dunbar's poems with their modernised spellings are largely taken from W. MacNeile Dixon's 1910 Edinburgh book of Scottish verse.

LAMENT FOR THE MAKARIS

‹When he was seik›

I that in heal was and glaidness,
Am troublit now with great seikness,
And feeblit with infirmitie;
Timor Mortis conturbat me.

Our plesance here is all vain-glory,
This false warld is bot transitory,
The flesh is brukill, the Fiend is sle:
Timor Mortis conturbat me.

The state of man dois change and vary,
Now sound, now seik, now blyth, now sary,
Now dansand merry, now like to die;
Timor Mortis conturbat me

No state in erd here standis siccar;
As with the wind wavis the wicker,
So wavis this warldis vanitie;
Timor Mortis conturbat me.

Unto the dede gois all Estatis,
Princes, Prelatis, and Potestatis,
Baith rich and puir of all degree;
Timor Mortis conturbat me.

He takis the knichtis in-to field,
Enarmit under helm and shield;
Victor he is at all melee;
Timor Mortis conturbat me.

That strang unmerciful tyrand
Takis on the moderis breist soukand
The babe, full of benignitie;
Timor Mortis conturbat me.

He takis the champion in the stour,
The capitane closit in the tour,
The lady in bour full of beautie;
Timor Mortis conturbat me.

He sparis no lord for his puissance,
Na clerk for his intelligence;
His awful straik may no man flee;
Timor Mortis conturbat me.

Art-magicianis, and astrologis,
Rethoris, logicianis, and theologis,
Them helpis no conclusionis sle;
Timor Mortis conturbat me.

In medicine the most practicianis,
Leechis, surigianis, and phisicianis,
Them self fra dede may not supple;
Timor Mortis conturbat me.

I see that makaris amang the laif
Playis here their pageant, syne gods to graif;
Sparit is nocht their facultie;
Timor Mortis conturbat me.

He has done piteously devour
The noble Chaucer, of makaris flour,
The Monk of Bery, and Gower, all three;
Timor Mortis conturbat me.

The gude Sir Hew of Eglintoun,
Ettrick, Heriot, and Wintoun,
He has ta'en out of this countrie;
Timor Mortis conturbat me.

That scorpion fell has done infec'
Maister John Clerk and James Afleck,
Fra ballad-making and tragedie;
Timor Mortis conturbat me.

Holland and Barbour he has bereavit;
Alas! that he has nocht with us leavit
Sir Mungo Lockhart of the Lea:
Timor Mortis conturbat me.

Clerk of Tranent eke he has ta'en,
That made the Aunteris of Gawain;
Sir Gilbert Hay endit has he;
Timor Mortis conturbat me.

He has Blind Harry, and Sandy Traill
Slain with his shot of mortal hail,
Whilk Patrick Johnstoun micht nocht flee;
Timor Mortis conturbat me.

He has reft Merser his endite,
That did in lufe so lively write,
So short, so quick, of sentence hie;
Timor Mortis conturbat me.

He has ta'en Roull of Aberdeen,
And gentle Roull of Corstorphin;
Two better fellowis did no man see;
Timor Mortis conturbat me.

In Dunfermline he has done roune
With Maister Robert Henryson;
Sir John the Ross embraced has he;
Timor Mortis conturbat me.

And he has now ta'en, last of a',
Gude gentle Stobo and Quintin Shaw,
Of wham all wichtis has pitie:
Timor Mortis conturbat me.

Gude Maister Walter Kennedy
In point of dede lies verily,
Great ruth it were that so suld be;
Timor Mortis conturbat me.

Sen he has all my brether ta'en
He will nocht lat me lif alane,
On force I maun his next prey be;
Timor Mortis conturbat me.

Sen for the dede remead is none,
Best is that we for dede dispone,
Eftir our dede that lif may we;
Timor Mortis conturbat me.

Glossary

HEAL: health; BRUKILL: frail; SLE: sly; SIKKAR: sure; WICKER: willow; SOUKAND: sucking; STOUR: struggle; STRAIK: stroke; SUPPLE: rescue; MAKARIS: poets; THE LAIF: the rest; GRAIF: grave; AUNTERIS: Adventures; ENDITE: poem, writings; DONE ROUNE: talked; WICHTIS: wights, person; SEN: since; DISPONE: prepare ourselves.

❧

OF THE NATIVITY OF CHRIST

Rorate celi desuper!
Heavens distil your balmy shouris,
For now is risen the bricht day ster,
Fro the rose Mary, flour of flouris;
The clear Son, whom no clud devouris,
Surmounting Phœbus in the east,
Is comen of his heavenly touris;
Et nobis Puer natus est.

Archangellis, angellis, and dompnationis.
Tronis, potestatis, and martyris seir,
And all ye heavenly operationis,
Ster, planet, firmament, and sphere,
Fire, erd, air, and water clear,
To him gife loving, most and least,
That come in-to so meek mannér;
Et nobis Puer natus est.

Sinneris be glaid, and penance do,
And thank your Maker hairtfully;

For he that ye micht nocht come to,
To you is comen full hum'ly,
Your saulis with his blude to buy,
And louse you of the Fiendis arrest,
And only of his awn mercy;
Pro nobis Puer natus est.

All clergy do to him incline,
And bow unto that bairn bening,
And do your observance divine
To him that is of kingis King;
Ensence his altar, read, and sing
In haly kirk with mind degest,
Him honouring attour all thing,
Qui nobis Puer natus est.

Celestial fowlis in the air,
Sing with your notis upon hicht;
In firthis and in forestis fair
Be mirthful now, at all your micht,
For passit is your dully nicht;
Aurora has the cludis pierc'd,
The sun is risen with glaidsome licht,
Et nobis Puer natus est.

Now spring up flouris fra the root,
Revert you upward naturally,
In honour of the blissit fruit
That raise up fro the rose Mary;
Lay out your leavës lustily,
Fro dede tak life now at the lest
In worship of that Prince worthy,
Qui nobis Puer natus est.

Sing heaven imperial, most of hicht,
Regions of air mak harmony;
All fish in flood and fowl of licht,
Be mirthful and mak melody:
All *Gloria in excelsis* cry,
Heaven, erd. sea, man, bird, and beast,
He that is crownit abune the sky
Pro nobis Puer natus est.

Glossary

SHOURIS: showers; ERD: earth; IN-TO: in; ENSENCE; cover with incense;
DIGEST: quiet, grave; ATTOUR: above; CLUDIS: clouds; AT THE LEST: at
last

THE DANCE OF THE SEVEN DEIDLY SINNIS

Of Februar the fifteen nicht,
Full lang before the dayis licht,
I lay in-till a trance;
And then I saw baith heaven and hell:
Me thocht, amangis the fiendis fell,
Mahoun gart cry ane dance
Of shrewis that were never shriven
Aganis the feast of Fasternis even,
To mak their observance;
He bade gallantis ga graith a guise,
And cast up gamountis in the skies,
That last came out of France.

Heilie harlottis on hawtane wise
Come in with mony sundry guise,
Bot yit leuch never Mahoun;
Whill priestis come in with bare shaven neckis,
Than all the fiendis leuch, and made geckis,
Black Belly, and Bawsy Brown.

'Lat see', quod he, 'Now wha beginnis';
with that the foul Seven Deidly Sinnis
Begouth to leap at anis.
And first of all in dance was Pride,
With bare wild back and bonnet on side,
Like to mak vaistie wanis;
And round about him, as a wheel,
Hang all in rumpillis to the heel
His kethat for the nanis:
Mony proud trumpour with him trippit
Throw skaldand fire, ay as they skippit
They girn'd with hideous granis.

Than Ire come in with sturt and strife;
His hand was ay upon his knife,
He brandiest like a beir:
Boasteris, braggeris, and bargaineris,
Eftir him passit in-to pairis
All bodin in feir of weir;
In jackis and scryppis and bonnettis of steel,
Their leggis were chainyit to the heel,
Frawart was their affeir:
Some upon other with brandis beft,
Some jaggit otheris to the heft,
With knivis that sharp culd shear.
[already arrayed in trappings of war

Next in the dance followit Envý,
Fill'd full of feid and felony,

Hid malice and despite;
For privy hatrent that traitor trem'lit
Him followit mony freik dissem'lit,
With feignèd wordis white;
And flatteris in-to menis faces;
And backbiteris of sundry races,
To lie that had delight;
And rounaris of false leasingis;
Alas! that courtis of noble kingis
Of them can never be quite.

Next him in dance come Covatice,
Root of all evil and grund of vice,
That never culd be content;
Caitivis, wretches and okkeraris,
Hud-pikis, hurdaris and gadderaris,
All with that warlo went:
Out of their throatis they shot on other
Het molten gold, me thocht a fudder,
As fireflaucht maist fervent;
Ay as they toomit them of shot,
Fiendis fill'd them new up to the throat
With gold of all kin prent.

Syne Sweirness, at the second bidding,
Come like a sow out of a midding,
Fully sleepy was his grunyie:
Mony sweir bumbard belly-huddroun,
Mony slute daw and sleepy duddroun,
Him servit ay with sounyie;
He drew them furth in-till a chainyie,
And Belial, with a bridle-reinyie,
Ever lasht them on the lunyie:
In dance they were so slaw of feet,
They gaif them in the fire a heat,
And made them quicker of cunyie.

Than Lechery, that laithly corse,
Come berand like a braggit horse,
And Idleness did him lead;
There was with him ane ugly sort,
And mony stikand foul tramort,
That had in sin been deid.
When they were entrit in the dance,
They were full strange of countenance.
Like turkass birnand reid;
All led they other by the tersis,
Suppose they fycket with their ersis,
It micht be na remead.

Than the foul monster Gluttony,
Of wame unsatiable and greedy,

To dance he did him dress:
Him followit mony foul drunkart,
With can and collep, cop and quart,
In surfeit and excess;
Full mony a waistless wallydrag,
With wamis unwieldable, did furth wag
In creish that did incress;
'Drink!' ay they cryit, with mony a gape,
The fiendis gaif them het leid to laip,
Their lovery was na less.

Na minstrellis playit to them but doubt,
For gleemen there were haldin out,
Be day, and eke by nicht;
Except a minstrel that slew a man,
Swa till his heritage he wan,
And enter'd be brief of richt.

Than cried Mahoun for a Hieland padyane;
Syne ran a fiend to fetch MacFadzen,
Far northward in a neuk;
Be he the coronach had done shout,
Ersemen so gadderit him about,
In Hell great room they tuk.
Thae termagantis, with tag and tatter,
Full loud in Erse begouth to clatter,
And roup like raven and rook:
The Devil sa deavit was with their yell,
That in the deepest pot of hell
He smoorit them with smoke.

Glossary

MAHOUN: Mahomet, i.e. the devil; FASTERNIS EVEN: 16 February;
GRAITH A GHISE: prepare a masquerade; GAMOUNTIS: capers; HEILIE:
disdainful; HAWTANE: haughty; LEUCH: laughed; GECKIS: mocking faces;
BEGOUTH: begin; AT ANIS: at once; VAISTIE WANIS: waste dwellings;
KETHAT: cassock; NANIS: nonce; TRUMPOUR: deceiver; BRANDIEST:
swaggered; BEIR: bear; ALL BODIN IN FEIR OF WEIR: already arrayed in
trappings of war; SCRYPPIS: bags; CHAINYIT: clothed in chain armour;
FRAWART: forward; AFFEIR: demeanour; BRANDIS BEFT: swords struck;
FEID: ill-will; HATRENT: hatred; FREIK: folk; MENIS: men's; ROUNARIS:
whisperers; LEASINGIS: lies; QUITE: quit; OKKERARIS: usurers; HUD-
PIKIS, HURDARIS AND GADDERARIS: misers, hoarders and gatherers;
WARLO: wizard; FUDDER: great amount; FIREFLAUCHT: wild-fire;
TOOMIT THEM: emptied themselves; ALL KIN PRINT: all kinds of stamp;
SWEIRNESS: Sloth; GRUNYIE: snout, face; MONY SWEIR BUMBARD
BELLY-HUDDROUN: many a lazy glutton; SLUTE DAW: dirty slattern;
DUDDROUN: sloven; WITH SOUNYIE: unwillingly; LUNYIE: loins;
CUNYIE: apprehension; BERAND: neighing; BRAGGIT HORSE: stallion;
SORT: company; TRAMORT: corpse; TURKASS: pincers; TERSIS: penises;
WAME: belly; COLLEP: drinking vessel; WALLYDRAG: weakling; WAG:
totter; CREISH: grease; HET LEID TO LAIP: hot lead to lap; LOVERY:
allowance; HALDIN OUT: kept out; SWA: so; PADYANE: pageant; BE HE:
by the time that; ERSEMAN: Gaels; ROUP: croak; DEAVIT: deafened;
SMOORIT: smothered

Anne Finch (1661–1720), Countess of Winchilsea, was a friend of Pope, Swift and Purcell (who set one of her poems to music), and her poems were much admired by Wordsworth, who described her style as 'chaste, tender and vigorous'. Her 'Nocturnal Reverie' particularly appealed to him, fitting his ideal of the poet with eyes 'steadily fixed upon his object ... that his feelings had urged him to work upon in the spirit of genuine imagination'.

Her superb poem, 'The Spleen', can only be represented by two short extracts here, but even in this truncated state displays her care and skill and the subtlety of her theme, now heroic, now domestic. My favourite of her poems, not included here, is 'The Petition for an Absolute Retreat', which depends for effect on the cumulative power of its 300 lines, and should not be fragmented – but let me recommend it strongly. Otherwise, I have chosen a range of her work which I hope will dispel the notion that she is relevant merely because she is a woman. The evidence of her poetry is enough to prove her distinctive and able to hold her own among her contemporaries.

The Spleen

◂A Pindaric Poem▸

(lines 1–24; 43–62)

What art thou, Spleen, which everything dost ape?
  Thou Proteus to abused mankind,
  Who never yet thy real cause could find
Or fix thee to remain in one continued shape.
  Still varying thy perplexing form
  Now a Dead Sea thou'lt represent,
  A calm of stupid discontent,
Then, dashing on the rocks, with rage into a storm.
  Trembling sometimes thou dost appear
  Dissolved into a panic fear;
  Or sleep intruding dost thy shadows spread
And crowd with boding dreams the melancholy head;
  Or when the midnight hour is told
  And drooping lids thou still dost waking hold,
  Thy fond delusions cheat the eyes;
  Before them antic spectres dance,
Unusual fires their pointed heads advance
  And airy phantoms rise.
  Such was the monstrous vision seen
When Brutus (now beneath his cares oppressed
And all Rome's fortunes rolling in his breast
  Before Philippi's latest field,
Before his fate did to Octavius yield)
  Was vanquished by the Spleen.

[. . .]

  In every one thou dost possess
  New are thy motions and thy dress;
  Now in some grove a listening friend
  Thy false suggestions must attend,
Thy whispered griefs, thy fancied sorrows hear,
Breathed in a sigh and witnessed by a tear;
  Whilst in the light and vulgar crowd
  Thy slaves, more clamorous and loud,
By laughters unprovoked thy influence too confess.
In the imperious wife thou Vapours art,
  Which from o'erheated passions rise
  In clouds to the attractive brain
  Until, descending thence again,
  Through the o'ercast and showering eyes,
  Upon her husband's softened heart,
  He the disputed point must yield,
Something resign of the contested field;
Till lordly man, born to imperial sway,
Compounds for peace, to make that right away
And woman, armed with spleen, does servilely obey.

❧

A Letter to Daphnis

This to the crown and blessing of my life,
The much loved husband of a happy wife;
To him whose constant passion found the art
To win a stubborn and ungrateful heart,
And to the world by tenderest proof discovers
They err, who say that husbands can't be lovers.
With such return of passion as is due,
Daphnis I love, Daphnis my thoughts pursue;
Daphnis, my hopes and joys are bounded all in you.
Even I, for Daphnis' and my promise' sake,
What I in women censure, undertake.
But this from love, not vanity proceeds;
You know who writes, and I who 'tis that reads.
Judge not my passion by my want of skill:
Many love well, though they express it ill;
And I your censure could with pleasure bear,
Would you but soon return, and speak it here.

April 2nd, 1685

❧

A Song of the Cannibals

Lovely viper, haste not on,
Nor curl, in various folds along,
Till from that figur'd coat of thine,
Which ev'ry motion, makes more fine.
I take, as near as art can do.
A draught, of what I wond'ring view;
Which, in a bracelet, for my Love
Shall be with careful mixtures wove.
So, may'st thou find thy beauties last,
As thou doest not, retard thy haste.
So, may'st thou, above all the snakes,
That harbour, in the neigh'bring brakes,
Be honour'd; and where thou do'st pass
The shades be close, and fresh the grass.

❧

A Nocturnal Reverie

In such a night, when every louder wind
Is to its distant cavern safe confined;
And only gentle zephyr fans his wings,
And lonely Philomel, still waking, sings;
Or from some tree, famed for the owl's delight,
She, hollowing clear, directs the wanderer right;

In such a night, when passing clouds give place,
Or thinly veil the heaven's mysterious face;
When in some river, overhung with green,
The waving moon and trembling leaves are seen;
When freshened grass now bears itself upright,
And makes cool banks to pleasing rest invite,
Whence springs the woodbine and the bramble-
      rose,
And where the sleepy cowslip sheltered grows;
Whilst now a paler hue the foxglove takes,
Yet chequers still with red the dusky brakes:
When scattered glow-worms, but in twilight fine,
Show trivial beauties watch their hour to shine;
When odours, which declined repelling day,
Through temperate air uninterrupted stray;
When darkened groves their softest shadows wear,
And falling waters we distinctly hear;
When through the gloom more venerable shows
Some ancient fabric, awful in repose,
While sunburnt hills their swarthy looks conceal,
And swelling haycocks thicken up the vale:
When the loosed horse now, as his pasture leads,
Comes slowly grazing through the adjoining meads,
Whose stealing pace, and lengthened shade we fear,
Till torn-up forage in his teeth we hear:
When nibbling sheep at large pursue their food,
And unmolested kine rechew the cud;
When curlews cry beneath the village walls,
And to her straggling brood the partridge calls;
Their short-lived jubilee the creatures keep,
Which but endures while tyrant man does sleep:
When a sedate content the spirit feels,
And no fierce light disturbs, whilst it reveals;
But silent musings urge the mind to seek
Something, too high for syllables to speak;
Till the free soul to a composedness charmed,
Finding the elements of rage disarmed,
O'er all below a solemn quiet grown,
Joys in the inferior world, and thinks it like her
      own:
In such a night let me abroad remain,
Till morning breaks, and all's confused again;
Our cares, our toils, our clamours are renewed,
Or pleasures, seldom reached, pursued.

❧

SIR PLAUSIBLE

Sir Plausible, as 'tis well known,
Has no opinions of his own;
But closes with each stander by,
Now in a truth, now in a lie,
Fast as chameleons change their dye;
Has still some applicable story
To gratify a Whig or Tory,
And even a Jacobite in tatters
If met alone he smoothly flatters;
Greets friend and foe with wishes fervent,
And lives and dies your humble servant.

A SONG ON THE SOUTH SEA, 1720

Ombre and basset laid aside,
New games employ the fair;
And brokers all those hours divide
Which lovers used to share.

The court, the park, the foreign song
And harlequin's grimace
Forlorn; amidst the city throng
Behold each blooming face.

With Jews and Gentiles undismayed
Young tender virgins mix;
Of whiskers nor of beards afraid,
Nor all the cozening tricks.

Bright jewels, polished once to deck
The fair one's rising breast,
Or sparkle round her ivory neck,
Lie pawned in iron chest.

The gayer passions of the mind
How avarice controls!
Even love does now no longer find
A place in female souls.

George Gascoigne (1539?–77) is one fine example of that body of Tudor poetry which has suffered in comparison with Sidney and the sonnet writers, but which is varied in form and subject matter. It belongs unmistakably to a native tradition, yet is open to international influences. Gascoigne has three main interests in his writing: the short poem, with a courtly theme; the satire, often including vivid personal experiences; and closely argued poems of self-criticism. He combines an alliterative strength which draws on earlier roots of English verse, with anticipation of the smoother musical qualities of a Sidney or a Spenser. With Gascoigne, however, the bluntness and directness is always more likely to take control. Most attractively, his writing has immediate physical qualities: 'An Absent Lover' looks conventional enough, but the sound of the sea is in it. 'The Steel Glass', the first non-dramatic poem in blank verse in English, also contains passages with forceful, almost incantatory qualities. Here he castigates the times for their confusion of 'seeming' with true 'being', and proposes that the age needs to be reflected in a 'Steel Glass', which will show things as they really are. Yet for all this bluff assertion of dealing with 'plain truth', Gascoigne often involves the reader in complexities of perspective. To complicate matters further, his authorship of some of the poems has been doubted, or he himself has deliberately made this obscure. Many of his poems are dramatic in the sense that they are addressed to a definite person, whether lover, patron, or himself. The Lord he addresses in 'Gascoigne's Woodmanship', is Lord Grey of Wilton, but the poet is also fictionalizing himself, and justifying his whole life to more than just his critics. If he seems too fond of praising his own qualities, he also avoids self pity. Gascoigne can be direct and moving but such directness – 'Old babe, now learn to suck' – is part of a style which is complex and subtle.

George Gascoigne

An Absent Lover, parted from his Lady by Sea, thus Complaineth.

Both deep and dreadful were the seas
Which held Leander from his love,
Yet could no doubts his mind appease,
Nor save his life for her behove:
But guiltless blood itself would spill
To please the waves and work his will.

O greedy gulf, o wretched waves,
O cruel floods, o sink of shames,
You hold true lovers bound like slaves
And keep them from their worthy dames:
Your open mouth gapes evermore
Till one or both be drowned therefore.

For proof whereof myself may sing
And shriek to pierce the lofty skies,
Whose Lady left me languishing
Upon the shore in woeful wise:
And crossed the seas out of my sight
Whereby I lost my chief delight.

She said that no such trustless flood
Should keep our loves long time in twain:
She swore no bread should do her good
Till she might see myself again.
She said and swore these words and mo
But now I find them nothing so.

What resteth then for me to do,
Thou salt sea foam, come, say thy mind:
Should I come drown within thee too
That am of true Leander's kind?
And headlong cast this corpse of mine
Into those greedy guts of thine?

No cruel, but in spite of thee
I will make seas where erst were none:
My tears shall flow in full degree
Till all my mirth may ebb to moan.
Into such drops I mean to melt
And in such seas my self to swelt.

Yet you, dear Dame, for whom I fade,
Thus starving still in wretched state:
Remember once your promise made,
Perform it now though all too late.

Come home to Mars who may you please,
Let Vulcan bide beyond the seas.

Gascoigne's Woodmanship

My worthy Lord, I pray you wonder not
To see your woodman shoot so oft awry,
Nor that he stands amazed like a sot
And lets the harmless deer unhurt go by.
Or if he strike a doe which is but carren,
Laugh not good Lord, but favour such a fault;
Take will in worth, he would fain hit the barren;
But though his heart be good, his hap is naught.
And therefore now I crave your Lordship's leave
To tell you plain what is the cause of this.
First if it please your honour to perceive
What makes your woodman shoot so oft amiss,
Believe me, Lord, the case is nothing strange.
He shoots awry almost at every mark;
His eyes have been so used for the range,
That now God knows they be both dim and dark.
For proof he bears the note of folly now,
Who shot sometimes to hit Philosophy,
And ask you why? forsooth I make avow
Because his wanton wits went all awry.
Next that, he shot to be a man in law,
And spent some time with learned Littleton,
Yet in the end, he proved but a daw,
For law was dark and he had quickly done.
Then could he wish Fitzherbert such a brain
As Tully had, to write the law by art,
So that with pleasure, or with little pain,
He might perhaps have caught a truant's part.
But all too late, he most misliked the thing,
Which most might help to guide his arrow straight;
He winked wrong, and so let slip the string,
Which cast him wide, for all his quaint conceit.
From thence he shot to catch a courtly grace,
And thought even there to wield the world at will,
But out, alas, he much mistook the place,
And shot awry at every rover still.
The blazing baits which draw the gazing eye
Unfeathered there his first affection;
No wonder then although he shot awry,
Wanting the feathers of discretion.
Yet more than them, the marks of dignity
He much mistook, and shot the wronger way,
Thinking the purse of prodigality

Had been best mean to purchase such a prey.
He thought the flattering face which fleereth still,
Had been full fraught with all fidelity,
And that such words as courtiers use at will,
Could not have varied from the verity.
But when his bonnet buttoned with gold,
His comely cape beguarded all with gay,
His bumbast hose, with linings manifold,
His knit silk stocks and all his quaint array,
Had picked his purse of all the Peter pence
Which might have paid for his promotion,
Then, all too late, he found that light expense
Had quite quenched out the court's devotion.
So that since then the taste of misery
Hath been always full bitter in his bit,
And why? forsooth because he shot awry,
Mistaking still the marks which others hit.
But now behold what mark the man doth find:
He shoots to be a soldier in his age;
Mistrusting all the virtues of the mind,
He trusts the power of his personage.
As though long limbs led by a lusty heart,
Might yet suffice to make him rich again,
But Flushing frays have taught him such a part
That now he thinks the wars yield no such gain.
And sure I fear, unless your lordship deign
To train him yet into some better trade,
It will be long before he hit the vein
Whereby he may a richer man be made.
He cannot climb as other catchers can,
To lead a charge before himself be led.
He cannot spoil the simple sakeless man,
Which is content to feed him with his bread.
He cannot pinch the painful soldier's pay,
And shear him out his share in ragged sheets.
He cannot stoop to take a greedy prey
Upon his fellows grovelling in the streets.
He cannot pull the spoil from such as pill,
And seem full angry at such foul offence,
Although the gain content his greedy will,
Under the cloak of contrary pretence:
And nowadays, the man that shoots not so,
May shoot amiss, even as your woodman doth:
But then you marvel why I let them go,
And never shoot, but say farewell forsooth:
Alas my Lord, while I do muse hereon,
And call the mind my youthful years misspent,
They give me such a bone to gnaw upon,
That all my senses are in silence pent.
My mind is rapt in contemplation,
Wherein my dazzled eyes only behold

The black hour of my constellation
Which framed me so luckless on the mould.
Yet therewithal I cannot but confess,
That vain presumption makes my heart to swell,
For thus I think, not all the world, I guess,
Shoots bet than I, nay some shoots not so well.
In Aristotle somewhat did I learn
To guide my manners all by comeliness,
And Tully taught me somewhat to discern
Between sweet speech and barbarous rudeness.
Old Parkins, Rastell, and Dan Bracton's books,
Did lend me somewhat of the lawless law;
The crafty courtiers with their guileful looks,
Must needs put some experience in my maw:
Yet cannot these with many maistries mo
Make me shoot straight at any gainful prick,
Where some that never handled such a bow
Can hit the white or touch it near the quick,
Who can nor speak nor write in pleasant wise,
Nor lead their life by Aristotle's rule,
Nor argue well on questions that arise,
Nor plead a case more than my Lord Mayor's mule.
Yet can they hit the marks that I do miss,
And win the mean which may the man maintain.
Now when my mind doth mumble upon this,
No wonder then although I pine for pain:
And whiles mine eyes behold this mirror thus,
The herd goeth by, and farewell gentle does:
So that your lordship quickly may discuss
What blinds mine eyes so oft, as I suppose.
But since my Muse can to my Lord rehearse
What makes me miss, and why I do not shoot,
Let me imagine in this worthless verse,
If right before me, at my standing's foot
There stood a doe, and I should strike her dead,
And then she prove a carrion carcass too,
What figure might I find within my head,
To scuse the rage which ruled me so to do?
Some might interpret with plain paraphrase,
That lack of skill or fortune led the chance,
But I must otherwise expound the case;
I say Jehovah did this doe advance,
And made her bold to stand before me so,
Till I had thrust mine arrow to her heart,
That by the sudden of her overthrow
I might endeavour to amend my part
And turn mine eyes that they no more behold
Such guileful marks as seem more than they be:
And though they glister outwardly like gold,
Are inwardly but brass, as men may see:
And when I see the milk hang in her teat,

Methinks it saith, old babe now learn to suck,
Who in thy youth couldst never learn the feat
To hide the whites which live with all good luck.
Thus have I told my Lord, God grant in season,
A tedious tale in rhyme, but little reason.

THE STEEL GLASS

That age is dead and vanished long ago
Which thought that steel both trusty was and true
And needed not a foil of contraries
But showed all things even as they were indeed.
Instead whereof our curious years can find
The crystal glass which glimseth brave and bright
And shows the thing much better than it is,
Beguiled with foils of sundry subtle sights
So that they seem and covet not to be.

This is the cause, believe me now my Lord,
That realms do rue from high prosperity,
That kings decline from princely government,
That Lords do lack their ancestors' good will,
That knights consume their patrimonies still,
That gentlemen do make the merchant rise,
That ploughmen beg and craftsmen cannot thrive
That clergy quails and hath small reverence,
That laymen live by moving mischief still,
That courtiers thrive at latter Lammas day
That officers can scarce enrich their heirs,
That soldiers starve or preach at Tyburn cross,
That lawyers buy and purchase deadly hate,
That merchants climb and fall again as fast,
That roisters brag above their betters' room,
That sycophants are counted jolly guests,
That Lais leads a lady's life aloft,
And Lucrece lurks with sober bashful grace.

Two extraordinary poems come to us from England's late-14th century revival of alliterative verse. *Pearl* and *Sir Gawain and the Green Knight*, written in the north-west midland dialect, are often presumed the work of a single author, 'The Gawain Poet'.

The general reader may prefer to ignore scholarly controversy and consider *Pearl* as told by a dreamer who has lost a 'precious pearl', an infant daughter. He sleeps on a mound and his spirit enters an earthly Paradise, where a maiden – the heaven-form of his daughter – comes to the far shore of a river. She instructs the dreamer how to regain the pearl of Christian salvation. As she joins a procession of virgins filing into the Holy City of *Revelation*, he attempts to cross the river but his dream vanishes.

Sir Gawain combines two traditional motifs, a 'Beheading Contest' and a 'Temptation'. A Green Knight enters Arthur's court and challenges Sir Gawain to strike off his head – providing this giant may return the blow. Decapitated, the Green Knight retrieves his head and sets a fateful rendezvous for Gawain. On his way there, Gawain, lodging in a castle, is persuaded by its seductive chatelaine to accept a magic girdle. In the final confrontation the Green Knight reveals himself as the lady's husband but gives the ashamed Gawain only a cautionary nick from the axe-blade for taking the girdle.

Both these poems glitter with brilliant sounds. *Pearl*, which has perhaps the most complex metrics of any English poem, has 101 closely-rhymed stanzas whose twelve lines are heavily alliterated and include a key word and refrain component. Sir Gawain's narrative drive comes from each stanza's 'stock', two-syllable 'bob', and rhymed quatrain, the 'wheel'.

My slightly compromised modernisations aim at readability along with minimum distortion to sound and meaning (with final 'e' left when necessary).

PEARL

(lines 1–180)

‹ I ›

Pearl, pleasant to prince's pay
To cleanly close in gold so clear:
Out of orient, I hardily say,
Nor proved I never her precious peer,
So round, so reken in each array,
So small, so smooth her sides were,
Wheresoever I judged gemmes gay,
I set her singly in singlere.
Alas! I lost her in an arbour;
Through grass to ground it from me got.
I dewyne, fordolked of luf-dangér
Of that private pearl without a spot.

Since in that spot it from me sprang,
Oft have I waited, wishing that weal,
That wont was while devoide my wrang
And heighten my hap and all my heal.
That does but thrych my heart thrang,
My breast in bale but borne and bele.
Yet thought me never so sweet a song
As stille stounde let to me steal.
For sooth there fleten to me fele,
To think her colour so clad in clot.
O mould, thou mars a merry jewel,
My private pearl without a spot.

That spot with spices must needs spread,
Where such riches to rot is run:
Bloomes blayke and blue and red
There shine full sheer against the sun.
Flower and fruit may not be fade
Where it down drove in mouldes dun;
For each grass must grow of graines dead –
No wheat were else to wones won.
Of good each good is ay begun:
So seemly a seed might faile not,
That springing spices up ne spun
Of that precious pearl without a spot.

To that spot that I in speech expoun'
I entered in that arbor green,
In August in a high season,
When corn is carven with crookes keen.
On hill where pearl it trundelled down
Shadowed these wortes full sheer and sheen –
Gilofre, ginger and gromylyoun,
And peonies powdered all between.

If it was seemly on to seen,
A fair reflair yet from it float.
There wones that worthy, I wot and ween,
My precious pearl without a spot.

Before that spot my hand I spenned
For care full cold that me had caught;
A devely dole in my heart denned,
Though reason set myselfen saght.
I plained my pearl that there was spenned
With fierce skills that faste fought;
Though kind of Christ me comfort kenned,
My wretched will in woe still wrought.
I fell upon that flowery flaght,
Such odour to my hernes shot;
I slid upon a sleeping-schlaghte
On that precious perle without a spot.

‹ II ›

From the spot my spirit there sprang in space;
My body on balke there abode in sweven.
My ghost is gone in Godes grace
In ádventure where marvels meven.
I nor wist in this world where that it was,
But I knew me cast where cliffes cleaven.
Toward a forest I bore my face,
Where rich rockes were to descreven.
The light of them might no man leven,
The gleaming glory that of them glent;
For were never webbes that wights weaven
Of half so dear adubbement.

Dubbed were all those downes sides
With crystal cliffs so clear of kind.
Holtwoods bright about them bides
Of boles as blue as ble of Inde.
As burnished silver the leaf onslides,
That thick could trill on each a tynde.
When gleam of glades against them glides,
With shimmering sheen full shrill they shined.
The gravel that on ground could grind
Were precious pearls of orient,
The sunne-beams but blo and blinde
In respect of that adubbement.

The adubbemente of those downes dear
Garten my ghost all grief forget.
So fresh flavours of fruites were,
As food it could me fair refete.
Fowls there flewen in frith in fere,
Of flaming hues, both small and great.

But citole-string and cithernere
Her reken mirth might not re-treat;
For when those birds their winges beat,
They songen with a sweet assent.
So gracious glee could no man get
As hear and see their adubbement.

So all was dubbed on dear assise
That frith where fortune forth me fares.
The dearth thereof for to devise
Is no wight worthy that tongue bears.
I walked ay forth in wely wise;
No bank so big that did me deres.
The further in the frith, the fairer could rise
The plain, the plants, the spice, the pears,
And rawes and rands and rich rivers –
As fil d'or fine her bankes brent.
I won to a water by shore that sheers;
Lord, dear was its adubbement!

The dubbements of those dear-worth deep
Were bankes bene of beryl bright.
Swingeing sweet the water could sweep,
With a rowning rourde raking aright.
In the founce there stonden stones steep,
As glint through glass that glowed and glight,
As streaming stars, when strothe-men sleep,
Staring in welkin in winter night.
For every pebble in pool there pight
Was emerald, sapphire, other gemme gente,
That all the lough gleamed of light,
So dear was its adubbement.

◄ III ►

The dubbement dear of down and dales,
Of wood and water and wlonk plains,
Built in me bliss, abated my bales.
Fordidden my stress, destroyed my pains.
Down after a stream that dryyle hales
I bowed in bliss, brimful my brains.
The further I followed those floaty vales,
The more strength of joy my hearte strains
As fortune fares, where as she fraynes,
Whether solace she send other else sore,
The wight to whom her will she waynes
Hyttes to have ay more and more.

[. . .]

More and more, and yet wel mare,
Me list to see the brook beyond;
For if it was fair where I could fare,

Well lovelier was the farther land.
About me could I stop and stare,
To finde a ford fast could I fonde;
But wothes more I wist there ware,
The further I stalked by the strond.
And ever me thought I should not wonde
For where there weals so winne wore.
Then newe note me came on hand
That moved my hand ay more and more.

More marvel could my dom adaunt:
I saw beyond that merry mere
A crystal cliff ful relusaunt;
Many royal ray could from it rear.
At the foot thereof there sat a faunt,
A maiden of menske, full debonaire;
Blistening white was her bleaunt.
I knew her well, I had seen her ere.
As glistening gold that man con shear,
So shone that sheen anunder shore.
On length I looked to her there;
The longer, I knew her more and more.

The more I frayste her faire face,
Her figure fine when I had fonte,
Such gladdening glory could to me glace
As little before thereto was wont.
To call her list could me enchase,
But basement gave my heart a brunt;
I saw her in so strange a place,
Such a burr might make my hearte blunt.
Then veres her up her faire front,
Her visage white as plain ivore:
That stung my heart full stray atount,
And ever the longer, the more and more.

Glossary

I

CLOSE: set; REKEN: radiant; IN SINGLERE: as unique I DWYNE . . .
DANGER: I pine mortally wounded by love's power; THAT WONT . . .
WRANG: Which once used to drive away my sorrow; HAP, HELE:
happiness, well-being; THAT DOES . . . THRANG: This weighs on my
heart and my breast swells and festers with grief; STOUNDE: hour;
FLETEN: flowed; FELE: many; COLOUR: (i.e., of her face); BLAYKE: pale;
WHERE IT DOWN . . . DUN: Where (the pearl) sank into brown soil;
WONES: dwellings; UP NE SPUN: would not spring up; CARVEN: cut;
TRUNDELLED: rolled; SHADOWED . . . SHINE: these bright, beautiful
plants cast shadow; GILOFRE: gillyflower; GROMYLYOUN: gromwell;
REFLAIR: fragrance; WONES . . . WORTHY: lies that precious one;
SPENNED: clasped; FULL COLD: chilling; DEVELY: desolating; DENNED:
lay deep; SET . . . SAGHT: tried to console me; SPENNED: imprisoned;
SKILLS: arguments; KENNED: taught; FLAGHT: turf; HERNES: head;
SLEEPING-SCHLAGHTE: deep sleep.

II

III

❧

Sir Gawain and the Green Knight

(lines 179–231)

Well gay was this gome geared in green,
And the hair of his head of his horse swete.
Fair fanning fax umbefoldes his shoulders;
As much beard as a bush over his breast hangs,
That with his highlich hair that from his head
        reaches
Was evesed all umbetorne above his elbows,
That half his arms thereunder were halched in the
        wise
Of a king's capados that closes his swyre.
The mane of that main horse much to it like,
Well crisped and combed, with knots full many
Folded in with fil d'or about the fair green,
Ay a herle of the hair, another of gold.
The tail and his topping twinning of a suit,
And binded both with a band of a bright green,
Dubbed with full dear stones, as the dock lasted;
Then thrawn with a thong, a thwarle-knot aloft,
There many bells full bright of brende gold ringen.
Such a foal upon folde, nor freke that it rides,
Was never seen in that salle with sight ere that time,
        with eye.

He looked as lightning light,
So said all that him syye;
It seemed as no man might
Under his dynttes dryye.

Whether had he no helm nor hauberk neither,
Nor no pysan, nor no plate that pented to armes,
Nor no schaft, nor no shield, to shove nor to smite,
But in his one hand he had a holly bobbe,
That is greatest in green when greaves are bare,
And an axe in his other, a huge and unmeet,
A spetos sparthe to expound in spell, whoso might.
The head of an ell-rod the large length had,
The grayn all of green steel and of golde hewen,
The bit burnished bright, with a broad edge
As well shapen to sheer as sharp razors.
The stele of a stiff staff the sturne it by grypte,
That was wounden with iron to the wand's ende,
And all engraven with green in gracious works;
A lace lapped around, that louked at the head,
And so after the halme halched full oft,
With tryed tassels thereto tacched enough
On buttons of the bright green embroidered full rich.
This hathel heldes him in and the hall enters,
Driving to the high dais, dut he no wothe.
Hailed he never one, but high he overlooked.
The first word that he warp: 'Where is,' he said,
'The governor of this gang? Gladly I would
See that segg in sight, and with himself speak
        reason.'
        To knights he cast his eye,
        And rolled it up and down,
        He stopped and could study
        Who walt there most renown.

Glossary

John Gay (1685–1732) was given to high-jinks and good humoured irony rather than satire, a temperament unsuited to his rather narrow times. That makes him enjoyable for the general reader though less available to university modules in Augustan Poetry. His reputation has suffered accordingly, though it's true that, *Beggar's Opera* apart, he rarely played to his strengths. A friend of Pope's, sometimes he wants – or feels he ought – to do what Pope would, when the poem would rather do something else. The moral of 'An Apparition', for instance, doesn't grow out of the atmospheric and brilliantly specific description, which is eloquent enough just being itself. You need to know 'the mark' is scatological to get the joke, one that rebounds on the reader and subverts the poem's convention. The 'garter' is the Order of the Garter.

I like Gay's spoof pastoral, 'The Shepherd's Week' ('Your herds for want of Water stand a'dry, They're weary of your Songs – and so am I') but plumped instead for an extra passage from his strongest poem, *Trivia*. It's a 1500-line London street-guide packed with advice: 'What Trades prejudicial to Walkers'; 'Of whom to enquire the Way'; 'Of Shoes'; 'Of avoiding Paint' and so on. It's also packed with classical allusion, and like much of his work follows – or plays with – literary models. I chose to ignore this, by and large, in favour of pungently vivid incident: 'An Episode of the great Frost', where a woman literally loses her head; 'The Dangers of Football'; the fire brigade in action; and the first example, as far as I know, of road-rage in heroic couplets. Some of the crowd-pleasing 'Fables' seem merely conventional, but in my favourite Gay enters the poem himself, a gesture that sums his best work up: tongue-in-cheek that really means it.

A TRUE STORY OF AN APPARITION

(lines 51–142)

It was an ancient lonely house, that stood
Upon the borders of the spacious wood;
Here towers and antique battlements arise,
And there in heaps the moulder'd ruine lyes;
Some Lord this mansion held in days of yore,
To chase the wolf, and pierce the foaming boar:
How chang'd, alas, from what it once had been!
'Tis now degraded to a publick Inn.
　　Strait he dismounts, repeats his loud commands;
Swift at the gate the ready landlord stands;
With frequent cringe he bows, and begs excuse,
His house was full, and ev'ry bed in use.
What not a garret, and no straw to spare?
Why then the kitchin fire, and elbow-chair
Shall serve for once to nod away the night.
The kitchin ever is the servant's right,
Replys the host; there, all the fire around,
The Count's tir'd footmen snore upon the ground.
　　The maid, who listen'd to this whole debate,
With pity learnt the weary stranger's fate.
Be brave, she crys, you still may be our guest,
Our haunted room was ever held the best:
If then your valour can the fright sustain
Of rattling curtains, and the clinking chain,
If your couragious tongue have power to talk,
When round your bed the horrid ghost shall walk;
If you dare ask it, why it leaves its tomb,
I'll see your sheets well-air'd, and show the room.
Soon as the frighted maid her tale had told,
The stranger enter'd, for his heart was bold.
　　The damsel led him through a spacious hall,
Where ivy hung the half-demolish'd wall;
She frequent look'd behind, and chang'd her hue,
While fancy tipt the candle's flame with blue.
And now they gain'd the winding stairs ascent,
And to the lonesome room of terrors went.
When all was ready, swift retir'd the maid,
The watch-lights burn, tuckt warm in bed was laid
The hardy stranger, and attends the sprite
Till his accustom'd walk at dead of night.
　　At first he hears the wind with hollow roar
Shake the loose lock, and swing the creaking door;
Nearer and nearer draws the dreadful sound
Of rattling chains, that dragg'd upon the ground:
When lo, the spectre came with horrid stride,
Approach'd the bed, and drew the curtains wide!
In human form the ghastful Phantom stood,
Expos'd his mangled bosom dy'd with blood,

Then silent pointing to his wounded breast,
Thrice wav'd his hand. Beneath the frighted guest
The bed-cords trembled, and with shudd'ring fear,
Sweat chill'd his limbs, high rose his bristled hair;
Then mutt'ring hasty pray'rs, he mann'd his heart,
And cry'd aloud; Say, whence and who thou art.
The stalking ghost with hollow voice replys,
Three years are counted, since with mortal eyes
I saw the sun, and vital air respir'd.
Like thee benighted, and with travel tir'd,
Within these walls I slept. O thirst of gain!
See, still the planks the bloody mark retain;
Stretch'd on this very bed, from sleep I start,
And see the steel impending o'er my heart;
The barb'rous hostess held the lifted knife,
The floor ran purple with my gushing life.
My treasure now they seize, the golden spoil
They bury deep beneath the grass-grown soil,
Far in the common field. Be bold, arise,
My steps shall lead thee to the secret prize;
There dig and find; let that thy care reward:
Call loud on justice, bid her not retard
To punish murder; lay my ghost at rest,
So shall with peace secure thy nights be blest;
And when beneath these boards my bones are
    found,
Decent interr them in some sacred ground.
  Here ceas'd the ghost. The stranger springs from
    bed,
And boldly follows where the Phantom led;
The half-worn stony stairs they now descend,
Where passages obscure their arches bend
Silent they walk; and now through groves they pass,
Now through wet meads their steps imprint the
    grass;
At length amidst a spacious field they came:
There stops the spectre, and ascends in flame.
Amaz'd he stood, no bush, no briar was found,
To teach his morning search to find the ground;
What cou'd he do? the night was hideous dark,
Fear shook his joints, and nature dropt the mark:
With that he starting wak'd, and rais'd his head,
But found the golden mark was left in bed.
  What is the statesman's vast ambitious scheme,
But a short vision, and a golden dream?
Power, wealth, and title elevate his hope;
He wakes. But for a garter finds a rope.

Trivia: Book II

(lines 319–98)

  Winter my theme confines; whose nitry wind
Shall crust the slabby mire, and kennels bind;
She bids the snow descend in flaky sheets,
And in her hoary mantle cloath the streets.
Let not the virgin tread these slipp'ry roads,
The gath'ring fleece the hollow patten loads;
But if thy footsteps slide with clotted frost,
Strike off the breaking balls against the post.
On silent wheel the passing coaches roll;
Oft' look behind and ward the threatning pole.
In harden'd orbs the school-boy moulds the snow,
To mark the coachman with a dextrous throw.
Why do ye, boys, the kennel's surface spread,
To tempt with faithless pass the matron's tread?
How can ye laugh, to see the damsel spurn,
Sink in your frauds and her green stocking mourn?
At White's, the harness'd chairman idly stands,
And swings, around his waist, his tingling hands:
The sempstress speeds to 'Change with red-tipt nose;
The Belgian stove beneath her footstool glows,
In half-whipt muslin needles useless lie,
And shuttle-cocks across the counter fly.
These sports warm harmless; why then will ye
    prove,
Deluded maids, the dang'rous flame of love?

Where Covent-garden's famous temple stands,
That boasts the work of Jones' immortal hands;
Columns, with plain magnificence, appear,
And graceful porches lead along the square:
Here oft' my course I bend, when lo! from far,
I spy the furies of the foot-ball war:
The 'prentice quits his shop, to join the crew,
Encreasing crowds the flying game pursue.
Thus, as you roll the ball o'er snowy ground,
The gath'ring globe augments with ev'ry round;
But whither shall I run? the throng draws nigh,
The ball now skims the street, now soars on high;
The dext'rous glazier strong returns the bound,
And jingling sashes on the pent-house sound.

O roving Muse, recal that wond'rous year,
When Winter reign'd in bleak Britannia's air;
When hoary Thames, with frosted oziers crown'd,
Was three long moons in icy fetters bound.
The waterman, forlorn along the shore,
Pensive reclines upon his useless oar,
Sees harness'd steeds desert the stony town;

And wander roads unstable, not their own:
Wheels o'er the harden'd waters smoothly glide,
And rase with whiten'd tracks the slipp'ry tide.
Here the fat cook piles high the blazing fire,
And scarce the spit can turn the steer entire.
Booths sudden hide the Thames, lone streets appear,
And num'rous games proclaim the crowded fair.
So when a gen'ral bids the martial train
Spread their encampment o'er the spacious plain;
Thick-rising tents a canvas city build,
And the loud dice resound thro' all the field.
'Twas here the matron found a doleful fate:
Let elegiac lay the woe relate,
Soft, as the breath of distant flutes, at hours,
When silent ev'ning closes up the flow'rs;
Lulling, as falling water's hollow noise;
Indulging grief, like Philomela's voice.

Doll ev'ry day had walk'd these treach'rous roads;
Her neck grew warpt beneath autumnal loads
Of various fruit; she now a basket bore,
That head, alas! shall basket bear no more.
Each booth she frequent past, in quest of gain,
And boys with pleasure heard her shrilling strain.
Ah Doll! all mortals must resign their breath,
And industry it self submit to death!
The cracking crystal yields, she sinks, she dies,
Her head, chopt off, from her lost shoulders flies:
Pippins she cry'd, but death her voice confounds,
And pip-pip-pip along the ice resounds.
So when the Thracian Furies Orpheus tore,
And left his bleeding trunk deform'd with gore,
His sever'd head floats down the silver tide,
His yet warm tongue for his lost consort cry'd;
Eurydice, with quiv'ring voice, he mourn'd,
And Heber's banks Eurydice return'd.

BOOK III
(lines 17–44; 353–76)

Where the fair columns of Saint Clement stand,
Whose straiten'd bounds encroach upon the Strand;
Where the low penthouse bows the walker's head,
And the rough pavement wounds the yielding tread,
Where not a post protects the narrow space,
And strung in twines, combs dangle in thy face;
Summon at once thy courage, rouze thy care,
Stand firm, look back, be resolute, beware.
Forth issuing from steep lanes, the collier's steeds
Drag the black load; another cart succeeds,

Team follows team, crowds heap'd on crowds
    appear,
And wait impatient, 'till the road grow clear.
Now all the pavement sounds with trampling feet,
And the mixt hurry barricades the street.
Entangled here, the waggon's lengthen'd team
Cracks the tough harness; here a pond'rous beam
Lies over-turn'd athwart; for slaughter fed,
Here lowing bullocks raise their horned head.
Now oaths grow loud, with coaches coaches jar,
And the smart blow provokes the sturdy war;
From the high box they whirl the thong around,
And with the twining lash their shins resound:
Their rage ferments, more dang'rous wounds they
    try,
And the blood gushes down their painful eye.
And now on foot the frowning warriors light,
And with their pond'rous fists renew the fight;
Blow answers blow, their cheeks are smear'd with
    blood
'Till down they fall, and grappling roll in mud.

[. . .]

But hark! Distress with screaming voice draws
    nigh'r,
And wakes the slumb'ring street with cries of fire.
At first a glowing red enwraps the skies,
And born by winds the scatt'ring sparks arise;
From beam to beam, the fierce contagion spreads;
The spiry flames now lift aloft their heads,
Through the burst sash a blazing deluge pours,
And splitting tiles descend in rattling show'rs.
Now with thick crowds th'enlighten'd pavement
    swarms,
The fire-man sweats beneath his crooked arms,
A leathern casque his vent'rous head defends,
Boldly he climbs where thickest smoke ascends;
Mov'd by the mother's streaming eyes and pray'rs.
The helpless infant through the flame he bears,
With no less virtue, than through hostile fire,
The Dardan hero bore his aged sire.
See forceful engines spout their levell'd streams,
To quench the blaze that runs along the beams;
The grappling hook plucks rafters from the walls
And heaps on heaps the smoky ruin falls.
Blown by strong winds the fiery tempest roars,
Bears down new walls, and pours along the floors:
The heav'ns are all a-blaze, the face of night
Is cover'd with a sanguine dreadful light . . .

FABLE L.

‹The Hare and many Friends. ›

Friendship, like love, is but a name
Unless to one you stint the flame.
The child, whom many fathers share,
Hath seldom known a father's care;
'Tis thus in friendships; who depend
On many rarely find a friend.

A Hare, who, in a civil way,
Comply'd with ev'ry thing, like *Gay*,
Was known by all the bestial train,
Who haunt the wood, or graze the plain:
Her care was, never to offend,
And ev'ry creature was her friend.

As forth she went at early dawn
To taste the dew-besprinkled lawn,
Behind she hears the hunter's cries,
And from the deep-mouth'd thunder flies;
She starts, she stops, she pants for breath,
She hears the near advance of death,
She doubles, to mis-lead the hound,
And measures back her mazy round;
'Till, fainting in the publick way,
Half dead with fear she gasping lay.

What transport in her bosom grew,
When first the horse appear'd in view!

Let me, says she, your back ascend,
And owe my safety to a friend,
You know my feet betray my flight,
To friendship ev'ry burthen's light.

The horse reply'd, poor honest puss,
It grieves my heart to see thee thus;
Be comforted, relief is near;
For all your friends are in the rear.

She next the stately bull implor'd;
And thus reply'd the mighty lord.
Since ev'ry beast alive can tell
That I sincerely wish you well,
I may, without offence, pretend
To take the freedom of a friend;
Love calls me hence; a fav'rite cow
Expects me near yon barley mow:
And when a lady's in the case,
You know, all other things give place.
To leave you thus might seem unkind;
But see, the goat is just behind.

The goat remark'd her pulse was high,
Her languid head, her heavy eye;

My back, says he, may do you harm;
The sheep's at hand, and wool is warm.

The sheep was feeble, and complain'd,
His sides a load of wool sustain'd,
Said he was slow, confest his fears;
For hounds eat sheep as well as hares.

She now the trotting calf addrest,
To save from death a friend distrest.

Shall I, says he, of tender age,
In this important care engage?
Older and abler past you by;
How strong are those! how weak am I!
Should I presume to bear you hence,
Those friends of mine may take offence.
Excuse me then. You know my heart.
But dearest friends, alas, must part!
How shall we all lament! Adieu.
For see the hounds are just in view.

People used to get Goldsmith at school, get him by heart. Bits and pieces of *The Deserted Village* survive in the speech of old people, even those whose schooling finished at the earliest possible legal age. Auburn's Parson and Schoolmaster were quite familiar characters once, and Auburn's public house was a familiar place. Clare and Crabbe look back to Goldsmith and in rhyming couplets with more edge and passion continue his lament and his polemic. 'The Deserted Village' is an important poem and we can't afford to let it lapse.

In his dedicatory letter Goldsmith anticipated the criticism 'that the depopulation [his poem] deplores is no where to be seen, and the disorders it laments are only to be found in the poet's own imagination'. He answered: 'I have taken all possible pains ... to be certain of what I alledge, and all my views and enquiries have led me to believe those miseries real, which I here attempt to display'. We may not need that assurance. He will have seen such things in his native Ireland. And poetry often imagines worse to come. In Clare's day in England, and in Scotland during the clearances, it duly came. The tyrant (l. 37) and the spoiler (l. 49) still do pretty much as they please and the poor and the voiceless suffer it. So Goldsmith had and his readers still have real material. But his poem does something more. It keeps alive the myth of innocence and simplicity and in so doing excites a longing for the sort of life that the love of money debars us from entering into. Achieving those two things – showing actual wrongs and reanimating an archetypal ideal – Goldsmith as a poet through the wit and musicality of his lines makes (see l. 422) some *redress*.

THE DESERTED VILLAGE

(lines 1–74; 113–62; 177–88; 193–250; 265–86; 303–44; 363–426)

Sweet Auburn, loveliest village of the plain,
Where health and plenty cheered the labouring
    swain,
Where smiling spring its earliest visit paid,
And parting summer's lingering blooms delayed,
Dear lovely bowers of innocence and ease,
Seats of my youth, when every sport could please,
How often have I loitered o'er thy green,
Where humble happiness endeared each scene;
How often have I paused on every charm,
The sheltered cot, the cultivated farm,
The never failing brook, the busy mill,
The decent church that topt the neighbouring hill,
The hawthorn bush, with seats beneath the shade,
For talking age and whispering lovers made.
How often have I blest the coming day,
When toil remitting lent its turn to play,
And all the village train from labour free
Led up their sports beneath the spreading tree,
While many a pastime circled in the shade,
The young contending as the old surveyed;
And many a gambol frolicked o'er the ground,
And slights of art and feats of strength went round.
And still as each repeated pleasure tired,
Succeeding sports the mirthful band inspired;
The dancing pair that simply sought renown
By holding out to tire each other down,
The swain mistrustless of his smutted face,
While secret laughter tittered round the place,
The bashful virgin's side-long looks of love,
The matron's glance that would those looks reprove.
These were thy charms, sweet village; sports like
    these,
With sweet succession, taught even toil to please;
These round thy bowers their cheerful influence
    shed,
These were thy charms – But all these charms are
    fled.

Sweet smiling village, loveliest of the lawn,
Thy sports are fled, and all thy charms withdrawn;
Amidst thy bowers the tyrant's hand is seen,
And desolation saddens all thy green:
One only master grasps the whole domain,
And half a tillage stints thy smiling plain;
No more thy glassy brook reflects the day,
But choaked with sedges, works its weedy way.

Along thy glades, a solitary guest,
The hollow sounding bittern guards its nest;
Amidst thy desert walks the lapwing flies,
And tires their ecchoes with unvaried cries.
Sunk are thy bowers in shapeless ruin all,
And the long grass o'ertops the mouldering wall,
And trembling, shrinking from the spoiler's hand,
Far far away thy children leave the land.

Ill fares the land, to hastening ills a prey,
Where wealth accumulates, and men decay;
Princes and lords may flourish, or may fade;
A breath can make them, as a breath has made.
But a bold peasantry, their country's pride,
When once destroyed, can never be supplied.

A time there was, ere England's griefs began,
When every rood of ground maintained its man;
For him light labour spread her wholesome store,
Just gave what life required, but gave no more.
His best companions, innocence and health;
And his best riches, ignorance of wealth.

But times are altered; trade's unfeeling train
Usurp the land and dispossess the swain;
Along the lawn, where scattered hamlets rose,
Unwieldy wealth, and cumbrous pomp repose;
And every want to oppulence allied,
And every pang that folly pays to pride.
These gentle hours that plenty bade to bloom,
Those calm desires that asked but little room,
Those healthful sports that graced the peaceful
    scene,
Lived in each look, and brightened all the green;
These far departing seek a kinder shore,
And rural mirth and manners are no more.

[. . .]

Sweet was the sound when oft at evening's close,
Up yonder hill the village murmur rose;
There as I past with careless steps and slow,
The mingling notes came softened from below;
The swain responsive as the milk-maid sung,
The sober herd that lowed to meet their young;
The noisy geese that gabbled o'er the pool,
The playful children just let loose from school;
The watch-dog's voice that bayed the whispering
    wind,
And the loud laugh that spoke the vacant mind,
These all in sweet confusion sought the shade,
And filled each pause the nightingale had made.

But now the sounds of population fail,
No chearful murmurs fluctuate in the gale,
No busy steps the grass-grown foot-way tread,
For all the bloomy flush of life is fled.
All but yon widowed, solitary thing
That feebly bends beside the plashy spring;
She, wretched matron, forced, in age, for bread,
To strip the brook with mantling cresses spread,
To pick her wintry faggot from the thorn,
To seek her nightly shed, and weep till morn;
She only left of all the harmless train,
The sad historian of the pensive plain.

Near yonder copse, where once the garden smil'd,
And still where many a garden flower grows wild;
There, where a few torn shrubs the place disclose,
The village preacher's modest mansion rose.
A man he was, to all the country dear,
And passing rich with forty pounds a year;
Remote from towns he ran his godly race,
Nor ere had changed, nor wish'd to change his
    place;
Unpractised he to fawn, or seek for power,
By doctrines fashioned to the varying hour;
Far other aims his heart had learned to prize,
More skilled to raise the wretched than to rise.
His house was known to all the vagrant train,
He chid their wanderings, but relieved their pain;
The long remembered beggar was his guest,
Whose beard descending swept his aged breast;
The ruined spendthrift, now no longer proud,
Claimed kindred there, and had his claims allowed;
The broken soldier, kindly bade to stay,
Sate by his fire, and talked the night away;
Wept o'er his wounds, or tales of sorrow done,
Shouldered his crutch, and shewed how fields were
    won.
Pleased with his guests, the good man learned to
    glow,
And quite forgot their vices in their woe;
Careless their merits, or their faults to scan,
His pity gave ere charity began.

[. . .]

At church, with meek and unaffected grace,
His looks adorned the venerable place;
Truth from his lips prevailed with double sway,
And fools, who came to scoff, remained to pray.
The service past, around the pious man,
With steady zeal each honest rustic ran;
Even children followed with endearing wile,

And plucked his gown, to share the good man's
    smile.
His ready smile a parent's warmth exprest,
Their welfare pleased him, and their cares distrest;
To them his heart, his love, his griefs were given,
But all his serious thoughts had rest in Heaven.

[. . .]

    Beside yon straggling fence that skirts the way,
With blossomed furze unprofitably gay,
There, in his noisy mansion, skill'd to rule,
The village master taught his little school;
A man severe he was, and stern to view,
I knew him well, and every truant knew;
Well had the boding tremblers learned to trace
The day's disasters in his morning face;
Full well they laugh'd with counterfeited glee,
At all his jokes, for many a joke had he;
Full well the busy whisper circling round,
Conveyed the dismal tidings when he frowned;
Yet he was kind, or if severe in aught,
The love he bore to learning was in fault;
The village all declared how much he knew;
'Twas certain he could write, and cypher too;
Lands he could measure, terms and tides presage,
And even the story ran that he could gauge.
In arguing too, the parson owned his skill,
For e'en tho' vanquished, he could argue still;
While words of learned length, and thundering
    sound,
Amazed the gazing rustics ranged around,
And still they gazed, and still the wonder grew,
That one small head could carry all he knew.

    But past is all his fame. The very spot
Where many a time he triumphed, is forgot.
Near yonder thorn, that lifts its head on high,
Where once the sign-post caught the passing eye,
Low lies that house where nut-brown draughts
    inspired,
Where grey-beard mirth and smiling toil retired,
Where village statesmen talked with looks profound,
And news much older than their ale went round.
Imagination fondly stoops to trace
The parlour splendours of that festive place;
The white-washed wall, the nicely sanded floor,
The varnished clock that clicked behind the door;
The chest contrived a double debt to pay,
A bed by night, a chest of drawers by day;
The pictures placed for ornament and use,
The twelve good rules, the royal game of goose;

The hearth, except when winter chill'd the day,
With aspen boughs, and flowers, and fennel gay,
While broken tea-cups, wisely kept for shew,
Ranged o'er the chimney, glistened in a row.

    Vain transitory splendours! Could not all
Reprieve the tottering mansion from its fall!
Obscure it sinks, nor shall it more impart
An hour's importance to the poor man's heart;
Thither no more the peasant shall repair
To sweet oblivion of his daily care;
No more the farmer's news, the barber's tale,
No more the wood-man's ballad shall prevail;
No more the smith his dusky brow shall clear,
Relax his ponderous strength, and lean to hear,
The host himself no longer shall be found
Careful to see the mantling bliss go round;
Nor the coy maid, half willing to be prest,
Shall kiss the cup to pass it to the rest.

[. . .]

    Ye friends to truth, ye statesmen who survey
The rich man's joy's encrease, the poor's decay,
'Tis yours to judge, how wide the limits stand
Between a splendid and an happy land.
Proud swells the tide with loads of freighted ore,
And shouting Folly hails them from her shore;
Hoards, even beyond the miser's wish abound,
And rich men flock from all the world around.
Yet count our gains. This wealth is but a name
That leaves our useful products still the same.
Not so the loss. The man of wealth and pride,
Takes up a space that many poor supplied;
Space for his lake, his park's extended bounds,
Space for his horses, equipage, and hounds;
The robe that wraps his limbs in silken sloth,
Has robbed the neighbouring fields of half their
    growth;
His seat, where solitary sports are seen,
Indignant spurns the cottage from the green;
Around the world each needful product flies,
For all the luxuries the world supplies.
While thus the land adorned for pleasure all
In barren splendour feebly waits the fall.

[. . .]

    Where then, ah, where shall poverty reside,
To scape the pressure of contiguous pride?
If to some common's fenceless limits strayed,
He drives his flock to pick the scanty blade,

Those fenceless fields the sons of wealth divide,
And even the bare-worn common is denied.

If to the city sped – What waits him there?
To see profusion that he must not share;
To see ten thousand baneful arts combined
To pamper luxury, and thin mankind;
To see those joys the sons of pleasure know,
Extorted from his fellow-creature's woe.
Here, while the courtier glitters in brocade,
There the pale artist plies the sickly trade;
Here, while the proud their long drawn pomps
    display,
There the black gibbet glooms beside the way.
The dome where pleasure holds her midnight reign,
Here richly deckt admits the gorgeous train,
Tumultuous grandeur crowds the blazing square,
The rattling chariots clash, the torches glare;
Sure scenes like these no troubles ere annoy!
Sure these denote one universal joy!
Are these thy serious thoughts? – Ah, turn thine
    eyes
Where the poor houseless shivering female lies.
She once, perhaps, in village plenty blest,
Has wept at tales of innocence distrest;
Her modest looks the cottage might adorn,
Sweet as the primrose peeps beneath the thorn;
Now lost to all; her friends, her virtue fled,
Near her betrayer's door she lays her head,
And pinch'd with cold, and shrinking from the
    shower,
With heavy heart deplores that luckless hour,
When idly first, ambitious of the town,
She left her wheel and robes of country brown.

Do thine, sweet AUBURN, thine, the loveliest
    train,
Do thy fair tribes participate her pain?
Even now, perhaps, by cold and hunger led,
At proud men's doors they ask a little bread!

Ah, no. To distant climes, a dreary scene,
Where half the convex world intrudes between,
Through torrid tracts with fainting steps they go,
Where wild Altama murmurs to their woe.
[. . .]

Good Heaven! what sorrows gloom'd that parting
    day,
That called them from their native walks away;
When the poor exiles, every pleasure past,

Hung round their bowers, and fondly looked their
    last,
And took a long farewell, and wished in vain
For seats like these beyond the western main;
And shuddering still to face the distant deep,
Returned and wept, and still returned to weep.
The good old sire, the first prepared to go
To new found worlds, and wept for others woe.
But for himself, in conscious virtue brave,
He only wished for worlds beyond the grave.
His lovely daughter, lovelier in her tears,
The fond companion of his helpless years,
Silent went next, neglectful of her charms,
And left a lover's for a father's arms.
With louder plaints the mother spoke her woes,
And blest the cot where every pleasure rose;
And kist her thoughtless babes with many a tear,
And claspt them close in sorrow doubly dear;
Whilst her fond husband strove to lend relief
In all the silent manliness of grief.

O luxury! Thou curst by heaven's decree,
How ill exchanged are things like these for thee!
How do thy potions with insidious joy,
Diffuse their pleasures only to destroy!
Kingdoms by thee, to sickly greatness grown,
Boast of a florid vigour not their own.
At every draught more large and large they grow,
A bloated mass of rank unwieldy woe;
Till sapped their strength, and every part unsound,
Down, down they sink, and spread a ruin round.

Even now the devastation is begun,
And half the business of destruction done;
Even now, methinks, as pondering here I stand,
I see the rural virtues leave the land.
Down where yon anchoring vessel spreads the sail
That idly waiting flaps with every gale,
Downward they move, a melancholy band,
Pass from the shore, and darken all the strand.
Contented toil, and hospitable care,
And kind connubial tenderness, are there;
And piety with wishes placed above,
And steady loyalty, and faithful love.
And thou, sweet Poetry, thou loveliest maid,
Still first to fly where sensual joys invade;
Unfit in these degenerate times of shame,
To catch the heart, or strike for honest fame;
Dear charming nymph, neglected and decried,
My shame in crowds, my solitary pride.
Thou source of all my bliss, and all my woe,

That found'st me poor at first, and keep'st me so;
Thou guide by which the nobler arts excell,
Thou nurse of every virtue, fare thee well.
Farewell, and O where'er thy voice be tried,
On Torno's cliffs, or Pambamarca's side,
Whether where equinoctial fervours glow,
Or winter wraps the polar world in snow,
Still let thy voice prevailing over time,
Redress the rigours of the inclement clime;
Aid slighted truth, with thy persuasive strain
Teach erring man to spurn the rage of gain;
Teach him that states of native strength possest,
Tho' very poor, may still be very blest,

Of the 'Ricardian' poets – the four major writers probably working during the reign of Richard II – Gower (c. 1330–1408) is the least commonly praised nowadays; yet he is as accomplished a stylist as Chaucer and writes in a tradition which has more in common with the later mainstream of English literature than have Langland and the *Gawain*-poet. Up to the seventeenth century he was praised as often as Chaucer; Ben Jonson uses him more than Chaucer as evidence in his *Grammar*. The explanation for all these facts is the same: Gower is a classical writer, conservative in temper and accomplishments. He wrote expertly in Latin and French as well as English, writing long poetic works in all three languages. Though he wrote short poems too in both English and French, his greatest work is unquestionably the *Confessio Amantis*, written mostly it seems in the 1380s and surviving in three manuscripts from the 1390s. An early manuscript has a dedication to his fellow-Londoner poet Chaucer, later apparently cancelled. Gower is a decidedly political writer by the standards of his age. His work contains encomia to both Richard II and Henry IV, and his long Latin work *Vox Clamantis* has a savage and insulting satirical attack on the leaders of the Peasants' Revolt of 1381, comparing them to animals as they made their fated way into the city.

Confessio Amantis, as its name suggests, is the confession of a lover Amans to a priest of Venus, organized into books under the headings of the Seven Deadly sins, with an extra encyclopaedic book describing pagan beliefs. Gower's greatest skill is his metrical ease with the octosyllabics he writes in, as evidenced by the much-admired story included below, Rosiphilee from Book 4, illustrative of Sloth in Love. He is capable of great graphic lyricism. The other extracts given here are the poem's opening with its declared intent to find a middle way between the sententious and the trivial, and the humane conclusion in which Amans accepts that lovers who spend all their life examining their consciences will end up too old for love, in keeping with the poem's theme of 'Kynde', Nature, which is a brilliant example of the way in which all the Ricardian writers introduce a balancing scepticism into their 'moral thyngs'.

JOHN GOWER

CONFESSIO AMANTIS

‹Prologus›

(lines 1–65)

Of hem that writen ous tofore
The bokes duelle, and we therfore
Ben tawht of that was write tho:
Forthi good is that we also
In oure tyme among ous hiere
Do wryte of newe som matiere,
Essampled of these olde wyse
So that it myhte in such a wyse,
Whan we ben dede and elleswhere,
Beleve to the worldes eere
In tyme comende after this.
Bot for men sein, and soth it is,
That who that al of wisdom writ
It dulleth ofte a mannes wit
To him that schal it aldai rede,
For thilke cause, if that ye rede,
I wolde go the middel weie
And wryte a bok betwen the tweie,
Somwhat of lust, somwhat of lore,
That of the lasse or of the more
Som man mai lyke of that I wryte:
And for that fewe men endite
In oure englissh, I thenke make
A bok for Engelondes sake,
The yer sextenthe of kyng Richard.
What schal befalle hierafterward
God wot, for now upon this tyde
Men se the world on every syde
In sondry wyse so diversed,
That it welnyh stant al reversed,
As forto speke of tyme ago.
The cause whi it changeth so
It needeth nought to specifie,
The thing so open is at ÿe
That every man it mai beholde:
And natheles be daies olde,
Whan that the bokes weren levere,
Wrytinge was beloved evere
Of hem that weren vertuous;
For hier in erthe amonges ous,
If noman write hou that it stode,
The pris of hem that weren goode
Scholde, as who seith, a gret partie
Be lost: so for to magnifie
The worthi princes that tho were,
The bokes schewen hiere and there,
Whereof the world ensampled is;

And tho that deden thanne amis
Thurgh tirannie and crualte,
Right as thei stoden in degre,
So was the wrytinge of here werk.
Thus I, which am a burel clerk,
Purpose forto wryte a bok
After the world that whilom tok
Long tyme in olde daies passed:
Bot for men sein it is now lassed,
In worse plit than it was tho,
I thenke forto touche also
The world which neweth every dai,
So as I can, so as I mai.
Thogh I seknesse have upon honde
And longe have had, yit woll I fonde
To wryte and do my bisinesse,
That in som part, so as I gesse,
The wyse man mai ben avised.

‹Book 4›

(lines 1254–446)

Of Armenye, I rede thus,
Ther was a king, which Herupus
Was hote, and he a lusti Maide
To dowhter hadde, and as men saide
Hire name was Rosiphelee;
Which tho was of gret renomee,
For sche was bothe wys and fair
And scholde ben hire fader hair.
Bot sche hadde o defalte of Slowthe
Towardes love, and that was rowthe;
For so wel cowde noman seie,
Which mihte sette hire in the weie
Of loves occupacion
Thurgh non ymaginacion;
That scole wolde sche noght knowe.
And thus sche was on of the slowe
As of such hertes besinesse,
Til whanne Venus the goddesse,
Which loves court hath forto reule,
Hath broght hire into betre reule,
Forth with Cupide and with his miht:
For thei merveille how such a wiht,
Which tho was in hir lusti age,
Desireth nother Mariage
Ne yit the love of paramours,
Which evere hath be the comun cours
Amonges hem that lusti were.
So was it schewed after there:
For he that hihe hertes loweth

With fyri Dartes whiche he throweth,
Cupide, which of love is godd,
In chastisinge hath mad a rodd
To dryve awei hir wantounesse;
So that withinne a while, I gesse,
Sche hadde on such a chance sporned,
That al hire mod was overtorned,
Which ferst sche hadde of slow manere:
For thus it fell, as thou schalt hiere.
Whan come was the Monthe of Maii,
Sche wolde walke upon a dai,
And that was er the Sonne Ariste;
Of wommen bot a fewe it wiste,
And forth sche wente prively
Unto the Park was faste by,
Al softe walkende on the gras,
Til sche cam ther the Launde was,
Thurgh which ther ran a gret rivere.
It thoghte hir fair, and seide, 'Here
I wole abide under the schawe':
And bad hire wommen to withdrawe,
And ther sche stod al one stille,
To thenke what was in hir wille.
Sche sih the swote floures springe,
Sche herde glade fouks singe,
Sche sih the bestes in her kinde,
The buck, the do, the hert, the hinde,
The madle go with the femele;
And so began ther a querele
Betwen love and hir oghne herte,
Fro which sche couthe noght asterte.
And as sche caste hire yhe aboute,
Sche syh clad in o suite a route
Of ladis, wher thei comen ryde
Along under the wodes syde:
On faire amblende hors thei sete,
That were al whyte, fatte and grete,
And everichon thei ride on side.
The Sadles were of such a Pride,
With Perle and gold so wel begon,
So riche syh sche nevere non;
In kertles and in Copes riche
Thei weren clothed, alle liche,
Departed evene of whyt and blew;
With alle lustes that sche knew
Thei were enbrouded overal.
Here bodies weren long and smal,
The beaute faye upon her face
Non erthly thing it may desface;
Corones on here hed thei beere,
As ech of hem a qweene weere,

That al the gold of Cresus halle
The leste coronal of alle
Ne mihte have boght after the worth:
Thus come thei ridende forth.
  The kinges dowhter, which this syh,
For pure abaissht drowh hire adryh
And hield hire clos under the bowh,
And let hem passen stille ynowh;
For as hire thoghte in hire avis,
To hem that were of such a pris
Sche was noght worthi axen there,
Fro when they come or what thei were:
Bot levere than this worldes good
Sche wolde have wist hou that it stod,
And putte hire hed alitel oute;
And as sche lokede hire aboute,
Sche syh comende under the linde
A womman up an hors behinde.
The hors on which sche rod was blak,
Al lene and galled on the back,
And haltede, as he were encluyed,
Wherof the womman was annuied;
Thus was the hors in sori plit,
Bot for al that a sterre whit
Amiddes in the front he hadde.
Hir Sadel ek was wonder badde,
In which the wofull womman sat,
And natheles ther was with that
A riche bridel for the nones
Of gold and preciouse Stones.
Hire cote was somdiel totore;
Aboute hir middel twenty score
Of horse haltres and wel mo
Ther hyngen ate time tho.
  Thus when sche cam the ladi nyh,
Than tok sche betre hiede and syh
This womman fair was of visage,
Freyssh, lusti, yong and of tendre age;
And so this ladi, ther sche stod,
Bethoghte hire wel and understod
That this, which com ridende tho,
Tidinges couthe telle of tho,
Which as sche sih tofore ryde,
And putte hir forth and preide abide,
And seide 'Ha, Suster, let me hiere,
What ben thei, that now riden hiere,
And ben so richeliche arraied?'
  This womman, which com so esmaied,
Ansuerde with ful softe speche,
And seith, 'Ma Dame, I schal you teche.
These ar of tho that whilom were

Servantz to love, and trowthe beere,
Ther as thei hadde here herte set.
Fare wel, for I mai noght be let:
Ma Dame, I go to mi servise,
So moste I haste in alle wise;
Forthi, ma Dame, yif me leve,
I mai noght longe with you leve,'

   'Ha, goode Soster, yit I preie,
Tell me whi ye ben so beseie
And with these haltres thus begon.'

   'Ma Dame, whilom I was on
That to mi fader hadde a king;
Bot I was slow, and for no thing
Me liste noght to love abeie,
And that I now ful sore abeie.
For I whilom no love hadde,
Min hors is now so fieble and badde,
And al totore is myn arai,
And every yeer this freisshe Maii
These lusti ladis ryde aboute,
And I mot nedes suie here route
In this manere as ye now se,
And trusse here haltres forth with me,
And am bot as here horse knave.
Non other office I ne have,
Hem thenkth I am worthi nomore,
For I was slow in loves lore,
Whan I was able forto lere,
And wolde noght the tales hiere
Of hem that couthen love teche.'

   'Now tell me thanne, I you beseche,
Wherof that riche bridel serveth.'

   With that hire chere awei sche swerveth,
And gan to wepe, and thus sche tolde:
'This bridel, which ye nou beholde
So riche upon myn horse hed, –
Ma Dame, afore, er I was ded,
Whan I was in mi lusti lif,
Ther fel into myn herte a strif
Of love, which me overcom,
So that therafter hiede I nom
And thoghte I wolde love a kniht:
That laste wel a fourtenyht,
For it no lengere mihte laste,
So nyh my lif was ate laste.
Bot now, allas, to late war
That I ne hadde him loved ar:
For deth cam so in haste bime,
Er I therto hadde eny time,
That it ne mihte ben achieved.
Bot for al that I am relieved,

Of that mi will was good therto,
That love soffreth it be so
That I schal swiche a bridel were.
Now have ye herd al myn ansuere:
To godd, ma Dame, I you betake,
And warneth alle for mi sake,
Of love that thei ben noght ydel,
And bidd hem thenke upon mi brydel,'
And with that word al sodeinly
Sche passeth, as it were a Sky,
Al clene out of this ladi sihte:
And tho for fere hire herte afflihte,
And seide to hirself, 'Helas!
I am riht in the same cas.
Bot if I live after this day,
I schal amende it, if I may.'
And thus homward this lady wente,
And changede al hire ferste entente,
Withinne hire herte and gan to swere
That sche none haltres wolde bere.

◄ Book 8 ►
(lines 2932–67)

'It were a thing unresonable,
A man to be so overseie.
Forthi tak hiede of that I seie;
For in the lawe of my comune
We be noght schape to comune,
Thiself and I, nevere after this.
Now have y seid al that ther is
Of love as for thi final ende:
Adieu, for y mot fro the wende.'
And with that word al sodeinly,
Enclosid in a sterred sky,
Venus, which is the qweene of love,
Was take in to hire place above,
More wiste y nought wher sche becam.
And thus my leve of hire y nam,
And forth with al the same tide
Hire prest, which wolde nought abide,
Or be me lief or be me loth,
Out of my sighte forth he goth,
And y was left with outen helpe.
So wiste I nought wher of to yelpe,
Bot only that y hadde lore
My time, and was sori ther fore.
And thus bewhapid in my thought,
Whan al was turnyd in to nought,
I stod amasid for a while,
And in my self y gan to smyle

Thenkende uppon the bedis blake,
And how they weren me betake,
For that ye schulde bidde and preie.
And whanne y sigh non othre weie
Bot only that y was refusid,
Unto the lif which y hadde usid
I thoughte nevere torne ayein:
And in this wise, soth to seyn,
Homward a softe pas y wente.

My choice of work by Thomas Gray
(1716–71) is, inevitably, the Elegy. The poem
has become so familiar, so much a part of
the language, that it is easy to take it for
granted and to forget what is being said.
How to get round this? My own way has
been to come back to the Elegy after reading
some of Gray's letters. It becomes possible
to hear his voice again behind the poem's
generalities, and to recognize how directly
he speaks out of his own experience of life.

The Elegy is many poems in one. I admire
the way that it unfolds and surprises itself.
The strong wayward current of its rhetoric
is exploratory. Just over half-way through
(with the stanza 'Yet ev'n these bones …')
Gray veers away from the conclusion he
had originally planned, and re-enters his
subject, to discover the unwritten poem
standing at the edge of the one he has been
writing, a preoccupation at variance with
his conscious theme. The lines that follow
open out in their turn, with Gray's dis-
tanced portrait of himself as seen through
the eyes of the 'hoary-headed swain'. Then
comes the surprise of 'The Epitaph'.
Impossible to take the poem further than
this.

Gray was possessed simultaneously by a
wondering sense of life's myriad possibility
and by a sad sense of the unrealizable
nature of this possibility, doomed – either
despite its richness or because of it – to be
smothered, misapplied, depraved. (His feel-
ing for the suppressed potential of obscure
village lives is connected with a suppression
which he himself felt, as a man of evidently
homosexual temperament.) The preoccu-
pation which steals up on this first theme,
changing the course of the Elegy, is the
need for answered affection and the pres-
ence of a 'kindred spirit', for the knowledge
that a real meeting has taken place this
side of the grave.

THOMAS GRAY

ELEGY WRITTEN IN A COUNTRY CHURCHYARD

The curfew tolls the knell of parting day,
The lowing herd wind slowly o'er the lea,
The ploughman homeward plods his weary way,
And leaves the world to darkness and to me.

Now fades the glimmering landscape on the sight,
And all the air a solemn stillness holds,
Save where the beetle wheels his droning flight,
And drowsy tinklings lull the distant folds;

Save that from yonder ivy-mantled tow'r
The moping owl does to the moon complain
Of such as, wand'ring near her secret bow'r,
Molest her ancient solitary reign.

Beneath those rugged elms, that yew-tree's shade,
Where heaves the turf in many a mould'ring heap,
Each in his narrow cell for ever laid,
The rude forefathers of the hamlet sleep.

The breezy call of incense-breathing morn,
The swallow twitt'ring from the straw-built shed,
The cock's shrill clarion or the echoing horn,
No more shall rouse them from their lowly bed.

For them no more the blazing hearth shall burn,
Or busy housewife ply her evening care:
No children run to lisp their sire's return,
Or climb his knees the envied kiss to share.

Oft did the harvest to their sickle yield,
Their furrow oft the stubborn glebe has broke;
How jocund did they drive their team afield!
How bowed the woods beneath their sturdy stroke!

Let not Ambition mock their useful toil,
Their homely joys and destiny obscure;
Nor Grandeur hear, with a disdainful smile,
The short and simple annals of the poor.

The boast of heraldry, the pomp of pow'r,
And all that beauty, all that wealth e'er gave,
Awaits alike the inevitable hour.
The paths of glory lead but to the grave.

Nor you, ye Proud, impute to these the fault,
If Mem'ry o'er their tomb no trophies raise,

Where through the long-drawn aisle and fretted
vault
The pealing anthem swells the note of praise.

Can storied urn or animated bust
Back to its mansion call the fleeting breath?
Can Honour's voice provoke the silent dust,
Or Flatt'ry soothe the dull cold ear of Death?

Perhaps in this neglected spot is laid
Some heart once pregnant with celestial fire;
Hands that the rod of empire might have swayed,
Or waked to ecstasy the living lyre.

But Knowledge to their eyes her ample page
Rich with the spoils of time did ne'er unroll;
Chill Penury repressed their noble rage,
And froze the genial current of the soul.

Full many a gem of purest ray serene
The dark unfathomed caves of ocean bear:
Full many a flower is born to blush unseen
And waste its sweetness on the desert air.

Some village-Hampden that with dauntless breast
The little tyrant of his fields withstood;
Some mute inglorious Milton here may rest,
Some Cromwell guiltless of his country's blood.

Th' applause of list'ning senates to command,
The threats of pain and ruin to despise,
To scatter plenty o'er a smiling land,
And read their hist'ry in a nation's eyes,

Their lot forbade: nor circumscribed alone
Their growing virtues, but their crimes confined;
Forbade to wade through slaughter to a throne,
And shut the gates of mercy on mankind.

The struggling pangs of conscious truth to hide,
To quench the blushes of ingenuous shame,
Or heap the shrine of Luxury and Pride
With incense kindled at the Muse's flame.

Far from the madding crowd's ignoble strife
Their sober wishes never learned to stray;
Along the cool sequestered vale of life
They kept the noiseless tenor of their way.

Yet ev'n these bones from insult to protect
Some frail memorial still erected nigh,

With uncouth rhymes and shapeless sculpture
    decked,
Implores the passing tribute of a sigh.

Their name, their years, spelt by th' unlettered
    muse,
The place of fame and elegy supply:
And many a holy text around she strews,
That teach the rustic moralist to die.

For who to dumb Forgetfulness a prey,
This pleasing anxious being e'er resigned,
Left the warm precincts of the cheerful day,
Nor cast one longing ling'ring look behind?

On some fond breast the parting soul relies,
Some pious drops the closing eye requires;
Ev'n from the tomb the voice of Nature cries,
Ev'n in our ashes live their wonted fires.

For thee who, mindful of th' unhonoured dead,
Dost in these lines their artless tale relate;
If chance, by lonely Contemplation led,
Some kindred spirit shall inquire thy fate,

Haply some hoary-headed swain may say,
'Oft have we seen him at the peep of dawn
Brushing with hasty steps the dews away
To meet the sun upon the upland lawn.

'There at the foot of yonder nodding beech
That wreathes its old fantastic roots so high,
His listless length at noontide would he stretch,
And pore upon the brook that babbles by.

'Hard by yon wood, now smiling as in scorn,
Mutt'ring his wayward fancies he would rove,
Now drooping, woeful wan, like one forlorn,
Or crazed with care, or crossed in hopeless love.

'One morn I missed him on the customed hill,
Along the heath and near his fav'rite tree;
Another came; nor yet beside the rill,
Nor up the lawn, nor at the wood was he;

'The next with dirges due in sad array
Slow through the church-way path we saw him
    borne.
Approach and read (for thou canst read) the lay,
Graved on the stone beneath yon aged thorn.'

‹ The Epitaph ›

Here rests his head upon the lap of earth
A youth to fortune and to fame unknown.
Fair Science frowned not on his humble birth,
And Melancholy marked him for her own.

Large was his bounty and his soul sincere,
Heaven did a recompense as largely send:
He gave to Mis'ry all he had, a tear,
He gained from heav'n ('twas all he wished) a friend.

No farther seek his merits to disclose,
Or draw his frailties from their dread abode
(There they alike in trembling hope repose),
The bosom of his Father and his God.

Born at Beauchamp Court, Warwick, educated at Shrewsbury and Cambridge, a Privy Councillor and friend of Sir Philip Sidney, servant to Queen Elizabeth I, knighted in 1597 and Chancellor of the Exchequer from 1614 to 1621, in which year he was raised to the peerage as Lord Brooke, Fulke Greville (1554–1628) can fairly be described as one of the élite, and it was presumably to please or impress the more literary members of that select group that he composed his poems and closet-dramas. Most of his works as we know them were published after his death. But resentment of élites is no reason to turn away from Greville's verses, which address the universal subjects of love and mortality. Though he wrote two tragedies, *Alaham* and *Mustapha* (1609), the work for which he will be remembered is the collection of 109 short poems, *Caelica*, begun in the 1580s and printed in 1633. In this the earlier pieces have the flavour of Petrarchan love poems, but spiritual and philosophical considerations crowd in as the years pass – and in handling these Greville reflected the prevailing beliefs of the English renaissance. His poems make their appeal to the ear and the intellect, not to the inner eye. While the verses, with their elaborate analogies and parallels, are always elegantly turned, he sometimes allowed the exigencies of rhyme and scansion to distort the syntax to a point at which two readings may be needed to discover his meaning, though the effort will usually be rewarded. Despite the wry undertone there are hints of a lighter side to Greville in 'Scoggin his wife', but he remains essentially a grave and reflective writer. What follows is a selection of his less abstract work.

CHORUS SACERDOTUM

◄ From Mustapha ►

Oh, wearisome condition of humanity!
    Born under one law, to another bound;
Vainly begot, and yet forbidden vanity;
    Created sick, commanded to be sound.
        What meaneth Nature by these diverse laws?
        Passion and Reason self-division cause.

Is it the mark or majesty of power
    To make offences that it may forgive?
Nature herself doth her own self deflower
    To hate those errors she herself doth give.
        But how should man think what he may not
          do,
        If Nature did not fail, and punish too?

Tyrant to others, to herself unjust,
    Only commands things difficult and hard,
Forbids us all things which it knows we lust,
    Makes easy pains, unpossible reward.
        If Nature did not take delight in blood,
        She would have made more easy ways to good.

We that are bound by vows and by promotion,
    With pomp of holy sacrifice and rites,
To lead belief in good and still devotion,
    To preach of heaven's wonders and delights;
        Yet, when each of us in his own heart looks,
        He find the God there far unlike his books.

❧

CAELICA: XXII

I, with whose colours Myra dress'd her head,
I, that wore posies of her own hand-making,
I, that mine own name in the chimneys read
By Myra finely wrought ere I was waking:
    Must I look on, in hope time coming may
    With change bring back my turn again to play?

I, that on Sunday at the church-stile found
A garland sweet, with true-love knots in flowers,
Which I to wear about mine arm was bound
That each of us might know that all was ours:
    Must I now lead an idle life in wishes,
    And follow Cupid for his loaves and fishes?

I, that did wear the ring her mother left,
I, for whose love she gloried to be blamed,
I, with whose eyes her eyes committed theft,
I, who did make her blush when I was named;
    Must I lose ring, flowers, blush, theft and go
      naked,
    Watching with sighs, till dead love be awaked?

I, that when drowsie Argus fell asleep,
Like jealousy o'erwatched with desire,
Was even warned modesty to keep,
While her breath speaking kindled Nature's fire:
    Must I look on a-cold while others warm
      them?
    Do Vulcan's brothers in such fine nets arm
      them?

Was it for this that I might Myra see,
Washing the water with her beauties white?
Yet would she never write her love to me;
Thinks wit of change while thoughts are in delight?
    Mad girls must safely love, as they may leave,
    No man can print a kiss, lines may deceive.

❧

CAELICA: XL

The nurse-life wheat within his green husk growing
Flatters our hope and tickles our desire,
Nature's true riches in sweet beauties showing,
Which sets all hearts, with labour's love, on fire.

No less fair is the wheat, when golden ear
Shows unto hope the joys of near enjoying:
Fair and sweet is the bud, more sweet and fair
The rose, which proves that time is not destroying.

Caelica, your youth, the morning of delight,
Enamel'd o'er with beauties white and red,
All sense and thoughts did to belief invite
That love and glory there are brought to bed;
    And your ripe year's love noon, he goes no
      higher,
    Turns all the spirits of man into desire.

❧

CAELICA: L

Scoggin his wife by chance mistook her bed;
Such chances oft befall poor womankind,
Alas poor souls, for when they miss their head,
What marvel it is, though the rest be blind?

This bed it was a lord's bed where she light,
Who nobly pitying this poor woman's hap,
Gave alms both to relieve and to delight,
And made the golden shower fall on her lap.

Then in a freedom asks her as they lay,
Whose were her lips and breasts: and she sware, his:
For hearts are open when thoughts fall to play.
At last he asks her, whose her backside is?
    She vow'd that it was Scoggin's only part,
    Who never yet came nearer to her heart.

Scoggin o'erheard; but taught by common use
That he who sees all those which do him harm,
Or will in marriage boast such small abuse,
Shall never have his nightgown furred warm:
    And was content, since all was done in play,
    To know his luck and bear his arms away.

Yet when his wife should to the market go,
Her breast and belly he in canvas dress'd,
And on her backside fine silk did bestow;
Joying to see it braver than the rest.

His neighbours ask'd him, why? and Scoggin sware
That part of all his wife was only his:
The lord should deck the rest, to whom they are,
For he knew not what lordly fashion is.
    If husbands now should only deck their own,
    Silk would make many by their backs be
      known.

❧

CAELICA: LV

Cynthia, because your horns look diverse ways,
Now darken'd to the East, now to the West,
Then at full glory once in thirty days,
Sense doth believe that change is Nature's rest.

Poor earth, that dare presume to judge the sky;
Cynthia is ever round, and never varies,

Shadows and distance do abuse the eye,
And in abused sense truth oft miscarries:
    Yet who this language to the people speaks,
    Opinion's empire, sense's idol breaks.

CAELICA: LXXXVI

The earth, with thunder torn, with fire blasted,
With waters drowned, with windy palsy shaken
Cannot for this with heaven be distasted,
Since thunder, rain and winds from earth are taken:
Man torn with love, with inward furies blasted,
Drown'd with despair, with fleshly lustings shaken,
Cannot for this with heaven be distasted;
Love, fury, lustings out of man are taken.
Then man, endure thyself, those clouds will vanish;
Life is a top which whipping sorrow driveth;
Wisdom must bear what our flesh cannot banish,
The humble lead, the stubborn bootless striveth:
    Or man, forsake thyself, to heaven turn thee,
    Her flames enlighten nature, never burn thee.

CAELICA: C

In night, when colours all to black are cast,
Distinction lost or gone down with the light,
The eye a watch to inward senses plac'd,
Not seeing, yet still having power of sight,

Gives vain alarums to the inward sense,
Where fear stirr'd up with witty tyranny
Confounds all powers, and thorough self-offence,
Doth forge and raise impossibility:

Such as in thick depriving darknesses
Proper reflections of the error be,
And images of self-confusednesses,
Which hurt imaginations only see;
    And from this nothing seen, tells news of
        devils,
    Which but expressions be of inward evils.

Thomas Hardy (1840–1928) spent the greater part of his life in his native Dorset. He wrote poetry throughout, starting in the 1860s while he was a practising architect, though he did not publish any till 1898, three years after his career as a novelist had come to an end decisively with *Jude the Obscure*: an unusual pattern of work for a writer.

From then on he wrote prolifically till the last: about 1000 poems altogether. As Philip Larkin declared, 'One can read him for years and years and still be surprised.' He wrote also with increasing mastery. The sequence provoked by his wife's death in 1912 contains some of his most powerful poems: 'The Voice', 'At Castle Boterel'.

In the early days of his reputation as a poet many leading critics such as T. S. Eliot, rather surprisingly, and F. R. Leavis, predictably, seemed not to see the point of Hardy's poetic aims and techniques and led their followers into similar myopia The liveliest explanation of this has been that Hardy was not difficult enough; in an era when scholars felt the need to decode and interpret, his themes were accessible and interesting, and expressed in language which, even when eccentric, was perfectly clear.

The tide of Hardy criticism has long since turned. There will always be people who can make nothing of him but by now we have among us significant poets of more than one generation who have been influenced by him, some unconsciously, others in a kind of deliberate conversion as described so well by Larkin. W. H. Auden has spoken of him as his 'poetical father'. David Wright has called his work 'a beginning of the end of Victorian poetry'. Donald Davie has analysed at length the effect he has had on the whole course of twentieth-century poetry.

Thomas Hardy

Friends Beyond

William Dewy, Tranter Reuben, Farmer Ledlow late
    at plough,
    Robert's kin, and John's, and Ned's,
And the Squire, and Lady Susan, lie in Mellstock
    churchyard now!

'Gone,' I call them, gone for good, that group of
    local hearts and heads;
    Yet at mothy curfew-tide.
And at midnight when the noon-heat breathes it
    back from walls and leads,

They've a way of whispering to me – fellow-wight
    who yet abide –
    In the muted, measured note
Of a ripple under archways, or a lone cave's stillicide:

'We have triumphed: this achievement turns the
    bane to antidote,
    Unsuccesses to success,
Many thought-worn eves and morrows to a morrow
    free of thought.

'No more need we corn and clothing, feel of old
    terrestial stress;
    Chill detraction stirs no sigh;
Fear of death has even bygone us: death gave all that
    we possess.'

W.D. – 'Ye mid burn the old bass-viol that I set such
    value by.'
Squire. – 'You may hold the manse in fee,
    You may wed my spouse, may let my children's
    memory of me die.'

Lady S. – 'You may have my rich brocades, my laces;
    take each household key;
    Ransack coffer, desk, bureau;
    Quiz the few poor treasures hid there, con the
    letters kept by me.'

Far. – 'Ye mid zell mv favourite heifer, ye mid let
    the charlock grow,
    Foul the grinterns, give up thrift.'
Far. Wife. – 'If ye break my best blue china, children,
    I shan't care or ho.'

All. – 'We've no wish to hear the tidings, how the
    people's fortunes shift;

What your daily doings are;
    Who are wedded, born, divided; if your lives beat
    slow or swift.

'Curious not the least are we if our intents you
    make or mar,
    If you quire to our old tune
If the City stage still passes, if the weirs still roar
    afar.'

– Thus, with very gods' composure, freed those
    crosses late and soon
    Which, in life, the Trine allow
(Why, none witteth), and ignoring all that haps
    beneath the moon,

William Dewy, Tranter Reuben, Farmer Ledlow late
    at plough,
    Robert's kin, and John's, and Ned's,
And the Squire, and Lady Susan, murmur mildly to
    me now.

'I Look into my glass'

I look into my glass,
And view my wasting skin,
And say, 'Would God it came to pass
My heart had shrunk as thin!'

For then, I, undistrest
By hearts grown cold to me,
Could lonely wait my endless rest
With equanimity.

But Time, to make me grieve,
Part steals, lets part abide;
And shakes this fragile frame at eve
With throbbings of noontide.

Drummer Hodge

◄ I ►

They throw in Drummer Hodge, to rest
    Uncoffined – just as found:
    His landmark is a kopje-crest

That breaks the veldt around;
And foreign constellations west
    Each night above his mound.

◄ II ►

Young Hodge the Drummer never knew –
    Fresh from his Wessex home –
The meaning of the broad Karoo,
    The Bush, the dusty loam,
And why uprose to nightly view
    Strange stars amid the gloam.

◄ III ►

Yet portion of that unknown plain
    Will Hodge for ever be;
His homely Northern breast and brain
    Grow to some Southern tree,
And strange-eyed constellations reign
    His stars eternally.

TO AN UNBORN PAUPER CHILD

◄ I ►

Breathe not, hid Heart: cease silently,
And though thy birth-hour beckons thee,
    Sleep the long sleep:
    The Doomsters heap
Travails and teens around us here,
And Time-wraiths turn our songsingings to fear.

◄ II ►

Hark, how the peoples surge and sigh,
And laughters fail, and greetings die:
    Hopes dwindle; yea,
    Faiths waste away,
Affections and enthusiasms numb;
Thou canst not mend these things if thou dost
    come.

◄ III ►

Had I the ear of wombèd souls
Ere their terrestrial chart unrolls,
    And thou wert free
    To cease, or be,
Then would I tell thee all I know,
And put it to thee: Wilt thou take Life so?

◄ IV ►

Vain vow! No hint of mine may hence
To theeward fly: to thy locked sense
    Explain none can
    Life's pending plan:
Thou wilt thy ignorant entry make
Though skies spout fire and blood and nations quake.

◄ V ►

Fain would I, dear, find some shut plot
Of earth's wide wold for thee, where not
    One tear, one qualm,
    Should break the calm.
But I am weak as thou and bare;
No man can change the common lot to rare.

◄ VI ►

Must come and bide. And such are we –
Unreasoning, sanguine, visionary –
    That I can hope
    Health, love, friends, scope
In full for thee; can dream thou wilt find
Joys seldom yet attained by humankind!

THE DARKLING THRUSH

I leant upon a coppice gate
    When Frost was spectre-grey,
And Winter's dregs made desolate
    The weakening eye of day.
The tangled bine-stems scored the sky
    Like strings of broken lyres,
And all mankind that haunted nigh
    Had sought their household fires.

The land's sharp features seemed to be
    The Century's corpse outleant,
His crypt the cloudy canopy,
    The wind his death-lament.
The ancient pulse of germ and birth
    Was shrunken hard and dry,
And every spirit upon earth
    Seemed fervourless as I.

At once a voice arose among
    The bleak twigs overhead
In a full-hearted evensong
    Of joy illimited;

An aged thrush, frail, gaunt, and small,
   In blast-beruffled plume,
Had chosen thus to fling his soul
   Upon the growing gloom.

So little cause for carolings
   Of such ecstatic sound
Was written on terrestrial things
   Afar or nigh around,
That I could think there trembled through
   His happy good-night air
Some blessed Hope, whereof he knew
   And I was unaware.

THE SELF-UNSEEING

Here is the ancient floor,
Footworn and hollowed and thin,
Here was the former door
Where the dead feet walked in.

She sat here in her chair,
Smiling into the fire;
He who played stood there,
Bowing it higher and higher.

Childlike, I danced in a dream;
Blessings emblazoned that day;
Everything glowed with a gleam;
Yet we were looking away!

A CHURCH ROMANCE

She turned in the high pew, until her sight
Swept the west gallery, and caught its row
Of music-men with viol, book, and bow
Against the sinking sad tower-window light.

She turned again; and in her pride's despite
One strenuous viol's inspirer seemed to throw
A message from his string to her below,
Which said: 'I claim thee as my own forthright!'

Thus their hearts' bond began, in due time signed.
And long years thence, when Age had scared
   Romance.

At some old attitude of his or glance
That gallery-scene would break upon her mind,
With him as minstrel, ardent, young, and trim,
Bowing 'New Sabbath' or 'Mount Ephraim.'

CHANNEL FIRING

That night your great guns, unawares,
Shook all our coffins as we lay,
And broke the chancel window-squares,
We thought it was the Judgment-day

And sat upright. While drearisome
Arose the howl of wakened hounds:
The mouse let fall the altar-crumb,
The worms drew back into the mounds,

The glebe cow drooled. Till God called, 'No;
It's gunnery practice out at sea
Just as before you went below;
The world is as it used to be:

'All nations striving strong to make
Red war yet redder. Mad as hatters
They do no more for Christés sake
Than you who are helpless in such matters.

'That this is not the judgment-hour
For some of them's a blessed thing,
For if it were they'd have to scour
Hell's floor for so much threatening. . . .

'Ha ha. It will be warmer when
I blow the trumpet (if indeed
I ever do; for you are men,
And rest eternal sorely need).'

So down we lay again. 'I wonder,
Will the world ever saner be,'
Said one, 'than when He sent us under
In our indifferent century!'

And many a skeleton shook his head.
'Instead of preaching forty year,'
My neighbour Parson Thirdly said,
'I wish I had stuck to pipes and beer.'

Again the guns disturbed the hour,
Roaring their readiness to avenge,
As far inland as Stourton Tower,
And Camelot, and starlit Stonehenge.
April 1914.

❧

The Voice

Woman much missed, how you call to me, call to
    me,
Saying that now you are not as you were
When you had changed from the one who was all to
    me,
But as at first, when our day was fair.

Can it be you that I hear? Let me view you, then,
Standing as when I drew near to the town
Where you would wait for me: yes, as I knew you
    then,
Even to the original air-blue gown!

Or is it only the breeze, in its listlessness
Travelling across the wet mead to me here,
You being ever dissolved to wan wistlessness,
Heard no more again far or near?

    Thus I; faltering forward,
    Leaves around me falling,
Wind oozing thin through the thorn from norward,
    And the woman calling.

❧

At Castle Boterel

As I drive to the junction of lane and highway,
    And the drizzle bedrenches the waggonette,
I look behind at the fading byway,
    And see on its slope, now glistening wet,
        Distinctly yet

Myself and a girlish form benighted
    In dry March weather. We climb the road
Beside a chaise. We had just alighted
    To ease the sturdy pony's load
        When he sighed and slowed.

What we did as we climbed, and what we talked of
    Matters not much, nor to what it led, –
Something that life will not be balked of
    Without rude reason till hope is dead,
        And feeling fled.

It filled but a minute. But was there ever
    A time of such quality, since or before,
In that hill's story? To one mind never,
    Though it has been climbed, foot-swift, foot-sore,
        By thousands more.

Primaeval rocks form the road's steep border,
    And much have they faced there, first and last.
Of the transitory in Earth's long order;
    But what they record in colour and cast
        Is – that we two passed.

And to me, though Time's unflinching rigour,
    In mindless rote, has ruled from sight
The substance now, one phantom figure
    Remains on the slope, as when that night
        Saw us alight.

I look and see it there, shrinking, shrinking,
    I look back at it amid the rain
For the very last time; for my sand is sinking,
    And I shall traverse old love's domain
        Never again.

❧

The Convergence of the Twain
(Lines on the loss of the 'Titanic')

        ◄ I ►
    In a solitude of the sea
    Deep from human vanity,
And the Pride of Life that planned her, stilly
        couches she.

        ◄ II ►
    Steel chambers, late the pyres
    Of her salamandrine fires,
Cold currents thrid, and turn to rhythmic tidal
        lyres.

        ◄ III ►
    Over the mirrors meant
    To glass the opulent

The sea-worm crawls – grotesque, slimed, dumb,
    indifferent.

    ◄ IV ►
Jewels in joy designed
  To ravish the sensuous mind
Lie lightless, all their sparkles bleared and black and
    blind.

    ◄ V ►
Dim moon-eyed fishes near
  Gaze at the gilded gear
And query: 'What does this vaingloriousness down
    here?' . . .

    ◄ VI ►
Well: while was fashioning
  This creature of cleaving wing,
The Immanent Will that stirs and urges everything

    ◄ VII ►
Prepared a sinister mate
  For her – so gaily great –
A Shape of Ice, for the time far and dissociate.

    ◄ VIII ►
And as the smart ship grew
  In stature, grace, and hue,
In shadowy silent distance grew the Iceberg too.

    ◄ IX ►
Alien they seemed to be:
  No mortal eye could see
The intimate welding of their later history.

    ◄ X ►
Or sign that they were bent
  By paths coincident
On being anon twin halves of one august event,

    ◄ XI ►
Till the Spinner of the Years
  Said 'Now!' And each one hears,
And consummation comes, and jars two
    hemispheres.

THE OXEN

Christmas Eve, and twelve of the clock.
  'Now they are all on their knees,'
An elder said as we sat in a flock
  By the embers in hearthside ease.

We pictured the meek mild creatures where
  They dwelt in their strawy pen,
Nor did it occur to one of us there
  To doubt they were kneeling then.

So fair a fancy few would weave
  In these years! Yet, I feel,
If somone said on Christmas Eve,
  'Come; see the oxen kneel

'In the lonely barton by yonder coomb
  Our childhood used to know,'
I should go with him in the gloom,
  Hoping it might be so.

LAST WORDS TO A DUMB FRIEND

Pet was never mourned as you,
Purrer of the spotless hue,
Plumy tail, and wistful gaze
While you humoured our queer ways,
Or outshrilled your morning call
Up the stairs and through the hall –
Foot suspended in its fall –
While, expectant, you would stand
Arched, to meet the stroking hand;
Till your way you chose to wend
Yonder, to your tragic end.

Never another pet for me!
Let your place all vacant be;
Better blankness day by day
Than companion torn away.
Better bid his memory fade,
Better blot each mark he made,
Selfishly escape distress
By contrived forgetfulness,
Than preserve his prints to make
Every morn and eve an ache.

From the chair whereon he sat
Sweep his fur, nor wince thereat;
Rake his little pathways out
Mid the bushes roundabout;
Smooth away his talons' mark
From the claw-worn pine-tree bark,
Where he climbed as dusk embrowned,
Waiting us who loitered round.

Strange it is this speechless thing,
Subject to our mastering,
Subject for his life and food
To our gift, and time, and mood;
Timid pensioner of us Powers,
His existence ruled by ours,
Should – by crossing at a breath
Into safe and shielded death,
By the merely taking hence
Of his insignificance –
Loom as largened to the sense,
Shape as part, above man's will,
Of the Imperturbable.

As a prisoner, flight debarred,
Exercising in a yard,
Still retain I, troubled, shaken,
Mean estate, by him forsaken;
And this home, which scarcely took
Impress from his little look,
By his faring to the Dim
Grows all eloquent of him.

Housemate, I can think you still
Bounding to the window-sill,
Over which I vaguely see
Your small mound beneath the tree,
Showing in the autumn shade
That you moulder where you played.

THE FROZEN GREENHOUSE

'There was a frost
Last night!' she said,
'And the stove was forgot
When we went to bed,
And the greenhouse plants
Are frozen dead!'

By the breakfast blaze
Blank-faced spoke she,
Her scared young look
Seeming to be
The very symbol
Of tragedy.

The frost is fiercer
Than then to-day,
As I pass the place
Of her once dismay,
But the greenhouse stands
Warm, tight, and gay,

While she who grieved
At the sad lot
Of her pretty plants –
Cold, iced, forgot –
Herself is colder,
And knows it not.

THE LAST SIGNAL
(Oct. 11, 1886)

‹A Memory of William Barnes›

Silently I footed by an uphill road
    That led from my abode to a spot yew-boughed
Yellowly the sun sloped low down to westward,
        And dark was the east with cloud.

Then, amid the shadow of that livid sad east,
    Where the light was least, and a gate stood wide,
Something flashed the fire of the sun that was facing it,
        Like a brief blaze on that side.

Looking hard and harder I knew what it meant –
    The sudden shine sent from the livid east scene;
It meant the west mirrored by the coffin of my friend
            there,
        Turning to the road from his green,

To take his last journey forth – he who in his prime
    Trudged so many a time from that gate athwart the
            land!
Thus a farewell to me he signalled on his grave-way,
        As with a wave of his hand.

AFTERWARDS

When the Present has latched its postern behind my
    tremulous stay,
  And the May month flaps its glad green leaves like
    wings,
Delicate-filmed as new-spun silk, will the neighbours
    say,
  'He was a man who used to notice such things'?

If it be in the dusk when, like an eyelid's soundless
    blink,
  The dewfall-hawk comes crossing the shades to
    alight
Upon the wind-warped upland thorn, a gazer may
    think,
  'To him this must have been a familiar sight.'

If I pass during some nocturnal blackness, mothy and
    warm,
  When the hedgehog travels furtively over the lawn,
One may say, 'He strove that such innocent creatures
    should come to no harm,
  But he could do little for them; and now he is gone.'

If, when hearing that I have been stilled at last, they
    stand at the door,
  Watching the full-starred heavens that winter sees,
Will this thought rise on those who will meet my face
    no more,
  'He was one who had an eye for such mysteries'?

And will any say when my bell of quittance is heard in
    the gloom,
  And a crossing breeze cuts a pause in its outrollings,
Till they rise again, as they were a new bell's boom,
  'He hears it not now, but used to notice such
    things'?

The *Testament of Cresseid*, conceived by Robert Henryson (?1424–?1506) as a sequel to Chaucer's long novelistic *Troylus and Cryseyde*, is undoubtedly one of the great poems of the age. From its beginnings in cold severe weather it maintains a wonderfully grave tone and an easy remorseless narrative. Cresseid offends Venus and Cupid by blaming them for Diomede's desertion of her and this calls down the wrath of the gods, especially Saturn. The judgment is pronounced that she be a beggar and leper.

I have selected the end of the poem, which shows Cresseid as leper meeting Troilus and that extraordinary moment when Troilus half thinks he knows her and throws money to her. This is one of the great moments in all poetry, And it well illustrates the medieval idea of Fortune as a wheel which turns from prosperity to adversity (and of course in the other direction as well).

In the closing section Cresseid blames herself and not the gods for her fate. Thus she learns insight into her own condition. The poem raises many issues, for instance women as sexual objects and victims (their stories written by male writers). Henryson, I think, shows pity for Cresseid but at the same time imposes a terrible sentence on her, totally destroying her beauty; Chaucer was a different kind of poet.

I chose two other poems to show Henryson's variety, first of all the fable of the two mice and secondly 'The Garment of Good Ladies'. The extract from 'The Two Mice' describes the dangers undergone in the town by the two mice in search of luxurious food, after the town mouse's denigration of her country cousin's more niggardly but safer existence. The poem has fine convincing detail and a wonderfully sustained tone. 'The Garment of Good Ladies' has a nice lyrical movement and though composed of moral sentiments, has a lovely music.

Robert Henryson

The Testament of Cresseid
(lines 470–616)

Thus chydand with hir drerie destenye,
Weiping, scho woik the nicht fra end to end;
Bot all in vane; hir dule, hir cairfull cry
Micht not remeid nor yit hir murning mend.
Ane lipper lady rais and till hir wend
And said, 'Quhy spurnis thou aganis the wall,
To sla thyself and mend nathing at all?'

Sen thy weiping doubillis bot thy wo,
I counsall the mak vertew of ane neid
To leir to clap thy clapper to and fro
And leif efter the law of lipper leid.
Thair was na buit bot furth with thame scho yeid
Fra place to place, quhill cauld and hounger sair
Compellit hir to be ane rank beggair.

That samin tyme of Troy the garnisoun,
Quhilk had to chiftane worthie Troylus,
Throw jeopardie of weir had strikken doun
Knichtis of Grece in number mervellous,
With greit tryumphe and laude victorious
Agane to Troy richt royallie they raid
The way quhair Cresseid with the lipper baid.

Seing that companie thai come, all with ane stevin;
Thay gaif ane cry, and shuik coppis gude speid:
Said: 'Worthie lordis, for goddis lufe of hevin,
To us lipper part of your almous deid.'
Than to thair cry nobill Troylus tuik heid,
Having pietie, neir by the place can pas
Quhair Cresseid sat, not witting quhat scho was.

Than upon him scho kest up baith hir ene,
And with ane blenk it come into his thocht,
That he sumtime hir face befoir had sene.
Bot scho was in sic plye he knew hir nocht,
Yit than hir luik into his mynd it brocht
The sweit visage and amorous blenking
Of fair Cresseid sumtyme his awin darling.

Na wonder was, suppois in mind that he
Tuik her figure sa sone, and lo, now quhy?
The idole of ane thing in cace may be
So deip imprentit in the fantasy
That it deludis the wittis outwardly,
And sa appeiris in forme and lyke estait,
Within the mynd as it was figurait.

Ane spark of lufe than till his hart culd spring,
And kendlit all his bodie in ane fyre.
With hait fevir ane sweit and trimbling
Him tuik, quhill he was reddie to expyre.
To beir his scheild his breist began to tyre.
Within ane quhyle he changit mony hew,
And nevertheles not ane ane uther knew.

For knichtlie pietie and memoriall
Of fair Cresseid, ane gyrdill can he tak,
Ane purs of gold, and mony gay jowall,
And in the skirt of Cresseid doun can swak:
Than raid away, and not ane word he spak,
Pensive in hart, quhill he come to the toun,
And for greit cair oft syis almaist fell doun.

The lipper folk to Cresseid than can draw,
To se the equall distributioun
Of the almous, bot quhen the gold thay saw,
Ilk ane to uther prevelie can roun,
And said: 'Yone lord hes mair affectioun,
How ever it be, unto yone Lazarous,
Than to us all, we knaw be his almous.

'Quhat lord is yone,' quod scho, 'have ye na feill
Hes done to us so greit humanitie?'
'Yes,' quod a lipper man, 'I knaw him weill.
Schir Troylus it is, gentill and fre.'
Quhen Cresseid understude that it was he,
Stiffer than steill their stert ane bitter stound
Throwout hir hart, and fell doun to the ground.

Quhen scho ovircome, with siching sair and sad.
With mony cairfull cry and cald ochane:
'Now is my breist with stormie stoundis stad,
Wrappit in wo, ane wretch full will of wane.'
Than swounit scho oft or scho culd refrane,
And ever in hir swouning cryit scho thus:
'O fals Cresseid and trew knicht Troylus!

Thy lufe, thy lawtie, and thy gentilnes,
I countit small in my prosperitie,
Sa elevait I was in wantones,
And clam upon the fickill quheill sa hie.
All faith and lufe I promissit to the,
Was in the self fickill and frivolous:
O fals Cresseid, and trew knicht Troylus!

For lufe of me thow keipt gude continence,
Honest and chaist in conversatioun.
Of all wemen protectour and defence

Thou was, and helpit thair opinioun.
My mynd in fleschelie foull affectioun
Was inclynit to lustis lecherous:
Fy, fals Cresseid, O trew knicht Troylus!

Lovers be war and tak gude heid about
Quhome that ye lufe, for quhome ye suffer paine.
I lat yow wit, thair is richt few thairout
Quhome ye may traist to have trew lufe agane:
Preif quhen ye will, your labour is in vaine.
Thairfoir, I reid, ye tak thame as ye find:
For they ar sad as widdercok in wind.

Becaus I knew the greit unstabilnes
Brukill as glas, into my self I say,
Traisting in uther als greit unfaithfulnes:
Als unconstant, and als untrew of fey.
Thocht sum be trew, I wait richt few ar thay.
Quha findis treuth let him his lady ruse:
Nane but my self as now I will accuse.'

Quhen this was said, with paper scho sat doun,
And on this maneir maid hir testament:
'Heir I beteiche my corps and carioun
With wormis and with taidis to be rent.
My cop and clapper and myne ornament,
And all my gold the lipper folk sall have
Quhen I am deid, to burie me in grave.

This royall ring, set with this ruby reid,
Quhilk Troylus in drowrie to me send,
To him agane I leif it quhen I am deid,
To mak my cairfull deid unto him kend:
Thus I conclude schortlie and mak ane end,
My spreit I leif to Diane quhair scho dwellis
To walk with hir in waist woddis and wellis.

O Diomeid, thou hes baith broche and belt,
Quhilk Troylus gave me in takning
Of his trew lufe'; and with that word scho swelt.
And sone ane lipper man tuik of the ring,
Syne buryit hir withouttin tarrying,
To Troylus furthwith the ring he bair,
And of Cresseid the deith he can declair.

Quhen he had hard hir greit infirmitie,
Hir legacie and lamentatioun,
And how scho endit in sic povertie,
He swelt for wo, and fell doun in ane swoun,
For greit sorrow his hart to brist was boun:

Siching full sadlie, said, 'I can no moir,
Scho was untrew, and wo is me thairfoir.'

Sum said he maid ane tomb of merbell gray,
And wrait hir name and superscriptioun,
And laid it on hir grave quhair that scho lay,
In goldin letteris, containing this ressoun:
'Lo, fair ladyis, Cresseid, of Troyis toun,
Sumtyme countit the flour of womanheid,
Under this stane, lait lipper, lyis deid.'

Now worthie wemen in this ballet schort,
Maid for your worschip and instructioun,
Of cheritie, I monische and exhort,
Ming not your lufe with fals deceptioun.
Beir in your mynd this schort conclusioun
Of fair Cresseid, as I have said befoir,
Sen scho is deid, I speik of hir no moir.

Glossary

WOIK: kept awake; NEID: necessity; LEIR: learn; LEIF: live; LEID: folk; BUIT: help; YEID: went; JEOPARDIE OF WEIR: fortune of war; RAID: rode; LIPPER: leprous; STEVIN: voice; GUDE SPEID: vigorously; PART OF YOUR ALMOUS DEID: give of your charity; PIETIE: pity; KEST: cast; BLENK: glance; PLYE: plight; IDOLE: mental image or impression; SWAK: toss; SYIS: times; ROUN: whisper; FEILL: notion; STERT: started; STOUND: throb; OVIRCOME: came to; OCHANE: alas; STAD: beset; WILL OF WANE: lost of hope; REFRANE: restrain herself; LAWTIE: loyalty; CLAM: climbed; OPINIOUN: reputation; PREIFE: make proof; REID: counsel; SAD: steadfast; BRUKILL: brittle; TRAISTING: expecting; RUSE: praise; BETEICHE: commit; TAIDIS: toads; DROWRIE: love-token; CAIRFUL DEID: miserable death; DIANE: goddess of chastity; TAKNING: token; SWELT: passed away; BOUN TO BRIST: ready to burst; RESSOUN: declaration; BALLET: simple poem; WORSCHIP: honour, credit; MING: mingle

THE TWO MICE
(lines 22–203)

In stowthry ay throw rankest gerss and corne
Under covert full prevely couth crepe,
The oldest mouss was gyde and yeid beforne,
The younger till hir wayis tuk gud kepe.
On nycht thai ran and on the day thai slepe;
Till in the morning or the laverock sang
Thai fande the toune and in gladly can gang.

Nocht fer fra this unto a worthy wane
The burgess brocht thaim syne quhar thai suld be;
Intill ane innes thair herbery was tane,
Intill a spence with vittale gret plente;

Cheiss and butter upon skelfis hie,
Flesche and fische eneuch, baith fresche and salt,
And sekis full of grotis meile and malt.

Eftir quhen thai disposit war to dyne,
Withoutin grace thai wesche and went to meit,
All kynd of courssis that cukis couth devyne,
Mutoune and beif strikin in talyeis grete;
A lordis fair thus can thai counterfeit,
Except a thing, thai drank the wattir cleire
Insteid of wyne, bot yit thai maid gud chere.

With blyth upcast and mery countenance
The eldest sister sperit at hir gest
Gif that scho thocht be ressoun differens
Betwix hir charmer and hir sary nest.
'Ye, dame,' quod scho, 'How lang now will this lest?
'Evirmore, I wait, and langer too.'
'Gif it sa be, ye ar at eiss,' quod scho.

Till eik their cheir ane subcharge furth scho brocht,
Ane plait of grotis, and ane dische full of meill;
Thraf caikis als I trow scho spairit nocht,
Aboundantlie about hir for to deill;
And mane full fyne scho brocht insteid of geill,
And ane quhyte candill out of ane coffer stall
Insteid of spyce to gust their mouth withall.

Thus maid thai mery quhill thai micht na mare
And, 'Haile, Yule, haile!' thai cryit upon hie.
Eftir joye ofttymes cummis caire
And truble eftir gret prosperitie.
Thus as thai sat in all their jolyte,
So come the spensar with keyis intill hand
Opinnit the dure and thaim at dynere fand.

Thai taryit nocht to wesche, as I supposs,
Bot unto go quha micht formast wyn.
The burgess had a hole and in scho gois;
Hir sister had no hole to hyde hir in:
To se this sely mouss it was gret syne;
So desolate and will of a gud reid;
For verray dreid scho fell in swoun nere deid.

Bot as God wald it fell a happy cass;
The spensar had na laser for to byd,
To serss, to seike, to char nor yit to chase,
Bot on he went and left the dure up wyde.
This bald burgess his passage wele has spyid;
Out of hir hoile scho come and cryit on hie,
'How, fair sister! cry pepe quharever ye be.'

This rurale mouss lay flatlingis on the ground
And for the deid full sore scho was dredand,
For till hir hart straike mony wilsome stound,
As in a fever trymblit fut and hand;
Quhen scho hir sister into sic plyte fand
For verray pete scho began to grete,
Syne comfort hir with wordis hony sweit.

'Quhy ly ye se? Rys up my sister deire;
Cum to your meit, this perrell is ourpast.'
The tother answerd with a hevy cheire,
'I may nocht eit, I am so sair agast;
I had lever thir fourtie dayis haf fast
With watter caile and gnawe benes and peiss
Than all this fest in this dreid and diseiss.'

With fair trety yit scho gart hir rys
And unto burd togiddir baith thai sat;
Scantlie had thai drunkin anys or twys,
Quhen in come Gib Hunter, our joly cat,
And bad God speid: the burgess up with that;
In at hir hole scho fled as fyre of flint;
Balderonis the tother be the bak has hynt.

Fra fut to fut scho kest hir to and fra
Quhile up, quhile doune, als tait as ony kid;
Quhilis wald scho let hir ryn under the stra,
Quhilis wald scho wynke and play with hir bukhed
Thus to the sely mouss gret pane scho did,
Till at the last, throw fair fortoune and hap.
Betwene the dosore and the wall scho crap.

Syne up in haist behynd the parrelling
So hie scho clame that Gilbert micht nocht get hir
And be the clukis richt craftely can hyng;
Till he was gone, hir cher was all the better.
Syne doune scho come quhen their was nane to let
    hir,
Upon the burgess mouss loude couth scho cry,
'Fair wele, sister, thi fest heir I defy!

'Thy mangery is mengit all with caire,
Thy gus is gud, thi ganesall soure as gall;
The suchardis of thi service is bot saire,
Sa sall thou fynd hereefterwart may fall.
I thank yone courting and yone parpell wall
Of my defence now fra yone cruell best.
Allmychty God, kepe me fra sic ane fest!

'War I anys in the kith that I come fra,
For weile and wa I suld never cum agane.'

With that scho tuke hir leif and furth can ga
Quhylis throw the corne and quhilis throw the plane:
Quhen scho was furth and fre, scho was full fane,
And merely scho merkit unto the mure.
I can nocht tell how eftirwart scho fure.

Bot I herd saye scho passit till hir den
Als warme in woll, suppose it was nocht grete,
Als benely stuffit baith but and ben
Of nutis, pess, benes, ry and quheit;
Quhenever scho list scho had eneuch till eit
In quyet and eiss withoutin dreid:
Bot till hir sisteris fest no mor scho yeid.

Glossary

STOWTHRY: stealth; KEPE: heed; FER: far; SYNE: thereupon; SPENCE: parlour; SKELFIS: shelves; SEKIS: sacks; STRIKIN IN TAILYEIS: cut in slices; FAIR: fare; UPCAST: banter; BE RESOUN: for good reason; SARY: sorry; WAIT: fancy; EISS: ease; SUBCHARGE: second course; THRAF: unleavened; MANE: fine bread; GEILL: jelly; STALL: stole; GUST: taste; SPENSAR: steward; WESCHE: wash; FORMAST WYN: get first; GRET SYN: great pity; WILL OF A GUD REID: at her wits' end; CASS: chance; LASER: leisure; SERSS: search; CHAR: turn aside; UP: open; THE DEID: death; STRAIK: struck; WILSOME STOUND: wild throb; LEVER: rather; WATTER CAILE: broth without meat stock; DISEISS: discomfort; TRETY: entreaty; UNTO BURD: at table; BALDERONIS: Pussy; HYNT: seized; KEST: cast; TAIT: merrily; BUKHED: hide and seek; DOSORE: curtain; PARRELLING: partition; CLAME: climbed; CLUKIS: claws; LET: stop; DEFY: renounce; SUCHARDIS: aftercourse; COURTING: curtain; PARPELL: partition; WA: woe; LEIF: leave; FURTH: in the open; FANE: glad; MERKIT UNTO: made for; FURE: fared; WOLL: wool; BENELY: comfortably

THE GARMONT OF GUDE LADEIS

Waid my gud lady lufe me best
And wirk eftir my will,
I suld ane garmond gudliest
Gar mak hir body till.

Of hie honour suld be hir hud
Upon hir heid to weir,
Garneist with governance so gud,
Na demying suld her deir.

Hir sark suld be hir body nixt,
Of chestetie so quhyt,
With schame and dreid togidder mixt,
The same suld be perfyt.

Hir kirtill suld be of clene constance,
Lasit with lesum lufe,

The mailyeis of continuance
For nevir to remufe.

Hir gown suld be of gudliness,
Weill ribband with renowne,
Purfillit with plesour in ilk place,
Furrit with fyne fassoun.

Hir belt suld be of benignitie
About hir middill meit;
Hir mantill of humilitie
To tholl bayth wind and weit.

Hir hat suld be of fair having
And hir tepat of trewth,
Hir patelet of gud pansing,
Hir hals ribbane of rewth.

Hir slevis suld be of esperance
To keip hir fra dispair,
Hir gluvis of gud govirnance
To gyd hir fyngearis fair.

Hir schone suld be of sickernes,
In syne that scho nocht slyd,
Hir hois of honestie, I gess,
I suld for hir provyd.

Wald scho put on this garmond gay,
I durst sweir by my seill,
That scho woir nevir grene nor gray
That set hir half so weill.

Glossary

GARNEIST: ornamented; DEMYNG: (harsh) opinion; DEIR: harm; DREID: timidity; LESUM: lawful; MAILYEIS: eyelets; CONTINUANCE: steadfastness; PURFILLIT: embroidered; FASSOUN: fashion; THOLL: endure; HAVING: deportment; TEPAT: tippet; PATALET: ruff; PANSING: thoughts; HALS: neck; REWTH: pity; SICKERNESS: sureness; SEILL: seal, bond

Addison pilloried George Herbert (1593–1633) as a 'false wit'. He suffered from the advocacy of early champions who sold the poet on the strength of his piety rather than his poetry. When his kind of piety became unfashionable, the poetry fell from favour until it was dusted down by Coleridge and revised by the Wesleys.

Herbert is the most figurative of poets. If in a poem an ornament glosses meaning and a conceit displaces it, a figure contains, develops and extends it. Herbert's figures, which at first may seem conventional, not only carry argument: often they *are* the argument, the inherent logic of the figure (from swaddling to winding sheet in 'Mortification', from 'host' to 'Host' in 'Love Bade Me Welcome') conveys a multiplicity of senses and yet is proof against paraphrase. What one critic calls the 'immanence' of Herbert's poems consists precisely in this: his ideas are bodied forth; they exist in and for a common world; they are enacted and therefore enabling.

The diction is generally simple. What is complex (because the thoughts and feelings are) is the syntax, and the ways in which it plays against extremely demanding verse forms, many of them of Herbert's own invention. Charles Cotton said Herbert had 'a soul composed of harmonies'. The figures are at times far-fetched but they are almost always made appropriate in the poem. The forms, too, are appropriate to the theme, invented as it were to embody them. ('Mortification' enacts in its contractions and expansions, from dimeter to pentameter, a rhythmic and visual process of mortification.)

When his secular ambitions were thwarted, Herbert turned to his pastoral vocation, taking to Bemerton, near Salisbury, the 'poor abilities' in poetry which he had consecrated at the age of sixteen to 'God's glory'. He wrote poems that strengthened Charles I in his final prison, that touched William Cowper as he trembled on the threshold of his early depression. A dependence on scripture, which he shared with the unlettered as with the learned, takes the brittleness from his erudition. His poems address a common source of wisdom in a common language. In a secular age they still – perhaps more than ever – touch the attentive reader on the quick.

Harken unto a Verser, who may chance
  Rhyme thee to good, and make a bait
    of pleasure.

THE AGONY

Philosophers have measured mountains,
Fathomed the depths of seas, of states, and kings,
Walked with a staff to heav'n, and traced fountains:
    But there are two vast, spacious things,
The which to measure it doth more behove:
Yet few there are that sound them; Sin and Love.

Who would know Sin, let him repair
Unto Mount Olivet; there shall he see
A man so wrung with pains, that all his hair,
    His skin, his garments bloody be.
Sin is that press and vice, which forceth pain
To hunt his cruel food through ev'ry vein.

Who knows not Love, let him assay
And taste that juice, which on the cross a pike
Did set again abroach; then let him say
    If ever he did taste the like.
Love is that liquor sweet and most divine,
Which my God feels as blood; but I, as wine.

❧

REDEMPTION

Having been tenant long to a rich Lord,
  Not thriving, I resolved to be bold,
  And make a suit unto him, to afford
A new small-rented lease, and cancel th' old.
In heaven at his manor I him sought:
  They told me there, that he was lately gone
  About some land, which he had dearly bought
Long since on earth, to take possession.
I straight returned, and knowing his great birth,
  Sought him accordingly in great resorts;
  In cities, theatres, gardens, parks, and courts:
At length I heard a ragged noise and mirth
  Of thieves and murderers: there I him espied,
  Who straight, *Your suit is granted*, said, and died.

❧

AFFLICTION (1)

When first thou didst entice to thee my heart,
　　I thought the service brave:
So many joys I writ down for my part,
　　Besides what I might have
Out of my stock of natural delights,
Augmented with thy gracious benefits.

I looked on thy furniture so fine,
　　And made it fine to me:
Thy glorious household-stuff did me entwine,
　　And 'tice me unto thee.
Such stars I counted mine: both heav'n and earth
Paid me my wages in a world of mirth.

What pleasures could I want, whose King I served?
　　Where joys my fellows were.
Thus argued into hopes, my thoughts reserved
　　No place for grief or fear.
Therefore my sudden soul caught at the place,
And made her youth and fierceness seek thy face,

At first thou gav'st me milk and sweetnesses;
　　I had my wish and way:
My days were strawed with flow'rs and happiness;
　　There was no month but May.
But with my years sorrow did twist and grow,
And made a party unawares for woe.

My flesh began unto my soul in pain,
　　Sicknesses cleave my bones;
Consuming agues dwell in ev'ry vein,
　　And tune my breath to groans.
Sorrow was all my soul; I scarce believed,
Till grief did tell me roundly, that I lived.

When I got health, thou took'st away my life,
　　And more; for my friends die:
My mirth and edge was lost; a blunted knife
　　Was of more use than I.
Thus thin and lean without a fence or friend,
I was blown through with ev'ry storm and wind.

Whereas my birth and spirit rather took
　　The way that takes the town;
Thou didst betray me to a ling'ring book,
　　And wrap me in a gown.
I was entangled in the world of strife,
Before I had the power to change my life.

Yet, for I threat'ned oft the siege to raise,
　　Not simp'ring all mine age,
Thou often didst with academic praise
　　Melt and dissolve my rage.
I took thy sweet'ned pill, till I came where
I could not go away, nor persevere.

Yet lest perchance I should too happy be
　　In my unhappiness,
Turning my purge to food, thou throwest me
　　Into more sickness.
Thus doth thy power cross-bias me, not making
Thine own gift good, yet me from my ways taking.

Now I am here, what thou wilt do with me
　　None of my books will show:
I read, and sigh, and wish I were a tree;
　　For sure then I should grow
To fruit or shade: at least some bird would trust
Her household to me, and I should be just.

Yet, though thou troublest me, I must be meek;
　　In weakness must be stout.
Well, I will change the service, and go seek
　　Some other master out.
Ah my dear God! though I am clean forgot,
Let me not love thee, if I love thee not.

❧

PRAYER (1)

Prayer the Church's banquet, Angels' age,
　　God's breath in man returning to his birth,
　　The soul in paraphrase, heart in pilgrimage,
The Christian plummet sounding heav'n and earth;
Engine against th' Almighty, sinners' tower,
　　Reversed thunder, Christ-side-piercing spear,
　　The six-days world-transposing in an hour,
A kind of tune, which all things hear and fear;
Softness, and peace, and joy, and love, and bliss,
　　Exalted Manna, gladness of the best;
　　Heaven in ordinary, man well dressed,
The milky way, the bird of Paradise,
　　Church-bells beyond the stars heard, the soul's
　　　　blood,
　　The land of spices; something understood.

❧

JORDAN (1)

Who says that fictions only and false hair
Become a verse? Is there in truth no beauty;
Is all good structure in a winding stair?
May no lines pass, except they do their duty,
    Not to a true, but painted chair?

Is it no verse, except enchanted groves
And sudden arbours shadow coarse-spun lines?
Must purling streams refresh a lover's loves?
Must all be veiled, while he that reads, divines,
    Catching the sense at two removes?

Shepherds are honest people; let them sing:
Riddle who list, for me, and pull for Prime:
I envy no man's nightingale or spring;
Nor let them punish me with loss of rhyme,
    Who plainly say, *My God, My King.*

❧

MATINS

    I cannot ope mine eyes,
  But thou art ready there to catch
  My morning-soul and sacrifice:
Then we must needs for that day make a match.

    My God, what is a heart?
  Silver, or gold, or precious stone,
  Or star, or rainbow, or a part
Of all these things, or all of them in one?

    My God, what is a heart,
  That thou shouldst it so eye, and woo,
  Pouring upon it all thy art,
As if that thou hadst nothing else to do?

    Indeed man's whole estate
  Amounts (and richly) to serve thee:
  He did not heav'n and earth create,
Yet studies them, not him by whom they be.

    Teach me thy love to know;
  That this new light, which now I see,
  May both the work and workman show:
Then by a sunbeam I will climb to thee.

❧

CHURCH-MONUMENTS

While that my soul repairs to her devotion,
Here I intomb my flesh, that it betimes
May take acquaintance of this heap of dust;
To which the blast of death's incessant motion,
Fed with the exhalation of our crimes,
Drives all at last. Therefore I gladly trust

My body to this school, that it may learn
To spell his elements, and find his birth
Written in dusty heraldry and lines:
Which dissolution sure doth best discern,
Comparing dust with dust, and earth with earth.
These laugh at Jet and Marble put for signs,

To sever the good fellowship of dust,
And spoil the meeting. What shall point out them,
When they shall bow, and kneel, and fall down flat
To kiss those heaps, which now they have in trust?
Dear flesh, while I do pray, learn here thy stem
And true descent; that when thou shalt grow fat,

And wanton in thy cravings, thou mayst know,
That flesh is but the glass, which holds the dust
That measures all our time; which also shall
Be crumbled into dust. Mark here below
How tame these ashes are, how free from lust,
That thou mayst fit thyself against thy fall.

❧

SIGHS AND GROANS

      O do not use me
After my sins! look not on my desert,
But on thy glory! then thou wilt reform
And not refuse me: for thou only art
The mighty God, but I a silly worm;
      O do not bruise me!

      O do not urge me!
For what account can thy ill steward make?
I have abused thy stock, destroyed thy woods,
Sucked all thy magazines: my head did ache,
Till it found out how to consume thy goods:
      O do not scourge me!

      O do not blind me!
I have deserved that an Egyptian night

Should thicken all my powers; because my lust
Hath still sewed fig-leaves to exclude thy light:
But I am frailty, and already dust;
         O do not grind me!

         O do not fill me
With the turned vial of thy bitter wrath!
For thou hast other vessels full of blood,
A part whereof my Saviour emptied hath,
Ev'n unto death: since he died for my good,
         O do not kill me!

         But O reprieve me!
For thou hast *life* and *death* at thy command;
Thou art both *Judge* and *Saviour, feast* and *rod,*
Cordial and *Corrosive:* put not thy hand
Into the bitter box; but O my God,
         My God, relieve me!

VIRTUE

Sweet day, so cool, so calm, so bright,
The bridal of the earth and sky:
The dew shall weep thy fall tonight;
         For thou must die.

Sweet rose, whose hue angry and brave
Bids the rash gazer wipe his eye:
Thy root is ever in its grave,
         And thou must die.

Sweet spring, full of sweet days and roses,
A box where sweets compacted lie;
My music shows ye have your closes,
         And all must die.

Only a sweet and virtuous soul,
Like seasoned timber, never gives;
But though the whole world turn to coal,
         Then chiefly lives.

MAN

         My God, I heard this day,
That none doth build a stately habitation,
         But he that means to dwell therein.
         What house more stately hath there been,
Or can be, than is Man? to whose creation
         All things are in decay.

         For Man is ev'ry thing,
And more: He is a tree, yet bears no fruit;
         A beast, yet is, or should be more:
         Reason and speech we only bring.
Parrots may thank us, if they are not mute,
         They go upon the score.

         Man is all symmetry,
Full of proportions, one limb to another,
         And all to all the world besides:
         Each part may call the farthest, brother:
For head with foot hath private amity,
         And both with moons and tides.

         Nothing hath got so far,
But Man hath caught and kept it, as his prey.
         His eyes dismount the highest star:
         He is in little all the sphere.
Herbs gladly cure our flesh; because that they
         Find their acquaintance there.

         For us the winds do blow,
The earth doth rest, heav'n move, and fountains flow.
         Nothing we see, but means our good,
         As our *delight,* or as our *treasure:*
The whole is, either our cupboard of *food,*
         Or cabinet of *pleasure.*

         The stars have us to bed;
Night draws the curtain, which the sun withdraws;
         Music and light attend our head.
         All things unto our *flesh* are kind
In their *descent* and *being;* to our *mind*
         In their *ascent* and *cause.*

         Each thing is full of duty:
Waters united are our navigation;
         Distinguished, our habitation;
         Below, our drink; above, our meat;
Both are our cleanliness. Hath one such beauty?
         Then how are all things neat?

More servants wait on Man,
Than he'll take notice of: in ev'ry path
        He treads down that which doth befriend
            him,
        When sickness makes him pale and wan.
O mighty love! Man is one world, and hath
        Another to attend him.

        Since then, my God, thou hast
So brave a Palace built; O dwell in it,
        That it may dwell with thee at last!
        Till then, afford us so much wit;
That, as the world serves us, we may serve thee,
        And both thy servants be.

❧

LIFE

I made a posy, while the day ran by;
Here will I smell my remnant out, and tie
        My life within this band.
But time did beckon to the flowers, and they
By noon most cunningly did steal away,
        And withered in my hand.

My hand was next to them, and then my heart:
I took, without more thinking, in good part
        Time's gentle admonition:
Who did so sweetly death's sad taste convey,
Making my mind to smell my fatal day;
        Yet sug'ring the suspicion.

Farewell dear flowers, sweetly your time ye spent,
Fit, while ye lived, for smell or ornament,
        And after death for cures.
I follow straight without complaints or grief,
Since if my scent be good, I care not, if
        It be as short as yours.

❧

MORTIFICATION

        How soon doth man decay!
When clothes are taken from a chest of sweets
    To swaddle infants, whose young breath
        Scarce knows the way;

Those clouts are little winding sheets,
Which do consign and send them unto death.

        When boys go first to bed,
They step into their voluntary graves,
    Sleep binds them fast; only their breath
        Makes them not dead:
    Successive nights, like rolling waves,
Convey them quickly, who are bound for death.

        When youth is frank and free,
And calls for music, while his veins do swell,
    All day exchanging mirth and breath
        In company;
    That music summons to the knell,
Which shall befriend him at the house of death.

        When man grows staid and wise,
Getting a house and home, where he may move
    Within the circle of his breath,
        Schooling his eyes;
    That dumb inclosure maketh love
Unto the coffin, that attends his death.

        When age grows low and weak,
Marking his grave, and thawing ev'ry year,
    Till all do melt, and drown his breath
        When he would speak;
    A chair or litter shows the bier,
Which shall convey him to the house of death.

        Man, ere he is aware,
Hath put together a solemnity,
    And dressed his hearse, while he has breath
        As yet to spare:
    Yet Lord, instruct us so to die,
That all these dyings may be life in death.

❧

HOPE

I gave to Hope a watch of mine: but he
        An anchor gave to me.
Then an old prayer-book I did present:
        And he an optic sent.
With that I gave a vial full of tears:
        But he a few green ears:

Ah Loiterer! I'll no more, no more I'll bring:
　　I did expect a ring.

THE COLLAR

I struck the board, and cried, No more.
　　　　I will abroad.
What? shall I ever sigh and pine?
My lines and life are free; free as the road,
　　Loose as the wind, as large as store.
　　　　Shall I be still in suit?
Have I no harvest but a thorn
To let me blood, and not restore
What I have lost with cordial fruit?
　　　　Sure there was wine
Before my sighs did dry it: there was corn
　　Before my tears did drown it.
Is the year only lost to me?
　　Have I no bays to crown it?
No flowers, no garlands gay? All blasted?
　　　　All wasted?
Not so, my heart: but there is fruit,
　　And thou hast hands.
Recover all thy sigh-blown age
On double pleasures: leave thy cold dispute
　　Of what is fit, and not. Forsake thy cage,
　　　　Thy rope of sands,
Which petty thoughts have made, and made to thee
　　Good cable, to enforce and draw,
　　　　And be thy law,
While thou didst wink and wouldst not see.
　　　　Away; take heed:
　　　　I will abroad.
Call in thy death's head there: tie up thy fears.
　　　　He that forbears
　　To suit and serve his need,
　　　　Deserves his load.
But as I raved and grew more fierce and wild
　　　　At every word,
Me thoughts I heard one calling, *Child*:
　　And I replied, *My Lord*.

THE FLOWER

How fresh, O Lord, how sweet and clear
Are thy returns! ev'n as the flowers in spring;
　　To which, besides their own demean,
The late-past frosts tributes of pleasure bring.
　　　　Grief melts away
　　　　Like snow in May,
　　As if there were no such cold thing.

Who would have thought my shrivelled heart
Could have recovered greenness? It was gone
　　Quite underground; as flowers depart
To see their mother-root, when they have blown;
　　　　Where they together
　　　　All the hard weather,
　　Dead to the world, keep house unknown.

These are thy wonders, Lord of power,
Killing and quick'ning, bringing down to hell
　　And up to heaven in an hour;
Making a chiming of a passing-bell.
　　　　We say amiss,
　　　　This or that is:
　　Thy word is all, if we could spell.

O that I once past changing were,
Fast in thy Paradise, where no flower can wither!
　　Many a spring I shoot up fair,
Off'ring at heav'n, growing and groaning thither:
　　　　Nor doth my flower
　　　　Want a spring-shower,
　　My sins and I joining together:

But while I grow in a straight line,
Still upwards bent, as if heav'n were mine own,
　　Thy anger comes, and I decline:
What frost to that? what pole is not the zone,
　　　　Where all things burn,
　　　　When thou dost turn,
　　And the least frown of thine is shown?

And now in age I bud again,
After so many deaths I live and write;
　　I once more smell the dew and rain,
And relish versing: O my only light,
　　　　It cannot be
　　　　That I am he
　　On whom thy tempests fell all night.

These are thy wonders, Lord of love;
To make us see we are but flowers that glide:
    Which when we once can find and prove,
Thou hast a garden for us, where to bide.
        Who would be more,
        Swelling through store,
    Forfeit their Paradise by their pride.

AARON

    Holiness on the head,
    Light and perfections on the breast,
Harmonious bells below, raising the dead
    To lead them unto life and rest.
        Thus are true Aarons dressed.

    Profaneness in my head,
    Defects and darkness in my breast,
A noise of passions ringing me for dead
    Unto a place where is no rest.
        Poor priest thus am I dressed.

    Only another head
    I have, another heart and breast,
Another music, making live not dead,
    Without whom I could have no rest
        In him I am well dressed.

    Christ is my only head,
    My alone only heart and breast,
My only music, striking me ev'n dead;
    That to the old man I may rest,
        And be in him new dressed.

    So holy in my head,
    Perfect and light in my dear breast,
My doctrine tuned by Christ (who is not dead,
    But lives in me while I do rest),
        Come people; Aaron's dressed.

DISCIPLINE

Throw away thy rod,
Throw away thy wrath:
        O my God
Take the gentle path.

For my heart's desire
Unto thine is bent:
        I aspire
To a full consent.

Not a word or look
I affect to own,
        But by book,
And thy book alone.

Though I fail, I weep:
Though I halt in pace,
        Yet I creep
To the throne of grace.

Then let wrath remove;
Love will do the deed:
        For with love
Stony hearts will bleed.

Love is swift of foot;
Love's a man of war,
        And can shoot,
And can hit from far.

Who can scape his bow?
That which wrought on thee,
        Brought thee low,
Needs must work on me.

Throw away thy rod;
Though man frailties hath,
        Thou art God:
Throw away thy wrath.

DEATH

Death, thou wast once an uncouth hideous thing,
        Nothing but bones,
    The sad effect of sadder groans:
Thy mouth was open, but thou couldst not sing.

For we considered thee as at some six
    Or ten years hence,
      After the loss of life and sense,
Flesh being turned to dust, and bones to sticks.

We looked on this side of thee, shooting short;
    Where we did find
      The shells of fledge souls left behind,
Dry dust, which sheds no tears, but may extort.

But since our Saviour's death did put some blood
    Into thy face;
      Thou art grown fair and full of grace,
Much in request, much sought for, as a good.

For we do now behold thee gay and glad,
    As at doomsday;
      When souls shall wear their new array,
And all thy bones with beauty shall be clad.

Therefore we can go die as sleep, and trust
    Half that we have
      Unto an honest faithful grave;
Making our pillows either down, or dust.

In the poems of Robert Herrick (1591–1674) there is a music that seems to belong exclusively, and naturally, to the English language but which has appeared nowhere before or since. It is as though this music had lain there in English words, somewhat like those ideal sculptural forms that Michelangelo believed lay hidden in the marble for him to discover and get out. If Herrick hadn't found it, it might have been forever unfound, since the seventeenth century seems the ideal time to have found it. The poetry of Ben Jonson (which Herrick so much admires) has a gorgeous music, but there is a kind of forcefulness in it that makes unlikely such butterfly-wing nuances as 'From whose happy spark here let / Spring the purple violet'.

Herrick's Muse seems to have offered him a choice of five or six subjects: the various beauties of young women, his poetry, the pleasures and pains of country life, erotic or paradisaical dreams and visions, the decay of beauty, his own ageing and approaching death. In some of his best poems, these themes are there together, as in 'The Bad Season Makes the Poet Sad', and the astonishing 'Corinna's Going A-Maying'.

LOVE (3)

Love bade me welcome: yet my soul drew back,
    Guilty of dust and sin.
But quick-eyed Love, observing me grow slack
    From my first entrance in,
Drew nearer to me, sweetly questioning,
    If I lacked anything.

A guest, I answered, worthy to be here:
    Love said, You shall be he.
I the unkind, ungrateful? Ah my dear,
    I cannot look on thee.
Love took my hand, and smiling did reply,
    Who made the eyes but I?

Truth Lord, but I have marred them: let my shame
    Go where it doth deserve.
And know you not, says Love, who bore the blame?
    My dear, then I will serve.
You must sit down, says Love, and taste my meat:
    So I did sit and eat.

ROBERT HERRICK

DISCONTENTS IN DEVON

More discontents I never had
 Since I was born, than here;
Where I have been, and still am sad,
 In this dull Devon-shire:
Yet justly too I must confess;
 I ne'er invented such
Ennobled numbers for the press,
 Than where I loath'd so much.

DELIGHT IN DISORDER

A sweet disorder in the dress
Kindles in clothes a wantonness:
A lawn about the shoulders thrown
Into a fine distraction:
An erring lace which here and there
Enthralls the crimson stomacher:
A cuff neglectful, and thereby
Ribands to flow confusedly:
A winning wave (deserving note)
In the tempestuous petticoat:
A careless shoestring, in whose tie
I see a wild civility:
Do more bewitch me, than when art
Is too precise in every part.

THE VISION

Sitting alone (as one forsook)
Close by a silver-shedding brook;
With hands held up to Love, I wept;
And after sorrows spent, I slept:
Then in a vision I did see
A glorious form appear to me:
A virgin's face she had; her dress
Was like a sprightly *Spartaness*.
A silver bow with green silk strung,
Down from her comely shoulders hung:
And as she stood, the wanton air
Dandled the ringlets of her hair.
Her legs were such *Diana* shows,
When tuckt up she a hunting goes;
With buskins shortened to descrie

The happy dawning of her thigh:
Which when I saw, I made access
To kiss that tempting nakedness:
But she forbad me, with a wand
Of myrtle she had in her hand:
And chiding me, said, Hence, remove,
Herrick, thou art too coarse to love.

TO DIANEME

Sweet, be not proud of those two eyes,
Which star-like sparkle in their skies;
Nor be you proud, that you can see
All hearts your captives, yours yet free:
Be you not proud of that rich hair
Which wantons with the love-sick air:
Whenas the ruby which you wear,
Sunk from the tip of your soft ear,
Will last to be a precious stone
When all your world of beauty's gone.

UPON JULIA'S BREASTS

Display thy breasts, my Julia, there let me
Behold that circummortal purity:
Between whose glories, there my lips I'll lay,
Ravished, in that fair *Via Lactea*.

TO ANTHEA, WHO MAY COMMAND HIM ANY THING

Bid me to live, and I will live
 Thy Protestant to be;
Or bid me love, and I will give
 A loving heart to thee.

A heart as soft, a heart as kind,
 A heart as sound and free
As in the whole world thou canst find,
 That heart I'll give to thee.

Bid me to weep, and I will weep
   While I have eyes to see:
And, having none, yet I will keep
   A heart to weep for thee.

Bid me despair, and I'll despair
   Under that *cypress* tree:
Or bid me die, and I will dare
   E'en death to die for thee.

Thou art my life, my love, my heart,
   The very eyes of me:
And hast command of every part
   To live and die for thee.

❧

A Nuptial Song

‹Or the Epithalamium on Sir Clipsby
Crew and his Lady›
(lines 111–160)

And to your more bewitching, see, the proud
Plump bed bear up, and swelling like a cloud,
   Tempting the two too modest; can
   Ye see it brusle like a swan,
      And you be cold
To meet it when it woos and seems to fold
   The arms to hug it? Throw, throw
Yourselves into the mighty overflow
      Of that white pride, and drown
   The night with you in floods of down.

The bed is ready, and the maze of love
Looks for the treaders; everywhere is wove
   Wit and new mystery; read, and
   Put in practice, to understand
      And know each wile,
Each hieroglyphic of a kiss or smile;
   And do it to the full; reach
High in your conceit, and some way teach
      Nature and art one more
   Play than they ever knew before.

If needs we must for ceremony's sake
Bless a sack-posset, luck go with it, take
   The night-charm quickly, you have spells
   And magics for to end, and hells
      To pass; but such
And of such torture as no one would grutch

To live therein for ever; fry
And consume, and grow again to die
      And live, and, in that case,
   Love the confusion of the place.

But since it must be done, despatch, and sew
Up in a sheet your bride, and what if so
   It be with rock or walls of brass
   Ye tower her up, as *Danae* was;
      Think you that this
Or hell itself a powerful bulwark is?
   I tell ye no; but like a
Bold bolt of thunder he will make his way
      And rend the cloud, and throw
   The sheets about like flakes of snow.

All now is hush'd in silence: midwife-moon
With all her owl-eyed issue begs a boon,
   Which you must grant; that's entrance; with
   Which extract, all we can call pith
      And quintessence
Of planetary bodies; so commence,
   All fair constellations
Looking upon ye, that two nations,
      Springing from two such fires
   May blaze the virtue of their sires.

❧

Her Legs

Fain would I kiss my Julia's dainty leg,
Which is as white and hairless as an egg.

❧

His Prayer to Ben Jonson

When I a verse shall make,
Know I have prayed thee,
For old religion's sake,
Saint Ben to aid me.

Make the way smooth for me
When I, thy Herrick,
Honouring thee, on my knee
Offer my lyric.

Candles I'll give to thee,
And a new altar;
And thou 'Saint Ben' shalt be
Writ in my psalter.

The Bad Season Makes the Poet Sad

Dull to my self, and almost dead to these
My many fresh and fragrant mistresses:
Lost to all music, now; since every thing
Puts on the semblance here of sorrow.
Sick is the land to'th' heart; and doth endure
More dangerous faintings by her desp'rate cure.
But if that golden age would come again,
And Charles here rule, as he before did reign;
If smooth and unperplext the Seasons were,
As when the Sweet Maria lived here:
I should delight to have my curls half drown'd
In Tyrian dews, and head with roses crown'd.
And once more yet (ere I am laid out dead)
Knock at a star with my exalted head.

Upon Prew His Maid

In this little urn is laid
Prewdence Baldwin (once my maid)
From whose happy spark here let
Spring the purple violet.

An Ode for Him

Ah Ben!
Say how, or when
Shall we thy guests
Meet at those lyric feasts
Made at the Sun,
The Dog, the Triple Tun?
Where we such clusters had
As made us nobly wild, not mad;
And yet each verse of thine
Outdid the meat, outdid the frolic wine.

My Ben,
Or come again,
Or send to us
Thy wit's great overplus;
But teach us yet
Wisely to husband it,
Lest we that talent spend,
And having once brought to an end
That precious stock, the store
Of such a wit the world should have no more.

His Tears To Thames

I send, I send here my supremest kiss
To thee, my silver-footed Thamasis.
No more shall I reiterate thy strand
Whereon so many stately structures stand:
Nor in the summer's sweeter evenings go
To bathe in thee, as thousand others do,
No more shall I along thy crystal glide
In barge, with boughs and rushes beautified,
With soft smooth virgins (for our chaste disport)
To Richmond, Kingston, and to Hampton Court:
Never again shall I with finny oar
Put from, or draw unto, the faithful shore:
And landing here, or safely landing there,
Make way to my belovèd Westminster:
Or to the golden Cheapside, where the earth
Of Julia Herrick gave to me my birth.
May all clean nymphs and curious water-dames,
With swanlike state, float up and down thy streams:
No drought upon thy wanton waters fall
To make them lean and languishing at all.
No ruffling winds come hither to disease
Thy pure and silver-wristed Naiades.
Keep up your state, ye streams; and as ye spring,
Never make sick your banks by surfeiting.
Grow young with tides, and though I see ye never,
Receive this vow, so fare ye well for ever.

ANOTHER GRACE FOR A CHILD

Here a little child I stand,
Heaving up my either hand;
Cold as paddocks though they be,
Here I lift them up to Thee,
For a benizon to fall
On our meat, and on us all. *Amen.*

❧

CORINNA'S GOING A-MAYING

Get up, get up for shame, the blooming morn
Upon her wings presents the god unshorn.
 See how Aurora throws her fair
 Fresh-quilted colours through the air:
 Get up, sweet slug-a-bed, and see
 The dew bespangling herb and tree.
Each flower has wept and bow'd towards the east
Above an hour since: yet you not dress'd;
 Nay! not so much as out of bed?
 When all the birds have matins said
 And sung their thankful hymns, 'tis sin,
 Nay, profanation to keep in,
Whenas a thousand virgins on this day
Spring, sooner than the lark, to fetch in May.

Rise and put on your foliage, and be seen
To come forth, like the spring-time, fresh and
 green.
 And sweet as Flora. Take no care
 For jewels for your gown or hair:
 Fear not; the leaves will strew
 Gems in abundance upon you:
Besides, the childhood of the day has kept,
Against you come, some orient pearls unwept;
 Come and receive them while the light
 Hangs on the dew-locks of the night:
 And Titan on the eastern hill
 Retires himself, or else stands still
Till you come forth. Wash, dress, be brief in
 praying:
Few beads are best when once we go a-Maying.

Come, my Corinna, come; and, coming, mark
How each field turns a street, each street a park
 Made green and trimm'd with trees: see how
 Devotion gives each house a bough
 Or branch: each porch, each door, ere this

An ark, a tabernacle is,
Made up of white-thorn neatly interwove;
As if here were those cooler shades of love.
 Can such delights be in the street
 And open fields and we not see't?
 Come, we'll abroad; and let's obey
 The proclamation made for May:
And sin no more, as we have done, by staying;
But, my Corinna, come, let's go a-Maying.

There's not a budding boy or girl this day
But is got up, and gone to bring in May.
 A deal of youth, ere this, is come
 Back, and with white-thorn laden home.
 Some have despatch'd their cakes and cream
 Before that we have left to dream:
And some have wept, and woo'd, and plighted
 troth,
And chose their priest, ere we can cast off sloth:
 Many a green-gown has been given;
 Many a kiss, both odd and even:
 Many a glance too has been sent
 From out the eye, love's firmament;
Many a jest told of the keys betraying
This night, and locks pick'd, yet we're not a-
 Maying.

Come, let us go while we are in our prime;
And take the harmless folly of the time.
 We shall grow old apace, and die
 Before we know our liberty.
 Our life is short, and our days run
 As fast away as does the sun;
And, as a vapour or a drop of rain,
Once lost, can ne'er be found again,
 So when or you or I are made
 A fable, song, or fleeting shade,
 All love, all liking, all delight
 Lies drowned with us in endless night.
Then while time serves, and we are but decaying,
Come, my Corinna, come, let's go a-Maying.

Of the small group of poets which used to be called 'English Chaucerians', Hoccleve (c. 1368–c. 1426) has been most defined by the association with Chaucer. The best known surviving illustration of Chaucer occurs in a manuscript of Hoccleve's *The Regiment of Princes*, a work which also contains Hoccleve's tribute to his 'mayster dere and fader reverent,/My mayster Chaucer, flour of eloquence,/Mirrour of fructuous entendement./O universyl fader in science!' (lines 1961–4). Yet of all Chaucer's early English followers, Hoccleve is the most distinctive. His great interest is to have written autobiographical poetry in medieval England. He worked as a clerk in the Privy Seal, and his absences from that work are compatible with the dates of the nervous breakdown he describes at the beginning of his *Complaint* (1421), given below. He wrote shorter poems, on both religious and profane subjects, but his principal works are *The Regiment of Princes* (1411), an encyclopaedic work of over 5000 lines, and a grouped 'Series' of poems, beginning with the *Complaint*, which are a set of narratives connected by a strikingly modern critical linking through a 'Dialogue' with a Friend. Attempts have been made to ascribe his not uncommon metrical awkwardnesses to an excess rather than a lack of virtuosity. But his great and enduring appeal lies in his vivid and colloquial evocations of London in the early fifteenth century, in the autobiographical passsages printed here from the *Complaint* and *La Male Regle de Thomas Hoccleve*, a description of the minor dissoluteness of his life centring on London taverns.

COMPLAINT

(lines 1–36; 50–77)

Aftir that hervest inned had hise sheves,
And that the broun sesoun of mihelmesse
Was come and gan the trees robbe of her leves
That grene hed teen and in lusty freisshenesse,
And hem into colour of yelownesse
Had died and doun thrown undir foote,
That chaunge sanke into myn herte roote.

For freisshly broughte it to my remembraunce
That stablenesse in this worlde is ther noon.
Ther is no thing but chaunge and variaunce.
Howe welthi a man be, or wel be goon,
Endure it shal not: he shal it forgoon.
Deeth undir foote shal him thriste adoun;
That is every wightes conclucioun,

Wiche for to weyve is in no mannes myght,
Howe riche he be, stronge, lusty, freissh and gay.
And in the ende of Novembre, uppon a night,
Sighynge sore as I in my bed lay
For this and othir thoughtis wiche many a day
Byforne I tooke, sleep cam noon in myn ye,
So vexid me the thoughtful maladie.

I sy wel, sithin I with siknesse last
Was scourgid, cloudy hath bene the favour
That shoon on me ful bright in times past.
The sunne abated, and the dirke shour
Hilded doun right on me, and in langour
Me made swymme, so that my spirite
To lyve no lust had ne no delite.

The greef aboute myn herte so sore swal
And bolned evere to and to so sore
That nedis oute I muste ther withal.
I thoughte I nolde kepe it cloos no more,
Ne lete it in me for to eelde and hore.
And, for to preve I cam of a womman,
I braste oute on the morwe and thus bigan.

Here endith my prolog: and folwith my
    compleinte. [. . .]

[. . .]

But although the substaunce of my memorie
Wente to pleie, as for a certein space,
Yit the lorde of vertue, the kyng of glorie,
Of his highe myght and his benigne grace,

Made it for to retourne into the place
Whens it cam; wiche at alle halwemesse
Was five yeere, neither more ne lesse.

And evere sithin (thankid be god oure lord
Of his good and gracious reconsiliacioun),
My wit and I have bene of suche acord
As we were or the alteracioun
Of it was. But, by my savacioun,
Sith that time have I be sore sette on fire
And lyved in greet turment and martire.

For, though that my wit were hoom come agein,
Men wolde it not so undirstonde or take.
With me to dele hadden they disdein.
A rietous persone I was, and forsake.
Min oolde frendshipe was al overshake;
No wight with me list make daliaunce.
The worlde me made a straunge countinuaunce.

With that myn herte sore gan to tourment.
For ofte, whanne I in Westmynstir halle
And eke in Londoun amonge the prees went
I sy the chere abaten and apalle
Of hem that weren wonte me for to calle
To companie. Her heed they caste awry
Whanne I hem mette, as they not me sy.

Glossary

DIED: dyed; HOWE: however; WEL BE GOON: well provided; WEYVE: avoid; BYFORNE I TOOKE: took heed of; THOUGHTFUL: worrying; SY: saw; SITHIN: since; HILDED: poured BOLNED: Swelled; TO EELDE AND HORE: to age, grow grey; BRASTE OUTE: burst out; MORWE: next day; WENTE TO PLEIE: went off duty; ALLE HALWEMESSE: All Saints' Day; OR: before; RIETOUS: dissolute; FORSAKE: abandoned; OVERSHAKE: passed away; DALIAUNCE: conversation; SY: saw; APALLE: grow dim

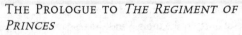

THE PROLOGUE TO *THE REGIMENT OF PRINCES*
(lines 995-1022)

'A wryter mote thre thynges to hym knytte,
And in tho may be no disseveraunse:
Mynde, ye and hande: non may from othyr flytte
But in hem mot be joynt continuance.
The mynde all hooll, wythouten varyaunse,
On yee and hand awayte mote alwaye,
And they too eke on hym, it ys no nay.

'Whoso schall wryght may not holde a tale
Wyth hym ne hym, ne synge thys ne that.
But all hys wyttes hole, grete and smale,
Ther most apere and halden them therat.
And syn he speke may ne synge nat
But bothe two he nedes most forbere,
Hys labor to hym ys the alengre.

'Thys artificers se y day be day
In the hottest of all theyr besynes
Talken and syng and make game and play,
And forthe her labour passeth wyth gladnesse.
But we labour in traveylous stylnesse.
We stope and stare uppon the schepys skynne,
And kepe most our songe and wordys wythyn.

'Wryting also dothe grete annoye thre
Off wyche ful fewe folkys taken hede
Sauf we oure self, and thys, lo, they be:
Stomak ys oon, whom stoppyng, oute of drede,
Annoyeth sore; and to oure bakkys nede
Mot yt be grevous; an the thrydde, oure yen
Uppon the wyte mochell sorowe dryen.

Glossary

ALENGRE: longer; OUTE OF DREDE: without doubt; DRYEN: suffer

LA MALE REGLE
(lines 177-202)

Wher was a gretter maister eeke than y
Or bet aqweyntid at Westmynstre yate,
Among the taverneres namely
And cookes when I cam, eerly or late?
I pynchid nat at hem in myn acate
But paied hem as that they axe wolde.
Wherfore I was the welcomere algate
And for 'a verray gentil man' yholde.

And if it happid on the Someres day
That I thus at the taverne hadde be,
Whan I departe sholde and go my way
Hoom to the privee seer, so wowed me
Hete and unlust and superfluitee
To walke unto the brigge and take a boot,
That nat durste I contrarie hem all three
But dide as that they stired me, god woot.

And in the wyntir, for the way was deep,
Unto the brigge I dressid me also,
And ther the bootmen took upon me keep
For they my riot kneewen fern ago.
With hem I was itugged to and fro,
So wel was him that I with wolde fare,
For riot paieth largely everemo;
He styntith nevere til his purs be bare.

Othir than 'maistir' callid was I nevere
Among this meynee – in myn audience.

Glossary

PYNCHID: underpaid; ACATE: purchases; VOWED: enticed; STIRED: prompted; DEEP: covered with mud

Two poets share the dates of Thomas Hood (1799–1845): the author of Serious Poems and the author of Poems of Wit and Humour (as Alfred Ainger sub-titled the two volumes of Poems of Thomas Hood that he edited and published in 1897). Hood was certainly witty and humorous, but light verse tends to have a shorter shelf-life than dark – or heavy – verse and, as my selection shows, I would take the first volume of his 1897 Poems to my desert island, but not the second.

Taking my choices in reverse order, I have chosen 'The Song of the Shirt' for its passionate indictment of sweated labour, the dark side of Victorian prosperity, a subject that most poets tended to leave to the novelists of the day.

'Ruth', another poem about labour, offers a happy rural contrast to the urban anguish of 'The Song of the Shirt', and shows in its closing stanza the more genial hand of the Poet of Wit and Humour. It also shows a debt to his more gifted contemporary, John Keats, in whose 'Ode to Autumn' we encounter 'Ruth, when sick for home,/She stood in tears amid the alien corn'.

The same process is initiated by 'I Remember, I Remember', a darker poem – its darkness intensified by memories of light – that would prompt a later and greater poet, Philip Larkin, to a still darker review of his own childhood, a poem he too called 'I Remember, I Remember'. So poets, like Olympic runners, pass the torch from hand to hand down the generations.

I have lived – gratefully – with these poems for fifty years, and it is a pleasure to pass them on.

Thomas Hood

I Remember, I Remember

I remember, I remember,
The house where I was born,
The little window where the sun
Came peeping in at morn;
He never came a wink too soon,
Nor brought too long a day,
But now, I often wish the night
Had borne my breath away!

I remember, I remember,
The roses, red and white,
The violets, and the lily-cups,
Those flowers made of light!
The lilacs where the robin built,
And where my brother set
The laburnum on his birthday, –
The tree is living yet!

I remember, I remember,
Where I was used to swing,
And thought the air must rush as fresh
To swallows on the wing;
My spirit flew in feathers then,
That is so heavy now,
And summer pools could hardly cool
The fever on my brow!

I remember, I remember,
The fir trees dark and high;
I used to think their slender tops
Were close against the sky:
It was a childish ignorance,
But now 'tis little joy
To know I'm farther off from heaven
Than when I was a boy.

Ruth

She stood breast high amid the corn,
Clasped by the golden light of morn,
Like the sweetheart of the sun,
Who many a glowing kiss had won.

On her cheek an autumn flush,
Deeply ripened; – such a blush

In the midst of brown was born,
Like red poppies grown with corn.

Round her eyes her tresses fell,
Which were blackest none could tell,
But long lashes veiled a light,
That had else been all too bright.

And her hat, with shady brim,
Made her tressy forehead dim; –
Thus she stood amid the stooks,
Praising God with sweetest looks: –

Sure, I said, heaven did not mean,
Where I reap thou shouldst but glean,
Lay thy sheaf adown and come,
Share my harvest and my home.

The Song of the Shirt

With fingers weary and worn,
    With eyelids heavy and red,
A woman sat, in unwomanly rags,
    Plying her needle and thread –
        Stitch! stitch! stitch!
In poverty, hunger, and dirt,
    And still with a voice of dolorous pitch
She sang the 'Song of the Shirt.'

'Work! work! work!
While the cock is crowing aloof!
    And work – work – work,
Till the stars shine through the roof!
It's Oh! to be a slave
    Along with the barbarous Turk,
Where woman has never a soul to save,
    If this is Christian work!

'Work – work – work
Till the brain begins to swim;
    Work – work – work
Till the eyes are heavy and dim!
Seam, and gusset, and seam,
Till over the buttons I fall asleep,
    And sew them on in a dream!

'Oh Men, with Sisters dear!
    Oh, Men, with Mothers and Wives!

It is not linen you're wearing out,
But human creatures' lives!
Stitch – stitch – stitch,
In poverty, hunger, and dirt,
Sewing at once, with a double thread,
A Shroud as well as a Shirt.

'But why do I talk of Death?
That Phantom of grisly bone,
I hardly fear his terrible shape,
It seems so like my own –
It seems so like my own,
Because of the fasts I keep;
Oh, God! that bread should be so dear,
And flesh and blood so cheap!

'Work – work – work!
My labour never flags;
And what are its wages? A bed of straw,
A crust of bread – and rags.
That shatter'd roof – and this naked floor –
A table – a broken chair –
And a wall so blank, my shadow I thank
For sometimes falling there!

'Work – work – work!
From weary chime to chime,
Work – work – work –
As prisoners work for crime!
Band, and gusset, and seam,
Seam, and gusset, and band,
Till the heart is sick, and the brain benumb'd,
As well as the weary hand.

'Work – work – work,
In the dull December light,
And work – work – work,
When the weather is warm and bright –
While underneath the eaves
The brooding swallows cling
As if to show me their sunny backs
And twit me with the spring.

'Oh! but to breathe the breath
Of the cowslip and primrose sweet –
With the sky above my head,
And the grass beneath my feet,
For only one short hour
To feel as I used to feel,
Before I knew the woes of want
And the walk that costs a meal!

'Oh! but for one short hour!
A respite however brief!
No blessed leisure for Love or Hope,
But only time for Grief!
A little weeping would ease my heart,
But in their briny bed
My tears must stop, for every drop
Hinders needle and thread!'

With fingers weary and worn,
With eyelids heavy and red,
A woman sat in unwomanly rags,
Plying her needle and thread –
Stitch! stitch! stitch!
In poverty, hunger, and dirt,
And still with a voice of dolorous pitch, –
Would that its tone could reach the Rich! –
She sang this 'Song of the Shirt!'

'To most readers it will not be surprising,' wrote Michael Roberts in the introduction to his *Faber Book of Modern Verse* (1936), 'that an anthology of modern poetry should begin with Hopkins.' Hopkins (1844–89) had already had a considerable influence on modern poetry, yet by his dates he was wholly Victorian and had died half a century before. The temporal dislocation of this posthumous converse which so many poets and readers have delightedly had with Hopkins is a useful reminder of the fact that continuities may have to arc across discontinuities. If Hopkins looked forward, with innovative deployments of imagery and syntax, he also looked back, sidestepping Chaucer and drawing sustenance from Anglo-Saxon and medieval alliterative poetry, which to him showed 'the naked thew and sinew of the English language'. His care for the language was never antiquarian, but was always devoted to inducing vigour and freshness. Poetry is a 'living art, made for performance'. A Jesuit priest with an Oxford First, who composed poetry in Welsh, Latin and Greek as well as English, might be thought to have given hostages to the esoteric, and indeed he did once speak of 'excellences higher than clearness at a first reading', but the lyrical lift and drive of his poetry, the energies of feeling which fuel it, are pervasive and unmistakable. Few lyric masters have exposed their joys, doubts, longings and despairs within such an iron inscape (to use his own word) of verbal and stanzaic control. Even the tincture of homoeroticism, which is today quite clear and does not have to be apologized for, is made all the more moving from the restraint of its distilling.

'The Wreck of the Deutschland', Hopkins's most famous poem, is absent from the present selection only because its length would have taken up too much of the space available.

'SEE HOW SPRING OPENS'

See how Spring opens with disabling cold,
And hunting winds and the long-lying snow.
Is it a wonder if the buds are slow?
Or where is strength to make the leaf unfold?
Chilling remembrance of my days of old
Afflicts no less, what yet I hope may blow,
That seed which the good sower once did sow,
So loading with obstruction that threshold
Which should ere now have led my feet to the field.
It is the waste done in unreticent youth
Which makes so small the promise of that yield
That I may win with late-learnt skill uncouth
From furrows of the poor and stinting weald.
Therefore how bitter, and learnt how late, the truth!

THE WINDHOVER:

◄ To Christ our Lord ►

I caught this morning morning's minion, king-
    dom of daylight's dauphin, dapple-dawn-drawn
        Falcon, in his riding
    Of the rolling level underneath him steady air, and
        striding
High there, how he rung upon the rein of a wimpling
        wing
In his ecstasy! then off, off forth on swing,
    As a skate's heel sweeps smooth on a bow-bend: the
        hurl and gliding
    Rebuffed the big wind. My heart in hiding
Stirred for a bird, – the achieve of, the mastery of the
        thing!

Brute beauty and valour and act, oh, air, pride, plume,
        here
    Buckle! AND the fire that breaks from thee then, a
        billion
Times told lovelier, more dangerous, O my chevalier!

    No wonder of it: shéer plód makes plough down
        sillion
Shine, and blue-bleak embers, ah my dear,
    Fall, gall themselves, and gash gold-vermilion.

Hurrahing in Harvest

Summer ends now; now, barbarous in beauty, the
    stooks rise
Around; up above, what wind-walks! what lovely
    behaviour
Of silk-sack clouds! has wilder, wilful-wavier
Meal-drift moulded ever and melted across skies?

I walk, I lift up, I lift up heart, eyes,
Down all that glory in the heavens to glean our
    Saviour;
And, éyes, heárt, what looks, what lips yet gave you a
Rapturous love's greeting of realer, of rounder replies?

And the azurous hung hills are his world-wielding
    shoulder
Majestic – as a stallion stalwart, very-violet-sweet! –
These things, these things were here and but the
    beholder
Wanting; which two when they once meet,
The heart rears wings bold and bolder
And hurls for him, O half hurls earth for him off
    under his feet.

❧

Binsey Poplars

‹ felled 1879 ›

My aspens dear, whose airy cages quelled,
Quelled or quenched in leaves the leaping sun,
All felled, felled, are all felled;
    Of a fresh and following folded rank
        Not spared, not one
           That dandled a sandalled
       Shadow that swam or sank
On meadow and river and wind-wandering
    weed-winding bank.

    O if we but knew what we do
      When we delve or hew –
    Hack and rack the growing green!
      Since country is so tender
    To touch, her being só slender,
    That, like this sleek and seeing ball
    But a prick will make no eye at all,
      Where we, even where we mean
        To mend her we end her,
    When we hew or delve:

After-comers cannot guess the beauty been.
    Ten or twelve, only ten or twelve
      Strokes of havoc únselve
        The sweet especial scene,
      Rural scene, a rural scene,
      Sweet especial rural scene.

❧

The Bugler's First Communion

A bugler boy from barrack (it is over the hill
There) – boy bugler, born, he tells me, of Irish
    Mother to an English sire (he
Shares their best gifts surely, fall how things will),

This very very day came down to us after a boon he on
My late being there begged of me, overflowing
    Boon in my bestowing,
Came, I say, this day to it – to a First Communion.

Here he knelt then ín regimental red.
Forth Christ from cupboard fetched, how fain I of feet
    To his youngster take his treat!
Low-latched in leaf-light housel his too huge godhead.

There ! and your sweetest seedings, ah divine,
By it, heavens, befall him! as a heart Christ's darling,
    dauntless;
    Tongue true, vaunt- and tauntless;
Breathing bloom of a chastity in mansex fine.

Frowning and forefending angel-warder
Squander the hell-rook ranks sally to molest him;
    March, kind comrade, abreast him;
Dress his days to a dexterous and starlight order.

How it dóes my heart good, visiting at that bleak hill,
When limber liquid youth, that to all I teach
    Yields tender as a pushed peach,
Hies headstrong to its wellbeing of a self-wise self-will!

Then though I should tread tufts of consolation
Dáys áfter, só I in a sort deserve to
    And do serve God to serve to
Just such slips of soldiery Christ's royal ration.

Nothing élse is like it, no, not all so strains
Us: fresh youth fretted in a bloomfall all portending

That sweet's sweeter ending;
Realm both Christ is heir to and thére réigns.

O now well work that sealing sacred ointment!
O for now charms, arms, what bans off bad
  And locks love ever in a lad!
Let mé though see no more of him, and not
  disappointment

Those sweet hopes quell whose least me quickenings
  lift,
In scarlet or somewhere of some day seeing
  That brow and bead of being,
An our day's God's own Galahad. Though this child's
  drift

Seems by a divíne doom chánnelled, nor do I cry
Disaster there; but may he not rankle and roam
  In backwheels though bound home? –
That left to the Lord of the Eucharist, I here lie by;

Recorded only, I have put my lips on pleas
Would brandle adamantine heaven with ride and jar,
  did
  Prayer go disregarded:
Forward-like, but however, and like favourable heaven
  heard these.

FELIX RANDAL

Felix Randal the farrier, O is he dead then? my duty all
  ended,
Who have watched his mould of man, big-boned and
  hardy-handsome
Pining, pining, till time when reason rambled in it and
  some
Fatal four disorders, fleshed there, all contended?

Sickness broke him. Impatient, he cursed at first, but
  mended
Being anointed and all; though a heavenlier heart
  began some
Months earlier, since I had our sweet reprieve and
  ransom
Tendered to him. Ah well, God rest him all road ever
  he offended!

This seeing the sick endears them to us, us too it
  endears.
My tongue had taught thee comfort, touch had
  quenched thy tears,
Thy tears that touched my heart, child, Felix, poor
  Felix Randal;

How far from then forethought of, all thy more
  boisterous years,
When thou at the random grim forge, powerful amidst
  peers,
Didst fettle for the great grey drayhorse his bright and
  battering sandal!

INVERSNAID

This darksome burn, horseback brown,
His rollrock highroad roaring down,
In coop and in comb the fleece of his foam
Flutes and low to the lake falls home.

A windpuff-bonnet of fáwn-fróth
Turns and twindles over the broth
Of a pool so pitchblack, féll-fequipping,
It rounds and rounds Despair to drowning.

Degged with dew, dappled with dew
Are the groins of the braes that the brook treads
  through,
Wiry heathpacks, flitches of fern,
And the beadbonny ash that sits over the burn.

What would the world be, once bereft
Of wet and of wildness? Let them be left,
O let them be left, wildness and wet;
Long live the weeds and the wilderness yet.

'AS KINGFISHERS CATCH FIRE'

As kingfishers catch fire, dragonflies draw flame;
  As tumbled over rim in roundy wells
  Stones ring; like each tucked string tells, each hung
   bell's
Bow swung finds tongue to fling out broad its name;
Each mortal thing does one thing and the same:

Deals out that being indoors each one dwells;
　Selves – goes itself; *myself* it speaks and spells,
Crying *What I do is me: for that I came.*

Í say more: the just man justices;
　Keeps gráce: thát keeps all his goings graces;
Acts in God's eye what in God's eye he is –
　Chríst. For Christ plays in ten thousand places,
Lovely in limbs, and lovely in eyes not his
　To the Father through the features of men's faces.

❧

THE LEADEN ECHO AND THE GOLDEN ECHO

‹Maidens' song from St. Winefred's Well›

‹The Leaden Echo›

How to kéep – is there ány any, is there none such,
　nowhere known some, bow or brooch or braid or
　brace, láce, latch or catch or key to keep
Back beauty, keep it, beauty, beauty, beauty, . . . from
　vanishing away?
Ó is there no frowning of these wrinkles, rankèd
　wrinkles deep,
Dówn? no waving off of these most mournful
　messengers, still messengers, sad and stealing
　messengers of grey? –
No there 's none, there 's none, O no there 's none,
Nor can you long be, what you now are, called fair,
Do what you may do, what, do what you may,
And wisdom is early to despair:
Be beginning; since, no, nothing can be done
To keep at bay
Age and age's evils, hoar hair,
Ruck and wrinkle, drooping, dying, death's worst,
　winding sheets, tombs and worms and tumbling to
　decay;
So be beginning, be beginning to despair.
O there 's none; no no no there 's none:
Be beginning to despair, to despair,
Despair, despair, despair, despair.

‹The Golden Echo›

　　　　　Spare!
There ís one, yes I have one (Hush there!),
Only not within seeing of the sun.
Not within the singeing of the strong sun,

Tall sun's tingeing, or treacherous the tainting of
　the earth's air,
Somewhere elsewhere there is ah well where! one,
Ońe. Yes I cán tell such a key, I dó know such a
　place,
Where whatever's prizèd and passes of us,
　everything that's fresh and fast flying of us, seems
　to us sweet of us and swiftly away with, done
　away with, undone,
Undone, done with, soon done with, and yet dearly
　and dangerously sweet
Of us, the wimpled-water-dimpled, not-by-
　morning-matchéd face,
The flower of beauty, fleece of beauty, too too apt
　to, ah! to fleet,
Never fleets móre, fastened with the tenderest truth
To its own best being and its loveliness of youth: it
　is an everlastingness of, O it is an all youth!
Come then, your ways and airs and looks, locks,
　maidengear, gallantry and gaiety and grace,
Winning ways, airs innocent, maiden manners,
　sweet looks, loose locks, long locks, lovelocks,
　gaygear, going gallant, girlgrace –
Resign them, sign them, seal them, send them,
　motion them with breath,
And with sighs soaring, soaring síghs, deliver
Them; beauty-in-the-ghost, deliver it, early now,
　long before death
Give beauty back, beauty, beauty, beauty, back to
　God, beauty's self and beauty's giver.
See; not a hair is, not an eyelash, not the least lash
　lost; every hair
Is, hair of the head, numbered.
Nay, what we had lighthanded left in surly the mere
　mould
Will have waked and have waxed and have walked
　with the wind what while we slept,
This side, that side hurling a heavyheaded
　hundredfold
What while we, while we slumbered.
O then, weary then whý should we tread? O why are
　we so haggard at the heart, so care-coiled, care-
　killed, so fagged, so fashed, so cogged, so
　cumbered,
When the thing we freely forfeit is kept with fonder
　a care,
Fonder a care kept than we could have kept it, kept
Far with fonder a care (and we, we should have lost
　it) finer, fonder
A care kept. – Where kept? do but tell us where
　kept, where. –

Yonder. – What high as that! We follow, now we
    follow. – Yonder, yes yonder, yonder,
Yonder.

🦗

'NO WORST, THERE IS NONE'

No worst, there is none. Pitched past pitch of grief,
More pangs will, schooled at forepangs, wilder wring.
Comforter, where, where is your comforting?
Mary, mother of us, where is your relief?
My cries heave, herds-long; huddle in a main, a chief-
woe, world-sorrow; on an age-old anvil wince and
    sing –
Then lull, then leave off. Fury had shrieked 'No ling-
ering! Let me be fell: force I must be brief'.
O the mind, mind has mountains; cliffs of fall
Frightful, sheer, no-man-fathomed. Hold them cheap
May who ne'er hung there. Nor does long our small
Durance deal with that steep or deep. Here! creep,
Wretch, under a comfort serves in a whirlwind: all
Life death does end and each day dies with sleep.

🦗

'TO SEEM THE STRANGER LIES MY LOT'

To seem the stranger lies my lot, my life
Among strangers. Father and mother dear,
Brothers and sisters are in Christ not near
And he my peace/my parting, sword and strife.

England, whose honour O all my heart woos, wife
To my creating thought, would neither hear
Me, were I pleading, plead nor do I: I wear-
y of idle a being but by where wars are rife.

I am in Ireland now; now I am at a thírd
Remove. Not but in all removes I can
Kind love both give and get. Only what word

Wisest my heart breeds dark heaven's baffling ban
Bars or hell's spell thwarts. This to hoard unheard,
Heard unheeded, leaves me a lonely began.

🦗

'I WAKE AND FEEL THE FELL OF DARK, NOT DAY'

I wake and feel the fell of dark, not day.
What hours, O what black hoúrs we have spent
This night! what sights you, heart, saw; ways you went
And more must, in yet longer light's delay.

With witness I speak this. But where I say
Hours I mean years, mean life. And my lament
Is cries countless, cries like dead letters sent
To dearest him that lives alas! away.

I am gall, I am heartburn. God's most deep decree
Bitter would have me taste: my taste was me;
Bones built in me, flesh filled, blood brimmed the
    curse.

Selfyeast of spirit a dull dough sours. I see
The lost are like this, and their scourge to be
As I am mine, their sweating selves; but worse.

🦗

'MY OWN HEART LET ME MORE HAVE PITY ON'

My own heart let me more have pity on; let
Me live to my sad self hereafter kind,
Charitable; not live this tormented mind
With this tormented mind tormenting yet.

I cast for comfort I can no more get
By groping round my comfortless, than blind
Eyes in their dark can day or thirst can find
Thirst's all-in-all in all a world of wet.

Soul, self; come, poor Jackself, I do advise
You, jaded, let be; call off thoughts awhile
Elsewhere: leave comfort root-room: let joy size

At God knows when to God knows what; whose smile
's not wrung, see you; unforeseen times rather – as skies
Betweenpie mountains – lights a lovely mile.

🦗

That Nature is a Heraclitean Fire and of the Comfort of the Resurrection

Cloud-puffball, torn tufts, tossed pillows flaunt forth,
   then chevy on an air-
built thoroughfare: heaven-roysterers, in gay-gangs
   they throng; they glitter in marches.
Down roughcast, down dazzling whitewash, wherever
   an elm arches,
Shivelights and shadowtackle in long lashes lace, lance,
   and pair.
Delightfully the bright wind boisterous ropes, wrestles,
   beats earth bare
Of yestertempest's creases; in pool and rutpeel parches
Squandering ooze to squeezed dough, crust, dust;
   stanches, starches
Squadroned masks and manmarks treadmire toil there
Footfretted in it. Million-fuelèd, nature's bonfire burns
   on.
But quench her bonniest, dearest to her, her clearest-
   selvèd spark
Man, how fast his firedint, his mark on mind, is gone!
Both are in an unfathomable, all is in an enormous
   dark
Drowned. O pity and indignation! Manshape, that
   shone
Sheer off, disseveral, a star, death blots black out; nor
   mark
        Is any of him at all so stark
But vastness blurs and time beats level. Enough! the
   Resurrection,
A heart's-clarion! Away grief's gasping, joyless days,
   dejection.
        Across my foundering deck shone
A beacon, an eternal beam. Flesh fade, and mortal trash
Fall to the residuary worm; world's wildfire, leave but
   ash:
        In a flash, at a trumpet crash,
I am all at once what Christ is, since he was what I am,
   and
This Jack, joke, poor potsherd, patch, matchwood,
   immortal diamond,
        Is immortal diamond.

'Thou art indeed just, Lord'

Justus quidem tu es, Domine, si disputem tecum; verumtamen
   justa loquar ad te: Quare via impiorum prosperatur? &c.

Thou art indeed just, Lord, if I contend
With thee; but, sir, so what I plead is just.
Why do sinners' ways prosper? and why must
Disappointment all I endeavour end?

Wert thou my enemy, O thou my friend,
How wouldst thou worse, I wonder, than thou dost
Defeat, thwart me? Oh, the sots and thralls of lust
Do in spare hours more thrive than I that spend,

Sir, life upon thy cause. See, banks and brakes
Now, leavèd how thick! lacèd they are again
With fretty chervil, look. and fresh wind shakes

Them; birds build – but not I build; no, but strain,
Time's eunuch, and not breed one work that wakes.
Mine, O thou lord of life, send my roots rain.

To R. B.

The fine delight that fathers thought; the strong
Spur, live and lancing like the blowpipe flame,
Breathes once and, quenchèd faster than it came,
Leaves yet the mind a mother of immortal song.

Nine months she then, nay years, nine years she long
Within her wears, bears, cares and combs the same:
The widow of an insight lost she lives, with aim
Now known and hand at work now never wrong.

Sweet fire the sire of muse, my soul needs this;
I want the one rapture of an inspiration.
O then if in my lagging lines you miss

The roll, the rise, the carol, the creation,
My winter world, that scarcely breathes that bliss
Now, yields you, with some sighs, our explanation.

EPITHALAMION (UNFINISHED)

Hark, hearer, hear what I do; lend a thought now,
    make believe
We are leafwhelmed somewhere with the hood
Of some branchy bunchy bushybowered wood,
Southern dean or Lancashire clough or Devon cleave,
That leans along the loins of hills, where a
    candycoloured, where a gluegold-brown
Marbled river, boisterously beautiful, between
Roots and rocks is danced and dandled, all in froth and
    water-blowballs, down.
We are there, when we hear a shout
That the hanging honeysuck, the dogeared hazels in
    the cover
Makes dither, makes hover
And the riot of a rout
Of, it must be, boys from the town
Bathing: it is summer's sovereign good.

By there comes a listless stranger: beckoned by the
    noise
He drops towards the river: unseen
Sees the bevy of them, how the boys
With dare and with downdolphinry and bellbright
    bodies huddling out,
Are earthworld, airworld, waterworld thorough hurled,
    all by turn and turn about.

This garland of their gambol flashes in his breast
Into such a sudden zest
Of summertime joys
That he hies to a pool neighbouring; sees it is the best
There; sweetest, freshest, shadowiest;
Fairyland; silk-beech, scrolled ash, packed sycamore,
    wild wychelm, hornbeam fretty overstood
By. Rafts and rafts of flake leaves light, dealt so,
    painted on the air,
Hang as still as hawk or hawkmoth, as the stars or as
    the angels there,
Like the thing that never knew the earth, never off
    roots
Rose. Here he feasts: lovely all is! No more: off with –
    down he dings
His bleachèd both and woolwoven wear:
Careless these in coloured wisp
All lie tumbled-to; then with loop-locks
Forward falling, forehead frowning, lips crisp
Over finger-teasing task, his twiny boots
Fast he opens, last he off wrings
Till walk the world he can with bare his feet

And come where lies a coffer, burly all of blocks
Built of chancequarrièd, selfquainèd, hoar-huskèd rocks
And the water warbles over into, filleted with glassy
    grassy quicksilvery shivès and shoots
And with heavenfallen freshness down from moorland
    still brims,
Dark or daylight on and on. Here he will then, here he
    will the fleet
Flinty kindcold element let break across his limbs
Long. Where we leave him, froliclavish, while he looks
    about him, laughs, swims.

Enough now; since the sacred matter that I mean
I should be wronging longer leaving it to float
Upon this only gambolling and echoing-of-earth note –

'THE CHILD IS FATHER TO THE MAN'
‹(Wordsworth)›

'The child is father to the man.'
How can he be? The words are wild.
Suck any sense from that who can:
'The child is father to the man.'
No; what the poet did write ran,
'The man is father to the child.'
'The child is father to the man!'
How can he be? The words are wild.

It has been said of A. E. Housman (1859–1936) that he made despair beautiful. The despair in these poems is that of a man facing life and death without religious belief, and without marriage or a lover. Housman was a homosexual, in an age when homosexual behaviour was punishable by imprisonment. The bleak music of his poems about lost, unrequited or impossible love moves many readers, including me, to tears. Clive James has written of Philip Larkin, 'He faces the worst on our behalf, and brings it to order.' This is certainly true of Housman, and it may explain the enduring popularity of his work.

Choosing my favourites has meant leaving out all the poems about lads going off to war (the kind of thing that inspired Hugh Kingsmill's well-known parody 'What still alive at twenty-two,/ A clean upstanding chap like you?'). With more misgivings, I put aside much-anthologised nature poems such as 'Tell me not now, it needs not saying' and 'On Wenlock Edge' – I like them less than the poems below.

Housman was a classical scholar, Professor of Latin at University College, London and, later, at Cambridge. He was a man of reserved and conventional demeanour. One of his sisters, on first reading his poems, expressed surprise at the discovery that 'Alfred has a heart'. Some time after I first discovered Alfred and his heart, I was delighted to find out that he also possessed a rather ruthless sense of humour. The parody 'Fragment of a Greek Tragedy' shows Housman at his funniest – I have included two extracts at the end of this selection.

EPIGRAPH TO *MORE POEMS*

They say my verse is sad: no wonder;
    Its narrow measure spans
Tears of eternity, and sorrow,
    Not mine, but man's.

This is for all ill-treated fellows
    Unborn and unbegot,
For them to read when they're in trouble
    And I am not.

❧

A SHROPSHIRE LAD

◄ II ►

Loveliest of trees, the cherry now
Is hung with bloom along the bough,
And stands about the woodland ride
Wearing white for Eastertide.

Now, of my threescore years and ten,
Twenty will not come again,
And take from seventy springs a score,
It only leaves me fifty more.

And since to look at things in bloom
Fifty springs are little room,
About the woodlands I will go
To see the cherry hung with snow.

◄ XIII ►

When I was one-and-twenty
    I heard a wise man say,
'Give crowns and pounds and guineas
    But not your heart away;
Give pearls away and rubies
    But keep your fancy free.'
But I was one-and-twenty,
    No use to talk to me.

When I was one-and-twenty
    I heard him say again,
'The heart out of the bosom
    Was never given in vain;
'Tis paid with sighs a plenty
    And sold for endless rue.'
And I am two-and-twenty,
    And oh, 'tis true, 'tis true.

‹ XVII ›

Twice a week the winter thorough
   Here stood I to keep the goal:
Football then was fighting sorrow
   For the young man's soul.

Now in Maytime to the wicket
   Out I march with bat and pad:
See the son of grief at cricket
   Trying to be glad.

Try I will; no harm in trying:
   Wonder 'tis how little mirth
Keeps the bones of man from lying
   On the bed of earth.

‹ XXXII ›

From far, from eve and morning
   And yon twelve-winded sky,
The stuff of life to knit me
   Blew hither: here am I.

Now – for a breath I tarry
   Nor yet disperse apart –
Take my hand quick and tell me,
   What have you in your heart.

Speak now, and I will answer;
   How shall I help you, say;
Ere to the wind's twelve quarters
   I take my endless way.

‹ XXXIII ›

If truth in hearts that perish
   Could move the powers on high,
I think the love I bear you
   Should make you not to die.

Sure, sure, if stedfast meaning,
   If single thought could save,
The world might end to-morrow,
   You should not see the grave.

This long and sure-set liking,
   This boundless will to please,
– Oh, you should live for ever
   If there were help in these.

But now, since all is idle,
   To this lost heart be kind,

Ere to a town you journey
   Where friends are ill to find.

‹ XXXVI ›

White in the moon the long road lies,
   The moon stands blank above;
White in the moon the long road lies
   That leads me from my love.

Still hangs the hedge without a gust,
   Still, still the shadows stay:
My feet upon the moonlit dust
   Pursue the ceaseless way.

The world is round, so travellers tell,
   And straight though reach the track,
Trudge on, trudge on, 'twill all be well,
   The way will guide one back.

But ere the circle homeward hies
   Far, far must it remove:
White in the moon the long road lie
   That leads me from my love.

‹ XL ›

Into my heart an air that kills
   From yon far country blows:
What are those blue remembered hills,
   What spires, what farms are those?

This is the land of lost content,
   I see it shining plain,
The happy highways where I went
   And cannot come again.

‹ LVII ›

You smile upon your friend to-day,
   To-day his ills are over;
You hearken to the lover's say,
   And happy is the lover.

'Tis late to hearken, late to smile,
   But better late than never:
I shall have lived a little while
   Before I die for ever.

‹ LIX

‹ The Isle of Portland ›

The star-filled seas are smooth to-night
   From France to England strown;

Black towers above the Portland light
   The felon-quarried stone.

On yonder island, not to rise,
   Never to stir forth free,
Far from his folk a dead lad lies
   That once was friends with me.

Lie you easy, dream you light,
   And sleep you fast for aye;
And luckier may you find the night
   Than ever you found the day.

❧

Last Poems

‹ X ›

Could man be drunk for ever
   With liquor, love, or fights,
Lief should I rouse at morning
   And lief lie down of nights.

But men at whiles are sober
   And think by fits and starts,
And if they think, they fasten
   Their hands upon their hearts.

‹ XII ›

   The laws of God, the laws of man,
He may keep that will and can;
Not I: let God and man decree
Laws for themselves and not for me;
And if my ways are not as theirs
Let them mind their own affairs.
Their deeds I judge and much condemn,
Yet when did I make laws for them?
Please yourselves, say I, and they
Need only look the other way.
But no, they will not; they must still
Wrest their neighbour to their will,
And make me dance as they desire
With jail and gallows and hell-fire.
And how am I to face the odds
Of man's bedevilment and God's?
I, a stranger and afraid
In a world I never made.
They will be master, right or wrong;
Though both are foolish, both are strong.
And since, my soul, we cannot fly

To Saturn nor to Mercury,
Keep we must, if keep we can,
These foreign laws of God and man.

❧

More Poems

‹ XV ›

Tarry, delight, so seldom met,
   So sure to perish, tarry still;
Forbear to cease or languish yet,
   Though soon you must and will.

By Sestos town, in Hero's tower,
   On Hero's heart Leander lies;
The signal torch has burned its hour
   And sputters as it dies.

Beneath him, in the nighted firth,
   Between two continents complain
The seas he swam from earth to earth
   And he must swim again.

‹ XXIII ›

Crossing alone the nighted ferry
   With the one coin for fee,
Whom, on the wharf of Lethe waiting,
   Count you to find? Not me.

The brisk fond lackey to fetch and carry,
   The true, sick-hearted slave,
Expect him not in the just city
   And free land of the grave.

‹ XXXI ›

Because I liked you better
   Than suits a man to say,
It irked you, and I promised
   To throw the thought away.

To put the world between us
   We parted, stiff and dry;
'Good-bye,' said you, 'forget me.'
   'I will, no fear,' said I.

If here, where clover whitens
   The dead man's knoll, you pass,
And no tall flower to meet you
   Starts in the trefoiled grass.

Halt by the headstone naming
  The heart no longer stirred,
And say the lad that loved you
  Was one that kept his word.

❧

ADDITIONAL POEMS

◄ IV ►

It is no gift I tender,
  A loan is all I can;
But do not scorn the lender;
  Man gets no more from man.

Oh, mortal man may borrow
  What mortal man can lend;
And 'twill not end to-morrow,
  Though sure enough 'twill end.

If death and time are stronger,
  A love may yet be strong;
The world will last for longer,
  But this will last for long.

❧

FRAGMENT OF A GREEK TRAGEDY

(lines 1–28; last 12 lines)

Alcmaeon.   Chorus.

Cho. O suitably attired in leather boots
  Head of a traveller, wherefore seeking whom
  Whence by what way how purposed art thou
    come
  To this well-nightingaled vicinity?
  My object in inquiring is to know.
  But if you happen to be deaf and dumb
  And do not understand a word I say,
  Nod with your hand to signify as much.
Alc. I journeyed hither a Boeotian road.
Cho. Sailing on horseback or with feet for oars?
Alc. Plying by turns my partnership of legs.
Cho. Beneath a shining or a rainy Zeus?
Alc. Mud's sister, not himself, adorns my shoes.
Cho. To learn your name would not displease me
    much.
Alc. Not all that men desire do they obtain.

Cho. Might I then hear at what your presence
    shoots?
Alc. A shepherd's questioned mouth informed me
    that –
Cho. What? for I know not yet what you will say.
Alc. Nor will you ever, if you interrupt.
Cho. Proceed, and I will hold my speechless tongue.
Alc. – This house was Eriphyla's, no one's else.
Cho. Nor did he shame his throat with hateful lies.
Alc. May I then enter, passing through the door?
Cho. Go, chase into the house a lucky foot.
  And, O my son, be, on the one hand, good,
  And do not, on the other hand, be bad;
  For that is very much the safest plan.
Alc. I go into the house with heels and speed.

[…]

Eriphyla (within). O, I am smitten with a hatchet's
    jaw;
  And that in deed and not in word alone.
Cho. I thought I heard a sound within the house
  Unlike the voice of one that jumps for joy.
Eri. He splits my skull, not in a friendly way,
  Once more: he purposes to kill me dead.
Cho. I would not be reputed rash, but yet
  I doubt if all be gay within the house.
Eri. O! O! another stroke! That makes the third.
  He stabs me to the heart against my wish.
Cho. If that be so, thy state of health is poor;
  But thine arithmetic is quite correct.

A hymn is not necessarily good poetry, and any critical judgement is clouded by the mass of associations clinging to those which are familiar from childhood. Moreover, hymns seem inextricably linked with their tunes, good or bad: when we look at them on the page instead of singing them we seem, as Donald Davie has put it (in his Penguin anthology The Psalms in English), to be 'scanning the libretti of vanished operas'. Perhaps this partly accounts for their poor representation in anthologies.

The brief given by the editors to their selectors speaks of 'vital continuities', and no doubt my love for the hymns used in Anglican liturgies forms part of the compost which nourished my poetry. But few of the poems I have chosen were favourites in my childhood (neither Baxter nor Crossman was known to me), and it is only in adult life that I have come to see Isaac Watts as the greatest of hymn-writers. None can equal him in the power to evoke the immensity of creation. Some would put Charles Wesley above him, and I had great difficulty in limiting my selection from Wesley to four poems. Even so, I could not print the whole of 'Wrestling Jacob', which Watts said was worth the whole of his own writings. (Much information about the hymns of these two writers is included in Ian Bradley's excellent Penguin Book of Hymns to which I am greatly indebted.)

Exclusion, of course, has been the hardest part, and the space given to Watts and Wesley has meant that the choice of the rest is somewhat arbitrary, with a bias in favour of earlier writers. I have saved a little space by printing two quatrains together as an eight-line stanza wherever it did not spoil the poem. I regret the absence of any of J. M. Neale's translations, and any version of the 23rd Psalm: this is because George Herbert's is the best, and he, like Cowper, is included elsewhere in the anthology.

'THOU ART MY LIFE'

‹ Francis Quarles (1592–1644) ›

Thou art my Life; if thou but turn away,
My life's a thousand deaths: thou art my Way;
Without thee, Lord, I travel not, but stray.

My Light thou art; without thy glorious sight
My eyes are darkened with perpetual night:
My God, thou art my Way, my Life, my Light.

Thou art my Way; I wander, if thou fly:
Thou art my Light; if hid, how blind am I!
Thou art my Life; if thou withdraw, I die.

Disclose thy sunbeams, close thy wings and stay;
See, see how I am blind, and dead, and stray.
O thou that art my Light, my Life, my Way.

From Emblemes, 1635, a sixteen-stanza poem beginning 'Why dost thou hide thy lovely face?'. I found these four stanzas used as a hymn in The Oxford Hymn Book.

A COLLOQUY WITH GOD

‹ Sir Thomas Browne (1605–1682) ›

The night is come, like to the day;
Depart not thou, great God, away.
Let not my sins, black as the night,
Eclipse the lustre of thy light.
Keep still in my horizon; for to me
The sun makes not the day, but thee.
Thou whose nature cannot sleep,
On my temples sentry keep;
Guard me 'gainst those watchful foes,
Whose eyes are open while mine close;
Let no dreams my head infest,
But such as Jacob's temples blessed.
While I do rest, my soul advance;
Make my sleep a holy trance,
That I may, my rest being wrought,
Awake into some holy thought;
And with as active vigour run
My course as doth the nimble sun.
Sleep is a death; O make me try,
By sleeping, what it is to die:
And as gently lay my head
On my grave, as now my bed.

Howe'er I rest, great God, let me
Awake again at last with thee.
And thus assured, behold I lie
Securely, or to wake or die.
These are my drowsy days; in vain
I do now wake to sleep again:
O come that hour, when I shall never
Sleep again, but wake for ever.

From *Religio Medici*, 1643.

THE COVENANT OF FAITH

‹Richard Baxter (1615–1691)›

Now it belongs not to my care
    Whether I die or live;
To love and serve thee is my share,
    And this thy grace must give.
If life be long, I will be glad
    That I may long obey,
If short, yet why should I be sad
    That shall have the same pay?

Christ leads me through no darker rooms
    Than he went through before;
He that into God's kingdom comes
    Must enter by this door.
Come, Lord, when grace hath made me meet
    Thy blessèd face to see
For if thy work on earth be sweet,
    What will thy glory be?

Then I shall end my sad complaints
    And weary sinful days,
And join with the triumphant saints
    That sing Jehovah's praise.
My knowledge of that life is small,
    The eye of faith is dim;
But it's enough that Christ knows all,
    And I shall be with him.

From *Poetical Fragments*, 1699, part of a longer poem.

LOVE UNKNOWN

‹Samuel Crossman (1624–1691)›

My song is love unknown,
    My Saviour's love to me,
Love to the loveless shown,
    That they might lovely be.
        O, who am I,
            That for my sake
            My Lord should take
        Frail flesh, and die?

He came from his blest throne,
    Salvation to bestow:
But men made strange, and none
    The longed-for Christ would know.
        But O, my Friend,
            My Friend indeed,
            Who at my need
        His life did spend!

Sometimes they strew his way,
    And his sweet praises sing,
Resounding all the day
    Hosannas to their King.
        Then 'Crucify!'
            Is all their breath,
            And for his death
        They thirst and cry.

Why, what hath my Lord done?
    What makes this rage and spite?
He made the lame to run,
    He gave the blind their sight.
        Sweet injuries!
            Yet they at these
            Themselves displease,
        And 'gainst him rise.

They rise, and needs will have
    My dear Lord made away;
A murderer they save,
    The Prince of Life they slay.
        Yet cheerful he
            To suffering goes,
            That he his foes
        From thence might free.

In life no house, no home,
    My Lord on earth might have;
In death no friendly tomb

But what a stranger gave.
    What may I say?
        Heav'n was his home
        But mine the tomb
    Wherein he lay.

Here might I stay and sing,
  No story so divine;
Never was love, dear King,
  Never was grief like thine!
    This is my Friend,
    In whose sweet praise
    I all my days
  Could gladly spend.

From *The Young Man's Meditation* ..., 1664. Not published as a hymn till 1868.

EVENING HYMN

‹Thomas Ken (1637–1711)›

All praise to thee, my God, this night
For all the blessings of the light;
Keep me, O keep me, King of kings,
Beneath thy own almighty wings.

Forgive me, Lord, for thy dear Son,
The ill that I this day have done,
That with the world, myself and thee,
I ere I sleep at peace may be.

Teach me to live, that I may dread
The grave as little as my bed;
To die, that this vile body may
Rise glorious at the awful day.

O may my soul on thee repose
And may sweet sleep mine eyelids close,
Sleep that may me more vigorous make
To serve my God when I awake.

When in the night I sleepless lie
My soul with heavenly thoughts supply,
Let no ill dreams disturb my rest,
No powers of darkness me molest.

Praise God from whom all blessings flow,
Praise him all creatures here below,
Praise him above, ye heavenly host,
Praise Father, Son and Holy Ghost.

From *Poems Devotional & Didactic*. No date given in British Museum or Bodleian copy.

PSALM XXXIV

‹Nahum Tate (1652–1715)›

Through all the changing scenes of life,
  In trouble and in joy,
The praises of my God shall still
  My heart and tongue employ.
Of his deliverance I will boast,
  Till all that are distressed
From my example courage take
  And soothe their griefs to rest.

O magnify the Lord with me,
  With me exalt his name;
When in distress to him I called
  He to my rescue came.
The hosts of God encamp around
  The dwellings of the just;
Deliverance he affords to all
  Who on his succour trust.

O make but trial of his love,
  Experience will decide
How blest they are, and only they
  Who in his truth confide.
Fear him, ye saints, and you will then
  Have nothing else to fear;
Make you his service your delight,
  Your wants shall be his care.

While hungry lions lack their prey
  The Lord will food provide
For such as put their trust in him,
  And see their needs supplied.

Part of an eighteen-verse hymn. *New Version of the Psalms of David* ... Tate & Brady, 1696.

ODE on the Creation

‹Joseph Addison (1672–1719)›

The spacious firmament on high,
With all the blue, ethereal sky,
And spangled heav'ns, a shining frame,
Their great Original proclaim.
Th'unwearied sun, from day to day,
Does his Creator's power display,
And publishes to every land
The work of an almighty Hand.

Soon as the evening shades prevail,
The moon takes up the wondrous tale,
And nightly to the listening earth
Repeats the story of her birth;
Whilst all the stars that round her burn,
And all the planets in their turn,
Confirm the tidings as they roll,
And spread the truth from pole to pole.

What though, in solemn silence all
Move round the dark terrestrial ball?
What though nor reäl voice nor sound
Amid their radiant orbs be found?
In reason's ear they all rejoice,
And utter forth a glorious voice,
For ever singing, as they shine,
'The hand that made us is Divine'.

From The Poetical Works, 1750.

FIVE HYMNS

‹Isaac Watts (1674–1748)›

Jesus shall reign where'er the sun
Does his successive journeys run,
His kingdom stretch from shore to shore
Till moons shall wax and wane no more.
Behold the Islands with their Kings,
And Europe her best tribute brings;
From North to South the Princes meet
To pay their homage at his feet.

There Persia glorious to behold,
There India stands in Eastern Gold,
And barbarous nations at his word
Submit and bow and own their Lord.

For him shall endless prayer be made,
And praises throng to crown his head,
His name like sweet perfume shall rise
With every morning sacrifice.

People and realms of every tongue
Dwell on his love with sweetest song;
And infant voices shall proclaim
Their early blessings on his name.
Blessings abound where'er he reigns,
The prisoner leaps to lose his chains,
The weary find eternal rest,
And all the sons of want are blest.

Where he displays his healing power
Death and the curse are known no more;
In him the tribes of Adam boast
More blessings than their father lost.
Let every creature rise and bring
Peculiar honours to our king;
Angels descend with songs again,
And earth repeat the long Amen.

From Paraphrase of Psalm 72, from The Psalms of David Imitated, 1719.

God is a name my soul adores,
The almighty Three, the eternal One:
Nature and Grace with all their Powers
Confess the infinite Unknown.
From thy great self thy Being springs;
Thou art thine own Original;
Made up of uncreated things,
And self-sufficience bears them all.

Thy Voice hath formed the seas and spheres,
Bid the waves roar, and planets shine;
But nothing like thy Self appears
Through all these spacious works of thine.
Still rolling Nature dies and grows;
From change to change the creatures run:
Thy Being no succession knows,
And all thy vast Designs are one.

A glance of thine runs through the Globes,
Rules the bright Worlds and moves their Frame:
Broad sheets of light compose thy Robes;
Thy Guards are formed of living flame.

Thrones and Dominions round thee fall
And worship in submissive forms;
Thy Presence shakes this lower ball,
This little dwelling place of worms.

Then how shall trembling mortals dare
To sing thy Glory or thy Grace?
Beneath thy Feet we lie so far,
And see but shadows of thy Face.
Who can behold the blazing light?
Who can approach consuming flame?
None but thy Wisdom knows thy Might;
None but thy Word can speak thy Name.

From *Hymns and Spiritual Songs*, 1707.

❧

There is a land of pure delight
    Where saints immortal reign,
Infinite day excludes the night
    And pleasures banish pain.
There everlasting spring abides,
    And never-withering flowers;
Death like a narrow sea divides
    That heavenly land from ours.

Sweet fields beyond the swelling flood
    Stand dressed in living green;
So to the Jews old Canaan stood
    While Jordan rolled between.
But timorous mortals start and shrink
    To cross the narrow sea,
And linger trembling on the brink,
    And fear to launch away.

O could we make our doubts remove,
    These gloomy doubts that rise,
And see the Canaan that we love
    With unbeclouded eyes!
Could we but climb where Moses stood,
    And view the landscape o'er,
Not Jordan's stream, nor death's cold flood,
    Should fright us from the shore.

From *Hymns and Spiritual Songs*, 1707.

❧

Our God, our help in ages past,
    Our hope for years to come,
Our shelter from the stormy blast
    And our eternal home.
Under the shadow of thy throne
    Thy saints have dwelt secure,
Sufficient is thine arm alone,
    And our defence is sure.

Before the hills in order stood
    Or earth received her frame,
From everlasting thou art God,
    To endless years the same.
Thy Word commands our flesh to dust,
    Return, ye sons of men;
All nations rose from Earth at first,
    And turn to earth again.

A thousand ages in thy sight
    Are like an evening gone,
Short as the watch that ends the night
    Before the rising sun.
The busy tribes of flesh and blood,
    With all their lives and cares,
Are carried downward by the flood
    And lost in following years.

Time, like an ever-rolling stream
    Bears all its sons away;
They fly, forgotten as a dream
    Dies at the opening day.
Like flowery fields the nations stand
    Pleased with the morning light;
The flowers beneath the Mower's hand
    Lie withering e'er 'tis night.

Our God, our help in ages past,
    Our hope for years to come,
Be thou our guard while troubles last,
    And our eternal home.

From *The Psalms of David Imitated*, 1719.

❧

When I survey the wondrous Cross,
    Where the young Prince of Glory died,
My richest gain I count but loss,
    And pour contempt on all my pride.

Forbid it, Lord, that I should boast
   Save in the death of Christ my God;
All the vain things that charm me most,
   I sacrifice them to his blood.

See from his head, his hands, his feet,
   Sorrow and love flow mingled down;
Did e'er such love and sorrow meet,
   Or thorns compose so rich a crown?

His dying crimson, like a robe,
   Spreads o'er his body on the Tree;
Then am I dead to all the globe,
   And all the globe is dead to me.

Were the whole realm of nature mine,
   That were a present far too small;
Love so amazing, so divine,
   Demands my soul, my life, my all.

From *Hymns and Spiritual Songs*, 1707, with the original second line.

THE DESPONDING SOUL'S WISH

‹ John Byrom (1692–1763) ›

My spirit longeth for Thee
   Within my troubled breast,
Although I be unworthy
   Of so divine a guest.

Of so divine a guest
   Unworthy though I be,
Yet has my heart no rest
   Unless it come from Thee.

Unless it come from Thee,
   In vain I look around;
In all that I can see,
   No rest is to be found.

No rest is to be found
   But in thy blessed Love;
O let my wish be crowned,
   And send it from above!

From *Miscellaneous Poems*, 1773.

FOUR HYMNS

‹ Charles Wesley (1707–1788) ›

O for a thousand tongues to sing
   My dear Redeemer's praise!
The glories of my God and King,
   The triumphs of his grace.
My gracious Master and my God,
   Assist me to proclaim,
To spread through all the earth abroad
   The honours of thy name.

Jesus, the name that charms our fears,
   That bids our sorrows cease;
'Tis music in the sinner's ears,
   Tis life and health and peace.
He breaks the power of cancelled sin,
   He sets the prisoner free,
His blood can make the foulest clean,
   His blood availed for me.

He speaks, and listening to his voice
   New life the dead receive,
The mournful broken hearts rejoice,
   The humble poor believe.
Hear him, ye deaf, his praise, ye dumb,
   Your loosened tongues employ,
Ye blind, behold your Saviour come,
   And leap, ye lame, for joy.

Look unto him, ye nations, own
   Your God, ye fallen race;
Look and be saved by faith alone,
   Be justified by grace!
See all your sins on Jesus laid;
   The Lamb of God was slain,
His soul was once an offering made
   For every soul of man.

Awake from guilty nature's sleep,
   And Christ shall give you light,
Cast all your sins into the deep,
   And wash the Aethiop white.
With me your chief you then shall know
   Shall feel your sins forgiven;
Anticipate your heaven below
   And own that love is heaven.

From *Hymns and Sacred Poems*, 1740; part of an eighteen-stanza hymn.

Love divine, all loves excelling,
　Joy of heaven, to earth come down,
Fix in us thy humble dwelling,
　All thy faithful mercies crown.
Jesu, thou art all compassion,
　Pure unbounded love thou art;
Visit us with thy salvation,
　Enter every trembling heart.

Breathe, O breathe thy loving spirit
　Into every troubled breast,
Let us all in thee inherit,
　Let us find that second rest.
Take away our bent to sinning
　Alpha and Omega be;
End of faith, as its beginning,
　Set our hearts at liberty.

Come, almighty to deliver,
　Let us all thy life receive;
Suddenly return, and never,
　Never more thy temples leave.
Thee we would be always blessing,
　Serve thee as thy hosts above,
Pray and praise thee without ceasing,
　Glory in thy perfect love.

Finish then thy new creation,
　Pure and sinless let us be;
Let us see thy great salvation
　Perfectly restored in thee:
Changed from glory into glory,
　Till in heaven we take our place,
Till we cast our crowns before thee,
　Lost in wonder, love and praise.

From *Hymns for those that seek, and those that have Redemption*, 1747.

＊

O Thou who camest from above,
　The pure celestial fire to impart,
Kindle a flame of sacred love
　On the mean altar of my heart.
There let it for thy glory burn
　With inextinguishable blaze,
And trembling to its source return
　In humble prayer and ardent praise.

Jesus, confirm my heart's desire
　To work and speak and think for thee;
Still let me guard the holy fire,

And still stir up thy gift in me.
Ready for all thy perfect will,
　My acts of faith and love repeat,
Till death thy endless mercies seal,
　And make my sacrifice complete.

Short Hymns on Selected Passages of Scripture, 1762.

＊

‹ Wrestling Jacob ›

Come, O thou Traveller unknown,
　Whom still I hold but cannot see;
My company before is gone,
　And I am left alone with thee:
With thee all night I mean to stay,
And wrestle till the break of day.

I need not tell thee who I am,
　My misery or sin declare;
Thyself hast called me by my name,
　Look on thy hands and read it there.
But who, I ask thee, who art thou?
Tell me thy name, and tell me now.

In vain thou strugglest to get free,
　I never will unloose my hold:
Art thou the man that died for me?
　The secret of thy love unfold.
Wrestling I will not let thee go
Till I thy name, thy nature know . . .

Yield to me now for I am weak,
　But confident in self-despair:
Speak to my heart, in blessings speak,
　Be conquered by my instant prayer.
Speak, or thou never hence shalt move,
And tell me if thy name is Love.

'Tis Love, 'tis Love! Thou diedst for me!
　I hear thy whisper in my heart.
The morning breaks, the shadows flee,
　Pure Universal Love thou art:
To me, to all, thy bowels move,
Thy nature and thy name is Love. . . .

Lame as I am, I take the prey,
　Hell, earth and sin with ease o'ercome;
I leap for joy, pursue my way,
　And as a bounding hart fly home,

Through all eternity to prove
Thy nature and thy name is Love.

From *Hymns for the people called Methodists*, 1780. This is part of
a longer hymn, which exists in various versions.

❧

'When God of old'

‹John Keble (1792–1866)›

When God of old came down from heaven,
   In power and wrath he came;
Before his feet the clouds were riven,
   Half darkness and half flame.
But when he came the second time,
   He came in power and love;
Softer than gale at morning prime,
   Hovered his holy dove.

The fires that rushed on Sinai down
   In sudden torrents dread,
Now gently light, a glorious crown,
   On every sainted head.
Like arrows went those lightnings forth
   Winged with the sinner's doom,
But these like tongues o'er all the earth
   Proclaiming life to come.

And as on Israel's awestruck ear
   The voice exceeding loud,
The trump that angels quake to hear,
   Thrilled from the deep dark cloud;
So, when the Spirit of our God
   Came down his flock to find,
A voice from heaven was heard abroad,
   A rushing mighty wind.

It fills the Church of God, it fills
   The sinful world around;
Only in stubborn hearts and wills
   No place for it is found.
Come Lord, come Wisdom, Love and Power,
   Open our ears to hear,
Let us not miss the accepted hour;
   Save, Lord, by love or fear.

The Christian Year, 1827. This has four quatrains which are omitted
from hymn-book versions: I include one of them.

❧

Praise to the Holiest

‹J. H. Newman (1801–1890)›

Praise to the Holiest in the height,
   And in the depth be praise;
In all his words most wonderful,
   Most sure in all his ways.
O loving wisdom of our God,
   When all was sin and shame,
A second Adam to the fight
   And to the rescue came.

O wisest love, that flesh and blood
   Which did in Adam fail,
Should strive afresh against the foe,
   Should strive and should prevail.
And that a higher gift than grace
   Should flesh and blood refine,
God's presence and his very self,
   And essence all-divine.

O generous love, that he who smote
   In Man for man the foe,
The double agony in Man
   For man should undergo.
And in the garden secretly,
   And on the Cross on high,
Should teach his brethren, and inspire
   To suffer and to die.

Praise to the Holiest in the height,
   And in the depth be praise,
In all his words most wonderful,
   Most sure in all his ways.

From *The Dream of Gerontius*, 1865. Extracted as a hymn by the
editors of *Hymns Ancient and Modern*.

❧

Dr Johnson (1709–84) is one of the giants of our literature, but his poetry has been overshadowed by his prose and the fame of his conversation and personality. This may be because he wrote very few poems, and most of them are occasional or freely translated from Latin. Yet at its best his verse is magnificent. If the epigrammatic closure of his couplets announces Pope as his master, it also points to the differences between them. Where Pope is waspish, mordant and suavely elegant, Johnson is grave, compassionate and severe. His poetic style has the same sturdy eloquence as his prose and has been praised for observing the prose virtues, though this should not blind us to his poetic qualities, above all memorability and concision.

Johnson's masterpiece, 'The Vanity of Human Wishes', and the earlier 'London' are satires on modern life adapted from the Roman poet Juvenal. In both, Johnson's Christian stoicism and the kindliness of his nature mitigate the Roman's proverbial ferocity while, if anything, increasing the severity. Both also provide occasions for reflections on English history and, through Thales, the angry satirist of 'London', Johnson gives expression to his own wounded patriotism. There is patriotism, too, in his prologue to the play *A Word to the Wise*, written for a benefit performance after the playwright's death. Here, weighing Christian charity against the importance of critical judgement (no light matter in his eyes), Johnson provides a warming example of his deep and subtle morality. The moving tributes to Claudy Phillips, an itinerant violinist, and Robert Levet, an aged physician whom Johnson supported financially, fix a similar generosity in lapidary forms. Finally, from the last month of Johnson's life comes a translation of Horace, which typically turns a classical model towards his own concerns: here with mortality and the ineluctable passing of time.

LONDON: A POEM

‹ In Imitation of the Third Satire of Juvenal ›
(lines 19–82)

While Thales waits the wherry that contains
Of dissipated wealth the small remains,
On Thames's banks, in silent thought we stood,
Where Greenwich smiles upon the silver flood:
Struck with the seat that gave Eliza birth,
We kneel, and kiss the consecrated earth;
In pleasing dreams the blissful age renew,
And call Britannia's glories back to view;
Behold her cross triumphant on the main,
The guard of commerce, and the dread of Spain,
Ere masquerades debauch'd, excise oppress'd,
Or English honour grew a standing jest.

A transient calm the happy scenes bestow,
And for a moment lull the sense of woe.
At length awaking, with contemptuous frown,
Indignant Thales eyes the neighb'ring town.

Since worth, he cries, in these degen'rate days
Wants ev'n the cheap reward of empty praise;
In those curs'd walls, devote to vice and gain,
Since unrewarded science toils in vain;
Since hope but sooths to double my distress,
And ev'ry moment leaves my little less;
While yet my steady steps no staff sustains,
And life still vig'rous revels in my veins;
Grant me, kind Heaven, to find some happier place,
Where honesty and sense are no disgrace;
Some pleasing bank where verdant osiers play,
Some peaceful vale with Nature's paintings gay;
Where once the harrass'd Briton found repose,
And safe in poverty defy'd his foes;
Some secret cell, ye pow'rs, indulgent give.
Let – live here, for – has learn'd to live.
Here let those reign, whom pensions can incite
To vote a patriot black, a courtier white;
Explain their country's dear-bought rights away,
And plead for pirates in the face of day;
With slavish tenets taint our poison'd youth,
And lend a lie the confidence of truth.

Let such raise palaces, and manors buy,
Collect a tax, or farm a lottery,
With warbling eunuchs fill a licens'd stage,
And lull to servitude a thoughtless age.

Heroes, proceed! What bounds your pride shall hold?
What check restrain your thirst for pow'r and gold?

Behold rebellious virtue quite o'erthrown,
Behold our fame, our wealth, our lives your own.
To such, a groaning nation's spoils are giv'n,
When publick crimes inflame the wrath of Heav'n:
But what, my friend, what hope remains for me,
Who start at theft, and blush at perjury?
Who scarce forbear, tho' Britain's court he sing,
To pluck a titled poet's borrow'd wing;
A statesman's logic, unconvinc'd can hear,
And dare to slumber o'er the *Gazetteer*;
Despise a fool in half his pension drest,
And strive in vain to laugh at Clodio's jest.

Others with softer smiles, and subtler art,
Can sap the principles, or taint the heart;
With more address a lover's note convey,
Or bribe a virgin's innocence away.
Well may they rise, while I, whose rustic tongue
Ne'er knew to puzzle right, or varnish wrong,
Spurn'd as a beggar, dreaded as a spy,
Live unregarded, unlamented die.

An Epitaph on Claudy Phillips, a Musician

Phillips, whose touch harmonious could remove
The pangs of guilty pow'r, and hapless love,
Rest here distress'd by poverty no more,
Find here that calm, thou gav'st so oft before.
Sleep, undisturb'd, within this peaceful shrine,
Till angels wake thee, with a note like thine.

The Vanity of Human Wishes

‹ The Tenth Satire of Juvenal Imitated ›
(lines 99–120; 135–64; 191–222; 343–68)

In full-blown dignity, see Wolsey stand,
Law in his voice, and fortune in his hand:
To him the Church, the Realm, their pow'rs
    consign,
Thro' him the rays of regal bounty shine,
Turn'd by his nod the stream of honour flows,
His smile alone security bestows;
Still to new heights his restless wishes tow'r,
Claim leads to claim, and pow'r advances pow'r;

Till conquest unresisted ceas'd to please,
And rights submitted, left him none to seize.
At length his Sov'reign frowns – the train of state
Mark the keen glance, and watch the sign to hate.
Where-e'er he turns he meets a stranger's eye,
His suppliants scorn him, and his followers fly;
At once is lost the pride of aweful state,
The golden canopy, the glitt'ring plate,
The regal palace, the luxurious board,
The liv'ried army, and the menial lord.
With age, with cares, with maladies oppress'd,
He seeks the refuge of monastic rest.
Grief aids disease, remember'd folly stings,
And his last sighs reproach the faith of kings.

[. . .]

When first the college rolls receive his name,
The young enthusiast quits his ease for fame;
Through all his veins the fever of renown
Burns from the strong contagion of the gown;
O'er Bodley's dome his future labours spread,
And Bacon's mansion trembles o'er his head;
Are these thy views? proceed, illustrious youth,
And virtue guard thee to the throne of truth,
Yet should thy soul indulge the gen'rous heat,
Till captive science yields her last retreat;
Should reason guide thee with her brightest ray,
And pour on misty doubt resistless day;
Should no false kindness lure to loose delight,
Nor praise relax, nor difficulty fright;
Should tempting novelty thy cell refrain,
And sloth effuse her opiate fumes in vain;
Should beauty blunt on fops her fatal dart,
Nor claim the triumph of a letter'd heart;
Should no disease thy torpid veins invade,
Nor melancholy's phantoms haunt thy shade;
Yet hope not life from grief or danger free,
Nor think the doom of Man revers'd for thee:
Deign on the passing world to turn thine eyes,
And pause awhile from letters to be wise;
There mark what ills the scholar's life assail,
Toil, envy, want, the patron, and the jail.
See nations slowly wise, and meanly just,
To buried merit raise the tardy bust.
If dreams yet flatter, once again attend,
Hear Lydiat's life and Galileo's end.

[. . .]

On what foundation stands the warrior's pride?
How just his hopes let Swedish Charles decide;
A frame of adamant, a soul of fire,

No dangers fright him, and no labours tire;
O'er love, o'er fear, extends his wide domain,
Unconquer'd lord of pleasure and of pain;
No joys to him pacific scepters yield,
War sounds the trump, he rushes to the field;
Behold surrounding kings their pow'rs combine,
And one capitulate, and one resign;
Peace courts his hand, but spreads her charms in
    vain;
'Think nothing gain'd, he cries, till nought remain,
On Moscow's walls till Gothic standards fly,
And all be mine beneath the polar sky.'
The march begins in military state,
And nations on his eye suspended wait;
Stern famine guards the solitary coast,
And winter barricades the realms of frost;
He comes, nor want nor cold his course delay; –
Hide, blushing glory, hide Pultowa's day:
The vanquish'd hero leaves his broken bands,
And shews his miseries in distant lands;
Condemn'd a needy supplicant to wait,
While ladies interpose, and slaves debate.
But did not chance at length her error mend?
Did no subverted empire mark his end?
Did rival monarchs give the fatal wound?
Or hostile millions press him to the ground?
His fall was destin'd to a barren strand,
A petty fortress, and a dubious hand;
He left the name, at which the world grew pale,
To point a moral, or adorn a tale.

[. . .]

   Where then shall hope and fear their objects find?
Must dull suspence corrupt the stagnant mind?
Must helpless Man, in ignorance sedate,
Roll darkling down the torrent of his fate?
Must no dislike alarm, no wishes rise,
No cries invoke the mercies of the skies?
Enquirer, cease, petitions yet remain,
Which Heav'n may hear, nor deem religion vain.
Still raise for good the supplicating voice,
But leave to Heav'n the measure and the choice.
Safe in his pow'r, whose eyes discern afar
The secret ambush of a specious pray'r.
Implore his aid, in his decisions rest,
Secure whate'er he gives, he gives the best.
Yet when the sense of sacred presence fires,
And strong devotion to the skies aspires,
Pour fourth thy fervours for a healthful mind,
Obedient passions, and a will resign'd;
For love, which scarce collective Man can fill;

For patience sov'reign o'er transmuted ill;
For faith, that panting for a happier seat,
Counts death kind Nature's signal of retreat:
These goods for Man the laws of Heav'n ordain,
These goods he grants, who grants the pow'r to gain;
With these celestial wisdom calms the mind,
And makes the happiness she does not find.

PROLOGUE TO HUGH KELLY'S *A WORD TO THE WISE*

This night presents a play, which publick rage,
Or right, or wrong, once hooted from the stage;
From zeal or malice now no more we dread,
For English vengeance *wars not with the dead.*
A generous foe regards, with pitying eye,
The man whom fate has laid, where all must lie.
To wit, reviving from its author's dust,
Be kind, ye judges, or at least be just:
Let no resentful petulance invade
Th'oblivious grave's inviolable shade.
Let one great payment every claim appease,
And him who cannot hurt, allow to please;
To please by scenes unconscious of offence,
By harmless merriment, or useful sense.
Where aught of bright, or fair, the piece displays,
Approve it only – 'tis too late to praise.
If want of skill, or want of care appear,
Forbear to hiss – the poet cannot hear.
By all, like him, must praise and blame be found;
At best, a fleeting gleam, or empty sound.
Yet then shall calm reflection bless the night,
When liberal pity dignify'd delight;
When pleasure fired her torch at virtue's flame,
And mirth was bounty with a humbler name.

ON THE DEATH OF DR ROBERT LEVET

Condemn'd to hope's delusive mine,
   As on we toil from day to day,
By sudden blasts, or slow decline,
   Our social comforts drop away.

Well tried through many a varying year,
   See LEVET to the grave descend;

Officious, innocent, sincere,
 Of ev'ry friendless name the friend.

Yet still he fills affection's eye,
 Obscurely wise, and coarsely kind;
Nor, letter'd arrogance, deny
 Thy praise to merit unrefin'd.

When fainting nature call'd for aid,
 And hov'ring death prepar'd the blow,
His vig'rous remedy display'd
 The power of art without the show.

In misery's darkest caverns known,
 His useful care was ever nigh,
Where hopeless anguish pour'd his groan,
 And lonely want retir'd to die.

No summons mock'd by chill delay,
 No petty gain disdain'd by pride,
The modest wants of ev'ry day
 The toil of ev'ry day supplied.

His virtues walk'd their narrow round,
 Nor made a pause, nor left a void;
And sure th'Eternal Master found
 The single talent well employed.

The busy day, the peaceful night,
 Unfelt, uncounted, glided by;
His frame was firm, his powers were bright,
 Tho' now his eightieth year was nigh.

Then with no throbbing fiery pain,
 No cold gradations of decay,
Death broke at once the vital chain,
 And free'd his soul the nearest way.

Proclaims mortality to Man.
Rough Winter's blasts to Spring give way
Spring yields to Summer's sovereign ray
Then Summer sinks in Autumn's reign
And Winter chills the world again
Her losses soon the moon supplies
But wretched Man, when once he lies
Where Priam and his sons are laid
Is nought but ashes and a shade.
Who knows if Jove who counts our score
Will toss us in a morning more?
What with your friend you nobly share
At least you rescue from your heir.
Not you, Torquatus, boast of Rome,
When Minos once has fix'd your doom,
Or eloquence, or splendid birth
Or virtue shall replace on earth.
Hippolytus unjustly slain
Diana calls to life in vain,
Nor can the might of Theseus rend
The chains of hell that hold his friend.

Translation of Horace: Odes IV, vii

‹(Diffugere nives)›

The snow dissolv'd no more is seen,
The fields, and woods, behold, are green,
The changing year renews the plain
The rivers know their banks again
The spritely nymph and naked grace
The mazy dance together trace.
The changing year's successive plan

To read Ben Jonson is to encounter many poets – poet as scholar, brawler, dramatist, court laureate, public moralist, private agonizer, and satirist. He lived at a time when it was not considered necessary to melt all one's styles into one: for Jacobeans, different needs called for different styles. The expression of personality was not important. The reader may marvel, then, that Jonson could write so well in so many ways. 'Her Triumph', for example – lines which haunted Ezra Pound throughout his career – is both lush and orderly; in its more compact manner it equals anything by Spenser for its joy in sound and elaborate image. It contrasts with others equally splendid in this selection, as they do with one another. 'Hymn to Diana', with all the 'classical' virtues, is hard, cool, and poised like its subject: this is the poetry of formality and explicitness. 'Gypsy Song', from a masque, has the sound of an improvised popular song – a rough knockabout piece considered appropriate to its gypsy singers. 'To Heaven' and 'On My First Son' are two of the best examples of poetry of statement found in the language, almost devoid of imagery but alert and sensitive to every dramatic modulation of feeling and thought. Last, the longest and most elaborate poem here, 'To the Immortal Memory', is like a great celebratory baroque painting full of artifice and realism, flattery and wisdom, scholarship and decoration: to succeed in getting inside of it is to enter another time.

HER TRIUMPH

See the chariot at hand here of Love,
    Wherein my lady rideth!
Each that draws is a swan or a dove,
    And well the car Love guideth.
As she goes, all hearts do duty
        Unto her beauty;
And enamoured, do wish, so they might
        But enjoy such a sight,
    That they still were to run by her side,
Thorough swords, thorough seas, whither she
    would ride.

Do but look on her eyes, they do light
    All that Love's world compriseth!
Do but look on her hair, it is bright
    As Love's star when it riseth!
Do but mark, her forehead's smoother
        Than words that soothe her!
And from her arched brows, such a grace
        Sheds itself through the face,
    As alone there triumphs to the life
All the gain, all the good, of the elements' strife.

Have you seen but a bright lily grow,
    Before rude hands have touched it?
Have you marked but the fall o' the snow,
    Before the soil hath smutched it?
Have you felt the wool o' the beaver?
        Or swan's down ever?
Or have smelled o' the bud o' the briar?
        Or the nard i' the fire?
    Or have tasted the bag o' the bee?
O so white! O so soft! O so sweet is she!

SONG

Still to be neat, still to be dressed,
As you were going to a feast;
Still to be powdered, still perfumed:
Lady, it is to be presumed,
Though art's hid causes are not found,
All is not sweet, all is not sound.

Give me a look, give me a face,
That makes simplicity a grace;
Robes loosely flowing, hair as free:

Such sweet neglect more taketh me
Than all the adulteries of art:
They strike mine eyes, but not my heart.

KAROLIN'S SONG

Though I am young and cannot tell
    Either what death or love is well,
Yet I have heard they both bear darts
    And both do aim at human hearts;
And then again I have been told
    Love wounds with heat, as death with cold:
So that I fear they do but bring
    Extremes to touch, and mean one thing.

As in a ruin, we it call
    One thing to be blown up, or fall;
Or to our end like way may have
    By a flash of lightning, or a wave;
So love's inflamed shaft or brand
    May kill as soon as death's cold hand:
Except love's fires the virtue have
    To fright the frost out of the grave.

SONG TO CELIA

Drink to me only with thine eyes,
    And I will pledge with mine;
Or leave a kiss but in the cup,
    And I'll not look for wine.
The thirst that from the soul doth rise
    Doth ask a drink divine;
But might I of Jove's nectar sup,
    I would not change for thine.
I sent thee late a rosy wreath,
    Not so much honouring thee
As giving it a hope that there
    It could not withered be.
But thou thereon didst only breathe,
    And sent'st it back to me;
Since when it grows, and smells, I swear,
    Not of itself, but thee.

A SONG

Oh, do not wanton with those eyes
    Lest I be sick with seeing;
Nor cast them down, but let them rise,
    Lest shame destroy their being.

Oh, be not angry with those fires,
    For then their threats will kill me;
Nor look too kind on my desires,
    For then my hopes will spill me.

Oh, do not steep them in thy tears,
    For so will sorrow slay me;
Nor spread them as distract with fears,
    Mine own enough betray me.

HYMN TO CYNTHIA

Queen and huntress, chaste and fair
Now the sun is laid to sleep,
Seated in thy silver chair,
State in wonted manner keep:
    Hesperus entreats thy light,
    Goddess excellently bright.

Earth, let not thy envious shade
Dare itself to interpose;
Cynthia's shining orb was made
Heaven to clear, when day did close:
    Bless us then with wished sight,
    Goddess excellently bright.

Lay thy bow of pearl apart,
And thy crystal-shining quiver;
Give unto the flying hart
Space to breathe, how short soever:
    Thou that mak'st a day of night,
    Goddess excellently bright.

GYPSY SONG

From the famous Peak of Derby
    And the Devil's Arse there hard by
    Where we yearly keep our musters,
    Thus the Egyptians throng in clusters.

Be not frighted with our fashion,
    Though we seem a tattered nation:
    We account our rags our riches,
    So our tricks exceed our stitches.

Give us bacon, rinds of walnuts,
    Shells of cockles and of small nuts,
    Ribbons, bells, and saffron linen,
    All the world is ours to win in.

Knacks we have that will delight you,
    Sleights of hand that will invite you
    To endure our tawny faces,
    And not cause you cut your laces.

All your fortunes we can tell ye,
    Be they for your back or belly,
    In the moods too, and the tenses,
    That may fit your fine five senses.

Draw but then your gloves, we pray you,
    And sit still, we will not fray you:
    For though we be here at Burley,
    We'd be loath to make a hurly.

❧

ON MY FIRST SON

Farewell, thou child of my right hand, and joy;
  My sin was too much hope of thee, loved boy.
Seven years thou wert lent to me, and I thee pay,
  Exacted by thy fate, on the just day.
Oh, could I lose all father now! For why
  Will man lament the state he should envy?
To have so soon 'scaped world's and flesh's rage,
  And, if no other misery, yet age?
Rest in soft peace, and, asked, say here doth lie
  Ben Jonson his best piece of poetry;
For whose sake, henceforth, all his vows be such,
  As what he loves may never like too much.

❧

INVITING A FRIEND TO SUPPER

Tonight, grave sir, both my poor house and I
    Do equally desire your company;
Not that we think us worthy such a guest,
    But that your worth will dignify our feast
With those that come; whose grace may make that
    seem
    Something, which else could hope for no esteem.
It is the fair acceptance, sir, creates
    The entertainment perfect, not the cates.
Yet shall you have, to rectify your palate,
    An olive, capers, or some better salad
Ushering the mutton; with a short-legged hen,
    If we can get her, full of eggs, and then
Lemons, and wine for sauce; to these, a coney
    Is not to be despaired of, for our money;
And though fowl now be scarce, yet there are clerks,
    The sky not falling, think we may have larks.
I'll tell you of more, and lie, so you will come:
    Of partridge, pheasant, woodcock, of which some
May yet be there; and god wit, if we can;
    Knat, rail and ruff, too. Howsoe'er, my man
Shall read a piece of Virgil, Tacitus,
    Livy, or of some better book to us,
Of which we'll speak our minds, amidst our meat;
    And I'll profess no verses to repeat;
To this, if aught appear which I not know of,
    That will the pastry, not my paper, show of.
Digestive cheese and fruit there sure will be;
    But that which most doth take my muse and me
Is a pure cup of rich Canary wine,
    Which is the Mermaid's now, but shall be mine;
Of which had Horace or Anacreon tasted,
    Their lives, as do their lines, till now had lasted.
Tobacco, nectar, or the Thespian spring
    Are all but Luther's beer to this I sing.
Of this we will sup free, but moderately;
    And we will have no Poley or Parrot by;
Nor shall our cups make any guilty men,
    But at our parting we will be as when
We innocently met. No simple word
    That shall be uttered at our mirthful board
Shall make us sad next morning, or affright
    The liberty that we'll enjoy tonight.

❧

On Gut

Gut eats all day, and lechers all the night,
    So all his meat he tasteth over, twice;
And striving so to double his delight,
    He makes himself a thoroughfare of vice.
Thus in his belly can he change a sin:
    Lust it comes out, that gluttony went in.

On Spies

Spies, you are lights in state, but of base stuff,
Who, when you've burnt yourselves down to the snuff,
Stink, and are thrown away. End fair enough.

To Heaven

Good and great God, can I not think of thee,
    But it must straight my melancholy be?
Is it interpreted in me disease
    That, laden with my sins, I seek for ease?
Oh, be thou witness, that the reins dost know
    And hearts of all, if I be sad for show;
And judge me after, if I dare pretend
    To aught but grace, or aim at other end.
As thou art all, so be thou all to me,
    First, midst, and last; converted one and three;
My faith, my hope, my love; and in this state,
    My judge, my witness, and my advocate.
Where have I been this while exiled from thee?
    And whither rapt, now thou but stoop'st to me?
Dwell, dwell here still: Oh, being everywhere,
    How can I doubt to find thee ever here?
I know my state, both full of shame and scorn,
    Conceived in sin, and unto labour born,
Standing with fear, and must with horror fall,
    And destined unto judgement, after all.
I feel my griefs too, and there scarce is ground
    Upon my flesh to inflict another wound.
Yet dare I not complain, or wish for death
    With holy Paul, lest it be thought the breath
Of discontent; or that these prayers be
    For weariness of life not love of thee.

An Ode. To Himself

Where dost thou careless lie,
    Buried in ease and sloth?
    Knowledge that sleeps doth die;
    And this security,
    It is the common moth
That eats on wits and arts, and oft destroys them
    both.

Are all the Aonian springs
    Dried up? Lies Thespia waste?
    Doth Clarius' harp want strings,
    That not a nymph now sings?
    Or droop they, as disgraced
To see their seats and bowers by chattering pies
    defaced?

If hence thy silence be,
    As 'tis too just a cause,
    Let this thought quicken thee:
    Minds that are great and free,
    Should not on fortune pause;
'Tis crown enough to virtue still, her own applause.

What though the greedy fry
    Be taken with false baits
    Of worded balladry,
    And think it poesy?
    They die with their conceits,
And only piteous scorn upon their folly waits.

Then take in hand thy lyre,
    Strike in thy proper strain;
    With Japhet's line, aspire
    Sol's chariot for new fire
    To give the world again;
Who aided him, will thee, the issue of Jove's brain.

And since our dainty age
    Cannot endure reproof,
    Make not thyself a page
    To that strumpet, the stage;
    But sing high and aloof,
Safe from the wolf's black jaw, and the dull ass's
    hoof.

My Picture Left in Scotland

I now think Love is rather deaf than blind,
   For else it could not be
        That she
Whom I adore so much should so slight me.
   And cast my love behind;
I'm sure my language to her was as sweet,
     And every close did meet
     In sentence of as subtle feet,
       As hath the youngest he
That sits in shadow of Apollo's tree.

Oh, but my conscious fears
    That fly my thoughts between,
    Tell me that she hath seen
    My hundred of grey hairs,
    Told seven-and-forty years,
Read so much waste, as she cannot embrace
   My mountain belly, and my rocky face;
And all these through her eyes have stopped her
   ears.

❧

To the Immortal Memory and Friendship of That Noble Pair, Sir Lucius Cary and Sr. H. Morison

‹The Turn›
Brave infant of Saguntum, clear
Thy coming forth in that great year
When the prodigious Hannibal did crown
His rage with razing your immortal town.
Thou, looking then about,
Ere thou wert half got out,
Wise child, didst hastily return,
And mad'st thy mother's womb thine urn.
How summed a circle didst thou leave mankind
Of deepest lore could we the centre find!

‹The Counter-Turn›
Did wiser nature draw thee back
From out the horror of that sack?
Where shame, faith, honour, and regard of right
Lay trampled on; the deeds of death and night
Urged, hurried forth, and hurled
Upon the affrighted world:
Sword, fire, and famine with fell fury met,
And all on utmost ruin set;

As, could they but life's miseries foresee,
No doubt all infants would return like thee.

‹The Stand›
For what is life, if measured by the space,
Not by the act?
Or masked man, if valued by his face
Above his fact?
Here's one outlived his peers
And told forth four-score years;
He vexed time, and busied the whole state;
Troubled both foes and friends,
But ever to no ends;
What did this stirrer, but die late?
How well at twenty had he fallen or stood!
For three of his four-score he did no good.

‹The Turn›
He entered well by virtuous parts,
Got up and thrived with honest arts;
He purchased friends and fame and honours then,
And had his noble name advanced with men;
But weary of that flight,
He stooped in all men's sight
To sordid flatteries, acts of strife,
And sunk in that dead sea of life
So deep, as he did then death's waters sup,
But that the cork of title buoyed him up.

‹The Counter-Turn›
Alas, but Morison fell young!
He never fell: thou fall'st, my tongue.
He stood, a soldier to the last right end,
A perfect patriot, and a noble friend;
But most, a virtuous son.
All offices were done
By him so ample, full, and round,
In weight, in measure, number, sound,
As, though his age imperfect might appear,
His life was of humanity the sphere.

‹The Stand›
Go now, and tell out days summed up with fears;
And make them years;
Produce thy mass of miseries on the stage,
To swell thine age;
Repeat of things a throng,
To show thou hast been long,
Not lived; for life does her great actions spell
By what was done and wrought
In season, and so brought

To light: her measures are, how well
Each syllabe answered, and was formed, how fair:
These make the lines of life, and that's her air.

‹The Turn›
It is not growing like a tree
In bulk, doth make man better be;
Or standing long an oak, three hundred year,
To fall a log at last, dry, bald, and sere:
A lily of a day
Is fairer far, in May,
Although it fall and die that night;
It was the plant and flower of light.
In small proportions we just beauty see,
And in short measures life may perfect be.

‹The Counter-Turn›
Call, noble Lucius, then for wine,
And let thy looks with gladness shine;
Accept this garland, plant it on thy head;
And think, nay know, thy Morison's not dead.
He leaped the present age,
Possessed with holy rage
To see that bright eternal day,
Of which we priests and poets say
Such truths as we expect for happy men;
And there he lives with memory, and Ben

‹The Stand›
Jonson, who sung this of him, ere he went
Himself to rest,
Or taste a part of that full joy he meant
To have expressed
In this bright asterism;
Where it were friendship's schism
(Were not his Lucius long with us to tarry)
To separate these twi-
Lights, the Dioscuri;
And keep the one half from his Harry.
But fate doth so alternate the design,
Whilst that in heaven, this light on earth must
    shine.

‹The Turn›
And shine as you exalted are;
Two names of friendship, but one star:
Of hearts the union. And those not by chance
Made, or indentured, or leased out to advance
The profits for a time.
No pleasures vain did chime,
Of rhymes, or riots, at your feasts,

Orgies of drink, or feigned protests:
But simple love of greatness, and of good;
That knits brave minds and manners, more than
    blood.

‹The Counter-Turn›
This made you first to know the why
You liked; then after to apply
That liking; and approach so one the tother
Till either grew a portion of the other:
Each styled, by his end,
The copy of his friend.
You lived to be the great surnames
And titles by which all made claims
Unto the virtue. Nothing perfect done
But as a Cary, or a Morison.

‹The Stand›
And such a force the fair example had,
As they that saw
The good and durst not practise it, were glad
That such a law
Was left yet to mankind;
Where they might read and find
Friendship in deed was written, not in words;
And with the heart, not pen,
Of two so early men
Whose lines her rolls were, and records.
Who, ere the first down bloomed on the chin,
Had sowed these fruits, and got the harvest in.

Keats died of tuberculosis in Rome on 23 February 1821, aged twenty-five. Two months later Shelley began writing his famous elegy 'Adonais' (which was first printed in Pisa the following June). Shelley's intention was to honour his dead friend, and to attack those – such as the Tory *Blackwood's Magazine* and the *Quarterly Review* – whose 'savage criticism' of *Endymion* had produced an 'agitation' which had led to Keats's 'rapid consumption'. It was a well-meant defence. But it transformed Keats – who in life had been robust, convivial and radical – into a beautiful weakling.

The first biography of Keats, which was published by Richard Monckton Milnes in 1848, tried to correct Shelley's distortion – to little avail. Throughout the nineteenth century, as Keats's reputation grew, he remained fixed in the popular imagination as 'the youngest of the martyrs'. (The phrase is Oscar Wilde's.) Even in the 1960s, when three excellent biographies (by Walter Jackson Bate, Robert Gittings, and Aileen Ward) finally filled in most of the details of Keats's short life, the received image remained substantially the same. Keats had been blighted by the world but had been separated from it by his devotion to 'the principle of Beauty'. He had certainly not shown a developed interest in contemporary social affairs, or in politics.

Not true. Keats was born into a lower-middle-class family which was deeply aware of its social insecurities, at a time of national and international crisis. He attended a school which, while not being precisely a Dissenting Academy, shared many of the radical aims of such an institution. During his training to be a doctor at Guy's, he was inspired by the progressive aims of that great Whig institution. When he turned from medicine to poetry, he brought to his writing the same ideals that had fed him in the early years of his life; he wanted to produce poems which were 'physicianly', and which came down on 'the liberal side of the question'.

My selection from Keats's poems is designed to illustrate these neglected aspects of his genius, as well as the much-praised sensuality of his work, of which it forms an important part.

ON FIRST LOOKING INTO CHAPMAN'S HOMER

Much have I travelled in the realms of gold,
    And many goodly states and kingdoms seen;
    Round many western islands have I been
Which bards in fealty to Apollo hold.
Oft of one wide expanse had I been told
    That deep-browed Homer ruled as his demesne;
    Yet did I never breathe its pure serene
Till I heard Chapman speak out loud and bold:
Then felt I like some watcher of the skies
    When a new planet swims into his ken;
Or like stout Cortez when with eagle eyes
    He stared at the Pacific – and all his men
Looked at each other with a wild surmise –
    Silent, upon a peak in Darien.

❧

SLEEP AND POETRY
(lines 96–104; 122–32)

O for ten years, that I may overwhelm
Myself in poesy; so I may do the deed
That my own soul has to itself decreed.
Then will I pass the countries that I see
In long perspective, and continually
Taste their pure fountains. First the realm I'll pass
Of Flora, and old Pan: sleep in the grass,
Feed upon apples red, and strawberries,
And choose each pleasure that my fancy sees;

[. . .]

And can I ever bid these joys farewell?
Yes, I must pass them for a nobler life,
Where I may find the agonies, the strife
Of human hearts: for lo! I see afar,
O'ersailing the blue cragginess, a car
And steeds with streamy manes – the charioteer
Looks out upon the winds with glorious fear:
And now the numerous tramplings quiver lightly
Along a huge cloud's ridge; and now with sprightly
Wheel downward come they into fresher skies,
Tipped round with silver from the sun's bright eyes.

❧

ENDYMION

‹Book I›
(lines 1–33)

A thing of beauty is a joy for ever:
Its loveliness increases; it will never
Pass into nothingness; but still will keep
A bower quiet for us, and a sleep
Full of sweet dreams, and health, and quiet
   breathing.
Therefore, on every morrow, are we wreathing
A flowery band to bind us to the earth,
Spite of despondence, of the inhuman dearth
Of noble natures, of the gloomy days,
Of all the unhealthy and o'er-darkened ways
Made for our searching: yes, in spite of all,
Some shape of beauty moves away the pall
From our dark spirits. Such the sun, the moon,
Trees old, and young, sprouting a shady boon
For simple sheep; and such are daffodils
With the green world they live in; and clear rills
That for themselves a cooling covert make
'Gainst the hot season; the mid forest brake,
Rich with a sprinkling of fair musk-rose blooms:
And such too is the grandeur of the dooms
We have imagined for the mighty dead;
All lovely tales that we have heard or read:
An endless fountain of immortal drink,
Pouring unto us from the heaven's brink.

Nor do we merely feel these essences
For one short hour; no, even as the trees
That whisper round a temple become soon
Dear as the temple's self, so does the moon,
The passion poesy, glories infinite,
Haunt us till they become a cheering light
Unto our souls, and bound to us so fast,
That, whether there be shine, or gloom o'ercast,
They alway must be with us, or we die.

‹Book III›
(lines 1–40)

There are who lord it o'er their fellow-men
With most prevailing tinsel: who unpen
Their baaing vanities, to browse away
The comfortable green and juicy hay
From human pastures; or, O torturing fact!
Who, through an idiot blink, will see unpacked
Fire-branded foxes to sear up and singe
Our gold and ripe-eared hopes. With not one tinge
Of sanctuary splendour, not a sight

Able to face an owl's, they still are dight
By the blear-eyed nations in empurpled vests,
And crowns, and turbans. With unladen breasts,
Save of blown self-applause, they proudly mount
To their spirit's perch, their being's high account,
Their tiptop nothings, their dull skies, their
   thrones –
Amid the fierce intoxicating tones
Of trumpets, shoutings, and belaboured drums,
And sudden cannon. Ah! how all his hums,
In wakeful ears, like uproar passed and gone –
Like thunder clouds that spake to Babylon,
And set those old Chaldeans to their tasks. –
Are then regalities all gilded masks?
No, there are thronèd seats unscalable
But by a patient wing, a constant spell,
Or by ethereal things that, unconfined,
Can make a ladder of the eternal wind,
And poise about in cloudy thunder-tents
To watch the abysm-birth of elements.
Aye, 'bove the withering of old-lipped Fate
A thousand Powers keep religious state,
In water, fiery realm, and airy bourne;
And, silent as a consecrated urn,
Hold sphery sessions for a season due.
Yet few of these far majesties, ah, few!
Have bared their operations to this globe –
Few, who with gorgeous pageantry enrobe
Our piece of heaven – whose benevolence
Shakes hand with our own Ceres; every sense
Filling with spiritual sweets to plenitude,
As bees gorge full their cells. [. . .]

❧

TO J. H. REYNOLDS, ESQ.
(lines 86–105)

Dear Reynolds! I have a mysterious tale,
And cannot speak it: the first page I read
Upon a lampit rock of green sea-weed
Among the breakers; 'twas a quiet eve,
The rocks were silent, the wide sea did weave
An untumultuous fringe of silver foam
Along the flat brown sand; I was at home
And should have been most happy, – but I saw
Too far into the sea, where every maw
The greater on the less feeds evermore. –
But I saw too distinct into the core
Of an eternal fierce destruction,
And so from happiness I far was gone.

Still I am sick of it, and though, to-day,
I've gather'd young spring-leaves, and flowers gay
Of periwinkle and wild strawberry,
Still do I that most fierce destruction see, –
The shark at savage prey, – the hawk at pounce, –
The gentle robin, like a pard or ounce,
Ravening a worm, – Away, ye horrid moods!

HYPERION

‹Book I›

(lines 164–200)

But one of the whole mammoth-brood still kept
His sovereignty, and rule, and majesty; –
Blazing Hyperion on his orbèd fire
Still sat, still snuffed the incense, teeming up
From man to the sun's God; yet unsecure:
For as among us mortals omens drear
Fright and perplex, so also shuddered he –
Not at dog's howl, or gloom-bird's hated screech,
Or the familiar visiting of one
Upon the first toll of his passing-bell,
Or prophesyings of the midnight lamp;
But horrors, portioned to a giant nerve,
Oft made Hyperion ache. His palace bright
Bastioned with pyramids of glowing gold,
And touched with shade of bronzèd obelisks,
Glared a blood-red through all its thousand courts,
Arches, and domes, and fiery galleries;
And all its curtains of Aurorian clouds
Flushed angerly: while sometimes eagle's wings,
Unseen before by Gods or wondering men,
Darkened the place; and neighing steeds were heard,
Not heard before by Gods or wondering men.
Also, when he would taste the spicy wreaths
Of incense, breathed aloft from sacred hills,
Instead of sweets, his ample palate took
Savour of poisonous brass and metal sick:
And so, when harboured in the sleepy west,
After the full completion of fair day, –
For rest divine upon exalted couch
And slumber in the arms of melody,
He paced away the pleasant hours of ease
With stride colossal, on from hall to hall;
While far within each aisle and deep recess,
His wingèd minions in close clusters stood,
Amazed and full of fear; like anxious men

Who on wide plains gather in panting troops,
When earthquakes jar their battlements and towers.

THE EVE OF ST AGNES

(lines 298–324)

‹XXXIV›

Her eyes were open, but she still beheld,
Now wide awake, the vision of her sleep:
There was a painful change, that nigh expelled
The blisses of her dream so pure and deep
At which fair Madeline began to weep,
And moan forth witless words with many a sigh;
While still her gaze on Porphyro would keep;
Who knelt, with joinèd hands and piteous eye,
Fearing to move or speak, she looked so dreamingly.

‹XXXV›

'Ah, Porphyro!' said she, 'but even now
Thy voice was at sweet tremble in mine ear,
Made tuneable with every sweetest vow;
And those sad eyes were spiritual and clear:
How changed thou art! how pallid, chill, and
    drear!
Give me that voice again, my Porphyro,
Those looks immortal, those complainings dear!
Oh leave me not in this eternal woe,
For if thou diest, my Love, I know not where to go.'

‹XXXVI›

Beyond a mortal man impassioned far
At these voluptuous accents, he arose,
Ethereal, flushed, and like a throbbing star
Seen mid the sapphire heaven's deep repose;
Into her dream he melted, as the rose
Blendeth its odour with the violet, –
Solution sweet: meantime the frost-wind blows
Like Love's alarum pattering the sharp sleet
Against the window-panes: St Agnes' moon hath set.

La Belle Dame Sans Merci

‹A Ballad›

‹ I ›

Oh, what can ail thee, knight-at-arms,
  Alone and palely loitering?
The sedge has withered from the lake,
  And no birds sing.

‹ II ›

Oh, what can ail thee, knight-at-arms,
  So haggard and so woe-begone?
The squirrel's granary is full,
  And the harvest's done.

‹ III ›

I see a lily on thy brow,
  With anguish moist and fever dew;
And on thy cheeks a fading rose
  Fast withereth too.

‹ IV ›

I met a lady in the meads,
  Full beautiful – a faery's child,
Her hair was long, her foot was light,
  And her eyes were wild.

‹ V ›

I made a garland for her head,
  And bracelets too, and fragrant zone;
She looked at me as she did love,
  And made sweet moan.

‹ VI ›

I set her on my pacing steed,
  And nothing else saw all day long;
For sidelong would she bend, and sing
  A faery's song.

‹ VII ›

She found me roots of relish sweet,
  And honey wild, and manna dew,
And sure in language strange she said –
  'I love thee true'.

‹ VIII ›

She took me to her elfin grot,
  And there she wept and sighed full sore,
And there I shut her wild wild eyes
  With kisses four.

‹ IX ›

And there she lullèd me asleep
  And there I dreamed – Ah! woe betide!
The latest dream I ever dreamt
  On the cold hill side.

‹ X ›

I saw pale kings and princes too,
  Pale warriors, death-pale were they all;
They cried – 'La Belle Dame sans Merci
  Hath thee in thrall!'

‹ XI ›

I saw their starved lips in the gloam,
  With horrid warning gapèd wide,
And I awoke and found me here,
  On the cold hill's side.

‹ XII ›

And this is why I sojourn here
  Alone and palely loitering,
Though the sedge has withered from the lake,
  And no birds sing.

Ode to Psyche

O Goddess! hear these tuneless numbers, wrung
  By sweet enforcement and remembrance dear,
And pardon that thy secrets should be sung
  Even into thine own soft-conchèd ear:
Surely I dreamt to-day, or did I see
  The wingèd Psyche with awakened eyes?
I wandered in a forest thoughtlessly,
  And, on the sudden, fainting with surprise,
Saw two fair creatures, couchèd side by side
  In deepest grass, beneath the whisp'ring roof
  Of leaves and trembled blossoms, where there
    ran
      A brooklet, scarce espied:
'Mid hushed, cool-rooted flowers, fragrant-eyed,
  Blue, silver-white, and budded Tyrian,
They lay calm-breathing on the bedded grass;
  Their arms embraced, and their pinions too;
  Their lips touched not, but had not bade adieu,
As if disjoined by soft-handed slumber,
And ready still past kisses to outnumber
  (At tender eye-dawn of aurorean love:)
    The wingèd boy I knew;

But who wast thou, O happy, happy dove?
　　His Psyche true!

O latest born and loveliest vision far
　　Of all Olympus' faded hierarchy!
Fairer than Phœbe's sapphire-regioned star,
　　Or Vesper, amorous glow-worm of the sky;
Fairer than these, though temple thou hast none,
　　　　Nor altar heaped with flowers;
Nor virgin-choir to make delicious moan
　　　　Upon the midnight hours;
No voice, no lute, no pipe, no incense sweet
　　From chain-swung censer teeming;
No shrine, no grove, no oracle, no heat
　　Of pale-mouthed prophet dreaming.

O brightest! thought too late for antique vows,
　　Too, too late for the fond believing lyre,
When holy were the haunted forest boughs,
　　Holy the air, the water, and the fire;
Yet even in these days so far retired
　　From happy pieties, thy lucent fans,
　　Fluttering among the faint Olympians,
I see, and sing, by my own eyes inspired.
So let me be thy choir, and make a moan
　　　　Upon the midnight hours;
Thy voice, thy lute, thy pipe, thy incense sweet
　　From swingèd censer teeming –
Thy shrine, thy grove, thy oracle, thy heat
　　Of pale-mouthed prophet dreaming.

Yes, I will be thy priest, and build a fane
　　In some untrodden region of my mind,
Where branchèd thoughts, new grown with pleasant
　　　　pain,
　　Instead of pines shall murmur in the wind:
Far, far around shall those dark-clustered trees
　　Fledge the wild-ridgèd mountains steep by steep;
And there by zephyrs, streams, and birds, and bees,
　　The moss-lain Dryads shall be lulled to sleep;
And in the midst of this wide quietness
　　A rosy sanctuary will I dress
With the wreathed trellis of a working brain,
　　With buds, and bells, and stars without a name,
With all the gardener Fancy e'er could feign,
　　Who breeding flowers, will never breed the
　　　　same:
And there shall be for thee all soft delight
　　That shadowy thought can win,

A bright torch, and a casement ope at night,
　　To let the warm Love in!

❧

ODE ON A GRECIAN URN

◄ I ►

Thou still unravished bride of quietness,
　　Thou foster-child of silence and slow time,
Sylvan historian, who canst thus express
　　A flowery tale more sweetly than our rhyme:
What leaf-fringed legend haunts about thy shape
　　Of deities or mortals, or of both,
　　　　In Tempe or the dales of Arcady?
　　What men or gods are these? What maidens loth?
What mad pursuit? What struggle to escape?
　　　　What pipes and timbrels? What wild ecstasy?

◄ II ►

Heard melodies are sweet, but those unheard
　　Are sweeter; therefore, ye soft pipes, play on;
Not to the sensual ear, but, more endeared,
　　Pipe to the spirit ditties of no tone:
Fair youth, beneath the trees, thou canst not leave
　　Thy song, nor ever can those trees be bare;
　　　Bold Lover, never, never canst thou kiss,
Though winning near the goal – yet, do not grieve;
　　She cannot fade, though thou hast not thy bliss,
　　　For ever wilt thou love, and she be fair!

◄ III ►

Ah, happy, happy boughs! that cannot shed
　　Your leaves, nor ever bid the Spring adieu;
And, happy melodist, unwearièd,
　　For ever piping songs for ever new;
More happy love! more happy, happy love!
　　For ever warm and still to be enjoyed,
　　　For ever panting, and for ever young;
All breathing human passion far above,
　　That leaves a heart high-sorrowful and cloyed,
　　　A burning forehead, and a parching tongue.

◄ IV ►

Who are these coming to the sacrifice?
　　To what green altar, O mysterious priest,
Lead'st thou that heifer lowing at the skies,
　　And all her silken flanks with garlands dressed?
What little town by river or sea shore,
　　Or mountain-built with peaceful citadel,

Is emptied of this folk, this pious morn?
And, little town, thy streets for evermore
    Will silent be; and not a soul to tell
    Why thou art desolate, can e'er return.

◄ V ►

O Attic shape! Fair attitude! with brede
  Of marble men and maidens overwrought,
With forest branches and the trodden weed;
    Thou, silent form, dost tease us out of thought
As doth eternity: Cold Pastoral!
    When old age shall this generation waste,
      Thou shalt remain in midst of other woe
Than ours, a friend to man, to whom thou say'st,
    'Beauty is truth, truth beauty, – that is all
      Ye know on earth, and all ye need to know.'

ODE TO A NIGHTINGALE

◄ I ►

My heart aches, and a drowsy numbness pains
  My sense, as though of hemlock I had drunk
Or emptied some dull opiate to the drains
    One minute past, and Lethe-wards had sunk:
'Tis not through envy of thy happy lot,
    But being too happy in thine happiness, –
      That thou, light-wingèd Dryad of the trees,
        In some melodious plot
  Of beechen green, and shadows numberless,
    Singest of summer in full-throated ease.

◄ II ►

O, for a draught of vintage! that hath been
  Cooled a long age in the deep-delvèd earth,
Tasting of Flora and the country green,
    Dance, and Provençal song, and sunburnt mirth!
O for a beaker full of the warm South,
    Full of the true, the blushful Hippocrene,
      With beaded bubbles winking at the brim,
        And purple-stainèd mouth;
  That I might drink, and leave the world unseen,
    And with thee fade away into the forest dim:

◄ III ►

Fade far away, dissolve, and quite forget
  What thou among the leaves hast never known,
The weariness, the fever, and the fret
  Here, where men sit and hear each other groan;

Where palsy shakes a few, sad, last gray hairs,
  Where youth grows pale, and spectre-thin, and
    dies;
    Where but to think is to be full of sorrow
      And leaden-eyed despairs,
    Where Beauty cannot keep her lustrous eyes,
      Or new Love pine at them beyond to-
        morrow.

◄ IV ►

Away! away! for I will fly to thee,
  Not charioted by Bacchus and his pards,
But on the viewless wings of Poesy,
    Though the dull brain perplexes and retards:
Already with thee! tender is the night,
    And haply the Queen-Moon is on her throne,
      Clustered around by all her starry Fays;
        But here there is no light,
  Save what from heaven is with the breezes blown
    Through verdurous glooms and winding
      mossy ways.

◄ V ►

I cannot see what flowers are at my feet,
  Nor what soft incense hangs upon the boughs,
But, in embalmèd darkness, guess each sweet
    Wherewith the seasonable month endows
The grass, the thicket, and the fruit-tree wild;
    White hawthorn, and the pastoral eglantine;
      Fast fading violets covered up in leaves;
        And mid-May's eldest child,
  The coming musk-rose, full of dewy wine,
    The murmurous haunt of flies on summer
      eves.

◄ VI ►

Darkling I listen; and, for many a time
  I have been half in love with easeful Death,
Called him soft names in many a musèd rhyme,
    To take into the air my quiet breath;
Now more than ever seems it rich to die,
    To cease upon the midnight with no pain,
      While thou art pouring forth thy soul abroad
        In such an ecstasy!
  Still wouldst thou sing, and I have ears in vain –
    To thy high requiem become a sod.

◄ VII ►

Thou wast not born for death, immortal Bird!
  No hungry generations tread thee down;

The voice I hear this passing night was heard
  In ancient days by emperor and clown:
Perhaps the self-same song that found a path
  Through the sad heart of Ruth, when, sick for
    home,
    She stood in tears amid the alien corn;
      The same that oft-times hath
  Charmed magic casements, opening on the foam
  Of perilous seas, in faery lands forlorn.

◄ VIII ►

Forlorn! the very word is like a bell
  To toll me back from thee to my sole self!
Adieu! the fancy cannot cheat so well
  As she is famed to do, deceiving elf.
Adieu! adieu! thy plaintive anthem fades
  Past the near meadows, over the still stream,
    Up the hill-side; and now 'tis buried deep
      In the next valley-glades:
    Was it a vision, or a waking dream?
      Fled is that music: – Do I wake or sleep?

LAMIA

◄ Part I ►
(lines 47–67)

She was a gordian shape of dazzling hue,
Vermilion-spotted, golden, green, and blue;
Striped like a zebra, freckled like a pard,
Eyed like a peacock, and all crimson barred;
And full of silver moons, that, as she breathed,
Dissolv'd, or brighter shone, or interwreathed
Their lustres with the gloomier tapestries –
So rainbow-sided, touched with miseries,
She seemed, at once, some penanced lady elf,
Some demon's mistress, or the demon's self.
Upon her crest she wore a wannish fire
Sprinkled with stars, like Ariadne's tiar:
Her head was serpent, but ah, bitter-sweet!
She had a woman's mouth with all its pearls
  complete:
And for her eyes: what could such eyes do there
But weep, and weep, that they were born so fair?
As Proserpine still weeps for her Sicilian air.
Her throat was serpent, but the words she spake
Came, as through bubbling honey, for Love's
  sake,

And thus; while Hermes on his pinions lay,
Like a stooped falcon ere he takes his prey.

TO AUTUMN

◄ I ►
Season of mists and mellow fruitfulness,
  Close bosom-friend of the maturing sun;
Conspiring with him how to load and bless
  With fruit the vines that round the thatch-eves
    run;
To bend with apples the mossed cottage-trees,
  And fill all fruit with ripeness to the core;
    To swell the gourd, and plump the hazel
    shells
  With a sweet kernel; to set budding more,
And still more, later flowers for the bees,
Until they think warm days will never cease,
    For Summer has o'er-brimmed their clammy
    cells.

◄ II ►
Who hath not seen thee oft amid thy store?
  Sometimes whoever seeks abroad may find
Thee sitting careless on a granary floor,
  Thy hair soft-lifted by the winnowing wind;
Or on a half-reaped furrow sound asleep,
  Drowsed with the fume of poppies, while thy
    hook
    Spares the next swath and all its twinèd
    flowers:
And sometimes like a gleaner thou dost keep
  Steady thy laden head across a brook;
  Or by a cider-press, with patient look,
    Thou watchest the last oozings hours by
    hours.

◄ III ►
Where are the songs of Spring? Ay, where are they?
  Think not of them, thou hast thy music too, –
While barrèd clouds bloom the soft-dying day,
  And touch the stubble-plains with rosy hue;
Then in a wailful choir the small gnats mourn
  Among the river sallows, borne aloft
    Or sinking as the light wind lives or dies;
And full-grown lambs loud bleat from hilly bourn;
  Hedge-crickets sing; and now with treble soft

The red-breast whistles from a garden-croft;
    And gathering swallows twitter in the skies.

❧

The Fall of Hyperion
A Dream

◄ [Canto I] ►

(lines 1–18; 237–71)

Fanatics have their dreams, wherewith they weave
A paradise for a sect; the savage too
From forth the loftiest fashion of his sleep
Guesses at Heaven; pity these have not
Traced upon vellum or wild Indian leaf
The shadows of melodious utterance.
But bare of laurel they live, dream, and die;
For Poesy alone can tell her dreams,
With the fine spell of words alone can save
Imagination from the sable charm
And dumb enchantment. Who alive can say,
'Thou art no Poet – may'st not tell thy dreams'?
Since every man whose soul is not a clod
Hath visions, and would speak, if he had loved,
And been well nurtured in his mother tongue.
Whether the dream now purposed to rehearse
Be poet's or fanatic's will be known
When this warm scribe my hand is in the grave.

[. . .]

I looked upon the altar, and its horns
Whitened with ashes, and its languorous flame,
And then upon the offerings again;
And so by turns – till sad Moneta cried,
'The sacrifice is done, but not the less
Will I be kind to thee for thy good will.
My power, which to me is still a curse,
Shall be to thee a wonder; for the scenes
Still swooning vivid through my globèd brain,
With an electral changing misery,
Thou shalt with those dull mortal eyes behold,
Free from all pain, if wonder pain thee not.'
As near as an immortal's spherèd words
Could to a mother's soften, were these last:
And yet I had a terror of her robes,
And chiefly of the veils, that from her brow
Hung pale, and curtained her in mysteries,
That made my heart too small to hold its blood.
This saw that Goddess, and with sacred hand
Parted the veils. Then saw I a wan face,

Not pined by human sorrows, but bright-blanched
By an immortal sickness which kills not;
It works a constant change, which happy death
Can put no end to; deathwards progressing
To no death was that visage; it had passed
The lily and the snow; and beyond these
I must not think now, though I saw that face –
But for her eyes I should have fled away.
They held me back, with a benignant light,
Soft mitigated by divinest lids
Half-closed, and visionless entire they seemed
Of all external things; – they saw me not,
But in blank splendour, beamed like the mild
    moon,
Who comforts those she sees not, who knows not
What eyes are upward cast. [. . .]

❧

'Bright star'

Bright star, would I were steadfast as thou art –
    Not in lone splendour hung aloft the night
And watching, with eternal lids apart,
    Like nature's patient, sleepless Eremite,
The moving waters at their priestlike task
    Of pure ablution round earth's human shores,
Or gazing on the new soft-fallen mask
    Of snow upon the mountains and the moors –
No – yet still steadfast, still unchangeable,
    Pillowed upon my fair love's ripening breast,
To feel for ever its soft fall and swell,
    Awake for ever in a sweet unrest,
Still, still to hear her tender-taken breath,
And so live ever – or else swoon to death.

❧

'This living hand'

This living hand, now warm and capable
Of earnest grasping, would, if it were cold
And in the icy silence of the tomb,
So haunt thy days and chill thy dreaming nights
That thou wouldst wish thine own heart dry of
    blood
So in my veins red life might stream again,
And thou be conscience-calmed – see here it is –
I hold it towards you.

Sometimes the experiences that yield most of us nothing but suffering can be for poets the source of their best work. Wilfred Owen went to the trenches. Henry King's wife died. Suddenly there is a conjunction between skill as a poet and the need to express powerful feelings. In his elegy, 'An Exequy To His Matchlesse never to be forgotten Friend', King (1592–1669) employs the stock techniques of the period. It is an argument in which each point is proved by a witty play with images that derive from the preoccupations of the seventeenth century: religion, cosmology, astronomy, navigation and war. What makes it so moving to a twentieth-century reader is that the voice of the poem comes over as that of a man genuinely struggling to understand and come to terms with his loss. The distortions of the poem's preposterous wit reflect the distortions of a mind overwhelmed by grief. The obsessiveness with which the poet's longing to be reunited with his wife becomes the principle informing his entire world seems natural. This is especially true of the ending, where there is an extraordinary fusion between the fantasies of the mind and the immediate sensations of the body as the poet hears his pulse beating like a drum in his own funeral procession. My other choice is the short poem 'Sic Vita'. Its subject is unoriginal: the brevity and fragility of life. What King does with it is stunning. He conjures a world that is at once cosmic and minute, from stars and eagles in the sky to the earth and seas and the bubbles wind creates on water. Then with a wonderful economy of wit he demolishes it, image by image, in a list that ends, in a little stab of inevitability, with man.

AN EXEQUY TO HIS MATCHLESS NEVER TO BE FORGOTTEN FRIEND

Accept, thou shrine of my dead saint,
Instead of dirges this complaint!
And for sweet flowers to crown thy hearse
Receive a strew of weeping verse
From thy grieved friend, whom thou mightst see
Quite melted into tears for thee.
    Dear loss! Since thy untimely fate
My task hath been to meditate
On thee, on thee: thou art the book,
The library whereon I look,
Though almost blind. For thee (loved clay!)
I languish out, not live the day,
Using no other exercise
But what I practise with mine eyes.
By which wet glasses I find out
How lazily time creeps about
The one that mourns. This, only this
My exercise and business is:
So I compute the weary hours
With sighs dissolvèd into showers.
    Nor wonder if my time go thus
Backward and most preposterous;
Thou has benighted me. Thy set
This eve of blackness did beget
Who wast my day (though overcast
Before thou hadst thy noontide passed)
And I remember must in tears
Thou scarce hadst seen so many years
As day tells hours. By thy clear sun
My love and fortune first did run;
But thou wilt never more appear
Folded within my hemisphere;
Since both thy light and motion
Like a fled star is fallen and gone,
And 'twixt me and my soul's dear wish
The Earth now interposed is
Which such a strange eclipse doth make
As ne'er was read in almanac.
    I could allow thee for a time
To darken me and my sad clime:
Were it a month, a year, or ten,
I would thy exile live till then,
And all that space my mirth adjourn
So thou wouldst promise to return,
And putting off thy ashy shrowd
At length disperse this sorrow's cloud.
    But woe is me! the longest date
Too narrow is to calculate

These empty hopes. Never shall I
Be so much blest as to descry
A glimpse of thee, till that day come
Which shall the Earth to cinders doom;
And a fierce fever must calcine
The body of this world, like thine
(My little world!). That fit of fire
Once off, our bodies shall aspire
To our souls' bliss: then we shall rise,
And view ourselves with clearer eyes
In that calm region, where no night
Can hide us from each other's sight.

    Meantime thou hast her, earth: much good
May my harm do thee. Since it stood
With heaven's will I might not call
Her longer mine, I give thee all
My short-lived right and interest
In her, whom living I loved best:
With a most free and bounteous grief
I give thee what I could not keep.
Be kind to her; and prithee look
Thou write into thy Domesday Book
Each parcel of this rarity,
Which in thy casket shrined doth lie:
See that thou make thy reck'ning straight,
And yield her back again by weight;
For thou must audit on thy trust
Each grain and atom of this dust,
As thou wilt answer him that lent,
Not gave thee, my dear monument.

    So close the ground, and about her shade
Black curtains draw: my bride is laid.
    Sleep on, my love, in thy cold bed,
Never to be disquieted.
My last good night! Thou wilt not wake
Till I thy fate shall overtake:
Till age, or grief, or sickness must
Marry my body to that dust
It so much loves, and fill the room
My heart keeps empty in thy tomb.
Stay for me there: I will not fail
To meet thee in that hollow vale.
And think not much of my delay:
I am already on the way,
And follow thee with all the speed
Desire can make, or sorrows breed.
Each minute is a short degree,
And every hour a step towards thee.
At night when I betake to rest,
Next morn I rise nearer my west
Of life, almost by eight hours' sail,

Than when sleep breathed his drowsy gale.
    Thus from the sun my bottom steers,
And my days' compass downward bears.
Nor labour I to stem the tide,
Through which to thee I swiftly glide.
    'Tis true; with shame and grief I yield:
Thou, like the van, first tookst the field,
And gotten hast the victory
In thus adventuring to die
Before me, whose more years might crave
A just precedence in the grave.
But hark! My pulse, like a soft drum,
Beats my approach, tells thee I come;
And, slow howe'er my marches be,
I shall at last sit down by thee.
    The thought of this bids me go on,
And wait my dissolution
With hope and comfort. Dear, forgive
The crime! I am content to live
Divided, with but half a heart,
Till we shall meet and never part.

SIC VITA

Like to the falling of a star;
Or as the flights of eagles are;
Or like the fresh spring's gaudy hue;
Or silver drops of morning dew;
Or like a wind that chafes the flood;
Or bubbles which on water stood:
Even such is man, whose borrowed light
Is straight called in, and paid to night.

The wind blows out, the bubble dries:
The spring entombed in autumn lies:
The dew dries up: the star is shot:
The flight is past: and man forgot.

Rudyard Kipling (1865–1936), a favourite poet of both Kaiser Wilhelm and Jorge Luis Borges, was tremendously popular during his lifetime, and was regarded by many as the unofficial Poet Laureate. He was certainly the only poet I ever heard my father quote and 'Boots' was the poem he would recite on our Sunday afternoon walks. I didn't much care for it myself, though, nor the other barrack-room ballads. At the age of seven I had had enough of war.

I confess to having read little of his verse over the years, and so, when recently I sat down with the 'compleat works' (Michael Schmidt being a persuasive sort of chap), I was taken with Kipling's virtuosity and fluency, and in particular, with his feeling for history and the landscape: the dizzy sense of the present falling into the past.

His poems – memorable and quotable – elicit a response from the reader. Not merely adorning the page, they almost demand to escape from it and be off into the real world. On Sunday afternoons I often go for a walk with my young son. I have learned 'Boots'.

A SMUGGLER'S SONG

If you wake at midnight, and hear a horse's feet,
Don't go drawing back the blind, or looking in the
    street.
Them that asks no questions isn't told a lie.
Watch the wall, my darling, while the Gentlemen go
    by!
    Five and twenty ponies,
    Trotting through the dark –
    Brandy for the Parson,
    'Baccy for the Clerk;
  Laces for a lady, letters for a spy,
And watch the wall, my darling, while the Gentlemen
    go by!

Running round the woodlump if you chance to find
Little barrels, roped and tarred, all full of brandy-wine,
Don't you shout to come and look, nor use 'em for
    your play.
Put the brushwood back again, – and they'll be gone
    next day!

If you see the stable-door setting open wide;
If you see a tired horse lying down inside;
If your mother mends a coat cut about and tore;
If the lining's wet and warm – don't you ask no more!

If you meet King George's men, dressed in blue and
    red,
You be careful what you say, and mindful what is said.
If they call you 'pretty maid', and chuck you 'neath the
    chin,
Don't you tell where no one is, nor yet where no one's
    been!

Knocks and footsteps round the house – whistles after
    dark –
You've no call for running out till the house-dogs
    bark.
Trusty's here, and *Pincher's* here, and see how dumb they
    lie –
They don't fret to follow when the Gentlemen go by!

If you do as you've been told, 'likely there's a chance
You'll be give a dainty doll, all the way from France,
With a cap of Valenciennes, and a velvet hood –
A present from the Gentlemen, along o' being good!
    Five and twenty ponies,
    Trotting through the dark –
    Brandy for the Parson,

'Baccy for the Clerk;
Them that asks no questions isn't told a lie –
Watch the wall, my darling, while the Gentlemen go
    by!

THE BALLAD OF MINEPIT SHAW

About the time that taverns shut
    And men can buy no beer,
Two lads went up by the keepers' hut
    To steal Lord Pelham's deer.

Night and the liquor was in their heads –
    They laughed and talked no bounds,
Till they waked the keepers on their beds,
    And the keepers loosed the hounds.

They had killed a hart, they had killed a hind,
    Ready to carry away,
When they heard a whimper down the wind
    And they heard a bloodhound bay.

They took and ran across the fern,
    Their crossbows in their hand,
Till they met a man with a green lantern
    That called and bade 'em stand.

'What are ye doing, O Flesh and Blood,
    And what's your foolish will,
That you must break into Minepit Wood
    And wake the Folk of the Hill?'

'Oh, we've broke into Lord Pelham's park,
    And killed Lord Pelham's deer,
And if ever you heard a little dog bark
    You'll know why we come here!

'We ask you let us go our way,
    As fast as we can flee,
For if ever you heard a bloodhound bay,
    You'll know how pressed we be.'

'Oh, lay your crossbows on the bank
    And drop the knife from your hand,
And though the hounds are at your flank
    I'll save you where you stand!'

They laid their crossbows on the bank
    They threw their knives in the wood,
And the ground before them opened and sank
    And saved 'em where they stood.

'Oh, what's the roaring in our ears
    That strikes us well-nigh dumb?'
'Oh, that is just how things appear!
    According as they come.'

'What are the stars before our eyes
    That strike us well-nigh blind?'
'Oh, that is just how things arise
    According as you find.'

'And why's our bed so hard to the bones
    Excepting where it's cold?'
'Oh, that's because it is precious stones
    Excepting where 'tis gold.

'Think it over as you stand,
    For I tell you without fail,
If you haven't got into Fairyland
    You're not in Lewes Gaol.'

All night long they thought of it,
    And, come the dawn, they saw
They'd tumbled into a great old pit,
    At the bottom of Minepit Shaw.

And the keepers' hound had followed 'em close
    And broke her neck in the fall;
So they picked up their knives and their crossbows
    And buried the dog. That's all.

But whether the man was a poacher too
    Or a Pharisee so bold –
I reckon there's more things told than are true,
    And more things true than are told.

The poet who is the author of perhaps the greatest of very short poems in English had a very long life (1775–1864). When Landor was a child, there was an old woman in his village who was said to have spoken with John Milton, when she was very young. Young Swinburne paid tribute on a visit to Landor as a young Pound paid tribute to Swinburne, so that Landor embodies a kind of link between Milton and the modern period.

The poems are suitable to this link: deeply romantic in feeling, classical in formal economy and bite, they have a sculptural clarity that appealed mightily to Pound.

It is a truism that Landor is a poet's poet. I once heard Elizabeth Bishop, in the course of a conversation with Robert Lowell, recite 'Past Ruin'd Ilion' for the edification of Lowell and me. 'That is the kind of poetry we all should write,' she told Lowell, rather scoldingly. The sounds of that poem, of his four brilliant lines on the hair of Lucrezia Borgia, and in particular of his poem 'Separation' ('There is a mountain and a wood between us') stand as a kind of measure for the best in poetic writing, for me.

Landor wrote wonderful poems longer than these ('The Fiesolan Idyl', 'To His Child Carlino'), but I have chosen to keep to the songs and epigrams in this selection. The great stylist kept his powers into his very old age, and I have included the extraordinary poem 'Memory', which along with the epigram beginning 'To my ninth decad I have tottered on' surely embodies some of the most powerful writing imaginable on the subject of feeling one's powers failing in old age.

PAST RUIN'D ILION

Past ruin'd Ilion Helen lives,
  Alcestis rises from the shades;
Verse calls them forth; 'tis verse that gives
  Immortal youth to mortal maids.

Soon shall Oblivion's deepening veil
  Hide all the peopled hills you see,
The gay, the proud, while lovers hail
  In distant ages you and me.

The tear for fading beauty check,
  For passing glory cease to sigh;
One form shall rise above the wreck,
  One name, Ianthe, shall not die.

❦

ON SEEING A HAIR OF LUCRETIA BORGIA

Borgia, thou once wert almost too august,
And high for adoration; – now thou 'rt dust!
All that remains of thee these plaits infold –
Calm hair, meand'ring with pellucid gold!

❦

WORMWOOD AND RUE

◄ 1 ►
Wormwood and rue be on his tongue
  And ashes on his head,
Who chills the feast and checks the song
  With emblems of the dead!

◄ 2 ►
By young and jovial, wise and brave,
  Such mummers are derided.
His sacred rites shall Bacchus have,
  Unspared and undivided.

◄ 3 ►
Coucht by my friends, I fear no mask
  Impending from above,
I only fear the later flask
  That holds me from my love.

❦

DEATH OF THE DAY

My pictures blacken in their frames
   As night comes on,
And youthful maids and wrinkled dames
   Are now all one.

Death of the day! a sterner Death
   Did worse before;
The fairest form, the sweetest breath,
   Away he bore.

SEPARATION

There is a mountain and a wood between us,
Where the lone shepherd and late bird have seen us
Morning and noon and even-tide repass.
Between us now the mountain and the wood
Seem standing darker than last year they stood,
And say we must not cross, alas! alas!

TO ROBERT BROWNING

   There is delight in singing, though none hear
   Beside the singer; and there is delight
   In praising, though the praiser sit alone
And see the prais'd far off him, far above.
   Shakespeare is not our poet, but the world's,
   Therefore on him no speech; and short for
      thee,
   Browning! Since Chaucer was alive and hale,
   No man hath walk'd along our roads with step
So active, so inquiring eye, or tongue
So varied in discourse. But warmer climes
Give brighter plumage, stronger wing; the breeze
   Of Alpine heights thou playst with, borne on
   Beyond Sorrento and Amalfi, where
   The Siren waits thee, singing song for song.

THE LEAVES ARE FALLING

   The leaves are falling; so am I;
The few late flowers have moisture in the eye;
     So have I too.
   Scarcely on any bough is heard
   Joyous, or even unjoyous, bird
     The whole wood through.

   Winter may come: he brings but nigher
His circle (yearly narrowing) to the fire
     Where old friends meet:
   Let him; now heaven is overcast,
   And spring and summer both are past,
     And all things sweet.

FROM SAPPHO

Mother, I cannot mind my wheel;
   My fingers ache, my lips are dry:
Oh! if you felt the pain I feel!
   But Oh, who ever felt as I?

No longer could I doubt him true;
   All other men may use deceit:
He always said my eyes were blue,
   And often swore my lips were sweet.

ROSE AYLMER

Ah what avails the sceptred race,
   Ah what the form divine!
What, every virtue, every grace!
   For, Aylmer, all were thine.

Sweet Aylmer, whom these wakeful eyes
   May weep, but never see,
A night of sorrows and of sighs
   I consecrate to thee.

MEMORY

The mother of the Muses, we are taught,
Is Memory: she has left me; they remain,
And shake my shoulder, urging me to sing
About the summer days, my loves of old.
Alas! alas! is all I can reply.
Memory has left with me that name alone,
Harmonious name, which other bards may sing,
But her bright image in my darkest hour
Comes back, in vain comes back, call'd or uncall'd.
Forgotten are the names of visitors
Ready to press my hand but yesterday;
Forgotten are the names of earlier friends
Whose genial converse and glad countenance
Are fresh as ever to mine ear and eye;
To these, when I have written, and besought
Remembrance of me, the word *Dear* alone
Hangs on the upper verge, and waits in vain.
A blessing wert thou, O oblivion,
If thy stream carried only weeds away,
But vernal and autumnal flowers alike
It hurries down to wither on the strand.

'TO MY NINTH DECAD I HAVE TOTTERED ON'

To my ninth decad I have tottered on,
 And no soft arm bends now my steps to steady;
She, who once led me where she would, is gone,
 So when he calls me, Death shall find me ready.

Although *Piers Plowman* is one of the few great masterpieces of medieval English poetry, and according to C. S. Lewis the only one capable of 'sublimity', we know very little about its author, William Langland (d. 1386?). We are not even certain of his name; anything that we do know is inferred from the poem itself. It is likely that he came, like many writers in Middle English, from the west Midlands. On the poem's evidence he seems to have lived in Cornhill: 'in London and off London both' There are 51 manuscripts of the poem, in at least three distinguishable textual stages, dating from the 1360s to 1386. The B-text is the one usually most favoured both because it is the most coherently completed of the full-length versions of the poem, and because it is richest in Lewis's passages of sublimity. The extracts given here are the poem's beautiful dream-vision opening; the fable of Belling the Cat which seems to have been introduced into this radical text as a somewhat conservative response to the Peasants' Revolt of 1381; the vision of 'great creating Nature' from the poem's centre; and Christ's great address at the Crucifixion.

William Langland

Piers Plowman

‹Prologue›

(lines 1–75)

In a somer seson, when softe was the sonne,
I shoop me into shroudes as I a sheep were,
In habite as an heremite unholy of werkes,
Wente wide in this world wondres to here.
Ac on a May morwenynge on Malverne hilles
Me bifel a ferly, of Fairye me thoghte.
I was wery forwandred and wente me to reste
Under a brood bank by a bourne syde;
And as I lay and lenede and loked on the watres,
I slombred into a slepyng, it sweyed so murye.

Thanne gan I meten a merveillous swevene –
That I was in a wildernesse, wiste I nevere where.
Ac as I biheeld into the eest an heigh to the sonne,
I seigh a tour on a toft trieliche ymaked,
A deep dale bynethe, a dongeon therinne,
With depe diches and derke and dredfulle of sighte.
A fair feeld ful of folk fond I ther bitwene –
Of alle manere of men, the meene and the riche,
Werchynge and wandrynge as the world asketh.
Somme putten hem to the plough, pleiden ful
selde,
In settynge and sowynge swonken ful harde,
And wonnen that thise wastours with glotonye
destruyeth.
And somme putten hem to pride, apparailed hem
therafter,
In contenaunce of clothynge comen disgised.
In preieres and penaunce putten hem manye,
Al for the love of Oure Lord lyveden ful streyte
In hope to have heveneriche blisse –
As ancres and heremites that holden hem in hire
selles,
Coveiten noght in contree to cairen aboute
For no likerous liflode hire likame to plese.
And somme chosen chaffare; they cheveden the
bettre –
As it semeth to oure sight that swiche men thryveth;
And somme murthes to make as mynstralles konne,
And geten gold with hire glee – giltlees, I leeve.
Ac japeres and jangeleres, Judas children,
Feynen hem fantasies, and fooles hem maketh –
And hen wit at wille to werken if they wolde.
That Poul precheth of hem I wol net preve it here:
Qui loquitur turpiloquium is Luciferes hyne.
Bidderes and beggeres faste aboute yede
Til hire bely and hire bagge were bredful ycrammed;
Faiteden for hire foode, foughten at the ale.

In glotonye, God woot, go thei to bedde,
And risen with ribaudie, tho Roberdes knaves;
Sleep and sory sleuthe seweth hem evere.
Pilgrymes and palmeres plighter hem togidere
For to seken Seint Jame and seintes at Rome;
Wenten forth in hire wey with many wise tales,
And hadden leve to lyen al hire lif after.
I seigh somme that seiden thei hadde ysought
seintes:
To ech a tale that thei tolde hire tonge was tempred
to lye
Moore than to seye sooth, it semed bi hire speche.
Heremytes on an heep with hoked staves
Wenten to Walsyngham – and hire wenches after:
Grete lobies and longe that lothe were to swynke
Clothed hem in copes to ben knowen from othere,
And shopen hem heremytes hire ese to have.
I fond there freres, alle the foure ordres,
Prechynge the peple for profit of the wombe:
Glosed the gospel as hem good liked;
For coveitise of copes construwed it as thei wolde.
Manye of thise maistres mowe clothen hem at likyng
For hire moneie and hire marchaundise marchen
togideres.
Sith charite hath ben chapman and chief to shryve
lordes
Manye ferlies han fallen in a fewe yeres.
But Holy Chirche and hii horde bettre togidres
The mooste meschief on molde is mountynge up
faste.
Ther preched a pardoner as he a preest were:
Broughte forth a bulle with bisshopes seles,
And seide that hymself myghte assoillen hem alle
Of falshede of fastynge, of avowes ybroken.
Lewed men leved hym wel and liked hise wordes,
Comen up knelynge to kissen his bulle.
He bonched hem with his brevet and blered hire
eighen,
And raughte with his rageman rynges and broches.

Glossary

false tales and play the fool, and have brains at their command to work if they want to. What St Paul says about them I dare not say here: *he who speaks obscenity is Lucifer's servant*; BIDDERES: mendicants; BREDFUL: chock-full; ROBERDES KNAVES: lawless vagabonds; SLEUTHE SEWETH: sloth follow; PALMERES . . . SEINT JAME: pilgrims to St James of Compostela; LYEN: tell lies; AN HEEP: a crowd; GRETE LOBIES . . . TO SWYNKE: great gangling louts that were loath to work, BEN KNOWEN: be distinguished; SHOPEN HEM: made themselves; FRERES: friars; WOMBE: belly; GLOSED . . . LIKED: interpreted the Gospel as it suited them; MAISTRES: gentry; SITH CHARITE . . . SHRYVE LORDES: since love has turned into a pedlar and been foremost in shriving lords; FERLIES HAN FALLEN: strange things have happened; BUT HOLY . . . TO GIDRES: unless Holy Church and they work together better; ASSOILLEN: absolve; FALSHEDE OF FASTYNGE: evading fasting; LEVED: believed; BONCHED: thumped; RAUGHTE . . . RAGEMAN: used his document to procure

‹ 'Belling the Cat' ›

(Prologue, lines 146–210)

With that ran ther a route of ratons at ones
And smale mees myd hem: mo than a thousand
Comen to a counseil for the commune profit;
For a cat of a court cam when hym liked
And overleep hem lightliche and laughte hem at his
     wille,
And pleide with hem perillousli and possed aboute.
     'For doute of diverse dredes we dar noght wel
     loke!
And if we grucche of his gamen he wol greven us
     alle –
Cracchen us or clawen us and in his clouches holde,
That us lotheth the lif er he late us passe.
Mighte we with any wit his wille withstonde,
We myghte be lordes olofte and lyven at oure ese'.
     A raton of renoun, moost renable of tonge,
Seide for a sovereyn salve to hem alle.
'I have yseyen segges', quod he, 'in the Cite of
     Londoun
Beren beighes ful brighte abouten hire nekkes,
And somme colers of crafty work; uncoupled they
     wenden
Bothe in wareyne and in waast where hem leve
     liketh,
And outher while thei arn elliswhere, as I here telle.
Were ther a belle on hire beighe, by Jesus, as me
     thynketh,
Men myghte witen wher their wente and away
     renne.
And right so', quod that raton, 'reson me sheweth
To bugge a belle of bras or of bright silver
And knytten it on a coler for oure commune profit
And hangen it upon the cattes hals – thanne here we
     mowen
Wher he ryt or rest or rometh to pleye;
And if hym list for to laike, thanne loke we mowen

And peeren in his presence the while hym pleye
     liketh,
And if hym wratheth, be war and his wey shonye'.
     Al the route of ratons to this reson assented;
Ac tho the belle was ybrought and on the beighe
     hanged
Ther ne was raton in al the route, for al the reaume
     of France,
That dorste have bounden the belle aboute the cattes
     nekke,
Ne hangen it aboute his hals al Engelond to wynne,
Ac helden hem unhardy and hir counseil feble,
And leten hire laboure lost and al hire longe studie.
     A mous that muche good kouthe, as me tho
     thoughte,
Strook forth sternely and stood bifore hem alle,
And to the route of ratons reherced thise wordes:
'Though we hadde ykilled the cat, yet sholde ther
     come another
To cracchen us and al oure kynde, though we cropen
     under benches.
Forthi I counseille al the commune to late the cat
     worthe,
And be we nevere so bolde the belle hym to shewe.
The while he caccheth conynges he coveiteth noght
     oure caroyne,
But fedeth hym al with venyson; defame we hym
     nevere.
For bettre is a litel los than a long sorwe:
The maze among us alle, theigh we mysse a sherewe!
For I herde my sire seyn, is seven yeer ypassed,
'Ther the cat is a kitoun, the court is ful elenge'.
That witnesseth Holy Writ, whoso wole it rede –
Ve terre ubi puer rex est, &c.
For may no renk ther reste have for ratons by nyghte.
For many mennes malt we mees wolde destruye,
And also ye route of ratons rende mennes clothes,
Nere the cat of the court that ken you overlepe;
For hadde ye rattes youre raik ye kouthe noght rule
     yowselve.
     'I seye for me', quod the mous, 'I se so muchel
     after,
Shal nevere the cat ne the kiton by my counseil be
     greved,
Ne carpynge of this coler that costed me nevere.
And though it costned me catel, biknowen it I nolde,
But suffren as hymself wolde so doon as hym
     liketh –
Coupled and uncoupled to cacche what thei mowe.
Forthi ech a wis wight I warne – wite wel his owene!'

(What this metels bymeneth, ye men that ben murye,
Devyne ye – for I ne dar, by deere God in hevene)!

Glossary

‹The Vision of Nature›

(passus 11, lines 320–66)

And slepynge I seigh al this; and sithen cam Kynde
And nempned me by my name, and bad me nymen hede,
And thorough the wondres of this world wit for to take.
And on a mountaigne that Myddelerthe highte, as me tho thoughte,
I was fet forth by ensaumples to knowe,
Thorough ech a creature, Kynde my creatour to lovye.
  I seigh the sonne and the see and the sond after,
And where that briddes and beestes by hir make thei yeden,
Wilde wormes in wodes, and wonderful foweles
With fleckede fetheres and of fele colours.
Man and his make I myghte se bothe;
Poverte and pientee, bothe pees and werre,
Blisse and bale – bothe I seigh at ones,
And how men token Mede and Mercy refused.
  Reson I seigh soothly sewen alle beestes
In etynge, in drynkynge and in engendrynge of kynde.
And after cours of concepcion noon took kepe of oother
As whan thei hadde ryde in rotey tyme; anoonright therafter
Males drowen hem to males amornynge by hemselve,
And femelles to femelles ferded and drowe.
Ther ne was cow ne cowkynde that conceyved hadde
That wolde belwe after bole, ne boor after sowe.

Bothe hors and houndes and alle othere beestes
Medled noght with hir makes that mid fole were.
  Briddes I biheld that in buskes made nestes;
Hadde nevere wye wit to werche the leeste.
I hadde wonder at whom and wher the pye
Lerned to legge the stikkes in which she leyeth and bredeth.
Ther nys wrighte, as I wene, sholde werche hir nest to paye;
If any mason made a molde therto, muche wonder it were.
  And yet me merveilled moore: many othere briddes
Hidden and hileden hir egges ful derne
In mareys and mores for men sholde hem noght fynde,
And hidden hir egges when thei therfro wente,
For fere of othere foweles and for wilde beestes.
  And some troden hir makes and on trees bredden
And broughten forth hir briddes so al above the grounde.
And some briddes at the bile thorugh brethyng conceyved,
And some caukede; I took kepe how pecokkes bredden.
Muche merveilled me what maister thei hadde,
And who taughte hem on trees to tymbre so heighe
That neither burn ne beest may hir briddes rechen.
  And sithen I loked on the see and so forth on the sterres;
Manye selkouthes I seigh, ben noght to seye nouthe.
I seigh floures in the fryth and hir faire colours,
And how among the grene gras growed so many hewes,
And some soure and some swete – selkouth me thoughte.

Glossary

tradesman; TO PAYE: to equal it; MOLDE: building-mould; HILEDEN: secreted; DERNE: hidden; MAREYS: marshes; FOR MEN SHOLDE: so that men would; THERFRO: away from; FOR WILDE BEESTES: from wild animals; TRODEN: copulated with; SO: in that way; BILE: bill; BRETHYNG: breathing; CAUKEDE: trod; MAISTER: instructor; TYMBRE: build; BURN: man; RECHEN: reach; SO FORTH; onwards; SELKOUTHES: wonders; NOUTHE: now; FRYTH; meadow; SELKOUTH; amazing.

◄ Christ dies on the Cross, and rebukes the Devil in Hell ►

(passus 18, lines 57–67; 362–73)

'*Consummatum est*,' quod Crist, and comsede for to
    swoune,
Pitousliche and pale as a prison that deieth;
The lord of lif and of light tho leide hise eighen
    togideres.
The day for drede withdrough and derk bicam the
    sonne.
The wal waggede and cleef, and al the world quaved.
Dede men for that dene come out of depe graves,
And tolde why that tempeste so longe tyme durede.
    'For a bitter bataille,' the dede body seide;
'Lif and Deeth in this derknesse, hir oon fordooth hir
    oother.
Shal no wight wite witterly who shal have the
    maistrie
Er Sonday aboute sonne risyng' – and sank with that
    til erthe.[. . .]

[. . .]

Now bigynneth thi gile ageyn thee to turne
And my grace to growe ay gretter and widder.
The bitternesse that thow hast browe, now brouke it
    thiselve;
That art doctour of deeth, drynk that thow madest!
    'For I that am lord of lif, love is my drynke,
And for that drynke today, I deide upon erthe.
I faughte so, me thursteth yet, for mannes soule sake;
May no drynke me moiste, ne my thurst slake,
Til the vendage falle in the vale of Josaphat,
That I drynke right ripe must, *resureccio mortuorum*.
And thanne shal I come as a kyng, crowned, with
    aungeles,
And have out of helle alle mennes soules.

Glossary

CONSUMMATUM EST: it is finished; COMSEDE: Began; PRISON: prisoner; LEIDE . . . TOGIDERES: closed his eyes; CLEEF: split; DENE: din; HIR OON . . . OOTHER: one of them is destroying the other; WITE WITTERLY: know truly; BROWE: brewed; BROUKE: enjoy; TIL THE VENDAGE . . . MORTUORUM: until the wine-harvest comes in the vale of Jehoshaphat, when I shall drink a well-matured new wine, the resurrection of the dead.

I have chosen these poems because they are my favourite poems by Edward Lear (1812–88) and Lewis Carroll (the pseudonym used by Charles Lutwidge Dodgson, 1832–98). When I was very young, I had a picture-book of *The Quangle Wangle's Hat* that I loved, so it had to be included. 'The Dong with a Luminous Note' and 'The Pobble Who Has No Toes' both make guest appearances in *The Quangle Wangle's Hat*, so I felt that these three poems belonged together. Almost the best thing about them is the nonsense vocabulary – the 'Great Gromboolian Plain', the 'Hills of the Chankly Bore', 'the Zemmery Fidd' and 'the Crumpetty Tree' make real life and real words seem boring. Carroll's 'mimsy borogoves' and 'frumious Bandersnatch' in 'Jabberwocky' are equally imaginative and memorable. 'The Mad Gardener's Song' and 'Father William' are surreal and hilarious, and I chose 'Evidence Read at the Trial of the Knave of Hearts' because of its strange, mysterious quality, and because I love the title.

THE DONG WITH A LUMINOUS NOSE

‹ Edward Lear ›

When awful darkness and silence reign
Over the great Gromboolian plain,
  Through the long, long wintry nights; –
When the angry breakers roar
As they beat on the rocky shore; –
  When Storm-clouds brood on the towering
    heights
Of the Hills of the Chankly Bore: –

Then, through the vast and gloomy dark,
There moves what seems a fiery spark,
  A lonely spark with silvery rays
  Piercing the coal-black night, –
  A Meteor strange and bright: –
Hither and thither the vision strays,
  A single lurid light.
Slowly it wanders, – pauses, – creeps, –
Anon it sparkles, – flashes and leaps;
And ever as onward it gleaming goes
A light on the Bong-tree stems it throws.
And those who watch at that midnight hour
From Hall or Terrace, or lofty Tower,
Cry, as the wild light passes along, –
    'The Dong! – the Dong!
  'The wandering Dong through the forest goes!
    'The Dong! the Dong!
    'The Dong with a luminous Nose!'

    Long years ago
  The Dong was happy and gay,
Till he fell in love with a Jumbly Girl
  Who came to those shores one day,
For the Jumblies came in a sieve, they did, –
Landing at eve near the Zemmery Fidd
    Where the Oblong Oysters grow,
  And the rocks are smooth and gray.
And all the woods and the valleys rang
With the Chorus they daily and nightly sang, –
    'Far and few, far and few,
    Are the lands where the Jumblies live;
    Their heads are green, and their hands are blue
    And they went to sea in a sieve.'

Happily, happily passed those days!
    While the cheerful Jumblies staid;
  They danced in circlets all night long,
  To the plaintive pipe of the lively Dong,
    In moonlight, shine, or shade.

For day and night he was always there
By the side of the Jumbly Girl so fair,
With her sky-blue hands, and her sea-green hair.
Till the morning came of that hateful day
When the Jumblies sailed in their sieve away,
And the Dong was left on the cruel shore
Gazing – gazing for evermore, –
Ever keeping his weary eyes on
That pea-green sail on the far horizon, –
Singing the Jumbly Chorus still
As he sate all day on the grassy hill, –
    'Far and few, far and few,
    Are the lands where the Jumblies live;
    Their heads are green, and their hands are blue,
    And they went to sea in a sieve.'

But when the sun was low in the West,
  The Dong arose and said; –
  – 'What little sense I once possessed
  Has quite gone out of my head!' –
And since that day he wanders still
By lake and forest, marsh and hill,
Singing – 'O somewhere, in valley or plain
'Might I find my Jumbly Girl again!
'For ever I'll seek by lake and shore
'Till I find my Jumbly Girl once more!'

    Playing a pipe with silvery squeaks,
    Since then his Jumbly Girl he seeks,
    And because by night he could not see,
    He gathered the bark of the Twangum Tree
      On the flowery plain that grows.
      And he wove him a wondrous Nose, –
    A Nose as strange as a Nose could be!
Of vast proportions and painted red,
And tied with cords to the back of his head.
    – In a hollow rounded space it ended
    With a luminous Lamp within suspended,
      All fenced about
      With a bandage stout
      To prevent the wind from blowing it out; –
    And with holes all round to send the light,
    In gleaming rays on the dismal night.

And now each night, and all night long,
Over those plains still roams the Dong;
And above the wail of the Chimp and Snipe
You may hear the squeak of his plaintive pipe
While ever he seeks, but seeks in vain
To meet with his Jumbly Girl again;
Lonely and wild – all night he goes, –

The Dong with a luminous Nose!
And all who watch at the midnight hour,
From Hall or Terrace, or lofty Tower,
Cry, as they trace the Meteor bright,
Moving along through the dreary night, –
    'This is the hour when forth he goes,
    'The Dong with a luminous Nose!
    'Yonder – over the plain he goes;
      'He goes!
      'He goes;
    'The Dong with a luminous Nose!'

THE POBBLE WHO HAS NO TOES
‹ Edward Lear ›

‹ I ›

The Pobble who has no toes
  Had once as many as we;
When they said, 'Some day you may lose them
    all;' –
  He replied, – 'Fish fiddle de-dee!'
And his Aunt Jobiska made him drink,
Lavender water tinged with pink,
For she said, 'The World in general knows
There's nothing so good for a Pobble's toes!'

‹ II ›

The Pobble who has no toes,
  Swam across the Bristol Channel;
But before he set out he wrapped his nose,
  In a piece of scarlet flannel.
For his Aunt Jobiska said, 'No harm
'Can come to his toes if his nose is warm;
'And it's perfectly known that a Pobble's toes
'Are safe, – provided he minds his nose.'

‹ III ›

The Pobble swam fast and well
  And when boats or ships came near him
He tinkledy-binkledy-winkled a bell
  So that all the world could hear him.
And all the Sailors and Admirals cried,
When they saw him nearing the further side, –
'He has gone to fish, for his Aunt Jobiska's
Runcible Cat with crimson whiskers!'

‹ IV ›

But before he touched the shore,
  The shore of the Bristol Channel,
A sea-green Porpoise carried away
  His wrapper of scarlet flannel.
And when he came to observe his feet
Formerly garnished with toes so neat
His face at once became forlorn
On perceiving that all his toes were gone!

‹ V ›

And nobody ever knew
  From that dark day to the present,
Whoso had taken the Pobble's toes,
  In a manner so far from pleasant.
Whether the shrimps or crawfish gray,
Or crafty Mermaids stole them away –
Nobody knew; and nobody knows
How the Pobble was robbed of his twice five toes!

‹ VI ›

The Pobble who has no toes
  Was placed in a friendly Bark,
And they rowed him back, and carried him up,
  To his Aunt Jobiska's Park.
And she made him a feast at his earnest wish
Of eggs and buttercups fried with fish; –
And she said, – 'It's a fact the whole world knows,
'That Pobbles are happier without their toes.'

THE QUANGLE WANGLE'S HAT
‹ Edward Lear ›

‹ I ›

On the top of the Crumpetty Tree
  The Quangle Wangle sat,
  But his face you could not see
    On account of his Beaver Hat.
  For his Hat was a hundred and two feet wide,
  With ribbons and bibbons on every side
And bells, and buttons, and loops and lace,
  So that nobody ever could see the face
    Of the Quangle Wangle Quee.

‹ II ›

The Quangle Wangle said
  To himself on the Crumpetty Tree, –

'Jam; and jelly; and bread;
   'Are the best food for me!
'But the longer I live on this Crumpetty Tree
'The plainer than ever it seems to me
'That very few people come this way
'And that life on the whole is far from gay!'
   Said the Quangle Wangle Quee.

     ◄ III ►

But there came to the Crumpetty Tree,
   Mr. and Mrs. Canary;
And they said, – 'Did you ever see
   'Any spot so charmingly airy?
'May we build a nest on your lovely Hat?
Mr. Quangle Wangle, grant us that!
'O please let us come and build a nest
'Of whatever material suits you best,
   'Mr. Quangle Wangle Quee!'

     ◄ IV ►

And besides, to the Crumpetty Tree
   Came the Stork, the Duck, and the Owl;
The Snail, and the Bumble-Bee,
   The Frog, and the Fimble Fowl;
(The Fimble Fowl, with a Corkscrew leg;)
And all of them said, – 'We humbly beg,
   'We may build our homes on your lovely Hat, –
   'Mr. Quangle Wangle, grant us that!
     'Mr. Quangle Wangle Quee!'

     ◄ V ►

And the Golden Grouse came there,
   And the Pobble who has no toes, –
And the small Olympian bear, –
   And the Dong with a luminous nose.
And the Blue Baboon, who played the flute, –
And the Orient Calf from the Land of Tute, –
And the Attery Squash, and the Bisky Bat, –
All came and built on the lovely Hat
   Of the Quangle Wangle Quee.

     ◄ VI ►

And the Quangle Wangle said
   To himself on the Crumpetty Tree, –
'When all these creatures move
   'What a wonderful noise there'll be!'
And at night by the light of the Mulberry moon
They danced to the Flute of the Blue Baboon,
On the broad green leaves of the Crumpetty Tree,

And all were as happy as happy could be,
   With the Quangle Wangle Quee.

❧

FATHER WILLIAM

◄ Lewis Carroll ►

'You are old Father William,' the young man said,
   'And your hair has become very white;
And yet you incessantly stand on your head –
   Do you think, at your age, it is right?'

'In my youth,' Father William replied to his son,
   'I feared it might injure the brain;
But, now that I'm perfectly sure I have none,
   Why, I do it again and again.'

'You are old,' said the youth, 'as I mentioned before,
   And have grown most uncommonly fat;
Yet you turned a back-somersault in at the door –
   Pray, what is the reason of that?'

'In my youth,' said the sage, as he shook his grey
     locks,
   'I kept all my limbs very supple
By the use of this ointment – one shilling a box –
   Allow me to sell you a couple?'

'You are old,' said the youth, 'and your jaws are too
     weak
   For anything tougher than suet;
Yet you finished the goose, with the bones and the
     beak –
   Pray, how did you manage to do it?'

'In my youth,' said his father, 'I took to the law,
   And argued each case with my wife;
And the muscular strength, which it gave to my
     jaw,
   Has lasted the rest of my life.'

'You are old,' said the youth, 'one would hardly
     suppose
   That your eye was as steady as ever;
Yet you balanced an eel on the end of your nose –
   What made you so awfully clever?'

'I have answered three questions, and that is
     enough,

Said his father; 'don't give yourself airs!
Do you think I can listen all day to such stuff?
Be off, or I'll kick you down stairs!'

🐦

EVIDENCE READ AT THE TRIAL OF THE KNAVE OF HEARTS

‹Lewis Carroll›

They told me you had been to her,
    And mentioned me to him:
She gave me a good character,
    But said I could not swim.

He sent them word I had not gone,
    (We know it to be true):
If she should push the matter on,
    What would become of you?

I gave her one, they gave him two,
    You gave us three or more;
They all returned from him to you,
    Though they were mine before.

If I or she should chance to be
    Involved in this affair,
He trusts to you to set them free,
    Exactly as we were.

My notion was that you had been
    (Before she had this fit)
An obstacle that came between
    Him, and ourselves, and it.

Don't let him know she liked them best,
    For this must ever be
A secret kept from all the rest,
    Between yourself and me.

🐦

THE MAD GARDENER'S SONG

‹Lewis Carroll›

He thought he saw an Elephant
    That practised on a fife:
He looked again, and found it was
    A letter from his wife.

'At length I realise,' he said,
    'The bitterness of Life!'

He thought he saw a Buffalo
    Upon the chimney-piece:
He looked again, and found it was
    His Sister's Husband's Niece.
'Unless you leave this house,' he said,
    'I'll send for the Police!'

He thought he saw a Rattlesnake
    That questioned him in Greek:
He looked again, and found it was
    The Middle of Next Week.
'The one thing I regret,' he said,
    'Is that it cannot speak!'

He thought he saw a Banker's Clerk
    Descending from the bus:
He looked again, and found it was
    A Hippopotamus:
'If this should stay to dine,' he said,
    'There won't be much for us!'

He thought he saw a Kangaroo
    That worked a coffee-mill:
He looked again, and found it was
    A Vegetable-Pill.
'Were I to swallow this,' he said,
    'I should be very ill!'

He thought he saw a Coach-and-Four
    That stood beside his bed:
He looked again, and found it was
    A Bear without a Head.
'Poor thing,' he said, 'poor silly thing!
    It's waiting to be fed!'

He thought he saw an Albatross
    That fluttered round the lamp:
He looked again, and found it was
    A Penny-Postage-Stamp.
'You'd best be getting home,' he said:
    'The nights are very damp!'

He thought he saw a Garden-Door
    That opened with a key:
He looked again, and found it was
    A Double Rule of Three:
'And all its mystery,' he said,
    'Is clear as day to me!'

He thought he saw an Argument
That proved he was the Pope:
He looked again, and found it was
A Bar of Mottled Soap.
'A fact so dread,' he faintly said,
'Extinguishes all hope!'

JABBERWOCKY

◄ Lewis Carroll ►

'Twas brillig, and the slithy toves
Did gyre and gimble in the wabe;
All mimsy were the borogoves,
And the mome raths outgrabe.

'Beware the Jabberwock, my son!
The jaws that bite, the claws that catch!
Beware the Jubjub bird, and shun
The frumious Bandersnatch!'

He took his vorpal sword in hand:
Long time the manxome foe he sought –
So rested he by the Tumtum tree,
And stood awhile in thought.

And as in uffish thought he stood,
The Jabberwock, with eyes of flame,
Came whiffling through the tulgey wood,
And burbled as it came!

One, two! One, two! And through and through
The vorpal blade went snicker-snack!
He left it dead, and with its head
He went galumphing back.

'And hast thou slain the Jabberwock?
Come to my arms, my beamish boy!
O frabjous day! Callooh! Callay!'
He chortled in his joy.

'Twas brillig, and the slithy toves
Did gyre and gimble in the wabe;
All mimsy were the borogoves,
And the mome raths outgrabe.

When Longfellow died in 1882, at seventy-five, he was at the height of his fame. He was widely regarded as not only the glory of American letters but was also loved as one of the greatest poets of the English language itself. Like Tennyson, his fame had spread throughout the English-reading world.

But for the past seventy or so years, perhaps rather more than that, he has been first derided, then neglected. A few fragments survive. Many people can at least recognise the sound of 'The Song of Hiawatha' when they hear it. 'A Psalm of Life' ('Lives of great men all remind us . . .'), 'The Wreck of the Hesperus' and 'The Village Blacksmith' maybe raise a wan, patronising smile.

The possible reasons for this derision and neglect, and the way in which both the general public and literary academics have lost interest in Longfellow, are complex. As someone who – after a Second World War childhood in the southern USA, where I was badly and unimaginatively schooled in such poems as 'The Courtship of Miles Standish' – has for several years enjoyed a number of Longfellow's poems, I have given space here to a dozen that for me pass the test of repeated readings. Two of them, 'The Fire of Drift-Wood' and 'The Jewish Cemetery at Newport', are medium-length poems of meditation: a third, 'My Lost Youth', is an extended elegiac lyric. But most of them are short, and four are sonnets, a form in which Longfellow worked particularly skilfully.

Several of Longfellow's best poems date from the last twenty years of his life, after the accidental death of his second wife, Fanny, in 1861 ('The Cross of Snow' is an elegy for her), at a time when his reputation seemed assured but when he was often deeply depressed. I agree with that fine American poet Howard Nemerov, who as long ago as 1963 unfashionably wrote: 'Longfellow, gentle as he is, maintains beneath his gentleness a fair share of that unyielding perception of reality which belongs to good poetry wherever and whenever written'.

HENRY WADSWORTH LONGFELLOW

THE RAINY DAY

The day is cold, and dark, and dreary;
It rains, and the wind is never weary;
The vine still clings to the mouldering wall,
But at every gust the dead leaves fall,
    And the day is dark and dreary.

My life is cold, and dark, and dreary;
It rains, and the wind is never weary;
My thoughts still cling to the mouldering Past,
But the hopes of youth fall thick in the blast,
    And the days are dark and dreary.

Be still, sad heart! and cease repining;
Behind the clouds is the sun still shining;
Thy fate is the common fate of all,
Into each life some rain must fall,
    Some days must be dark and dreary.

THE FIRE OF DRIFT-WOOD

We sat within the farm-house old,
    Whose windows, looking o'er the bay,
Gave to the sea-breeze, damp and cold,
    An easy entrance, night and day.

Not far away we saw the port,
    The strange, old-fashioned, silent town,
The lighthouse, the dismantled fort,
    The wooden houses, quaint and brown.

We sat and talked until the night,
    Descending, filled the little room;
Our faces faded from the sight,
    Our voices only broke the gloom.

We spake of many a vanished scene,
    Of what we once had thought and said,
Of what had been, and might have been,
    And who was changed, and who was dead;

And all that fills the hearts of friends,
    When first they feel, with secret pain,
Their lives thenceforth have separate ends,
    And never can be one again;

The first slight swerving of the heart,
    That words are powerless to express,

And leave it still unsaid in part,
    Or say it in too great excess.

The very tones in which we spake
    Had something strange, I could but mark;
The leaves of memory seemed to make
    A mournful rustling in the dark.

Oft died the words upon our lips,
    As suddenly, from out the fire
Built of the wreck of stranded ships,
    The flames would leap and then expire.

And, as their splendor flashed and failed,
    We thought of wrecks upon the main,
Of ships dismasted, that were hailed
    And sent no answer back again.

The windows, rattling in their frames,
    The ocean, roaring up the beach,
The gusty blast, the bickering flames,
    All mingled vaguely in our speech;

Until they made themselves a part
    Of fancies floating through the brain,
The long-lost ventures of the heart,
    That send no answers back again.

O flames that glowed! O hearts that yearned!
    They were indeed too much akin,
The drift-wood fire without that burned,
    The thoughts that burned and glowed within.

THE JEWISH CEMETERY AT NEWPORT

How strange it seems! These Hebrews in their
        graves,
    Close by the street of this fair seaport town,
Silent beside the never-silent waves,
    At rest in all this moving up and down!

The trees are white with dust, that o'er their sleep
    Wave their broad curtains in the south wind's
        breath,
While underneath these leafy tents they keep
    The long, mysterious Exodus of Death.

And these sepulchral stones, so old and brown,
    That pave with level flags their burial-place,

Seem like the tablets of the Law, thrown down
    And broken by Moses at the mountain's base.

The very names recorded here are strange,
    Of foreign accent, and of different climes;
Alvares and Rivera interchange
    With Abraham and Jacob of old times.

'Blessed be God, for he created Death!'
    The mourners said, 'and Death is rest and peace';
Then added, in the certainty of faith,
    'And giveth Life that nevermore shall cease.'

Closed are the portals of their Synagogue,
    No Psalms of David now the silence break,
No Rabbi reads the ancient Decalogue
    In the grand dialect the Prophets spake.

Gone are the living, but the dead remain,
    And not neglected; for a hand unseen,
Scattering its bounty, like a summer rain,
    Still keeps their graves and their remembrance
        green.

How came they here? What burst of Christian hate,
    What persecution, merciless and blind,
Drove o'er the sea – that desert desolate –
    These Ishmaels and Hagars of mankind?

They lived in narrow streets and lanes obscure,
    Ghetto and Judenstrass, in mirk and mire;
Taught in the school of patience to endure
    The life of anguish and the death of fire.

All their lives long, with the unleavened bread
    And bitter herbs of exile and its fears,
The wasting famine of the heart they fed,
    And slaked its thirst wirh marah of their tears.

Anathema maranatha! was the cry
    That rang from town to town, from street to
        street:
At every gate the accursed Mordecai
    Was mocked and jeered, and spurned by
        Christian feet.

Pride and humiliation hand in hand
    Walked with them through the world where'er
        they went;
Trampled and beaten were they as the sand,
    And yet unshaken as the continent.

For in the background figures vague and vast
    Of patriarchs and of prophets rose sublime,
And all the great traditions of the Past
    They saw reflected in the coming time.

And thus forever with reverted look
    The mystic volume of the world they read,
Spelling it backward, like a Hebrew book,
    Till life became a Legend of the Dead.

But ah! what once has been shall be no more!
    The groaning earth in travail and in pain
Brings forth its races, but does not restore,
    And the dead nations never rise again.

MY LOST YOUTH

Often I think of the beautiful town
    That is seated by the sea;
Often in thought go up and down
The pleasant streets of that dear old town,
    And my youth comes back to me.
        And a verse of a Lapland song
        Is haunting my memory still:
    'A boy's will is the wind's will,
And the thoughts of youth are long, long thoughts.'

I can see the shadowy lines of its trees,
    And catch, in sudden gleams,
The sheen of the far-surrounding seas,
And islands that were the Hesperides
    Of all my boyish dreams.
        And the burden of that old song,
        It murmurs and whispers still:
    'A boy's will is the wind's will,
And the thoughts of youth are long, long thoughts.'

I remember the black wharves and the slips,
    And the sea-tides tossing free;
And Spanish sailors with bearded lips,
And the beauty and mystery of the ships,
    And the magic of the sea.
        And the voice of that wayward song
        Is singing and saying still:
    'A boy's will is the wind's will,
And the thoughts of youth are long, long thoughts.'

I remember the bulwarks by the shore,
  And the fort upon the hill;
The sunrise gun, with its hollow roar,
The drum-beat repeated o'er and o'er,
  And the bugle wild and shrill.
    And the music of that old song
    Throbs in my memory still:
    'A boy's will is the wind's will,
And the thoughts of youth are long, long thoughts.'

I remember the sea-fight far away,
  How it thundered o'er the tide!
And the dead captains, as they lay
In their graves, o'erlooking the tranquil bay
  Where they in battle died.
    And the sound of that mournful song
    Goes through me with a thrill:
    'A boy's will is the wind's will,
And the thoughts of youth are long, long thoughts.'

I can see the breezy dome of groves,
  The shadows of Deering's Woods;
And the friendships old and the early loves
Come back with a Sabbath sound, as of doves
  In quiet neighborhoods.
    And the verse of that sweet old song,
    It flutters and murmurs still:
    'A boy's will is the wind's will,
And the thoughts of youth are long, long thoughts.'

I remember the gleams and glooms that dart
  Across the school-boy's brain;
The song and the silence in the heart,
  That in part are prophecies, and in part
  Are longings wild and vain.
    And the voice of that fitful song
    Sings on, and is never still:
    'A boy's will is the wind's will,
And the thoughts of youth are long, long thoughts.'

There are things of which I may not speak;
  There are dreams that cannot die;
There are thoughts that make the strong heart
    weak,
  And bring a pallor into the cheek,
  And a mist before the eye.
    And the words of that fatal song
    Come over me like a chill:
    'A boy's will is the wind's will,
And the thoughts of youth are long, long thoughts.'

Strange to me now are the forms I meet
  When I visit the dear old town;
But the native air is pure and sweet,
And the trees that o'ershadow each well-known
    street,
  As they balance up and down,
    Are singing the beautiful song,
    Are sighing and whispering still:
    'A boy's will is the wind's will,
And the thoughts of youth are long, long thoughts.'

And Deering's Woods are fresh and fair,
  And with joy that is almost pain
My heart goes back to wander there,
And among the dreams of the days that were,
  I find my lost youth again.
    And the strange and beautiful song,
    The groves are repeating it still:
    'A boy's will is the wind's will,
And the thoughts of youth are long, long thoughts.'

❦

VOX POPULI

When Mazárvan the Magician
  Journeyed westward through Cathay.
Nothing heard he but the praises
  Of Badoura on his way.

But the lessening rumor ended
  When he came to Khaledan,
There the folk were talking only
  Of Prince Camaralzaman.

So it happens with the poets:
  Every province hath its own;
Camaralzaman is famous
  Where Badoura is unknown.

❦

AFTERMATH

When the summer fields are mown,
When the birds are fledged and flown,
  And the dry leaves strew the path:
With the falling of the snow,
With the cawing of the crow,

Once again the fields we mow
   And gather in the aftermath.

Not the sweet, new grass with flowers
Is this harvesting of ours;
   Not the upland clover bloom;
But the rowen mixed with weeds,
Tangled tufts from marsh and meads,
Where the poppy drops its seeds
   In the silence and the gloom.

❧

NATURE

As a fond mother, when the day is o'er,
   Leads by the hand her little child to bed,
   Half willing, half reluctant to be led,
   And leave his broken playthings on the floor,
Still gazing at them through the open door,
   Nor wholly reassured and comforted
   By promises of others in their stead,
   Which, though more splendid, may not please
     him more;
So Nature deals with us, and takes away
   Our playthings one by one, and by the hand
   Leads us to rest so gently, that we go
Scarce knowing if we wish to go or stay,
   Being too full of sleep to understand
   How far the unknown transcends the what we
     know.

❧

FOUR BY THE CLOCK

Four by the clock! and yet not day;
But the great world rolls and wheels away,
With its cities on land, and its ships at sea,
Into the dawn that is to be!

Only the lamp in the anchored bark
Sends its glimmer across the dark,
And the heavy breathing of the sea
Is the only sound that comes to me.

❧

MEZZO CAMMIN

Half of my life is gone, and I have let
   The years slip from me and have not fulfilled
   The aspiration of my youth, to build
   Some tower of song with lofty parapet.
Not indolence, nor pleasure, nor the fret
   Of restless passions that would not be stilled,
   But sorrow, and a care that almost killed,
   Kept me from what I may accomplish yet;
Though, half-way up the hill, I see the Past
   Lying beneath me with its sounds and sights, –
   A city in the twilight dim and vast,
With smoking roofs, soft bells, and gleaming
     lights, –
   And hear above me on the autumnal blast
   The cataract of Death far thundering from the
     heights.

❧

THE CROSS OF SNOW

In the long, sleepless watches of the night,
   A gentle face – the face of one long dead –
   Looks at me from the wall, where round its head
   The night-lamp casts a halo of pale light.
Here in this room she died; and soul more white
   Never through martyrdom of fire was led
   To its repose; nor can in books be read
   The legend of a life more benedight.
There is a mountain in the distant West
   That, sun-defying, in its deep ravines
   Displays a cross of snow upon its side.
Such is the cross I wear upon my breast
   These eighteen years, through all the changing
     scenes
   And seasons, changeless since the day she died.

❧

CHAUCER

An old man in a lodge within a park;
   The chamber walls depicted all around
   With portraitures of huntsman, hawk, and
     hound,
   And the hurt deer. He listeneth to the lark,

Whose song comes with the sunshine through the
    dark
  Of painted glass in leaden lattice bound;
  He listeneth and he laugheth at the sound,
  Then writeth in a book like any clerk.
He is the poet of the dawn, who wrote
  The Canterbury Tales, and his old age
  Made beautiful with song; and as I read
I hear the crowing cock, I hear the note
  Of lark and linnet, and from every page
  Rise odours of ploughed field or flowery mead.

❧

THE TIDE RISES, THE TIDE FALLS

The tide rises, the tide falls,
The twilight darkens, the curlew calls;
Along the sea-sands damp and brown
The traveller hastens toward the town,
    And the tide rises, the tide falls.

Darkness settles on roofs and walls,
But the sea in the darkness calls and calls;
The little waves, with their soft, white hands,
Efface the footprints in the sands,
    And the tide rises, the tide falls.

The morning breaks; the steeds in their stalls
Stamp and neigh, as the hostler calls;
The day returns, but nevermore
Returns the traveller to the shore,
    And the tide rises, the tide falls.

Richard Lovelace (1628–57) is best known for short lyrics such as 'To Lucasta, Going to the Wars' that brilliantly epitomise the Cavalier ideal of the lover-poet-soldier: 'I could not love thee (Dear) so much, / Loved I not honour more.' Heroic flourishes of this kind are typical of poets like Lovelace, Suckling, Herrick, and Carew. Lovelace was, however, the youngest of the Cavalier poets, and his work shares with that of Andrew Marvell, born three years later, an acute self-consciousness about its own rhetorical procedures. Like Marvell, Lovelace often makes surreptitious but telling use of political idioms. These aspects of his writing are particularly evident in 'The Grasshopper', a poem dedicated to his friend Charles Cotton, in which Lovelace contrasts the grasshopper's demise at the coming of winter ('Poor verdant fool! and now green ice') with the warming, sustaining powers of friendship. In expanding this conceit Lovelace's metaphors insistently gesture towards the plight of Charles I ('usurping of his reign [1.30] ... he hath his crown again [1.32] ... richer than untempted kings [1.36]'). At his best Lovelace is an extraordinarily subtle writer, and even his bawdier poems like 'Ellinda's Glove' or 'The Scrutiny' exhibit a certain gallantry and finesse. Sex was never for Lovelace the annihilating experience of nothingness it became for Restoration poets such as Rochester. On the contrary, in a number of poems, like 'Calling Lucasta from her Retirement. Ode' or the much longer 'Amarantha. A Pastoral' (a poem that greatly influenced Marvell's 'Upon Appleton House'), Lovelace attempts to figure the regeneration of England in terms of a redemptive union between Lucasta and the poet. Such restorations were not to happen in Lovelace's own lifetime. He died in 1657 in extreme poverty, just three years before the collapse of the Protectorate and the return of Charles II.

RICHARD LOVELACE

TO LUCASTA, GOING TO THE WARS

Tell me not (Sweet) I am unkind,
   That from the nunnery
Of thy chaste breast, and quiet mind,
   To war and arms I fly.

True; a new mistress now I chase,
   The first foe in the field;
And with a stronger faith embrace
   A sword, a horse, a shield.

Yet this inconstancy is such,
   As you too shall adore;
I could not love thee (Dear) so much,
   Loved I not honour more.

❧

THE GRASSHOPPER. TO MY NOBLE FRIEND, MR CHARLES COTTON. ODE.

Oh thou that swing'st upon the waving hair
   Of some well-filléd oaten beard,
Drunk every night with a delicious tear
   Dropped thee from heaven, where now th'art
      reared.

The joys of earth and air are thine entire,
   That with thy feet and wings dost hop and fly;
And when thy poppy works thou dost retire
   To thy carved acorn-bed to lie.

Up with the day, the sun thou welcom'st then,
   Sport'st in the gilt-plaits of his beams,
And all these merry days mak'st merry men,
   Thyself, and melancholy streams.

But ah the sickle! Golden ears are cropped;
   Ceres and Bacchus bid good night;
Sharp frosty fingers all your flowers have topped,
   And what scythes spared, winds shave off quite.

Poor verdant fool! and now green ice: thy joys
   Large and as lasting, as thy perch of grass,
Bid us lay in 'gainst winter, rain, and poise
   Their floods, with an o'erflowing glass.

Thou best of men and friends! we will create
   A genuine summer in each other's breast;

And spite of this cold time and frozen fate
   Thaw us a warm seat to our rest.

Our sacred hearths shall burn eternally
   As vestal flames, the North-wind, he
Shall strike his frost-stretched wings, dissolve and
      fly
   This Etna in epitome.

Dropping December shall come weeping in,
   Bewail th' usurping of his reign;
But when in showers of old Greek we begin,
   Shall cry, he hath his crown again!

Night as clear Hesper shall our tapers whip
   From the light casements where we play,
And the dark hag from her black mantle strip,
   And stick there everlasting day.

Thus richer than untempted kings are we,
   That asking nothing, nothing need:
Though lord of all what seas embrace; yet he
   That wants himself, is poor indeed.

❧

THE SCRUTINY

Why should you swear I am forsworn,
   Since thine I vowed to be?
Lady it is already morn,
   And 'twas last night I swore to thee
That fond impossibility.

Have I not loved thee much and long,
   A tedious twelve hours' space?
I must all other beauties wrong,
   And rob thee of a new embrace;
Could I still dote upon thy face.

Not, but all joy in thy brown hair,
   By others may be found;
But I must search the black and fair
   Like skilful min'ralists that sound
For treasure in unploughed-up ground.

Then, if when I have loved my round,
   Thou prov'st the pleasant she;
With spoils of meaner beauties crowned,

I laden will return to thee,
Ev'n sated with variety.

❧

ELLINDA'S GLOVE

Thou snowy farm with thy five tenements!
  Tell thy white mistress here was one
  That called to pay his daily rents:
But she a gathering flowers and hearts is gone,
And thou left void to rude possession.

But grieve not pretty ermine cabinet,
  Thy alablaster lady will come home;
  If not, what tenant can there fit
The slender turnings of thy narrow room,
But must ejected be by his own doom?

Then give me leave to leave my rent with thee;
  Five kisses, one unto a place:
  For though the lute's too high for me;
Yet servants knowing minikin nor base,
Are still allowed to fiddle with the case.

❧

CALLING LUCASTA FROM HER
RETIREMENT. ODE.

From the dire monument of thy black room
Where now that vestal flame thou dost entomb
As in the inmost cell of all Earth's womb,

Sacred Lucasta like the pow'rful ray
Of Heavenly Truth pass this Cimmerian way,
Whilst all the standards of your beams display:

Arise and climb our whitest highest hill,
There your sad thoughts with joy and wonder fill,
And see seas calm as Earth, Earth as your will.

Behold how lightning like a taper flies
And gilds your chari't, but ashaméd dies
Seeing itself out-gloried by your eyes.

Threat'ning and boistrous tempests gently bow,
And to your steps part in soft paths, when now
There nowhere hangs a cloud, but on your brow.

No show'rs but 'twixt your lids, nor gelid snow,
But what your whiter chaster breast doth owe,
Whilst winds in chains colder your sorrow blow.

Shrill trumpets now do only sound to eat,
Artillery hath loaden every dish with meat,
And drums at every health alarms beat.

All things LUCASTA, but LUCASTA call,
Trees borrow tongues, waters in accents fall,
The air doth sing, and fire's musical.

Awake from the dead vault in which you dwell,
All's loyal here, except your thoughts rebel,
Which so let loose, often their gen'ral quell.

See! She obeys! by all obeyéd thus;
No storms, heats, colds, no souls contentious,
Nor civil war is found – I mean, to us.

Lovers and angels, though in heaven they show
And see the woes and discords here below,
What they not feel, must not be said to know.

Lydgate (c. 1370–1449), a monk of Bury St Edmunds, was the most ambitious and prolific of Chaucer's immediate followers with 145,000 lines of poetry to his credit, and he was much the most admired of them in his own day. As his best critic Derek Pearsall says, his debt to Chaucer is enormous. Often he just copies him badly, as in the description of Criseyde lifted for his *Troy Book*; he took on the challenge of the master most confidently by starting the return journey from Canterbury with his *Siege of Thebes* (1420–22). Up to 1600 his name was usually mentioned with those of the masters, Chaucer and Gower; and it is worth noting that there are 29 manuscripts of *The Siege of Thebes* (as against 16 of Chaucer's *Troilus*, for example). But when reaction against him set in, it did so with a vengeance. The most familiar critical judgement on him is Ritson's from 1800: 'a most prolix and voluminous poetastor... prosaick and driveling monk'. Although this judgement has to be seen in the context of Ritson's splenetic insanity, it must be conceded that Lydgate is the first of the English poets whose modern standing would be higher if he had written less. Even in his best writings, such as the opening section of *The Temple of Glas*, the impact of a beginning which can be brilliant and strange is often dissipated by what strikes the modern reader as a garrulous looseness. The problem is that Lydgate's work is very often a series of set-piece exercises in rhetorical *amplificatio*, the expansiveness of which is deeply inimical to modern ideals of brevity. He is able to produce a line of sweep and gracefulness, such as this on the requirement of children forced to become clerics, 'In wide copes perfeccion to feine' (*Temple of Glas*, 204). But, as the extracts here testify, what is most characteristic of him is a style compounded of a Latinate richness with a surprisingly modern-sounding syntactic force.

A COMPLAYNT OF A LOVERES LYFE

(lines 36–84)

And by a ryver forth I gan costey
Of water clere as berel or cristal
Til at the last I founde a lytil wey
Towarde a parke enclosed with a wal
In compas round; and by a gate smal
Whoso that wolde frely myghte goon
Into this parke walled with grene stoon.

And in I went to her the briddes songe
Which on the braunches bothe in pleyn and vale
So loude song that al the wode ronge
Lyke as hyt shold shever in pesis smale.
And, as me thoghte, that the nyghtyngale
With so grete myght her voys gan out wrest
Ryght as her hert for love wolde brest.

The soyle was pleyn, smothe and wonder softe,
Al oversprad wyth tapites that Nature
Had made herselfe, celured eke alofte
With bowys grene the floures for to cure
That in her beaute they may long endure
Fro al assaute of Phebus fervent fere
Which in his spere so hote shone and clere.

The eyre atempre and the smothe wynde
Of Zepherus among the blosmes whyte
So holsom was and norysshing be kynde
That smale buddes and round blomes lyte
In maner gan of her brethe delyte
To yif us hope that their frute shal take
Ayens autumpne redy for to shake.

I saw ther Daphene closed under rynde,
Grene laurer and the holsom pyne,
The myrre also that wepeth ever of kynde,
The cedre high, upryght as a lyne,
The philbert eke that lowe doth enclyne
Her bowes grene to the erthe doune
Unto her knyght icalled Demophoune.

Ther saw I eke the fresshe hawethorne
In white motele that so soote doth smelle,
Asshe, firre and oke with mony a yonge acorne,
And mony a tre mo than I can telle.
And me berforne I saw a litel welle
That had his course (as I gan beholde)
Under an hille with quyke stremes colde.

The gravel gold, the water pure as glas,
The bankys round, the welle environyng,
And soft as veluet the yonge gras
That thereupon lustely cam spryngyng.
The sute of trees aboute compassyng
Her shadow cast, closyng the welle round
And al the erbes growyng on the grounde.

THE TEMPLE OF GLAS
(lines 166–233)

And some also that putten ful grete wite
On double louers that love thingis new,
Thurgh whos falsnes hindred be the trew.
And some ther were, as it is ofte found,
That for her ladi meny a blodi wounde
Endurid hath in mani a regioun
Whiles that another hath poscessioun
Al of his ladi and berith awai the fruyte
Of his labur and of al his suyte.
And other eke compleyned on Riches:
Hou he with Tresour doth his besines
To wynnen al, againes kynd and ryght,
Wher trew lovers have noon force ne myght.
And some ther were, as maydens yung of age,
That pleined sore with peping and with rage
That thei were coupled, againes al nature,
With croked elde that mai not long endure
Forto perfourme the lust of loves plai:
For it ne sit not unto fresshe May
Forto be coupled to oold Januari.
Thei ben so divers that thei moste varie,
For eld is grucching and malencolious,
Ay ful of ire and suspecious,
And youth entendeth to ioy and lustines,
To myrth and plai and to al gladnes.
Allas that ever that it shulde fal,
So suote sugre icoupled be with gal.
These yonge folk criden ofte sithe
And praied Venus hir power forto kithe
Vpon this myschef and shape remedie.
And right anon I herd othir crie
With sobbing teris and with ful pitous soune,
Tofore the goddess, bi lamentacioun,
That conseiles in hir tender youthe
And in childhode (as it is ofte couthe)
Yrendred were into religioun
Or thei hade yeris of discresioun,

That al her life cannot but complein,
In wide copis perfeccion to feine:
Ful covertli to curen al hir smert
And shew the contrarie outward of her hert.
Thus saugh I wepen many a faire maide,
That on hir freendis al the wite thei leide.
And other next I saugh there in gret rage
That thei were married in her tendir age
Withoute fredom of eleccioun,
Wher love hath seld domynacioun,
For love, at laarge and at liberte,
Would freli chese and not with such trete.
And other saugh I ful oft wepe and wring
That they in men founde swych variynge,
To love a seisoun, while that beaute floureth,
And bi disdein so ungoodli loureth
On hir that whilom he callid his ladi dere,
That was to him so plesaunt and entere.
But lust with fairnes is so overgone
That in her hert trouth abideth none.
And some alo I saugh in teris reyne
And pitousli on God and Kynde pleyne,
That ever thei would on eny creature
So mych beaute, passing bi mesure,
Set on a woman, to yeue occasioun
A man to love to his confusioun:
And nameli there where he shall have no grace,
For with a loke, forthbi as he doth pace,
Ful oft falleth, thurugh casting of an yghe
A man is woundid that he most nedis deye
That never efter, peraurenture, shal hir se.

THOMAS KINSELLA ◂ on ▸ JAMES CLARENCE MANGAN

James Clarence Mangan (1803–49) was born in Dublin into a very poor family. Working first in a scrivener's office, and later as an occasional journalist, he led a life of misery and deprivation, with alcohol contributing to an early death.

His works include, besides some personal poems of great bleakness, a body of early important translations from the Irish. Mangan knew no Irish himself; his 'versions' were made from texts produced by others, including the scholars Eugene O'Curry and John O. Donovan.

Yeats thought 'The Nameless One' 'quite wonderful'. He names Mangan, in 'To Ireland in the Coming Times', with Davis and Ferguson, as a precursor in the Irish poetic tradition.

Joyce chose Mangan as the subject of his student paper before the University Literary and Historical Society. He drew attention many times in his career to Mangan's work.

THE NAMELESS ONE

◂ Ballad ▸

Roll forth, my song, like the rushing river,
    That sweeps along to the mighty sea;
God will inspire me while I deliver
        My soul of thee!

Tell thou the world, when my bones lie whitening
    Amid the last homes of youth and eld,
That there was once one whose veins ran lightning
        No eye beheld.

Tell how his boyhood was one drear night-hour,
    How shone for him, through his griefs and gloom,
No star of all heaven sends to light our
        Path to the tomb.

Roll on, my song, and to after ages
    Tell how, disdaining all earth can give,
He would have taught men, from wisdom's pages,
        The way to live.

And tell how trampled, derided, hated,
    And worn by weakness, disease, and wrong,
He fled for shelter to God, who mated
        His soul with song –

With song which alway, sublime or vapid,
    Flowed like a rill in the morning beam,
Perchance not deep, but intense and rapid –
        A mountain stream.

Tell how this Nameless. condemned for years long
    To herd with demons from hell beneath,
Saw things that made him, with groans and tears,
        long
            For even death.

Go on to tell how, with genius wasted,
    Betrayed in friendship, befooled in love,
With spirit shipwrecked, and young hopes blasted,
        He still, still strove.

Till, spent with toil, dreeing death for others,
    And some whose hands should have wrought for
        him
(If children live not for sires and mothers),
        His mind grew dim.

And he fell far through that pit abysmal
   The gulf and grave of Maginn and Burns,
And pawned his soul for the devil's dismal
      Stock of returns.

But yet redeemed it in days of darkness,
   And shapes and signs of the final wrath,
When death, in hideous and ghastly starkness,
      Stood on his path.

And tell how now, amid wreck and sorrow,
   And want, and sickness, and houseless nights,
He bides in calmness the silent morrow,
      That no ray lights.

And lives he still, then? Yes! Old and hoary
   At thirty-nine, from despair and woe,
He lives endunng what future story
      Will never know.

Him grant a grave to, ye pitying noble,
   Deep in your bosoms! There let him dwell!
He, too, had tears for all souls in trouble,
      Here and in hell.

O'Hussey's Ode to the Maguire

‹(From the Irish of O'Hussey)›

Where is my Chief, my Master, this bleak night,
   mavrone!
O, cold, cold, miserably cold is this bleak night for
   Hugh,
Its showery, arrowy, speary sleet pierceth one through
   and through,
Pierceth one to the very bone!

Rolls real thunder? Or was that red, livid light
Only a meteor? I scarce know; but through the
   midnight dim
The pitiless ice-wind streams. Except the hate that
   persecutes *him*
Nothing hath crueller venomy might.

An awful, a tremendous night is this, meseems!
The flood-gates of the rivers of heaven, I think, have
   been burst wide –

Down from the overcharged clouds, like unto headlong
   ocean's tide,
Descends grey rain in roaring streams.

Though he were even a wolf ranging the round green
   woods,
Though he were even a pleasant salmon in the
   unchainable sea,
Though he were a wild mountain eagle, he could
   scarce bear, he,
This sharp, sore sleet, these howling floods.

O, mournful is my soul this night for Hugh Maguire!
Darkly, as in a dream, he strays! Before him and
   behind
Triumphs the tyrannous anger of the wounding wind,
The wounding wind, that burns as fire!

It is my bitter grief – it cuts me to the heart –
That in the country of Clan Darry this should be his
   fate!
O, woe is me, where is he? Wandering, houseless,
   desolate,
Alone, without or guide or chart!

Medreams I see just now his face, the strawberry
   bright,
Uplifted to the blackened heavens, while the
   tempestuous winds
Blow fiercely over and round him, and the smiting
   sleet-shower blinds
The hero of Galang tonight!

Large, large affliction unto me and mine it is,
That one of his majestic bearing, his fair, stately form,
Should thus be tortured and o'erborne – that this
   unsparing storm
Should wreak its wrath on head like his!

That his great hand, so oft the avenger of the oppressed,
Should this chill, churlish night, perchance, be
   paralysed by frost –
While through some icicle-hung thicket – as one lorn
   and lost –
He walks and wanders without rest.

The tempest-driven torrent deluges the mead,
It overflows the low banks of the rivulets and ponds –
The lawns and pasture-grounds lie locked in icy bonds
So that the cattle cannot feed.

The pale bright margins of the streams are seen by
    none.
Rushes and sweeps along the untameable flood on
    every side –
It penetrates and fills the cottagers' dwellings far and
    wide –
Water and land are blent in one.

Through some dark woods, 'mid bones of monsters,
    Hugh now strays,
As he confronts the storm with anguished heart, but
    manly brow –
O! what a sword-wound to that tender heart of his
    were now
A backward glance at peaceful days.

But other thoughts are his – thoughts that can still
    inspire
With joy and an onward-bounding hope the bosom of
    Mac-Nee –
Thoughts of his warriors charging like bright billows
    of the sea,
Borne on the wind's wings, flashing fire!

And though frost glaze tonight the clear dew of his
    eyes,
And white ice-gauntlets glove his noble fine fair fingers
    o'er,
A warm dress is to him that lightning-garb he ever
    wore,
The lightning of the soul, not skies.

◄Avran►

Hugh marched forth to the fight – I grieved to see him
    so depart;
And lo! to-night he wanders frozen, rain-drenched,
    sad, betrayed –
But the memory of the lime-white mansions his right hand hath
    laid
In ashes warms the hero's heart!

❦

LAMENT OVER THE RUINS OF THE ABBEY OF TEACH MOLAGA

◄(From the Irish)►

    I wandered forth at night alone
Along the dreary, shingly, billow-beaten shore;

Sadness that night was in my bosom's core,
    My soul and strength lay prone.

    The thin wan moon, half overveiled
By clouds, shed her funereal beams upon the scene;
While in low tones, with many a pause between,
    The mournful night-wind wailed.

    Musing of Life, and Death, and Fate,
I slowly paced along, heedless of aught around,
Till on the hill, now, alas! ruin-crowned,
    Lo! the old Abbey-gate!

    Dim in the pallid moonlight stood,
Crumbling to slow decay, the remnant of that pile
Within which dwelt so many saints erewhile
    In loving brotherhood!

    The memory of the men who slept
Under those desolate walls – the solitude – the
    hour –
Mine own lorn mood of mind – all joined to
    o'erpower
    My spirit – and I wept!

    In yonder Goshen once – I thought –
Reigned Piety and Peace: Virtue and Truth were
    there;
With Charity and the blessed spirit of Prayer
    Was each fleet moment fraught!

    There, unity of Work and Will
Blent hundreds into one: no jealousies or jars
Troubled their placid lives; their fortunate stars
    Had triumphed o'er all Ill!

    There, kneeled each morn and even
The Bell for Matin – Vesper: Mass was said or
    sung –
From the bright silver censer as it swung
    Rose balsamy clouds to Heaven.

    Through the round cloistered corridors
A many a midnight hour, bareheaded and unshod,
Walked the Grey Friars, beseeching from their God
    Peace for these western shores.

    The weary pilgrim bowed by Age
Oft found asylum there – found welcome, and
    found wine.

Oft rested in its halls the Paladine,
   The Poet and the Sage!

Alas! alas! how dark the change!
Now round its mouldering walls, over its pillars low,
The grass grows rank, the yellow gowans blow,
   Looking so sad and strange!

Unsightly stones choke up its wells;
The owl hoots all night long under the altar-stairs;
The fox and badger make their darksome lairs
   In its deserted cells!

Tempest and Time – the drifting sands –
The lightning and the rains – the seas that sweep
   around
These hills in winter-nights, have awfully crowned
   The work of impious hands!

The sheltering, smooth-stoned massive wall –
The noble figured roof – the glossy marble piers –
The monumental shapes of elder years –
   Where are they? Vanished all!

Rite, incense, chant, prayer, mass, have ceased –
All, all have ceased! Only the whitening bones half
   sunk
In the earth now tell that ever here dwelt monk,
   Friar, acolyte, or priest.

Oh! woe, that Wrong should triumph thus!
Woe that the olden right, the rule and the renown
Of the Pure-souled and Meek should thus go down
   Before the Tyrannous!

Where wert thou, Justice, in that hour?
Where was thy smiting sword? What had those good
   men done,
That thou shouldst tamely see them trampled on
   By brutal England's Power?

Alas! I rave! . . . If Change is here,
Is it not o'er the land? Is it not too in me?
Yes! I am changed even more than what I see.
   Now is my last goal near!

My worn limbs fail – my blood moves cold –
Dimness is on mine eyes – I have seen my children
   die;
They lie where I too in brief space shall lie –
   Under the grassy mould!

I turned away, as toward my grave,
And, all my dark way homeward by the Atlantic's
   verge,
Resounded in mine ears like to a dirge
   The roaring of the wave.

A Vision of Connaught in the Thirteenth Century

I walked entranced
   Through a land of Morn;
The sun, with wondrous excess of light,
   Shone down and glanced
     Over seas of corn
And lustrous gardens aleft and right.
   Even in the clime
     Of resplendent Spain,
Beams no such sun upon such a land;
   But it was the time,
     'Twas in the reign,
Of Cáhal Mór of the Wine-red Hand.

Anon stood nigh
   By my side a man
Of princely aspect and port sublime.
   Him queried I –
   'O, my Lord and Khan,
What clime is this, and what golden time?'
   When he – 'The clime
     Is a clime to praise,
The clime is Erin's, the green and bland;
   And it is the time,
     These be the days,
Of Cáhal Mór of the Wine-red Hand!'

Then saw I thrones,
   And circling fires,
And a Dome rose near me, as by a spell,
   Whence flowed the tones
     Of silver lyres,
And many voiced in wreathèd swell;
   And their thrilling chime
     Fell on mine ears
As the heavenly hymn of an angel-band –
   'It is now the time,
     These be the years,
Of Cáhal Mór of the Wine-red Hand!'

I sought the hall,
      And, behold! – a change
From light to darkness, from joy to woe!
    King, nobles, all,
      Looked aghast and strange;
The minstrel-group sate in dumbest show!
    Had some great crime
      Wrought this dread amaze,
This terror? None seemed to understand
    'Twas then the time,
      We were in the days,
Of Cáhal Mór of the Wine-red Hand.

I again walked forth;
    But lo! the sky
Showed fleckt with blood, and an alien sun
    Glared from the north,
      And there stood on high,
Amid his shorn beams, a skeleton!
    It was by the stream
      Of the castled Maine,
One Autumn eve, in the Teuton's land,
    That I dreamed this dream
      Of the time and reign
Of Cáhal Mór of the Wine-red Hand!

❧

GOOD COUNSEL

◄(From the Ottoman)►

Tutor not thyself in science: go to masters for
      perfection;
      Also speak thy thoughts aloud:
Whoso in the glass beholdeth nought besides his
      own reflection
      Bides both ignorant and proud.

Study not in one book only: bee-like, rather, at a
      hundred
      Sources gather honeyed lore:
Thou art else that helpless bird which, when her
      nest has once been plundered.
      Ne'er can build another more.

❧

SIBERIA

In Siberia's wastes
    The Ice-wind's breath
Woundeth like the toothèd steel;
Lost Siberia doth reveal
    Only blight and death.

Blight and death alone.
    No Summer shines.
Night is interblent with Day.
In Siberia's wastes alway
    The blood blackens, the heart pines.

In Siberia's wastes
    No tears are shed,
For they freeze within the brain.
Nought is felt but dullest pain,
    Pain acute, yet dead;

Pain as in a dream,
    When years go by
Funeral-paced, yet fugitive,
When man lives, and doth not live,
    Doth not live – nor die.

In Siberia's wastes
    Are sands and rocks.
Nothing blooms of green or soft,
But the snow-peaks rise aloft
    And that gaunt ice-blocks.

And the exile there
    Is one with those;
They are part, and he is part,
For the sands are in his heart,
    And the killing snows.

Therefore, in those wastes
    None curse the Czar.
Each man's tongue is cloven by
The North Blast, that heweth nigh
    With sharp scymitar.

And such doom each drees,
    Till, hunger-gnawn,
And cold-slain, he at length sinks there,
Yet scarce more a corpse than ere
    His last breath was drawn.

Hero and Leander is about love's folly. From the beginning, the poem is busy with images of destruction: the Hellespont, on whose opposite banks these lovers dwell, and in whose waters Leander perishes, is introduced immediately as 'guilty of true-loves' blood', and Hero's kirtle is covered with stains, 'Made with the blood of wretched lovers slain'. Love robs us of free will, the one faculty that sets us apart from the animals. It even makes fools of the gods. Moreover, while we are told that true love does not dissemble (that it is, in fact, mute), a large part of Book I is dedicated to Leander's persuasions, which, while they may be sincere, are nevertheless exercises in pure rhetoric. Indeed, though all the romantic myths are here, the poem itself constantly undermines them. (Love is too full of faith, too credulous, / With folly and false hope deluding us.)

The unreliability of appearances will also play a part in the eventual outcome, (though the poem does not reach its conclusion, and was probably still work in progress when Marlowe died, aged 29, in 1593). In Book I, we are told that Leander resembles 'a maid in man's attire'; in his encounter with Neptune, in Book II, he is mistaken for Ganymede, another icon of male beauty, whom Neptune has loved and lost, (to Jove, naturally). Leander immediately rebuts Neptune's love-talk, thinking, in his innocence, the mistake is not one of identity, but of gender, 'You are deceiv'd, I am no woman, I'. On this occasion, Neptune lets him go but, unlike Leander, we know he will be back.

HERO AND LEANDER

◀ Book I ▶

(lines 167–385)

It lies not in our power to love or hate,
For will in us is overrul'd by fate.
When two are stripp'd, long ere the course begin
We wish that one should lose, the other win;
And one especially do we affect
Of two gold ingots like in each respect.
The reason no man knows: let it suffice,
What we behold is censur'd by our eyes.
Where both deliberate, the love is slight;
Who ever lov'd, that lov'd not at first sight?
He kneel'd, but unto her devoutly pray'd;
Chaste Hero to herself thus softly said:
'Were I the saint he worships, I would hear him',
And as she spake those words, came somewhat near
    him.
He started up, she blush'd as one asham'd;
Wherewith Leander much more was inflam'd.
He touch'd her hand, in touching it she trembled:
Love deeply grounded hardly is dissembled.
These lovers parled by the touch of hands;
True love is mute, and oft amazed stands.
Thus while dumb signs their yielding hearts
    entangled,
The air with sparks of living fire was spangled,
And Night, deep-drench'd in misty Acheron,
Heav'd up her head, and half the world upon
Breath'd darkness forth (dark night is Cupid's day).
And now begins Leander to display
Love's holy fire, with words, with sighs and tears,
Which like sweet music ent'red Hero's ears,
And yet at every word she turn'd aside,
And always cut him off as he replied.
At last, like to a bold sharp sophister,
With cheerful hope thus he accosted her.
  'Fair creature, let me speak without offence,
I would my rude words had the influence
To lead thy thoughts, as thy fair looks do mine,
Then shouldst thou be his prisoner who is thine.
Be not unkind and fair; misshapen stuff
Are of behaviour boisterous and rough.
O shun me not, but hear me ere you go,
God knows I cannot force love, as you do.
My words shall be as spotless as my youth,
Full of simplicity and naked truth.
This sacrifice (whose sweet perfume descending
From Venus' altar to your footsteps bending)
Doth testify that you exceed her far

To whom you offer, and whose nun you are.
Why should you worship her? Her you surpass
As much as sparkling diamonds flaring glass.
A diamond set in lead his worth retains;
A heavenly nymph, belov'd of human swains,
Receives no blemish, but oft-times more grace,
Which makes me hope, although I am but base,
Base in respect of thee, divine and pure,
Dutiful service may thy love procure;
And I in duty will excel all other,
As thou in beauty dost exceed Love's mother.
Nor heaven, nor thou, were made to gaze upon;
As heaven preserves all things, so save thou one.
A stately builded ship, well-rigg'd and tall,
The ocean maketh more majestical:
Why vowest thou then to live in Sestos here,
Who on Love's seas more glorious wouldst appear?
Like untun'd golden strings all women are,
Which long time lie untouch'd will harshly jar.
Vessels of brass oft handled brightly shine;
What difference betwixt the richest mine
And basest mould but use? For both, not us'd,
Are of like worth. Then treasure is abus'd
When misers keep it; being put to loan,
In time it will return us two for one.
Rich robes themselves and others do adorn;
Neither themselves nor others, if not worn.
Who builds a palace and rams up the gate,
Shall see it ruinous and desolate.
Ah, simple Hero, learn thyself to cherish;
Lone women like to empty houses perish.
Less sins the poor rich man that starves himself
In heaping up a mass of drossy pelf
Than such as you: his golden earth remains,
Which, after his decease, some other gains;
But this fair gem, sweet in the loss alone,
When you fleet hence, can be bequeath'd to none.
Or if it could, down from th'enamell'd sky
All heaven would come to claim this legacy,
And with intestine broils the world destroy,
And quite confound nature's sweet harmony.
Well therefore by the gods decreed it is,
We human creatures should enjoy that bliss.
One is no number; maids are nothing, then,
Without the sweet society of men.
Wilt thou live single still? One shalt thou be,
Though never-singling Hymen couple thee.
Wild savages that drink of running springs
Think water far excels all earthly things:
But they that daily taste neat wine, despise it.
Virginity, albeit some highly prize it,

Compar'd with marriage, had you tried them both,
Differs as much as wine and water doth.
Base bullion for the stamp's sake we allow,
Even so for men's impression do we you.
By which alone, our reverend fathers say,
Women receive perfection every way.
This idol which you term virginity
Is neither essence subject to the eye,
No, nor to any one exterior sense,
Nor hath it any place of residence,
Nor is't of earth or mould celestial,
Or capable of any form at all.
Of that which hath no being, do not boast;
Things that are not at all, are never lost.
Men foolishly do call it virtuous:
What virtue is it that is born with us?
Much less can honour be ascrib'd thereto;
Honour is purchas'd by the deeds we do.
Believe me, Hero, honour is not won
Until some honourable deed be done.
Seek you for chastity, immortal fame,
And know that some have wrong'd Diana's name?
Whose name is it, if she be false or not,
So she be fair, but some vile tongues will blot?
But you are fair (ay me) so wondrous fair,
So young, so gentle, and so debonair,
As Greece will think, if thus you live alone,
Some one or other keeps you as his own.
Then, Hero, hate me not, nor from me fly,
To follow swiftly blasting infamy.
Perhaps thy sacred priesthood makes thee loth,
Tell me, to whom mad'st thou that heedless oath?'
   'To Venus', answered she, and as she spake,
Forth from those two tralucent cisterns brake
A stream of liquid pearl, which down her face
Made milk-white paths, whereon the gods might
      trace
To Jove's high court. He thus replied: 'The rites
In which love's beauteous empress most delights,
Are banquets, Doric music, midnight revel,
Plays, masques, and all that stern age counteth evil.
Thee as a holy idiot doth she scorn,
For thou in vowing chastity hast sworn
To rob her name and honour, and thereby
Commit'st a sin far worse than perjury,
Even sacrilege against her deity,
Through regular and formal purity.
To expiate which sin, kiss and shake hands,
Such sacrifice as this Venus demands.'
   Thereat she smil'd, and did deny him so
As put thereby yet might he hope for mo.

Which makes him quickly reinforce his speech,
And her in humble manner thus beseech:
　'Though neither gods nor men may thee deserve,
Yet for her sake whom you have vow'd to serve,
Abandon fruitless cold virginity,
The gentle queen of love's sole enemy.
Then shall you most resemble Venus' nun
When Venus' sweet rites are perform'd and done.
Flint-breasted Pallas joys in single life,
But Pallas and your mistress are at strife.
Love, Hero, then, and be not tyrannous,
But heal the heart that thou hast wounded thus,
Nor stain thy youthful years with avarice;
Fair fools delight to be accounted nice.
The richest corn dies if it be not reap'd;
Beauty alone is lost, too warily kept.'
These arguments he us'd, and many more,
Wherewith she yielded that was won before.
Hero's looks yielded, but her words made war;
Women are won when they begin to jar.
Thus having swallow'd Cupid's golden hook,
The more she striv'd, the deeper was she strook.
Yet evilly feigning anger, strove she still,
And would be thought to grant against her will.
So having paus'd a while, at last she said:
'Who taught thee rhetoric to deceive a maid?
Ay me, such words as these should I abhor,
And yet I like them for the orator.'
　With that, Leander stoop'd to have embrac'd her,
But from his spreading arms away she cast her,
And thus bespake him: 'Gentle youth, forbear
To touch the sacred garments which I wear.
Upon a rock, and underneath a hill,
Far from the town (where all is whist and still,
Save that the sea, playing on yellow sand,
Sends forth a rattling murmur to the land,
Whose sound allures the golden Morpheus
In silence of the night to visit us)
My turret stands, and there God knows I play
With Venus' swans and sparrows all the day.
A dwarfish beldam bears me company,
That hops about the chamber where I lie,
And spends the night (that might be better spent)
In vain discourse and apish merriment.
Come thither.' As she spake this, her tongue tripp'd,
For unawares 'Come thither' from her slipp'd,
And suddenly her former colour chang'd,
And here and there her eyes through anger rang'd.
And like a planet, moving several ways
At one self instant, she poor soul assays,
Loving, not to love at all, and every part

Strove to resist the motions of her heart.
And hands so pure, so innocent, nay such
As might have made heaven stoop to have a touch,
Did she uphold to Venus, and again
Vow'd spotless chastity, but all in vain.
Cupid beats down her prayers with his wings,
Her vows above the empty air he flings;
All deep enrag'd, his sinewy bow he bent,
And shot a shaft that burning from him went,
Wherewith she strooken looked so dolefully
As made Love sigh to see his tyranny.
And as she wept, her tears to pearl he turn'd,
And wound them on his arm, and for her mourn'd.
Then towards the palace of the Destinies
Laden with languishment and grief he flies,
And to those stern nymphs humbly made request
Both might enjoy each other, and be blest.
But with a ghastly dreadful countenance,
Threat'ning a thousand deaths at every glance,
They answered Love, nor would vouchsafe so much
As one poor word, their hate to him was such.
Hearken awhile, and I us I tell you why.

‹ Book II ›

(lines 1–262)

By this, sad Hero, with love unacquainted,
Viewing Leander's face, fell down and fainted.
He kiss'd her, and breath'd life into her lips,
Wherewith, as one displeas'd, away she trips.
Yet as she went, full often look'd behind,
And many poor excuses did she find
To linger by the way, and once she stay'd,
And would have turn'd again, but was afraid,
In off'ring parley, to be counted light.
So on she goes, and in her idle flight
Her painted fan of curled plumes let fall,
Thinking to train Leander therewithal.
He being a novice, knew not what she meant,
But stay'd, and after her a letter sent,
Which joyful Hero answer'd in such sort
As he had hope to scale the beauteous fort
Wherein the liberal Graces lock'd their wealth,
And therefore to her tower he got by stealth.
Wide open stood the door, he need not climb,
And she herself before the pointed time
Had spread the board, with roses strew'd the room
And oft look'd out, and mus'd he did not come.
At last he came; O who can tell the greeting
These greedy lovers had at their first meeting?
He ask'd, she gave, and nothing was denied;

Both to each other quickly were allied.
Look how their hands, so were their hearts united,
And what he did she willingly requited.
(Sweet are the kisses, the embracements sweet,
When like desires and affections meet,
For from the earth to heaven is Cupid rais'd,
Where fancy is in equal balance pais'd.)
Yet she this rashness suddenly repented,
And turn'd aside, and to herself lamented,
As if her name and honour had been wrong'd
By being possess'd of him for whom she long'd;
Ay, and she wish'd, albeit not from her heart,
That he would leave her turret and depart.
The mirthful god of amorous pleasure smil'd
To see how he this captive nymph beguil'd;
For hitherto he did but fan the fire,
And kept it down that it might mount the higher.
Now wax'd she jealous, lest his love abated,
Fearing her own thoughts made her to be hated.
Therefore unto him hastily she goes,
And, like light Salmacis, her body throws
Upon his bosom, where with yielding eyes
She offers up herself a sacrifice
To slake his anger, if he were displeas'd.
O what god would not therewith be appeas'd?
Like Aesop's cock, this jewel he enjoyed,
And as a brother with his sister toyed,
Supposing nothing else was to be done,
Now he her favour and good will had won.
But know you not that creatures wanting sense
By nature have a mutual appetence,
And wanting organs to advance a step,
Mov'd by love's force, unto each other leap?
Much more in subjects having intellect
Some hidden influence breeds like effect.
Albeit Leander, rude in love, and raw,
Long dallying with Hero, nothing saw
That might delight him more, yet he suspected
Some amorous rites or other were neglected.
Therefore unto his body hers he clung;
She, fearing on the rushes to be flung,
Striv'd with redoubled strength; the more she
    strived
The more a gentle pleasing heat revived,
Which taught him all that elder lovers know.
And now the same 'gan so to scorch and glow,
As in plain terms (yet cunningly) he crav'd it;
Love always makes those eloquent that have it.
She, with a kind of granting, put him by it,
And ever as he thought himself most nigh it,
Like to the tree of Tantalus she fled,

And, seeming lavish, sav'd her maidenhead.
Ne'er king more sought to keep his diadem,
Than Hero this inestimable gem.
Above our life we love a steadfast friend,
Yet when a token of great worth we send,
We often kiss it, often look thereon,
And stay the messenger that would be gone:
No marvel, then, though Hero would not yield
So soon to part from that she dearly held.
Jewels being lost are found again, this never;
'Tis lost but once, and once lost, lost for ever.
    Now had the Morn espied her lover's steeds,
Whereat she starts, puts on her purple weeds,
And red for anger that he stay'd so long,
All headlong throws herself the clouds among.
And now Leander, fearing to be miss'd,
Embrac'd her suddenly, took leave, and kiss'd.
Long was he taking leave, and loth to go,
And kiss'd again, as lovers use to do.
Sad Hero wrung him by the hand and wept,
Saying, 'Let your vows and promises be kept.'
Then standing at the door she turn'd about,
As loth to see Leander going out.
And now the sun that through th'horizon peeps,
As pitying these lovers, downward creeps,
So that in silence of the cloudy night,
Though it was morning, did he take his flight.
But what the secret trusty night conceal'd,
Leander's amorous habit soon reveal'd.
With Cupid's myrtle was his bonnet crown'd,
About his arms the purple riband wound
Wherewith she wreath'd her largely spreading hair;
Nor could the youth abstain, but he must wear
The sacred ring wherewith she was endow'd
When first religious chastity she vow'd;
Which made his love through Sestos to be known,
And thence unto Abydos sooner blown
Than he could sail; for incorporeal Fame,
Whose weight consists in nothing but her name,
Is swifter than the wind, whose tardy plumes
Are reeking water, and dull earthly fumes.
Home when he came, he seem'd not to be there,
But like exiled air thrust from his sphere,
Set in a foreign place; and straight from thence,
Alcides-like, by mighty violence,
He would have chas'd away the swelling main
That him from her unjustly did detain.
Like as the sun in a diameter
Fires and inflames objects removed far
And heateth kindly, shining lat'rally,
So beauty sweetly quickens when 'tis nigh,

But being separated and removed,
Burns where it cherish'd, murders where it loved.
Therefore even as an index to a book,
So to his mind was young Leander's look.
O none but gods have power their love to hide,
Affection by the count'nance is descried.
The light of hidden fire itself discovers,
And love that is conceal'd betrays poor lovers.
His secret flame apparently was seen,
Leander's father knew where he had been,
And for the same mildly rebuk'd his son,
Thinking to quench the sparkles new begun.
But love, resisted once, grows passionate,
And nothing more than counsel lovers hate.
For as a hot proud horse highly disdains
To have his head controll'd, but breaks the reins,
Spits forth the ringled bit, and with his hooves
Checks the submissive ground, so he that loves,
The more he is restrain'd, the worse he fares.
What is it now but mad Leander dares?
'O Hero, Hero!' thus he cried full oft,
And then he got him to a rock aloft,
Where having spied her tower, long stared he on't,
And prayed the narrow toiling Hellespont
To part in twain, that he might come and go,
But still the rising billows answered 'No.'
With that he stripp'd him to the ivory skin,
And crying, 'Love, I come', leapt lively in.
Whereat the sapphire-visag'd god grew proud,
And made his cap'ring Triton sound aloud,
Imagining that Ganymede, displeas'd,
Had left the heavens; therefore on him he seiz'd.
Leander striv'd, the waves about him wound,
And pull'd him to the bottom, where the ground
Was strew'd with pearl, and in low coral groves
Sweet singing mermaids sported with their loves
On heaps of heavy gold, and took great pleasure
To spurn in careless sort the shipwreck treasure.
For here the stately azure palace stood
Where kingly Neptune and his train abode.
The lusty god embrac'd him, call'd him love,
And swore he never should return to love.
But when he knew it was not Ganymede,
For under water he was almost dead,
He heav'd him up, and looking on his face,
Beat down the bold waves with his triple mace,
Which mounted up, intending to have kiss'd him,
And fell in drops like tears because they miss'd him.
Leander being up, began to swim,
And, looking back, saw Neptune follow him;
Whereat aghast, the poor soul 'gan to cry,

'O let me visit Hero ere I die.'
The god put Helle's bracelet on his arm,
And swore the sea should never do him harm.
He clapp'd his plump cheeks, with his tresses play'd,
And smiling wantonly, his love bewray'd.
He watch'd his arms, and as they open'd wide
At every stroke, betwixt them would he slide
And steal a kiss, and then run out and dance,
And as he turn'd, cast many a lustful glance,
And throw him gaudy toys to please his eye,
And dive into the water, and there pry
Upon his breast, his thighs, and every limb,
And up again, and close beside him swim,
And talk of love. Leander made reply,
'You are deceiv'd, I am no woman, I.'
Thereat smil'd Neptune, and then told a tale,
How that a shepherd, sitting in a vale,
Play'd with a boy so fair and unkind
As for his love both earth and heaven pin'd;
That of the cooling river durst not drink,
Lest water-nymphs should pull him from the brink;
And when he sported in the fragrant lawns,
Goat-footed satyrs and up-staring fauns
Would steal him thence. Ere half this tale was done,
'Ay me,' Leander cried, 'th'enamoured sun,
That now should shine on Thetis' glassy bower,
Descends upon my radiant Hero's tower.
O that these tardy arms of mine were wings!'
And as he spake, upon the waves he springs.
Neptune was angry that he gave no ear,
And in his heart revenging malice bare;
He flung at him his mace, but as it went,
He call'd it in, for love made him repent.
The mace returning back, his own hand hit,
As meaning to be veng'd for darting it.
When this fresh-bleeding wound Leander view'd,
His colour went and came, as if he ru'd
The grief which Neptune felt. In gentle breasts
Relenting thoughts, remorse and pity rests.
And who have hard hearts and obdurate minds
But vicious, harebrain'd, and illit'rate hinds?
The god, seeing him with pity to be moved,
Thereon concluded that he was beloved.
(Love is too full of faith, too credulous,
With folly and false hope deluding us.)
Wherefore Leander's fancy to surprise,
To the rich Ocean for gifts he flies.
'Tis wisdom to give much, a gift prevails
When deep-persuading oratory fails.
    By this, Leander, being near the land,

Cast down his weary feet, and felt the sand.
Breathless albeit he were, he rested not
Till to the solitary tower he got,
And knock'd and call'd, at which celestial noise
The longing heart of Hero much more joys
Than nymphs and shepherds when the timbrel
    rings,
Or crooked dolphin when the sailor sings.
She stay'd not for her robes, but straight arose,
And drunk with gladness to the door she goes,
Where seeing a naked man she screech'd for fear –
Such sights as this to tender maids are rare –
And ran into the dark herself to hide;
Rich jewels in the dark are soonest spied.
Unto her was he led, or rather drawn,
By those white limbs, which sparkled through the
    lawn.
The nearer that he came, the more she fled,
And seeking refuge, slipp'd into her bed.
Whereon Leander sitting thus began,
Through numbing cold all feeble, faint and wan:
'If not for love, yet, love, for pity sake,
Me in thy bed and maiden bosom take;
At least vouchsafe these arms some little room,
Who, hoping to embrace thee, cheerly swum.
This head was beat with many a churlish billow,
And therefore let it rest upon thy pillow.'
Herewith affrighted Hero shrunk away,
And in her lukewarm place Leander lay,
Whose lively heat, like fire from heaven fet,
Would animate cross clay, and higher set
The drooping thoughts of base-declining souls
Than dreary Mars carousing nectar bowls.
His hands he cast upon her like a snare;
She, overcome with shame and sallow fear,
Like chaste Diana when Actaeon spied her,
Being suddenly betray'd, div'd down to hide her.

Of all the momentous choices which confronted me as a schoolboy in the 1960s – ale or lager, boys or girls, Beatles or Stones – none was more vexatious than that between metaphysicality and romanticism; or, as an English teacher brilliantly put it, between cerebration and celebration. It seemed to me, then as now, a choice which ideally needn't be made; and the poets I most admire are those who balance intellect and emotion in ways which transcend the necessary imbalances of their historical moments: Greville, Marvell, Coleridge, Auden, Gunn.

Those five poets, and Andrew Marvell (1621–78) especially, possess another, more mysterious quality: they combine a tone of close-up intimacy and candour with an extraordinary degree of personal self-effacement. We may happen to know various things about them, and information about their families or lovers or friends may turn up in their poems, but they neither bore us with their own egos nor send us scurrying to footnotes and biographies to complete their poems. 'The Definition of Love', unspecific and ungendered (apart from Fate), transforms lived-in authenticity into universality; 'To His Coy Mistress' is as intimate and, in its wonderful closing paragraph, as urgent a *carpe diem* as any, yet it's of absolutely no importance who the coy mistress may have been or whether she existed at all.

From 'Upon Appleton House', Marvell's longest non-political poem, I've included the opening series of observations on scale and proportion (stanzas 1–7) and the central 'meadow-sequence' (stanzas 47–69), which finds him moving, with no loss of assurance, into wilder terrain than the more familiar formal garden at Nun Appleton. That, of course, provides the setting for 'The Garden' itself, an inexhaustible poem whose verbal textures and stanzaic form have been gratefully echoed by later writers – for instance, in Robert Lowell's 'Waking Early Sunday Morning' (and, indeed, in my own 'The Stones on Thorpeness Beach'). Lastly, as a coda, I've added a short and less well-known poem, Marvell's song of praise to 'music, the mosaic of the air'.

ANDREW MARVELL

THE DEFINITION OF LOVE

My love is of a birth as rare
As 'tis for object strange and high:
It was begotten by Despair
Upon Impossibility.

Magnanimous Despair alone
Could show me so divine a thing,
Where feeble Hope could ne'er have flown
But vainly flapped its tinsel wing.

And yet I quickly might arrive
Where my extended soul is fixed,
But Fate does iron wedges drive,
And always crowds itself betwixt.

For Fate with jealous eye does see
Two perfect loves, nor lets them close:
Their union would her ruin be,
And her tyrannic power depose.

And therefore her decrees of steel
Us as the distant Poles have placed,
(Though Love's whole world on us doth wheel)
Not by themselves to be embraced,

Unless the giddy heaven fall,
And earth some new convulsion tear;
And, us to join, the world should all
Be cramped into a planisphere.

As lines (so loves) oblique may well
Themselves in every angle greet:
But ours so truly parallel,
Though infinite, can never meet.

Therefore the love which us doth bind,
But Fate so enviously debars,
Is the conjunction of the mind,
And opposition of the stars.

❧

TO HIS COY MISTRESS

Had we but world enough, and time,
This coyness, Lady, were no crime.
We would sit down, and think which way
To walk, and pass our long love's day.

Thou by the Indian Ganges' side
Shouldst rubies find: I by the tide
Of Humber would complain. I would
Love you ten years before the flood:
And you should, if you please, refuse
Till the conversion of the Jews.
My vegetable love should grow
Vaster than empires, and more slow.
An hundred years should go to praise
Thine eyes, and on thy forehead gaze.
Two hundred to adore each breast:
But thirty thousand to the rest.
An age at least to every part,
And the last age should show your heart:
For, Lady, you deserve this state;
Nor would I love at lower rate.
    But at my back I always hear
Time's wingèd chariot hurrying near:
And yonder all before us lie
Deserts of vast eternity.
Thy beauty shall no more be found;
Nor, in thy marble vault, shall sound
My echoing song: then worms shall try
That long-preserved virginity:
And your quaint honour turn to dust;
And into ashes all my lust.
The grave's a fine and private place,
But none, I think, do there embrace.
    Now, therefore, while the youthful glue
Sits on thy skin like morning dew,
And while thy willing soul transpires
At every pore with instant fires,
Now let us sport us while we may;
And now, like amorous birds of prey,
Rather at once our time devour,
Than languish in his slow-chapped power.
Let us roll all our strength, and all
Our sweetness, up into one ball:
And tear our pleasures with rough strife,
Thorough the iron grates of life.
Thus, though we cannot make our sun
Stand still, yet we will make him run.

❧

UPON APPLETON HOUSE

‹To my Lord Fairfax›

(lines 1–56; 369–552)

Within this sober frame expect
Work of no foreign architect,
That unto caves the quarries drew,
And forests did to pastures hew,
Who of his great design in pain
Did for a model vault his brain,
Whose columns should so high be raised
To arch the brows that on them gazed.

Why should of all things man unruled
Such unproportioned dwellings build?
The beasts are by their dens expressed:
And birds contrive an equal nest;
The low-roofed tortoises do dwell
In cases fit of tortoise shell:
No creature loves an empty space;
Their bodies measure out their place.

But he, superfluously spread,
Demands more room alive than dead;
And in his hollow palace goes
Where winds (as he) themselves may lose;
What need of all this marble crust
T'impark the wanton mote of dust,
That thinks by breadth the world t'unite
Though the first builders failed in height?

But all things are composèd here
Like Nature, orderly and near:
In which we the dimensions find
Of that more sober age and mind,
When larger-sizèd men did stoop
To enter at a narrow loop;
As practising, in doors so strait,
To strain themselves through heaven's gate.

And surely when the after age
Shall hither come in pilgrimage,
These sacred places to adore,
By Vere and Fairfax trod before,
Men will dispute how their extent
Within such dwarfish confines went:
And some will smile at this, as well
As Romulus his bee-like cell.

Humility alone designs
Those short but admirable lines,

By which, ungirt and unconstrained,
Things greater are in less contained.
Let others vainly strive t'immure
The circle in the quadrature!
These holy mathematics can
In every figure equal man.

Yet thus the laden house does sweat,
And scarce endures the Master great:
But where he comes the swelling hall
Stirs, and the square grows spherical,
More by his magnitude distressed,
Then he is by its straitness pressed:
And too officiously it slights
That in itself which him delights.

[...]

And now to the abyss I pass
Of that unfathomable grass,
Where men like grasshoppers appear,
But grasshoppers are giants there:
They, in their squeaking laugh, contemn
Us as we walk more low than them:
And, from the precipices tall
Of the green spires, to us do call.

To see men through this meadow dive,
We wonder how they rise alive,
As, under water, none does know
Whether he fall through it or go.
But, as the mariners that sound,
And show upon their lead the ground,
They bring up flowers so to be seen,
And prove they've at the bottom been.

No scene that turns with engines strange
Does oftener than these meadows change.
For when the sun the grass hath vexed,
The tawny mowers enter next;
Who seem like Israelites to be,
Walking on foot through a green sea.
To them the grassy deeps divide,
And crowd a lane to either side.

With whistling scythe, and elbow strong.
These massacre the grass along:
While one, unknowing, carves the rail,
Whose yet unfeathered quills her fail.
The edge all bloody from its breast
He draws, and does his stroke detest,

Fearing the flesh untimely mowed
To him a fate as black forebode.

But bloody Thestylis, that waits
To bring the mowing camp their cates,
Greedy as kites, has trussed it up,
And forthwith means on it to sup:
When on another quick she lights,
And cries, 'He called us Israelites;
But now, to make his saying true,
Rails rain for quails, for manna, dew.'

Unhappy birds! what does it boot
To build below the grass's root;
When lowness is unsafe as height,
And chance o'ertakes, what 'scapeth spite?
And now your orphan parents' call
Sounds your untimely funeral.
Death-trumpets creak in such a note,
And 'tis the sourdine in their throat.

Or sooner hatch or higher build:
The mower now commands the field,
In whose new traverse seemeth wrought
A camp of battle newly fought:
Where, as the meads with hay, the plain
Lies quilted o'er with bodies slain:
The women that with forks it fling,
Do represent the pillaging.

And now the careless victors play,
Dancing the triumphs of the hay;
Where every mower's wholesome heat
Smells like an Alexander's sweat.
Their females fragrant as the mead
Which they in fairy circles tread:
When at their dance's end they kiss,
Their new-made hay not sweeter is.

When after this 'tis piled in cocks,
Like a calm sea it shows the rocks,
We wondering in the river near
How boats among them safely steer.
Or, like the desert Memphis sand,
Short pyramids of hay do stand.
And such the Roman camps do rise
In hills for soldiers' obsequies.

This scene again withdrawing brings
A new and empty face of things,
A levelled space, as smooth and plain

As cloths for Lely stretched to stain.
The world when first created sure
Was such a table rase and pure.
Or rather such is the *toril*
Ere the bulls enter at Madril.

For to this naked equal net,
Which Levellers take pattern at,
The villagers in common chase
Their cattle, which it closer rase;
And what below the scythe increased
Is pinched yet nearer by the beast.
Such, in the painted world, appeared
D'Avenant with the universal herd.

They seem within the polished grass
A landskip drawn in looking-glass,
And shrunk in the huge pasture show
As spots, so shaped, on faces do –
Such fleas, ere they approach the eye,
In multiplying glasses lie.
They feed so wide, so slowly move,
As constellations do above.

Then, to conclude these pleasant acts
Denton sets ope its cataracts,
And makes the meadow truly be
(What it but seemed before) a sea.
For, jealous of its Lord's long stay,
It tries t'invite him thus away.
The river in itself is drowned,
And isles the astonished cattle round.

Let others tell the paradox,
How eels now bellow in the ox;
How horses at their tails do kick,
Turned as they hang to leeches quick;
How boats can over bridges sail;
And fishes do the stables scale.
How salmons trespassing are found;
And pikes are taken in the pound.

But I, retiring from the flood,
Take sanctuary in the wood,
And, while it lasts, myself embark
In this yet green, yet growing ark,
Where the first carpenter might best
Fit timber for his keel have pressed.
And where all creatures might have shares,
Although in armies, not in pairs.

The double wood of ancient stocks,
Linked in so thick, an union locks,
It like two pedigrees appears,
On th' one hand Fairfax, th' other Vere's:
Of whom though many fell in war,
Yet more to heaven shooting are:
And, as they Nature's cradle decked,
Will in green age her hearse expect.

When first the eye this forest sees
It seems indeed as wood not trees:
As if their neighbourhood so old
To one great trunk them all did mould.
There the huge bulk takes place, as meant
To thrust up a fifth element,
And stretches still so closely wedged
As if the night within were hedged.

Dark all without it knits; within
It opens passable and thin;
And in as loose an order grows,
As the Corinthean porticoes.
The arching boughs unite between
The columns of the temple green;
And underneath the wingèd choirs
Echo about their tunèd fires.

The nightingale does here make choice
To sing the trials of her voice.
Low shrubs she sits in, and adorns
With music high the squatted thorns.
But highest oaks stoop down to hear,
And listening elders prick the ear.
The thorn, lest it should hurt her, draws
Within the skin its shrunken claws.

But I have for my music found
A sadder, yet more pleasing sound:
The stock-doves, whose fair necks are graced
With nuptial rings, their ensigns chaste;
Yet always, for some cause unknown,
Sad pair unto the elms they moan.
O why should such a couple mourn,
That in so equal flames do burn!

Then as I careless on the bed
Of gelid strawberries do tread,
And through the hazels thick espy
The hatching throstles shining eye,
The heron from the ash's top,
The eldest of its young lets drop,

As if it stork-like did pretend
That tribute to its Lord to send.

But most the hewel's wonders are,
Who here has the holtfelster's care.
He walks still upright from the root,
Measuring the timber with his foot,
And all the way, to keep it clean,
Doth from the bark the woodmoths glean.
He, with his beak, examines well
Which fit to stand and which to fell.

The good he numbers up, and hacks,
As if he marked them with the axe.
But where he, tinkling with his beak,
Does find the hollow oak to speak,
That for his building he designs,
And through the tainted side he mines.
Who could have thought the tallest oak
Should fall by such a feeble stroke!

THE GARDEN

How vainly men themselves amaze
To win the palm, the oak, or bays,
And their uncessant labours see
Crowned from some single herb or tree,
Whose short and narrow vergèd shade
Does prudently their toils upbraid,
While all flow'rs and all trees do close
To weave the garlands of repose.

Fair Quiet, have I found thee here,
And Innocence, thy sister dear!
Mistaken long, I sought you then
In busy companies of men.
Your sacred plants, if here below,
Only among the plants will grow.
Society is all but rude,
To this delicious solitude.

No white nor red was ever seen
So am'rous as this lovely green.
Fond lovers, cruel as their flame,
Cut in these trees their mistress' name.
Little, alas, they know, or heed,
How far these beauties hers exceed!

Fair trees! wheres'e'er your barks I wound,
No name shall but your own be found.

When we have run our passion's heat,
Love hither makes his best retreat.
The gods, that mortal beauty chase,
Still in a tree did end their race.
Apollo hunted Daphne so,
Only that she might laurel grow.
And Pan did after Syrinx speed,
Not as a nymph, but for a reed.

What wondrous life is this I lead!
Ripe apples drop about my head;
The luscious clusters of the vine
Upon my mouth do crush their wine;
The nectarene, and curious peach,
Into my hands themselves do reach;
Stumbling on melons, as I pass,
Ensnared with flowers, I fall on grass.

Meanwhile the mind, from pleasures less,
Withdraws into its happiness:
The mind, that ocean where each kind
Does straight its own resemblance find,
Yet it creates, transcending these,
Far other worlds, and other seas,
Annihilating all that's made
To a green thought in a green shade.

Here at the fountain's sliding foot,
Or at some fruit-tree's mossy root,
Casting the body's vest aside,
My soul into the boughs does glide:
There like a bird it sits, and sings,
Then whets, and combs its silver wings;
And, till prepared for longer flight,
Waves in its plumes the various light.

Such was that happy garden-state,
While man there walked without a mate:
After a place so pure, and sweet,
What other help could yet be meet!
But 'twas beyond a mortal's share
To wander solitary there:
Two paradises 'twere in one
To live in paradise alone.

How well the skilful gardener drew
Of flowers and herbs this dial new,
Where from above the milder sun

Does through a fragrant zodiac run;
And, as it works, the industrious bee
Computes its time as well as we.
How could such sweet and wholesome hours
Be reckoned but with herbs and flowers!

MUSIC'S EMPIRE

First was the world as one great cymbal made,
Where jarring winds to infant Nature played.
All music was a solitary sound,
To hollow rocks and murmuring fountains bound.

Jubal first made the wilder notes agree;
And Jubal tuned music's first jubilee:
He called the echoes from their sullen cell,
And built the organ's city where they dwell.

Each sought a consort in that lovely place;
And virgin trebles wed the manly base.
From whence the progeny of numbers new
Into harmonious colonies withdrew.

Some to the lute, some to the viol went,
And others chose the cornet eloquent,
These practising the wind, and those the wire,
To sing men's triumphs, or in heaven's choir.

Then music, the mosaic of the air,
Did of all these a solemn noise prepare:
With which she gained the empire of the ear,
Including all between the earth and sphere.

Victorious sounds! Yet here your homage do
Unto a gentler conqueror than you:
Who though he flies the music of his praise,
Would with you heaven's hallelujahs raise.

The poems written by John Milton (1608–74) before the Civil War are enchanting, as if Shakespearean comedy could last forever, so I represent them fully; but he worked for Cromwell's cause, went blind, and only then wrote his *Paradise Lost*, an 'epic' of some sadness and terrifying greatness.

His sonnets bridge the two phases of his life, and in them he has almost too much to say. 'On the late Massacre in Piedmont' is a powerful, committed poem which says in terms as exact as a propaganda poster just what Milton has to say: it is horrifying to find that it is quite realistic, and the truth. It was by this force of passion and thought that he became the great poet of his age and language, though his victory seemed wildly unlikely at the time, and some of his poems had to wait many years for publication. The fact remains that John Milton, Andrew Marvell and John Dryden all walked behind Cromwell's coffin. Today, what tugs us more is the masque-like poetry of his youth and innocence.

I have chosen an extract from *Paradise Lost* that expresses Milton's sadness and religion, and a longer one in which his old flame still sparkles: his description of Paradise. He is a complex poet, and he needs his vast length.

L'ALLEGRO

Hence, loathed Melancholy,
 Of Cerberus and blackest Midnight born
In Stygian cave forlorn
 'Mongst horrid shapes, and shrieks, and sights
  unholy!
Find out some uncouth cell,
 Where brooding Darkness spreads his jealous
  wings,
And the night-raven sings;
 There, under ebon shades and low-browed rocks,
As ragged as thy locks,
 In dark Cimmerian desert ever dwell.
But come, thou Goddess fair and free,
In heaven yclept Euphrosyne,
And by men heart-easing Mirth;
Whom lovely Venus, at a birth,
With two sister Graces more,
To ivy-crowned Bacchus bore:
Or whether (as some sager sing)
The frolic wind that breathes the spring,
Zephyr, with Aurora playing,
As he met her once a-Maying,
There, on beds of violets blue,
And fresh-blown roses washed in dew,
Filled her with thee, a daughter fair,
So buxom, blithe, and debonair.
 Haste thee, Nymph, and bring with thee
Jest, and youthful Jollity,
Quips and Cranks and wanton Wiles,
Nods and Becks and wreathed Smiles,
Such as hang on Hebe's cheek,
And love to live in dimple sleek;
Sport that wrinkled Care derides,
And Laughter holding both his sides.
Come, and trip it, as you go,
On the light fantastic toe;
And in thy right hand lead with thee
The mountain-nymph, sweet Liberty;
And, if I give thee honour due,
Mirth, admit me of thy crew,
To live with her, and live with thee,
In unreproved pleasures free;
To hear the lark begin his flight,
And, singing, startle the dull night,
From his watch-tower in the skies,
Till the dappled dawn doth rise;
Then to come, in spite of sorrow,
And at my window bid good morrow,
Through the sweet-briar or the vine,

Or the twisted eglantine;
While the cock, with lively din,
Scatters the rear of darkness thin;
And to the stack, or the barn door.
Stoutly struts his dames before:
Oft list'ning how the hounds and horn
Cheerly rouse the slumb'ring morn,
From the side of some hoar hill,
Through the high wood echoing shrill:
Sometime walking, not unseen,
By hedgerow elms, on hillocks green,
Right against the eastern gate
Where the great Sun begins his state,
Robed in flames and amber light,
The clouds in thousand liveries dight;
While the ploughman, near at hand,
Whistles o'er the furrowed land,
And the milkmaid singeth blithe,
And the mower whets his scythe,
And every shepherd tells his tale
Under the hawthorn in the dale.
Straight mine eye hath caught new pleasures,
Whilst the landskip round it measures:
Russet lawns, and fallows grey,
Where the nibbling flocks do stray;
Mountains on whose barren breast
The labouring clouds do often rest;
Meadows trim with daisies pied;
Shallow brooks, and rivers wide;
Towers and battlements it sees
Bosomed high in tufted trees,
Where perhaps some beauty lies,
The cynosure of neighbouring eyes.
Hard by a cottage chimney smokes
From betwixt two aged oaks,
Where Corydon and Thyrsis met
Are at their savoury dinner set
Of herbs and other country messes,
Which the neat-handed Phillis dresses;
And then in haste her bower she leaves,
With Thestylis to bind the sheaves;
Or, if the earlier season lead,
To the tanned haycock in the mead.
Sometimes, with secure delight,
The upland hamlets will invite,
When the merry bells ring round,
And the jocund rebecks sound
To many a youth and many a maid
Dancing in the chequered shade,
And young and old come forth to play
On a sunshine holiday,

Till the livelong daylight fail:
Then to the spicy nut-brown ale,
With stories told of many a feat,
How Faëry Mab the junkets eat.
She was pinched and pulled, she said;
And by the Friars' lantern led,
Tells how drudging goblin sweat
To earn his cream-bowl duly set,
When in one night, ere glimpse of morn,
His shadowy flail hath threshed the corn
That ten day-labourers could not end;
Then lies him down the lubber fiend,
And, stretched out all the chimney's length,
Basks at the fire his hairy strength,
And crop-full out of doors he flings,
Ere the first cock his matin rings.
Thus done the tales, to bed they creep,
By whispering winds soon lulled asleep.
Towered cities please us then,
And the busy hum of men,
Where throngs of knights and barons bold,
In weeds of peace, high triumphs hold,
With store of ladies, whose bright eyes
Rain influence, and judge the prize
Of wit or arms, while both contend
To win her grace whom all commend.
There let Hymen oft appear
In saffron robe, with taper clear,
And pomp, and feast, and revelry,
With mask and antique pageantry;
Such sights as youthful poets dream
On summer eves by haunted stream.
Then to the well-trod stage anon,
If Jonson's learned sock be on,
Or sweetest Shakespeare, Fancy's child,
Warble his native wood-notes wild.
    And ever, against eating cares,
Lap me in soft Lydian airs,
Married to immortal verse,
Such as the meeting soul may pierce,
In notes with many a winding bout
Of linked sweetness long drawn out
With wanton heed and giddy cunning,
The melting voice through mazes running,
Untwisting all the chains that tie
The hidden soul of harmony;
That Orpheus' self may heave his head
From golden slumber on a bed
Of heaped Elysian flowers, and hear
Such strains as would have won the ear
Of Pluto to have quite set free

His half-regained Eurydice.
     These delights if thou canst give,
Mirth, with thee I mean to live.

LYCIDAS

In this Monody the Author bewails a learned Friend,
unfortunately drowned in his passage from Chester on the Irish
Seas, 1637; and, by occasion, foretells the ruin of our corrupted
Clergy, then in their height.

Yet once more, O ye laurels, and once more,
Ye myrtles brown, with ivy never sere,
I come to pluck your berries harsh and crude,
And with forced fingers rude
Shatter your leaves before the mellowing year.
Bitter constraint and sad occasion dear
Compels me to disturb your season due;
For Lycidas is dead, dead ere his prime,
Young Lycidas, and hath not left his peer.
Who would not sing for Lycidas? he knew
Himself to sing, and build the lofty rhyme.
He must not float upon his watery bier
Unwept, and welter to the parching wind,
Without the meed of some melodious tear.
     Begin, then, Sisters of the sacred well
That from beneath the seat of Jove doth spring;
Begin, and somewhat loudly sweep the string.
Hence with denial vain and coy excuse:
So may some gentle Muse
With lucky words favour my destined urn,
And as he passes turn,
And bid fair peace be to my sable shroud!
For we were nursed upon the self-same hill,
Fed the same flock, by fountain, shade, and rill;
Together both, ere the high lawns appeared
Under the opening eyelids of the Morn,
We drove a-field, and both together heard
What time the grey-fly winds her sultry horn,
Batt'ning our flocks with the fresh dews of night,
Oft till the star that rose at evening bright
Toward heaven's descent had sloped his westering
     wheel.
Meanwhile the rural ditties were not mute,
Tempered to th' oaten flute;
Rough Satyrs danced, and Fauns with cloven heel
From the glad sound would not be absent long;
And old Damætas loved to hear our song.

     But, oh, the heavy change, now thou art gone,
Now thou art gone, and never must return!
Thee, Shepherd, thee the woods, and desert caves,
With wild thyme and the gadding vine o'ergrown,
And all their echoes, mourn.
The willows, and the hazel copses green,
Shall now no more be seen,
Fanning their joyous leaves to thy soft lays.
As killing as the canker to the rose,
Or taint-worm to the weanling herds that graze,
Or frost to flowers, that their gay wardrobe wear,
When first the white-thorn blows;
Such, Lycidas, thy loss to shepherd's ear.
     Where were ye, Nymphs, when the remorseless
          deep
Closed o'er the head of your loved Lycidas?
For neither were ye playing on the steep,
Where your old bards, the famous Druids, lie,
Nor on the shaggy top of Mona high,
Nor yet where Deva spreads her wizard stream.
Ay me! I fondly dream
Had ye been there, . . . for what could that have
          done?
What could the Muse herself that Orpheus bore,
The Muse herself, for her enchanting son,
Whom universal nature did lament,
When, by the rout that made the hideous roar,
His gory visage down the stream was sent,
Down the swift Hebrus to the Lesbian shore?
     Alas! what boots it with incessant care
To tend the homely, slighted, shepherd's trade,
And strictly meditate the thankless Muse?
Were it not better done, as others use,
To sport with Amaryllis in the shade,
Or with the tangles of Neæra's hair?
Fame is the spur that the clear spirit doth raise
(That last infirmity of noble mind)
To scorn delights, and live laborious days;
But the fair guerdon when we hope to find,
And think to burst out into sudden blaze,
Comes the blind Fury with th' abhorred shears,
And slits the thin-spun life. 'But not the praise,'
Phœbus replied, and touched my trembling ears:
'Fame is no plant that grows on mortal soil,
Nor in the glistering foil
Set off to the world, nor in broad rumour lies,
But lives and spreads aloft by those pure eyes
And perfect witness of all-judging Jove;
As he pronounces lastly on each deed,
Of so much fame in heaven expect thy meed.'
     O fountain Arethuse, and thou honoured flood,

Smooth-sliding Mincius, crowned with vocal reeds,
That strain I heard was of a higher mood.
But now my oat proceeds,
And listens to the Herald of the Sea
That came in Neptune's plea.
He asked the waves, and asked the felon winds,
What hard mishap hath doomed this gentle swain?
And questioned every gust of rugged winds
That blows from off each beaked promontory.
They knew not of his story;
And sage Hippotades their answer brings;
That not a blast was from his dungeon strayed,
The air was calm, and on the level brine
Sleek Panope with all her sisters played.
It was that fatal and perfidious bark,
Built in th' eclipse, and rigged with curses dark,
That sunk so low that sacred head of thine.
  Next, Camus, reverend sire, went footing slow,
His mantle hairy, and his bonnet sedge,
Inwrought with figures dim, and on the edge
Like to that sanguine flower inscribed with woe.
'Ah! who hath reft,' quoth he, 'my dearest pledge?'
Last came, and last did go,
The Pilot of the Galilean Lake;
Two massy keys he bore of metals twain
(The golden opes, the iron shuts amain).
He shook his mitred locks, and stern bespake: –
'How well could I have spared for thee, young
      swain,
Enow of such as, for their bellies' sake,
Creep, and intrude, and climb into the fold!
Of other care they little reck'ning make
Than how to scramble at the shearers' feast,
And shove away the worthy bidden guest.
Blind mouths! that scarce themselves know how to
      hold
A sheep-hook, or have learned aught else the least
That to the faithful herdman's art belongs!
What recks it them? What need they? They are sped;
And, when they list, their lean and flashy songs
Grate on their scrannel pipes of wretched straw;
The hungry sheep look up, and are not fed,
But, swoln with wind and the rank mist they draw,
Rot inwardly, and foul contagion spread:
Besides what the grim wolf with privy paw
Daily devours apace, and nothing said.
But that two-handed engine at the door
Stands ready to smite once, and smite no more.'
  Return, Alpheus, the dread voice is past
That shrunk thy streams; return, Sicilian Muse,
And call the vales, and bid them hither cast

Their bells and flowrets of a thousand hues.
Ye valleys low, where the mild whispers use
Of shades, and wanton winds, and gushing brooks,
On whose fresh lap the swart star sparely looks,
Throw hither all your quaint enamelled eyes,
That on the green turf suck the honied showers,
And purple all the ground with vernal flowers.
Bring the rathe primrose that forsaken dies,
The tufted crow-toe, and pale jessamine,
The white pink, and the pansy freaked with jet,
The glowing violet,
The musk-rose, and the well-attired woodbine,
With cowslips wan that hang the pensive head,
And every flower that sad embroidery wears:
Bid amaranthus all his beauty shed,
And daffadillies fill their cups with tears,
To strew the laureate hearse where Lycid lies.
For so, to interpose a little ease,
Let our frail thoughts dally with false surmise.
Ay me! whilst thee the shores and sounding seas
Wash far away, where'er thy bones are hurled;
Whether beyond the stormy Hebrides,
Where thou perhaps under the whelming tide
Visit'st the bottom of the monstrous world;
Or whether thou, to our moist vows denied,
Sleep'st by the fable of Bellerus old,
Where the great Vision of the guarded mount
Looks toward Namancos, and Bayona's hold.
Look homeward, Angel, now, and melt with ruth:
And, O ye dolphins, waft the hapless youth.
  Weep no more, woeful shepherds, weep no more,
For Lycidas, your sorrow, is not dead,
Sunk though he be beneath the wat'ry bed,
And yet anon repairs his drooping head,
And tricks his beams, and with new-spangled ore
Flames in the forehead of the morning sky:
So Lycidas sunk low, but mounted high,
Through the dear might of Him that walked the
      waves;
Where, other groves and other streams along,
With nectar pure his oozy locks he laves,
And hears the unexpressive nuptial song,
In the blest kingdoms meek of joy and love.
There entertain him all the Saints above,
In solemn troops, and sweet societies,
That sing, and singing in their glory move,
And wipe the tears for ever from his eyes.
Now, Lycidas, the shepherds weep no more;
Henceforth thou art the Genius of the shore,
In thy large recompense, and shalt be good
To all that wander in that perilous flood.

Thus sang the uncouth swain to th' oaks and
    rills,
While the still morn went out with sandals grey:
He touched the tender stops of various quills,
With eager thought warbling his Doric lay:
And now the sun had stretched out all the hills,
And now was dropt into the western bay;
At last he rose, and twitched his mantle blue:
To-morrow to fresh woods, and pastures new.

ON THE MORNING OF CHRIST'S NATIVITY

‹ I ›

This is the month, and this the happy morn,
Wherein the Son of Heaven's eternal King,
Of wedded Maid and Virgin Mother born,
Our great redemption from above did bring;
For so the holy sages once did sing,
    That He our deadly forfeit should release,
And with His Father work us a perpetual peace.

‹ II ›

That glorious Form, that Light unsufferable,
And that far-beaming blaze of Majesty,
Wherewith He wont at Heaven's high council-table
To sit the midst of Trinal Unity,
He laid aside; and here with us to be
    Forsook the courts of everlasting day,
And chose with us a darksome house of mortal
    clay.

‹ III ›

Say, Heavenly Muse, shall not thy sacred vein
Afford a present to the Infant God?
Hast thou no verse, no hymn, or solemn strain,
To welcome Him to this His new abode,
Now while the Heaven, by the Sun's team untrod,
    Hath took no print of the approaching light,
And all the spangled host keep watch in squadrons
    bright?

‹ IV ›

See how from far upon the eastern road
The star-led wizards haste with odours sweet!
O run, prevent them with thy humble ode,
And lay it lowly at His blessed feet;
Have thou the honour first thy Lord to greet,

And join thy voice unto the angel quire,
From out His secret altar touched with hallowed
    fire.

‹ The hymn ›

‹ I ›

It was the winter wild,
While the Heaven-born Child
    All meanly wrapt in the rude manger lies;
Nature in awe to Him
Had doffed her gaudy trim,
    With her great Master so to sympathize:
It was no season then for her
To wanton with the sun her lusty paramour.

‹ II ›

Only with speeches fair
She woos the gentle air
    To hide her guilty front with innocent snow,
And on her naked shame,
Pollute with sinful blame,
    The saintly veil of maiden white to throw,
Confounded that her Maker's eyes
Should look so near upon her foul deformities.

‹ III ›

But He, her fears to cease,
Sent down the meek-eyed Peace;
    She crowned with olive green came softly sliding
Down through the turning sphere,
His ready harbinger,
    With turtle wing the amorous clouds dividing,
And waving wide her myrtle wand,
She strikes a universal peace through sea and land.

‹ IV ›

No war or battle's sound
Was heard the world around,
    The idle spear and shield were high up-hung:
The hooked chariot stood
Unstained with hostile blood,
    The trumpet spake not to the armed throng,
And kings sat still with awful eye,
As if they surely knew their sovran Lord was by.

‹ V ›

But peaceful was the night
Wherein the Prince of Light
    His reign of peace upon the earth began:
The winds with wonder whist,

Smoothly the waters kissed,
  Whispering new joys to the mild Ocean,
Who now hath quite forgot to rave,
While birds of calm sit brooding on the charmed
    wave.

‹ VI ›

The stars with deep amaze
Stand fixed in steadfast gaze,
  Bending one way their precious influence,
And will not take their flight,
For all the morning light,
  Or Lucifer that often warned them thence;
But in their glimmering orbs did glow,
Until their Lord Himself bespake, and bid them go.

‹ VII ›

And though the shady gloom
Had given day her room,
  The sun himself withheld his wonted speed,
And hid his head for shame,
As his inferior flame
  The new-enlightened world no more should
    need;
He saw a greater Sun appear
Than his bright throne or burning axle-tree could
    bear.

‹ VIII ›

The shepherds on the lawn,
Or ere the point of dawn,
  Sat simply chatting in a rustic row;
Full little thought they then
That the mighty Pan
  Was kindly come to live with them below;
Perhaps their loves or else their sheep,
Was all that did their silly thoughts so busy keep.

‹ IX ›

When such music sweet
Their hearts and ears did greet,
  As never was by mortal finger strook,
Divinely warbled voice
Answering the stringed noise,
  As all their souls in blissful rapture took:
The air such pleasure loth to lose,
With thousand echoes still prolongs each heavenly
    close.

‹ X ›

Nature that heard such sound
Beneath the hollow round
  Of Cynthia's seat, the airy region thrilling
Now was almost won
To think her part was done,
  And that her reign had here its last fulfilling;
She knew such harmony alone
Could hold all Heaven and Earth in happier union.

‹ XI ›

At last surrounds their sight
A globe of circular light,
  That with long beams the shame-faced night
    arrayed,
The helmed cherubim
And sworded seraphim
  Are seen in glittering ranks with wings displayed,
Harping in loud and solemn quire,
With unexpressive notes to Heaven's new-born Heir.

‹ XII ›

Such music (as 'tis said)
Before was never made,
  But when of old the sons of morning sung,
While the Creator great
His constellations set,
  And the well-balanced world on hinges hung,
And cast the dark foundations deep,
And bid the welt'ring waves their oozy channel
    keep.

‹ XIII ›

Ring out, ye crystal spheres,
Once bless our human ears
  (If ye have power to touch our senses so),
And let your silver chime
Move in melodious time,
  And let the base of Heaven's deep organ blow;
And with your ninefold harmony
Make up full consort to th' angelic symphony.

‹ XIV ›

For if such holy song
Enwrap our fancy long.
  Time will run back and fetch the age of gold,
And speckled vanity
Will sicken soon, and die,
  And lep'rous sin will melt from earthly mould,
And Hell itself will pass away
And leave her dolorous mansions to the peering day.

‹ XV ›

Yea, Truth and Justice then
Will down return to men,
   Orbed in a rainbow; and, like glories wearing,
Mercy will sit between,
Throned in celestial sheen,
    With radiant feet the tissued clouds down-
      steering,
And Heaven, as at some festival,
Will open wide the gates of her high palace-hall.

‹ XVI ›

But wisest Fate says No,
This must not yet be so,
   The Babe lies yet in smiling infancy,
That on the bitter cross
Must redeem our loss,
   So both Himself and us to glorify:
Yet first to those ychained in sleep,
The wakeful trump of doom must thunder through
    the deep,

‹ XVII ›

With such a horrid clang
As on Mount Sinai rang,
   While the red fire and smould'ring clouds out-
    brake:
The aged Earth aghast
With terror of that blast
   Shall from the surface to the centre shake;
When at the world's last session,
The dreadful Judge in middle air shall spread His
    throne.

‹ XVIII ›

And then at last our bliss
Full and perfect is,
   But now begins; for from this happy day
Th' old Dragon under-ground
In straiter limits bound,
   Not half so far casts his usurped sway,
And, wroth to see his kingdom fail,
Swinges the scaly horror of his folded tail.

‹ XVIX ›

The oracles are dumb,
No voice or hideous hum
   Runs through the arched roof in words deceiving.
Apollo from his shrine
Can no more divine,
   With hollow shriek the steep of Delphos leaving.

No nightly trance or breathed spell
Inspires the pale-eyed priest from the prophetic cell.

‹ XX ›

The lonely mountains o'er,
And the resounding shore,
   A voice of weeping heard, and loud lament;
From haunted spring and dale,
Edged with poplar pale,
   The parting Genius is with sighing sent,
With flower-inwoven tresses torn
The nymphs in twilight shade of tangled thickets
    mourn.

‹ XXI ›

In consecrated earth,
And on the holy hearth,
   The Lars and Lemures moan with midnight
    plaint;
In urns and altars round,
A drear and dying sound
   Affrights the Flamens at their service quaint;
And the chill marble seems to sweat,
While each peculiar power forgoes his wonted seat.

‹ XXII ›

Peor and Baalim
Forsake their temples dim,
   With that twice-battered god of Palestine;
And mooned Ashtaroth,
Heaven's queen and mother both,
   Now sits not girt with tapers' holy shrine;
The Libyc Hammon shrinks his horn,
In vain the Tyrian maids their wounded Thammuz
    mourn.

‹ XXIII ›

And sullen Moloch fled,
Hath left in shadows dread
   His burning idol all of blackest hue;
In vain with cymbals' ring
They call the grisly king,
   In dismal dance about the furnace blue;
The brutish gods of Nile as fast,
Isis and Orus, and the dog Anubis, haste.

‹ XXIV ›

Nor is Osiris seen
In Memphian grove or green,
   Trampling the unshowered grass with lowings
    loud:

Nor can he be at rest
Within his sacred chest,
   Nought but profoundest Hell can be his shroud,
In vain with timbrelled anthems dark
The sable-stoled sorcerers bear his worshipped ark.

◄ XXV ►

He feels from Juda's land
The dreaded Infant's hand,
   The rays of Bethlehem blind his dusky eyn;
Nor all the gods beside,
Longer dare abide,
   Not Typhon huge ending in snaky twine:
Our Babe, to show His Godhead true,
Can in His swaddling bands control the damned
    crew.

◄ XXVI ►

So when the sun in bed,
Curtained with cloudy red,
   Pillows his chin upon an orient wave,
The flocking shadows pale
Troop to th' infernal jail,
   Each fettered ghost slips to his several grave,
And the yellow-skirted fays
Fly after the night-steeds, leaving their moon-loved
    maze.

◄ XXVII ►

But see, the Virgin blest
Hath laid her Babe to rest:
   Time is our tedious song should here have
    ending,
Heaven's youngest teemed star,
Hath fixed her polished car,
   Her sleeping Lord with handmaid lamp
    attending:
And all about the courtly stable,
Bright-harnessed angels sit in order serviceable.

❧

ON SHAKESPEARE

What needs my Shakespeare for his honoured bones,
The labour of an age in piled stones,
Or that his hallowed relics should be hid
Under a star-ypointing pyramid?
Dear son of memory, great heir of fame,
What need'st thou such weak witness of thy name?

Thou in our wonder and astonishment
Hast built thyself a live-long monument.
For whilst to th' shame of slow-endeavouring art,
Thy easy numbers flow, and that each heart
Hath from the leaves of thy unvalued book
Those delphic lines with deep impression took;
Then thou, our fancy of itself bereaving,
Dost make us marble with too much conceiving;
And so sepulchered in such pomp dost lie,
That kings for such a tomb would wish to die.

❧

TO THE NIGHTINGALE

O Nightingale that on yon bloomy spray
   Warbl'st at eve, when all the woods are still,
   Thou with fresh hope the lover's heart dost fill,
   While the jolly hours lead on propitious May.
Thy liquid notes that close the eye of day,
   First heard before the shallow cuckoo's bill,
   Portend success in love. O, if Jove's will
   Have linked that amorous power to thy soft lay,
Now timely sing, ere the rude bird of hate
   Foretell my hopeless doom, in some grove nigh;
   As thou from year to year hast sung too late
For my relief, yet hadst no reason why.
   Whether the Muse or Love call thee his mate,
   Both them I serve, and of their train am I.

❧

ON HIS DECEASED WIFE

Methought I saw my late espoused saint
   Brought to me like Alcestis from the grave,
   Whom Jove's great son to her glad husband gave,
   Rescued from Death by force, though pale and
    faint,
Mine, as whom washed from spot of childbed taint
   Purification in the Old Law did save,
   And such as yet once more I trust to have
   Full sight of her in Heaven without restraint,
Came vested all in white, pure as her mind.
   Her face was veiled; yet to my fancied sight
   Love, sweetness, goodness, in her person shined
So clear as in no face with more delight.
   But, O! as to embrace me she inclined,

I waked, she fled, and day brought back my
     night.

❧

ON THE LATE MASSACRE IN PIEDMONT

Avenge, O Lord, thy slaughtered saints, whose bones
     Lie scattered on the Alpine mountains cold;
     Even them who kept thy truth so pure of old,
     When all our fathers worshipped stocks and
          stones,
Forget not: in thy book record their groans
     Who were thy sheep, and in their ancient fold
     Slain by the bloody Piedmontese, that rolled
     Mother with infant down the rocks. Their moans
The vales redoubled to the hills, and they
     To Heaven. Their martyred blood and ashes sow
     O'er all th' Italian fields, where still doth sway
The triple Tyrant; that from these may grow
     A hundredfold, who, having learnt thy way,
     Early may fly the Babylonian woe.

❧

PARADISE LOST

‹Book III›

(lines 1–55)

    Hail, holy Light, offspring of Heaven first-born!
Or of th' Eternal coeternal beam
May I express thee unblamed? since God is light,
And never but in unapproached light
Dwelt from eternity, dwelt then in thee,
Bright effluence of bright essence increate!
Or hear'st thou rather pure ethereal stream,
Whose fountain who shall tell? before the Sun,
Before the Heavens, thou wert, and at the voice
Of God, as with a mantle, didst invest
The rising world of waters dark and deep,
Won from the void and formless Infinite!
Thee I revisit now with bolder wing,
Escaped the Stygian Pool, though long detained
In that obscure sojourn, while in my flight,
Through utter and thorough middle darkness
     borne,
With other notes than to th' Orphean lyre
I sung of Chaos and eternal Night,
Taught by the Heavenly Muse to venture down

The dark descent, and up to reascend,
Though hard and rare: thee I revisit safe,
And feel thy sovran vital lamp; but thou
Revisit'st not these eyes, that roll in vain
To find thy piercing ray, and find no dawn;
So thick a drop serene hath quenched their orbs,
Or dim suffusion veiled. Yet not the more
Cease I to wander where the Muses haunt
Clear spring, or shady grove, or sunny hill,
Smit with the love of sacred song; but chief
Thee, Sion, and the flowery brooks beneath,
That wash thy hallowed feet, and warbling flow,
Nightly I visit: nor sometimes forget
Those other two equalled with me in fate,
So were I equalled with them in renown,
Blind Thamyris and blind Maeonides,
And Tiresias and Phineus, prophets old:
Then feed on thoughts that voluntary move
Harmonious numbers; as the wakeful bird
Sings darkling, and, in shadiest covert hid,
Tunes her nocturnal note. Thus with the year
Seasons return; but not to me returns
Day, or the sweet approach of even or morn,
Or sight of vernal bloom, or summer's rose,
Or flocks, or herds, or human face divine;
But cloud instead and ever-during dark
Surrounds me, from the cheerful way of men
Cut off, and, for the book of knowledge fair,
Presented with a universal blank
Of Nature's works, to me expunged and rased,
And wisdom at one entrance quite shut out.
So much the rather thou, Celestial Light,
Shine inward, and the mind through all her powers
Irradiate; there plant eyes; all mist from thence
Purge and disperse, that I may see and tell
Of things invisible to mortal sight.

‹Book IV›

(lines 194–355)

Thence up he flew, and on the Tree of Life,
The middle tree and highest there that grew,
Sat like a cormorant; yet not true life
Thereby regained, but sat devising death
To them who lived; nor on the virtue thought
Of that life-giving plant, but only used
For prospect what, well used, had been the pledge
Of immortality. So little knows
Any, but God alone, to value right
The good before him, but perverts best things
To worst abuse, or to their meanest use.

Beneath him, with new wonder, now he views,
To all delight of human sense exposed,
In narrow room Nature's whole wealth; yea. more! –
A Heaven on Earth: for blissful Paradise
Of God the garden was, by him in the east
Of Eden planted; Eden stretched her line
From Auran eastward to the royal towers
Of great Seleucia, built by Grecian kings,
Or where the sons of Eden long before
Dwelt in Telassar. In this pleasant soil
His far more pleasant garden God ordained.
Out of the fertile ground he caused to grow
All trees of noblest kind for sight, smell, taste;
And all amid them stood the Tree of Life,
High eminent, blooming ambrosial fruit
Of vegetable gold; and, next to life,
Our death, the Tree of Knowledge, grew fast by –
Knowledge of good, bought dear by knowing ill.
Southward through Eden went a river large,
Nor changed his course, but through the shaggy hill
Passed underneath ingulfed; for God had thrown
That mountain, as his garden-mould, high raised
Upon the rapid current, which through veins
Of porous earth with kindly thirst updrawn
Rose a fresh fountain, and with many a rill
Watered the garden; thence united fell
Down the steep glade, and met the nether flood,
Which from his darksome passage now appears,
And now, divided into four main streams,
Runs diverse, wandering many a famous realm
And country whereof here needs no account;
But rather to tell how, if Art could tell
How, from that sapphire fount the crisped brooks,
Rolling on orient pearl and sands of gold,
With mazy error under pendent shades
Ran nectar, visiting each plant, and fed
Flowers worthy of Paradise, which not nice Art
In beds and curious knots, but Nature boon
Poured forth profuse on hill, and dale, and plain,
Both where the morning sun first warmly smote
The open field, and where the unpierc'd shade
Embrowned the noontide bowers. Thus was this
    place,
A happy rural seat of various view:
Groves whose rich trees wept odorous gums and
    balm;
Others whose fruit, burnished with golden rind,
Hung amiable – Hesperian fables true,
If true, here only – and of delicious taste.
Betwixt them lawns, or level downs, and flocks
Grazing the tender herb, were interposed,

Or palmy hillock; or the flowery lap
Of some irriguous valley spread her store,
Flowers of all hue, and without thorn the rose.
Another side, umbrageous grots and caves
Of cool recess, o'er which the mantling vine
Lays forth her purple grape, and gently creeps
Luxuriant; meanwhile murmuring waters fall
Down the slope hills, dispersed, or in a lake,
That to the fringed bank with myrtle crowned
Her crystal mirror holds, unite their streams.
The birds their quire apply; airs, vernal airs,
Breathing the smell of field and grove, attune
The trembling leaves, while universal Pan,
Knit with the Graces and the Hours in dance,
Led on th' eternal Spring. Not that fair field
Of Enna, where Proserpin gathering flowers,
Herself a fairer flower, by gloomy Dis
Was gathered – which cost Ceres all that pain
To seek her through the world – nor that sweet
    grove
Of Daphne, by Orontes and th' inspired
Castalian spring, might with this Paradise
Of Eden strive; nor that Nyseian isle,
Girt with the river Triton, where old Cham,
Whom Gentiles Ammon call, and Libyan Jove,
Hid Amalthea, and her florid son,
Young Bacchus, from his stepdame Rhea's eye;
Nor, where Abassin kings their issue guard,
Mount Amara (though this by some supposed
True Paradise) under the Ethiop line
By Nilus' head, enclosed with shining rock,
A whole day's journey high, but wide remote
From this Assyrian garden, where the Fiend
Saw undelighted all delight, all kind
Of living creatures, new to sight and strange
Two of far nobler shape, erect and tall,
God-like erect, with native honour clad
In naked majesty, seemed lords of all,
And worthy seemed; for in their looks divine
The image of their glorious Maker shone,
Truth, wisdom, sanctitude severe and pure –
Severe, but in true filial freedom placed;
Whence true authority in men: though both
Not equal, as their sex not equal seemed;
For contemplation he and valour formed,
For softness she and sweet attractive grace;
He for God only, she for God in him.
His fair large front and eye sublime declared
Absolute rule; and hyacinthine locks
Round from his parted forelock manly hung
Clustering, but not beneath his shoulders broad:

She, as a veil down to the slender waist,
Her unadorned golden tresses wore
Dishevelled, but in wanton ringlets waved
As the vine curls her tendrils, which implied
Subjection, but required with gentle sway,
And by her yielded, by him best received,
Yielded with coy submission, modest pride,
And sweet, reluctant amorous delay.
Nor those mysterious parts were then concealed;
Then was not guilty shame: dishonest Shame
Of Nature's works, Honour dishonourable,
Sin-bred, how have ye troubled all mankind
With shows instead, mere show of seeming pure,
And banished from man's life his happiest life
Simplicity and spotless innocence!
So passed they naked on, nor shunned the sight
Of God or Angel; for they thought no ill;
So hand in hand they passed, the loveliest pair
That ever since in love's embraces met –
Adam, the goodliest man of men since born
His sons; the fairest of her daughters Eve.
Under a tuft of shade that on a green
Stood whispering soft, by a fresh fountain-side,
They sat them down; and, after no more toil
Of their sweet gard'ning labour than sufficed
To recommend cool Zephyr, and made ease
More easy, wholesome thirst and appetite
More grateful, to their supper-fruits they fell –
Nectarine fruits, which the compliant boughs
Yielded them, sidelong as they sat recline
On the soft downy bank damasked with flowers.
The savoury pulp they chew, and in the rind,
Still as they thirsted, scoop the brimming stream;
Nor gentle purpose, nor endearing smiles
Wanted, nor youthful dalliance, as beseems
Fair couple linked in happy nuptial league,
Alone as they. About them frisking played
All beasts of th' earth, since wild, and of all chase
In wood or wilderness, forest or den;
Sporting the lion ramped, and in his paw
Dandled the kid; bears, tigers, ounces, pards,
Gambolled before them; th' unwieldy elephant.
To make them mirth, used all his might, and
    wreathed
His lithe proboscis; close the serpent sly,
Insinuating, wove with Gordian twine
His braided train, and of his fatal guile
Gave proof unheeded. Others on the grass
Coouched, and, now filled with pasture, gazing sat,
Or bedward ruminating; for the sun,
Declined, was hasting now with prone career

To th' Ocean Isles, and in th' ascending scale
Of Heaven the stars that usher evening rose;

‹Book XI›
(lines 625–end)

    So spake our mother Eve; and Adam heard
Well pleased, but answered not; for now too high
Th' Archangel stood, and from the other hill
To their fixed station, all in bright array
The Cherubim descended, on the ground
Gliding meteorous, as evening mist,
Risen from a river, o'er the marish glides,
And gathers ground fast at the labourer's heel
Homeward returning. High in front advanced,
The brandished sword of God before them blazed.
Fierce as a comet, which with torrid heat,
And vapour as the Libyan air adust,
Began to parch that temperate clime; whereat
In either hand the hast'ning Angel caught
Our lingering parents, and to th' eastern gate
Led them direct, and down the cliff as fast
To the subjected plain; then disappeared.
They, looking back, all the eastern side beheld
Of Paradise, so late their happy seat,
Waved over by that flaming brand, the gate
With dreadful faces thronged and fiery arms:
Some natural tears they dropped, but wiped them
    soon;
The world was all before them, where to choose
Their place of rest, and Providence their guide:
They, hand in hand, with wandering steps and slow,
Through Eden took their solitary way.

PARADISE REGAINED
‹Book I›
(lines 280–313)

'But, as I rose out of the laving stream,
Heaven opened her eternal doors, from whence
The Spirit descended on me like a dove;
And last, the sum of all, my Father's voice,
Audibly heard from Heaven, pronounced me his,
Me his beloved Son, in whom alone
He was well pleased: by which I knew the time
Now full, that I no more should live obscure,
But openly begin, as best becomes
The authority which I derived from Heaven.
And now by some strong motion I am led

Into this wilderness; to what intent
I learn not yet, perhaps I need not know;
For what concerns my knowledge God reveals.'

　So spake our Morning Star, then in his rise,
And, looking round, on every side beheld
A pathless desert, dusk with horrid shades.
The way he came not having marked, return
Was difficult, by human steps untrod;
And he still on was led, but with such thoughts
Accompanied by things past and to come
Lodged in his breast, as well might recommend
Such solitude before choicest society.
Full forty days he passed – whether on hill
Sometimes, anon in shady vale, each night
Under the covert of some ancient oak
Or cedar to defend him from the dew,
Or harboured in one cave, is not revealed;
Nor tasted human food, nor hunger felt,
Till those days ended; hungered then at last
Among wild beasts. They at his sight grew mild,
Nor sleeping him nor waking harmed; his walk
The fiery serpent fled and noxious worm;
The lion and fierce tiger glared aloof.

‹Book IV›
(lines 236–90)

'Look once more, ere we leave this specular mount,
Westward, much nearer by south-west; behold
Where on th' Ægean shore a city stands,
Built nobly, pure the air and light the soil –
Athens, the eye of Greece, mother of arts
And eloquence, native to famous wits
Or hospitable, in her sweet recess,
City or suburban studious walks and shades;
See there the olive-grove of Academe,
Plato's retirement, where the Attic bird
Trills her thick-warbled notes the summer long;
There, flow'ry hill, Hymettus, with the sound
Of bees' industrious murmur, oft invites
To studious musing; there Ilissus rolls
His whispering stream; within the walls then view
The schools of ancient sages – his who bred
Great Alexander to subdue the world,
Lyceum there: and painted Stoa next:
There thou shalt hear and learn the secret power
Of harmony, in tones and numbers hit
By voice or hand, and various-measured verse,
Æolian charms and Dorian lyric odes,
And his who gave them breath, but higher sung,
Blind Melesigenes, thence Homer called,

Whose poem Phœbus challenged for his own.
Thence what the lofty grave Tragedians taught
In chorus or iambic, teachers best
Or moral prudence, with delight received
In brief sententious precepts, while they treat
Of fate, and chance, and change in human life,
High actions and high passions best describing:
Thence to the famous Orators repair,
Those ancient, whose resistless eloquence
Wielded at will that fierce democracy,
Shook the Arsenal, and fulmin'd over Greece
To Macedon and Artaxerxes' throne;
To sage Philosophy next lend thine ear,
From Heaven descended to the low-roofed house
Of Socrates – see there his tenement –
Whom, well inspired, the oracle pronounced
Wisest of men; from whose mouth issued forth
Mellifluous streams, that watered all the schools
Of Academics old and new, with those
Surnamed Peripatetics, and the sect
Epicurean, and the Stoic severe;
These here revolve, or, as thou lik'st, at home,
Till time mature thee to a kingdom's weight;
These rules will render thee a king complete
Within thyself, much more with empire joined.'

　To whom our Saviour sagely thus replied: –
'Think not but that I know these things; or think
I know them not, not therefore am I short
Of knowing what I ought: he who receives
Light from above, from the Fountain of Light,
No other doctrine needs, though granted true [...]

PETER SCUPHAM ◄ on ► WILLIAM MORRIS

When William Morris (1834–96) read his first poem, 'The Willow and the Red Cliff', to his friends in the Pre-Raphaelite Brotherhood, he is said to have responded to their enthusiasm with 'Well, if this is poetry it is very easy to write.' The early lyrics evoke the decorative sorrows of a medieval never-never land, but his extraordinary, bluff facility soon found a course for its energy in such sprawling secondary epics as *The Earthly Paradise* and *Jason*.

There are two major works, though, which leap free from the somnolent tapestries which were Morris's bane: *Sigurd the Volsung* and *The Pilgrims of Hope*. I was brought up on the Matter of the North; my imagination first caught by Padraic Column's retelling of Norse Legends in *The Children of Odin*. *Sigurd*, which draws from the Old Norse *Edda* and the German *Niebelungenlied* demonstrates Morris's architectural skill as a poet and shows his lolloping lines pulled into a kind of energetic ferocity under the pressure of a theme which stirred his own psyche. In this extract Sigurd, having killed the dwarf Fafnir, now metamorphosed into a serpent, and gained wisdom by eating his heart, claims the treasure Fafnir guarded.

Morris is always at his best when stirred by the sense of event and purpose. This crusading Utopian, weaver, typographer, what-have-you, put something of the ardour which made him a political idealist into a narrative sequence, *The Pilgrims of Hope*, which tracks the progress of a pair of lovers into social awareness and the Paris Commune. Loosely written, the same old lollopers, but no fustian.

THE PILGRIMS OF HOPE

◄ V: New Birth ►

(lines 67–end)

So passed the world on its ways, and weary with
    waiting we were.
Men ate and drank and married; no wild cry smote the
    air,
No great crowd ran together to greet the day of doom;
And ever more and more seemed the town like a
    monstrous tomb
To us, the Pilgrims of Hope, until to-night it came,
And Hope on the stones of the street is written in
    letters of flame.

This is how it befel: a workmate of mine had heard
Some bitter speech in my mouth, and he took me up
    at the word,
And said, 'Come over to-morrow to our Radical
    spouting-place;
For there, if we hear nothing new, at least we shall see
    a new face;
He is one of those Communist chaps, and 'tis like that
    you two may agree.'
So we went, and the street was as dull and as common
    as aught you could see;
Dull and dirty the room. Just over the chairman's chair
Was a bust, a Quaker's face with nose cocked up in the
    air;
They were common prints on the wall of the heads of
    the party fray,
And Mazzini dark and lean amidst them gone astray.
Some thirty men we were of the kind that I knew full
    well,
Listless, rubbed down to the type of our easy-going
    hell.
My heart sank down as I entered, and wearily there I
    sat
While the chairman strove to end his maunder of this
    and of that.
And partly shy he seemed, and partly indeed ashamed
Of the grizzled man beside him as his name to us he
    named.
He rose, thickset and short, and dressed in shabby
    blue,
And even as he began it seemed as though I knew
The thing he was going to say, though I never heard it
    before.
He spoke, were it well, were it ill, as though a message
    he bore,

A word that he could not refrain from many a million
of men.
Nor aught seemed the sordid room and the few that
were listening then
Save the hall of the labouring earth and the world
which was to be.
Bitter to many the message, but sweet indeed unto
me,
Of man without a master, and earth without a strife,
And every soul rejoicing in the sweet and bitter of life:
Of peace and good-will he told, and I knew that in
faith he spake,
But his words were my very thoughts, and I saw the
battle awake,
And I followed from end to end; and triumph grew in
my heart
As he called on each that heard him to arise and play
his part
In the tale of the new-told gospel, lest as slaves they
should live and die.

He ceased, and I thought the hearers would rise up
with one cry,
And bid him straight enrol them; but they, they
applauded indeed,
For the man was grown full eager, and had made them
hearken and heed:
But they sat and made no sign, and two of the glibber
kind
Stood up to jeer and to carp, his fiery words to blind.
I did not listen to them, but failed not his voice to
hear
When he rose to answer the carpers, striving to make
more clear
That which was clear already; not overwell, I knew,
He answered the sneers and the silence, so hot and
eager he grew;
But my hope full well he answered, and when he called
again
On men to band together lest they live and die in vain,
In fear lest he should escape me, I rose ere the meeting
was done,
And gave him my name and my faith – and I was the
only one.
He smiled as he heard the jeers, and there was a shake
of the hand,
He spoke like a friend long known; and lo! I was one
of the band.

And now the streets seem gay and the high stars
glittering bright;

And for me, I sing amongst them, for my heart is full
and light.
I see the deeds to be done and the day to come on the
earth,
And riches vanished away and sorrow turned to
mirth;
I see the city squalor and the country stupor gone.
And we a part of it all – we twain no longer alone
In the days to come of the pleasure, in the days that
are of the fight –
I was born once long ago: I am born again to-night.

❧

THE STORY OF SIGURD THE VOLSUNG

◄ Book II: How Sigurd took to him the treasure of the Elf Andvari ►

Now Sigurd eats of the heart that once in the Dwarf-
king lay,
The hoard of the wisdom begrudged, the might of the
earlier day.
Then wise of heart was he waxen, but longing in him
grew
To sow the seed he had gotten, and till the field he
knew.
So he leapeth aback of Greyfell, and rideth the desert
bare,
And the hollow slot of Fafnir, that led to the Serpent's
lair.
Then long he rode adown it, and the ernes flew
overhead,
And tidings great and glorious of that Treasure of old
they said.
So far o'er the waste he wended, and when the night
was come
He saw the earth-old dwelling, the dread Gold-
wallower's home:
On the skirts of the Heath it was builded by a tumbled
stony bent;
High went that house to the heavens, down 'neath the
earth it went,
Of unwrought iron fashioned for the heart of a greedy
king:
'Twas a mountain, blind without, and within was its
plenishing
But the Hoard of Andvari the ancient, and the sleeping
Curse unseen,
The Gold of the Gods that spared not and the greedy
that have been.

Through the door strode Sigurd the Volsung, and the grey moon and the sword
Fell on the tawny gold-heaps of the ancient hapless Hoard:
Gold gear of hosts unburied, and the coin of cities dead,
Great spoil of the ages of battle, lay there on the Serpent's bed:
Huge blocks from mid-earth quarried, where none but the Dwarfs have mined,
Wide sands of the golden rivers no foot of man may find
Lay 'neath the spoils of the mighty and the ruddy rings of yore:
But amidst was the Helm of Aweing that the Fear of earth-folk bore,
And there gleamed a wonder beside it, the Hauberk all of gold,
Whose like is not in the heavens nor has earth of its fellow told:
There Sigurd seeth moreover Andvari's Ring of Gain,
The hope of Loki's finger, the Ransom's utmost grain;
For it shone on the midmost gold-heap like the first star set in the sky
In the yellow space of even when moon-rise draweth anigh.
Then laughed the Son of Sigmund, and stooped to the golden land,
And gathered that first of the harvest and set it on his hand;
And he did on the Helm of Aweing, and the Hauberk all of gold,
Whose like is not in the heavens, nor has earth of its fellow told:
Then he praised the day of the Volsungs amid the yellow light,
And he set his hand to the labour and put forth his kingly might;
He dragged forth gold to the moon, on the desert's face he laid
The innermost earth's adornment, and rings for the nameless made;
He toiled and loaded Greyfell, and the cloudy war-steed shone
And the gear of Sigurd rattled in the flood of moonlight wan;
There he toiled and loaded Greyfell, and the Volsung's armour rang
Mid the yellow bed of the Serpent: but without the eagles sang:

'Bind the red rings, O Sigurd! let the gold shine free and clear!
For what hath the Son of the Volsungs the ancient Curse to fear?'

'Bind the red rings, O Sigurd! for thy tale is well begun,
And the world shall be good and gladdened by the Gold lit up by the sun.'

'Bind the red rings, O Sigurd! and gladden all thine heart
For the world shall make thee merry ere thou and she depart.'

'Bind the red rings, O Sigurd! for the ways go green below,
Go green to the dwelling of Kings, and the halls that the Queen-folk know.'

'Bind the red rings, O Sigurd! for what is there bides by the way,
Save the joy of folk to awaken, and the dawn of the merry day?'

'Bind the red rings, O Sigurd! for the strife awaits thine hand,
And a plenteous war-field's reaping, and the praise of many a land.'

'Bind the red rings, O Sigurd! But how shall storehouse hold
That glory of thy winning and the tidings to be told?'

Now the moon was dead, and the star-worlds were great on the heavenly plain,
When the steed was fully laden; then Sigurd taketh the rein
And turns to the ruined rock-wall that the lair was built beneath,
For there he deemed was the gate and the door of the Glittering Heath,
But not a whit moved Greyfell for aught that the King might do;
Then Sigurd pondered a while, till the heart of the beast he knew,
And clad in all his war-gear he leaped to the saddle-stead,
And with pride and mirth neighed Greyfell and tossed aloft his head,

And sprang unspurred o'er the waste, and light and
swift he went,
And breasted the broken rampart, the stony tumbled
bent;
And over the brow he clomb, and there beyond was
the world,
A place of many mountains and great crags together
hurled.
So down to the west he wendeth, and goeth swift and
light,
And the stars are beginning to wane, and the day is
mingled with night;
For full fain was the sun to arise and look on the Gold
set free,
And the Dwarf-wrought rings of the Treasure and the
gifts from the floor of the sea.

Coventry Patmore (1823–96) is now the least read of the Victorian poets. His most popular work in his own lifetime was *The Angel in the House*, a sequence in praise of married love, too successfully of its age to be of more than historical interest, but some of the irregular odes collected as *The Unknown Eros* (1877) are a different matter. These poems found little favour with most of Patmore's contemporaries, but in the best of them exalted thought is expressed in verse whose rhythm is responsive to deep feeling. Harking back to Donne and Crashaw, they sound a note not otherwise heard in nineteenth-century poetry. Significantly, Gerard Manley Hopkins admired some of them, and Patmore himself wrote well about that other original verse craftsman of his day, William Barnes.

Patmore wrote always in the grand manner – which has not endeared him to our century. His diction is less lively than his pulse. But there is a core of sincerity to him, and his voice in such poems as 'A Farewell' and 'The Toys' is not quite like any other. He has a way of making you remember what he says when you have forgotten who said it. Just before his untimely death in 1991 the poet Terence Hards repeated the opening lines of 'Winter' to me, saying he did not know who had written them but that for years he had been unable to get them out of his head.

An anti-clerical Roman Catholic convert who read Swedenborg and once destroyed a whole prose book he had written on the Virgin Mary because Hopkins spoke a word of moral disapproval, Patmore was three times married. The preface he wrote for the collected edition of his poems which appeared in 1886 puts his case decently. 'I have written little,' it runs, 'but it is all my best; I have never spoken when I had nothing to say, nor spared time or labour to make my words true. I have respected posterity; and should there be a posterity which cares for letters, I dare to hope that it will respect me.'

A Farewell

With all my will, but much against my heart,
We two now part.
My Very Dear,
Our solace is, the sad road lies so clear.
It needs no art,
With faint, averted feet
And many a tear,
In our opposèd paths to persevere.
Go thou to East, I West.
We will not say
There's any hope, it is so far away.
But, O, my Best,
When the one darling of our widowhead,
The nursling Grief,
Is dead,
And no dews blur our eyes
To see the peach-bloom come in evening skies,
Perchance we may,
Where now this night is day,
And even through faith of still averted feet,
Making full circle of our banishment,
Amazèd meet;
The bitter journey to the bourne so sweet
Seasoning the termless feast of our content
With tears of recognition never dry.

The Toys

My little Son, who look'd from thoughtful eyes
And moved and spoke in quiet grown-up wise,
Having my law the seventh time disobey'd,
I struck him, and dismiss'd
With hard words and unkiss'd,
– His Mother, who was patient, being dead.
Then, fearing lest his grief should hinder sleep,
I visited his bed,
But found him slumbering deep,
With darken'd eyelids, and their lashes yet
From his late sobbing wet.
And I, with moan,
Kissing away his tears, left others of my own;
For, on a table drawn beside his head,
He had put, within his reach,
A box of counters and a red-vein'd stone,
A piece of glass abraded by the beach,
And six or seven shells,

A bottle with bluebells,
And two French copper coins, ranged there with
    careful art,
To comfort his sad heart.
So when that night I pray'd
To God, I wept, and said:
Ah! when at last we lie with trancèd breath,
Not vexing Thee in death,
And Thou rememberest of what toys
We made our joys,
How weakly understood
Thy great commanded good,
Then, fatherly not less
Than I whom Thou hast moulded from the clay,
Thou'lt leave Thy wrath, and say,
'I will be sorry for their childishness.'

Magna Est Veritas

Here, in this little Bay,
Full of tumultuous life and great repose,
Where, twice a day,
The purposeless, glad ocean comes and goes,
Under high cliffs, and far from the huge town,
I sit me down.
For want of me the world's course will not fail:
When all its work is done, the lie shall rot;
The truth is great, and shall prevail,
When none cares whether it prevail or not.

Winter

I, singularly moved
To love the lovely that are not beloved,
Of all the Seasons, most
Love Winter, and to trace
The sense of the Trophonian pallor on her face.
It is not death, but plenitude of peace;
And the dim cloud that does the world enfold
Hath less the characters of dark and cold
Than warmth and light asleep,
And correspondent breathing seems to keep
With the infant harvest, breathing soft below
Its eider coverlet of snow.
Nor is in field or garden anything

But, duly looked into, contains serene
The substance of things hoped for, in the Spring,
And evidence of Summer not yet seen.
On every chance-mild day
That visits the moist shaw,
The honeysuckle, 'sdaining to be crost
In urgence of sweet life by sleet or frost,
'Voids the time's law
With still increase
Of leaflet new, and little, wandering spray;
Often, in sheltering brakes,
As one from rest disturbed in the first hour,
Primrose or violet bewildered wakes,
And deems 'tis time to flower;
Though not a whisper of her voice he hear,
The buried bulb does know
The signals of the year,
And hails far Summer with his lifted spear;
The gorse-field dark, by sudden, gold caprice,
Turns, here and there, into a Jason's fleece;
Lilies, that soon in Autumn slipped their gowns of
    green
And vanished into earth,
And came again, ere Autumn died, to birth,
Stand full-arrayed, amidst the wavering shower,
And perfect for the Summer, less the flower;
In nook of pale or crevice of crude bark,
Thou canst not miss,
If close thou spy, to mark
The ghostly chrysalis,
That, if thou touch it, stirs in its dream dark;
And the flushed Robin, the evenings hoar,
Does of Love's Day, as if he saw it, sing;
But sweeter yet than dream or song of Summer or
    Spring
Are Winter's sometime smiles, that seem to well
From infancy ineffable;
Her wandering, languorous gaze,
So unfamiliar, so without amaze,
On the elemental, chill adversity,
The uncomprehended rudeness; and her sigh
And solemn, gathering tear,
And look of exile from some great repose, the sphere
Of ether, moved by ether only, or
By something still more tranquil.

I have chosen the following poems of Edgar Allan Poe (1809–49) – here chronologically offered – because they are both accomplished and representative. For the fullness of Poe's vision, one must go to the prose, but certain poems are partial distillations of it. 'The Haunted Palace' has the symbolism of many of Poe's tales of psychic conflict; 'The Conqueror Worm' describes a phase of the cosmic history proposed in *Eureka*; 'Annabel Lee' is related to all those stories, such as 'Ligeia', in which a lost beloved signifies a lost spiritual wholeness which the hero strives to recover through imagination and dream.

Poe described poetry as 'a wild effort to reach the beauty above', and the movement of many of his poems, in space or time, is away from this present world. 'Sonnet to Science' says that poetry must abandon this planet for 'some happier star'; 'Evening Star' rejects our Earth's moon in favour of a 'distant fire'; 'To Helen' yearns back in time, and 'Eldorado' says that only beyond the grave will desire be answered. Not only do Poe's poems speak of transcending the here and now; they also, even when they have a spine of narrative or argument, continually seek to estrange the reader from everyday earthly consciousness, and thus presumably to impel him in the direction of supernal beauty. The magic means employed include vagueness and paradox, a stress on such ideas as dissolution and disappearance, and an incantatory repetition which one finds at its most powerful in 'Annabel Lee' or the final stanza of 'To One in Paradise'.

'Fairyland' is unlike any other poem of Poe's. It deals – with much verve – in his customary themes and devices, yet breaks its flow with self-mocking collapses into a prosaic, commonsensical tone. The result is a poignancy unique in his work. 'Fairyland' was Elizabeth Bishop's favourite Poe poem, and it is a favourite of mine as well.

Edgar Allan Poe

Evening Star

'Twas noontide of summer,
   And mid-time of night;
And stars, in their orbits,
   Shone pale, thro' the light
Of the brighter, cold moon,
   'Mid planets her slaves,
Herself in the Heavens,
   Her beam on the waves.
   I gaz'd awhile
   On her cold smile;
Too cold – too cold for me –
   There pass'd, as a shroud,
   A fleecy cloud,
And I turn'd away to thee,
   Proud Evening Star,
   In thy glory afar,
And dearer thy beam shall be;
   For joy to my heart
   Is the proud part
Thou bearest in Heav'n at night,
   And more I admire
   Thy distant fire,
Than that colder, lowly light.

Sonnet to Science

Science! true daughter of Old Time thou art!
   Who alterest all things with thy peering eyes.
Why preyest thou thus upon the poet's heart,
   Vulture, whose wings are dull realities?
How should he love thee? or how deem thee wise,
   Who wouldst not leave him in his wandering
To seek for treasure in the jewelled skies,
   Albeit he soared with an undaunted wing?
Hast thou not dragged Diana from her car?
   And driven the Hamadryad from the wood
To seek a shelter in some happier star?
   Hast thou not torn the Naiad from her flood,
The Elfin from the green grass, and from me
   The summer dream beneath the tamarind tree?

Fairyland

Dim vales – and shadowy floods –
And cloudy-looking woods,
Whose forms we can't discover
For the tears that drip all over:
Huge moons there wax and wane
Again – again – again –
Every moment of the night –
For ever changing places –
And they put out the star-light
With the breath from their pale faces.
About twelve by the moon-dial
One more filmy than the rest
(A kind which, upon trial,
They have found to be the best)
Comes down – still down – and down
With its centre on the crown
Of a mountain's eminence,
While its wide circumference
In easy drapery falls
Over hamlets, over halls,
Wherever they may be –
O'er the strange woods – o'er the sea –
Over spirits on the wing –
Over every drowsy thing –
And buries them up quite
In a labyrinth of light –
And then how deep! – O, deep!
Is the passion of their sleep.
In the morning they arise,
And their moony covering
Is soaring in the skies,
With the tempests as they toss,
Like – almost any thing –
Or a yellow Albatross.
They use that moon no more
For the same end as before –
Videlicet a tent –
Which I think extravagant.
Its atomies, however,
Into a shower dissever,
Of which those butterflies,
Of Earth, who seek the skies,
And so come down again
(Never-contented things!)
Have brought a specimen
Upon their quivering wings.

To Helen

Helen, thy beauty is to me
    Like those Nicéan barks of yore,
That gently, o'er a perfumed sea,
    The weary, wayworn wanderer bore
    To his own native shore.

On desperate seas long wont to roam,
    Thy hyacinth hair, thy classic face,
Thy Naiad airs have brought me home
    To the glory that was Greece,
    And the grandeur that was Rome.

Lo! in yon brilliant window niche
    How statue-like I see thee stand,
    The agate lamp within thy hand!
Ah, Psyche, from the regions which
    Are Holy Land!

The City in the Sea

Lo! Death has reared himself a throne
In a strange city lying alone
Far down within the dim West,
Where the good and the bad and the worst and
    the best,
Have gone to their eternal rest.
Their shrines and palaces and towers
(Time-eaten towers that tremble not!)
Resemble nothing that is ours.
Around, by lifting winds forgot,
Resignedly beneath the sky
The melancholy waters lie.

No rays from the holy heaven come down
On the long night-time of that town;
But light from out the lurid sea
Streams up the turrets silently –
Gleams up the pinnacles far and free –
Up domes – up spires – up kingly halls –
Up fanes – up Babylon-like walls –
Up shadowy long-forgotten bowers
Of sculptured ivy and stone flowers –
Up many and many a marvellous shrine
Whose wreathéd friezes intertwine
The viol, the violet, and the vine.

Resignedly beneath the sky
The melancholy waters lie.

So blend the turrets and shadows there
That all seem pendulous in air,
While from a proud tower in the town
Death looks gigantically down.

There open fanes and gaping graves
Yawn level with the luminous waves;
But not the riches there that lie
In each idol's diamond eye –
Not the gaily-jewelled dead
Tempt the waters from their bed;
For no ripples curl, alas!
Along that wilderness of glass –
No swellings tell that winds may be
Upon some far-off happier sea –
No heavings hint that winds have been
On seas less hideously serene.

But lo, a stir is in the air!
The wave – there is a movement there!
As if the towers had thrust aside,
In slightly sinking, the dull tide –
As if their tops had feebly given
A void within the filmy Heaven.
The waves have now a redder glow –
The hours are breathing faint and low –
And when, amid no earthly moans,
Down, down that town shall settle hence,
Hell, rising from a thousand thrones,
Shall do it reverence.

To One in Paradise

Thou wast that all to me, love,
    For which my soul did pine –
A green isle in the sea, love,
    A fountain and a shrine,
All wreathed with fairy fruits and flowers,
    And all the flowers were mine.

Ah, dream too bright to last!
    Ah, starry Hope! that didst arise
But to be overcast!
    A voice from out the Future cries,
'On! on!' – but o'er the Past
    (Dim gulf!) my spirit hovering lies
Mute, motionless, aghast!

For, alas! alas! with me
    The light of Life is o'er!

No more – no more – no more –
(Such language holds the solemn sea
   To the sands upon the shore)
Shall bloom the thunder-blasted tree,
   Or the stricken eagle soar!

And all my days are trances,
   And all my nightly dreams
Are where thy grey eye glances,
   And where thy footstep gleams –
In what ethereal dances,
   By what eternal streams.

THE HAUNTED PALACE

In the greenest of our valleys
   By good angels tenanted,
Once a fair and stately palace –
   Radiant palace – reared its head.
In the monarch Thought's dominion –
   It stood there!
Never seraph spread a pinion
   Over fabric half so fair!

Banners yellow, glorious, golden,
   On its roof did float and flow,
(This – all this – was in the olden
   Time long ago);
And every gentle air that dallied,
   In that sweet day,
Along the ramparts plumed and pallid,
   A wingéd odour went away.

Wanderers in that happy valley,
   Through two luminous windows, saw
Spirits moving musically,
   To a lute's well-tunéd law,
Round about a throne where, sitting
   (Porphyrogene!)
In state his glory well-befitting,
   The ruler of the realm was seen.

And all with pearl and ruby glowing
   Was the fair palace door,
Through which came flowing, flowing, flowing,
   And sparkling evermore,
A troop of Echoes, whose sweet duty
   Was but to sing,

In voices of surpassing beauty,
   The wit and wisdom of their king.

But evil things, in robes of sorrow,
   Assailed the monarch's high estate.
(Ah, let us mourn! – for never morrow
   Shall dawn upon him, desolate!)
And round about his home the glory
   That blushed and bloomed,
Is but a dim-remembered story
   Of the old time entombed.

And travellers, now, within that valley,
   Through the red-litten windows see
Vast forms, that move fantastically
   To a discordant melody,
While, like a ghastly rapid river,
   Through the pale door
A hideous throng rush out forever,
   And laugh – but smile no more.

THE CONQUEROR WORM

Lo! 'tis a gala night
   Within the lonesome latter years!
An angel throng, bewinged, bedight
   In veils, and drowned in tears,
Sit in a theatre, to see
   A play of hopes and fears,
While the orchestra breathes fitfully
   The music of the spheres.

Mimes, in the form of God on high,
   Mutter and mumble low,
And hither and thither fly –
   Mere puppets they, who come and go
At bidding of vast formless things
   That shift the scenery to and fro,
Flapping from out their Condor wings
   Invisible Wo!

That motley drama – oh, be sure
   It shall not be forgot!
With its Phantom chased for evermore
   By a crowd that seize it not,
Through a circle that ever returneth in
   To the self-same spot,
And much of Madness, and more of Sin,
   And Horror the soul of the plot.

But see, amid the mimic rout
   A crawling shape intrude!
A blood-red thing that writhes from out
   The scenic solitude!
It writhes! – it writhes! – with mortal pangs
   The mimes become its food,
And the seraphs sob at vermin fangs
   In human gore imbued.

Out – out are the lights – out all!
   And, over each quivering form,
The curtain, a funeral pall,
   Comes down with the rush of a storm,
And the angels, all pallid and wan,
   Uprising, unveiling, affirm
That the play is the tragedy 'Man,'
   And its hero the Conqueror Worm.

ELDORADO

   Gaily bedight,
   A gallant knight,
In sunshine and in shadow,
   Had journeyed long,
   Singing a song,
In search of Eldorado.

   But he grew old –
   This knight so bold –
And o'er his heart a shadow
   Fell as he found
   No spot of ground
That looked like Eldorado.

   And as his strength
   Failed him at length,
He met a pilgrim shadow –
   'Shadow,' said he,
   'Where can it be –
This land of Eldorado?'

   'Over the Mountains
   Of the Moon,
Down the Valley of the Shadow,
   Ride, boldly ride,'
   The shade replied, –
'If you seek for Eldorado!'

ANNABEL LEE

It was many and many a year ago,
   In a kingdom by the sea,
That a maiden there lived whom you may know
   By the name of ANNABEL LEE;
And this maiden she lived with no other thought
   Than to love and be loved by me.

I was a child and *she* was a child,
   In this kingdom by the sea:
But we loved with a love that was more than love –
   I and my ANNABEL LEE;
With a love that the wingèd seraphs of heaven
   Coveted her and me.

And this was the reason that, long ago,
   In this kingdom by the sea,
A wind blew out of a cloud, chilling
   My beautiful ANNABEL LEE;
So that her highborn kinsmen came
   And bore her away from me,
To shut her up in a sepulchre
   In this kingdom by the sea.

The angels, not half so happy in Heaven,
   Went envying her and me: –
Yes! – that was the reason (as all men know,
   In this kingdom by the sea)
That the wind came out of the cloud by night,
   Chilling and killing my ANNABEL LEE.

But our love it was stronger by far than the love
   Of those who were older than we –
   Of many far wiser than we –
And neither the angels in heaven above,
   Nor the demons down under the sea,
Can ever dissever my soul from the soul
   Of the beautiful ANNABEL LEE: –

For the moon never beams, without bringing me
    dreams
   Of the beautiful ANNABEL LEE;
And the stars never rise, but I feel the bright eyes
   Of the beautiful ANNABEL LEE;
And so, all the night-tide, I lie down by the side
Of my darling, – my darling, – my life and my
    bride,
   In her sepulchre there by the sea,
   In her tomb by the side of the sea.

By the time Byron praised Pope as 'the moral poet of all civilisation', to praise Pope was already to defend him. Byron would be going out of his way here to make what, from him, initially seems an unexpected point – the less so, admittedly, since no satirist worth his salt could claim a lineage that didn't go through Pope; but the potential irony remains that Byron was hardly the most moral of poets himself. Satirists have always had a hard time. Pope, taking up his self-appointed role as defender of Truth after 1731, had trouble defending himself as a moral poet, as did Horace before him. Not that the critical orthodoxies of the period didn't allow satirists to claim to be moral, and at the same time delight with their wit (in the sense that the word then had), for they did. The problem really, is trying to work out who genuinely claimed it, and who genuinely believed it. Well, not Pope, I'd like to argue. Rather, far from being too moral for a wit, as he describes himself in the epilogue to the satires, Pope was, as I've enjoyed reading him, too witty for a moralist. Strange, at first sight, that some of the most exciting satirists should be those least suited to the moral injunctions they should be compelled to profess; but lucky then that Truth (in whatever proportion to *delectare*) should provide so perfect a cover for the exercising of their wit, to guard the poet, and sanctify the line and make 'Immortal, Verse as mean as mine.' Pope's moments of restraint, even in the moral essays and epistles, are quite rare. Most of the time he is thoroughly conquered by the ruling passion: in his case, an extravagantly inventive, abundantly energetic, absorptive engaged and engaging sensibility, which identifies him as a member of the school of rational amphibii, and a link in one possible chain joining Marvell, to Byron, to Auden.

AN ESSAY ON CRITICISM
(lines 289–383)

Some to conceit alone their taste confine,
And glitt'ring thoughts struck out at ev'ry line;
Pleas'd with a work where nothing's just or fit;
One glaring chaos and wild heap of wit:
Poets like painters, thus, unskill'd to trace
The naked nature and the living grace,
With gold and jewels cover ev'ry part,
And hide with ornaments their want of art.
True wit is nature to advantage drest,
What oft was thought, but ne'er so well exprest,
Something, whose truth convinc'd at sight we find,
That gives us back the image of our mind:
As shades more sweetly recommend the light,
So modest plainness sets off sprightly wit:
For works may have more wit than does 'em good,
As bodies perish through excess of blood.
　　Others for language all their care express,
And value books, as women men, for dress:
Their praise is still – the style is excellent;
The sense, they humbly take upon content.
Words are like leaves; and where they most abound,
Much fruit of sense beneath is rarely found.
False eloquence, like the prismatic glass,
Its gawdy colours spreads on ev'ry place;
The face of nature we no more survey,
All glares alike, without distinction gay:
But true expression, like th' unchanging sun,
Clears, and improves whate'er it shines upon,
It gilds all objects, but it alters none.
Expression is the dress of thought, and still
Appears more decent as more suitable;
A vile conceit in pompous words exprest,
Is like a clown in regal purple drest;
For diff'rent styles with diff'rent subjects sort,
As several garbs with country, town, and court.
Some by old words to fame have made pretence;
Ancients in phrase, mere moderns in their sense!
Such labour'd nothings, in so strange a style,
Amaze th'unlearn'd, and make the learned smile.
Unlucky, as Fungoso in the play,
These sparks with awkward vanity display
What the fine gentleman wore yesterday!
And but so mimic ancient wits at best,
As apes our grandsires in their doublets drest.
In words, as fashions, the same rule will hold;
Alike fantastic, if too new, or old;
Be not the first by whom the new are tried,
Nor yet the last to lay the old aside.

But most by numbers judge a poet's song,
And smooth or rough, with them, is right or wrong;
In the bright Muse tho' thousand charms conspire,
Her voice is all these tuneful fools admire,
Who haunt Parnassus but to please their ear,
Not mend their minds; as some to church repair,
Not for the doctrine, but the music there.
These equal syllables alone require,
Tho' oft the ear the open vowels tire,
While expletives their feeble aid *do* join,
And ten low words oft creep in one dull line,
While they ring round the same unvary'd chimes,
With sure returns of still expected rhymes.
Where-e'er you find 'the cooling western breeze',
In the next line, it 'whispers thro' the trees';
If crystal streams 'with pleasing murmurs creep',
The reader's threaten'd (not in vain) with 'sleep'.
Then, at the last, and only couplet fraught
With some unmeaning thing they call a thought,
A needless Alexandrine ends the song,
That like a wounded snake, drags its slow length along.
Leave such to tune their own dull rhymes, and know
What's roundly smooth, or languishingly slow;
And praise the easy vigour of a line,
Where Denham's strength, and Waller's sweetness
    join.
True ease in writing comes from art, not chance,
As those move easiest who have learn'd to dance.
'Tis not enough no harshness gives offence,
The sound must seem an echo to the sense.
Soft is the strain when Zephyr gently blows,
And the smooth stream in smoother numbers flows;
But when loud surges lash the sounding shore,
The hoarse, rough verse should like the torrent roar.
When Ajax strives, some rock's vast weight to throw,
The line too labours, and the words move slow;
Not so, when swift Camilla scours the plain,
Flies o'er th'unbending corn, and skims along the
    main.
Hear how Timotheus' vary'd lays surprize,
And bid alternate passions fall and rise!
While, at each change, the son of Lybian Jove
Now burns with glory, and then melts with love;
Now his fierce eyes with sparkling fury glow;
Now sighs steal out, and tears begin to flow:
Persians and Greeks like turns of nature found,
And the world's victor stood subdu'd by sound!
The pow'r of music all our hearts allow;
And what Timotheus was, is Dryden now.

THE RAPE OF THE LOCK

‹ Canto iii ›

(lines 1–160)

Close by those meads for ever crown'd with flow'rs,
Where Thames with pride surveys his rising tow'rs,
There stands a structure of majestic frame,
Which from the neighb'ring Hampton takes its name.
Here Britain's statesmen oft the fall foredoom
Of foreign tyrants, and of nymphs at home;
Here thou, great Anna! whom three realms obey,
Dost sometimes counsel take – and sometimes tea.
   Hither the heroes and the nymphs resort,
To taste awhile the pleasures of a court;
In various talk th' instructive hours they past,
Who gave the ball, or paid the visit last:
One speaks the glory of the British Queen,
And one describes a charming Indian screen;
A third interprets motions, looks, and eyes;
At ev'ry word a reputation dies.
Snuf, or the fan, supply each pause of chat,
With singing, laughing, ogling, and all that.
   Mean while declining from the noon of day,
The sun obliquely shoots his burning ray;
The hungry judges soon the sentence sign,
And wretches hang that jury-men may dine;
The merchant from th' Exchange returns in peace,
And the long labours of the toilette cease –
Belinda now, whom thirst of fame invites,
Burns to encounter two adventrous knights,
At ombre singly to decide their doom;
And swells her breast with conquests yet to come.
Strait the three bands prepare in arms to join,
Each band the number of the sacred Nine.
Soon as she spreads her hand, th' aerial guard
Descend and sit on each important card:
First Ariel perch'd upon a matadore,
Then each, according to the rank they bore;
For sylphs, yet mindful of their ancient race,
Are, as when women, wondrous fond of place.
   Behold, four kings in majesty rever'd,
With hoary whiskers and a forky beard;
And four fair queens whose hands sustain a flow'r,
Th' expressive emblem of their softer pow'r;
Four knaves in garbs succinct, a trusty band,
Caps on their heads, and halberds in their hand;
And particolour'd troops, a shining train,
Draw forth to combat on the velvet plain.
   The skilful nymph reviews her force with care;
'Let spades be trumps!' she said, and trumps they
    were.

Now move to war her sable matadores,
In show like leaders of the swarthy Moors.
Spadillio first, unconquerable lord!
Led off two captive trumps, and swept the board.
As many more Manillio forc'd to yield,
And march'd a victor from the verdant field.
Him Basto follow'd, but his fate more hard
Gain'd but one trump and one plebeian card.
With his broad sabre next, a chief in years,
The hoary majesty of spades appears;
Puts forth one manly leg, to sight reveal'd;
The rest his many-colour'd robe conceal'd.
The rebel-knave, who dares his prince engage,
Proves the just victim of his royal rage.
Ev'n mighty Pam that kings and queens o'erthrew,
And mow'd down armies in the fights of Lu,
Sad chance of war! now, destitute of aid,
Falls undistinguish'd by the victor spade!
    Thus far both armies to Belinda yield;
Now to the Baron fate inclines the field.
His warlike Amazon her host invades,
Th' imperial consort of the crown of spades.
The club's black tyrant first her victim dy'd,
Spite of his haughty mien, and barb'rous pride:
What boots the regal circle on his head,
His giant limbs in state unwieldy spread ?
That long behind he trails his pompous robe,
And of all monarchs only grasps the globe?
    The Baron now his diamonds pours apace;
Th' embroider'd king who shows but half his face,
And his refulgent queen, with pow'rs combin'd,
Of broken troops an easy conquest find.
Clubs, diamonds, hearts, in wild disorder seen,
With throngs promiscuous strow the level green.
Thus when dispers'd a routed army runs,
Of Asia's troops, and Africk's sable sons,
With like confusion different nations fly,
Of various habit and of various dye,
The pierc'd battalions dis-united fall,
In heaps on heaps; one fate o'erwhelms them all.
    The knave of diamonds tries his wily arts,
And wins (oh shameful chance!) the queen of hearts.
At this, the blood the virgin's cheek forsook,
A livid paleness spreads o'er all her look;
She sees, and trembles at th' approaching ill,
Just in the jaws of ruin, and codille.
And now, (as oft in some distemper'd state)
On one nice trick depends the gen'ral fate.
An ace of hearts steps forth: the king unseen
Lurk'd in her hand, and mourn'd his captive queen.
He springs to vengeance with an eager pace,

And falls like thunder on the prostrate ace.
The nymph exulting fills with shouts the sky,
The walls, the woods, and long canals reply.
    Oh thoughtless mortals! ever blind to fate,
Too soon dejected, and too soon elate!
Sudden these honours shall be snatch'd away,
And curs'd for ever this victorious day.
    For lo! the board with cups and spoons is
        crown'd,
The berries crackle, and the mill turns round.
On shining altars of Japan they raise
The silver lamp; the fiery spirits blaze.
From silver spouts the grateful liquors glide,
While China's earth receives the smoking tide.
At once they gratify their scent and taste,
And frequent cups prolong the rich repast.
Strait hover round the fair her airy band;
Some, as she sip'd, the fuming liquor fann'd,
Some o'er her lap their careful plumes display'd,
Trembling, and conscious of the rich brocade.
Coffee, (which makes the politician wise,
And see thro' all things with his half-shut eyes)
Sent up in vapours to the Baron's brain
New stratagems, the radiant lock to gain.
Ah cease rash youth! desist ere 'tis too late,
Fear the just gods, and think of Scylla's fate!
Chang'd to a bird, and sent to flit in air,
She dearly pays for Nisus' injur'd hair!
    But when to mischief mortals bend their will
How soon they find fit instruments of ill!
Just then, Clarissa drew with tempting grace
A two-edg'd weapon from her shining case;
So ladies in romance assist their knight,
Present the spear, and arm him for the fight.
He takes the gift with rev'rence, and extends
The little engine on his fingers' ends,
This just behind Belinda's neck he spread,
As o'er the fragrant steams she bends her head:
Swift to the lock a thousand sprights repair,
A thousand wings, by turns, blow back the hair,
And thrice they twitch'd the diamond in her ear,
Thrice she look'd back, and thrice the foe drew near.
Just in that instant, anxious Ariel sought
The close recesses of the virgin's thought;
As on the nosegay in her breast reclin'd,
He watch'd th' ideas rising in her mind,
Sudden he view'd, in spite of all her art,
An earthly lover lurking at her heart.
Amaz'd, confus'd, he found his pow'r expir'd,
Resign'd to fate, and with a sigh retir'd.
    The peer now spreads the glitt'ring forfex wide,

T'inclose the lock; now joins it, to divide.
Ev'n then, before the fatal engine clos'd,
A wretched sylph too fondly interpos'd;
Fate urg'd the sheers, and cut the sylph in twain,
(But airy substance soon unites again)
The meeting points the sacred hair dissever
From the fair head, for ever and for ever!

    Then flash'd the living lightning from her eyes,
And screams of horror rend th' affrighted skies.
Not louder shrieks to pitying heav'n are cast,
When husbands or when lap-dogs breathe their last,
Or when rich china vessels, fal'n from high,
In glittring dust and painted fragments lie!

THE DUNCIAD VARIORUM

‹Book iii›

(lines 275–358)

In Lud's old walls, tho' long I rul'd renown'd,
Far, as loud Bow's stupendous bells resound;
Tho' my own aldermen conferr'd my bays,
To me committing their eternal praise,
Their full-fed heroes, their pacific may'rs,
Their annual trophies, and their monthly wars.
Tho' long my party built on me their hopes,
For writing pamphlets, and for burning popes;
(Diff'rent our parties, but with equal grace
The Goddess smiles on Whig and Tory race,
'Tis the same rope at sev'ral ends they twist,
To Dulness, Ridpath is as dear as mist.)
Yet lo! in me what authors have to brag on!
Reduc'd at last to hiss in my own dragon.
Avert it, heav'n! that thou or Cibber e'er
Should wag two serpent tails in Smithfield fair.
Like the vile straw that's blown about the streets
The needy poet sticks to all he meets,
Coach'd, carted, trod upon, now loose, now fast.
In the dog's tail his progress ends at last.
Happier thy fortunes! like a rolling stone,
Thy giddy dulness still shall lumber on,
Safe in its heaviness, can never stray,
And licks up every blockhead in the way.
Thy dragons magistrates and peers shall taste,
And from each show rise duller than the last:
Till rais'd from booths to theatre, to court,
Her seat imperial, Dulness shall transport.
Already, opera prepares the way,
The sure fore-runner of her gentle sway.

To aid her cause, if heav'n thou can'st not bend,
Hell thou shalt move; for Faustus is thy friend:
Pluto with Cato thou for her shalt join,
And link the Mourning-Bride to Proserpine.
Grubstreet! thy fall should men and gods conspire,
Thy stage shall stand, ensure it but from fire.
Another Æschylus appears! prepare
For new abortions, all ye pregnant fair!
In flames, like Semeles, be brought to bed,
While opening Hell spouts wild-fire at your head.

    'Now Bavius, take the poppy from thy brow,
And place it here! here all ye heroes bow!
This, this is He, foretold by ancient rhymes,
Th' Augustus born to bring Saturnian times:
Beneath his reign, shall Eusden wear the bays,
Cibber preside Lord-Chancellor of Plays,
B * * sole Judge of Architecture sit,
And Namby Pamby be prefer'd for wit!
While naked mourns the dormitory wall,
And Jones' and Boyle's united labours fall,
While Wren with sorrow to the grave descends,
Gay dies un-pension'd with a hundred friends,
Hibernian politics, O Swift, thy doom,
And Pope's, translating three whole years with
      Broome.

    'Proceed great days! till learning fly the shore,
Till birch shall blush with noble blood no more,
Till thanes see Eton's sons for ever play,
Till Westminster's whole year be holiday;
Till Isis' elders reel, their pupils' sport;
And Alma Mater lie dissolv'd in port!

    'Signs following signs lead on the mighty year;
See! the dull stars roll round and re-appear.
She comes! the cloud-compelling pow'r, behold!
With night primæval, and with chaos old.
Lo! the great anarch's ancient reign restor'd,
Light dies before her uncreating word:
As one by one, at dread Medæa's strain,
The sick'ning stars fade off th' æthereal plain;
As Argus' eyes, by Hermes' wand opprest,
Clos'd one by one to everlasting rest:
Thus at her felt approach, and secret might,
Art after art goes out, and all is night.
See sculking Truth in her old cavern lye,
Secur'd by mountains of heap'd casuistry:
Philosophy, that touch'd the heavens before,
Shrinks to her hidden cause, and is no more:
See Physic beg the Stagyrite's defence!
See Metaphysic call for aid on Sense!
See Mystery to Mathematics fly!
In vain! they gaze, turn giddy, rave, and die.

Thy hand great Dulness! lets the curtain fall,
And universal Darkness covers all.'

'Enough! enough!' the raptur'd monarch cries;
And thro' the Ivory Gate the vision flies.

AN ESSAY ON MAN

‹Epistle II›

(lines 1–52)

Know then thyself, presume not God to scan;
The proper study of mankind is man.
Plac'd on this isthmus of a middle state,
A being darkly wise, and rudely great:
With too much knowledge for the Sceptic side,
With too much weakness for the Stoic's pride,
He hangs between; in doubt to act, or rest,
In doubt to deem himself a god, or beast;
In doubt his mind or body to prefer,
Born but to die, and reas'ning but to err;
Alike in ignorance, his reason such,
Whether he thinks too little, or too much:
Chaos of thought and passion, all confus'd;
Still by himself abus'd, or disabus'd;
Created half to rise, and half to fall;
Great lord of all things, yet a prey to all;
Sole judge of truth, in endless error hurl'd:
The glory, jest, and riddle of the world!
   Go, wond'rous creature! mount where Science
      guides
Go, measure earth, weigh air, and state the tides;
Instruct the planets in what orbs to run,
Correct old time, and regulate the sun;
Go, soar with Plato to th' empyreal sphere,
To the first good, first perfect, and first fair;
Or tread the mazy round his follow'rs trod,
And quitting sense call imitating God;
As Eastern priests in giddy circles run,
And turn their heads to imitate the sun.
Go, teach Eternal Wisdom how to rule –
Then drop into thyself, and be a fool!
   Superior beings, when of late they saw
A mortal man unfold all Nature's law,
Admir'd such wisdom in an earthly shape,
And shew'd a NEWTON as we shew an ape.
   Could he, whose rules the rapid comet bind,
Describe or fix one movement of his mind?
Who saw its fires here rise, and there descend,

Explain his own beginning, or his end?
Alas what wonder! Man's superior part
Uncheck'd may rise, and climb from art to art:
But when his own great work is but begun,
What reason weaves, by passion is undone.
   Trace Science then, with modesty thy guide;
First strip off all her equipage of pride,
Deduct what is but vanity, or dress,
Or learning's luxury, or idleness;
Or tricks to shew the stretch of human brain,
Mere curious pleasure, or ingenious pain:
Expunge the whole, or lop th' excrescent parts
Of all, our vices have created arts:
Then see how little the remaining sum,
Which serv'd the past, and must the times to come!

‹Epistle III›

(lines 7–78)

Look round our world; behold the chain of love
Combining all below and all above.
See plastic Nature working to this end,
The single atoms each to other tend,
Attract, attracted to, the next in place
Form'd and impell'd its neighbour to embrace.
See matter next, with various life endu'd,
Press to one centre still, the gen'ral good.
See dying vegetables life sustain,
See life dissolving vegetate again:
All forms that perish other forms supply,
(By turns we catch the vital breath, and die)
Like bubbles on the sea of matter born,
They rise, they break, and to that sea return.
Nothing is foreign: parts relate to whole;
One all-extending all-preserving soul
Connects each being, greatest with the least;
Made beast in aid of man, and man of beast;
All serv'd, all serving! nothing stands alone;
The chain holds on, and where it ends, unknown.
   Has God, thou fool! work'd solely for thy good,
Thy joy, thy pastime, thy attire, thy food?
Who for thy table feeds the wanton fawn,
For him as kindly spread the flow'ry lawn.
Is it for thee the lark ascends and sings?
Joy tunes his voice, joy elevates his wings:
Is it for thee the linnet pours his throat?
Loves of his own and raptures swell the note:
The bounding steed you pompously bestride,
Shares with his lord the pleasure and the pride:
Is shine alone the seed that strews the plain ?
The birds of heav'n shall vindicate their grain:

Thine the full harvest of the golden year?
Part pays, and justly, the deserving steer:
The hog, that plows not nor obeys thy call,
Lives on the labours of this lord of all.

    Know, Nature's children all divide her care;
The fur that warms a monarch, warm'd a bear.
While man exclaims, 'See all things for my use!'
'See man for mine!' replies a pamper'd goose;
And just as short of reason he must fall,
Who thinks all made for one, not one for all.

    Grant that the pow'rful still the weak controul,
Be man the wit and tyrant of the whole:
Nature that tyrant checks; he only knows,
And helps, another creature's wants and woes.
Say, will the falcon, stooping from above,
Smit with her varying plumage, spare the dove?
Admires the jay the insect's gilded wings?
Or hears the hawk when Philomela sings?
Man cares for all: to birds he gives his woods,
To beasts his pastures, and to fish his floods;
For some his int'rest prompts him to provide,
For more his pleasure, yet for more his pride;
All feed on one vain patron, and enjoy
Th'extensive blessing of his luxury.
That very life his learned hunger craves,
He saves from famine, from the savage saves;
Nay, feasts the animal he dooms his feast,
And, 'till he ends the being, makes it blest;
Which sees no more the stroke, or feels the pain,
Than favour'd man by touch etherial slain.
The creature had his feast of life before;
Thou too must perish, when thy feast is o'er!

    To each unthinking being, Heav'n a friend,
Gives not the useless knowledge of its end:
To man imparts it; but with such a view
As, while he dreads it, makes him hope it too:
The hour conceal'd, and so remote the fear,
Death still draws nearer, never seeming near.
Great standing miracle! that Heav'n assign'd
Its only thinking thing this turn of mind.

❧

EPISTLE II. TO ALLEN LORD BATHURST

(lines 1–100)

Who shall decide, when doctors disagree,
And soundest casuists doubt, like you and me?
You hold the word, from Jove to Momus giv'n,
That man was made the standing jest of Heav'n

And gold but sent to keep the fools in play,
For some to heap, and some to throw away.

    But I, who think more highly of our kind,
(And surely, Heav'n and I are of a mind)
Opine, that Nature, as in duty bound,
Deep hid the shining mischief under ground:
But when by man's audacious labour won,
Flam'd forth this rival to, its sire, the sun.
Then careful Heav'n supply'd two sorts of men,
To squander these, and those to hide agen.

    Like doctors thus, when much dispute has past,
We find our tenets just the same at last.
Both fairly owning, riches in effect
No grace of Heav'n or token of th'elect;
Giv'n to the fool, the mad, the vain, the evil,
To Ward, to Waters, Chartres, and the Devil.

    What Nature wants, commodious gold bestows,
'Tis thus we eat the bread another sows:
But how unequal it bestows, observe,
'Tis thus we riot, while who sow it, starve.
What Nature wants (a phrase I much distrust)
Extends to luxury, extends to lust:
And if we count among the needs of life
Another's toil, why not another's wife?
Useful, I grant, it serves what life requires,
But dreadful too, the dark assassin hires:
Trade it may help, society extend;
But lures the pirate, and corrupts the friend:
It raises armies in a nation's aid,
But bribes a senate, and the land's betray'd.

    Oh! that such bulky bribes as all might see,
Still, as of old, incumber'd villainy!
In vain may heroes fight, and patriots rave;
If secret gold saps on from knave to knave.
Could France or Rome divert our brave designs,
With all their brandies or with all their wines?
What could they more than knights and squires
      confound,
Or water all the quorum ten miles round?
A statesman's slumbers how this speech would
      spoil!
'Sir, Spain has sent a thousand jars of oil;
Huge bales of British cloth blockade the door;
A hundred oxen at your levee roar.'

    Poor Avarice one torment more would find;
Nor could Profusion squander all in kind.
Astride his cheese Sir Morgan might we meet,
And Worldly crying coals from street to street,
(Whom with a wig so wild, and mien so maz'd,
Pity mistakes for some poor tradesman craz'd).
Had Colepepper's whole wealth been hops and hogs,

Could he himself have sent it to the dogs?
His Grace will game: to White's a bull be led,
With spurning heels and with a butting head.
To White's be carried, as to ancient games,
Fair coursers, vases, and alluring dames.
Shall then Uxorio, if the stakes he sweep,
Bear home six whores, and make his lady weep?
Or soft Adonis, so perfum'd and fine,
Drive to St. James's a whole herd of swine?
Oh filthy check on all industrious skill,
To spoil the nation's last great trade, quadrille!

    Once, we confess, beneath the patriot's cloak,
From the crack'd bag the dropping guinea spoke,
And gingling down the back-stairs, told the crew,
'Old Cato is as great a rogue as you.'
Blest paper-credit! last and best supply!
That lends corruption lighter wings to fly!
Gold imp'd by thee, can compass hardest things,
Can pocket states, can fetch or carry kings;
A single leaf shall waft an army o'er,
Or ship off senates to a distant shore;
A leaf, like Sibyl's, scatter to and fro
Our fates and fortunes, as the winds shall blow:
Pregnant with thousands flits the scrap unseen,
And silent sells a king, or buys a queen.

    Since then, my lord, on such a world we fall,
What say you ? 'Say? Why take it, gold and all.'

    What riches give us let us then enquire:
Meat, fire, and clothes. What more? Meat, clothes,
    and fire.
Is this too little? would you more than live?
Alas! 'tis more than Turner finds they give.
Alas! 'tis more than (all his visions past)
Unhappy Wharton, waking, found at last!
What can they give? to dying Hopkins heirs;
To Chartres, vigour; Japhet, nose and ears?
Can they, in gems bid pallid Hippia glow,
In Fulvia's buckle case the throbs below,
Or heal, old Narses, thy obscener ail,
With all th' embroid'ry plaister'd at thy tail?
They might (were Harpax not too wise to spend)
Give Harpax self the blessing of a friend;
Or find some doctor that would save the life
Of wretched Shylock, spite of Shylock's wife:
But thousands die, without or this or that,
Die, and endow a college, or a cat:
To some, indeed, Heav'n grants the happier fate,
T' enrich a bastard, or a son they hate.

    ❦

AN EPISTLE FROM MR POPE, TO DR ARBUTHNOT

(lines 1–108)

Shut, shut the door, good John! fatigu'd I said,
Tie up the knocker, say I'm sick, I'm dead,
The Dog-star rages! nay 'tis past a doubt,
All Bedlam, or Parnassus, is let out:
Fire in each eye, and papers in each hand,
They rave, recite, and madden round the land.
    What walls can guard me, or what shades can
      hide?
They pierce my thickets, thro' my grot they glide,
By land, by water, they renew the charge,
They stop the chariot, and they board the barge.
No place is sacred, not the church is free,
Ev'n Sunday shines no sbbath-day to me:
Then from the Mint walks forth the man of rhyme,
Happy! to catch me, just at dinner-time.

    Is there a parson, much be-mus'd in beer,
A maudlin poetess, a rhyming peer,
A clerk, foredoom'd his father's soul to cross,
Who pens a stanza when he should engross?
Is there, who lock'd from ink and paper, scrawls
With desp'rate charcoal round his darken'd walls ?
All fly to Twit'nam, and in humble strain
Apply to me, to keep them mad or vain.
Arthur, whose giddy son neglects the laws,
Imputes to me and my damn'd works the cause:
Poor Cornus sees his frantic wife elope,
And curses wit, and poetry, and Pope.

    Friend to my life, (which did not you prolong,
The world had wanted many an idle song)
What drop or nostrum can this plague remove?
Or which must end me, a fool's wrath or love?
A dire dilemma! either way I'm sped,
If foes, they write, if friends, they read me dead.
Seiz'd and tied down to judge, how wretched I!
Who can't be silent, and who will not lie;
To laugh, were want of goodness and of grace,
And to be grave, exceeds all pow'r of face.
I sit with sad civility, I read
With honest anguish, and an aching head;
And drop at last, but in unwilling ears,
This saving counsel, 'Keep your piece nine years.'

    Nine years! cries he, who high in Drury-lane
Lull'd by soft zephyrs thro' the broken pane,
Rhymes e're he wakes, and prints before term ends,
Oblig'd by hunger and request of friends:
'The piece you think is incorrect: why take it,
I'm all submission, what you'd have it, make it.'

Three things another's modest wishes bound,
My friendship, and a prologue, and ten pound.

Pitholeon sends to me: 'You know his Grace,
I want a patron; ask him for a place.'
Pitholeon libell'd me – 'but here's a letter
Informs you sir, 'twas when he knew no better.
Dare you refuse him? Curl invites to dine,
He'll write a journal, or he'll turn divine.'

Bless me! a packet. – "Tis a stranger sues,
A virgin tragedy, an orphan muse.'
If I dislike it, 'Furies, death and rage!'
If I approve, 'Commend it to the stage.'
There (thank my stars) my whole commission ends,
The play'rs and I are, luckily, no friends.
Fir'd that the house reject him, "Sdeath I'll print it
And shame the fools – your int'rest, sir, with Lintot.'
Lintot, dull rogue! will think your price too much.
'Not sir, if you revise it, and retouch.'
All my demurrs but double his attacks,
At last he whispers 'Do, and we go snacks.'
Glad of a quarrel, strait I clap the door,
Sir, let me see your works and you no more.

'Tis sung, when Midas' ears began to spring,
(Midas, a sacred person and a king)
His very minister who spied them first,
(Some say his queen) was forc'd to speak, or burst.
And is not mine, my friend, a sorer case,
When ev'ry coxcomb perks them in my face?
'Good friend forbear! you deal in dang'rous things,
I'd never name queens, ministers, or kings;
Keep close to ears, and those let asses prick,
'Tis nothing' – Nothing? if they bite and kick?
Out with it, Dunciad! let the secret pass,
That secret to each fool, that he's an ass:
The truth once told, (and wherefore should we lie)
The queen of Midas slept, and so may I.

You think this cruel? take it for a rule,
No creature smarts so little as a fool.
Let peals of laughter, Codrus! round thee break,
Thou unconcern'd canst hear the mighty crack.
Pit, box and gall'ry in convulsions hurl'd,
Thou stand'st unshook amidst a bursting world.
Who shames a scribler? break one cobweb thro',
He spins the slight, self-pleasing thread anew;
Destroy his fib, or sophistry; in vain,
The creature's at his dirty work again;
Thron'd in the centre of his thin designs;
Proud of a vast extent of flimzy lines.
Whom have I hurt? has poet yet, or peer,
Lost the arch'd eye-brow, or Parnassian sneer?
And has not Colly still his lord, and whore?

His butchers Henley, his free-masons Moor?
Does not one table Bavius still admit?
Still to one Bishop Philips seem a wit?
Still Sapho – 'Hold! for God-sake – you'll offend:
No names – be calm – learn prudence of a friend:
I too could write, and I am twice as tall,
But foes like these!' – one flatt'rer's worse than all;
Of all mad creatures, if the learn'd are right,
It is the slaver kills, and not the bite.
A fool quite angry is quite innocent;
Alas! 'tis ten times worse when they repent.

❧

THE FIRST SATIRE OF THE SECOND BOOK OF HORACE IMITATED

(lines 1–80)

P. There are (I scare can think it, but am told)
There are to whom my satire seems too bold,
Scarce to wise Peter complaisant enough,
And something said of Chartres much too rough.
The lines are weak, another's pleas'd to say,
Lord Fanny spins a thousand such a day.
Tim'rous by nature, of the rich in awe,
I come to council learned in the law.
You'll give me, like a friend both sage and free,
Advice; and (as you use) without a fee.
F. I'd write no more.
                        P. Not write? but then I think,
And for my soul I cannot sleep a wink.
I nod in company, I wake at night,
Fools rush into my head, and so I write.
    F. You could not do a worse thing for your life.
Why, if the nights seem tedious – take a wife;
Or rather truly, if your point be rest,
Lettuce and cowslip wine; *Probatum est.*
But talk with Celsus, Celsus will advise
Hartshorn, or something that shall close your eyes.
Or if you needs must write, write Caesar's praise:
You'll gain at least a knighthood, or the bays.
    P. What? like Sir Richard, rumbling, rough and
        fierce,
With arms, and George, and Brunswick crowd the
        verse?
Rend with tremendous sound your ears asunder,
With gun, drum, trumpet, blunderbuss & thunder?
Or nobly wild, with Budgell's fire and force,
Paint angels trembling round his falling horse?
    F. Then all your Muse's softer art display,

Let Carolina smooth the tuneful lay,
Lull with Amelia's liquid name the Nine,
And sweetly flow through all the royal line.

P. Alas! few verses touch their nicer ear;
They scarce can bear their laureate twice a year:
And justly Caesar scorns the poet's lays,
It is to history he trusts for praise.

F. Better be Cibber, I'll maintain it still,
Than ridicule all taste, blaspheme quadrille,
Abuse the city's best good men in metre,
And laught at peers that put their trust in Peter.
Ev'n those you touch not, hate you.
       P. What should ail
  'em?

F. A hundred smart in Timon and in Balaam:
The fewer still you name, you wound the more;
Bond is but one, but Harpax is a score.

P. Each mortal has his pleasure: none deny
Scarsdale his bottle, Darty his ham-pie;
Ridotta sips and dances, till she see
The doubling lustres dance as fast as she;
F– loves the senate, Hockley-Hole his brother
Like in all else, as one egg to another.
I love to pour out all myself, as plain
As downright Shippen, or as old Montaigne.
In them, as certain to be lov'd as seen,
The soul stood forth, nor kept a thought within;
In me what spots (for spots I have) appear,
Will prove at least the medium must be clear.
In this impartial glass, my Muse intends
Fair to expose myself, my foes, my friends;
Publish the present age, but where my text
Is vice too high, reserve it for the next:
My foes shall wish my life a longer date,
And ev'ry friend the less lament my fate.

My head and heart thus flowing thro' my quill,
Verse-man or prose-man, term me which you will,
Papist or Protestant, or both between,
Like good Erasmus in an honest mean,
In moderation placing all my glory,
While Tories call me Whig, and Whigs a Tory.

Satire's my weapon, but I'm too discreet
To run a muck, and tilt at all I meet;
I only wear it in a land of Hectors,
Thieves, supercargoes, sharpers, and directors.
Save but our army! and let Jove encrust
Swords, pikes, and guns, with everlasting rust!
Peace is my dear delight – not Fleury's more:
But touch me, and no minister so sore.
Who-e'er offends, at some unlucky time
Slides into verse, and hitches in a rhyme,

Sacred to ridicule! his whole life long,
And the sad burthen of some merry song.

EPILOGUE TO THE SATIRES

‹Dialogue II›

(lines 205–55)

      P. So proud, I am no slave:
So impudent, I own myself no knave:
So odd, my country's ruin makes me grave.
Yes, I am proud; I must be proud to see
Men not afraid of God, afraid of me:
Safe from the bar, the pulpit, and the throne,
Yet touch'd and sham'd by ridicule alone.

O sacred weapon! left for truth's defence,
Sole dread of folly, vice, and insolence!
To all but Heav'n-directed hands denied,
The Muse may give thee, but the gods must guide.
Rev'rent I touch thee! but with honest zeal;
To rouse the watchmen of the publick weal,
To virtue's work provoke the tardy Hall,
And goad the prelate slumb'ring in his stall.

Ye tinsel insects! whom a court maintains,
That counts your beauties only by your stains,
Spin all your cobwebs o'er the eye of day!
The Muse's wing shall brush you all away:
All his Grace preaches, all his Lordship sings,
All that makes saints of queens, and gods of kings,
All, all but truth, drops dead-born from the press,
Like the last gazette, or the last address.

When black ambition stains a public cause,
A monarch's sword when mad vain-glory draws,
Not Waller's wreath can hide the nation's scar,
Nor Boileau turn the feather to a star.

Not so, when diadem'd, with rays divine,
Touch'd with the flame that breaks from virtue's
    shrine,
Her priestess muse forbids the good to die,
And ope's the Temple of Eternity;
There other trophies deck the truly brave,
Than such as Anstis casts into the grave;
Far other stars than * and ** wear,
And may descend to Mordington from Stair:
Such as on Hough's unsully'd mitre shine,
Or beam, good Digby! from a heart like thine.
Let envy howl while Heav'n's whole chorus sings,
And bark at honour not confer'd by kings;
Let flatt'ry sickening see the incense rise,

Sweet to the world, and grateful to the skies:
Truth guards the poet, sanctifies the line,
And makes immortal, verse as mean as mine.

   Yes, the last pen for freedom let me draw,
When truth stands trembling on the edge of law:
Here, last of Britons! let your names be read;
Are none, none living ? Let me praise the dead,
And for that cause which made your fathers shine,
Fall, by the Votes of their degen'rate line!

   Fr. Alas! alas! pray end what you began,
And write next winter more *Essays on Man*.

❧

The Dunciad

‹ Book IV ›

(lines 1–80)

Yet, yet a moment, one dim ray of light
Indulge, dread chaos, and eternal night!
Of darkness visible so much be lent,
As half to shew, half veil the deep intent.
Ye pow'rs! whose mysteries restor'd I sing,
To whom time bears me on his rapid wing,
Suspend a while your force inertly strong,
Then take at once the poet and the song.
   Now flam'd the Dog-star's unpropitious ray,
Smote ev'ry brain, and wither'd ev'ry bay;
Sick was the sun, the owl forsook his bow'r,
The moon-struck prophet felt the madding hour
Then rose the seed of chaos, and of night,
To blot out order, and extinguish light,
Of dull and venal a new world to mold,
And bring Saturnian days of lead and gold.
   She mounts the throne: her head a cloud
      conceal'd,
In broad effulgence all below reveal'd,
('Tis thus aspiring Dulness ever shines)
Soft on her lap her laureat son reclines.
   Beneath her foot-stool, Science groans in chains,
And Wit dreads exile, penalties and pains.
There foam'd rebellious Logic, gagg'd and bound,
There, stript, fair Rhet'ric languish'd on the ground;
His blunted arms by Sophistry are born,
And shameless Billingsgate her robes adorn.
Morality, by her false guardians drawn,
Chicane in furs, and Casuistry in lawn,
Gasps, as they straiten at each end the cord,
And dies, when Dulness gives her page the word.
Mad Mathesis alone was unconfin'd,

Too mad for mere material chains to bind,
Now to pure space lifts her extatic stare,
Now running round the circle, finds it square.
But held in ten-fold bonds the Muses lie,
Watch'd both by Envy's and by Flatt'ry's eye:
There to her heart sad Tragedy addrest
The dagger wont to pierce the tyrant's breast;
But sober History restrain'd her rage,
And promis'd vengeance on a barb'rous age.
There sunk Thalia, nerveless, cold, and dead,
Had not her sister satyr held her head:
Nor cou'd'st thou, Chesterfield! a tear refuse,
Thou wept'st, and with thee wept each gentle Muse.
   When lo! a harlot form soft sliding by,
With mincing step, small voice, and languid eye;
Foreign her air, her robe's discordant pride
In patch-work flutt'ring, and her head aside.
By singing peers up-held on either hand,
She tripp'd and laugh'd, too pretty much to stand;
Cast on the prostrate Nine a scornful look,
Then thus in quaint recitativo spoke.
   'O Cara! Cara! silence all that train:
Joy to great chaos! let division reign:
Chromatic tortures soon shall drive them hence,
Break all their nerves, and fritter all their sense:
One trill shall harmonize joy, grief, and rage,
Wake the dull church, and lull the ranting stage;
To the same notes thy sons shall hum, or snore,
And all thy yawning daughters cry, encore.
Another Phœbus, thy own Phœbus, reigns,
Joys in my jiggs, and dances in my chains.
But soon, ah soon rebellion will commence.
If music meanly borrows aid from sense:
Strong in new arms, lo! giant Handel stands,
Like bold Briareus, with a hundred hands;
To stir, to rouze, to shake the soul he comes,
And Jove's own thunders follow Mars's drums.
Arrest him, Empress; or you sleep no more' –
She heard, and drove him to th' Hibernian shore.
   And now had fame's posterior trumpet blown,
And all the nations summon'd to the throne.
The young, the old, who feel her inward sway,
One instinct seizes, and transports away.
None need a guide, by sure attraction led,
And strong impulsive gravity of head:
None want a place, for all their centre found,
Hung to the Goddess, and coher'd around.
Not closer, orb in orb, conglob'd are seen
The buzzing bees about their dusky queen.

Proud, ambitious, in high royal favour: little wonder that Walter Ralegh (1552–1618) had enemies. But pride in adversity – and Ralegh had plenty of that: imprisonment, the doomed expedition to South America, the death of his son, execution – has more appeal, and it is from the perspective of being cast down or out that the poems speak. For 'As you came from the holy land' he takes a ballad – known to, among others, Ophelia: see *Hamlet* IV. v – and transforms it with deftly varied rhythms into the setting for the jewel of his last stanza. The imperative, disillusioned 'The Lie' is a gauntlet thrown down in the face of a corrupt world by one who has only his integrity to lose. Both these poems are built upon conventional oppositions – seeming versus true love, worldly hypocrisy versus the soul's candour – and are achievements of artful simplicity, exquisite craft. 'The Ocean to Cynthia' is something entirely else. The passages printed here are from a manuscript of more than 500 lines that was not discovered until the 1860s, and which purports to be a fragment of a work many times its own size. It is private, obsessional, a teasing out of unresolved emotions; it veers towards and away from self-pity; it changes tack abruptly from present pain to the 'cordial sweetness' of memories, from praise of the lost beloved to despair at the vanity of writing itself; and it ends with no brave rhetorical flourish but in resignation. In contrast to the first two poems, it lacks both finish and shaping instinct, yet this contributes to its cumulative effect. It is a singular, troubling poem that questions our notions of what a good poem is.

AS YOU CAME FROM THE HOLY LAND

As you came from the holy land
   Of Walsinghame,
Met you not with my true love
   By the way as you came?

How shall I know your true love,
   That have met many one
As I went to the holy land,
   That have come, that have gone?

She is neither white nor brown,
   But as the heavens fair,
There is none hath a form so divine
   In the earth or the air.

Such an one did I meet, good sir,
   Such an angel-like face,
Who like a queen, like a nymph, did appear
   By her gait, by her grace.

She hath left me here all alone,
   All alone as unknown,
Who sometimes did me lead with herself,
   And me loved as her own.

What's the cause that she leaves you alone
   And a new way doth take,
Who loved you once as her own
   And her joy did you make?

I have loved her all my youth,
   But now old as you see;
Love likes not the falling fruit
   From the withered tree.

Know that Love is a careless child,
   And forgets promise past;
He is blind, he is deaf when he list
   And in faith never fast.

His desire is a cureless content
   And a trustless joy;
He is won with a world of despair
   And is lost with a toy.

Of womenkind such indeed is the love
   Or the word love abused,
Under which many childish desires
   And conceits are excused.

But true love is a durable fire
   In the mind ever burning,
Never sick, never old, never dead,
   From itself never turning.

THE LIE

Go, soul, the body's guest,
   Upon a thankless arrant;
Fear not to touch the best;
   The truth shall be thy warrant.
      Go, since I needs must die,
      And give the world the lie.

Say to the court, it glows
   And shines like rotten wood;
Say to the church, it shows
   What's good, and doth no good:
      If church and court reply,
      Then give them both the lie.

Tell potentates, they live
   Acting by others' action,
Not loved unless they give,
   Not strong but by affection.
      If potentates reply,
      Give potentates the lie.

Tell men of high condition
   That manage the estate,
Their purpose is ambition,
   Their practice only hate:
      And if they once reply,
      Then give them all the lie.

Tell them that brave it most,
   They beg for more by spending,
Who, in their greatest cost,
   Seek nothing but commending:
      And if they make reply,
      Then give them all the lie.

Tell zeal it wants devotion;
   Tell love it is but lust;
Tell time it metes but motion;
   Tell flesh it is but dust:
      And wish them not reply,
      For thou must give the lie.

Tell age it daily wasteth;
   Tell honour how it alters;
Tell beauty how she blasteth;
   Tell favour how it falters:
      And as they shall reply,
      Give every one the lie.

Tell wit how much it wrangles
   In tickle points of niceness;
Tell wisdom she entangles
   Herself in over-wiseness:
      And when they do reply,
      Straight give them both the lie.

Tell physic of her boldness;
   Tell skill it is prevention;
Tell charity of coldness;
   Tell law it is contention:
      And as they do reply,
      So give them still the lie.

Tell fortune of her blindness;
   Tell nature of decay;
Tell friendship of unkindness;
   Tell justice of delay:
      And if they will reply,
      Then give them all the lie.

Tell arts they have no soundness,
   But vary by esteeming;
Tell schools they want profoundness,
   And stand too much on seeming:
      If arts and schools reply,
      Give arts and schools the lie.

Tell faith it's fled the city;
   Tell how the country erreth;
Tell, manhood shakes off pity;
   Tell, virtue least preferreth:
      And if they do reply,
      Spare not to give the lie.

So when thou hast, as I
   Commanded thee, done blabbing,
Although to give the lie
   Deserves no less than stabbing,
      Stab at thee he that will,
      No stab thy soul can kill.

from THE OCEAN TO CYNTHIA

And as the icicles in a winter's day,
    Whenas the sun shines with unwonted warm,

So did my joys melt into secret tears,
    So did my heart dissolve in wasting drops;
And as the season of the year outwears,
    And heaps of snow from off the mountain tops

With sudden streams the valleys overflow,
    So did the time draw on my more despair;
Then floods of sorrow and whole seas of woe
    The banks of all my hope did overbear,

And drowned my mind in depths of misery.
    Sometime I died, sometime I was distract,
My soul the stage of fancy's tragedy;
    Then furious madness, where true reason lacked,

Wrote what it would, and scourged mine own
    conceit.
O heavy heart, who can thee witness bear?
What tongue, what pen, could thy tormenting treat,
    But thine own mourning thoughts which present
    were?

What stranger mind believe the meanest part?
    What altered sense conceive the weakest woe,
That tare, that rent, that pierced thy sad heart?
    And as a man distract, with treble might,

Bound in strong chains doth strive and rage in vain,
    Till, tired and breathless, he is forced to rest,
Finds by contention but increase of pain,
    And fiery heat inflamed in swollen breast;

So did my mind in change of passion
    From woe to wrath, from wrath return to woe,
Struggling in vain from love's subjection. [. . .]

A queen she was to me, no more Belphebe,
    A lion then, no more a milk-white dove;
A prisoner in her breast I could not be;
    She did untie the gentle chains of love.

Love was no more the love of hiding . . .

All trespass and mischance for her own glory.
    It had been such; it was still for the elect;

But I must be th'example in love's story;
    This was of all forepast the sad effect.

But thou, my weary soul and heavy thought,
    Made by her love a burden to my being,
Dost know my error never was forethought,
    Or ever could proceed from sense of loving.

Of other cause if then it had proceeding,
    I leave th'excuse, sith judgement hath been given;
The limbs divided, sundered, and a-bleeding,
    Cannot complain the sentence was uneven.

This did that nature's wonder, virtue's choice,
    The only paragon of time's begetting,
Divine in words, angelical in voice,
    That spring of joys, that flower of love's own
    setting,

The Idea remaining of those golden ages,
    That beauty, braving heaven's and earth
    embalming,
Which after worthless worlds but play on stages;
    Such didst thou her long since describe, yet
    sighing

That thy unable spirit could not find aught
    In heaven's beauties or in earth's delight,
For likeness fit to satisfy thy thought.
    But what hath it availed thee so to write?

She cares not for thy praise, who knows not theirs:
    It's now an idle labour, and a tale
Told out of time, that dulls the hearer's ears,
    A merchandise whereof there is no sale. [. . .]

She is gone, she is lost, she is found, she is ever fair.
    Sorrow draws weakly, where love draws not too;
Woe's cries sound nothing, but only in love's ear;
    Do then by dying what life cannot do. [. . .]

Ezra Pound finished the Rhymers – John Davidson (1857–1909), Ernest Dowson (1867–1900), Lionel Johnson (1867–1902), Arthur Symons (1865–1945) – for me with his deadly reference to 'the softness of the "nineties"'. Who would want to associate with softies? be touched by the palp of 'Only the rest! the rest! Only the gloom, / Soft and long gloom!'? As I fell in with Pound's bracing, purgative and aggressively masculine rhetoric, their satiric dismissal in 'Hugh Selwyn Mauberley' seemed entirely just.

It is still hard to read them other than through the lens of modernism. Pound complained of Johnson's 'curial speech' as against 'our aim' of 'the language as spoken'. Pound himself seems now in partial eclipse, but the contemporary demand for poetry to employ only 'language as spoken' gets ever bluffer. In the face of this I'm drawn back to the nineties poets for their refusal to steep their poetry in the ordinary, their sense that there is no shortage of common speech and conversational sensibility and that therefore the value of poetry is in the extraordinary cadence.

For them this was part of their hankering for a transcendent realm far above Davidson's moles on the Underground or the 'noise and glare' of Johnson's London. It is 'the image of our long desire' that draws them – 'desire', always a word to melt to. It is Platonist, mystical, and equally obviously sexual. It is fascinating to follow the sexual struggle of Johnson's 'Dark Angel' or Symons' striving to transmute the actuality of 'tumbled skirts upon a chair' into the 'ghost of memory' he evidently conceives of as a finer thing. That he thought so may have been a pose or the real matter of 'love's unrest', but it certainly drags his poem down towards mere convention. Ironically I find some of the most beautiful rhythms in these poems not where the poets are most eager for transcendence, but in the simplest of their earthly descriptions: Dowson's 'I watched the river grow more white and strange', or Johnson's 'Lean from the window to the air'. The world about them had more to offer than they allowed.

SPLEEN

◄ Ernest Dowson ►

I was not sorrowful, I could not weep,
And all my memories were put to sleep.

I watched the river grow more white and strange,
All day till evening I watched it change.

All day till evening I watched the rain
Beat wearily upon the window pane.

I was not sorrowful, but only tired
Of everything that ever I desired.

Her lips, her eyes, all day became to me
The shadow of a shadow utterly.

All day mine hunger for her heart became
Oblivion, until the evening came,

And left me sorrowful, inclined to weep,
With all my memories that could not sleep.

AD MANUS PUELLAE

◄ Ernest Dowson ►

for Leonard Smithers

I was always a lover of ladies' hands!
    Or ever mine heart came here to tryst,
For the sake of your carved white hands' commands;
    The tapering fingers, the dainty wrist;
    The hands of a girl were what I kissed.

I remember an hand like a *fleur-de-lys*
    When it slid from its silken sheath, her glove;
With its odours passing ambergris:
    And that was the empty husk of a love.
    Oh, how shall I kiss your hands enough?

They are pale with the pallor of ivories;
    But they blush to the tips like a curled sea-
        shell:
What treasure, in kingly treasuries,
    Of gold, and spice for the thurible,
    Is sweet as her hands to hoard and tell?

I know not the way from your finger-tips,
    Nor how I shall gain the higher lands,
The citadel of your sacred lips:
    I am captive still of my pleasant bands,
    The hands of a girl, and most your hands.

😈

PLATO IN LONDON

‹Lionel Johnson›

to Campbell Dodgson

The pure flame of one taper fall
Over the old and comely page:
No harsher light disturb at all
This converse with a treasured sage.
Seemly, and fair, and of the best,
    If Plato be our guest,
    Should things befall.

Without, a world of noise and cold:
Here, the soft burning of the fire.
And Plato walks, where the heavens unfold,
About the home of his desire.
From his own city of high things,
    He shows to us, and brings,
    Truth of fine gold.

The hours pass; and the fire burns low;
The clear flame dwindles into death:
Shut then the book with care; and so,
Take leave of Plato, with hushed breath
A little, by the falling gleams,
    Tarry the gracious dreams:
    And they too go.

Lean from the window to the air:
Hear London's voice upon the night!
Thou hast held converse with things rare:
Look now upon another sight!
The calm stars, in their living skies:
    And then, these surging cries,
    This restless glare!

That starry music, starry fire,
High above all our noise and glare:
The image of our long desire,
The beauty, and the strength, are there.
And Plato's thought lives, true and clear,

In as august a sphere:
Perchance, far higher.

😈

THE DARK ANGEL

‹Lionel Johnson›

Dark Angel, with thine aching lust
To rid the world of penitence:
Malicious Angel, who still dost
My soul such subtle violence!

Because of thee, no thought, no thing,
Abides for me undesecrate:
Dark Angel, ever on the wing,
Who never reaches me too late!

When music sounds, then changest thou
Its silvery to a sultry fire:
Nor will thine envious heart allow
Delight untutored by desire.

Through thee, the gracious Muses turn
To Furies, O mine Enemy!
And all the things of beauty burn
With flames of evil ecstasy.

Because of thee, the land of dreams
Becomes a gathering place of fears:
Until tormented slumber seems
One vehemence of useless tears.

When sunlight glows upon the flowers,
Or ripples down the dancing sea:
Thou, with thy troop of passionate powers,
Beleaguerest, bewilderest, me.

Within the breath of autumn woods,
Within the winter silences:
Thy venomous spirit stirs and broods,
O master of impieties!

The ardour of red flame is thine,
And thine the steely soul of ice:
Thou poisonest the fair design
Of nature, with unfair device.

Apples of ashes, golden bright;
Waters of bitterness, how sweet!

O banquet of a foul delight,
Prepared by thee, dark Paraclete!

Thou art the whisper in the gloom,
The hinting tone, the haunting laugh:
Thou art the adorner of my tomb,
The minstrel of mine epitaph.

I fight thee, in the Holy Name!
Yet, what thou dost, is what God saith:
Tempter! should I escape thy flame,
Thou wilt have helped my soul from Death:

The second Death, that never dies,
That cannot die, when time is dead:
Live Death, wherein the lost soul cries,
Eternally uncomforted.

Dark Angel, with thine aching lust!
Of two defeats, of two despairs:
Less dread, a change to drifting dust,
Than shine eternity of cares.

Do what thou wilt, thou shalt not so,
Dark Angel! triumph over me:
Lonely, unto the Lone, I go;
Divine, to the Divinity.

❦

A Northern Suburb

‹ John Davidson ›

Nature selects the longest way,
　And winds about in tortuous grooves;
A thousand years the oaks decay;
　The wrinkled glacier hardly moves.

But here the whetted fangs of change
　Daily devour the old demesne –
The busy farm, the quiet grange,
　The wayside inn, the village green.

In gaudy yellow brick and red,
　With rooting pipes, like creepers rank,
The shoddy terraces o'erspread
　Meadow and garth, and daisied bank.

With shelves for rooms the houses crowd,
　Like draughty cupboards in a row –

Ice-chests when wintry winds are loud,
　Ovens when summer breezes blow.

Roused by the fee'd policeman's knock,
　And sad that day should come again,
Under the stars the workmen flock
　In haste to reach the workmen's train.

For here dwell those who must fulfil
　Dull tasks in uncongenial spheres,
Who toil through dread of coming ill,
　And not with hope of happier years –

The lowly folk who scarcely dare
　Conceive themselves perhaps misplaced,
Whose prize for unremitting care
　Is only not to be disgraced.

❦

from Thirty Bob a Week

‹ John Davidson ›

For like a mole I journey in the dark,
　A-travelling along the underground
From my Pillar'd Halls and broad Suburbean Park,
　To come the daily dull official round;
And home again at night with my pipe all alight,
　A-scheming how to count ten bob a pound.

And it's often very cold and very wet,
　And my missis stitches towels for a hunks;
And the Pillar'd Halls is half of it to let –
　Three rooms about the size of travelling
　　trunks.
And we cough, my wife and I, to dislocate a sigh,
　When the noisy little kids are in their bunks.

But you never hear her do a growl or whine,
　For she's made of flint and roses, very odd;
And I've got to cut my meaning rather fine,
　Or I'd blubber, for I'm made of greens and
　　sod:
So p'r'aps we are in hell for all that I can tell,
　And lost and damn'd and served up hot to
　　God.

[…]

They say it daily up and down the land
　As easy as you take a drink, it's true;

But the difficultest go to understand,
    And the difficultest job a man can do,
Is to come it brave and meek with thirty bob a
      week,
    And feel that that's the proper thing for you.

It's a naked child against a hungry wolf;
    It's playing bowls upon a spluttering wreck;
It's walking on a string across a gulf
    With millstones fore-and-aft about your neck;
But the thing is daily done by many and many a
      one;
    And we fall, face forward, fighting, on the
      deck.

Stella Maris

‹Arthur Symons›

Why is it I remember yet
You, of all women one has met,
In random wayfare, as one meets
The chance romances of the streets,
The Juliet of a night? I know
Your heart holds many a Romeo.
And I, who call to mind your face
In so serene a pausing-place,
Where the pure bright expanse of sea,
The shadowy shore's austerity,
Seem a reproach to you and me,
I too have sought on many a breast
The ecstasy of love's unrest,
I too have had my dreams, and met
(Ah me!) how many a Juliet.
Why is it, then, that I recall
You, neither first nor last of all?
For, surely as I see to-night
The phantom of the lighthouse light,
Against the sky across the bay,
Fade, and return, and fade away,
So surely do I see your eyes
Out of the empty night arise;
Child, you arise and smile to me
Out of the night, out of the sea,
The Nereid of a moment there,
And is it sea-weed in your hair?
O lost and wrecked, how long ago,
Out of the drowning past, I know
You come to call me, come to claim

My share of your delicious shame.
Child, I remember, and can tell
One night we loved each other well,
And one night's love, at least or most
Is not so small a thing to boast.
You were adorable, and I
Adored you to infinity,
The nuptial night too briefly borne
To the oblivion of morn.
Ah! no oblivion, for I feel
Your lips deliriously steal
Along my neck, and fasten there;
I feel the perfume of your hair,
I feel your breast that heaves and dips
Desiring my desirous lips,
And that ineffable delight
When souls turn bodies, and unite
In the intolerable, the whole
Rapture of the embodied soul.
That joy was ours, we passed it by;
You have forgotten me, and I
Remember you thus, strangely won
An instant from oblivion.
And, I remembering, would declare
That joy, not shame is ours to share
Joy that we had the frank delight
To choose the chances of one night,
Out of vague nights, and days at strife,
So infinitely full of life.
What shall it profit me to know
Your heart holds many a Romeo?
Why should I grieve, though I forget
How many another Juliet?
Let us be glad to have forgot
That roses fade, and loves are not,
As dreams immortal, though they seem
Almost as real as a dream.
It is for this I see you rise,
A wraith, with starlight in your eyes,
Where calm hours weave, for such a mood
Solitude out of solitude;
For this, for this, you come to me
Out of the night, out of the sea.

WHITE HELIOTROPE

‹Arthur Symons›

The feverish room and that white bed,
The tumbled skirts upon a chair,
The novel flung half-open where
Hat, hair-pins, puffs, and paints, are spread;

The mirror that has sucked your face
Into its secret deep of deeps,
And there mysteriously keeps
Forgotten memories of grace;

And you, half dressed and half awake,
Your slant eyes strangely watching me,
And I, who watch you drowsily,
With eyes that, having slept not, ache;

This (need one dread? nay, dare one hope?)
Will rise, a ghost of memory, if
Ever again my handkerchief
Is scented with White Heliotrope.

POSTHUMOUS COQUETRY

‹Arthur Symons›

(from Théophile Gautier)

Let there be laid, when I am dead,
Ere 'neath the coffin lid I lie,
Upon my cheek a little red,
A little black about the eye.

For I in my close bier would fain,
As on the night his vows were made,
Rose-red eternally remain,
With kohl beneath my blue eye laid.

Wind me no shroud of linen down
My body to my feet, but fold
The white folds of my muslin gown
With thirteen flounces, as of old.

This shall go with me where I go:
I wore it when I won his heart;
His first look hallowed it, and so,
For him, I laid the gown apart.

No immortelles, no broidered grace
Of tears upon my cushion be;
Lay me on my own pillow's lace,
My hair across it, like the sea.

CITY NIGHTS

‹Arthur Symons›

In the Temple

The grey and misty night,
Slim trees that hold the night among
Their branches, and, along
The vague Embankment, light on light.

The sudden, racing lights!
I can just hear, distinct, aloof,
The gaily clattering hoof
Beating the rhythm of festive nights.

The gardens to the weeping moon
Sigh back the breath of tears.
O the refrain of years on years
'Neath the weeping moon!

IDEALISM

‹Arthur Symons›

I know the woman has no soul, I know
    The woman has no possibilities
    Of soul or mind or heart, but merely is
The masterpiece of flesh: well, be it so.
It is her flesh that I adore; I go
    Thirsting afresh to drain her empty kiss.
    I know she cannot love: it is not this
My vanquished heart implores in overthrow.
Tyrannously I crave, I crave alone,
    Her perfect body, Earth's most eloquent
    Music, divinest human harmony;
    Her body now a silent instrument,
        That 'neath my touch shall wake and make for
        me
The strains I have but dreamed of, never known.

Adored in his lifetime, banished for two hundred years, except for an occasional anthologised song, as simply too obscene to reprint in full, the poetry of John Wilmot, Earl of Rochester (1647–80) can at last be looked at afresh in all its brilliant, obsessive complexity. My aim in this brief selection has been to show as many sides of his work as possible which has meant leaving out the longer satires with their need for extensive annotation. I've therefore chosen 'The Imperfect Enjoyment' as my example of his longer poems not only because I think it one of his most accomplished but also because of its accessibility and true eroticism. Impotence in an age of sexual freedom with its concommitant diseases is a constant theme for Rochester and his contemporaries, including Aphra Behn who wrote a version of it from the woman's viewpoint.

'On His Prick' explores the same ground but in the rougher style which Rochester used for his sharpest satire. He rages against its failure to stand and his humiliation yet he can be tender, too, as in the verse 'To His More than Meritorious Wife' or 'Absent from Thee I Languish Still', an example of the songs that were part of his great appeal to women in his guise as the Arcadian poet-shepherd Strephon, in spite of the underlying misogyny of 'The Maidenhead' or 'A Song of a Young Lady: To Her Ancient Lover' or the rollicking 'Signior Dildo'.

Not surprisingly in the almost too clever son of a puritan mother, Rochester's lifestyle exacted an emotional as well as a physical toll. 'After Death' and the self castigatory 'To the Postboy' show him exploring nihilism, violent self-disgust and the fear of extinction which finally drove him from an adult profession of atheism to his death-bed conversion.

The Imperfect Enjoyment

Naked she lay, clasped in my longing arms,
I filled with love, and she all over charms,
Both equally inspired with eager fire,
Melting through kindness, flaming in desire:
With arms, legs, lips, close clinging to embrace,
She clips me to her breast, and sucks me to her face.
The nimble tongue (love's lesser lightning) played
Within my mouth, and to my thoughts conveyed
Swift orders, that I should prepare to throw
The all-dissolving thunderbolt below.
My fluttering soul, sprung with the pointed kiss,
Hangs hovering o'er her balmy brinks of bliss.
But whilst her busy hand would guide that part,
Which should convey my soul up to her heart,
In liquid raptures I dissolve all o'er,
Melt into sperm, and spend at every pore:
A touch from any part of her had done't,
Her hand, her foot, her very look's a cunt.
Smiling, she chides in a kind murmuring noise,
And from her body wipes the clammy joys:
When with a thousand kisses, wand'ring o'er
My panting bosom, and 'Is there then no more?'
She cries. 'All this to love and rapture's due;
Must we not pay a debt to pleasure too?'
But I, the most forlorn, lost man alive,
To show my wished obedience vainly strive.
I sigh, alas! and kiss, but cannot swive.
Eager desires confound my first intent,
Succeeding shame does more success prevent,
And rage, at last, confirms me impotent.
Even her fair hand, which might bid heat return
To frozen age, and make cold hermits burn,
Applied to my dead cinder, warms no more,
Than fire to ashes could past flames restore,
Trembling, confused, limber, dry,
A wishing, weak, unmoving lump I lie.
This dart of love, whose piercing point oft tried
With virgin blood, ten thousand maids has dyed:
Which Nature still directed with such art,
That it through every cunt reached every heart.
Stiffly resolved, 'twould carelessly invade
Woman or man, nor aught its fury stayed,
Where'er it pierced, a cunt it found, or made.
Now languid lies, in this unhappy hour,
Shrunk up, and sapless, like a withered flower.
Thou treacherous, base deserter of my flame,
False to my passion, fatal to my fame;
Through what mistaken magic does thou prove
So true to lewdness, so untrue to love?

What oyster, cinder, beggar, common whore,
Didst thou ere fail in all thy life before?
When vice, disease and scandal lead the way,
With what officious haste dost thou obey?
Like a rude roaring hector, in the streets,
That scuffles, cuffs, and ruffles all he meets;
But if his king and country claim his aid,
The rakehell villain shrinks, and hides his head:
Even so thy brutal valour is displayed;
Breaks every stew, does each small whore invade,
But when great Love the onset does command,
Base recreant to thy prince, thou darest not stand.
Worst part of me, and henceforth hated most
Through all the town: a common fucking-post,
On whom each whore relieves her tingling cunt,
As hogs on goats do rub themselves and grunt
May'st thou to ravenous cankers be a prey,
Or in consuming weepings waste away.
May strangury and stone thy days attend,
May'st thou ne'er piss, who did refuse to spend,
When all my joys did on false thee depend.
And may ten thousand abler pricks agree
To do the wronged Corinna right for thee.

ON HIS PRICK

Base mettle hanger by thy master's thigh,
Shame and disgrace to all prick heraldry,
Hide thy despised head and do not dare
To peep, no not so much as take the air
But through a buttonhole, but pine and die,
Confined within thy codpiece monastery.
The little childish boy that scarcely knows
The channel through which his water flows,
Touched by mistress's most magnetic hand
His little needle presently will stand,
And turn to her: but thou, in spite of that,
As oft cocks flopping like an old wife's hat.
Did she not take you in her ivory hand?
Doubtless stroked thee, yet thou would not stand?
Did she not raise thy drooping head on high
As it lay nodding on her wanton thigh?
Did she not clasp her legs about thy back,
Her porthole open? Prick, what didst thou lack?
Henceforth stand stiff, regain thy credit lost,
Or I'll ne'er draw thee but against a post.

TO HIS MORE THAN MERITORIOUS WIFE

I am by Fate slave to your will,
And I will be obedient still,
To show my love I will compose ye,
For your fair finger's ring a poesie,
In which shall be expressed my duty,
And how I'll be forever true t'ye,
With low-made legs and sugared speeches,
Yielding to your fair bum the breeches,
And show myself in all I can
Your very humble servant,

John.

THE MAIDENHEAD

Have you not in a chimney seen
A sullen faggot wet and green,
How coyly it received the heat,
And at both ends does fume and sweat?

So goes it with the harmless maid
When first upon her back she's laid:
But the well-experienced dame,
Cracks and rejoices in the flame.

'ABSENT FROM THEE I LANGUISH STILL'

Absent from thee I languish still
    Then ask me not when I return?
The straying fool 'twill plainly kill,
    To wish all day, all night to mourn.

Dear, from shine arms then let me fly,
    That my fantastic mind may prove,
The torments it deserves to try,
    That tears my fixed heart from my love.

When wearied with a world of woe,
    To thy safe bosom I retire,
Where love and peace and truth does flow,
    May I contented there expire.

Lest once more wand'ring from that heaven
    I fall on some base heart unblessed:

Faithless to thee, false, unforgiven,
  And lose my everlasting rest.

❦

A Song of a Young Lady: To her Ancient Lover

Ancient Person, for whom I
All the flattering youth defy;
Long be it ere thou grow old,
Aching, shaking, crazy, cold.
But still continue as thou art,
  Ancient Person of my heart.

On thy withered lips, and dry,
Which like barren furrows lie;
Brooding kisses I will pour,
Shall thy youthful heat restore.
Such kind showers in autumn fall,
And a second spring recall:
Nor from thee will ever part,
  Ancient Person of my heart.

Thy nobler part, which but to name
In our sex would be counted shame,
By age's frozen grasp possessed,
From his ice shall be released;
And, soothed by my reviving hand,
In former warmth and vigour stand,
All a lover's wish can reach,
For thy joy my love shall teach:
And for thy pleasure shall improve,
All that art can add to love.
Yet still I love thee without art,
  Ancient Person of my heart.

❦

'My dear mistress has a heart'

My dear mistress has a heart,
  Soft as those kind looks she gave me,
When, with love's resistless art
  And her eyes, she did enslave me.
But her constancy's so weak,
  She's so wild and apt to wander,
That my jealous heart would break
  Should we live one day asunder.

Melting joys about her move,
  Killing pleasures, wounding blisses,
She can dress her eyes in love,
  And her lips can arm with kisses;
Angels listen when she speaks,
  She's my delight, all mankind's wonder;
But my jealous heart would break,
  Should we live one day asunder.

❦

Love and Life

All my past life is mine no more,
  The flying hours are gone,
Like transitory dreams given o'er,
Whose images are kept in store
  By memory alone.

What ever is to come is not,
  How can it then be mine?
The present moment's all my lot,
And that as fast as it is got,
  Phyllis, is wholly thine.

Then talk not of inconstancy,
  False hearts, and broken vows,
If I, by miracle, can be,
This live-long minute true to thee,
  'Tis all that heaven allows.

❦

Translation: from Seneca's Troades

After death nothing is, and nothing, death;
The utmost limit of a gasp of breath.
Let the ambitious zealot lay aside
His hopes of heaven, whose faith is but his pride;
  Let slavish souls lay by their fear,
  Nor be concerned which way nor where
  After this life they shall be hurled.
Dead we become the lumber of the world,
And to that mass of matter shall be swept
Where things destroyed with things unborn are
    kept.
  Devouring time swallows us whole;
  Impartial death confounds body and soul.
  For Hell and the foul fiend that rules

God's everlasting fiery jails
(Devised by rogues, dreaded by fools).
With his grim, grisly dog that keeps the door,
Are senseless stories, idle tales.
Dreams, whimseys, and no more.

~

TO THE POST-BOY

Son of a whore, God damn you, can you tell
A peerless peer the readiest way to Hell?
I've outswilled Bacchus, sworn of my own
   make
Oaths would fright Furies and make Pluto
   quake.
I've swived more whores more ways than
   Sodom's walls
E'er knew, or the College of Rome's Cardinals.
Witness heroic scars, look here, ne'er go,
Cerecloths and ulcers from the top to toe.
Frighted at my own mischiefs I have fled
And bravely left my life's defender dead.
Broke houses to break chastity, and dyed
That floor with murder which my lust denied.
Pox on it, why do I speak of these poor things?
I have blasphemed my God and libelled Kings;
The readiest way to hell, come quick –
BOY: Ne'er stir,
The readiest way, my lord, 's by Rochester.

I have long been drawn to the simple directness of Christina Rossetti's language, what C. H. Sisson calls 'the intimate fall of her rhythms'. She is available to any reader: subtle in form and those thoughts that take the shape of feelings, direct in emotional charge.

Christina Rossetti (1830–94) was a poet who started writing early, and her earliest poems have some of the merits of her best work; and she continued writing almost to the end. If her life is not full of biographical interest of the kind which fascinates modern readers, it was full of deep human commitments, friendships, courtships, fears and regrets. It was also fuelled by a faith which felt wonder, doubt and moments of intense penetration of mystery, of a kind not common among her contemporaries. The religion of the later poems has not the flashes of the earlier. It feels a little doctrinaire, catcheistic or catechised. But all through the large body of poems which are rather narrow in their range, there are moments of complete mastery. A great critic and writer who knew her and who lived well into this century spoke of her as 'the most valuable poet that the Victorian age produced', a forerunner of much of the poetry of this century. This overstates her merits, but perhaps the overstatement will continue to draw attention to this quiet woman whose very quietness is a source of strength. She is the Gwen John to Dante Gabriel's Augustus, the one we turn to when the artful and the artificial weary us and the true voice of feeling is what we seek.

CHRISTINA ROSSETTI

MARY MAGDALENE

She came in deep repentance,
   And knelt down at His feet
Who can change the sorrow into joy.
   The bitter into sweet.

She had cast away her jewels
   And her rich attire,
And her breast was filled with a holy shame,
   And her heart with a holy fire.

Her tears were more precious
   Than her precious pearls –
Her tears that fell upon His feet
   As she wiped them with her curls.

Her youth and her beauty
   Were budding to their prime;
But she wept for the great transgression,
   The sin of other time.

Trembling betwixt hope and fear,
   She sought the King of Heaven,
Forsook the evil of her ways,
   Loved much, and was forgiven.

SONG

When I am dead, my dearest,
   Sing no sad songs for me:
Plant thou no roses at my head,
   Nor shady cypress tree:
Be the green grass above me
   With showers and dewdrops wet:
And if thou wilt, remember,
   And if thou wilt, forget.

I shall not see the shadows,
   I shall not fear the rain;
I shall not hear the nightingale
   Sing on as if in pain:
And dreaming through the twilight
   That doth not rise nor set,
Haply I may remember,
   And haply may forget.

ONE CERTAINTY

Vanity of vanities, the Preacher saith,
   All things are vanity. The eye and ear
   Cannot be filled with what they see and hear.
Like early dew or like the sudden breath
Of wind, or like the grass that withereth,
   Is man, tossed to and fro by hope and fear:
   So little joy hath he, so little cheer,
Till all things end in the long dust of death.
To-day is still the same as yesterday,
   To-morrow also even as one of them;
     And there is nothing new under the sun:
     Until the ancient race of Time be run.
   The old thorns shall grow out of the old stem,
And morning shall be cold and twilight grey.

SONG

Oh roses for the flush of youth,
   And laurel for the perfect prime;
But pluck an ivy branch for me
   Grown old before my time.

Oh violets for the grave of youth,
   And bay for those dead in their prime;
Give me the withered leaves I chose
   Before in the old time.

REMEMBER

Remember me when I am gone away,
   Gone far away into the silent land;
   When you can no more hold me by the hand,
Nor I half turn to go yet turning stay.
Remember me when no more day by day
   You tell me of our future that you plann'd:
Only remember me; you understand
It will be late to counsel then or pray.
Yet if you should forget me for a while
   And afterwards remember, do not grieve:
   For if the darkness and corruption leave
   A vestige of the thoughts that once I had,

Better by far you should forget and smile
    Than that you should remember and be sad.

❧

ENDURANCE

Yes, I too could face death and never shrink.
    But it is harder to bear hated life;
    To strive with hands and knees weary of strife;
To drag the heavy chain whose every link
    Galls to the bone; to stand upon the brink
    Of the deep grave, nor drowse tho' it be rife
    With sleep; to hold with steady hand the knife
Nor strike home: – this is courage, as I think.
Surely to suffer is more than to do.
    To do is quickly done: to suffer is
        Longer and fuller of heart-sicknesses.
    Each day's experience testifies of this.
Good deeds are many, but good lives are few:
        Thousands taste the full cup; who drains the
          lees?

❧

A WISH

I wish I were a little bird
    That out of sight doth soar;
I wish I were a song once heard
    But often pondered o'er,
Or shadow of a lily stirred
    By wind upon the floor,
Or echo of a loving word
    Worth all that went before,
Or memory of a hope deferred
    That springs again no more.

❧

A CHILLY NIGHT

I rose at the dead of night.
    And went to the lattice alone
To look for my Mother's ghost
    Where the ghostly moonlight shone.

My friends had failed one by one,
    Middle-aged, young, and old.
Till the ghosts were warmer to me
    Than my friends that had grown cold.

I looked and I saw the ghosts
    Dotting plain and mound:
They stood in the blank moonlight,
    But no shadow lay on the ground:
They spoke without a voice
    And they leaped without a sound.

I called: 'O my Mother dear,' –
    I sobbed: 'O my Mother kind,
Make a lonely bed for me
    And shelter it from the wind.

'Tell the others not to come
    To see me night or day:
But I need not tell my friends
    To be sure to keep away.'

My Mother raised her eyes,
    They were blank and could not see:
Yet they held me with their stare
    While they seemed to look at me.

She opened her mouth and spoke;
    I could not hear a word,
While my flesh crept on my bones
    And every hair was stirred.

She knew that I could not hear
    The message that she told
Whether I had long to wait
    Or soon should sleep in the mould:
I saw her toss her shadowless hair
    And wring her hands in the cold.

I strained to catch her words,
    And she strained to make me hear;
But never a sound of words
    Fell on my straining ear.

From midnight to the cockcrow
    I kept my watch in pain
While the subtle ghosts grew subtler
    In the sad night on the wane.

From midnight to the cockcrow
    I watched till all were gone,

Some to sleep in the shifting sea
  And some under turf and stone:
Living had failed and dead had failed,
  And I was indeed alone.

A Better Resurrection

I have no wit, no words, no tears:
  My heart within me like a stone
Is numbed too much for hopes or fears.
  Look right, look left, I dwell alone;
I lift mine eyes, but dimmed with grief
  No everlasting hills I see;
My life is in the falling leaf:
  O Jesus, quicken me.

My life is like a faded leaf,
  My harvest dwindled to a husk:
Truly my life is void and brief
  And tedious in the barren dusk;
My life is like a frozen thing,
  No bud nor greenness can I see;
Yet rise it shall – the sap of Spring:
  O Jesus, rise in me.

My life is like a broken bowl,
  A broken bowl that cannot hold
One drop of water for my soul
  Or cordial in the searching cold:
Cast in the fire the perished thing;
  Melt and remould it, till it be
A royal cup for Him, my King:
  O Jesus, drink of me.

A Birthday

My heart is like a singing bird
  Whose nest is in a watered shoot:
My heart is like an apple-tree
  Whose boughs are bent with thickset fruit;
My heart is like a rainbow shell
  That paddles in a halcyon sea;
My heart is gladder than all these
  Because my love is come to me.

Raise me a dais of silk and down;
  Hang it with vair and purple dyes;
Carve it in doves and pomegranates,
  And peacocks with a hundred eyes;
Work it in gold and silver grapes,
  In leaves and silver fleurs-de-lys;
Because the birthday of my life
  Is come, my love is come to me.

At Home

When I was dead, my spirit turned
  To seek the much-frequented house.
I passed the door, and saw my friends
  Feasting beneath green orange-boughs;
From hand to hand they pushed the wine,
  They sucked the pulp of plum and peach;
They sang, they jested, and they laughed,
  For each was loved of each.

I listened to their honest chat.
  Said one: 'To-morrow we shall be
Plod plod along the featureless sands,
  And coasting miles and miles of sea.'
Said one: 'Before the turn of tide
  We will achieve the eyrie-seat.'
Said one: 'To-morrow shall be like
  To-day, but much more sweet.'

'To-morrow,' said they, strong with hope,
  And dwelt upon the pleasant way:
'To-morrow,' cried they one and all,
  While no one spoke of yesterday.
Their life stood full at blessed noon;
  I, only I, had passed away:
'To-morrow and to-day,' they cried;
  I was of yesterday.

I shivered comfortless, but cast
  No chill across the tablecloth;
I all-forgotten shivered, sad
  To stay and yet to part how loth:
I passed from the familiar room,
  I who from love had passed away,
Like the remembrance of a guest
  That tarrieth but a day.

MIRAGE

The hope I dreamed of was a dream,
    Was but a dream; and now I wake,
Exceeding comfortless, and worn, and old,
    For a dream's sake.

I hang my harp upon a tree,
    A weeping willow in a lake;
I hang my silenced harp there, wrung and snapt
    For a dream's sake.

Lie still, lie still, my breaking heart;
    My silent heart, lie still and break:
Life, and the world, and mine own self are changed
    For a dream's sake.

❧

SHALL I FORGET?

Shall I forget on this side of the grave?
I promise nothing: you must wait and see,
    Patient and brave.
(O my soul, watch with him, and he with me.)

Shall I forget in peace of Paradise?
I promise nothing: follow, friend, and see,
    Faithful and wise.
(O my soul, lead the way he walks with me.)

❧

ITALIA, IO TI SALUTO

To come back from the sweet South, to the North
    Where I was born, bred, look to die;
Come back to do my day's work in its day.
      Play out my play –
    Amen, amen, say I.

To see no more the country half my own,
    Nor hear the half familiar speech,
Amen, I say; I turn to that bleak North
     Whence I came forth –
    The South lies out of reach.

But when our swallows fly back to the South,
    To the sweet South, to the sweet South,

The tears may come again into my eyes
    On the old wise,
    And the sweet name to my mouth.

❧

A DIRGE

Why were you born when the snow was falling?
You should have come to the cuckoo's calling,
Or when grapes are green in the cluster,
Or at least when lithe swallows muster
    For their far off flying
    From summer dying.

Why did you die when the lambs were cropping?
You should have died at the apples' dropping.
When the grasshopper comes to trouble,
And the wheat-fields are sodden stubble,
    And all winds go sighing
    For sweet things dying.

❧

A CHRISTMAS CAROL

In the bleak mid-winter
    Frosty wind made moan,
Earth stood hard as iron,
    Water like a stone;
Snow had fallen, snow on snow,
    Snow on snow,
In the bleak mid-winter
    Long ago.

Our God, Heaven cannot hold Him
    Nor earth sustain;
Heaven and earth shall flee away
    When he comes to reign:
In the bleak mid-winter
    A stable-place sufficed
The Lord God Almighty
    Jesus Christ.

Enough for Him, whom cherubim
    Worship night and day,
A breastful of milk

And a mangerful of hay;
Enough for Him, whom angels
   Fall down before,
The ox and ass and camel
   Which adore.

Angels and archangels
   May have gathered there,
Cherubim and seraphim
   Thronged the air;
But only His mother
   In her maiden bliss
Worshipped the Beloved
   With a kiss.

What can I give Him,
   Poor as I am?
If I were a shepherd
   I would bring a lamb,
If I were a Wise Man
   I would do my part, –
Yet what I can I give Him,
   Give my heart.

'I WISH I COULD REMEMBER'

'Era già l'ora che volge il desio.' – Dante
'Ricorro al tempo ch' io vi vidi prima.' – Petrarca

I wish I could remember that first day,
   First hour, first moment of your meeting me,
   If bright or dim the season, it might be
Summer or Winter for aught I can say;
So unrecorded did it slip away,
   So blind was I to see and to foresee,
   So dull to mark the budding of my tree
That would not blossom yet for many a May.
If only I could recollect it, such
   A day of days! I let it come and go
   As traceless as a thaw of bygone snow;
It seemed to mean so little, meant so much;
If only now I could recall that touch,
   First touch of hand in hand – Did one but know!

The poems of Dante Gabriel Rossetti (1828–82) have fallen out of favour as his sister's reputation has grown: perhaps that sense of coterie – the Pre-Raphaelite Brotherhood, The Germ – surrounds him with an attenuated air of clique, a theatricality in which Elizabeth Siddall is for ever being exhumed, his own poems rescued from the corruptions of her grave, Burne-Jones fixes the spears and wings of his anorexic knights and angels and 'Topsy' Morris bounds and roars about his task of regenerating England aesthetically and politically. He is more than this. 'The Orchard-Pit', which may stand here for that medievalising, chivalric streak which runs through so much of the century's verse is a true haunting, the more so for its fragmentary nature. The enigmatic female figure there is a sister to David Jones' Queen of the Wood wedding the dead soldiers of the Western Front to the natural world in his In Parenthesis; 'The Woodspurge' and 'Sudden Light' in themselves bear out Robert Frost's remark that a poet is someone who in a lifetime of standing in thunderstorms gets struck by lightning once or twice, and 'A Superscription' from the huge, untidy sonnet sequence The House of Life has a wonderful opening and a wonderful last line.

The Victorians frequently cry out to us for rescue from their diction, but the sequence Rossetti wrote about his continental excursion, A Trip to Paris and Belgium, shows the formal, musical, archaic patterning giving way to something much more impressionistic, the constant movement of train and coach encouraging a more risky sense of vivid jotting down without too exact a finish. Finally, the sonnet 'Dawn on the Night-Journey', with that strangely apposite moth, reaches out, surely, in tone and diction, to Edward Thomas some forty years later.

Dante Gabriel Rossetti

The Orchard-Pit

Piled deep below the screening apple-branch
   They lie with bitter apples in their hands:
And some are only ancient bones that blanch,
And some had ships that last year's wind did
     launch,
   And some were yesterday the lords of lands.

In the soft dell, among the apple-trees,
   High up above the hidden pit she stands,
And there for ever sings, who gave to these,
That lie below, her magic hour of ease,
   And those her apples holden in their hands.

This in my dreams is shown me; and her hair
   Crosses my lips and draws my burning breath;
Her song spreads golden wings upon the air,
Life's eyes are gleaming from her forehead fair,
   And from her breasts the ravishing eyes of Death.

Men say to me that sleep hath many dreams,
   Yet I knew never but this dream alone:
There, from a dried-up channel, once the stream's,
The glen slopes up; even such in sleep it seems
   As to my waking sight the place well known.
    *   *   *   *   *
My love I call her, and she loves me well:
   But I love her as in the maelstrom's cup
The whirled stone loves the leaf inseparable
That clings to it round all the circling swell,
   And that the same last eddy swallows up.

The Woodspurge

The wind flapped loose, the wind was still,
Shaken out dead from tree and hill:
I had walked on at the wind's will, –
I sat now, for the wind was still.

Between my knees my forehead was, –
My lips, drawn in, said not Alas!
My hair was over in the grass,
My naked ears heard the day pass.

My eyes, wide open, had the run
Of some ten weeds to fix upon;

Among those few, out of the sun,
The woodspurge flowered, three cups in one.

From perfect grief there need not be
Wisdom or even memory:
One thing then learnt remains to me, –
The woodspurge has a cup of three.

Sudden Light

   I have been here before,
      But when or how I cannot tell:
   I know the grass beyond the door,
      The sweet keen smell,
The sighing sound, the lights around the shore.

   You have been mine before, –
      How long ago I may not know:
   But just when at that swallow's soar
      Your neck turned so,
Some veil did fall, – I knew it all of yore.

   Has this been thus before?
      And shall not thus time's eddying flight
   Still with our lives our love restore
      In death's despite,
And day and night yield one delight once more?

The House of Life

‹Sonnet XCVII: A Superscription›

Look in my face; my name is Might-have-been;
   I am also called No-more, Too-late, Farewell;
   Unto thine ear I hold the dead-sea shell
Cast up thy Life's foam-fretted feet between;
Unto thine eyes the glass where that is seen
   Which had Life's form and Love's, but by my spell
   Is now a shaken shadow intolerable,
Of ultimate things unuttered the frail screen.

Mark me, how still I am! But should there dart
   One moment through thy soul the soft surprise
   Of that winged Peace which lulls the breath of
     sighs, –

Then shalt thou see me smile, and turn apart
Thy visage to mine ambush at thy heart
   Sleepless with cold commemorative eyes.

❧

A Trip to Paris and Belgium

‹I: London to Folkestone›

A constant keeping-past of shaken trees,
And a bewildered glitter of loose road;
Banks of bright growth, with single blades atop
Against white sky: and wires – a constant chain –
That seem to draw the clouds along with them
(Things which one stoops against the light to see
Through the low window; shaking by at rest,
Or fierce like water as the swiftness grows);
And, seen through fences or a bridge far off,
Trees that in moving keep their intervals
Still one 'twixt bar and bar; and then at times
Long reaches of green level, where one cow,
Feeding among her fellows that feed on,
Lifts her slow neck, and gazes for the sound.

   Fields mown in ridges; and close garden-crops
Of the earth's increase; and a constant sky
Still with clear trees that let you see the wind;
And snatches of the engine-smoke, by fits
Tossed to the wind against the landscape, where
Rooks stooping heave their wings upon the day.

   Brick walls we pass between, passed so at once
That for the suddenness I cannot know
Or what, or where begun, or where at end.
Sometimes a station in grey quiet; whence,
With a short gathered champing of pent sound,
We are let out upon the air again.
Pauses of water soon, at intervals,
That has the sky in it; – the reflexes
O' the trees move towards the bank as we go by,
Leaving the water's surface plain. I now
Lie back and close my eyes a space; for they
Smart from the open forwardness of thought
Fronting the wind.

     *   *   *   *   *

          I did not scribble more,
Be certain, after this; but yawned, and read,
And nearly dozed a little, I believe;
Till, stretching up against the carriage-back,

I was roused altogether, and looked out
To where the pale sea brooded murmuring.

❧

Dawn on the Night-Journey

Till dawn the wind drove round me. It is past
   And still, and leaves the air to lisp of bird,
   And to the quiet that is almost heard
Of the new-risen day, as yet bound fast
In the first warmth of sunrise. When the last
   Of the sun's hours to-day shall be fulfilled,
   There shall another breath of time be stilled
For me, which now is to my senses cast
As much beyond me as eternity,
   Unknown, kept secret. On the newborn air
The moth quivers in silence. It is vast,
Yea, even beyond the hills upon the sea,
   The day whose end shall give this hour as sheer
As chaos to the irrevocable Past.

In the nineteeth century, the poetical tales of Walter Scott (1771–1832) crammed with fair maidens, Scottish baronial heroics and blood-drenched battle, were best sellers – not despite the tetrameter couplets in which they canter along but because of them. Like the border ballads that inspired them, Scott's epics were predictably memorable; read aloud once or twice, they could be got 'by heart'. Scott himself possessed a formidable memory. When in 1802 he began to write The Lay of the Last Minstrel, he had heard Coleridge's 'Christabel' recited to him once; yet when Scott's Lay appeared in 1805, even its admirers noted that it owed its 'Pindaric' meters and even an entire line or two to Coleridge's unpublished fragment. Thirteen years later, Scott was still able to recite 'Christabel' from memory to Lord Byron.

Memorability, like narrative flow, is so little a property of poetry today that it is difficult for us to value Scott's ease of metrical utterance. Even in his own day, Coleridge found the jogging pace of The Lady of the Lake 'like a dog, mechanically lifting its leg six times to piss a canto.' Yet Scott was as responsible for the making of Romantic Scotland as Wordsworth was for the invention of the Lake District. The passages from Marmion and The Lady of the Lake I have selected are some that, despite their old-fashioned gait, show Scott as a poet whose accurate eye and love of his own countryside compare with John Clare's. As for Scott the minstrel, I have tried to represent him at his most natural. 'Young Lochinvar' is a fine recitation piece, but so well known that it hardly seems fair to reprint it yet again. And though 'The Eve of Saint John' is an almost perfect ballad, it is too long. So I have chosen some of Madge Wildfire's 'rude songs' from The Heart of Midlothian as being as close to genuine folk-balladry as Scott comes.

'November'

◄ Marmion: Introduction to Canto First ►
(lines 15–20; 23–6; 31–6)

No longer Autumn's glowing red
Upon our Forest hills is shed;
No more beneath the evening beam,
Fair Tweed reflects their purple gleam;
Away has pass'd the heather-bell
That bloomed so rich on Needpath-fell [. . .]

The sheep, before the pinching heaven,
To shelter'd dale and down are driven,
Where yet some faded herbage pines
And yet a watery sunbeam shines [. . .]

The shepherd shifts his mantle's fold,
And wraps him closer from the cold;
His dogs no merry circles wheel,
But, shivering, follow at his heel;
A cowering glance they often cast,
As deeper moans the gathering blast.

'Saint Mary's Lake'

◄ Marmion: Introduction to Canto Second ►
(lines 148–68)

Thou know'st it well, – nor fen, nor sedge
Pollute the pure lake's crystal edge;
Abrupt and sheer, the mountains sink
At once upon the level brink;
And just a trace of silver sand
Marks where the water meets the land.
Far in the mirror, bright and blue,
Each hill's huge outline you may view;
Shaggy with heath, but lonely bare,
Nor tree, nor bush, nor brake is there,
Save where, of land, yon slender line
Bears thwart the lake the scatter'd pine.
Yet even this nakedness has power,
And aids the feeling of the hour;
Nor thicket, dell, nor copse you spy,
Where living thing conceal'd might lie;
Nor point, retiring, hides a dell
Where swain, or woodman lone, might dwell

There's nothing left to fancy's guess,
You see that all is loneliness[. . .]

❧

THE LADY OF THE LAKE

‹ Canto First ›

‹ XI ›

The western waves of ebbing day
Roll'd o'er the glen their level way;
Each purple peak, each flinty spire,
Was bathed in floods of living fire.
But not a setting beam could glow
Within the dark ravines below,
Where twined the path in shadow hid,
Round many a rocky pyramid,
Shooting abruptly from the dell
Its thunder-splinter'd pinnacle;
Round many an insulated mass,
The native bulwarks of the pass
Huge as the tower which builders vain
Presumptuous piled on Shinar's plain.
The rocky summits, split and rent,
Form'd turret, dome, or battlement,
Or seemed fantastically set
With cupula or minaret . . .
Nor were these earth-born castles bare,
Nor lack'd they many a banner fair;
For, from their shriver'd brows display'd
Far o'er the unfathomable glade,
All twinkling with the dewdrops sheen,
The briar-rose fell in streamers green,
And creeping shrubs, of thousand dyes,
Waved in the west-wind's summer sighs.

Boon nature scatter'd, free and wild,
Each plant or flower, the mountain's child.
Here eglantine embalm 'd the air,
Hawthorn and hazel mingled there;
The primrose pale and violet flower,
Found in each cliff a narrow bower;
Fox-glove and night-shade, side by side,
Emblems of punishment and pride,
Grouped their dark hues with every stain
The weather-beaten crags retain.
With boughs that quaked at every breath,
Grey birch and aspen wept beneath;
Aloft, the ash and warrior oak

Cast anchor in the rifted rock;
And higher yet, the pine-tree hung
His shatter'd trunk, and frequent flung,
Where seemed the cliff to meet on high,
His boughs athwart the narrow'd sky.
Highest of all, where white peaks glanced,
Where glist'ning streamers waved and danced,
The wanderer's eye could barely view
The summer heaven's delicious blue;
So wondrous wild, the whole might seem
The scenery of a fairy dream.

❧

MADGE WILDFIRE'S SONGS

‹ from *The Heart of Midlothian* ›

When the glede's in the blue cloud,
    The lavrock lies still;
When the hound's in the greenwood
    The hind keeps the hill.

❧

O sleep ye sound, Sir James, she said,
    When ye suld rise and ride!
There's twenty men wi' blow and blade,
    Are seeking where ye hide.

❧

What did ye wi' the bridal ring,
    bridal ring, bridal ring?
What did ye wi' your wedding ring,
    ye little cutty quean, O?
I gied it till a sodger, a sodger, a sodger,
I gied it till a sodger, an auld true love o' mine, O.

❧

In the bonnie cells of Bedlam,
    Ere I was ane and twenty,
I had hempen bracelets strong,
And merry whips, ding-dong,
    And prayer and fasting plenty.

My banes are buried in yon kirk-yard
    Sae far ayont the sea,

And it is but my blithesome ghaist
  That's speaking now to thee.

❧

Proud Masie is in the wood,
    Walking so early;
Sweet Robin sits on the bush,
    Singing so rarely.

'Tell me, thou bonny bird,
When shall I marry me?'
'When six braw gentlemen
Kirkward shall carry ye.'

'Who makes the bridal bed,
Birdie say truly?'
'The gray-headed sexton
That delves the grave duly.'

'The glow-worm o'er grave and stone
Shall light thee steady.
The owl from the steeple sing,
"Welcome, proud lady."'

Love is the theme of all the non-dramatic poetry of Shakespeare (1564–1616). It is as if he wanted to leave to posterity a great opencast mine of everything he had discovered, learned, or imagined about the riches of that subject. And rich it is: frustration, worship, betrayal, obsession, abasement, jealousy, tenderness, lust; aggressive males and passive females, aggressive females and passive males; whiffs of homosexuality and bisexuality; a range of behaviour from toying with curls to violent death; a range of exempla from the pure flame of the highest chastity to the burning of venereal disease. And as attitudes to love and sex alter from age to age, this body of poetry retains a far from transient ability to engage later generations, perhaps because it transforms or flouts many of the conventions it acknowledges and uses. Not always: the tedious iterations of *The Rape of Luorece* have now little interest. On the other hand, *A Lover's Complaint*, long neglected, comes at us with a curiously strong, awkward appeal. The *Sonnets* remain central, and continue new agendas of discussion, both in areas of historical linguistics and in the context of gay and feminist reconsideration. Whether autobiographical or semi-dramatic, they hold a fascination for the ordinary reader that transcends any impatience about the identities of the Young Man, the Rival Poet, or the Dark Lady, while recognizing the power of the passions that wash around these figures and their finally mysterious relations. Few people today would share Shakespeare's belief in the immortality of verse – 'So long as men can breathe or eyes can see, / So long lives this, and this gives life to thee' – but the *Sonnets* have so many moving things to say about time and change, about decay and ageing and the search for permanence, that we are almost persuaded by those moments of sublime self-confidence, and hope that he may be right.

VENUS AND ADONIS

(lines 769–822; 1111–64)

'Nay, then,' quoth Adon, 'you will fall again
Into your idle over-handled theme;
The kiss I gave you is bestowed in vain,
And all in vain you strive against the stream;
    For, by this black-faced night, desire's foul nurse,
    Your treatise makes me like you worse and worse.

'If love have lent you twenty thousand tongues,
And every tongue more moving than your own,
Bewitching like the wanton mermaid's songs,
Yet from mine ear the tempting tune is blown;
    For know, my heart stands arméd in mine ear,
    And will not let a false sound enter there,

'Lest the deceiving harmony should run
Into the quiet closure of my breast;
And then my little heart were quite undone,
In his bedchamber to be barred of rest.
    No, lady, no; my heart longs not to groan,
    But soundly sleeps, while now it sleeps alone.

'What have you urged that I cannot reprove?
The path is smooth that leadeth on to danger;
I hate not love, but your device in love
That lends embracements unto every stranger.
    You do it for increase: O strange excuse,
    When reason is the bawd to lust's abuse!

'Call it not love, for Love to heaven is fled
Since sweating Lust on earth usurped his name;
Under whose simple semblance he hath fed
Upon fresh beauty, blotting it with blame;
    Which the hot tyrant stains and soon bereaves,
    As caterpillars do the tender leaves.

'Love comforteth like sunshine after rain,
But Lust's effect is tempest after sun;
Love's gentle spring doth always fresh remain,
Lust's winter comes ere summer half be done;
    Love surfeits not, Lust like a glutton dies;
    Love is all truth, Lust full of forgéd lies.

'More I could tell, but more I dare not say;
The text is old, the orator too green.
Therefore, in sadness, now I will away;
My face is full of shame, my heart of teen:
    Mine ears that to your wanton talk attended
    Do burn themselves for having so offended.'

With this, he breaketh from the sweet embrace
Of those fair arms which bound him to her breast,
And homeward through the dark laund runs apace;
Leaves Love upon her back deeply distressed.
    Look how a bright star shooteth from the sky,
    So glides he in the night from Venus' eye;

Which after him she darts, as one on shore
Gazing upon a late-embarkéd friend,
Till the wild waves will have him seen no more,
Whose ridges with the meeting clouds contend;
    So did the merciless and pitchy night
    Fold in the object that did feed her sight.

[. . .]

'Tis true, 'tis true; thus was Adonis slain:
He ran upon the boar with his sharp spear,
Who did not whet his teeth at him again,
But by a kiss thought to persuade him there;
    And nuzzling in his flank, the loving swine
    Sheathed unaware the tusk in his soft groin.

'Had I been toothed like him, I must confess,
With kissing him I should have killed him first;
But he is dead, and never did he bless
My youth with his; the more am I accurst.'
    With this, she falleth in the place she stood,
    And stains her face with his congealéd blood.

She looks upon his lips, and they are pale;
She takes him by the hand, and that is cold;
She whispers in his ears a heavy tale,
As if they heard the woeful words she told;
    She lifts the coffer-lids that close his eyes,
    Where, lo, two lamps, burnt out, in darkness lies;

Two glasses, where herself herself beheld
A thousand times, and now no more, reflect;
Their virtue lost wherein they late excelled,
And every beauty robbed of his effect.
    'Wonder of time,' quoth she, 'this is my spite,
    That, thou being dead, the day should yet be
        light.

'Since thou art dead, lo, here I prophesy
Sorrow on love hereafter shall attend;
It shall be waited on with jealousy,
Find sweet beginning but unsavoury end;
    Ne'er settled equally, but high or low,
    That all love's pleasure shall not match his woe.

'It shall be fickle, false and full of fraud;
Bud, and be blasted, in a breathing while;
The bottom poison, and the top o'erstrawed
With sweets that shall the truest sight beguile;
 The strongest body shall it make most weak,
 Strike the wise dumb, and teach the fool to
  speak.

'It shall be sparing, and too full of riot,
Teaching decrepit age to tread the measures;
The staring ruffian shall it keep in quiet,
Pluck down the rich, enrich the poor with treasures;
 It shall be raging-mad, and silly-mild,
 Make the young old, the old become a child.

'It shall suspect where is no cause of fear;
It shall not fear where it should most mistrust;
It shall be merciful and too severe,
And most deceiving when it seems most just;
 Perverse it shall be where it shows most toward,
 Put fear to valour, courage to the coward.

'It shall be cause of war and dire events,
And set dissension 'twixt the son and sire;
Subject and servile to all discontents,
As dry combustious matter is to fire.
 Sith in his prime death doth my love destroy,
 They that love best their loves shall not enjoy.'

❧

A Lover's Complaint

(lines 253–329)

'"How mighty then you are, O hear me tell!
The broken bosoms that to me belong
Have emptied all their fountains in my well,
And mine I pour your ocean all among.
I strong o'er them, and you o'er me being strong,
Must for your victory us all congest,
As compound love to physic your cold breast.

'"My parts had power to charm a sacred nun,
Who, disciplin'd, ay, dieted in grace,
Believ'd her eyes when they t'assail begun,
All vows and consecrations giving place.
O most potential love: vow, bond, nor space
In thee hath neither sting, knot, nor confine,
For thou art all, and all things else are thine.

'"When thou impresses't, what are precepts worth
Of stale example? When thou wilt inflame,
How coldly those impediments stand forth
Of wealth, of filial fear, law, kindred, fame.
Love's arms are peace, 'gainst rule, 'gainst sense,
 'gainst shame;
And sweetens in the suff'ring pangs it bears
The aloes of all forces, shocks, and fears.

'"Now all these hearts that do on mine depend,
Feeling it break, with bleeding groans they pine,
And, supplicant, their sighs to you extend
To leave the batt'ry that you make 'gainst mine,
Lending soft audience to my sweet design,
And credent soul to that strong-bonded oath
That shall prefer and undertake my troth."

'This said, his wat'ry eyes he did dismount,
Whose sights till then were levell'd on my face.
Each cheek a river running from a fount
With brinish current downward flow'd apace.
O, how the channel to the stream gave grace,
Who glaz'd with crystal gate the glowing roses
That flame through water which their hue encloses.

'O father, what a hell of witchcraft lies
In the small orb of one particular tear!
But with the inundation of the eyes
What rocky heart to water will not wear?
What breast so cold that is not warmed here?
O cleft effect! Cold modesty, hot wrath,
Both fire from hence and chill extincture hath.

'For lo, his passion, but an art of craft,
Even there resolv'd my reason into tears.
There my white stole of chastity I daff'd,
Shook off my sober guards and civil fears;
Appear to him as he to me appears,
All melting, though our drops this diff'rence bore:
His poison'd me, and mine did him restore.

'In him a plenitude of subtle matter,
Applied to cautels, all strange forms receives,
Of burning blushes or of weeping water,
Or sounding paleness; and he takes and leaves,
In either's aptness, as it best deceives –
To blush at speeches rank, to weep at woes,
Or to turn white and sound at tragic shows;

'That not a heart which in his level came
Could 'scape the hail of his all-hurting aim,

Showing fair nature is both kind and tame,
And, veil'd in them, did win whom he would maim.
Against the thing he sought he would exclaim;
When he most burn'd in heart-wish'd luxury,
He preach'd pure maid and prais'd cold chastity.

'Thus merely with the garment of a grace
The naked and concealed fiend he cover'd,
That th'unexperient gave the tempter place,
Which like a cherubin above them hover'd.
Who, young and simple, would not be so lover'd?
Ay me, I fell, and yet do question make
What I should do again for such a sake.'

'O, that infected moisture of his eye,
O, that false fire which in his cheek so glow'd,
O, that forc'd thunder from his heart did fly,
O, that sad breath his spongy lungs bestow'd,
O, all that borrow'd motion, seeming ow'd,
Would yet again betray the fore-betray'd,
And new pervert a reconciled maid.'

SPRING

◄ from *Love's Labour's Lost* ►

When daisies pied and violets blue
And lady-smocks all silver-white
And cuckoo-buds of yellow hue
Do paint the meadows with delight,
The cuckoo then on every tree
Mocks married men, for thus sings he:
'Cuckoo;
Cuckoo, cuckoo' – O word of fear,
Unpleasing to a married ear!

When shepherds pipe on oaten straws
And merry larks are ploughmen's clocks,
When turtles tread, and rooks and daws,
And maidens bleach their summer smocks;
The cuckoo then on every tree
Mocks married men, for thus sings he:
'Cuckoo;
Cuckoo, cuckoo' – O word of fear,
Unpleasing to a married ear!

SONG

◄ from *As You Like It* ►

Blow, blow, thou winter wind,
Thou art not so unkind
    As man's ingratitude;
Thy tooth is not so keen,
Because thou art not seen,
    Although thy breath be rude.
Heigh-ho! sing heigh-ho! unto the green holly.
Most friendship is feigning, most loving mere folly.
    Then, heigh-ho, the holly!
        This life is most jolly.

Freeze, freeze, thou bitter sky,
That dost not bite so nigh
    As benefits forgot;
Though thou the waters warp,
Thy sting is not so sharp
    As friend rememb'red not,
Heigh-ho! sing, &c.

'O MISTRESS MINE'

◄ from *Twelfth Night* ►

O mistress mine, where are you roaming?
O, stay and hear; your true love's coming,
    That can sing both high and low.
    Trip no further, pretty sweeting;
    Journeys end in lovers meeting,
    Every wise man's son doth know.

What is love? 'Tis not hereafter;
Present mirth hath present laughter;
    What's to come is still unsure.
In delay there lies no plenty,
Then come kiss me, sweet and twenty;
    Youth's a stuff will not endure.

SONG

◄ from *Cymbeline* ►

Fear no more the heat o' th' sun
    Nor the furious winter's rages;
Thou thy worldly task hast done,

Home art gone, and ta'en thy
   wages.
Golden lads and girls all must,
As chimney-sweepers, come to dust.

Fear no more the frown o' th' great;
   Thou art past the tyrant's stroke.
Care no more to clothe and eat;
   To thee the reed is as the oak.
The sceptre, learning, physic, must
All follow this and come to dust.

Fear no more the lightning flash,
   Nor th' all-dreaded thunder-stone;
Fear not slander, censure rash;
   Thou hast finish'd joy and moan.
All lovers young, all lovers must
Consign to thee and come to dust.

No exorciser harm thee!
Nor no witchcraft charm thee!
Ghost unlaid forbear thee!
Nothing ill come near thee!
Quiet consummation have,
And renowned be thy grave!

❧

ARIEL'S SONG

‹from *The Tempest*›

Full fathom five thy father lies;
   Of his bones are coral made;
Those are pearls that were his eyes;
   Nothing of him that doth fade
But doth suffer a sea-change
Into something rich and strange.
Sea-nymphs hourly ring his knell:
       Burden. Ding-dong.
Hark! now I hear them – Ding-dong bell.

❧

THE SONNETS

‹17›
Who will believe my verse in time to come,
If it were fill'd with your most high deserts?
– Though yet, heaven knows, it is but as a tomb

Which hides your life, and shows not half your
   parts.
If I could write the beauty of your eyes
And in fresh numbers number all your graces,
The age to come would say 'This poet lies;
Such heavenly touches ne'er touch'd earthly faces.'
So should my papers, yellow'd with their age,
Be scorn'd, like old men of less truth than tongue,
And your true rights be term'd a poet's rage
And stretched metre of an antique song.
   But were some child of yours alive that time,
   You should live twice: in it, and in my rhyme.

‹18›
Shall I compare thee to a summer's day?
Thou art more lovely and more temperate.
Rough winds do shake the darling buds of May,
And summer's lease hath all too short a date;
Sometime too hot the eye of heaven shines,
And often is his gold complexion dimm'd,
And every fair from fair sometime declines,
By chance or nature's changing course untrimm'd;
But thy eternal summer shall not fade
Nor lose possession of that fair thou ow'st,
Nor shall death brag thou wander'st in his shade,
When in eternal lines to time thou grow'st.
   So long as men can breathe or eyes can see,
   So long lives this, and this gives life to thee.

‹20›
A woman's face with Nature's own hand painted
Hast thou, the master-mistress of my passion;
A woman's gentle heart, but not acquainted
With shifting change as is false women's fashion;
An eye more bright than theirs, less false in rolling,
Gilding the object whereupon it gazeth;
A man in hue, all hues in his controlling,
Which steals men's eyes and women's souls
   amazeth.
And for a woman wert thou first created,
Till Nature as she wrought thee fell a-doting,
And by addition me of thee defeated
By adding one thing to my purpose nothing.
   But since she prick'd thee out for women's
      pleasure,
   Mine be thy love, and thy love's use their
      treasure.

‹29›
When, in disgrace with Fortune and men's eyes,
I all alone beweep my outcast state,

And trouble deaf heaven with my bootless cries,
And look upon myself and curse my fate,
Wishing me like to one more rich in hope,
Featur'd like him, like him with friends possess'd,
Desiring this man's art and that man's scope,
With what I most enjoy contented least;
Yet in these thoughts myself almost despising,
Haply I think on thee, and then my state,
Like to the lark at break of day arising,
From sullen earth sings hymns at heaven's gate;
   For thy sweet love remember'd such wealth
   brings
   That then I scorn to change my state with kings.

◄ 30 ►

When to the sessions of sweet silent thought
I summon up remembrance of things past,
I sigh the lack of many a thing I sought,
And with old woes new wail my dear time's waste.
Then can I drown an eye, unus'd to flow,
For precious friends hid in death's dateless night,
And weep afresh love's long since cancell'd woe,
And moan th'expense of many a vanish'd sight.
Then can I grieve at grievances foregone,
And heavily from woe to woe tell o'er
The sad account of fore-bemoaned moan,
Which I new pay as if not paid before.
   But if the while I think on thee, dear friend,
   All losses are restor'd, and sorrows end.

◄ 41 ►

Those pretty wrongs that liberty commits,
When I am sometime absent from thy heart,
Thy beauty and thy years full well befits,
For still temptation follows where thou art.
Gentle thou art, and therefore to be won,
Beauteous thou art, therefore to be assail'd;
And when a woman woos, what woman's son
Will sourly leave her till she have prevail'd?
Ay me! but yet thou mightst my seat forbear,
And chide thy beauty and thy straying youth,
Who lead thee in their riot even there
Where thou art forc'd to break a two-fold troth:
   Hers, by thy beauty tempting her to thee,
   Thine, by thy beauty being false to me.

◄ 42 ►

That thou hast her, it is not all my grief,
And yet it may be said I lov'd her dearly;
That she hath thee is of my wailing chief,
A loss in love that touches me more nearly.

Loving offenders, thus I will excuse ye:
Thou dost love her because thou know'st I love her,
And for my sake even so doth she abuse me,
Suff'ring my friend for my sake to approve her.
If I lose thee, my loss is my love's gain,
And losing her, my friend hath found that loss:
Both find each other, and I lose both twain,
And both for my sake lay on me this cross.
   But here's the joy: my friend and I are one.
   Sweet flattery! Then she loves but me alone.

◄ 55 ►

Not marble nor the gilded monuments
Of princes shall outlive this powerful rhyme,
But you shall shine more bright in these contents
Than unswept stone besmear'd with sluttish time.
When wasteful war shall statues overturn
And broils root out the work of masonry,
Nor Mars his sword nor war's quick fire shall burn
The living record of your memory.
'Gainst death and all oblivious enmity
Shall you pace forth; your praise shall still find
   room
Even in the eyes of all posterity
That wear this world out to the ending doom.
   So, till the judgement that yourself arise,
   You live in this, and dwell in lovers' eyes.

◄ 66 ►

Tir'd with all these, for restful death I cry,
As, to behold desert a beggar born,
And needy nothing trimm'd in jollity,
And purest faith unhappily forsworn,
And gilded honour shamefully misplac'd,
And maiden virtue rudely strumpeted,
And right perfection wrongfully disgrac'd,
And strength by limping sway disabled,
And art made tongue-tied by authority,
And folly, doctor-like, controlling skill,
And simple truth miscall'd simplicity,
And captive good attending captain ill:
   Tir'd with all these, from these would I be gone,
   Save that to die I leave my love alone.

◄ 73 ►

That time of year thou mayst in me behold
When yellow leaves, or none, or few, do hang
Upon those boughs which shake against the cold,
Bare ruin'd choirs where late the sweet birds sang.
In me thou seest the twilight of such day
As after sunset fadeth in the west;

Which by and by black night doth take away,
Death's second self, that seals up all in rest.
In me thou seest the glowing of such fire
That on the ashes of his youth doth lie,
As the death-bed whereon it must expire,
Consum'd with that which it was nourish'd by.
   This thou perceiv'st, which makes thy love more
      strong,
   To love that well which thou must leave ere long.

◄ 86 ►

Was it the proud full sail of his great verse,
Bound for the prize of all-too-precious you
That did my ripe thoughts in my brain inhearse,
Making their tomb the womb wherein they grew?
Was it his spirit, by spirits taught to write
Above a mortal pitch, that struck me dead?
No, neither he nor his compeers by night
Giving him aid my verse astonished.
He nor that affable familiar ghost
Which nightly gulls him with intelligence,
As victors of my silence cannot boast;
I was not sick of any fear from thence.
   But when your countenance fill'd up his line,
   Then lack'd I matter; that enfeebled mine.

◄ 87 ►

Farewell, thou art too dear for my possessing,
And like enough thou know'st thy estimate.
The charter of thy worth gives thee releasing;
My bonds in thee are all determinate.
For how do I hold thee but by thy granting?
And for that riches where is my deserving?
The cause of this fair gift in me is wanting,
And so my patent back again is swerving.
Thyself thou gav'st, thy own worth then not
      knowing,
Or me to whom thou gav'st it else mistaking;
So thy great gift, upon misprision growing,
Comes home again, on better judgement making.
   Thus have I had thee as a dream doth flatter:
   In sleep a king, but waking no such matter.

◄ 90 ►

Then hate me when thou wilt; if ever, now;
Now, while the world is bent my deeds to cross,
Join with the spite of fortune, make me bow,
And do not drop in for an after-loss.
Ah, do not, when my heart hath scap'd this sorrow,
Come in the rearward of a conquer'd woe;
Give not a windy night a rainy morrow,

To linger out a purpos'd overthrow.
If thou wilt leave me, do not leave me last,
When other petty griefs have done their spite,
But in the onset come; so shall I taste
At first the very worst of fortune's might,
   And other strains of woe, which now seem woe,
   Compar'd with loss of thee will not seem so.

◄ 94 ►

They that have power to hurt, and will do none,
That do not do the thing they most do show,
Who, moving others, are themselves as stone,
Unmoved, cold, and to temptation slow –
They rightly do inherit heaven's graces,
And husband nature's riches from expense;
They are the lords and owners of their faces,
Others but stewards of their excellence.
The summer's flower is to the summer sweet,
Though to itself it only live and die,
But if that flower with base infection meet,
The basest weed outbraves his dignity;
   For sweetest things turn sourest by their deeds:
   Lilies that fester smell far worse than weeds.

◄ 97 ►

How like a winter hath my absence been
From thee, the pleasure of the fleeting year!
What freezings have I felt, what dark days seen,
What old December's bareness everywhere!
And yet this time remov'd was summer's time,
The teeming autumn big with rich increase,
Bearing the wanton burden of the prime
Like widow'd wombs after their lords' decease.
Yet this abundant issue seem'd to me
But hope of orphans and unfather'd fruit,
For summer and his pleasures wait on thee,
And thou away, the very birds are mute;
   Or if they sing, 'tis with so dull a cheer
   That leaves look pale, dreading the winter's near.

◄ 107 ►

Not mine own fears, nor the prophetic soul
Of the wide world dreaming on things to come,
Can yet the lease of my true love control,
Suppos'd as forfeit to a confin'd doom.
The mortal moon hath her eclipse endur'd,
And the sad augurs mock their own presage;
Incertainties now crown themselves assur'd,
And peace proclaims olives of endless age.
Now with the drops of this most balmy time
My love looks fresh, and Death to me subscribes,

Since spite of him I'll live in this poor rhyme
While he insults o'er dull and speechless tribes.
   And thou in this shalt find thy monument
   When tyrants' crests and tombs of brass are spent.

◄ 109 ►

O never say that I was false of heart,
Though absence seem'd my flame to qualify.
As easy might I from myself depart
As from my soul, which in thy breast doth lie;
That is my home of love. If I have rang'd,
Like him that travels, I return again,
Just to the time, not with the time exchang'd,
So that myself bring water for my stain.
Never believe, though in my nature reign'd
All frailties that besiege all kinds of blood,
That it could so preposterously be stain'd
To leave for nothing all thy sum of good;
   For nothing this wide universe I call,
   Save thou, my rose; in it thou art my all.

◄ 116 ►

Let me not to the marriage of true minds
Admit impediments. Love is not love
Which alters when it alteration finds,
Or bends with the remover to remove.
O no, it is an ever-fixed mark
That looks on tempests and is never shaken;
It is the star to every wand'ring bark,
Whose worth's unknown although his height be
   taken.
Love's not Time's fool, though rosy lips and cheeks
Within his bending sickle's compass come;
Love alters not with his brief hours and weeks,
But bears it out even to the edge of doom.
   If this be error and upon me prov'd,
   I never writ, nor no man ever lov'd.

◄ 121 ►

'Tis better to be vile than vile esteem'd,
When not to be receives reproach of being,
And the just pleasure lost, which is so deem'd
Not by our feeling but by others' seeing.
For why should others' false adulterate eyes
Give salutation to my sportive blood?
Or on my frailties why are frailer spies,
Which in their wills count bad what I think good?
No, I am that I am, and they that level
At my abuses reckon up their own;
I may be straight, though they themselves be bevel

By their rank thoughts my deeds must not be
   shown,
   Unless this general evil they maintain:
   All men are bad and in their badness reign.

◄ 127 ►

In the old age black was not counted fair,
Or if it were, it bore not beauty's name;
But now is black beauty's successive heir,
And beauty slander'd with a bastard shame:
For since each hand hath put on nature's power,
Fairing the foul with art's false borrow'd face,
Sweet beauty hath no name, no holy bower,
But is profan'd, if not lives in disgrace.
Therefore my mistress' eyes are raven-black,
Her brow so suited, and they mourners seem
At such who, not born fair, no beauty lack,
Sland'ring creation with a false esteem.
   Yet so they mourn, becoming of their woe,
   That every tongue says beauty should look so.

◄ 129 ►

Th'expense of spirit in a waste of shame
Is lust in action; and till action, lust
Is perjur'd, murd'rous, bloody, full of blame,
Savage, extreme, rude, cruel, not to trust,
Enjoy'd no sooner but despised straight,
Past reason hunted, and no sooner had
Past reason hated as a swallowed bait
On purpose laid to make the taker mad;
Mad in pursuit and in possession so,
Had, having, and in quest to have, extreme;
A bliss in proof and prov'd, a very woe;
Before, a joy propos'd; behind, a dream.
   All this the world well knows, yet none knows
   well
   To shun the heaven that leads men to this hell.

◄ 134 ►

So, now I have confess'd that he is thine,
And I myself am mortgag'd to thy will,
Myself I'll forfeit, so that other mine
Thou wilt restore to be my comfort still.
But thou wilt not, nor he will not be free,
For thou art covetous, and he is kind.
He learn'd but surety-like to write for me
Under that bond that him as fast doth bind.
The statute of thy beauty thou wilt take,
Thou usurer that put'st forth all to use,
And sue a friend came debtor for my sake;
So him I lose through my unkind abuse.

Him have I lost; thou hast both him and me;
He pays the whole, and yet am I not free.

◄ 138 ►

When my love swears that she is made of truth,
I do believe her, though I know she lies,
That she might think me some untutor'd youth
Unlearned in the world's false subtleties.
Thus vainly thinking that she thinks me young,
Although she knows my days are past the best,
Simply I credit her false-speaking tongue;
On both sides thus is simple truth suppress'd.
But wherefore says she not she is unjust?
And wherefore say not I that I am old?
O, love's best habit is in seeming trust,
And age in love loves not to have years told.
    Therefore I lie with her, and she with me,
    And in our faults by lies we flatter'd be.

◄ 144 ►

Two loves I have, of comfort and despair,
Which like two spirits do suggest me still.
The better angel is a man right fair,
The worser spirit a woman colour'd ill.
To win me soon to hell my female evil
Tempteth my better angel from my side,
And would corrupt my saint to be a devil,
Wooing his purity with her foul pride.
And whether that my angel be turn'd fiend
Suspect I may, yet not directly tell;
But being both from me, both to each friend,
I guess one angel in another's hell.
    Yet this shall I ne'er know, but live in doubt
    Till my bad angel fire my good one out.

◄ 147 ►

My love is as a fever, longing still
For that which longer nurseth the disease,
Feeding on that which doth preserve the ill,
Th'uncertain sickly appetite to please.
My reason, the physician to my love,
Angry that his prescriptions are not kept,
Hath left me, and I desperate now approve
Desire is death, which physic did except.
Past cure I am, now reason is past care,
And frantic mad with evermore unrest.
My thoughts and my discourse as madmen's are,
At random from the truth, vainly express'd;
    For I have sworn thee fair, and thought thee
        bright,
    Who art as black as hell, as dark as night.

◄ 152 ►

In loving thee thou know'st I am forsworn,
But thou art twice forsworn, to me love swearing:
In act thy bed-vow broke, and new faith torn
In vowing new hate after new love bearing.
But why of two oaths' breach do I accuse thee
When I break twenty? I am perjur'd most,
For all my vows are oaths but to misuse thee,
And all my honest faith in thee is lost.
For I have sworn deep oaths of thy deep kindness,
Oaths of thy love, thy truth, thy constancy;
And to enlighten thee gave eyes to blindness,
Or made them swear against the thing they see.
    For I have sworn thee fair – more perjur'd eye,
    To swear against the truth so foul a lie.

❧

THE PHOENIX AND THE TURTLE

Let the bird of loudest lay,
On the sole Arabian tree,
Herald sad and trumpet be,
To whose sound chaste wings obey.

But thou shrieking harbinger,
Foul precurrer of the fiend,
Augur of the fever's end,
To this troop come thou not near!

From this session interdict
Every fowl of tyrant wing,
Save the eagle, feath'red king:
Keep the obsequy so strict.

Let the priest in surplice white,
That defunctive music can,
Be the death-divining swan,
Lest the requiem lack his right.

And thou treble-dated crow,
That thy sable gender mak'st
With the breath thou giv'st and tak'st,
'Mongst our mourners shalt thou go.

Here the anthem doth commence:
Love and constancy is dead;
Phoenix and the turtle fled
In a mutual flame from hence.

So they loved, as love in twain
Had the essence but in one:
Two distincts, division none:
Number there in love was slain.

Hearts remote, yet not asunder;
Distance, and no space was seen
'Twixt this turtle and his queen:
But in them it were a wonder.

So between them love did shine,
That the turtle saw his right
Flaming in the phoenix'sight;
Either was the other's mine.

Property was thus appalléd,
That the self was not the same;
Single nature's double name
Neither two nor one was calléd

Reason, in itself confounded,
Saw division grow together,
To themselves yet either neither,
Simple were so well compounded;

That it cried, How true a twain
Seemeth this concordant one!
Love hath reason, reason none,
If what parts can so remain.

Whereupon it made this threne
To the phoenix and the dove,
Co-supremes and stars of love,
As chorus to their tragic scene.

‹ Threnos ›

Beauty, truth, and rarity,
Grace in all simplicity,
Here enclosed, in cinders lie.

Death is now the phoenix' nest;
And the turtle's loyal breast
To eternity doth rest.

Leaving no posterity,
'Twas not their infirmity,
It was married chastity.

Truth may seem, but cannot be;
Beauty brag, but 'tis not she;
Truth and beauty buried be.

To this urn let those repair
That are either true or fair;
For these dead birds sigh a prayer.

Shelley (1792–1822), born into a landed Sussex family and prospective heir to a great estate, was a rebel against all existing institutions and accepted social values. He believed that human life, and even Nature and the universe, could be transformed – and would be transformed – if mankind had faith in freedom, justice and love, and acted out their principles. All of Shelley's longer poems are intended to contribute to the desired revolution and transformation, and he attached no importance to his wonderful lyrical poetry because most of it had no such purpose. The 'Ode to the West Wind', however, presents him in his chosen function as a prophet of revolution.

In *Prometheus Unbound*, the defeated and tortured champion of mankind brings about the fall of the old order under the tyrant Jupiter (God) by his refusal to submit. Shelley has no dramatic gift and there is no sense of struggle; the poem is rather a lyrical celebration of the triumph of good over evil. In *The Mask of Anarchy*, the attempt to deal more directly with political events (the massacre of Peterloo, when troops fired on rioting workers) fails to convince, because Shelley is committed to non-violent resistance.

From his boyhood Shelley tried to act out the belief in Free Love which he expounds in *Epipsychidion*. He fell in love with Mary Godwin, daughter of the philosopher William Godwin (whose *Political Justice* provided a basis for Shelley's more extreme philosophy) and the feminist Mary Wollstonecraft. Shelley eloped with Mary, abandoning his wife Harriet; he was denied custody of his children and left for the Continent. In *Julian and Maddalo* we have a glimpse of life in the 'Paradise of exiles, Italy', with Byron-Maddalo rejecting Shelley-Julian's notions of human perfectability.

Adonais is Shelley's tribute to Keats, using Greek mythology and echoes of Greek pastoral elegies to build a vision of poets and their fate. he refers to Keats's grave in the Protestant cemetery in Rome, where his own ashes were to be buried a year later. The conclusion is strangely prophetic of the manner of his own death, drowned in a storm off the Ligurian coast, to be united to 'the soul of Adonais like a star'.

Shelley's verse has a unique speed; it gives the sensation of soaring, plunging, floating. He seems to me to have had the most extraordinary genius, even if it was not given time to mature. Auden used to make a point of declaring that he had never been able to enjoy, or perhaps even read, a single line of Shelley. To which the best answer is, 'so much the worse for you'.

OZYMANDIAS

I met a traveller from an antique land
Who said: Two vast and trunkless legs of stone
Stand in the desert . . . Near them, on the sand,
Half sunk, a shattered visage lies, whose frown,
And wrinkled lip, and sneer of cold command,
Tell that its sculptor well those passions read
Which yet survive, stamped on these lifeless things,
The hand that mocked them, and the heart that fed:
And on the pedestal these words appear:
'My name is Ozymandias, king of kings:
Look on my works, ye Mighty, and despair!'
Nothing beside remains. Round the decay
Of that colossal wreck, boundless and bare
The lone and level sands stretch far away.

ODE TO THE WEST WIND

◄ I ►
O wild West Wind, thou breath of Autumn's being.
Thou, from whose unseen presence the leaves dead
Are driven, like ghosts from an enchanter fleeing,

Yellow, and black, and pale, and hectic red,
Pestilence-stricken multitudes: O thou,
Who chariotest to their dark wintry bed

The wingèd seeds, where they lie cold and low,
Each like a corpse within its grave, until
Thine azure sister of the Spring shall blow

Her clarion o'er the dreaming earth, and fill
(Driving sweet buds like flocks to feed in air)
With living hues and odours plain and hill:

Wild Spirit, which art moving everywhere;
Destroyer and preserver; hear, oh, hear!

◄ II ►
Thou on whose stream, mid the steep sky's
    commotion,
Loose clouds like earth's decaying leaves are shed,
Shook from the tangled boughs of Heaven and Ocean,

Angels of rain and lightning: there are spread
On the blue surface of thine aëry surge,
Like the bright hair uplifted from the head

Of some fierce Maenad, even from the dim verge
Of the horizon to the zenith's height,
The locks of the approaching storm. Thou dirge

Of the dying year, to which this closing night
Will be the dome of a vast sepulchre,
Vaulted with all thy congregated might

Of vapours, from whose solid atmosphere
Black rain, and fire, and hail will burst: oh, hear!

◄ III ►

Thou who didst waken from his summer dreams
The blue Mediterranean, where he lay,
Lulled by the coil of his crystàlline streams,

Beside a pumice isle in Baiae's bay
And saw in sleep old palaces and towers
Quivering within the wave's intenser day,

All overgrown with azure moss and flowers
So sweet, the sense faints picturing them! Thou
For whose path the Atlantic's level powers

Cleave themselves into chasms, while far below
The sea-blooms and the oozy woods which wear
The sapless foliage of the ocean, know

Thy voice, and suddenly grow grey with fear,
And tremble and despoil themselves: oh, hear!

◄ IV ►

If I were a dead leaf thou mightest bear;
If I were a swift cloud to fly with thee;
A wave to pant beneath thy power, and share

The impulse of thy strength, only less free
Than thou, O uncontrollable! If even
I were as in my boyhood, and could be

The comrade of thy wanderings over Heaven,
As then, when to outstrip thy skiey speed
Scarce seemed a vision; I would ne'er have striven

As thus with thee in prayer in my sore need.
Oh, lift me as a wave, a leaf, a cloud!
I fall upon the thorns of life! I bleed!

A heavy weight of hours has chained and bowed
One too like thee: tameless, and swift, and proud.

◄ V ►

Make me thy lyre, even as the forest is:
What if my leaves are falling like its own!
The tumult of thy mighty harmonies

Will take from both a deep, autumnal tone,
Sweet though in sadness. Be thou, Spirit fierce,
My spirit! Be thou me, impetuous one!

Drive my dead thoughts over the universe
Like withered leaves to quicken a new birth!
And, by the incantation of this verse,

Scatter, as from an unextinguished hearth
Ashes and sparks, my words among mankind!
Be through my lips to unawakened earth

The trumpet of a prophecy! O, Wind,
If Winter comes, can Spring be far behind?

TO THE MOON

Art thou pale for weariness
Of climbing heaven and gazing on the earth,
Wandering companionless
Among the stars that have a different birth –
And ever changing, like a joyless eye
That finds no object worth its constancy?

TO NIGHT

◄ I ►

Swiftly walk o'er the western wave,
Spirit of Night!
Out of the misty eastern cave,
Where, all the long and lone daylight,
Thou wovest dreams of joy and fear,
Which make thee terrible and dear, –
Swift be thy flight!

◄ II ►

Wrap thy form in a mantle gray,
Star-inwrought!
Blind with thine hair the eyes of Day;
Kiss her until she be wearied out,

Then wander o'er city, and sea, and land,
Touching all with thine opiate wand –
    Come, long-sought!

◄ III ►

When I arose and saw the dawn,
    I sighed for thee;
When light rode high, and the dew was gone,
And noon lay heavy on flower and tree,
And the weary Day turned to his rest,
Lingering like an unloved guest,
    I sighed for thee.

◄ IV ►

Thy brother Death came, and cried,
    Wouldst thou me?
Thy sweet child Sleep, the filmy-eyed,
Murmured like a noontide bee,
Shall I nestle near thy side?
Wouldst thou me? – And I replied,
    No, not thee!

◄ V ►

Death will come when thou art dead,
    Soon, too soon –
Sleep will come when thou art fled;
Of neither would I ask the boon
I ask of thee, belovèd Night –
Swift be thine approaching flight,
    Come soon, soon!

❧

'MUSIC, WHEN SOFT VOICES DIE'

Music, when soft voices die,
Vibrates in the memory –
Odours, when sweet violets sicken,
Live within the sense they quicken.

Rose leaves, when the rose is dead,
Are heaped for the belovèd's bed;
And so thy thoughts, when thou art gone,
Love itself shall slumber on.

❧

'ONE WORD IS TOO OFTEN PROFANED'

◄ I ►

One word is too often profaned
    For me to profane it,
One feeling too falsely disdained
    For thee to disdain it;
One hope is too like despair
    For prudence to smother,
And pity from thee more dear
    Than that from another.

◄ II ►

I can give not what men call love,
    But wilt thou accept not
The worship the heart lifts above
    And the Heavens reject not, –
The desire of the moth for the star,
    Of the night for the morrow,
The devotion to something afar
    From the sphere of our sorrow?

❧

LOVE'S PHILOSOPHY

◄ I ►

The fountains mingle with the river
    And the rivers with the Ocean,
The winds of Heaven mix for ever
    With a sweet emotion;
Nothing in the world is single;
    All things by a law divine
In one spirit meet and mingle.
    Why not I with thine? –

◄ II ►

See the mountains kiss high Heaven
    And the waves clasp one another;
No sister-flower would be forgiven
    If it disdained its brother;
And the sunlight clasps the earth
    And the moonbeams kiss the sea:
What is all this sweet work worth
    If thou kiss not me?

❧

ADONAIS

(lines 352–495)

◄ XL ►

He has outsoared the shadow of our night;
Envy and calumny and hate and pain,
And that unrest which men miscall delight
Can touch him not and torture not again;
From the contagion of the world's slow stain
He is secure, and now can never mourn
A heart grown cold, a head grown grey in vain;
Nor, when the spirit's self has ceased to burn
With sparkless ashes load an unlamented urn.

◄ XLI ►

He lives, he wakes – 'tis Death is dead, not he;
Mourn not for Adonais. – Thou young Dawn,
Turn all thy dew to splendour, for from thee
The spirit thou lamentest is not gone;
Ye caverns and ye forests, cease to moan!
Cease, ye faint flowers and fountains, and thou Air,
Which like a mourning veil thy scarf hadst thrown
O'er the abandoned Earth, now leave it bare
Even to the joyous stars which smile on its despair!

◄ XLII ►

He is made one with Nature: there is heard
His voice in all her music, from the moan
Of thunder, to the song of night's sweet bird;
He is a presence to be felt and known
In darkness and in light, from herb and stone,
Spreading itself where'er that Power may move
Which has withdrawn his being to its own;
Which wields the world with never-wearied love,
Sustains it from beneath, and kindles it above.

◄ XLIII ►

He is a portion of the loveliness
Which once he made more lovely: he doth bear
His part, while the one Spirit's plastic stress
Sweeps through the dull dense world, compelling
    there,
All new successions to the forms they wear;
Torturing th' unwilling dross that checks its flight
To its own likeness, as each mass may bear;
And bursting in its beauty and its might
From trees and beasts and men into the Heaven's
    light.

◄ XLIV ►

The splendours of the firmament of time
May be eclipsed, but are extinguished not;
Like stars to their appointed height they climb,
And death is a low mist which cannot blot
The brightness it may veil. When lofty thought
Lifts a young heart above its mortal lair,
And love and life contend in it, for what
Shall be its earthly doom, the dead live there
And move like winds of light on dark and stormy air.

◄ XLV ►

The inheritors of unfulfilled renown
Rose from their thrones, built beyond mortal
    thought,
Far in the Unapparent. Chatterton
Rose pale, – his solemn agony had not
Yet faded from him; Sidney, as he fought
And as he fell and as he lived and loved
Sublimely mild, a Spirit without spot,
Arose; and Lucan, by his death approved:
Oblivion as they rose shrank like a thing reproved.

◄ XLVI ►

And many more, whose names on Earth are dark,
But whose transmitted effluence cannot die
So long as fire outlives the parent spark,
Rose, robed in dazzling immortality.
'Thou art become as one of us,' they cry,
'It was for thee yon kingless sphere has long
Swung blind in unascended majesty,
Silent alone amid an Heaven of Song.
Assume thy wingèd throne, thou Vesper of our
    throng!'

◄ XLVII ►

Who mourns for Adonais? Oh, come forth,
Fond wretch! and know thyself and him aright.
Clasp with thy panting soul the pendulous Earth;
As from a centre, dart thy spirit's light
Beyond all worlds, until its spacious might
Satiate the void circumference: then shrink
Even to a point within our day and night;
And keep thy heart light lest it make thee sink
When hope has kindled hope, and lured thee to the
    brink.

◄ XLVIII ►

Or go to Rome, which is the sepulchre,
Oh, not of him, but of our joy: 'tis nought
That ages, empires, and religions there

Lie buried in the ravage they have wrought;
For such as he can lend, – they borrow not
Glory from those who made the world their prey;
And he is gathered to the kings of thought
Who waged contention with their time's decay,
And of the past are all that cannot pass away.

◄ XLIX ►

Go thou to Rome, – at once the Paradise,
The grave, the city, and the wilderness;
And where its wrecks like shattered mountains
    rise,
And flowering weeds, and fragrant copses dress
The bones of Desolation's nakedness
Pass, till the spirit of the spot shall lead
Thy footsteps to a slope of green access
Where, like an infant's smile, over the dead
A light of laughing flowers along the grass is spread:

◄ L ►

And grey walls moulder round, on which dull
    Time
Feeds, like slow fire upon a hoary brand;
And one keen pyramid with wedge sublime,
Pavilioning the dust of him who planned
This refuge for his memory, doth stand
Like flame transformed to marble; and beneath,
A field is spread, on which a newer band
Have pitched in Heaven's smile their camp of
    death,
Welcoming him we lose with scarce extinguished
    breath.

◄ LI ►

Here pause: these graves are all too young as yet
To have outgrown the sorrow which consigned
Its charge to each; and if the seal is set,
Here, on one fountain of a mourning mind,
Break it not thou! too surely shalt thou find
Thine own well full, if thou returnest home,
Of tears and gall. From the world's bitter wind
Seek shelter in the shadow of the tomb.
What Adonais is, why fear we to become?

◄ LII ►

The One remains, the many change and pass;
Heaven's light forever shines, Earth's shadows fly;
Life, like a dome of many-coloured glass,
Stains the white radiance of Eternity,
Until Death tramples it to fragments. – Die,
If thou wouldst be with that which thou dost seek!

Follow where all is fled! – Rome's azure sky,
Flowers, ruins, statues, music, words, are weak
The glory they transfuse with fitting truth to speak,

◄ LIII ►

Why linger, why turn back, why shrink, my
    Heart?
Thy hopes are gone before: from all things here
They have departed; thou shouldst now depart!
A light is passed from the revolving year,
And man, and woman; and what still is dear
Attracts to crush, repels to make thee wither.
The soft sky smiles, – the low wind whispers near:
'Tis Adonais calls! oh, hasten thither,
No more let Life divide what Death can join
    together.

◄ LIV ►

That Light whose smile kindles the Universe,
That Beauty in which all things work and move,
That Benediction which the eclipsing Curse
Of birth can quench not, that sustaining Love
Which through the web of being blindly wove
By man and beast and earth and air and sea,
Burns bright or dim, as each are mirrors of
The fire for which all thirst; now beams on me,
Consuming the last clouds of cold mortality.

◄ LV ►

The breath whose might I have invoked in song
Descends on me; my spirit's bark is driven,
Far from the shore, far from the trembling throng
Whose sails were never to the tempest given;
The massy earth and spherèd skies are riven!
I am borne darkly, fearfully, afar;
Whilst, burning through the inmost veil of
    Heaven,
The soul of Adonais, like a star,
Beacons from the abode where the Eternal are.

❧

EPIPSYCHIDION
(lines 149–89)

I never was attached to that great sect,
Whose doctrine is, that each one should select
Out of the crowd a mistress or a friend,
And all the rest, though fair and wise, commend
To cold oblivion, though it is in the code

Of modern morals, and the beaten road
Which those poor slaves with weary footsteps tread,
Who travel to their home among the dead
By the broad highway of the world, and so
With one chained friend, perhaps a jealous foe,
The dreariest and the longest journey go.

   True Love in this differs from gold and clay,
That to divide is not to take away.
Love is like understanding, that grows bright,
Gazing on many truths; 'tis like thy light,
Imagination! which from earth and sky,
And from the depths of human fantasy,
As from a thousand prisms and mirrors, fills
The Universe with glorious beams, and kills
Error, the worm, with many a sun-like arrow
Of its reverberated lightning. Narrow
The heart that loves, the brain that contemplates,
The life that wears, the spirit that creates
One object, and one form, and builds thereby
A sepulchre for its eternity.

   Mind from its object differs most in this:
Evil from good; misery from happiness;
The baser from the nobler; the impure
And frail, from what is clear and must endure.
If you divide suffering and dross, you may
Diminish till it is consumed away;
If you divide pleasure and love and thought,
Each part exceeds the whole; and we know not
How much, while any yet remains unshared,
Of pleasure may be gained, of sorrow spared:
This truth is that deep well, whence sages draw
The unenvied light of hope; the eternal law
By which those live, to whom this world of life
Is as a garden ravaged, and whose strife
Tills for the promise of a later birth
The wilderness of this Elysian earth.

JULIAN AND MADDALO

(lines 1–140)

I rode one evening with Count Maddalo
Upon the bank of land which breaks the flow
Of Adria towards Venice: a bare strand
Of hillocks, heaped from ever-shifting sand,
Matted with thistles and amphibious weeds,
Such as from earth's embrace the salt ooze breeds,

Is this; an uninhabited sea-side,
Which the lone fisher, when his nets are dried,
Abandons; and no other object breaks
The waste, but one dwarf tree and some few stakes
Broken and unrepaired, and the tide makes
A narrow space of level sand thereon,
Where 'twas our wont to ride while day went down.
This ride was my delight. I love all waste
And solitary places; where we taste
The pleasure of believing what we see
Is boundless, as we wish our souls to be:
And such was this wide ocean, and this shore
More barren than its billows; and yet more
Than all, with a remembered friend I love
To ride as then I rode; – for the winds drove
The living spray along the sunny air
Into our faces; the blue heavens were bare,
Stripped to their depths by the awakening north;
And, from the waves, sound like delight broke forth
Harmonising with solitude, and sent
Into our hearts aereal merriment.
So, as we rode, we talked; and the swift thought,
Winging itself with laughter, lingered not,
But flew from brain to brain, – such glee was ours,
Charged with light memories of remembered hours,
None slow enough for sadness: till we came
Homeward, which always makes the spirit tame.
This day had been cheerful but cold, and now
The sun was sinking, and the wind also.
Our talk grew somewhat serious, as may be
Talk interrupted with such raillery
As mocks itself, because it cannot scorn
The thoughts it would extinguish: – 'twas forlorn,
Yet pleasing, such as once, so poets tell,
The devils held within the dales of Hell
Concerning God, freewill and destiny:
Of all that earth has been or yet may be,
All that vain men imagine or believe,
Or hope can paint or suffering may achieve,
We descanted, and I (for ever still
Is it not wise to make the best of ill?)
Argued against despondency, but pride
Made my companion take the darker side.
The sense that he was greater than his kind
Had struck, methinks, his eagle spirit blind
By gazing on its own exceeding light.
Meanwhile the sun paused ere it should alight,
Over the horizon of the mountains; – Oh,
How beautiful is sunset, when the glow
Of Heaven descends upon a land like thee,
Thou Paradise of exiles, Italy!

Thy mountains, seas, and vineyards, and the towers
Of cities they encircle! – it was ours
To stand on thee, beholding it: and then,
Just where we had dismounted, the Count's men
Were waiting for us with the gondola. –
As those who pause on some delightful way
Though bent on pleasant pilgrimage, we stood
Looking upon the evening, and the flood
Which lay between the city and the shore,
Paved with the image of the sky . . . the hoar
And aëry Alps towards the North appeared
Through mist, an heaven-sustaining bulwark reared
Between the East and West; and half the sky
Was roofed with clouds of rich emblazonry
Dark purple at the zenith, which still grew
Down the steep West into a wondrous hue
Brighter than burning gold, even to the rent
Where the swift sun yet paused in his descent
Among the many-folded hills: they were
Those famous Euganean hills, which bear,
As seen from Lido thro' the harbour piles,
The likeness of a clump of peakèd isles –
And then – as if the Earth and Sea had been
Dissolved into one lake of fire, were seen
Those mountains towering as from waves of flame
Around the vaporous sun, from which there came
The inmost purple spirit of light, and made
Their very peaks transparent 'Ere it fade,'
Said my companion, 'I will show you soon
A better station' – so, o'er the lagune
We glided; and from that funereal bark
I leaned, and saw the city, and could mark
How from their many isles, in evening's gleam,
Its temples and its palaces did seem
Like fabrics of enchantment piled to Heaven.
I was about to speak, when – 'We are even
Now at the point I meant,' said Maddalo,
And bade the gondolieri cease to row.
Look, Julian, on the west, and listen well
If you hear not a deep and heavy bell.'
I looked, and saw between us and the sun
A building on an island; such a one
As age to age might add, for uses vile,
A windowless, deformed and dreary pile;
And on the top an open tower, where hung
A bell, which in the radiance swayed and swung;
We could just hear its hoarse and iron tongue:
The broad sun sunk behind it, and it tolled
In strong and black relief. – 'What we behold
Shall be the madhouse and its belfry tower,'
Said Maddalo, 'and ever at this hour

Those who may cross the water, hear that bell
Which calls the maniacs, each one from his cell,
To vespers.' – 'As much skill as need to pray
In thanks or hope for their dark lot have they
To their stern maker,' I replied. 'O ho!
You talk as in years past,' said Maddalo.
''Tis strange men change not. You were ever still
Among Christ's flock a perilous infidel,
A wolf for the meek lambs – if you can't swim
Beware of Providence.' I looked on him,
But the gay smile had faded in his eye.
'And such,' – he cried, 'is our mortality,
And this must be the emblem and the sign
Of what should be eternal and divine! –
And like that black and dreary bell, the soul,
Hung in a heaven-illumined tower, must toll
Our thoughts and our desires to meet below
Round the rent heart and pray – as madmen do
For what? they know not, – till the night of death
As sunset that strange vision, severeth
Our memory from itself, and us from all
We sought and yet were baffled.' I recall
The sense of what he said, although I mar
The force of his expressions. The broad star
Of day meanwhile had sunk behind the hill,
And the black bell became invisible,
And the red tower looked gray, and all between
The churches, ships and palaces were seen
Huddled in gloom; – into the purple sea
The orange hues of heaven sunk silently.
We hardly spoke, and soon the gondola
Conveyed me to my lodging by the way.

PROMETHEUS UNBOUND
(lines 554–end)

This is the day, which down the void abysm
At the Earth-born's spell yawns for Heaven's
    despotism.
  And Conquest is dragged captive through the
    deep:
Love, from its awful throne of patient power
In the wise heart, from the last giddy hour
  Of dread endurance, from the slippery, steep,
And narrow verge of crag-like agony; springs
And folds over the world its healing wings.

Gentleness, Virtue, Wisdom, and Endurance,
These are the seals of that most firm assurance
    Which bars the pit over Destruction's strength;
And if, with infirm hand, Eternity,
Mother of many acts and hours, should free
    The serpent that would clasp her with his length;
These are the spells by which to reassume
An empire o'er the disentangled doom: –

To suffer woes which Hope thinks infinite;
To forgive wrongs darker than death or night;
    To defy Power, which seems omnipotent;
To love, and bear; to hope till Hope creates
From its own wreck the thing it contemplates;
    Neither to change, nor falter, nor repent;
This, like thy glory, Titan, is to be
Good, great and joyous, beautiful and free;
This is alone Life, Joy, Empire, and Victory.

THE MASK OF ANARCHY
(lines 5–28; 146–55)

◄ II ►
I met Murder on the way –
He had a mask like Castlereagh –
Very smooth he looked, yet grim;
Seven blood-hounds followed him:

◄ III ►
All were fat; and well they might
Be in admirable plight,
For one by one, and two by two,
He tossed them human hearts to chew
Which from his wide cloak he drew.

◄ IIV ►
Next came Fraud, and he had on,
Like Eldon an ermined gown;
His big tears, for he wept well,
Turned to millstones as they fell.

◄ V ►
And the little children, who
Round his feet played to and fro,
Thinking every tear a gem,
Had their brains knocked out by them.

◄ VI ►
Clothed with the Bible, as with light,
And the shadows of the night,
Like Sidmouth, next, Hypocrisy
On a crocodile rode by.

◄ VII ►
And many more Destructions played
In this ghastly masquerade,
All disguised, even to the eyes,
Like Bishops, lawyers, peers, or spies.

[. . .]

◄ XXXVII ►
'Men of England, heirs of Glory,
Heroes of unwritten story,
Nurslings of one mighty Mother,
Hopes of her, and one another;

◄ XXXVIII ►
'Rise like Lions after slumber
In unvanquishable number,
Shake your chains to earth like dew
Which in sleep had fallen on you –
Ye are many – they are few.

SONG

◄ I ►
Rarely, rarely, comest thou,
    Spirit of Delight!
Wherefore hast thou left me now
    Many a day and night?
Many a weary night and day
'Tis since thou art fled away.

◄ II ►
How shall ever one like me
    Win thee back again?
With the joyous and the free
    Thou wilt scoff at pain.
Spirit false! thou hast forgot
All but those who need thee not.

◄ III ►
As a lizard with the shade
    Of a trembling leaf,

Thou with sorrow art dismayed;
   Even the sighs of grief
Reproach thee, that thou art not near,
And reproach thou wilt not hear.

◄ IV ►

Let me set my mournful ditty
   To a merry measure;
Thou wilt never come for pity,
   Thou wilt come for pleasure;
Pity then will cut away
Those cruel wings, and thou wilt stay.

◄ V ►

I love all that thou lovest,
   Spirit of Delight!
The fresh Earth in new leaves dressed,
   And the starry night;
Autumn evening, and the morn
When the golden mists are born.

◄ VI ►

I love snow, and all the forms
   Of the radiant frost
I love waves, and winds, and storms,
   Everything almost
Which is Nature's, and may be
Untainted by man's misery.

◄ VII ►

I love tranquil solitude
   And such society
As is quiet, wise, and good;
   Between thee and me
What difference? but thou dost possess
The things I seek, not love them less.

◄ VIII ►

I love Love – though he has wings,
   And like light can flee,
But above all other things,
   Spirit, I love thee –
Thou art love and life! Oh, come,
Make once more my heart thy home.

❧

WITH A GUITAR, TO JANE

Ariel to Miranda: – Take
This slave of Music, for the sake
Of him who is the slave of thee,
And teach it all the harmony
In which thou canst, and only thou,
Make the delighted spirit glow,
Till joy denies itself again,
And, too intense, is turned to pain;
For by permission and command
Of thine own Prince Ferdinand,
Poor Ariel sends this silent token
Of more than ever can be spoken;
Your guardian spirit, Ariel, who,
From life to life, must still pursue
Your happiness; – for thus alone
Can Ariel ever find his own.
From Prospero's enchanted cell,
As the mighty verses tell,
To the throne of Naples, he
Lit you o'er the trackless sea,
Flitting on, your prow before,
Like a living meteor.
When you die, the silent Moon,
In her interlunar swoon,
Is not sadder in her cell
Than deserted Ariel.
When you live again on earth,
Like an unseen star of birth,
Ariel guides you o'er the sea
Of life from your nativity.
Many changes have been run
Since Ferdinand and you begun
Your course of love, and Ariel still
Has tracked your steps, and served your will;
Now, in humbler, happier lot,
This is all remembered not;
And now, alas! the poor sprite is
Imprisoned, for some fault of his,
In a body like a grave; –
From you he only dares to crave,
For his service and his sorrow,
A smile to-day, a song to-morrow.

The artist who this idol wrought,
To echo all harmonious thought,
Felled a tree, while on the steep
The woods were in their winter sleep,
Rocked in that repose divine
On the wind-swept Apennine;

And dreaming, some of Autumn past
And some of Spring approaching fast,
And some of April buds and showers,
And some of songs in July bowers,
And all of love; and so this tree, –
O that such our death may be! –
Died in sleep, and felt no pain,
To live in happier form again:
From which, beneath Heaven's fairest star,
The artist wrought this loved Guitar,
And taught it justly to reply,
To all who question skilfully,
In language gentle as thine own;
Whispering in enamoured tone
Sweet oracles of woods and dells,
And summer winds in sylvan cells;
For it had learned all harmonies
Of the plains and of the skies
Of the forests and the mountains,
And the many-voicèd fountains;
The clearest echoes of the hills,
The softest notes of falling rills,
The melodies of birds and bees,
The murmuring of summer seas,
And pattering rain, and breathing dew,
And airs of evening; and it knew
That seldom-heard mysterious sound,
Which, driven on its diurnal round,
As it floats through boundless day,
Our world enkindles on its way. –
All this it knows, but will not tell
To those who cannot question well
The Spirit that inhabits it;
It talks according to the wit
Of its companions; and no more
Is heard than has been felt before,
By those who tempt it to betray
These secrets of an elder day:
But, sweetly as its answers will
Flatter hands of perfect skill,
It keeps its highest, holiest tone
For our belovèd Jane alone.

It occurred to me, in making this selection from Sir Philip Sidney (1554–86), to confine myself to his best-known work – along with his *Defence of Poetry* – and choose twenty-odd sonnets from *Astrophil and Stella*. That, however, would have been to deny the formal variety and metrical experimentation he brought to English poetry, and thus further diminish an outstanding man of the Renaissance: he was a soldier and a diplomat as well as a poet.

I therefore chose a stanza from 'O sweet woods' – a timelessly English hymn to nature, with notably strong phrasings – and stanzas from the wonderfully unremitting black pageantry of 'Corona', with its almost campy insistence on misery, the tiny and charming 'Sleep, baby mine', in which the poet's desire is a baby that will not settle, and the superb 'aristophanic', 'When to my deadly pleasure', whose last lines go in like nails. This still left me, I am glad to say, over half the allotted space for *Astrophil and Stella*.

The sonnets I gravitated towards were those I thought were the least rhetorical, the ones where you could sense real passion and real experience and the real man, who, 'overmastered by some thoughts' as he wrote in the *Defence*, 'yielded an inky tribute unto them.' What I probably mean though is the poems with the most effective rhetoric ('I am not I, pity the tale of me.').

I chose sonnets that show Sidney writing against artifice and empty tradition (1 and 6), show him preoccupied (27) as he goes on living in a highly-pressured world dominated by *Realpolitik* (30), content to name names (Stella, his 'star', was married to one Rich: 37), hearing her read him back his poems (58), loving it, as we would say in contemporary parlance, when she's angry (73), being out of sorts and frightened and desperate to hear news of her (76, 92, 99).

'O SWEET WOODS...'

(lines 15–28)

O sweet woods, the delight of solitariness,
O how much I do like your solitariness!
Here no treason is hid, veiled in innocence,
Nor envy's snaky eye finds any harbour here,
Nor flatterers' venomous insinuations,
Nor cunning humorists' puddled opinions,
Nor courteous ruin of proffered usury,
Nor time prattled away, cradle of ignorance,
Nor causeless duty, nor cumber of arrogance,
Nor trifling title of vanity dazzleth us,
Nor golden manacles, stand for a paradise:
Here wrong's name is unheard; slander a monster
    is.
Keep thy sprite from abuse, here no abuse doth
    haunt.
What man grafts in a tree dissimulation?

'I JOY IN GRIEF...'

◄ The Corona or 'double complaint' ►

(lines 1–60)

Strephon: I joy in grief, and do detest all joys;
    Despise delight, am tired with thought of ease.
    I turn my mind to all forms of annoys,
    And with the change of them my fancy please.
    I study that which most may me displease,
    And in despite of that displeasure's might
    Embrace that most that most my soul destroys;
    Blinded with beams, fell darkness is my sight;
    Dwell in my ruins, feed with sucking smart,
    I think from me, not from my woes, to part.

Klaius: I think from me, not from my woes, to part,
    And loathe this time called life, nay think that
        life
    Nature to me for torment did impart;
    Think my hard haps have blunted death's sharp
        knife,
    Not sparing me in whom his works be rife;
    And thinking this, think nature, life, and death
    Place sorrow's triumph on my conquered heart.
    Whereto I yield, and seek no other breath
    But from the scent of some infectious grave;
    Nor of my fortune aught but mischief crave.

Strephon: Nor of my fortune aught but mischief
        crave,
    And seek to nourish that which now contains
    All what I am; if I myself will save,
    Then I must save what in me chiefly reigns,
    Which is the hateful web of sorrow's pains.
    Sorrow, then cherish me, for I am sorrow;
    No being now but sorrow I can have;
    Then deck me as thine own; thy help I borrow,
    Since thou my riches art, and that thou has
    Enough to make a fertile mind lie waste.

Klaius: Enough to make a fertile mind lie waste
    Is that huge storm, which pours itself on me;
    Hailstones of tears, of sighs a monstrous blast,
    Thunders of cries; lightnings my wild looks be;
    The darkened heaven, my soul, which naught can
        see;
    The flying sprites which trees by roots up tear
    Be those despairs, which have my hopes quite
        waste.
    The difference is: all folks those storms forbear,
    But I cannot, who then my self should fly,
    So close unto my self my wracks do lie.

Strephon: So close unto my self my wracks do lie,
    Both cause, effect, beginning and the end
    Are all in me; what help then can I try?
    My ship, my self, whose course to love doth
        bend,
    Sore beaten, doth her mast of comfort spend;
    Her cable, reason, breaks from anchor, hope;
    Fancy, her tackling, torn away doth fly;
    Ruin, the wind, hath blown her from my scope;
    Bruised with the waves of care, but broken is
    On rock, despair, the burial of my bliss.

Klaius: On rock, despair, the burial of my bliss,
    I long do plough with plough of deep desire;
    The seed fast-meaning is, no truth to miss;
    I harrow it with thoughts, which all conspire
    Favour to make my chief and only hire.
    But woe is me, the year is gone about,
    And now I fain would reap, I reap but this:
    Hate fully grown, absence new sprongen out,
    So that I see, although my sight impair,
    Vain is their pain, who labour in despair.

SONG: 'SLEEP, BABY MINE, DESIRE'

To the tune of *Basciami vita mia*

Sleep, baby mine, desire; nurse beauty singeth;
Thy cries, O baby, set mine head on aching:
The babe cries: 'Way, thy love doth keep me waking.'

Lully, fully, my babe; hope cradle bringeth,
Unto my children alway good rest taking:
The babe cries: 'Way, thy love doth keep me waking.'

Since, baby mine, from me thy watching springeth;
Sleep then a little, pap content is making:
The babe cries: 'Nay, for that abide I waking.'

'WHEN TO MY DEADLY PLEASURE'

When to my deadly pleasure,
When to my lively torment,
Lady, mine eyes remained,
Joined, alas, to your beams,
With violence of heavenly
Beauty tied to virtue,
Reason abashed retired,
Gladly my senses yielded.
Gladly my senses yielding
Thus to betray my heart's fort
Left me devoid of all life.
They to the beamy suns went,
Where, by the death of all deaths,
Find to what harm they hastened;
Like to the silly sylvan
Burned by the light he best liked,
When with a fire he first met.
Yet, yet, a life to their death,
Lady, you have reserved;
Lady, the life of all love;
For though my sense be from me,
And I be dead, who want sense;
Yet do we both live in you;
Turned anew by your means
Unto the flower that aye turns,
As you, alas, my sun bends.
Thus do I fall, to rise thus;
Thus do I die, to live thus;
Changed to a change, I change not.
Thus may I not be from you;
Thus be my senses on you;

Thus what I think is of you;
Thus what I seek is in you;
All what I am, it is you.

ASTROPHIL AND STELLA

◄ 1 ►

Loving in truth, and fain in verse my love to show,
That she (dear she) might take some pleasure to my
    pain:
Pleasure might cause her read, reading might make her
    know;
Knowledge might pity win, and pity grace obtain;
   I sought fit words to paint the blackest face of woe,
Studying inventions fine, her wits to entertain:
Oft turning others' leaves to see if thence would flow
Some fresh and fruitful showers upon my sun-burn'd
    brain.
   But words came halting forth, wanting Invention's
    stay,
Invention, Nature's child, fled step-dame Study's blows,
And others' feet still seem'd but strangers in my way.
Thus great with child to speak, and helpless in my
    throes,
   Biting my truant pen, beating myself for spite,
   'Fool,' said my Muse to me, 'look in thy heart and
    write'.

◄ 6 ►

Some lovers speak when they their Muses entertain,
Of hopes begot by fear, of wot not what desires:
Of force of heav'nly beams, infusing hellish pain:
Of living deaths, dear wounds, fair storms and freezing
    fires:
   Some one his song in Jove, and Jove's strange tales
    attires,
Bordered with bulls and swans, powdered with golden
    rain:
Another humbler wit to shepherd's pipe retires,
Yet hiding royal blood full oft in rural vein.
   To some a sweetest plaint, a sweetest style affords,
   While tears pour out his ink, and sighs breathe out
    his words:
His paper, pale despair, and pain his pen doth move.
   I can speak what I feel, and feel as much as they,
   But think that all the map of my state I display,
When trembling voice brings forth that I do Stella love.

‹ 27 ›

Because I oft in dark abstracted guise,
    Seem most alone in greatest company,
    With dearth of words, or answers quite awry,
To them that would make speech of speech arise,
They deem, and of their doom the rumour flies,
    That poison foul of bubbling pride doth lie
    So in my swelling breast that only I
Fawn on myself, and others do despise:
    Yet pride I think doth not my soul possess,
Which looks too oft in his unflatt'ring glass:
But one worse fault, ambition, I confess,
That makes me oft my best friends overpass,
    Unseen, unheard, while thought to highest place
    Bends all his powers, even unto Stella's grace.

‹ 30 ›

Whether the Turkish new-moon minded be
    To fill his horns this year on Christian coast:
    How Pole's right king means, without leave of host,
To warm with ill-made fire cold Muscovy;
If French can yet three parts in one agree;
    What now the Dutch in their full diets boast;
    How Holland hearts, now so good towns be lost,
Trust in the pleasing shade of Orange tree;
    How Ulster likes of that same golden bit,
Wherewith my father once made it half tame;
If in the Scottish Court be welt'ring yet;
These questions busy wits to me do frame,
    I, cumb'red with good manners, answer do,
    But know not how, for still I think of you.

‹ 37 ›

My mouth doth water, and my breast doth swell,
    My tongue doth itch, my thoughts in labour be:
    Listen then, lordings, with good ear to me,
For of my life a riddle I must tell.
Towards Aurora's Court a nymph doth dwell,
    Rich in all beauties which man's eye can see:
    Beauties so far from reach of words that we
Abase her praise, saving she doth excel:
    Rich in the treasure of deserv'd renown,
Rich in the riches of a royal heart,
Rich in those gifts which give th'eternal crown:
Who though most rich in these and every part.
    Which make the patents of true worldly bliss,
    Hath no misfortune, but that Rich she is.

‹ 45 ›

Stella oft sees the very face of woe
    Painted in my beclouded stormy face:

But cannot skill to pity my disgrace,
Not though thereof the cause herself she know:
Yet hearing late a fable, which did show
    Of lovers never known a grievous case,
    Pity thereof gat in her breast such place,
That from that sea deriv'd, tears' spring did flow.
    Alas, if Fancy drawn by imag'd things,
Though false, yet with free scope more grace doth breed
Than servant's wrack, where new doubts honour brings;
Then think my dear, that you in me do read
    Of lover's ruin some sad tragedy:
    I am not I, pity the tale of me.

‹ 58 ›

Doubt there hath been, when with his golden chain
    The orator so far men's hearts doth bind,
    That no pace else their guided steps can find,
But as he them more short or slack doth rein,
Whether with words this sovereignty he gain,
    Cloth'd with fine tropes, with strongest reasons lin'd,
    Or else pronouncing grace, wherewith his mind
Prints his own lively form in rudest brain:
    Now judge by this, in piercing phrases late,
    Th'anatomy of all my woes I wrate,
Stella's sweet breath the same to me did read.
    O voice, O face, maugre my speech's might,
    Which wooed woe, most ravishing delight,
Even those sad words even in sad me did breed.

‹ 73 ›

Love still a boy, and oft a wanton is,
School'd only by his mother's tender eye.
What wonder then if he his lesson miss,
When for so soft a rod dear play he try?
    And yet my star, because a sug'red kiss
In sport I suckt, while she asleep did lie,
Doth lour, nay, chide; nay, threat for only this:
Sweet, it was saucy Love, not humble I.
    But no 'scuse serves, she makes her wrath appear
    In Beauty's throne, see now who dares come near
Those scarlet judges, threat'ning bloody pain?
    O heav'nly fool, thy most kiss-worthy face,
    Anger invests with such a lovely grace,
That Anger's self I needs must kiss again.

‹ 76 ›

She comes, and straight therewith her shining twins do
    move
    Their rays to me, who in her tedious absence lay
    Benighted in cold woe; but now appears my day,
The only light of joy, the only warmth of love.

She comes with light and warmth, which like Aurora
    prove
  Of gentle force, so that mine eyes dare gladly play
  With such a rosy morn, whose beams most freshly gay
Scorch not, but only do dark chilling sprites remove.
  But lo, while I do speak, it groweth noon with me;
Her flamy glist'ring lights increase with time and place;
Her heart cries 'Ah, it burns', mine eyes now dazzled be:
No wind, no shade, can cool, what help then in my
    case,
  But with short breath, long looks, stay'd feet and
    walking head,
  Pray that my sun go down with meeker beams to bed.

    ‹ 92 ›

Be your words made (good sir) of Indian ware,
  That you allow me them by so small a rate?
  Or do you cutted Spartans imitate?
Or do you mean my tender ears to spare,
That to my questions you so total are?
  When I demand of phoenix Stella's state,
  You say, forsooth, you left her well of late.
O God, think you that satisfies my care?
  I would know whether she did sit or walk,
How cloth'd, how waited on? Sigh'd she or smil'd?
Wherof, with whom, how often did she talk?
With what pastime, time's journey she beguil'd?
  If her lips deign'd to sweeten my poor name?
  Say all, and all, well said, still say the same.

    ‹ 99 ›

When far spent night persuades each mortal eye,
  To whom nor art nor nature granteth light,
  To lay his then mark wanting shafts of sight,
Clos'd with their quivers in sleep's armory;
With windows ope then most my mind doth lie,
  Viewing the shape of darkness and delight,
  Takes in that sad hue, which with th'inward night
Of his maz'd powers keeps perfit harmony:
  But when birds charm, and that sweet air, which is
Morn's messenger, with rose enamel'd skies
Calls each wight to salute the flower of bliss;
In tomb of lids then buried are mine eyes,
  Forc'd by their lord, who is asham'd to find
  Such light in sense, with such a dark'ned mind.

Skelton wrote rude, mad, beautiful, spry verse in the English alliterative tradition (though not pedantically so). He used mainly Rhyme Royal and a short two- or three-stress line with emphatic, repetitive rhyme.

He wanted to remake English as a literary language. He was excited about its words: shurvy, glaimy, werrin, fuck-sails, titivels, crakers, tavelles, hiddles, twible, noddipol, gramatoll, hoddipole, paltock, whipslovens, hardy dardy, skrike, loathly lusk, windshaken shanks, gene and gasp, jest ye movell, ye sluffered up souce, vertability, folability, coinquinate, isagogical, gressops, friskajolly, youkerkins...

Some poets elicit and gather their language, some command and pattern it. Skelton commands; he pecks and shakes his words, only to find they've come alive and are running away with the rhyme: 'Master Sophista, ye simplex syllogista, ye devillish dogmatista, your hawk on your fista, to hawk when you lista in ecclesia ista, Domine concupisti, with thy hawk on thy fisty? Numquid sic dixisti? Numquid sic fecisti? Sed ubi hoc legisti, aut unde hoc, Doctor Dawcock?' This can only be described as Rhyme writing skelton.

His voice is made of tags and refrains, much Latin and a scattering of nonsense. He had a parrot presiding over his verse: 'with my beke bent, my little wanton eye ... Parrot can mew and cry in Latin, Hebrew, Araby and Chaldy ... when Parrot is dead she cloth not putrefy ... pray you, let Parrot have liberty to speak!' It was the parrot's liberty (I once had a parrot shout 'Fool!' at me through an open window) that enabled him to criticise the Church and the Court in the person of Wolsey. As somebody once said, all art constantly aspires towards the condition of birdsong...

John Skelton

Woefully Arrayed

Woefully arrayed,
My blood, man,
For thee ran,
It may not be nay'd:
My body blo and wan,
woefully arrayed.

Behold me, I pray thee, with all thy whole reason,
And be not so hard-hearted, and for this encheason,
Sith I for thy soul's sake was slain in good season,
Beguiled and betrayed by Judas' false treason:
Unkindly entreated,
with sharp cord sore freted,
The lewes me threted:
They mowed, they grinned, they scorned me,
condemned to death, as thou mayest see,
Woefully arrayed.

Thus naked am I nailed, O man, for thy sake!
I love thee, then love me; why sleepest thou? awake!
Remember my tender heart-root for thee brake,
with paines my veines constrained to crake:
Thus tugged to and fro,
Thus wrapped all in woe,
Whereas never man was so,
Entreated thus in most cruel wise,
was like a lamb offered in sacrifice,
Woefully arrayed.

Of sharp thorn I have worn a crown on my head,
So pained, so strained, so rueful, so red,
Thus bobbed, thus robbed, thus for thy love dead,
Unfeigned I deigned my blood for to shed:
My feet and handes sore
The sturdy nailes bore:
What might I suffer more
Than I have done, O man, for thee?
Come when thou list, welcome to me,
woefully arrayed.

Of record thy good Lord I have been and shall be:
I am thine, thou art mine, my brother I call thee.
Thee love I entirely – see what is befall'n me!
Sore beating, sore threating, to make thee, man, all
    free:
Why art thou unkind?
Why hast not me in mind?
Come yet and thou shalt find
Mine endless mercy and grace –

See how a spear my heart did race,
Woefully arrayed.

Dear brother, no other thing I of thee desire
But give me thine heart free to reward mine hire:
I wrought thee, I bought thee from eternal fire:
I pray thee array thee toward my high empire
above the orient,
whereof I am regent,
Lord God omnipotent,
with me to reign in endless wealth:
Remember, man, thy soules health.

Woefully arrayed,
My blood, man,
For thee ran,
It may not be nay'd:
My body blo and wan,
Woefully arrayed.

The Tunning of Elinor Rumming
(lines 133–8; 351–81)

Some wenches come unlaced,
Some housewives come unbraced,
With their naked pappes,
That flippes and flappes,
That wigges and wagges
Like tawny saffron bagges . . .

[. . .]

Then thither came drunken Alice,
And she was full of tales,
Of tidings in Wales,
And of Saint James in Gales,
And of the Portingales,
With 'Lo, gossip, ywis,
Thus and thus it is:
There hath been great war
Between Temple Bar
And the Cross in Cheap,
And there came an heap
Of mill-stones in a rout . . .'
She speaketh thus in her snout,
Snivelling in her nose
As though she had the pose.
'Lo, here is an old tippet,
An ye will give me a sippet

Of your stale ale,
God send you good sale!'
And as she was drinking
She fell in a winking
With a barlichood,
She pissed where she stood.
Then began she to weep,
And forthwith fell asleep.
Elinour took her up
And blesed her with a cup
Of newe ale in cornes:
Alice found therein no thornes,
But supped it up at ones,
She found therein no bones . . .

PHILIP SPARROW
(lines 386–494; 550–70)

Lauda, anima mea, Dominum!
To weep with me look that ye come
All manner of birdes in your kind;
See none be left behind.
To mourning looke that ye fall
With dolorous songes funeral!,
Some to sing, and some to say,
Some to weep, and some to pray,
Every bird in his lay.
The goldfinch, the wagtail;
The jangling jay to rail,
The flecked pie to chatter
Of this dolorous matter;
And robin redbreast,
He shall be the priest
The requiem mass to sing,
Softly warbeling,
With help of the reed sparrow,
And the chatteringe swallow,
This hearse for to hallow;
The lark with his long toe;
The spink and the martinet also;
The shoveller with his broad beak;
The dotterel, that foolish peke,
And also the mad coot,
With balde face to toot;
The fieldfare and the snite;
The crow and the kite;
The raven, called Rolfe,
His plain-song to sol-fa;

The partridge, the quail;
The plover with us to wail;
The woodhack that singeth 'chur'
Hoarsely, as he had the mur;
The lusty chanting nightingale;
The popinjay to tell her tale,
That toteth oft in a glass,
Shall read the Gospel at mass;
The mavis with her whistle
Shall read there the Epistle.
But with a large and a long
To keep just plain-song,
Our chanters shall be the cuckoo,
The culver, the stockdowe,
With 'peewit' the lapwing
The versicles shall sing.
The bittern with his bumpe,
The crane with his trumpe,
The swan of Maeander,
The goose and the gander,
The duck and the drake,
Shall watch at this wake;
The peacock so proud,
Because his voice is loud,
And hath a glorious tail,
He shall sing the Grail;
The owl, that is so foul,
Must help us to howl;
The heron so gaunt,
And the cormorant,
With the pheasant,
And the gaggling gant,
And the churlish chough;
The knot and the ruff;
The barnacle, the buzzard,
With the mild mallard;
The divendop to sleep;
The water-hen to weep;
The puffin and the teal
Money they shall deal
To poore folk at large,
That shall be their charge,
The seamew and the titmouse;
The woodcock with the longe nose
The throstle with her warbling;
The starling with her brabling;
The rook with the osprey
That putteth fishes to a fray;
And the dainty curlew,
With turtle most true.

At this *Placebo*
We may not well forgo
The countering of the coe;
The stork also,
that maketh his nest
in chimneys to rest;
Within those walls
No broken galls
May there abide
Of cuckoldry side,
Or else philosophy
Maketh a great lie.
The Ostrich that will eat
An horseshoe so great,
In the stead of meat,
Such fervent heat
His stomach cloth frete;
He cannot well fly,
Nor sing tunably,
Yet at a brayd
He hath well assayed
To sol-fa above E-la.
Fa, lorell, *fa, fa!*
Ne quando
Male cantando.
The best that ever we can,
To make him our bell-man,
And let him ring the bells.
He can do no hing else

[…]

But for the eagle doth fly
Highest in the sky,
He shall be the sub-dean,
The choir to demean,
As provost principal,
To teach them their Ordinal;
Also the noble falcon,
With the ger-falcon,
The tarsil gentil,
They shall mourn soft and still
In their amice of grey;
The saker with them shall say
Dirige for Philip's soul;
The goshawk shall have a role
The choristers to control;
The lanners and the merlions
Shall stand in their mourning-gowns;
The hobby and the musket
The censers and the cross shall fet;

The kestrel in all this wark
Shall be holy water clerk.

❧

Speak, Parrot
(lines 204–24; 449–end)

For Parrot is no churlish chough, nor no flecked pie,
Parrot is no pendugum, that men call a carling,
Parrot is no woodcock, nor no butterfly,
Parrot is no stammering stare, that men call a
   starling.
But Parrot is my own dear heart and my dear darling.
Melpomene, that fair maid, she burnished his beak:

Parrot is a fair bird for a lady:
God of his goodness him framed and wrought;
When Parrot is dead she doth not putrefy.
Yea all things mortal shall turn unto nought,
Except man's soul, that Christ so deare bought;
That never may die, nor never die shall –
Make much of Parrot, the popinjay royall.

For that peerles Prince that Parrot did create,
He made you of nothing by his Majesty.
Point well this problem that Parrot doth prate,
And remember among how Parrot and ye
Shall leap from this life, as merry as we be:
Pomp, pride, honour, riches, and worldly lust,
Parrot saith plainly, shall turn all to dust.

[…]

So many moral matters, and so little used;
So much new making, and so mad time spent;
So much translation into English confused;
So much noble preaching, and so little amendment;
So much consultation, almost to none intent;
So much provision, and so little wit at need –
Since Deucalion's flood there can no clerkes rede.

So little discretion and so much reasoning;
So much hardy dardy and so little manliness;
So prodigal expense, and so shameful reckoning;
So gorgeous garments, and so much wretchedness;
So much portly pride, with purses penniless;
So much spent before, and so much unpaid behind –
Since Deucalion's flood there can no clerkes find.

So much forecasting and so far an after deal;
So much politic prating, and so little standeth in
  stead;
So little secretness, and so much great counsel;
So many bold barons, their hearts as dull as lead;
So many noble bodies under a daw's head;
So royal a king as reigneth upon us all –
Since Deucalion's flood was never seen nor shall.

So many complaintes, and so small redress;
So much calling on, and so small taking heed;
So much loss of merchandise, and so remediless;
So little care for the common weal, and so much
  need;
So much doubtful danger, and so little drede;
So much pride of prelates, so cruel and so keen –
Since Deucalian's flood, I trow, was never seen.

So many thieves hanged, and thieves never the less;
So much prisonment for matters not worth an haw;
So much papers wering for right a small excess;
So much pillory pageants under colour of good law;
So much turning on the cuck-stool for every gee-gaw;
So much mockish making of statutes of array –
Since Deucalion's flood was never, I dare say.

So brainless calves' heads, so many sheepes tails;
So bold a bragging butcher, and flesh sold so dear;
So many plucked partridges, and so fatte quails;
So mangy a mastiff cur, the great greyhound's peer;
So big a bulk of brow-antlers cabbaged that year;
So many swans dead, and so small revel –
Since Deucalion's flood, I trow, no man can tell.

So many truces taken and so little perfite truth;
So much belly-joy and so wasteful banqueting;
So pinching and sparing, and so little profit groweth;
So many hugy houses building and so small
  householding;
Such statutes upon diets, such pilling and polling;
So is all thing wrought wilfully withoute reason and
  skill –
Since Deucalion's flood, the world was never so ill.

So many vagabonds, so many beggars bold;
So much decay of monasteries and of religious places;
So hot hatred against the Church, and charity so cold;
So much of 'my Lord's Grace' and in him no graces;
So many hollow hearts and so double faces;
So much sanctuary-breaking, and privilege barred –
Since Deuealion's flood was never seen nor lyerd.

So much ragged right of a rammes horn;
So rigorous ruling in a prelate specially;
So bold and so bragging, and was so basely born;
So lordly in his looks and so disdainously;
So fat a maggot, bred of a fleshe-fly;
Was never such a filthy Gorgon, nor such an epicure,
Since Deucalion's flood, I make thee fast and sure.

So much privy watching in cold winters' nights;
So much searching of losers, and is himself so lewd;
So much conjurations for elfish mid-day sprites;
So many bulls of pardon published and shewed;
So much crossing and blessing, and him all
  beshrewed;
Such pole-axes and pillars, such mules traps with
  gold –
Since Deucalion's flood in no chronicle is told.

Dixit, quod Parrot.

Some time after leaving Cambridge for London, to try his luck as an independent writer, Christopher Smart (1722–71), the poet, Anglican and friend of Samuel Johnson, began to take certain of his doctrines so seriously that it was thought necessary to incarcerate him as a lunatic. He was eventually released, only to be later arrested and committed to a debtor's prison, where he died.

Much of his work is religious or liturgical in nature, and requires a considerable coincidence of outlook if it is to be read with much profit or pleasure. No-one, however, can question his industry. In a brief, representative selection this side of his work must be reduced almost to a case of samples. However, the immense *Jubilate Agno*, perhaps his strangest production, exists in such a chaotic and provisional state as almost to invite the free use of the scalpel. This invitation, or near invitation, I have taken up. For the rest, it may be said that for those who want hymns, or versifications of edifying material, Smart is certainly their man. He did all the Psalms into metrics, sometimes more than once; and among his completed projects are versifications of the Fables of Phaedrus and the Parables of Jesus Christ, both principally designed for children.

Much of Smart's work is so sanely and diligently well done that one only wishes it were more worth doing, My own selection is, by bulk, certainly weighted towards the unhymnic non-assembly-line side of the man, although, to shift the metaphor, I doubt whether it shifts the cargo to a dangerous degree, But be things what they may, all these items are certainly part of what this strange, affable and not undelightful oddbodkin did actually create.

To Ethelinda

(On her doing my verses the honour of wearing them in her bosom. Written at Thirteen.)

Happy verses! that were prest
In fair Ethelinda's breast!
Happy muse, that didst embrace
The sweet, the heav'nly fragrant place!
Tell me, is the omen true:
Shall the bard arrive there too?

Oft thro' my eyes my soul has flown,
And wantoned on that ivory throne:
There with extatic transport burned,
And thought it was to heaven returned.
Tell me, is the omen true:
Shall the body follow too?

When first at nature's early birth
Heav'n sent a man upon the earth,
Ev'n Eden was more fruitful found
When Adam came to till the ground:
Shall then those breasts be fair in vain,
And only rise to fall again?

No, no, fair nymph – for no such end
Did heav'n to thee its bounty lend;
That breast was ne'er designed by fate
For verse, or things inanimate;
Then throw them from that downy bed –
And take the poet in their stead.

The Immensity of the Supreme Being
(lines 46–64)

    Oh! could I search the bosom of the sea,
Down the great depth descending; there thy works
Would also speak thy residence; and there
Would I thy servant, like the still profound,
Astonished into silence muse thy praise!
Behold! behold! th' unplanted garden round
Of vegetable coral, sea-flowers gay,
And shrubs of amber from the pearl-paved bottom
Rise richly varied, where the finny race
In blithe security their gambols play:
While high above their heads Leviathan
The terror and the glory of the main

His pastime takes with transport, proud to see
The ocean's vast dominion all his own.
   Hence thro' the genial bowels of the earth
Easy may fancy pass; till at thy mines
Gani or Raolconda she arrive;
And from the adamant's imperial blaze
Form weak ideas of her maker's glory.

THE PRETTY BAR-KEEPER OF THE MITRE

‹(Written at College, 1741)›

"Relax, sweet girl, your wearied mind,
   And to hear the poet talk,
Gentlest creature of your kind,
   Lay aside your spunge and chalk;
Cease, cease the bar-bell, nor refuse
To hear the jingle of the Muse.

Hear your numerous vot'ries prayers,
   Come, O come and bring with thee
Giddy whimsies, wanton airs,
   And all love's soft artillery;
Smiles and throbs, and frowns, and tears,
With all the little hopes and fears.'

She heard – she came – and ere she spoke,
   Not unravished you might see
Her wanton eyes that winked the joke
   Ere her tongue could set it free.
While her forced blush her cheeks inflamed,
And seemed to say she was ashamed.

No handkerchief her bosom hid;
   No tippet from our sight debars
Her heaving breasts with moles o'erspread,
   Marked, little hemispheres, with stars;
While on them all our eyes we move,
Our eyes that meant immoderate love.

In every gesture, every air,
   Th' imperfect lisp, the languid eye,
In every motion of the fair
   We awkward imitators vie,
And, forming our own from her face,
Strive to look pretty, as we gaze.

If e'er she sneezed, the mimic crowd
   Sneezed too, and all their pipes laid down;

If she but stooped, we lowly bowed,
   And sullen, if she 'gan to frown,
In solemn silence sat profound –
But did she laugh? – the laugh went round.

Her snuff-box if the nymph pulled out,
   Each Johnian in responsive airs
Fed with the tickling dust his snout,
   With all the politesse of bears.
Dropped she her fan beneath her hoop?
Ev'n stake-stuck Clarians strove to stoop.

The sons of culinary Kay's,
   Smoking from the eternal treat,
Lost in ecstatic transport, gaze,
   As tho' the fair was good to eat.
Ev'n gloomiest King's-men, pleased awhile,
'Grin horribly a ghastly smile'.

But hark; she cries, 'my mamma calls',
   And strait, she's vanished from our sight.
'Twas then we saw the empty bowls;
   'Twas then we first perceived it night.
While all, sad synod, silent moan,
Both that she went – and went alone.

PROLOGUE TO A COMEDY CALLED
THE GRATEFUL FAIR

In ancient days (as jovial Horace sings)
When laurelled bards were lawgivers and kings,
Bold was the comic muse, without restraint,
To name the vicious, and the vice to paint;
Th' enlivened picture from the canvas flew,
And the strong likeness crowded on the view.
Our author practices more general rules,
He is no niggard of his knaves and fools.
Both small and great, both dull and pert he shews,
That every gentleman may pick and choose.
The laws dramatic, tho', he scarcely knows
Of time and place, and all the piteous prose
Which pedant Frenchmen snuffle thro' their nose.
Fools! – who prescribe what Homer should have
      done;
Like tattling watches, they correct the sun.
Critics, like posts, undoubtedly may show
The way to Pindus – but they cannot go:
For to delight and elevate the mind,

To heav'n-directed GENIUS is assigned.
Whene'er immortal Shakespear's works we read,
He wins the heart, before he strikes the head;
Swift to the soul the piercing image flies,
More swift than Celia's wit, or Celia's eyes;
More swift than some romantic traveller's thought;
More swift than British fire, where Marlbro' fought.
Fancy precedes and conquers all the mind,
Deliberating judgment slowly lags behind,
Comes to the field with blunderbuss and gun,
Like heavy Falstaff when the work is done;
Fights when the battle's o'er, with wondrous pain,
By Shrewsbury clock, and nobly slays the slain. –
– But critic censures are beneath his care,
Who strives to please the honest and the fair.
Their approbation is much more than fame,
He speaks – he writes – he breathes not – but for
    THEM.

WHERE'S THE POKER? – A TALE.

The poker lost, poor Susan stormed
And all the rites of rage performed;
As scolding, crying, swearing, sweating,
Abusing, fidgetting and fretting.
'Nothing but villainy and thieving;
Good heavens! What a world we live in!
If I don't find it in the morning,
I'll surely give my master warning.
He'd better far shut up his doors
Than keep such good-for-nothing whores,
For wheresoe'er their trade they drive,
We *vartuous* bodies cannot thrive.'
Well may poor Susan grunt and groan;
Misfortunes never come alone,
But tread each other's heels in throngs –
For the next day she lost the tongs.
The salt-box, cullender and grate,
Soon shared the same untimely fate.
In vain the vails and wages spent
On new ones – for the new ones went.
They'd been (she swore) some dev'l or witch in
To rob and plunder all the kitchen.
One night she to her chamber crept
(Where for a month she had not slept,
Her master being to her seeming
A better playfellow than dreaming).
Curse on the author of these wrongs!

In her own bed she found the tongs.
(Hang Thomas for an idle joker!)
And there, good lack! she found the poker,
With salt-box, pepper-box and kettle,
And all the culinary mettle. –
Be warned, ye fair, by Susan's crosses,
Keep chaste, and guard yourself from losses;
For if young girls delight in kissing,
No wonder, that the poker's missing.

from JUBILATE AGNO

◄ 1. ►

Let Arodi rejoice with the Royston Crow, there is a
    society of them at Trumpington and Cambridge.
For I bless the Lord Jesus from the bottom of
    Royston Cave to the top of King's Chapel.
Let Areli rejoice with the Criel, who is a dwarf that
    towereth above others.
For I am a little fellow, which is entitled to the
    great mess by the benevolence of God my father.
Let Phuvah rejoice with Platycerotes, whose weapons
    of defence keep them innocent.
For I this day made over my inheritance to my
    mother in consideration of her infirmities.
Let Shimron rejoice with the Kite, who is of more
    value than many sparrows.
For I this day made over my inheritance to my
    mother in consideration of her age.
Let Sered rejoice with the Wittal – a silly bird is wise
    unto his own preservation.
For I this day made over my inheritance to my
    mother in consideration of her poverty.
Let Elon rejoice with Attelabus, who is the locust
    without wings.
For I bless the thirteenth of August, in which I had
    the grace to obey the voice of Christ in my
    conscience.

◄ 2. ►

Let Shobi rejoice with the Kastrel – blessed be the
    name JESUS in falconry and in the MALL.
For I blessed God in St James's Park till I routed all
    the the company.
Let Elkanah rejoice with Cymindis – the Lord
    illuminate us against the powers of darkness.
For the officers of the peace are at variance with me,
    and the watchman smites me with his staff.

Let Ziba rejoice with Glottis whose tongue is
wreathed in his throat.
For I am the seed of the WELCH WOMAN and
speak the truth from my heart.

◄ 3. ►

Let The Eunuch rejoice with the Thorn-Back – It is
good to be discovered reading the BIBLE.
For Newton nevertheless is more of error than of
the truth, but I am of the WORD of GOD.

◄ 4. ►

Let Sergius Paulus rejoice with Dentex – Blessed be
the name of Jesus for my teeth.
For the AIR-PUMP weakens and dispirits but cannot
wholly exhaust.

◄ 5. ►

For I will consider my Cat Jeoffrey.
For he is the servant of the Living God duly and
daily serving him.

. . .

For he will not do destruction, if he is well-fed,
neither will he spit without provocation.
For he purrs with thankfulness, when God tells him
he's a good Cat

. . .

For he knows that God is his Saviour.

. . .

For he can spraggle upon waggle at the word of
command.
For he can jump from an eminence into his master's
bosom.
For he can catch the cork and toss it again.

. . .

For by stroking of him I have found out electricity.

◄ 6. ►

Let Hizkijah rejoice with the Dwarf American Sun-
Flower.
For the art of Agriculture is improving.

◄ 7. ►

Let Ross, house of Ross, rejoice with the Great
Flabber Dabber Flat Clapping Fish with hands.
Vide Anson's Voyage and Psalm 98th ix.

. . .

Let Johnson, House of Johnson, rejoice with
Omphalocarpa a type of bur. God be gracious to
Samuel Johnson.

. . .

Let Woodward, House of Woodward, rejoice with
Nerium the Rose-Laurel – God make the
professorship of fossils in Cambridge a useful
thing.

. . .

Let Quarme, House of Quarme, rejoice with
Thyosiris yellow Succory – I pray God bless all my
Subscribers.

◄ 8. ►

For I am come home again, but there is nobody to
kill the calf or to play the music.

THE LONG NOSED FAIR

Once on a time I fair Dorinda kissed,
Whose *nose* was too distinguished to be missed.
My dear, says I, I fain would kiss you closer,
But tho' your lips say *Aye* – your nose says, No, sir.
The maid was equally to fun inclined,
And placed her lovely lilly-hand BEHIND.
Here, swain, she cry'd, may'st thou securely kiss,
Where there's no nose to interrupt thy bliss.

from A SONG TO DAVID

◄ 1 ►

O Thou, that sit'st upon a throne,
With harp of high majestic tone,
   To praise the King of Kings;
And voice of heaven-ascending swell
Which, while its deeper notes excel,
   Clear as a clarion rings:

◄ 2 ►

To bless each valley, grove and coast,
And charm the cherubs to the post
   Of gratitude in throngs;
To keep the days on Zion's mount,
And send the year to his account,
   With dances and with songs:

◄ 3 ►

O servant of God's holiest charge,
The minister of praise at large,

Which thou may 'st now receive;
From thy blest mansion hail and hear,
From topmost eminence appear
   To this the wreath I weave.

<4>
Great, valiant, pious, good, and clean,
Sublime, contemplative, serene,
   Strong, constant, pleasant, wise!
Bright effluence of exceeding grace;
Best man! – the swiftness and the race,
   The peril, and the prize!

<5>
Great – from the lustre of his crown,
From Samuel's horn and God's renown,
   Which is the people's voice;
For all the host, from rear to van,
Applauded and embraced the man –
   The man of God's own choice.

<18>
He sung of God – the mighty source
Of all things – the stupendous force
   On which all strength depends;
From whose right arm, beneath whose eyes,
All period, power, and enterprise
   Commences, reigns, and ends.

<27>
Blest was the tenderness he felt
When to his graceful harp he knelt,
   And did for audience call;
When Satan with his hand he quelled,
And in serene suspense he held
   The frantic throes of Saul.

<49>
O DAVID, highest in the list
Of worthies, on God's ways insist,
   The genuine word repeat:
Vain are the documents of men,
And vain the flourish of the pen
   That keeps the fool's conceit.

<51>
For ADORATION all the ranks
Of angels yield eternal thanks,
   And DAVID in the midst;
With God's good poor, which, last and least
In man's esteem, thou to thy feast,
   O blessed bride-groom, bidst.

<58>
For ADORATION rip'ning canes
And cocoa's purest milk detains
   The western pilgrim's staff;
Where rain in clasping boughs inclosed,
And vines with oranges disposed,
   Embower the social laugh.

<63>
The cheerful holly, pensive yew,
And holy thorn, their trim renew;
   The squirrel hoards his nuts:
All creatures batten o'er their stores,
And careful nature all her doors
   For ADORATION shuts.

<66>
For ADORATION, in the skies,
The Lord's philosopher espies
   The Dog, the Ram, the Rose;
The planet's ring, Orion's sword;
Nor is his greatness less ador'd
   In the vile worm that glows.

<72>
Sweet is the dew that falls betimes,
And drops upon the leafy limes;
   Sweet Hermon's fragrant air:
Sweet is the lily's silver bell,
And sweet the wakeful tapers smell
   That watch for early prayer.

<78>
Beauteous the fleet before the gale;
Beauteous the multitudes in mail,
   Ranked arms and crested heads.
Beauteous the garden's umbrage mild,
Walk, water, meditated wild,
   And all the bloomy beds.

<84>
Glorious the sun in mid career;
Glorious th' assembled fires appear;
   Glorious the comet's train:
Glorious the trumpet and alarm;
Glorious th' almighty stretched-out arm;
   Glorious th' enraptured main.

<85>
Glorious the northern lights astream;
Glorious the song, when God's the theme;

Glorious the thunder's roar:
Glorious hosanna from the den;
Glorious the catholic amen;
    Glorious the martyr's gore.

‹86›

Glorious – more glorious is the crown
Of Him that brought salvation down
    By meekness, called thy Son;
Thou at stupendous truth believed,
And now the matchless deed's atchieved,
    DETERMINED, DARED and DONE.

ON A BED OF GUERNSEY LILIES

‹(Written in September 1763)›

Ye beauties! O how great the sum
    Of sweetness that ye bring;
On what a charity ye come
    To bless the latter spring!
How kind the visit that ye pay,
Like strangers on a rainy day,
    When heartiness despaired of guests:
No neighbour's praise your pride alarms,
No rival flower surveys your charms,
    Or heightens, or contests!

Lo, thro' her works gay nature grieves
    How brief she is and frail,
As ever o'er the falling leaves
    Autumnal winds prevail.
Yet still the philosophic mind
Consolatory food can find,
    And hope her anchorage maintain:
We never are deserted quite;
'Tis by succession of delight
    That love supports his reign.

[EPISTLE TO DR NARES]

Smart sends his compliments and pray'rs,
Health and long life to Dr Nares –
But the chief business of the card
Is 'come to dinner with the bard',
Who makes a mod 'rate share of wit

Put on the pot, and turn the spit.
'Tis said the Indians teach their sons
The use of bows instead of guns,
And, ere the striplings dare to dine,
They shoot their victuals off a pine.
The Public is as kind to me
As to his child a Cherokee;
And, if I chance to hit my aim,
I choose to feast upon the game;
For panegyric or abuse
Shall make the quill procure the goose
With apple-sauce and Durham mustard
And coaling pie o'erlaid with custard.
Pray please to signify with this
My love to Madam, Bob, and Miss,
Likewise to nurse and little Poll,
Whose praise so justly you extol.
P.S.
I have (don't think it a chimera)
Some good sound port and right Madeira.

29: LONG-SUFFERING OF GOD

‹from *Hymns for the Amusement of Children*›

One hundred feet from off the ground
That noble Aloe blows;
But mark ye by what skill profound
His charming grandeur rose.

One hundred years of patient care
The gard'ners did bestow;
Toil and hereditary prayer
Made all this glorious show.

Thus man goes on from year to year,
And bears no fruit at all;
But gracious God, still unsevere,
Bids showers of blessings fall.

The beams of mercy, dews of grace,
Our Saviour still supplies –
Ha! ha! the soul regains her place,
And sweetens all the skies.

[HORACE'S] ODES I, 38: TO HIS SERVANT

◂(He would have him bring nothing for the gracing of his banquet but myrtle.)▸

In the original metre exactly

Persian pomps, boy, ever I renounce them:
Scoff o' the plaited coronet's refulgence;
Seek not in fruitless vigilance the rose-tree's
    Tardier offspring.

Mere honest myrtle, that alone is ordered;
Me the mere myrtle decorates, as also
Thee, the prompt waiter to a jolly toper
    Housed in an arbour.

37: PRAY REMEMBER THE POOR

◂from *Hymns for the Amusement of Children*▸

I just came by the prison-door,
I gave a penny to the poor;
Papa did this good act approve
And poor Mamma cried out for love.

Whene'er the poor comes to my gate,
Relief I will communicate;
And tell my Sire his sons shall be
As charitably great as he.

THE HILLIAD

(lines 61–2)

The chequered world's before thee – go – farewell,
Beware of Irishmen – and learn to spell . . .

Spenser (1552–99) is the first great poet of the English Renaissance. *The Shepheardes Calender* is our earliest important series of pastorals. It owes much to Greek, Latin, Italian and French models. *Mother Hubberds Tale*, in the form of a Chaucerian beast-fable, points the way to the couplet satire of the Augustans.

In *Muiopotmos*, Spenser produced our first mock-heroic poem, in some ways anticipating Pope's *The Rape of The Lock*. His elegy on Philip Sidney, 'Astrophel', points towards the pastoral elegy as exemplified by Milton's *Lycidas* and Shelley's 'Adonais'. In his *Amoretti* and his *Epithalamion*, he shows himself a great love poet.

The Faerie Queene, though unfinished, is an epic poem which synthesizes the English traditions of Chaucer and Langland ('the Pilgrim that the Ploughman playde a whyle') with the italian romantic epic tradition of Ariosto and Tasso. It is also a profound philosophical poem, combining courtly flattery of the Queen with Protestant theology and Renaissance Platonism.

Although Ben Jonson strictured Spenser for writing 'no language', the diction in *The Faerie Queene*, derived from Chaucer, is an attempt to produce something analogous to the epic dialect of Homer; while that of *The Shepheardes Calender*, derived from English vernacular rustic speech, aims to imitate the Doric of Theocritus.

Spenser has been called 'the Poets' Poet' and in fact was a primary influence on such varied successors as Milton, Pope, Wordsworth, Keats, Tennyson and Yeats, among others. For the modern reader, he may at first appear to present difficulties. But as one reads his work, one is continually astonished and delighted by his complexity and variety and (sometimes) by the philosophical profundity of his thought.

Edmund Spenser

The Shepherd's Calendar

‹March›
(lines 61–117)

Thomalin It was upon a holiday,
  When shepherds' grooms han leave to play,
    I cast to go a shooting.
  Long wand'ring up and down the land,
  With bow and bolts in either hand,
    For birds in bushes tooting,
  At length within an ivy tod
  (There shrouded was the little god)
    I heard a busy bustling.
  I bent my bolt against the bush,
  Listening if anything did rush,
    But then heard no more rustling.
  Then, peeping close into the thick,
  Might see the moving of some quick,
    Whose shape appearéd not:
  But were it faery, fiend, or snake,
  My courage yearned it to awake,
    And manfully thereat shot.
  With that sprang forth a naked swain
  With spotted wings, like peacock's train,
    And laughing lope to a tree;
  His gilden quiver at his back,
  And silver bow, which was but slack,
    Which lightly he bent at me.
  That seeing, I levelléd again
  And shot at him with might and main,
    As thick as it had hailed.
  So long I shot, that all was spent;
  Then pumice stones I hastly hent
    And threw; but nought availed:
  He was so wimble and so wight,
  From bough to bough he leppéd light,
    And oft the pumice latched.
  Therewith affrayed, I ran away;
  But he, that erst seemed but to play,
    A shaft in earnest snatched,
  And hit me running in the heel:
  For then I little smart did feel,
    But soon it sore increaséd;
  And now it rankleth more and more,
  And inwardly it fest'reth sore,
    Ne wot I how to cease it.
Wil. Thomalin, I pity thy plight,
  Perdie with Love thou diddest fight;
    I know him by a token;
  For once I heard my father say,
  How he him caught upon a day,

Entangled in a fowling net,
  Which he for carrion crows had set
    That in our pear-tree haunted:
  Then said, he was a wingéd lad,
  But bow and shafts as then none had,
    Else had he sore been daunted.
  But see, the welkin thicks apace,
  And stooping Phœbus steeps his face:
    It's time to haste us homeward.

‹April›
(lines 37–153)

'Ye dainty nymphs, that in this blessed brook
    Do bathe your breast,
  Forsake your wat'ry bowers, and hither look,
    At my request:
  And eke you virgins, that on Parnasse dwell,
  Whence floweth Helicon, the learned well,
    Help me to blaze
    Her worthy praise,
  Which in her sex doth all excel.

'Of fair Elisa be your silver song,
    That blessed wight,
  The flower of virgins: may she flourish long
    In princely plight!
  For she is Syrinx' daughter without spot,
  Which Pam, the shepherds' god, of her begot:
    So sprong her grace
    Of heavenly race,
  No mortal blemish may her blot.

'See, where she sits upon the grassy green,
    (O seemly sight!)
  Yclad in scarlet, like a maiden queen,
    And ermines white:
  Upon her head a cremosin coronet,
  With damask roses and daffadillies set:
    Bay leaves between,
    And primroses green
    Embellish the sweet violet.

'Tell me, have ye seen her angelic face,
    Like Phœbe fair?
  Her heavenly 'haviour, her princely grace,
    Can you well compare?
  The red rose medled with the white yfere,
  In either cheek depeincten lively cheer:
    Her modest eye,
    Her majesty,
  Where have you seen the like but there?

'I saw Phœbus thrust out his golden head,
    Upon her to gaze:
But, when he saw how broad her beams did spread,
    It did him amaze.
He blushed to see another sun below,
Ne durst again his fiery face out show:
    Let him, if he dare,
    His brightness compare
With hers, to have the overthrow.

'Shew thyself, Cynthia, with thy silver rays,
    And be not abasht;
When she the beams of her beauty displays,
    O, how art thou dasht!
But I will not match her with Latona's seed,
Such folly great sorrow to Niobe did breed:
    Now she is a stone,
    And makes daily moan,
Warning all other to take heed.

'Pan may be proud that ever he begot,
    Such a bellibone;
And Syrinx rejoice that ever was her lot
    To bear such an one.
Soon as my younglings crien for the dam
To her will I offer a milkwhite lamb:
    She is my goddess plain,
    And I her shepherd's swain,
Albe forswonk and forswat I am.

'I see Calliope speed her to the place,
    Where my goddess shines;
And after her the other Muses trace,
    With their violines.
Bene they not bay branches which they do bear,
All for Elisa in her hand to wear?
    So sweetly they play,
    And sing all the way,
That it a heaven is to hear.

'Lo! how finely the Graces can it foot
    To the instrument:
They dancen deffly, and singen soot,
    In their merriment,
Wants not a fourth Grace, to make the dance even?
Let that room to my lady be yeven:
    She shall be a Grace,
    To fill the fourth place,
And reign with the rest in heaven.

'And whither runs this bevy of ladies bright,
    Ranged in a row?
They bene all Ladies of the Lake behight,
    That unto her go.
Chloris, that is the chiefest nymph of all,
Of olive branches bears a coronal:
    Olives bene for peace,
    When wars do surcease:
Such for a princess bene principal.

'Ye shepherds' daughters, that dwell on the green,
    Hie you there apace:
Let none come there but that virgins bene,
    To adorn her grace:
And when you come, whereas she is in place,
See that your rudeness do not you disgrace:
    Bind your fillets fast,
    And gird in your waist,
For more finnesse, with a tawdry lace.

'Bring hither the pink and purple columbine,
    With gillyflowers;
Bring coronations, and sops in wine,
    Worn of paramours:
Strow me the ground with daffadowndillies,
And cowslips, and kingcups, and lovéd lilies:
    The pretty paunce,
    And the chevisaunce,
Shall match with the fair flower-de-lis.

'Now rise up, Elisa, deckéd as thou art
    In royal array;
And now ye dainty damsels may depart
    Each one her way.
I fear I have troubléd your troops too long:
Let dame Elisa thank you for her song:
    And if you come hether
    When damsons I gether,
I will part them all you among.'

◄ December ►

(lines 19–72)

'Whilom in youth, when flowered my joyful spring,
Like swallow swift I wand'red here and there:
For heat of heedless lust me so did sting,
That I of doubted danger had no fear:
    I went the wasteful woods and forest wide,
    Withouten dread of wolves to bene espied.

'I wont to range amid the mazy thicket,
And gather nuts to make me Christmas game,
And joyéd oft to chase the trembling pricket,
Or hunt the heartless hare till she were tame.
    What reckéd I of wintry age's waste? –
    Then deeméd I my spring would ever last.

'How often have I scaled the craggy oak,
All to dislodge the raven of her nest?
How have I weariéd with many a stroke
The stately walnut-tree, the while the rest
    Under the tree fell all for nuts at strife?
    For ylike to me was liberty and life.

'And for I was in thilk same looser years,
(Whether the Muse so wrought me from my birth,
Or I too much believed my shepherd peers,)
Somedeal ybent to song and music's mirth,
    A good old shepherd, Wrenock was his name,
    Made me by art more cunning in the same.

'From thence I durst in derring-do compare
With shepherd's swain whatever fed in field;
And, if that Hobbinol right judgement bear,
To Pan his own self pipe I need not yield:
    For, if the flocking nymphs did follow Pan,
    The wiser Muses after Colin ran.

'But, ah! such pride at length was ill repaid:
The shepherds' god (perdie god was he none)
My hurtless pleasance did me ill upbraid;
My freedom lorn, my life he left to moan:
    Love they him called that gave me checkmate.
    But better mought they have behote him Hate.

'Then gan my lovely spring bid me farewell,
And summer season sped him to display
(For love then in the Lion's house did dwell)
The raging fire that kindled at his ray.
    A comet stirred up that unkindly heat,
    That reignéd (as men said) in Venus' seat.

'Forth was I led, not as I wont afore,
When choice I had to choose my wand'ring way,
But whither luck and love's unbridled lore
Would lead me forth on Fancy's bit to play:
    The bush my bed, the bramble was my bower,
    The woods can witness many a woeful stour.

'Where I was wont to seek the honey bee,
Working her formal rooms in waxen frame,

The grisly toad-stool grown there mought I see,
And loathéd paddocks lording on the same:
    And where the chanting birds lulled me asleep,
    The ghastly owl her grievous inn doth keep.

AMORETTI

◄ LXVIII ►

Most glorious Lord of life! that, on this day,
Didst make Thy triumph over death and sin;
And, having harrowed hell, didst bring away
Captivity thence captive, us to win:
This joyous day, dear Lord, with joy begin;
And grant that we, for whom Thou diddest die,
Being with Thy dear blood clean washed from sin,
May live for ever in felicity!
And that Thy love we weighing worthily,
May likewise love Thee for the same again:
And for Thy sake, that all like dear didst buy,
With love may one another entertain!
    So let us love, dear love, like as we ought:
    Love is the lesson which the Lord us taught.

EPITHALAMION

Ye learned sisters, which have oftentimes
Been to me aiding, others to adorn,
Whom ye thought worthy of your graceful rhymes
That even the greatest did not greatly scorn
To hear their names sung in your simple lays,
But joyéd in their praise;
And when ye list your own mishaps to mourn,
Which death. or love, or fortune's wreck did raise,
Your string could soon to sadder tenor turn,
And teach the woods and waters to lament
Your doleful dreariment.
Now lay those sorrowful complaints aside,
And having ail your heads with girlands crowned,
Help me mine own love's praises to resound;
Ne let the same of any be envide:
So Orpheus did for his own bride!
So I unto myself alone will sing
The woods shall to me answer, and my echo ring.

Early, before the world's light-giving lamp
His golden beam upon the hills doth spread.
Having dispersed the night's uncheerful damp,
Do ye awake: and with fresh lustihead
Go to the bower of my belovéd love,
My truest turtle-dove,
Bid her awake: for Hymen is awake,
And long since ready forth his mask to move,
With his bright tead that flames with many a flake,
And many a bachelor to wait on him,
In their fresh garments trim.
Bid her awake therefore, and soon her dight,
For lo! the wishéd day is come at last,
That shall, for all the pains and sorrows past,
Pay to her usury of long delight:
And whilst she doth her dight,
Do ye to her of joy and solace sing,
That all the woods may answer, and your echo ring.

Bring with you all the nymphs that you can hear
Both of the rivers and the forests green,
And of the sea that neighbours to her near:
All with gay girlands goodly well beseen,
And let them also with them bring in hand
Another gay girland,
For my fair love, of lilies and of roses,
Bound true-love wise, with a blue silk riband.
And let them make great store of bridal posies,
And let them eke bring store of other flowers,
To deck the bridal bowers.
And let the ground whereas her foot shall tread,
For fear the stones her tender foot should wrong,
Be strewed with fragrant flowers all along,
And diap'red like the discoloured mead.
Which done, do at her chamber door await,
For she will waken straight;
The whiles do ye this song unto her sing,
The woods shall to you answer, and your echo ring.

Ye nymphs of Mulla, which with careful heed
The silver scaly trouts do tend full well,
And greedy pikes which use therein to feed
(Those trouts and pikes all others do excel);
And ye likewise, which keep the rushy lake,
Where none do fishes take:
Bind up the locks the which hang scattered light,
And in his waters, which your mirror make,
Behold your faces as the crystal bright,
That when you come whereas my love doth lie,
No blemish she may spy.
And eke, ye lightfoot maids, which keep the deer,

That on the hoary mountain used to tower;
And the wild wolves, which seek them to devour,
With your steel darts do chase from coming near;
Be also present here,
To help to deck her, and to help to sing,
That all the woods may answer, and your echo ring.

Wake now, my love, awake! for it is time;
The rosy Morn long since left Tithone's bed,
All ready to her silver coach to climb;
And Phœbus gins to shew his glorious head.
Hark! how the cheerful birds do chant their lays
And carol of Love's praise.
The merry lark her matins sings aloft;
The thrush replies; the mavis descant plays:
The ouzel shrills, the ruddock warbles soft;
So goodly all agree, with sweet consent,
To this day's merriment.
Ah! my dear love, why do ye sleep thus long,
When meeter were that ye should now awake,
T' await the coming of your joyous make,
And hearken to the birds' love-learnd song,
The dewy leaves among!
For they of joy and pleasance to you sing,
That all the woods them answer, and their echo ring.

My love is now awake out of her dreams,
And her fair eyes, like stars that dimméd were
With darksome cloud, now shew their goodly beams
More bright than Hesperus his head doth rear.
Come now, ye damsels, daughters of delight,
Help quickly her to dight:
But first come, ye fair hours, which were begot
In Jove's sweet paradise of Day and Night;
Which do the seasons of the year allot,
And all, that ever in this world is fair,
Do make and still repair:
And ye three handmaids of the Cyprian Queen,
The which do still adorn her beauty's pride,
Help to adorn my beautifullest bride:
And, as ye her array, still throw between
Some graces to be seen;
And, as ye use to Venus, to her sing,
The whiles the woods shall answer, and your echo
    ring.

Now is my love all ready forth to come:
Let all the virgins therefore well await:
And ye fresh boys, that tend upon her groom,
Prepare yourselves, for he is coming straight.
Set all your things in seemly good array,

Fit for so joyful day:
The joyfull'st day that ever sun did see.
Fair sun! shew forth thy favourable ray,
And let thy lifeful heat not fervent be,
For fear of burning her sunshiny face,
Her beauty to disgrace.
O fairest Phœbus! father of the Muse!
If ever I did honour thee aright,
Or sing the thing that mote thy mind delight,
But let this day, let this one day, be mine;
Let all the rest be thine.
Then I thy sovereign praises loud will sing,
That all the woods shall answer, and their echo ring.

Hark: how the minstrels gin to shrill aloud
Their merry music that resounds from far,
The pipe, the tabor, and the trembling croud,
That well agree withouten breach or jar.
But, most of all, the damsels do delight
When they their timbrels smite,
And thereunto do dance and carol sweet,
That all the senses they do ravish quite;
The whiles the boys run up and down the street,
Crying aloud with strong confuséd noise,
As if it were one voice,
Hymen, to Hymen, Hymen, they do shout;
Doth reach, and all the firmament doth fill;
To which the people standing all about,
As in approvance, do thereto applaud,
And loud advance her laud;
And evermore they Hymen, Hymen sing,
That all the woods them answer, and their echo
   ring.

Lo! where she comes along with portly pace,
Like Phœbe, from her chamber of the east,
Arising forth to run her mighty race,
Clad all in white, that 'seems a virgin best.
So well it her beseems, that ye would ween
Some angel she had been.
Her long loose yellow locks like golden wire,
Sprinkled with pearl, and purling flowers atween,
Do like a golden mantle her attire;
And, being crownéd with a girland green,
Seem like some maiden queen.
Her modest eyes, abashéd to behold
So many gazers as on her do stare,
Upon the lowly ground affixéd are;
Ne dare lift up her countenance too bold,
But blush to hear her praises sung so loud,
So far from being proud.

Nathless do ye still loud her praises sing,
That all the woods may answer, and your echo ring.

Tell me, ye merchants' daughters, did ye see
So fair a creature in your town before;
So sweet, so lovely, and so mild as she,
Adorned with beauty's grace and virtue's store?
Her goodly eyes like sapphires shining bright,
Her forehead ivory white,
Her cheeks like apples which the sun hath rudded,
Her lips like cherries charming men to bite,
Her breast like to a bowl of cream uncrudded,
Her paps like lilies budded,
Her snowy neck like to a marble tower;
And all her body like a palace fair,
Ascending up, with many a stately stair,
To honour's seat and chastity's sweet bower.
Why stand ye still, ye virgins, in amaze,
Upon her so to gaze,
Whiles ye forget your former lay to sing,
To which the woods did answer, and your echo
   ring?

But if ye saw that which no eyes can see,
The inward beauty of her lively sprite,
Garnisht with heavenly gifts of high degree,
Much more then would ye wonder at that sight,
And stand astonisht like to those which read
Medusa's mazeful head.
There dwells sweet love, and constant chastity,
Unspotted faith, and comely womanhood,
Regard of honour, and mild modesty,
There virtue reigns as queen in royal throne,
And giveth laws alone,
The which the base affections do obey
And yield their services unto her will;
Ne thought of thing uncomely ever may
Thereto approach to tempt her mind to ill.
Had ye once seen these her celestial treasures.
And unrevealéd pleasures,
Then would ye wonder, and her praises sing,
That all the woods should answer, and your echo
   ring

Open the temple gates unto my love,
Open them wide that she may enter in,
And all the posts adorn as doth behove,
And all the pillars deck with girlands trim,
For to receive this saint with honour due,
That cometh in to you.
With trembling steps, and humble reverence,

She cometh in, before th' Almighty's view;
Of her ye virgins learn obedience,
When so ye come into those holy places,
To humble your proud faces:
Bring her up to th' high altar, that she may
The sacred ceremonies there partake,
The which do endless matrimony make;
And let the roaring organs loudly play
The praises of the Lord in lively notes;
The whiles, with hollow throats,
The choristers the joyous anthem sing,
That all the woods may answer, and their echo ring.

Behold, whiles she before the altar stands,
Hearing the holy priest that to her speaks,
And blesseth her with his two happy hands,
How the red roses flush up in her cheeks,
And the pure snow, with goodly vermeil stain
Like crimson dyed in grain:
That even th' angels, which continually,
About the sacred altar do remain,
Forget their service and about her fly,
Oft peeping in her face, that seems more fair
The more they on it stare.
But her sad eyes, still fastened on the ground,
Are governéd with goodly modesty,
That suffers not one look to glance awry,
Which may let in a little thought unsound.
Why blush ye, love, to give to me your hand,
The pledge of all our band!
Sing, ye sweet angels, Alleluia sing.
That all the woods may answer, and your echo ring.

Now all is done: bring home the bride again;
Bring home the triumph of our victory:
Bring home with you the glory of her gain,
With joyance bring her and with jollity.
Never had man more joyful day than this,
Whom heaven would heap with bliss.
Make feast therefore now all this livelong day;
This day for ever to me holy is.
Pour out the wine without restraint or stay,
Pour not by cups, but by the bellyful.
Pour out to all that wull,
And sprinkle all the posts and walls with wine,
That they may sweat, and drunken be withal.
Crown ye God Bacchus with a coronal,
And Hymen also crown with wreaths of vine;
And let the Graces dance unto the rest.
For they can do it best:
The whiles the maidens do their carol sing,

To which the woods shall answer, and their echo
ring.

Ring ye the bells, ye young men of the town,
And leave your wonted labours for this day:
This day is holy; do ye write it down,
That ye for ever it remember may.
This day the sun is in his chiefest height,
With Barnaby the bright,
From whence declining daily by degrees,
He somewhat loseth of his heat and light,
When once the Crab behind his back he sees.
But for this time it ill ordainéd was,
To choose the longest day in all the year,
And shortest night, when longest fitter were:
Yet never day so long, but late would pass.
Ring ye the bells, to make it wear away,
And bonfires make all day;
And dance about them, and about them sing,
That all the woods may answer, and your echo ring.

Ah! when will this long weary day have end,
And lend me leave to come unto my love?
How slowly do the hours their numbers spend!
How slowly does sad Time his feathers move!
Haste thee, O fairest planet, to thy home,
Within the western foam:
Thy tired steeds long since have need of rest.
Long though it be, at last I see it gloom,
And the bright evening star with golden crest
Appear out of the east.
Fair child of beauty! glorious lamp of love!
That all the host of heaven in ranks dost lead,
And guidest lovers through the night's sad dread,
How cheerfully thou lookest from above,
And seem'st to laugh atween thy twinkling light,
As joying in the sight
Of these glad many, which for joy do sing,
That all the woods them answer, and their echo ring!

Now cease, ye damsels, your delights forepast;
Enough it is that all the day was yours;
Now day is done, and night is nighing fast,
Now bring the bride into the bridal bowers.
The night is come, now soon her disarray,
And in her bed her lay;
Lay her in lilies and in violets,
And silken curtains over her display.
And odoured sheets, and arras coverlets.
Behold how goodly my fair love does lie,
In proud humility!

Like unto Maia, whenas Jove her took
In Tempe, lying on the flow'ry grass,
'Twixt sleep and wake, after she weary was,
With bathing in the Acidalian brook.
Now it is night, ye damsels may be gone,
And leave my love alone,
And leave likewise your former lay to sing:
The woods no more shall answer, nor your echo ring.

Now welcome, night! thou night so long expected,
That long day's labour dost at last defray,
And all my cares, which cruel Love collected,
Hast summed in one, and cancelléd for aye:
Spread thy broad wing over my love and me,
That no man may us see;
And in thy sable mantle us enwrap,
From fear of peril and foul horror free.
Let no false treason seek us to entrap,
Nor any dread disquiet once annoy
The safety of our joy;
But let the night be calm, and quietsome,
Without tempestuous storms or sad affray:
Like as when Jove with fair Alcmena lay,
When he begot the great Tirynthian groom
Or like as when he with thyself did lie
And begot Majesty.
And let the maids and young men cease to sing,
Ne let the woods them answer, nor their echo ring.

Let no lamenting cries, nor doleful tears,
Be heard all night within, nor yet without:
Ne let false whispers, breeding hidden fears,
Break gentle sleep with misconceivéd doubt.
Let no deluding dreams, nor dreadful sights,
Make sudden sad affrights;
Ne let house-fires, nor lightning's helpless harms,
Ne let the Pouke, nor other evil sprites,
Ne let mischievous witches with their charms,
Ne let hobgoblins, names whose sense we see not,
Fray us with things that be not:
Let not the shriek-owl nor the stork be heard,
Nor the night-raven, that still deadly yells;
Nor damnéd ghosts, called up with mighty spells,
Nor grisly vultures, make us once afeard:
Ne let th' unpleasant quire of frogs still croaking
Make us to wish their choking.
Let none of these their dreary accents sing;
Ne let the woods them answer, nor their echo ring.

But let still silence true night-watches keep,
That sacred peace may in assurance reign,

And timely sleep, when it is time to sleep,
May pour his limbs forth on your pleasant plain;
The whiles an hundred little wingéd loves,
Like divers-feathered doves,
Shall fly and flutter round about your bed,
And in the secret dark, that none reproves,
Their pretty stealths shall work, and snares shall
  spread
To filch away sweet snatches of delight,
Concealed through covert night.
Ye sons of Venus, play your sports at will!
For greedy pleasure, careless of your toys,
Thinks more upon her paradise of joys,
Than what ye do, albeit good or ill.
All night therefore attend your merry play,
For it will soon be day:
Now none doth hinder you, that say or sing;
Ne will the woods now answer, nor your echo ring.

Who is the same, which at my window peeps?
Or whose is that fair face that shines so bright?
Is it not Cynthia, she that never sleeps,
But walks about high heaven all the night?
O! fairest goddess. do thou not envý
My love with me to spy:
For thou likewise didst love, though now unthought,
And for a fleece of wool, which privily
The Latmian shepherd once unto thee brought,
Therefore to us be favourable now;
And sith of women's labours thou best charge,
And generation goodly cost enlarge,
Incline thy will t' effect our wishful vow,
And the chaste womb inform with timely seed,
That may our comfort breed:
Till which we cease our hopeful hap to sing;
Ne let the woods us answer, nor our echo ring.

And thou, great Juno! which with awful might
The laws of wedlock still dost patronize;
And the religion of the faith first plight
With sacred rites hast taught to solemnize;
And eke for comfort often calléd art
Of women in their smart;
Eternally bind thou this lovely band,
And all thy blessings unto us impart.
And thou, glad Genius! in whose gentle hand
The bridal bower and genial bed remain,
Without blemish or stain:
And the sweet pleasures of their love's delight
With secret aid dost succour and supply,
Till they bring forth the fruitful progeny;

Send us the timely fruit of this same night.
And thou fair Hebe! and thou, Hymen free!
Grant that it may so be.
Till which we cease your further praise to sing;
Ne any woods shall answer, nor your echo ring.

And ye high heavens, the temple of the gods,
In which a thousand torches flaming bright
Do burn, that to us wretched earthly clods
In dreadful darkness lend desiréd light;
And all ye powers which in the same remain,
More than we men can feign,
Pour out your blessing on us plenteously,
And happy influence upon us rain,
That we may raise a large posterity,
Which from the earth, which they may long possess
With lasting happiness,
Up to your haughty palaces may mount;
And, for the guerdon of their glorious merit,
May heavenly tabernacles there inherit,
Of blessed saints for to increase the count.
So let us rest, sweet love, in hope of this,
And cease till then our timely joys to sing;
The woods no more us answer, nor our echo ring!

Song I made in lieu of many ornaments,
With which my love should duly have been deckt,
Which cutting off through hasty accidents,
Ye could not stay your due time to expect,
But promised both to recompense;
Be unto her a goodly ornament,
And for short time an endless monument.

❧

The Faerie Queene

‹Book I: Canto I›

‹I›
A gentle knight was pricking on the plaine.
Y cladd in mightie armes and silver shielde,
Wherein old dints of deepe wounds did remaine,
The cruel markes of many a bloudy fielde;
Yet armes till that time did he never wield:
His angry steede did chide his foming bitt,
As much disdayning to the curbe to yield:
Full jolly knight he seemd, and faire did sit,
As one for knightly jousts and fierce encounters fitt.

‹II›
But on his brest a bloudie Crosse he bore,
The deare remembrance of his dying Lord,
For whose sweet sake that glorious badge he wore,
And dead as living ever him ador'd:
Upon his shield the like was also scor'd,
For soveraine hope, which in his helpe he had:
Right faithful true he was in deed and word,
But of his cheere did seeme too solemne sad;
Yet nothing did he dread, but ever was ydrad.

‹III›
Upon a great adventure he was bond,
That greatest Gloriana to him gave,
That greatest glorious Queen of Faerie lond,
To winne him worship, and her grace to have,
Which of all earthly things he most did crave;
And ever as he rode, his hart did yearne
To prove his puissance in battell brave
Upon his foe, and his new force to learne;
Upon his foe, a dragon horrible and stern.

‹Book I: Canto IX›

‹XXXVIII›
'What franticke fit,' (quoth he) 'hath thus distraught
Thee, foolish man, so rash a doome to give?
What justice ever other judgement taught,
But he should dye who merites not to live?
None els to death this man despayring drive
But his owne guiltie mind, deserving death.
Is then unjust to each his dew to give?
Or let him dye, that loatheth living breath?
Or let him die at ease, that liveth here uneath?

‹Book I: Canto IX›

‹XXXIX›
'Who travailes by the wearie wandring way,
To come unto his wished home in haste,
And meetes a flood that doth his passage stay,
Is not great grace to helpe him over past,
Or free his feet that in the myre sticke fast?
Most envious man, that grieves at neighbours good;
And fond, that joyest in the woe thou hast!
Why wilt not let him passe, that long hath stood
Upon the bancke, yet wilt thy selfe not pas the
    flood?

‹ Book II: Canto VII ›

‹ XLVI ›

There, as in glistring glory she did sitt,
She held a great gold chaine ylincked well,
Whose upper end to highest heven was knitt
And lower part did reach to lowest Hell;
And all that preace did rownd about her swell
To catchen hold of that long chaine, thereby
To climbe aloft, and others to excell:
That was Ambition, rash desire to sty,
And every linck thereof a step of dignity.

‹ XLVII ›

Some thought to raise themselves to high degree
By riches and unrighteous reward;
Some by close shouldring; some by flatteree:
Others through friendes; others for base regard,
And all by wrong waies for themselves prepard:
Those that were up themselves kept others low;
Those that were low themselves held others hard,
Ne suffred them to ryse or greater grow;
But every one did strive his fellow downe to throw.

‹ Book II: Canto VIII ›

‹ I ›

And is there care in heaven? And is there love
In heavenly spirits to these creatures bace
That may compassion of their evilles move?
There is: else much more wretched were the cace
Of men then beasts. But O! th' exceeding grace
Of highest God that loves his creatures so,
And all his workes with mercy doth embrace,
That blessed Angels he sends to and fro,
To serve to wicked man, to sense his wicked foe.

‹ II ›

How oft do they their silver bowers leave,
To come to succour us that succour want!
How oft do they with golden pineons cleave
The flitting skyes, like flying Pursuivant,
Against fowle feendes to ayd us militant!
They for us fight, they watch and dewly ward,
And their bright Squadrons round about us plant;
And all for love, and nothing for reward.
O! why should hevenly God to men have such
    regard?

‹ Book III: Canto VI ›

‹ XXXI ›

It sited was in fruitfull soyle of old,
And girt in with two walls on either side;
The one of yron, the other of bright gold,
That none might thorough breake, nor overstride:
And double gates it had which opened wide,
By which both in and out men moten pas:
Th' one faire and fresh, the other old and dride.
Old Genius the porter of them was,
Old Genius, the which a double nature has.

‹ XXXII ›

He letteth in, he letteth out to wend
All that to come into the world desire:
A thousand thousand naked babes attend
About him day and night, which doe require
That he with fleshly weeds would them attire:
Such as him list, such as eternall fate
Ordained hath, he clothes with sinfull mire,
And sendeth forth to live in mortall state,
Till they agayn returne backe by the hinder gate,

‹ XXXIII ›

After that they againe retourned beene,
They in that Gardin planted bee agayne,
And grow afresh, as they had never seene
Fleshly corruption, nor mortall payne.
Some thousand yeares so doen they there remayne,
And then of him are clad with other hew,
Or sent into the chaungefull world agayne,
Till thither they retourne where first they grew:
So, like a wheele, arownd they ronne from old to
    new.

‹ Book IV: Canto X ›

‹ XLIV ›

'"Great Venus! Queene of beautie and of grace,
The joy of Gods and men, that under skie
Doest fayrest shine, and most adorne thy place;
That with thy smyling looke doest peaifie
The raging seas, and makst the stormes to flie;
Thee, goddesse, thee the winds, the clouds doe
    feare,
And, when thou spredst thy mantle forth on hie,
The waters play, and pleasant lands appeare,
And heavens laugh, and al the world shews joyous
    cheare.

‹XLV›

'"Then doth the dædale earth throw forth to thee
Out of her fruitfull lap aboundant flowres;
And then all living wights, soone as they see
The spring breake forth out of his lusty bowers,
They all doe learne to play the Paramours;
First doe the merry birds, thy prety pages,
Privily pricked with thy lustfull powres,
Chirpe loud to thee out of their leavy cages,
And thee their mother call to coole their kindly rages.

‹XLVI›

'"Then doe the salvage beasts begin to play
Their pleasant friskes, and loath their wonted food:
The Lyons rore; the Tygres loudly bray;
The raging Buls rebellow through the wood,
And breaking forth dare tempt the deepest flood
To come where thou doest draw them with desire.
So all things else, that nourish vitall blood,
Soone as with fury thou doest them inspire,
In generation seeke to quench their inward fire.

‹Book VI: Canto X›

‹XII›

All they without were raunged in a ring,
And daunced round; but in the midst of them
Three other Ladies did both daunce and sing,
The whilest the rest them round about did hemme,
And like a girlond did in compasse stemme:
And in the middest of those same three was placed
Another Damzell, as a precious gemme
Amidst a ring most richly well enchaced,
That with her goodly presence all the rest much
    graced.

‹XIV›

Such was the beauty of this goodly band,
Whose sundry parts were here too long to tell;
But she that in the midst of them did stand
Seem'd all the rest in beauty to excell,
Crownd with a rosie girlond that right well
Did her beseeme: And ever, as the crew
About her daunst, sweet flowres that far did smell
And fragrant odours they uppon her threw;
But most of all those three did her with gifts endew.

‹XV›

Those were the Graces, daughters of delight,
Handmaides of Venus, which are wont to haunt
Uppon this hill, and daunce there day and night:

Those three to men all gifts of grace do graunt;
And all that Venus in her selfe doth vaunt
Is borrowed of them. But that faire one,
That in the midst was placed paravaunt,
Was she to whom that shepheard pypt alone;
That made him pipe so merrily, as never none.

‹XVI›

She was, to weete, that jolly Shepheards lasse,
Which piped there unto that merry rout;
That jolly shepheard, which there piped, was
Poore Colin Clout, (who knowes not Colin Clout?)
He pypt apace, whilest they him daunst about.
Pype, jolly shepheard, pype thou now apace
Unto thy love that made thee low to lout:
Thy love is present there with thee in place;
Thy love is there advaunst to be another Grace.

Much of the poetry of R. L. Stevenson (1850–94) is so filled with death that people feel it is safer left to their children. However it holds many rewards for the brave adult, not least among these the *après vu*, prequel trailers for Housman, Yeats, even Eliot and Beckett. Yet Stevenson himself remained diffident about his poetry, writing to Mrs Sitwell that he had 'the poetic character and no poetic talent', and later to Henley, 'I am a weak brother in verse.' I believe that even the following short selection demonstrates how powerful a brother poet he could really be.

Stevenson certainly prepared himself; 'in my innumerable gouty-footed lyrics I followed many masters'. He loved Horace, Martial and Herrick, but translated Baudelaire and Heine, and retained a snooty enthusiasm for raw Walt Whitman. In his essay on Whitman he declared 'style is the essence of thinking', which relates to his idea that he wrote narrative before poetry or fiction – Alastair Gray reminds us that poetry isn't a form of writing but a form of speech. In such interests he wrote in French sometimes, in English usually and never better than in Scots. Scots was spoken in the Edinburgh of his youth, and he broadened his with Lothians speech, particularly from the shepherd John Todd in summers spent in Swanston. He called it 'that very dark oracular medium', which it is in his terrifying short story 'Thrawn Janet', but here in his poetry it handles lyric and satirical themes, often written to tunes in the manner of Burns. It is notable how free his Scots octosyllabics are in comparison with those he wrote in English, where playfulness is carried inside a more rigid form. This can give his English verse a po-faced, subversive quality which was much imitated, not least by Belloc and 'Saki'. Yet 'Light foot...' is affecting as anything Stevenson wrote.

It is one of the purposes of anthologies to inspire an interest in their omissions, and that is my hope for this selection of Stevenson. The choice is personal, not representative; if you don't like it go to the original.

'WHEN AINCE APRILE HAS FAIRLY COME ...'

When aince Aprile has fairly come,
An' birds may bigg in winter's lum,
An' pleasure's spreid for a' and some
    O' whatna state,
Love, wi' her auld recruitin' drum,
    Than taks the gate.

The heart plays dunt wi' main an' micht;
The lasses' een are a' sae bricht,
Their dresses are sae braw an' ticht,
    The bonny birdies! –
Puir winter virtue at the sicht
    Gangs heels ower hurdies.

An' aye as love frae land to land
Tirls the drum wi' eident hand,
A' men collect at her command,
    Toun-bred or land 'art,
An' follow in a denty band
    Her gaucy standart.

An' I, wha sang o' rain an' snaw,
An' weary winter weel awa',
Noo busk me in a jacket braw,
    An' tak my place
I' the ram-stam, harum-scarum raw,
    Wi' smilin' face.

Glossary

BIGG: build; LUM: chimney; RAM-STAM: headstrong, reckless

THE CELESTIAL SURGEON

If I have faltered more or less
In my great task of happiness;
If I have moved among my race
And shown no glorious morning face;
If beams from happy human eyes
Have moved me not; if morning skies,
Books, and my food, and summer rain
Knocked on my sullen heart in vain –
Lord, thy most pointed pleasure take
And stab my spirit broad awake;

Or, Lord, if too obdurate I,
Choose thou, before that spirit die,
A piercing pain, a killing sin,
And to my dead heart run them in!

THE SPAEWIFE

O, I wad like to ken – to the beggar-wife says I –
Why chops are guid to brander and nane sae guid to
    fry.
An' siller, that's see braw to keep, is brawer still to gie.
– It's *gey an' easy speirin'*, says the beggar-wife to me.

O, I wad like to ken – to the beggar-wife says I –
Hoo a' things come to be whaur we find them when
    we try,
The lasses in their claes an' the fishes in the sea.
– It's *gey an' easy speirin'*, says the beggar-wife to me.

O, I wad like to ken – to the beggar-wife says I –
Why lads are a' to sell an' lasses a' to buy;
An' naebody for dacency but barely twa or three
– It's *gey an' easy speirin'*, says the beggar-wife to me.

O, I wad like to ken – to the beggar-wife says I –
Gin death as shure to men as killin' is to kye,
Why God has filled the yearth sae fu' o' tasty things to
    pree.
– It's *gey an' easy speirin'*, says the beggar-wife to me.

O, I wad like to ken – to the beggar-wife says I –
The reason o' the cause an' the wherefore o' the why,
Wi' mony anither riddle brings the tear into my e'e.
– It's *gey an' easy speirin'*, says the beggar-wife to me.

Glossary

SPAEWIFE: wisewoman; GEY AN': very; SPEIRIN': asking

NOT I

Some like drink
In a pint pot,

Some like to think;
    Some not.

Strong Dutch cheese,
Old Kentucky Rye,
Some like these:
    Not I.

Some like Poe
And others like Scott,
Some like Mrs. Stowe;
    Some not.

Some like to laugh,
Some like to cry.
Some like chaff;
    Not I.

TRAVEL
(lines 1–12)

I should like to rise and go
Where the golden apples grow;
Where below another sky
Parrot islands anchored lie,
And, watched by cockatoos and goats,
Lonely Crusoes building boats;.
Where in sunshine reaching out
Eastern cities, miles about,
Are with mosque and minaret
Among sandy gardens set,
And the rich goods from near and far
Hang for sale in the bazaar ...

A MILE AN' A BITTOCK

A mile an' a bittock, a mile or twa,
Abune the burn, ayont the law
Davie an' Donal' an' Cherlie an' a',
    An' the mune was shinin' clearly!

Ane went hame wi' the ither, an' then
The ither went hame wi' the ither twa men,
An' baith wad return him the service again,
    An' the mune was shinin' clearly!

The clocks were chappin' in house an' ha',
Eleeven, twal' an' ane an' twa;
An' the guidman's face was turns to the wa',
    An' the mune was shinin' clearly!

A wind got up frae affa the sea,
It blew the stars as clear's could be,
It blew in the een of a' o' the three,
    An' the mune was shinin' clearly!

Noo, Davie was first to get sleep in his head,
'The best o' frien's maun twine,' he said;
'I'm weariet, an' here I'm awe' to my bed.'
    An' the mune was shinin' clearly!

Twa o' them walkin' an' crackin' their lane,
The mornin' licht came grey an' plain,
An' the birds they yammert on stick an' stane,
    An' the mune was shinin' clearly!

O years ayont, O years awa',
My lads, ye'll mind whate'er befa' –
My lads, ye'll mind on the bield o' the law
    When the mune was shinin' clearly.

Glossary

LAW: hill; YAMMERT sang; BIELD: shelter

from EPITAPHS

◄ II ►

The angler rose, he took his rod,
He kneeled and made his prayers to God.
The living God sat overhead:
The angler tripped, the eels were fed.

from MORAL EMBLEMS

◄ III ►

The Abbot for a walk went out
A wealthy cleric, very stout,
And Robin has that Abbot stuck
As the red hunter spears the buck.

The djavel or the javelin
Has, you observe, gone bravely in,
And you may hear that weapon whack
Bang through the middle of his back.
Hence we may learn that abbots should
Never go walking in a wood.

THE SCOTSMAN'S RETURN FROM ABROAD

In mony a foreign pairs I've been,
An' mony an unco ferlie seen,
Since, Mr. Johnstone, you and I
Last walkit upon Cocklerye.
Wi' gleg, observant een, I pass't
By sea an' land, through East an' Wast,
And still in ilka age an' station
Saw naething but abomination.
In thir uncovenantit lands
The gangrel Scot uplifts his hands
At lack of a' sectarian fush'n,
An' cauld religious destitution.
He rins, puir man, frae place to place,
Tries a' their graceless means o' grace,
Preacher on preacher, kirk on kirk –
This yin a stot an' thon a stirk –
A bletherin' clan, no warth a preen,
As bad as Smith of Aiberdeen!

At last, across the weary faem,
Frae far, outlandish pairts I came.
On ilka side o' me I fand
Fresh tokens o' my native land.
Wi' whatna joy I hailed them a' –
The hilltaps standin' raw by raw,
The public house, the Hielan' birks,
And a' the bonny U.P. kirks!
But maistly thee, the bluid o' Scots,
Frae Maidenkirk to John o' Grots,
The king o' drinks, as I conceive it,
Talisker, Isla or Glenlivet!

For after years wi' a pockmantie
Frae Zanzibar to Alicante,
In mony a fash and sair affliction
I gie't as my sincere conviction –
Of a' their foreign tricks an' pliskies,
I maist abominate their whiskies.
Nae doot, themsel's they ken it weel,

An' wi' a hash o' leemon peel,
And ice an' siccan filth, they ettle
The stawsome kind o' goo to settle;
Sic wersh apothecary's broos wi'
As Scotsmen scorn to fyle their moo's wi'.

An' man, I was a blithe hame-comer
Whan first I syndit out my rummer.
Ye should hae seen me then, wi' care
The less important pairts prepare;
Syne, weel contentit wi' it a',
Pour in the speerits wi' a jaw!
I didnae drink, I didnae speak -
I only snowkit up the reek.
I was sae pleased therein to paddle,
I sat an' plowtered wi' my ladle.

An' blithe was I, the morrow's morn,
To daunder through the stookit corn,
And after a' my strange mishanters,
Sit doun amang my ain dissenters.
An', man, it was a joy to me
The pu'pit an' the pews to see,
The pennies dirlin' in the plate,
The elders lookin' on in state;
An' 'mang the first, as it befell,
Wha should I see, sir, but yoursel'.

I was, and I will no deny it,
At the first gliff a hantle tryit.
To see yoursel' in sic a station -
It seemed a doubtfu' dispensation.
The feelin' was a mere digression;
For shune I understood the session,
An' mindin' Aiken an' M'Neil,
I wondered they had done so weel.
I saw I had mysel' to blame;
For had I but remained at hame
Aiblins - though no ava' deservin' 't -
They micht hae named your humble servant.

The kirk was filled, the door was sleeked;
Up to the pu'pit ance I keeked;
I was mair pleased than I can tell -
It was the minister himsel'!
Proud, proud was I to see his face,
After sae lang awa' frae grace.
Pleased as I was, I'm no denyin'
Some maitters were not edifyin';
For first I fand - an' here was news! -
Mere hymn-books cockin' in the pews -

A humanised abomination,
Unfit for ony congregation.
Syne, while I still was on the tenter,
I scunnered at the new prezentor;
I thocht him gesterin' an' cauld -
A sair declension free the auld.
Syne, as though a' the faith was wreckit,
The prayer was not what I'd exspeckit.
Himsel', as it appeared to me,
Was no the man he used to be.
But just as I was growin' vext
He waled a maist judeecious text,
An', launchin' into his prelections,
Swoopt, wi' a skirl, on a' defections.

O what a gale was on my speerit
To hear the p'ints o' doctrine clearit,
And a' the horrors o' damnation
Set furth wi' faithfu' ministration!
Nae shauchlin' testimony here -
We were a' damned, an' that was clear.
I owned, wi' gratitude an' wonder,
He was a pleisure to sit under.

Glossary

JAW: pour, dash, throw; AIBLINS perhaps

TO S. R. CROCKETT

Blows the wind today, and the sun and the rain are
     flying,
   Blows the wind on the moors today and now,
Where about the graves of the martyrs the whaups are
     crying,
   My heart remembers how!

Grey recumbent tombs of the dead in desert places,
   Standing stones on the vacant wine-red moor,
Hills of sheep, and the homes of the silent vanished
     races.
   And winds austere and pure:

Be it granted me to behold you again in dying,
   Hills of home! and to hear again the call;

Hear about the graves of the martyrs the peewees
    crying,
  And hear no more at all.

THE LAST SIGHT

Once more I saw him. In the lofty room,
Where oft with lights and company his tongue
Was trump to honest laughter, sate attired
A something in his likeness. – 'Look!' said one,
Unkindly kind, 'look up, it is your boy!'
And the dread changeling gazed on me in vain.

LIGHT FOOT

Light foot and tight foot
  And green grass spread,
Early in the morning –
  But hope is on ahead.

Stout foot and proud foot
  And grey dust spread,
Early in the evening –
  And hope lies dead.

Long life and short life,
  The last word said,
Early in the evening
  There lies the bed.

Brief day and bright day
  And sunset red,
Early in the evening
  The stars are overhead.

A portrait shows Henry Howard (1517–47) as a sullen-looking youth with a pudding-bowl haircut. Surrey's brief, tempestuous life saw him repeatedly arrested, imprisoned (once at Windsor, as described in 'When Windsor walls'), and, in the end, executed for treason. 'Earl of Surrey' was a courtesy title given him in 1524 when his father became Duke of Norfolk. He was for most of his life in or about the suspicious, faction-ridden court of Henry VIII. He attended Anne Boleyn's trial; he was Catherine Howard's cousin. He served as a soldier at home and in France, but his Catholic sympathies made him appear unreliable. Perhaps he was: his son was to be executed for conspiring with Mary Queen of Scots.

Yet at the edges of his life he was a radically innovative poet. The blank verse (unrhymed iambic pentameters) of his version of parts of the *Aeneid* was a new invention, and it became the standard English verse line. He regularised the English sonnet, on which others would also seize.

Choosing from his work, I avoided his more overtly Petrarchan sonnets (often imitations), except for the beautiful 'Alas, so all things now', which is a direct imitation. Rather, I looked for Surrey's more personal note. None the less, a passage from his *Aeneid* seemed necessary not only for its vigour but because of its monumental historical importance. The sonnet on Sardanapalus shows the energy with which Surrey could treat a classical subject for himself. The elegy for Wyatt has a passionate gravity which I find compelling. In the other love poems I've picked, I hear a robust sangfroid at odds with Petrarchan convention, and one very definitely Surrey's own.

I have modernised spelling, edited some punctuation and provided titles, annotation and metrical accents as appropriate. Like all admirers of Surrey, I am indebted to Emrys Jones's edition of the poems, published in 1964.

'WHEN RAGING LOVE'

When raging love with extreme pain
Most cruelly distrains my heart;
When that my tears, as floods of rain,
Bear witness of my woeful smart;
When sighs have wasted so my breath
That I lie at the point of death:

I call to mind the navy great
That the Greeks brought to Troy town,
And how the boysteous winds did beat
Their ships and rent their sails adown,
Till Agamemnon's daughter's blood
Appeased the gods that them withstood.

And how that in those ten years' war
Full many a bloody deed was done,
And many a lord, that came full far,
There caught his bane, alas, too soon,
And many a good knight overrun,
Before the Greeks had Helen won.

Then think I thus: since such repair,
So long time war of valiant men,
Was all to win a lady fair,
Shall I not learn to suffer then,
And think my life well spent to be
Serving a worthier wight than she?

Therefore I never will repent,
But pains contented still endure:
For like as when, rough winter spent,
The pleasant spring straight draws in ure,
So after raging storms of care
Joyful at length may be my fare.

Glossary

BOYSTEOUS: rough; AGAMEMNON'S DAUGHTER: Iphigenia, sacrificed
at Aulis; DRAWS IN URE: comes into being; FARE: journey

'ALAS, SO ALL THINGS NOW'

Alas, so all things now do hold their peace,
Heaven and earth disturbèd in nothing;
The beasts, the air, the birds their song do cease;

The nightès chare the stars about doth bring.
Calm is the sea, the waves work less and less;
So am not I, whom love alas doth wring,
Bringing before my face the great increase
Of my desires, whereat I weep and sing
In joy and woe as in a doubtful ease.
For my sweet thoughts sometime do pleasure bring,
But by and by the cause of my disease
Gives me a pang that inwardly doth sting,
    When that I think what grief it is again
    To live and lack the thing should rid my pain.

Glossary

NIGHTÈS CHARE: night's chariot

'WHEN WINDSOR WALLS'

When Windsor walls sustained my wearied arm,
My hand my chin, to ease my restless head,
Each pleasant plot revested green with warm,
The blossomed boughs with lusty Ver yspread,
The flowered meads, the wedded birds so late
Mine eyes discovered. Then did to mind resort
The jolly woes, the hateless short debate,
The rakehell life that longs to love's disport.
Wherewith, alas, mine heavy charge of care,
Heaped in my breast, broke forth against my will,
And smoky sighs that overcast the air.
My vapoured eyes such dreary tears distil
    The tender spring to quicken where they fall,
    And I half bent to throw me down withal.

Glossary

LONGS: belongs

[ELEGY FOR SIR THOMAS WYATT]

W. resteth here, that quick could never rest;
Whose heavenly gifts increasèd by disdain
And virtue sank the deeper in his breast:
Such profit he by envy could obtain.

A head, where wisdom mysteries did frame,
Whose hammers beat still in that lively brain
As on a stithe, where that some work of fame
Was daily wrought to turn to Britain's gain.

A visage stern and mild, where both did grow
Vice to contemn, in virtue to rejoice;
Amid great storms whom grace assurèd so
To live upright and smile at fortune's choice.

A hand that taught what might be said in rhyme,
That reft Chaucer the glory of his wit;
A mark the which, unparfited for time,
Some may approach, but never none shall hit.

A tongue that served in foreign realms his king;
Whose courteous talk to virtue did inflame
Each noble heart; a worthy guide to bring
Our English youth by travail unto fame.

An eye whose judgement none affect could blind,
Friends to allure and foes to reconcile,
Whose piercing look did represent a mind
With virtue fraught, reposèd, void of guile.

A heart where dread was never so impressed
To hide the thought that might the truth advance;
In neither fortune loft nor yet repressed,
To swell in wealth, or yield into mischance.

A valiant corps, where force and beauty met;
Happy, alas, too happy, but for foes;
Lived and ran the race that nature set;
Of manhood's shape, where she the mould did lose.

But to the heavens that simple soul is fled,
Which left with such as covet Christ to know
Witness of faith that never shall be dead;
Sent for our health, but not receivèd so.

Thus, for our guilt, this jewel we have lost.
The earth his bones, the heavens possess his ghost.

Glossary

STITHE: anvil; REFT: stole from; UNPARFITED FOR TIME: uncompleted
for lack of time; AFFECT: liking, partiality; LOFT: arrogant; COPRS (living)
body

[SARDANAPALUS]

Th' Assyrians' king, in peace with foul desire
And filthy lust that stained his regal heart,
In war that should set princely hearts afire
Vanquished did yield for want of martial art.
The dent of swords from kisses seemèd strange,
And harder than his lady's side his targe;
From glutton feasts to soldiers' fare a change,
His helmet far above a garland's charge.
Who scarce the name of manhood did retain,
Drenchèd in sloth and womanish delight,
Feeble of sprete, unpatient of pain,
When he had lost his honour and his right,
   Proud time of wealth, in storms appalled with
     dread,
    Murdered himself to show some manful deed.

Glossary

TARGE: shield; CHARGE: weight; SPRETE: spirit; UNPATIENT: four
syllables

from THE AENEID II

◄(Aeneas is narrating)►

Whiles Laocon, that chosen was by lot
Neptunus' priest, did sacrifice a bull
Before the holy altar, suddenly
From Tenedon, behold, in circles great
By the calm seas come floating adders twain
Which plied towards the shore (I loathe to tell)
With rearèd breast lift up above the seas,
Whose bloody crests aloft the waves were seen.
The hinder part swam hidden in the flood;
Their grisly backs were linkèd manifold.
With sound of broken waves they gate the strand,
With glowing eyes, tainted with blood and fire;
Whose waltring tongues did lick their hissing
    mouths.
We fled away, our face the blood forsook.
But they with gate direct to Lacon ran.
And first of all each serpent doth enwrap
The bodies small of his two tender sons,
Whose wretched limbs they bit, and fed thereon.
Then raught they him, who had his weapon caught
To rescue them; twice winding him about,
With folded knots and circled tails, his waist.

Their scalèd backs did compass twice his neck,
With rearèd heads aloft and stretchèd throats.
He with his hands strove to unloose the knots;
Whose sacred fillets all besprinkled were
With filth of gory blood and venom rank.
And to the stars such dreadful shouts he sent,
Like to the sound the roaring bull forth lows
Which from the altar wounded doth astart,
The swerving axe when he shakes from his neck.
The serpents twain with hastèd trail they glide
To Pallas' temple and her towers of height;
Under the feet of which the goddess stern,
Hidden behind her target's boss, they crept.
New grips of dread then pierce our trembling
   breasts.
They said Lacon's deserts had dearly bought
His heinous deed, that piercèd had with steel
The sacred bulk, and thrown the wicked lance.
The people cried with sundry greeing shouts
To bring the horse to Pallas' temple blive,
In hope thereby the goddess' wrath t'appease.
We cleft the walls and closures of the town,
Whereto all help, and underset the feet
With sliding rolls, and bound his neck with ropes.
This fatal gin thus overclamb our walls,
Stuffed with armed men, about the which there ran
Children and maids that holy carols sang;
And well were they whose hands might touch the
   cords.
With threat'ning cheer thus slidèd through our town
The subtle tree, to Pallas' temple ward.
O native land! Ilion! And of the gods
The mansion place! O warlike walls of Troy!
Four times it stopped in th'entry of our gate,
Four times the harness clattered in the womb.
But we go on, unsound of memory,
And blinded eke by rage persèver still.
This fatal monster in the fane we place.

Glossary

GATE: reached; WALTRING: wavering; GATE: path; RAUGHT: seized;
FILLETS: headbands; TARGET: shield; GREEING: unanimous; BLIVE:
quickly; GIN: engine, machine; TREE: construction of wood – the Horse;
TO PALLAS' TEMPLE WARD: toward Pallas' temple; HARNESS: military
equipment; EKE: also; FANE: temple

❧

'GIVE PLACE, YE LOVERS'

Give place, ye lovers, here before
That spent your boasts and brags in vain:
My lady's beauty passeth more
The best of yours, I dare well sayn,
Than doth the sun the candle light
Or brightest day the darkest night.

And thereto hath a truth as just
As had Penelope the fair:
For what she saith, ye may it trust
As it by writing sealèd were.
And virtues hath she many moe
Than I with pen have skill to show.

I could rehearse, if that I would,
The whole effect of nature's plaint
When she had lost the perfect mould,
The like to whom she could not paint;
With wringing hands how she did cry,
And what she said, I know it, I.

I know she swore with raging mind,
Her kingdom only set apart,
There was no loss, by law of kind,
That could have gone so near her heart.
And this was chiefly all her pain:
She could not make the like again.

Since Nature thus gave her the praise
To be the chiefest work she wrought,
In faith, me think some better ways
On your behalf might well be sought
Than to compare, as ye have done,
To match the candle with the sun.

A DESCRIPTION OF A CITY SHOWER

'Cousin Swift,' said Dryden, 'you will never be a poet.' The remark was delivered from a confident height and is hard to argue with even now. Useless to reply that Swift's true 'poetry' was reserved for the prose, though no doubt it was, as the word has come to be understood; Dryden was talking about something different. And, in all honesty, the greater part of Swift's surprisingly large output of squibs, fables, epigrams, verse letters, and occasional or political rhymes makes disappointing reading, flavourless and thin.

Yet there are items that defy Dryden's put-down. The descriptive exercises, for instance: short-winded they may be, but compare any one of them with Dryden's heroically long-winded attempt to trap the Fire of London within the, boxy quatrains of 'Annus Mirabilis', and then ask which feels more real, which has more life.

Almost all Swift's best poems have an air of hastily rattled-off inventory-making about them. The lists of things that aggrieved, or disgusted, or simply amused him are disarmingly frank and fresh. Perhaps they appeal to a modern taste for the sketchy and the spontaneous which Dryden could never have allowed. Their structural looseness, too, now seems a form of eloquence, and the cruder strokes, the brutality, relate them to the Expressionism of two hundred years later. 'A Beautiful Young Nymph Going to Bed' – an inventory with a vengeance – could have been written for Otto Dix to illustrate.

Swift's misogyny is impossible either to ignore or to excuse. There is, however, complicating evidence in another poem, 'The Humble Petition of Frances Harris', where his delight in the feat of mimicry is wonderfully catching; where mockery and sympathy will not be easily disentangled; and where the prattling, unruly couplets read like an inspired extension of the method that makes 'A Description of a City Shower' so immediate. The maid's outpouring has the force of sheer, teeming, ungainsayable reality. In his notation of it, Swift pays tribute.

Careful observers may foretel the hour
(By sure prognosticks) when to dread a show'r.
While rain depends, the pensive cat gives o'er
Her frolicks, and pursues her tail no more.
Returning home at night you find the sink
Strike your offended sense with double stink.
If you be wise, then go not far to dine,
You spend in coach-hire more than save in wine.
A coming show'r your shooting corns presage;
Old aches throb, your hollow tooth will rage:
Saunt'ring in coffee-house is Dulman seen;
He damns the climate, and complains of spleen.

Mean while the South, rising with dabbled wings,
A sable cloud athwart the welkin flings;
That swill'd more liquor than it could contain,
And like a drunkard gives it up again.
Brisk Susan whips her linnen from the rope,
While the first drizzling show'r is born aslope:
Such is that sprinkling, which some careless quean
Flirts on you from her mop; but not so clean:
You fly, invoke the gods; then turning, stop
To rail; she singing, still whirls on her mop.
Nor yet the dust had shun'd the unequal strife,
But aided by the wind, fought still for life;
And wafted with its foe by vi'lent gust,
'Twas doubtful which was rain, and which was dust.
Ah! where must needy poet seek for aid,
When dust and rain at once his coat invade?
Sole coat, where dust, cemented by the rain,
Erects the nap, and leaves a cloudy stain.

Now, in contiguous drops the flood comes down,
Threat'ning with deluge this devoted town.
To shops in crowds the daggled females fly,
Pretend to cheapen goods; but nothing buy.
The Templar spruce, while ev'ry spout's abroach,
Stays till 'tis fair, yet seems to call a coach.
The tuck'd-up sempstress walks with hasty strides,
While streams run down her oil'd umbrella's sides.
Here various kinds by various fortunes led,
Commence acquaintance underneath a shed.
Triumphant Tories, and desponding Whigs,
Forget their feuds, and join to save their wigs.
Box'd in a chair the beau impatient sits,
While spouts run clatt'ring o'er the roof by fits;
And ever and anon with frightful din
The leather sounds; he trembles from within.
So, when Troy chair-men bore the wooden steed,

Pregnant with Greeks, impatient to be freed;
(Those bully Greeks, who, as the moderns do,
Instead of paying chair-men, run them thro')
Laocoon struck the out-side with his spear,
And each imprison'd hero quak'd for fear.

Now from all parts the swelling kennels flow,
And bear their trophies with them, as they go:
Filths of all hues and odours seem to tell
What streets they sail'd from, by the sight and smell.
They, as each torrent drives with rapid force,
From Smithfield, or St. Pulchre's shape their course;
And in huge confluent join at Snow-Hill Ridge,
Fall from the Conduit prone to Holbourn Bridge.

Sweepings from butcher's stall, dung, guts, and
    blood,
Drown'd puppies, stinking sprats, all drench'd in
    mud,
Dead cats, and turnip-tops come tumbling down
    the flood.

ON POETRY: A RAPSODY

(lines 319–56)

Hobbes clearly proves that ev'ry creature
Lives in a state of war by nature.
The greater for the smaller watch,
But meddle seldom with their match.
A whale of mod'rate size will draw
A shole of herrings down his maw;
A fox with geese his belly crams;
A wolf destroys a thousand lambs.
But, search among the rhiming race,
The brave are worry'd by the base.
If, on Parnassus' top you sit,
You rarely bite, are always bit:
Each poet of inferior size
On you shall rail and criticize;
And try to tear you limb from limb,
While others do as much for him:
The vermin only teaze and pinch
Their foes superior by an inch.
So, nat'ralists observe, a flea
Hath smaller fleas that on him prey,
And these have smaller yet to bite 'em,
And so proceed ad infinitum:
Thus ev'ry poet in his kind,

Is bit by him that comes behind;
Who, tho' too little to be seen,
Can teaze, and gall, and give the spleen;
Call dunces, fools, and sons of whores,
Lay Grub-street at each others doors:
Extol the Greek and Roman masters,
And curse our modern poetasters:
Complain, as many an ancient bard did,
How genius is no more rewarded:
How wrong a taste prevails among us;
How much our ancestors out-sung us;
Can personate an awkward scorn
For those who are not poets born:
And all their brother dunces lash,
Who crowd the press with hourly trash.

A BEAUTIFUL YOUNG NYMPH GOING TO BED

Corinna, pride of Drury-Lane,
For whom no shepherd sighs in vain;
Never did Covent-Garden boast
So bright a batter'd, stroling toast;
No drunken rake to pick her up,
No cellar where on tick to sup;
Returning at the midnight hour;
Four stories climbing to her bow'r;
Then, seated on a three-leg'd chair,
Takes off her artificial hair:
Now, picking out a chrystal eye,
She wipes it clean, and lays it by.
Her eye-brows from a mouse's hyde,
Stuck on with art on either side,
Pulls off with care, and first displays 'em,
Then in a play-book smoothly lays 'em.
Now dext'rously her plumpers draws,
That serve to fill her hollow jaws.
Untwists a wire; and from her gums
A set of teeth compleatly comes.
Pulls out the rags, contriv'd to prop
Her flabby dugs, and down they drop.
Proceeding on, the lovely goddess,
Unlaces next her steel-ribb'd bodice;
Which by the operator's skill,
Press down the lumps, the hollows fill.
Up goes her hand, and off she slips
The bolsters that supply her hips.
With gentlest touch, she next explores

Her shankers, issues, running sores;
Effects of many a sad disaster,
And then to each applies a plaister.
But must, before she goes to bed,
Rub off the dawbs of white and red;
And smooth the furrows in her front,
With greasy paper stuck upon't.
She takes a bolus e'er she sleeps;
And then between two blankets creeps.
With pains of love tormented lies;
Or, if she chance to close her eyes,
Of Bridewell and the compter dreams,
And feels the lash, and faintly screams;
Or, by a faithless bully drawn,
At some hedge-tavern lies in pawn.
Or, to Jamaica seems transported,
Alone, and by no planter courted.
Or, near Fleet-Ditch's oozy brinks,
Surrounded with a hundred stinks:
Belated, seems on watch to lye,
And snap some cully passing by.
Or, struck with fear, her fancy runs
On watchmen, constables, and duns,
From who she meets with frequent rubs;
But never from religious clubs;
Whose favour she is sure to find,
Because she pays them all in kind.

Corinna wakes. A dreadful sight!
Behold the ruins of the night!
A wicked rat her plaister stole,
Half eat, and dragg'd it to his hole.
The chrystal eye, alas, was miss't;
And puss had on her plumpers p – st.
A pidgeon pick't her issue-peas;
And shock her tresses fill'd with fleas.

The nymph, though in this mangled plight,
Must ev'ry morn her limbs unite;
But, how shall I describe her arts
To recollect the scatter'd parts?
Or, shew the anguish, toyl, and pain,
Of gathering up her self again.
The bashful muse will never bear,
In such a scene to interfere.
Corinna in the morning dizen'd,
Who sees will spew; who smells, be poison'd.

To their Excellencies the Lords Justices of Ireland The Humble Petition of Frances Harris

‹Who must starve, and die a Maid if it miscarries›

Humbly Sheweth,
That I went to warm my self in Lady Betty's chamber, because I was cold;
And I had in a purse seven pounds, four shillings and six pence, (besides farthings,) in money and gold;
So, because I had been buying things for my Lady last night,
I was resolv'd to tell my money, to see if it was right.
Now you must know, because my trunk has a very bad lock,
Therefore all the money I have, (which, GOD knows, is a very small stock,)
I keep in my pocket, ty'd about my middle, next my smock,
So, when I went to put up my purse, as GOD would have it, my smock was unript;
And instead of putting it into my pocket, down it slipt:
Then the bell rung, and I went down to put my Lady to bed;
And, GOD knows, I thought my money was as safe as my maidenhead.
So, when I came up again, I found my pocket feel very light,
But when I search'd and miss'd my purse, Lord! I thought, I should have sunk outright:
Lord! Madam, says Mary, how d'ye do? Indeed, said I, never worse.
But pray, Mary, can you tell what I have done with my purse:
Lord help me, said Mary, I never stirr'd out of this place:
Nay, said I, I had it in Lady Betty's chamber, that's a plain case.
So, Mary got me to bed, and cover'd me up warm:
However, she stole away my garters that I might do my self no harm.
So, I tumbled and toss'd all night, as you may very well think;
But hardly ever set my eyes together, or slept a wink.
So, I was adream'd, methought, that we went and search'd the folks round:
And in a corner of Mrs. Duke's box, ty'd in a rag, the money was found.
So, next morning we told Whittle, and he fell a swearing;

Then my Dame Wadgar came, and she, you know, is
thick of hearing:
Dame, said I, as loud as I could bawl, do you know
what a loss I have had?
Nay, said she, my Lord Collway's folks are all very sad
For my Lord Dromedary comes a Tuesday without fail;
Pugh; said I, but that's not the business that I ail.
Says Cary, says he, I have been a servant this five and
twenty years come spring;
And in all the places I liv'd, I never heard of such a
thing.
Yes, says the Steward, I remember, when I was at my
Lady Shrewsbury's,
Such a thing as this happen'd, just about the time of
gooseberries.
So I went to the party suspected, and I found her full
of grief;
(Now you must know, of all things in the world I hate
a thief.)
However, I was resolv'd to bring the discourse slily
about;
Mrs. Dukes, said I, here's an ugly accident has
happen'd out:
'Tis not that I value the money three skips of a louse;
But the thing I stand upon is, the credit of the house:
'Tis true, seven pounds, four shillings, and six pence,
makes a great hole in my wages;
Besides, as they say, service is no inheritance in these
ages.
Now, Mrs. Dukes, you know, and every body
understands,
That tho' 'tis hard to judge, yet money can't go
without hands.
The Devil take me, said she, (blessing her self,) if ever I
saw't!
So she roar'd like a Bedlam, as tho' I had call'd her all
to naught:
So you know, what could I say to her any more?
I e'en left her, and came away as wise as I was before.
Well: But then they would have had me gone to the
Cunning-man:
No, said I, 'tis the same thing, the Chaplain will be
here anon.
So the Chaplain came in. Now the servants say he is
my sweet-heart,
Because he's always in my chamber, and I always take
his part;
So, as the Devil would have it, before I was aware, out I
blunder'd,
Parson, said I, can you cast a nativity, when a body's
plunder'd?

(Now you must know, he hates to be call'd Parson like
the Devil.)
Truly, says he, Mrs. Nab, it might become you to be
more civil:
If your money be gone, as a learned Divine says, d'ye
see,
You are no text for my handling, so take that from me:
I was never taken for a conjurer before, I'd have you
know:
Lord, said I, don't be a angry, I am sure I never
thought you so:
You know, I honour the cloth; I design to be a parson's
wife;
I never took one in your coat for a conjurer in all my
life.
With that, he twisted his girdle at me like a rope; as
who should say,
Now you may go hang your self for me; and so went
away.
Well; I thought, I should have swoon'd: Lord, said I,
what shall I do?
I have lost my money; and I shall lose my true-love
too.
So, my lord call'd me, Harry, said my lord, don't cry,
I'll give something towards thy loss: And says my lady,
so will I.
Oh! but said I; what if after all, the chaplain won't
come to?
For that, he said, (an't please your Excellencies,) I must
petition you.

The Premisses tenderly consider'd, I desire your
Excellencies protection:
And that I may have a share in next Sunday's
collection:
And over and above, that I may have your Excellencies
letter,
With an order for the Chaplain aforesaid; or instead of
him a better.
And then your poor petitioner, both night and day,
Of the Chaplain (for 'tis his trade,) as in duty bound,
shall ever pray.

Swinburne (1837–1909) was both celebrated and notorious in his lifetime. Memorably described by one critic as 'the libidinous laureate of a pack of satyrs', he was defiantly pagan in his poetic expression, and his flirtation with the sadistic and the sexually ambiguous could have been expressly designed to scandalise the more easily scandalised of his contemporaries. Yet it would be easy to exaggerate Swinburne's outsider status. He was, in many ways, a typical Victorian. Indeed Queen Victoria herself once remarked, 'I am told that Mr. Swinburne is the best poet in my dominions.' The modern reader, whether entangled in the thickets of Swinburne's often demanding syntax or chasing down the meanings of his often recondite vocabulary and allusions, might be tempted to believe that the queen had been misled. However Swinburne should not be consigned to the ranks of the Great Unread; acknowledged as great in all the histories of English literature, unread by all but a few specialist scholars. Despite what he himself recognised as 'a tendency to the dulcet and luscious form of verbosity', a lushness which falls unsympathetically on the modern ear, his fluency and musicality, his skilful manipulation of exacting metrical forms and his rich imagery repay close reading. Inconveniently for an anthologist, Swinburne's gifts are best seen in longer poems, from which it is difficult to make excerpts. The selection offered here tries to show the range of his poetic writing, from the slightly sinister lyricism of 'A Match' to the skilful use – half in earnest, half in pastiche – of the ballad form in 'A Reiver's Neck-Verse', from the elegy in memory of his father ('Inferiae') to the parody and humour of 'The Higher Pantheism in a Nutshell'. Interested readers should move on to the longer verse.

THE GARDEN OF PROSERPINE

Here where the world is quiet;
Here, where all trouble seems
Dead winds' and spent waves' riot
In doubtful dreams of dreams;
I watch the green field growing
For reaping folk and sowing,
For harvest-time and mowing,
A sleepy world of streams.

I am tired of tears and laughter,
And men that laugh and weep;
Of what may come hereafter
For men that sow to reap:
I am weary of days and hours,
Blown buds of barren flowers,
Desires and dreams and powers
And everything but sleep.

Here life has death for neighbour,
And far from eye or ear
Wan waves and wet winds labour,
Weak ships and spirits steer;
They drive adrift, and whither
They wot not who make thither;
But no such winds blow hither,
And no such things grow here.

No growth of moor or coppice,
No heather-flower or vine,
But bloomless buds of poppies,
Green grapes of Proserpine,
Pale beds of blowing rushes
Where no leaf blooms or blushes
Save this whereout she crushes
For dead men deadly wine.

Pale, without name or number,
In fruitless fields of corn,
They bow themselves and slumber
All night till light is born;
And like a soul belated,
In hell and heaven unmated,
By cloud and mist abated
Comes out of darkness morn.

Though one were strong as seven,
He too with death shall dwell,
Nor wake with wings in heaven,
Nor weep for pains in hell;

Though one were fair as roses,
His beauty clouds and closes;
And well though love reposes,
In the end it is not well.

Pale, beyond porch and portal,
Crowned with calm leaves, she stands
Who gathers all things mortal
With cold immortal hands;
Her languid lips are sweeter
Than love's who fears to greet her
To men that mix and meet her
From many times and lands.

She waits for each and other,
She waits for all men born;
Forgets the earth her mother,
The life of fruits and corn;
And spring and seed and swallow
Take wing for her and follow
Where summer song rings hollow
And flowers are put to scorn.

There go the loves that wither,
The old loves with wearier wings;
And all dead years draw thither,
And all disastrous things;
Dead dreams of days forsaken,
Blind buds that snows have shaken,
Wild leaves that winds have taken,
Red strays of ruined springs.

We are not sure of sorrow,
And joy was never sure;
To-day will die to-morrow;
Time stoops to no man's lure;
And love, grown faint and fretful,
With lips but half regretful
Sighs, and with eyes forgetful
Weeps that no loves endure.

From too much love of living,
From hope and fear set free,
We thank with brief thanksgiving
Whatever gods may be
That no life lives for ever;
That dead men rise up never;
That even the weariest river
Winds somewhere safe to sea.

Then star nor sun shall waken,
Nor any change of light:

Nor sound of waters shaken,
Nor any sound or sight:
Nor wintry leaves nor vernal,
Nor days nor things diurnal;
Only the sleep eternal
In an eternal night.

INFERIAE

Spring, and the light and sound of things on earth
Requickening, all within our green sea's girth;
A time of passage or a time of birth
    Fourscore years since as this year, first and last.

The sun is all about the world we see,
The breath and strength of very spring; and we
Live, love, and feed on our own hearts; but he
    Whose heart fed mine has passed into the past.

Past, all things born with sense and blood and
    breath;
The flesh hears nought that now the spirit saith.
If death be like as birth and birth as death,
    The first was fair – more fair should be the last.

Fourscore years since, and come but one month more
The count were perfect of his mortal score
Whose sail went seaward yesterday from shore
    To cross the last of many an unsailed sea.

Light, love and labour up to life's last height,
These three were stars unsettling in his sight;
Even as the sun is life and heat and light
    And sets not nor is dark when dark are we.

The life, the spirit, and the work were one
That here – ah, who shall say, that here are done?
Not I, that know not; father, not thy son,
    For all the darkness of the night and sea.

A Reiver's Neck-Verse

Some die singing, and some die swinging,
   And weel mot a' they be:
Some die playing, and some die praying,
   And I wot sae winna we, my dear,
   And I wot sae winna we.

Some die sailing, and some die wailing,
   And some die fair and free:
Some die flyting, and some die fighting,
   But I for a fause love's fee, my dear,
   But I for a fause love's fee.

Some die laughing, and some die quaffing,
   And some die high on tree:
Some die spinning, and some die sinning,
   But faggot and fire for ye, my dear,
   Faggot and fire for ye.

Some die weeping, and some die sleeping,
   And some die under sea:
Some die ganging, and some die hanging,
   And a twine of a tow for me, my dear,
   A twine of a tow for me.

A Match

If love were what the rose is,
   And I were like the leaf,
Our lives would grow together
In sad or singing weather,
Blown fields or flowerful closes,
   Green pleasure or grey grief;
If love were what the rose is,
   And I were like the leaf.

If I were what the words are,
   And love were like the tune,
With double sound and single
Delight our lips would mingle,
With kisses glad as birds are
   That get sweet rain at noon;
If I were what the words are,
   And love were like the tune.

If you were life, my darling,
   And I your love were death,

We'd shine and snow together
Ere March made sweet the weather
With daffodil and starling
   And hours of fruitful breath;
If you were life, my darling,
   And I your love were death.

If you were thrall to sorrow,
   And I were page to joy,
We'd play for lives and seasons
With loving looks and treasons
And tears of night and morrow
   And laughs of maid and boy;
If you were thrall to sorrow,
   And I were page to joy.

If you were April's lady,
   And I were lord in May,
We'd throw with leaves for hours
And draw for days with flowers,
Till day like night were shady
   And night were bright like day;
If you were April's lady,
   And I were lord in May.

If you were queen of pleasure,
   And I were king of pain,
We'd hunt down love together,
Pluck out his flying-feather,
And teach his feet a measure,
   And find his mouth a rein;
If you were queen of pleasure,
   And I were king of pain.

The Higher Pantheism in a Nutshell

One, who is not, we see: but one, whom we see not, is:
Surely this is not that: but that is assuredly this.

What, and wherefore, and whence? for under is over
   and under:
If thunder could be without lightning, lightning could
   be without thunder.

Doubt is faith in the main: but faith, on the whole, is
   doubt:
We cannot believe by proof but could we believe
   without?

Why, and whither, and how? for barley and rye are not
    clover:
Neither are straight lines curves: yet over is under and
    over.

Two and two may be four: but four and four are not
    eight:
Fate and God may be twain: but God is the same thing
    as fate.

Ask a man what he thinks, and get from a man what
    he feels:
God, once caught in the fact, shows you a fair pair of
    heels.

Body and spirit are twins: God only knows which is
    which:
The soul squats down in the flesh, like a tinker drunk
    in a ditch.

More is the whole than a part: but half is more than
    the whole:
Clearly, the soul is the body: but is not the body the
    soul?

One and two are not one but one: and nothing is two:
Truth can hardly be false, if falsehood cannot be true.

Once the mastodon was: pterodactyls were common as
    cocks:
Then the mammoth was God: now is He a prize ox.

Parallels all things are: yet many of these are askew:
You are certainly I: but certainly I am not you.

Springs the rock from the plain, shoots the stream
    from the rock:
Cocks exist for the hen: but hens exist for the cock.

God, whom we see not, is: and God, who is not, we see:
Fiddle, we know, is diddle: and diddle, we take it, is dee.

Tennyson's reputation is entirely misleading. He has come down to us as a scion of Victorianism (born in 1809, he died in 1892), a voice of Empire, a clever metrician who was more the prisoner of form than its arbiter. But almost the reverse is true on all these counts. He is a wonderful, playful and challenging technician. He is an oblique, rather than direct product of his age. And far from being the voice of the Victorian era, he actually subverted an age of faith with a subtle poetry of doubt.

It was T. S. Eliot who first pointed this out in his essay on In Memoriam. The faith in that poem is nothing special, he argued. The doubt, on the other hand, is 'an intense experience'. This is true of a great deal of Tennyson's poetry. In fact the poems assembled here show that the dialogue between faith and doubt – a visceral struggle mediated by the music he was so celebrated for – is at the centre of his work. Nor is it a simple dialogue. It can be a painful engagement, with an ugly undertow of defeatism, just audible in the gorgeous, cranky rhythms of 'The Lady of Shalott'. But it is a dialogue that explains a great deal about the stresses in the mid-nineteenth century poem. For this reason, a long poem like Tennyson's 'Two Voices' is as important a register of the energies of his age as Arnold's 'The Buried Life'. Just as 'Tears Idle Tears' with its marvellous stanzaic movement from refrain to regret and back again is the first, defining lyric of pure pessimism which survives that time.

But it is in his most ambitious work – In Memoriam – that the argument between faith and doubt finds its true form. Tennyon's erotic, angry love for his lost friend is neither affirming nor easily dealt with in the poem. Arthur's Hallam's early death left him desolate and sceptical. The achievement of the poem is not only that it makes a powerful architecture out of the seasons of grief, but that it does so in stanzas so reminiscent of the Church of England hymnal, and yet so de-stabilizing of it at the same time, that it remains one of the darkest and most ambiguous elegies of the nineteenth century.

The Lady of Shalott

‹Part I›

On either side the river lie
Long fields of barley and of rye,
That clothe the wold and meet the sky;
And thro' the field the road runs by
    To many-tower'd Camelot;
And up and down the people go,
Gazing where the lilies blow
Round an island there below,
    The island of Shalott.

Willows whiten, aspens quiver,
Little breezes dusk and shiver
Thro' the wave that runs for ever
By the island in the river
    Flowing down to Camelot.
Four grey walls, and four grey towers,
Overlook a space of flowers,
And the silent isle imbowers
    The Lady of Shalott.

By the margin, willow-veil'd,
Slide the heavy barges trail'd
By slow horses: and unhail'd
The shallop flitteth silken-sail'd
    Skimming down to Camelot:
But who hath seen her wave her hand?
Or at the casement seen her stand?
Or is she known in all the land,
    The Lady of Shalott?

Only reapers, reaping early
In among the bearded barley,
Hear a song that echoes cheerly
From the river winding clearly,
    Down to tower'd Camelot;
And by the moon the reaper weary,
Piling sheaves in uplands airy,
Listening, whispers 'Tis the fairy
    Lady of Shalott

‹Part II›

There she weaves by night and day
A magic web with colours gay.
She has heard a whisper say,
A curse is on her if she stay
    To look down to Camelot.
She knows not what the curse may be,
And so she weaveth steadily.
And little other care hath she,
    The Lady of Shalott.

And moving thro' a mirror clear
That hangs before her all the year,
Shadows of the world appear.
There she sees the highway near
    Winding down to Camelot;
There the river eddy whirls,
And there the surly village-churls,
And the red cloaks of market girls,
    Pass onward from Shalott.

Sometimes a troop of damsels glad,
An abbot on an ambling pad.
Sometimes a curly shepherd-lad.
Or long-hair d page in crimson clad,
    Goes by to tower'd Camelot;
And sometimes thro the mirror blue
The knights come riding two and two:
She hath no loyal knight and true,
    The Lady of Shalott.

But in her web she still delights
To weave the mirror's magic sights,
For often thro' the silent nights
A funeral, with plumes and lights
    And music, went to Camelot;
Or when the moon was overhead,
Came two young lovers lately wed:
'I am half sick of shadows,' said
    The Lady of Shalott.

‹Part III›

A bow-shot from her bower-eaves,
He rode between the barley-sheaves,
The sun came dazzling thro' the leaves,
And flamed upon the brazen greaves
    Of bold Sir Lancelot.
A red-cross knight for ever kneel'd
To a lady in his shield,
That sparkled on the yellow field,
    Beside remote Shalott.

The gemmy bridle glitter'd free,
Like to some branch of stars we see
Hung in the golden Galaxy.
The bridle bells rang merrily
    As he rode down to Camelot;

And from his blazon'd baldric slung
A mighty silver bugle hung,
And as he rode his armour rung,
 Beside remote Shalott.

All in the blue unclouded weather
Thick-jewell'd shone the saddle-leather,
The helmet and the helmet-feather
Burn'd like one burning flame together,
 As he rode down to Camelot;
As often thro' the purple night,
Below the starry clusters bright,
Some bearded meteor, trailing light,
 Moves over still Shalott.

His broad clear brow in sunlight glow'd;
On burnish'd hooves his war-horse bode;
From underneath his helmet flow'd
His coal-black curls as on he rode,
 As he rode down to Camelot.
From the bank and from the river
He flash d into the crystal mirror,
'Tirra lirra,' by the river
 Sang Sir Lancelot.

She left the web, she left the loom,
She made three paces thro' the room,
She saw the water lily bloom,
She saw the helmet and the plume,
 She look'd down to Camelot.
Out flew the web and floated wide;
The mirror crack'd from side to side;
'The curse is come upon me,' cried
 The Lady of Shalott.

◄Part IV►

In the stormy east-wind straining,
The pale yellow woods were waning,
The broad stream in his banks complaining,
Heavily the low sly raining
 Over tower'd Camelot:
Down she came and found a boat
Beneath a willow left afloat,
And round about the prow she wrote
 The Lady of Shalott.

And down the river a dim expanse
Like some bold seer in a trance,
Seeing all his own mischance –
With a glassy countenance

Did she look to Camelot.
And at the closing of the day
She loosed the chain, and down she lay;
The broad stream bore her far away,
 The Lady of Shalott.

Lying, robed in snowy white
That loosely flew to left and right –
The leaves upon her falling light –
Thro' the noises of the night
 She floated down to Camelot:
And as the boat-head wound along
The willowy hills and fields among,
They heard her singing her last song,
 The Lady of Shalott.

Heard a carol, mournful, holy,
Chanted loudly, chanted lowly,
Till her blood was frozen slowly,
And her eyes were darken'd wholly,
 Turn'd to tower'd Cameiot.
For ere she reach'd upon the the tide
The first house by the water-side,
Singing in her song she died,
 The Lady of Shalott.

Under tower and balcony,
By garden-wall and gallery,
A gleaming shape she floated by,
Dead-pale between the houses high,
 Silent into Camelot.
Out upon the wharfs they came,
Knight and burgher, lord and dame,
And round the prow they read her name,
 The Lady of Shalott.

Who is this? and what is here?
And in the lighted palace near
Died the sound of royal cheer:
And they cross'd themselves for fear,
 All the knights at Camelot:
But Lancelot mused a little space;
He said, 'She has a lovely face;
God in his mercy lend her grace,
 The Lady of Shalott.'

ULYSSES

It little profits that an idle king,
By this still hearth, among these barren crags,
Match'd with an aged wife, I mete and dole
Unequal laws unto a savage race,
That hoard, and sleep, and feed. and know not me.
I cannot rest from travel: I will drink
Life to the lees. All times I have enjoy'd
Greatly, have suffer'd greatly, both with those
That loved me, and alone; on shore, and when
Thro' scudding drifts the rainy Hyades
Vext the dim sea. I am become a name;
For always roaming with a hungry heart
Much have I seen and known, – cities of men
And manners, climates, councils, governments,
Myself not least, but honour'd of them all, –
And drunk delight of battle with my peers,
Far on the ringing plains of windy Troy.
I am a part of all that I have met;
Yet all experience is an arch wherethro'
Gleams that untravell'd world whose margin fades
For ever and for ever when I move.
How dull it is to pause, to make an end,
To rust unburnish'd, not to shine in use!
As tho' to breathe were life! Life piled on life
Were all too little, and of one to me
Little remains; but every hour is saved
From that eternal silence, something more,
A bringer of new things; and vile it were
For some three suns to store and hoard myself,
And this gray spirit yearning in desire
To follow knowledge like a sinking star,
Beyond the utmost bound of human thought.

   This is my son, mine own Telemachus
To whom I leave the sceptre and the isle, –
Well-loved of me, discerning to fulfill
This labour, by slow prudence to make mild
A rugged people, and thro' soft degrees
Subdue them to the useful and the good.
Most blameless is he, centred in the sphere
Of common duties, decent not to fail
In offices of tenderness, and pay
Meet adoration to mv household gods,
When I am gone. He works his work, I mine.

   There lies the port: the vessel puffs her sail;
There gloom the dark, broad seas. My mariners,
Souls that have toil'd, and wrought, and thought
      with me. –
That ever with a frolic welcome took
The thunder and the sunshine, and opposed

Free hearts, free foreheads, – you and I are old;
Old age hath yet his honour and his toil.
Death closes all; but something ere the end,
Some work of noble note, may yet be done,
Not unbecoming men that strove with Gods.
The lights begin to twinkle from the rocks;
The long day wanes; the slow moon climbs: the deep
Moans round with many voices. Come, my friends.
'Tis not too late to seek a newer world.
Push off, and sitting well in order smite
The sounding furrows; for mv purpose holds
To sail beyond the sunset, and the baths
Of all the western stars, until I die.
It may be that the gulfs will wash us down;
It may be we shall touch the Happy Isles.
And see the great Achilles, whom we knew.
Tho' much is taken, much abides; and tho'
We are not now that strength which in old days
Moved earth and heaven, that which we are, we
      are, –
One equal temper of heroic hearts,
Made weak by time and fate, but strong in will
To strive, to seek, to find, and not to yield.

TITHONUS

The woods decay, the woods decay and fall,
The vapors weep their burthen to the ground,
Man comes and tills the field and lies beneath,
And after many a summer dies the swan.
Me only cruel immortality
Consumes; I wither slowly in thine arms,
Here at the quiet limit of the world,
A white-hair'd shadow roaming like a dream
The ever-silent spaces of the East,
Far-folded mists, and gleaming halls of morn.
   Alas! for this gray shadow, once a man –
So glorious in his beauty and thy choice,
Who madest him thy chosen, that he seem'd
To his great heart none other than a God!
I ask'd thee, 'Give me immortality.'
Then didst thou grant mine asking with a smile,
Like wealthy men who care not how they give.
But thy strong Hours indignant work'd their wills,
And beat me down and marr'd and wasted me,
And tho' they could not end me, left me maim'd
To dwell in presence of immortal youth,
Immortal age beside immortal youth,

And all I was in ashes. Can thy love,
Thy beauty, make amends, tho' even now,
Close over us, the silver star, thy guide,
Shines in those ttremulous eyes that fill with tears
To hear me? Let me go; take back thy gift.
Why should a man desire in any way
To vary from the kindly race of men,
Or pass beyond the goal of ordinance
Where all should pause, as is most meet for all?

    A soft air fans the cloud apart; there comes
A glimpse of that dark world where I was born.
Once more the old mysterious glimmer steals
From thy pure brows, and from thy shoulders pure,
And bosom beating with a heart renew'd.
Thy cheek begins to redden thro' the gloom,
Thy sweet eyes brighten slowly close to mine,
Ere yet they blind the stars, and the wild team
Which love thee, yearning for thy yoke, arise
And shake the darkness from their loosen'd manes,
And beat the twilight into flakes of fire.

    Lo! ever thus thou growest beautiful
In silence, then before shine answer given
Departest, and thy tears are on my cheek.
Why wilt thou ever scare me with thy tears,
And make me tremble lest a saying learnt,
In days far-off, on that dark earth, be true?
'The Gods themselves cannot recall their gifts.'

    Ay me! ay me! with what another heart
In days far-off, and with what other eyes
I used to watch – if I be he that watch'd –
The lucid outline forming round thee; saw
The dim curls kindle into sunny rings;
Changed with thy mystic change, and felt my blood
Glow with the glow that slowly crimson'd all
Thy presence and thy portals, while I lay,
Mouth, forehead, eyelids, growing dewy-warm
With kisses balmier than half-opening buds
Of April, and could hear the lips that kiss'd
Whispering I knew not what of wild and sweet,
Like that strange song I heard Apollo sing,
While Ilion like a mist rose into towers.

    Yet hold me not for ever in thine East;
How can my nature longer mix with shine?
Coldly thy rosy shadows bathe me, cold
Are all thy lights, and cold my wrinkled feet
Upon thy glimmering thresholds, when the steam
Floats up from those dim fields about the homes
Of happy men that have the power to die,
And grassy barrows of the happier dead.
Release me, and restore me to the ground.
Thou seest all things, thou wilt see my grave;

Thou wilt renew thy beauty morn by morn,
I earth in earth forget these empty courts,
And thee returning on thy silver wheels.

'TEARS, IDLE TEARS'

‹ from *The Princess* ›

'Tears, idle tears, I know not what they mean,
Tears from the depth of some divine despair
Rise in the heart, and gather to the eyes,
In looking on the happy autumn-fields,
And thinking of the days that are no more.

    'Fresh as the first beam glittering on a sail
That brings our friends up from the underworld,
Sad as the last which reddens over one
That sinks with all we love below the verge;
So sad, so fresh, the days that are no more.

'Ah, sad and strange, as in dark summer dawns
The earliest pipe of half-awaken'd birds
To dying ears, when unto dying eyes
The casement slowly grows a glimmering square;
So sad, so strange, the days that are no more.

'Dear as remember'd kisses after death
And sweet as those by hopeless fancy feign'd
On lips that are for others; deep as love
Deep as first love, and wild with all regret;
O Death in Life, the days that are no more!'

MAUD

‹ I ›

Come into the garden, Maud,
  For the black bat, night, has flown,
Come into the garden, Maud,
  I am here at the gate alone;
And the woodbine spices are wafted abroad,
  And the musk of the rose is blown.

‹ II ›

For a breeze of morning moves,
  And the planet of Love is on high,
Beginning to faint in the light that she loves

On a bed of daffodil sky,
To faint in the light of the sun she loves,
 To faint in his light, and to die.

◄ III ►

All night have the roses heard
 The flute, violin, bassoon;
All night has the casement jessamine stirr'd
 To the dancers dancing in tune;
Till a silence fell with the waking bird,
 And a hush with the setting moon.

◄ IV ►

I said to the lily, 'There is but one,
 With whom she has heart to be gay.
When will the dancers leave her alone?
 She is weary of dance and play
Now half to the setting moon are gone,
 And half to the rising day;
Low on the sand and loud on the stone
 The last wheel echoes away.

◄ V ►

I said to the rose, 'The brief night goes
 In babble and revel and wine.
O young lord-lover, what sighs are those,
 For one that will never be shine?
But mine, but mine,' so I sware to the rose,
 'For ever and ever, mine.'

◄ VI ►

And the soul of the rose went into my blood,
 As the music clash'd in the hall;
And long by the garden lake I stood,
 For I heard your rivulet fall
From the lake to the meadow and on to the wood,
 Our wood, that is dearer than all;

◄ VII ►

From the meadow your walks have left so sweet
 That whenever a March-wind sighs
He sets the jewel-print of your feet
 In violets blue as your eyes,
To the woody hollows in which we meet
 And the valleys of Paradise.

◄ VIII ►

The slender acacia would not shake
 One long milk-bloom on the tree;
That white lake-blossom fell into the lake
 As the pimpernel dozed on the lea;

But the rose was awake all night for your sake,
 Knowing your promise to me;
The lilies and roses were all awake,
 They sigh'd for the dawn and thee.

◄ IX ►

Queen rose of the rosebud garden of girls,
 Come hither, the dancers are done,
In gloss of satin and glimmer of pearls,
 Queen lily and rose in one;
Shine out, little head, sunning over with curls,
 To the flowers, and be their sun.

◄ X ►

There has fallen a splendid tear
 From the passion-flower at the gate.
She is coming, my dove, my dear;
 She is coming, my life, my fate.
The red rose cries, 'She is near, she is near;
 And the white rose weeps, 'She is late ;'
The larkspur listens, 'I hear, I hear;'
 And the lily whispers, 'I wait.'

◄ XI ►

She is coming, my own, my sweet;
 Were it ever so airy a tread,
My heart would hear her and beat,
 Were it earth in an earthy bed;
My dust would hear her and beat.
 Had I lain for a century dead,
Would start and tremble under her feet,
 And blossom in purple and red.

❧

THE LOTOS-EATERS

'Courage!' he said, and pointed toward the land,
'This mounting wave will roll us shoreward soon.'
In the afternoon they came unto a land
In which it seemed always afternoon.
All round the coast the languid air did swoon,
Breathing like one that hath a weary dream.
Full-faced above the valley stood the moon;
And, like a downward smoke, the slender stream
Along the cliff to fall and pause and fall did seem.

A land of streams! some, like a downward smoke,
Slow-dropping veils of thinnest lawn, did go;
And some thro' wavering lights and shadows broke,

Rolling a slumbrous sheet of foam below.
They saw the gleaming river seaward flow
From the inner land; far off, three mountain-tops,
Three silent pinnacles of aged snow,
Stood sunset-flush'd; and dew'd with showery drops,
Up-clomb the shadowy pine above the woven copse.

The charmed sunset linger'd low adown
In the red West; thro' mountain clefts the dale
Was seen far inland, and the yellow down
Border'd with pahn. and many a winding vale
And meadow, set with slender galingale;
A land where all things always seem'd the same!
And round about the keel with faces pale,
Dark faces pale against that rosy flame,
The mild-eyed melancholy Lotos-eaters came.

Branches they bore of that enchanted stem,
Laden with flower and fruit, whereof they gave
To each, but whoso did receive of them
And taste, to him the gushing of the wave
Far far away did seem to mourn and rave
On alien shores; and if his fellow spake,
His voice was thin, as voices from the grave;
And deep-asleep he seem'd, yet all awake,
And music in his ears his beating heart did make.

They sat them down upon the yellow sand,
Between the sun and the moon upon the shore:
And sweet it was to dream of Fatherland,
Of child, and wife, and slave; but evermore
Most weary seem'd the sea, weary the oar,
Weary the wandering fields of barren foam.
Then some one said, 'We will return no more;'
And all at once they sang, 'Our island home
Is far beyond the wave; we will no longer roam.'

❧

IN MEMORIAM

◄ 7 ►

Dark house, by which once more I stand
    Here in the long unlovely street,
    Doors, where my heart was used to beat
So quickly, waiting for a hand,

A hand that can be clasp'd no more –
    Behold me, for I cannot sleep,
    And like a guilty thing I creep
At earliest morning to the door.

He is not here; but far away
    The noise of life begins again,
    And ghastly thro' the drizzling rain
On the bald street breaks the blank day.

◄ 11 ►

Calm is the morn without a sound,
    Calm as to suit a calmer grief,
    And only thro' the faded leaf
The chestnut pattering to the ground:

Calm and deep peace on this high wold,
    And on these dews that drench the furze,
    And all the silvery gossamers
That twinkle into green and gold:

Calm and still light on yon great plain
    That sweeps with all its autumn bowers,
    And crowded farms and lessening towers,
To mingle with the bounding main:

Calm and deep peace in this wide air,
    These leaves that redden to the fall;
    And in my heart, if calm at all,
If any calm, a calm despair:

Calm on the seas, and silver sleep,
    And waves that sway themselves in rest,
    And dead calm in that noble breast
Which heaves but with the heaving deep.

◄ 19 ►

The Danube to the Severn gave
    The darken'd heart that beat no more;
    They laid him by the pleasant shore,
And in the hearing of the wave.

There twice a day the Severn fills;
    The salt sea-water passes by,
    And hustles half the babbling Wye,
And makes a silence in the hills.

The Wye is hush'd nor moved along,
    And hush'd my deepest grief of all,
    When fill'd with tears that cannot fall,
I brim with sorrow drowning song.

The tide flows down, the wave again
    Is vocal in its wooded walls;
    My deeper anguish also falls,
And I can speak a little then.

‹24›

And was the day of my delight
　　As pure and perfect as I say?
　　The very source and fount of Day
Is dash'd with wandering isles of night.

If all was good and fair we met,
　　This earth had been the Paradise
　　It never look'd to human eyes
Since our first Sun arose and set.

And is it that the haze of grief
　　Makes former gladness loom so great?
　　The lowness of the present state
That sets the past in this relief?

Or that the past will always win
　　A glory from its being far;
　　And orb into the perfect star
We saw not, when we moved therein?

‹27›

I envy not in any moods
　　The captive void of noble rage,
　　The linnet born within the cage,
That never knew the summer woods:

I envy not the beast that takes
　　His license in the field of time,
　　Unfetter'd bv the sense of crime,
To whom a conscience never wakes;

Nor, what may count itself as blest
　　The heart that never plighted troth
　　But stagnates in the weeds of sloth:
Nor any want-begotten rest.

‹28›

The time draws near the birth of Christ:
　　The moon is hid, the night is still;
　　The Christmas bells from hill to hill
Answer each other in the mist.

Four voices of four hamlets round,
　　From far and near, on mead and moor,
　　Swell out and fail, as if a door
Were shut between me and the sound:

Each voice four changes on the wind,
　　That now dilate, and now decrease,

Peace and goodwill, goodwill and peace,
Peace and goodwill, to all mankind.

This year I slept and woke with pain,
　　I almost wish'd no more to wake,
　　And that my hold on life would break
Before I heard those bells again:

But they my troubled spirit rule,
　　For they controll'd me when a boy;
　　They bring me sorrow touch'd with joy,
The merry merry bells of Yule.

‹39›

Old warder of these buried bones,
　　And answering now my random stroke
　　With fruitful cloud and living smoke,
Dark yew, that graspest at the stones

And dipppest toward the dreamless head,
　　To thee too comes the golden hour
　　When flower is feeling after flower;
But Sorrow – fixt upon the dead,

And darkening dark graves of men, –
　　What whisper'd from her lying lips?
　　Thy gloom is kindled at the tips,
And passes into gloom again.

‹44›

How fares it with the happy dead?
　　For here the man is more and more;
　　But he forgets the days before
God shut the doorways of his head.

The days have vanish'd, tone and tint,
　　And yet perhaps the hoarding sense
　　Gives out at times (he knows not whence)
A little flash, a mystic hint;

And in the long harmonious years
　　(If Death so taste Lethean springs),
　　May some dim touch of earthly things
Surprise thee ranging with thy peers.

If such a dreamy touch should fall,
　　O turn thee round, resolve the doubt;
　　My guardian angel will speak out
In that high place, and tell thee all.

Be near me when my light is low,
⠀⠀When the blood creeps, and the nerves prick
⠀⠀And tingle; and the heart is sick,
And all the wheels of Being slow.

Be near me when the sensuous frame
⠀⠀Is rack'd with pangs that conquer trust;
⠀⠀And Time, a maniac scattering dust,
And Life, a Fury slinging flame.

Be near me when my faith is dry,
⠀⠀And men the flies of latter spring,
⠀⠀That lay their eggs, and sting and sing
And weave their petty cells and die.

Be near me when I fade away,
⠀⠀To point the term of human strife,
⠀⠀And on the low dark verge of life
The twilight of eternal day.

‹59›

O Sorrow, wilt thou live with me
⠀⠀No casual mistress, but a wife
⠀⠀My bosom friend and half of life;
As I confess it needs must be;

O Sorrow, wilt thou rule my blood,
⠀⠀Be sometimes lovely like a bride
⠀⠀And put thy harsher moods aside,
If thou wilt have me wise and good.

My centered passion cannot move,
⠀⠀Nor will it lessen from to-day;
⠀⠀But I'll have leave at times to play
As with the creature of my love;

And set thee forth, for thou art mine,
⠀⠀With so much hope for years to come.
⠀⠀That, howsoe'er I know thee, some
Could hardly tell what name were thine.

‹69›

I dream'd there would be Spring no more,
⠀⠀That Nature's ancient power was lost
⠀⠀The streets were black with smoke and frost,
They chatter'd trifles at the door:

I wander'd from the noisy town
⠀⠀I found a wood with thorny boughs:

I took the thorns to bind my brows
I wore them like a civic crown:

I met with scoffs, I met with scorns
⠀⠀From youth and babe and hoary hairs:
⠀⠀They call'd me in the public squares
The fool that wears a crown of thorns:

They call'd me fool, they call'd me child.
⠀⠀I found an angel of the night
⠀⠀The voice was low, the look was bright
He look'd upon my crown and smiled:

He reach'd the glory of a hand
⠀⠀That seem'd to touch it into leaf:
⠀⠀The voice was not the voice of grief
The words were hard to understand.

‹77›

What hope is here for modern rhyme
⠀⠀To him, who turns a musing eye
⠀⠀On songs, and deeds, and lives, that lie
Foreshorten'd in the tract of time?

These mortal lullabies of pain
⠀⠀May bind a book, may line a box,
⠀⠀May serve to curl a maiden's locks
Or when a thousand moons shall wane

A man upon a stall may find,
⠀⠀And, passing, turn the page that tells
⠀⠀A grief, then changed to something else
Sung by a long-forgotten mind.

But what of that? My darken'd ways
⠀⠀Shall ring with music all the same;
⠀⠀To breathe my loss is more than fame,
To utter love more sweet than praise.

‹78›

Again at Christmas did we weave
⠀⠀The holly round the Christmas hearth;
⠀⠀The silent snow possess'd the earth,
And calmly fell our Christmas-eve:

The yule-clog sparkled keen with frost,
⠀⠀No wing of wind the region swept,
⠀⠀But over all things brooding slept
The quiet sense of something lost.

As in the winters left behind
    Again our ancient games had place,
    The mimic picture's breathing grace,
And dance and song and hoodman-blind.

Who show'd a token of distress?
    No single tear, no mark of pain:
    O sorrow, then can sorrow wane?
O grief, can grief be changed to less?

O last regret, regret can die!
    No – mixt with all this mystic frame,
    Her deep relations are the same,
But with long use her tears are dry.

‹89›

Witch-elms that counterchange the floor
    Of this flat lawn with dusk and bright,
    And thou, with all thy breadth and height
Of foliage, towering sycamore;

How often, hither wandering down
    My Arthur found your shadows fair,
    And shook to all the liberal air
The dust and din and steam of town:

He brought an eye for all he saw;
    He mixt in all our simple sports;
    They pleased him, fresh from brawling courts
And dusty purlieus of the law.

O joy to him in this retreat,
    Immantled in ambrosial dark,
    To drink the cooler air, and mark
The landscape winking thro' the heat:

O sound to rout the brood of cares,
    The sweep of scythe in morning dew,
    The gust that round the garden flew,
And tumbled half the mellowing pears!

O bliss, when all in circle drawn
    About him, heart and ear were fed
    To hear him, as he lay and read
The Tuscan poets on the lawn:

Or in the all-golden afternoon
    A guest, or happy sister, sung,
    Or here she brought the harp and flung
A ballad to the brightening moon:

Nor less it pleased in livelier moods,
    Beyond the bounding hill to stray
    And break the livelong summer day
With banquet in the distant woods;

Whereat we glanced from theme to theme,
    Discuss'd the books to love or hate,
    Or touch'd the changes of the state.
Or threaded some Socratic dream,

But if I praised the busy town,
    He loved to rail against it still,
    For 'ground in yonder social mill
We rub each other's angles down,

'And merge' he said 'in form and gloss
    The picturesque of man and man.'
    We talk'd: the stream beneath us ran,
The wine-flask lying couch'd in moss,

Or cool'd within the glooming wave;
    And last, returning from afar,
    Before the crimson-circled star
Had fall'n into her father's grave,

And brushing ankle-deep in flowers,
    We heard behind the woodbine veil
    The milk that bubbled in the pail,
And buzzings of the honied hours.

‹95›

By night we linger'd on the lawn,
    For underfoot the herb was dry;
    And genial warmth; and o'er the sky
The silvery haze of summer drawn;

And calm that let the tapers burn
    Unwavering: not a cricket chirr'd:
    The brook alone far-off was heard,
And on the board the fluttering urn:

And bats went round in fragrant skies,
    And wheel'd or lit the filmy shapes
    That haunt the dusk, with ermine capes
And woolly breasts and beaded eyes;

While now we sang old songs that peal'd
    From knoll to knoll, where, couch'd at ease,
    The white kine glimmer'd, and the trees
Laid their dark arms about the field.

But when those others, one by one,
    Withdrew themselves from me and night
    And in the house light after light
Went out, and I was all alone,

A hunger seized my heart; I read
    Of that glad year which once had been,
    In those fall'n leaves which kept their green,
The noble letters of the dead:

And strangely on the silence broke
    The silent-speaking words, and strange
    Was love's dumb cry defying change
To test his worth: and strangely spoke

The faith, the vigour, bold to dwell
    On doubts that drive the coward back,
    And keen thro' wordy snares to track
Suggestion to her inmost cell.

So word by word, and line by line,
    The dead man touch'd me from the past.
    And all at once it seem'd at last
The living soul was flash'd on mine,

And mine in this was wound, and whirl'd
    About empyreal heights of thought,
    And came on that which is, and caught
The deep pulsations of the world,

Aeonian music measuring out
    The steps of Time – the shocks of Chance –
    The blows of Death. At length my trance
Was cancell'd, stricken thro' with doubt

Vague words! but ah, how hard to frame
    In matter moulded forms of speech,
    Or ev'n for intellect to reach
Thro' memory that which I became:

Till now the doubtful dusk reveal'd
    The knolls once more where, couch'd at ease,
    The white kine glimmer'd, and the trees
Laid their dark arms about the field:

And suck'd from out the distant gloom
    A breeze began to tremble o'er
    The large leaves of the sycamore,
And fluctuate all the still perfume,

And gathering freshlier overhead,
    Rock'd the full foliaged elms, and swung
    The heavy-folded rose, and flung
The lilies to and fro, and said

'The dawn, the dawn,' and died away;
    And East and West, without a breath,
    Mixt their dim lights, like life and death,
To broaden into boundless day.

‹ 104 ›

The time draws near the birth of Christ;
    The moon is hid, the night is still;
    A single church below the hill
Is pealing, folded in the mist.

A single peal of bells below,
    That wakens at this hour of rest
    A single murmur in the breast
That these are not the bells I know.

Like strangers' voices here they sound,
    In lands where not a memory strays,
    Nor landmark breathes of other days,
But all is new unhallow'd ground.

‹ 107 ›

It is the day when he was born,
    A bitter day that early sank
    Behind a purple-frosty bank
Of vapour, leaving night forlorn.

The time admits not flowers or leaves
    To deck the banquet. Fiercely flies
    The blast of North and East, and ice
Makes daggers at the sharpen'd eaves,

And bristles all the brakes and thorns
    To yon hard crescent, as she hangs
    Above the wood which grides and clangs
Its leafless ribs and iron horns

Together, in the drifts that pass
    To darken on the rolling brine
    That breaks the coast. But fetch the wine
Arrange the board and brim the glass;

Bring in great logs and let them lie
    To make a solid core of heat
    Be cheerful-minded, talk and treat
Of all things ev'n as he were by;

We keep the day. With festal cheer,
    With books and music, surely we
    Will drink to him, whate'er he be
And sing the songs he loved to hear.

June Bracken and Heather

There on the top of the down,
The wild heather round me and over me June's high
    blue,
When I looked at the bracken so bright and the
    heather so brown,
I thought to myself I would offer this book to you,
This, and my love together,
To you that are seventy-seven,
With a faith as clear as the heights of the June-blue
    heaven,
And a fancy as summer-new
As the green of the bracken amid the gloom of the
    heather.

Crossing the Bar

Sunset and evening star,
    And one clear call for me!
And may there be no moaning of the bar,
    When I put out to sea,

But such a tide as moving seems asleep.
    Too full for sound and foam,
When that which drew from out the boundless deep
    Turns again home.

Twilight and evening bell,
    And after that the dark!
And may there be no sadness of farewell,
    When I embark;

For tho' from out our bourne of TIme and Place
    The flood may bear me far,
I hope to see my Pilot face to face
    When I have crost the bar.

James Thomson (1700–48) excels at the long poem, a genre which can present problems for the anthologist. In fact, though, his greatest work, *The Seasons*, is a kind of anthology in itself, fascinatingly readable in its variety of interests and loosely constructed enough to lend itself easily to the selection of extracts. I have chosen lengthy ones in an attempt to give a sense of the leisurely movement of his writing. Like Keats, Thomson finds 'every thing, every place interesting'. The birds and insects in the passages from 'Spring' and 'Summer' included here are described with affectionate attentiveness, and the evocation of the complexity of microscopic life which concludes the latter seems quite modern. But he was a man of his time, and his delightful portrayal of drunken huntsmen in 'Autumn' has all the verve one expects from Augustan satire. Even here, though, he cannot refrain from a haunting simile drawn from the natural world:

> . . . Before their maudlin eyes,
> Seen dim and blue, the double tapers
>   dance,
> Like the sun wading through the misty
>   sky.

The most memorable characters in *The Seasons* are its birds, animals and insects. The vignette of the robin in 'Winter' is touching without being sentimental because the creature is allowed to retain its otherness. Thomson is a celebrator, excited by the world. At times his enthusiasm seems naïve, and we may wonder about the political correctness of a Scot who was so fervent a supporter of the Union that he wrote the words to 'Rule, Britannia'. But his appetite for knowledge is a rare and admirable trait in a poet. In a passage which fuses science and poetry, he celebrates Newton for revealing the rainbow hidden inside the plain light of day. Thomson, too, was a man who discovered unexpected colours in the ordinary.

JAMES THOMSON

‹from *The Seasons*›

SPRING

(lines 604–60)

The blackbird whistles from the thorny brake,
The mellow bullfinch answers from the grove;
Nor are the linnets, o'er the flowering furze
Poured out profusely, silent. Joined to these
Innumerous songsters, in the freshening shade
Of new-sprung leaves, their modulations mix
Mellifluous. The jay, the rook, the daw,
And each harsh pipe, discordant heard alone,
Aid the full concert; while the stock-dove breathes
A melancholy murmur through the whole.
　　'Tis love creates their melody, and all
This waste of music is the voice of love,
That even to birds and beasts the tender arts
Of pleasing teaches. Hence the glossy kind
Try every winning way inventive love
Can dictate, and in courtship to their mates
Pour forth their little souls. First, wide around,
With distant awe, in airy rings they rove,
Endeavouring by a thousand tricks to catch
The cunning, conscious, half-averted glance
Of their regardless charmer. Should she seem
Softening the least approvance to bestow,
Their colours burnish, and, by hope inspired,
They brisk advance; then, on a sudden struck,
Retire disordered; then again approach,
In fond rotation spread the spotted wing,
And shiver every feather with desire.
　　Connubial leagues agreed, to the deep woods
They haste away, all as their fancy leads,
Pleasure, or food, or secret safety prompts;
That Nature's great command may be obeyed,
Nor all the sweet sensations they perceive
Indulged in vain. Some to the holly-hedge
Nestling repair, and to the thicket some;
Some to the rude protection of the thorn
Commit their feeble offspring. The cleft tree
Offers its kind concealment to a few,
Their food its insects, and its moss their nests.
Others apart far in the grassy dale,
Or roughening waste, their humble texture weave
But most in woodland solitudes delight,
In unfrequented glooms, or shaggy banks,
Steep, and divided by a babbling brook
Whose murmurs soothe them all the live-long day
When by kind duty fixed. Among the roots
Of hazel, pendent o'er the plaintive stream,

They frame the first foundation of their domes –
Dry sprigs of trees, in artful fabric laid,
And bound with clay together. Now 'tis nought
But restless hurry through the busy air,
Beat by unnumbered wings. The swallow sweeps
The slimy pool, to build his hanging house
Intent. And often, from the careless back
Of herds and flocks, a thousand tugging bills
Pluck hair and wool; and oft, when unobserved,
Steal from the barn a straw – till soft and warm
Clean and complete, their habitation grows.

SUMMER

(lines 246–317)

　　　　Nor shall the muse disdain
To let the little noisy summer-race
Live in her lay and flutter through her song:
Not mean though simple – to the sun allied,
From him they draw their animating fire.
　　Waked by his warmer ray, the reptile young
Come winged abroad, by the light air upborne,
Lighter, and full of soul. From every chink
And secret corner, where they slept away
The wintry storms, or rising from their tombs
To higher life, by myriads forth at once
Swarming they pour, of all the varied hues
Their beauty-beaming parent can disclose.
Ten thousand forms, ten thousand different tribes
People the blaze. To sunny waters some
By fatal instinct fly; where on the pool
They sportive wheel, or, sailing down the stream,
Are snatched immediate by the quick-eyed trout
Or darting salmon. Through the green-wood glade
Some love to stray; there lodged, amused, and fed
In the fresh leaf. Luxurious, others make
The meads their choice, and visit every flower
And every latent herb: for the sweet task
To propagate their kinds, and where to wrap
In what soft beds their young, yet undisclosed,
Employs their tender care. Some to the house,
The fold, and dairy hungry bend their flight;
Sip round the pail, or taste the curdling cheese:
Oft, inadvertent, from the milky stream
They meet their fate, or, weltering in the bowl
With powerless wings around them wrapt, expire.
　　But chief to heedless flies the window proves
A constant death; where, gloomily retired,

The villain spider lives, cunning and fierce,
Mixture abhorred! Amid a mangled heap
Of carcases in eager watch he sits,
O'erlooking all his waving snares around.
Near the dire cell the dreadless wanderer oft
Passes; as oft the ruffian shows his front.
The prey at last ensnared, he dreadful darts
With rapid glide along the leaning line;
And, fixing in the wretch his cruel fangs,
Strikes backward grimly pleased: the fluttering wing
And shriller sound declare extreme distress,
And ask the helping hospitable hand.

    Resounds the living surface of the ground:
Nor undelightful is the ceaseless hum
To him who muses through the woods at noon,
Or drowsy shepherd as he lies reclined,
With half-shut eyes, beneath the floating shade
Of willows grey, close-crowding o'er the brook.

    Gradual from these what numerous kinds descend,
Evading even the microscopic eye!
Full Nature swarms with life; one wondrous mass
Of animals, or atoms organized
Waiting the vital breath when Parent-Heaven
Shall bid his spirit blow. The hoary fen
In putrid streams emits the living cloud
Of pestilence. Through subterranean cells,
Where searching sunbeams scarce can find a way,
Earth animated heaves. The flowery leaf
Wants not its soft inhabitants. Secure
Within its winding citadel the stone
Holds multitudes. But chief the forest boughs,
That dance unnumbered to the playful breeze,
The downy orchard, and the melting pulp
Of mellow fruit the nameless nations feed
Of evanescent insects. Where the pool
Stands mantled o'er with green, invisible
Amid the floating verdure millions stray.
Each liquid too, whether it pierces, soothes,
Inflames, refreshes, or exalts the taste,
With various forms abounds. Nor is the stream
Of purest crystal, nor the lucid air,
Though one transparent vacancy it seems,
Void of their unseen people. These, concealed
By the kind art of forming Heaven, escape
The grosser eye of man: for, if the worlds
In worlds inclosed should on his senses burst,
From cates ambrosial and the nectared bowl
He would abhorrent turn; and in dead night,
When Silence sleeps o'er all, be stunned with noise.

AUTUMN
(lines 503–69)

    But first the fuelled chimney blazes wide;
The tankards foam; and the strong table groans
Beneath the smoking sirloin, stretched immense
From side to side, in which with desperate knife
They deep incision make, and talk the while
Of England's glory, ne'er to be defaced
While hence they borrow vigour; or, amain
Into the pasty plunged, at intervals,
If stomach keen can intervals allow,
Relating all the glories of the chase.
Then sated Hunger bids his brother Thirst
Produce the mighty bowl: the mighty bowl,
Swelled high with fiery juice, steams liberal round
A potent gale, delicious as the breath
Of Maia to the love-sick shepherdess
On violets diffused, while soft she hears
Her panting shepherd stealing to her arms.
Nor wanting is the brown October, drawn
Mature and perfect from his dark retreat
Of thirty years; and now his honest front
Flames in the light refulgent, not afraid
Even with the vineyard's best produce to vie.
To cheat the thirsty moments, whist a while
Walks his grave round beneath a cloud of smoke,
Wreathed fragrant from the pipe; or the quick
    dice,
In thunder leaping from the box, awake
The sounding gammon; while romp-loving miss
Is hauled about in gallantry robust.

    At last these puling idlenesses laid
Aside, frequent and full, the dry divan
Close in firm circle; and set ardent in
For serious drinking. Nor evasion sly
Nor sober shift is to the puking wretch
Indulged apart; but earnest brimming bowls
Lave every soul, the table floating round,
And pavement faithless to the fuddled foot.
Thus as they swim in mutual swill, the talk,
Vociferous at once from twenty tongues,
Reels first from theme to theme – from horses,
    hounds,
To church or mistress, politics or ghost –
In endless mazes, intricate, perplext.
Meantime, with sudden interruption, loud
The impatient catch bursts from the joyous heart.
That moment touched is each congenial soul;
And, opening in a full-mouthed cry of joy,
The laugh, the slap, the jocund curse goes round;

While, from their slumbers shook, the kennelled
  hounds
Mix in the music of the day again.
As when the tempest, that has vexed the deep
The dark night long, with fainter murmurs falls;
So gradual sinks their mirth. Their feeble tongues,
Unable to take up the cumbrous word,
Lie quite dissolved. Before their maudlin eyes,
Seen dim and blue, the double tapers dance,
Like the sun wading through the misty sky.
Then, sliding soft, they drop. Confused above,
Glasses and bottles, pipes and gazetteers,
As if the table even itself was drunk,
Lie a wet broken scene: and wide, below,
Is heaped the social slaughter – where astride
The lubber Power in filthy triumph sits,
Slumbrous, inclining still from side to side,
And steeps them drenched in potent sleep till morn.
Perhaps some doctor of tremendous paunch,
Awful and deep, a black abyss of drink,
Outlives them all; and, from his buried flock
Retiring, full of rumination sad,
Laments the weakness of these latter times.

❧

WINTER

(lines 223–64)

The keener tempests come: and, fuming dun
From all the livid east or piercing north,
Thick clouds ascend in whose capacious womb
A vapoury deluge lies, to snow congealed.
Heavy they roll their fleecy world along,
And the sky saddens with the gathered storm.
Through the hushed air the whitening shower
  descends,
At first thin-wavering; till at last the flakes
Fall broad and wide and fast, dimming the day
With a continual flow. The cherished fields
Put on their winter-robe of purest white.
'Tis brightness all; save where the new snow melts
Along the mazy current. Low the woods
Bow their hoar head; and, ere the languid sun
Faint from the west emits his evening ray,
Earth's universal face, deep-hid and chill,
Is one wild dazzling waste, that buries wide
The works of man. Drooping, the labourer-ox
Stands covered o'er with snow, and then demands
The fruit of all his toil. The fowls of heaven,

Tamed by the cruel season, crowd around
The winnowing store, and claim the little boon
Which Providence assigns them. One alone,
The redbreast, sacred to the household gods,
Wisely regardful of the embroiling sky,
In joyless fields and thorny thickets leaves
His shivering mates, and pays to trusted man
His annual visit. Half afraid, he first
Against the window beats; then brisk alights
On the warm hearth; then, hopping o'er the floor,
Eyes all the smiling family askance,
And pecks, and starts, and wonders where he is –
Till, more familiar grown, the table-crumbs
Attract his slender feet. The foodless wilds
Pour forth their brown inhabitants. The hare,
Though timorous of heart, and hard beset
By death in various forms, dark snares, and dogs,
And more unpitying men, the garden seeks,
Urged on by fearless want. The bleating kind
Eye the bleak heaven, and next the glistening earth,
With looks of dumb despair; then, sad-dispersed,
Dig for the withered herb through heaps of snow.

❧

TO THE MEMORY OF SIR ISAAC NEWTON

(lines 96–124)

Even Light itself, which every thing displays,
Shone undiscovered, till his brighter mind
Untwisted all the shining robe of day;
And, from the whitening undistinguished blaze,
Collecting every ray into his kind,
To the charmed eye educed the gorgeous train
Of parent colours. First the flaming red
Sprung vivid forth; the tawny orange next;
And next delicious yellow; by whose side
Fell the kind beams of all-refreshing green.
Then the pure blue, that swells autumnal skies,
Ethereal played; and then, of sadder hue,
Emerged the deepened indigo, as when
The heavy-skirted evening droops with frost;
While the last gleamings of refracted light
Died in the fainting violet away.
These, when the clouds distil the rosy shower,
Shine out distinct adown the watery bow;
While o'er our heads the dewy vision bends
Delightful, melting on the fields beneath.
Myriads of mingling dyes from these result,
And myriads still remain – infinite source

Of beauty, ever flushing, ever new.
　　Did ever poet image aught so fair,
Dreaming in whispering groves by the hoarse
　　brook?
Or prophet, to whose rapture heaven descends?
Even now the setting sun and shifting clouds,
Seen, Greenwich, from thy lovely heights, declare
How just, how beauteous the refractive law.

Henry Vaughan (1621–95) is a poet of extremes, writing in order to survive personal and public trauma. Knowing that much of life 'is loose and spills' yet glimpsing 'bright shoots of everlastingless', he produced in his twenties an outpouring of Shamanic art which appears to have saved his own life and was later offered to the Church in case it might help others. 'Make these mountains flow, / These mountains of cold ice in me . . .' Although I can share neither Vaughan's specifically Christian faith nor his royalist politics, I have been for several years deeply affected by the molten truth to experience of these poems. Vaughan saw poetry as healing: when the struggles traced in *Silex Scintillans* were over, he set most writing aside to work as a Breconshire doctor.

I regret that I have not been able to represent here Vaughan's exploration of processes of mourning, both his unblinking recognition of death – 'nothing but the snuff to me / Appeareth plain' . . . 'I have out-lived / My life' – and his realisation that, to be worthy of what love reveals, the mourner must continue to grow in contact with the dead. Trying to grasp the full sense of this intuition, I find myself thinking above all of the *Phaedrus*, in which Plato (through Socrates) evokes 'a reality without colour or shape, intangible but utterly real', reluctantly and inadequately to be conveyed through words, yet the essential ground of that form of love which is truthful communication.

Plato's concern with rhetoric is centrally relevant to Vaughan's work for, as well as being a poet of spiritual intuitions – which lie beyond all dogma, as they lie beyond language itself – Vaughan is a poet's poet, one for whom writing and publishing is not a matter of 'self-ends' but a sacred task.

Distraction

O knit me, that am crumbled dust! the heap
    Is all dispersed, and cheap;
      Give for a handful, but a thought
        And it is bought;
          Hadst thou
Made me a star, a pearl, or a rain-bow,
    The beams I then had shot
    My light had lessened not,
      But now
I find my self the less, the more I grow;
      The world
Is full of voices; Man is called, and hurled
    By each, he answers all,
    Knows every note, and call,
      Hence, still
Fresh dotage tempts, or old usurps his will.
Yet, hadst thou clipped my wings, when coffined in
    This quickened mass of sin,
    And saved that light, which freely thou
      Didst then bestow,
      I fear
I should have spurned, and said thou didst forbear;
    Or that thy store was less,
    But now since thou didst bless
      So much,
I grieve, my God! that thou hast made me such.
      I grieve?
O, yes! thou know'st I do; come, and relieve
    And tame, and keep down with thy light
    Dust that would rise, and dim my sight,
      Lest left alone too long
      Amidst the noise, and throng,
        Oppressed I
Striving to save the whole, by parcels die.

Vanity of Spirit

Quite spent with thoughts I left my cell, and lay
Where a shrill spring tuned to the early day.
    I begged here long, and groaned to know
    Who gave the clouds so brave a bow,
    Who bent the spheres, and circled in
    Corruption with this glorious ring,
    What is his name, and how I might
    Descry some part of his great light.
I summoned nature: pierced through all her store,

Broke up some seals, which none had touched before,
    Her womb, her bosom, and her head
    Where all her secrets lay a bed
    I rifled quite, and having passed
    Through all the creatures, came at last
    To search my self, where I did find
    Traces, and sounds of a strange kind.
Here of this mighty spring, I found some drills,
With echoes beaten from the eternal hills;
    Weak beams, and fires flashed to my sight,
    Like a young east, or moon-shine night,
    Which showed me in a nook cast by
    A piece of much antiquity,
    With hieroglyphics quite dismembered,
    And broken letters scarce remembered.
I took them up, and (much joyed,) went about
T' unite those pieces, hoping to find out
    The mystery; but this near done,
    That little light I had was gone:
    It grieved me much. At last, said I,
    Since in these veils my eclipsed eye
    May not approach thee, (for at night
    Who can have commerce with the light?)
    I'll disapparel, and to buy
    But one half glance, most gladly die.

The Water-fall

With what deep murmurs through time's silent
      stealth
Doth thy transparent, cool and watery wealth
    Here flowing fall,
    And chide, and call,
As if his liquid, loose retinue stayed
Ling'ring, and were of this steep place afraid,
    The common pass
    Where, clear as glass,
    All must descend
    Not to an end:
But quickened by this deep and rocky grave,
Rise to a longer course more bright and brave.
Dear stream! dear bank, where often I
Have sat, and pleased my pensive eye,
Why, since each drop of thy quick store
Runs thither, whence it flowed before,
Should poor souls fear a shade or night,
Who came (sure) from a sea of light?
Or since those drops are all sent back

So sure to thee, that none doth lack,
Why should frail flesh doubt any more
That what God takes, he'll not restore?
O useful element and clear!
My sacred wash and cleanser here,
My first consigner unto those
Fountains of life, where the Lamb goes?
What sublime truths, and wholesome themes,
Lodge in thy mystical, deep streams!
Such as dull man can never find
Unless that Spirit lead his mind,
Which first upon thy face did move,
And hatched all with his quickening love.
As this loud brook's incessant fall
In streaming rings restagnates all,
Which reach by course the bank, and then
Are no more seen, just so pass men.
O my invisible estate,
My glorious liberty, still late!
Thou art the channel my soul seeks,
Not this with cataracts and creeks.

THE MORNING-WATCH

O joys! Infinite sweetness! with what flowers,
And shoots of glory, my soul breaks, and buds!
            All the long hours
            Of night, and rest
            Through the still shrouds
            Of sleep, and clouds,
        This dew fell on my breast;
            O how it *bloods*,
And *spirits* all my earth! hark! In what rings,
And *hymning circulations* the quick world
            Awakes, and sings;
            The rising winds,
            And falling springs,
            Birds, beasts, all things
        Adore him in their kinds.
            Thus all is hurled
In sacred *hymns*, and order, the great *chime*
And *symphony* of nature. Prayer is
            The world in tune,
            A spirit-voice,
            And vocal joys
        Whose *echo* is heaven's bliss.
            O let me climb
When I lie down! The pious soul by night

Is like a clouded star, whose beams though said
            To shed their light
            Under some cloud
            Yet are above,
            And shine, and move
        Beyond that misty shroud.
            So in my bed
That curtained grave, though sleep, like ashes, hide
My lamp, and life, both shall in thee abide.

RESURRECTION AND IMMORTALITY
(lines 31–4)

For a preserving spirit doth still pass
            Untainted through this mass,
Which doth resolve, produce, and ripen all
            That to it fall [. . .]

The reader will notice immediately that I have not included sections from *Song of Myself*. The reason is that the poem should be read in its entirety (and in its entirety the poem far exceeds the number of lines allotted to poets in this anthology), that its acretions are central to its identity, and that editing it or leaving out certain parts undermines the poem's fundamental gesture of inclusiveness. I have chosen instead poems that have some of the anaphoral power of Whitman's epic, some of its 'democratic' syntax (the nonsubordination of clauses), but are much more efficient in their use of these characteristics.

'Crossing Brooklyn Ferry', in which Whitman (1819–92) carves out a place for himself in the lives of those who will come later ... but as an absence, one who will be missed, is an elegy written for himself – a crossing into the future, an anticipation of his posthumous literary presence. 'Out of the Cradle Endlessly Rocking', a magnificent poem on the 'calling' of poetry, is another attempt to transcend death. But in this poem, since death appears as a word 'lisped' by the sea, Whitman is not frightened by it: 'A word then, (for I will conquer it.)' The third poem I have included that bears some resemblance to *Song of Myself* is 'When Lilacs Last in the Dooryard Bloom'd', the lament for the death of President Lincoln, and one of the greatest elegies of the English language.

In 'As I Ebb'd with the Ocean of Life' Whitman sings a different song of himself than we usually hear in his poetry. It is full of self-doubt and uncertainty over what his poems will accomplish. It is not a Whitman who seems primarily the creation of his own rhetoric (the Whitman who contains multitudes), but another Whitman, perhaps the real one, the one who unashamedly admits that 'amid all the blab whose echoes recoil upon me / I have not once had the least idea who or what I am.' Finally, I have included 'Vigil Strange I Kept on the Field One Night'. This poem, charged with intimacy and subdued by helplessness, in which the death of a young soldier is eroticized, seems a far cry from the operatic 'Out of the Cradle Endlessly Rocking', and shows the sweep of Whitman's poetic voice.

CROSSING BROOKLYN FERRY

‹ 1 ›

Flood-tide below me! I see you face to face!
Clouds of the west – sun there half an hour high – I
     see you also face to face.

Crowds of men and women attired in the usual
     costumes, how curious you are to me!
On the ferry-boats the hundreds and hundreds that
     cross? returning home, are more curious to me than
     you suppose,
And you that shall cross from shore to shore years
     hence are more to me, and more in my meditations,
     than you might suppose.

‹ 2 ›

The impalpable sustenance of me from all things at all
     hours of the day,
The simple, compact, well-join'd scheme, myself
     disintegrated, every one disintegrated yet part of the
     scheme,
The similitudes of the past and those of the future,
The glories strung like beads on my smallest sights
     and hearings, on the walk in the street and the
     passage over the river,
The current rushing so swiftly and swimming with me
     far away,
The others that are to follow me, the ties between me
     and them,
The certainty of others, the life, love, sight, hearing of
     others.

Others will enter the gates of the ferry and cross from
     shore to shore,
Others will watch the run of the flood-tide,
Others will see the shipping of Manhattan north and
     west, and the heights of Brooklyn to the south and
     east,
Others will see the islands large and small;
Fifty years hence, others will see them as they cross,
     the sun half an hour high,
A hundred years hence, or ever so many hundred years
     hence, others will see them,
Will enjoy the sunset, the pouring-in of the flood-tide,
     the falling-back to the sea of the ebb-tide.

‹ 3 ›

It avails not, time nor place – distance avails not,
I am with you, you men and women of a generation,
     or ever so many generations hence,

Just as you feel when you look on the river and sky, so
    I felt,
Just as any of you is one of a living crowd, I was one of
    a crowd,
Just as you are refresh'd by the gladness of the river
    and the bright flow, I was refresh'd,
Just as you stand and lean on the rail, yet hurry with
    the swift current, I stood yet was hurried,
Just as you look on the numberless masts of ships and
    the thick-stemm'd pipes of steamboats, I look'd.

I too many and many a time cross'd the river of old,
Watched the Twelfth-month sea-gulls, saw them high
    in the air floating with motionless wings, oscillating
    their bodies,
Saw how the glistening yellow lit up parts of their
    bodies and left the rest in strong shadow,
Saw the slow-wheeling circles and the gradual edging
    toward the south,
Saw the reflection of the summer sky in the water,
Had my eyes dazzled by the shimmering track of beams,
Look'd at the fine centrifugal spokes of light round the
    shape of my head in the sunlit water,
Look'd on the haze on the hills southward and south-
    westward,
Look'd on the vapor as it flew in fleeces tinged with
    violet,
Look'd toward the lower bay to notice the vessels
    arriving,
Saw their approach, saw aboard those that were near
    me,
Saw the white sails of schooners and sloops, saw the
    ships at anchor,
The sailors at work in the rigging or out astride the
    spars,
The round masts, the swinging motion of the hulls,
    the slender serpentine pennants,
The large and small steamers in motion, the pilots in
    their pilot-houses,
The white wake left by the passage, the quick
    tremulous whirl of the wheels,
The flags of all nations, the falling of them at sunset,
The scallop-edged waves in the twilight, the ladled
    cups, the frolicsome crests and glistening,
The stretch afar growing dimmer and dimmer, the
    gray walls of the granite storehouses by the docks,
On the river the shadowy group, the big steam-tug
    closely flank'd on each side by the barges, the hay-
    boat, the belated lighter,
On the neighboring shore the fires from the foundry
    chimneys burning high and glaringly into the night,

Casting their flicker of black contrasted with wild red
    and yellow light over the tops of houses, and down
    into the clefts of streets.

‹ 4 ›
These and all else were to me the same as they are to
    you,
I loved well those cities, loved well the stately and
    rapid river,
The men and women I saw were all near to me,
Others the same – others who look back on me
    because I look'd forward to them,
(The time will come, though I stop here to-day and to-
    night.)

‹ 5 ›
What is it then between us?
What is the count of the scores or hundreds of years
    between us?

Whatever it is, it avails not – distance avails not, and
    place avails not,
I too lived, Brooklyn of ample hills was mine,
I too walk'd the streets of Manhattan island, and
    bathed in the waters around it,
I too felt the curious abrupt questionings stir within
    me,
In the day among crowds of people sometimes they
    came upon me,
In my walks home late at night or as I lay in my bed
    they came upon me,
I too had been struck from the float forever held in
    solution,
I too had receiv'd identity by my body,
That I was I knew was of my body, and what I should
    be I knew I should be of my body.

‹ 6 ›
It is not upon you alone the dark patches fall,
The dark threw its patches down upon me also,
The best I had done seem'd to me blank and
    suspicious,
My great thoughts as I supposed them, were they not
    in reality meagre?
Nor is it you alone who know what it is to be evil,
I am he who knew what it was to be evil,
I too knitted the old knot of contrariety,
Blabb'd, blush'd, resented, lied, stole, grudg'd,
Had guile, anger, lust, hot wishes I dared not speak,
Was wayward, vain, greedy, shallow, sly, cowardly,
    malignant,

The wolf, the snake, the hog, not wanting in me,
The cheating look, the frivolous word, the adulterous
     wish, not wanting,
Refusals, hates, postponements, meanness, laziness,
     none of these wanting,
Was one with the rest, the days and haps of the rest,
Was call'd by my nighest name by clear loud voices of
     young men as they saw me approaching or passing,
Felt their arms on my neck as I stood, or the negligent
     leaning of their flesh against me as I sat,
Saw many I loved in the street or ferry-boat or public
     assembly, yet never told them a word,
Lived the same life with the rest, the same old
     laughing, gnawing, sleeping,
Play'd the part that still looks back on the actor or
     actress,
The same old role, the role that is what we make it, as
     great as we like,
Or as small as we like, or both great and small.

‹7›
Closer yet I approach you,
What thought you have of me now, I had as much of
     you – I laid in my stores in advance,
I consider'd long and seriously of you before you were
     born.

Who was to know what should come home to me?
Who knows but I am enjoying this?
Who knows, for all the distance, but I am as good as
     looking at you now, for all you cannot see me?

‹8›
Ah, what can ever be more stately and admirable to me
     than mast-hemm'd Manhattan?
River and sunset and scallop-edg'd waves of flood-tide?
The sea-gulls oscillating their bodies, the hay-boat in
     the twilight, and the belated lighter?
What gods can exceed these that clasp me, the hand,
     and with voices I love call me promptly and loudly
     by my nighest name as I approach?
What is more subtle than this which ties me to the
     woman or man that looks in my face?
Which fuses me into you now, and pours my meaning
     into you?

We understand then do we not?
What I promis'd without mentioning it, have you not
     accepted?
What the study could not teach – what the preaching
     could not accomplish is accomplish'd, is it not?

‹9›
Flow on, river! flow with the flood-tide, and ebb with
     the ebb-tide!
Frolic on, crested and scallop-edg'd waves!
Gorgeous clouds of the sunset! drench with your
     splendor me, or the men and women generations
     after me!
Cross from shore to shore, countless crowds of
     passengers!
Stand up, tall masts of Mannahatta! stand up, beautiful
     hills of Brooklyn!
Throb, baffled and curious brain! throw out questions
     and answers!
Suspend here and everywhere, eternal float of solution!
Gaze, loving and thirsting eyes, in the house or street
     or public assembly!
Sound out, voices of young men! loudly and musically
     call me by my nighest name!
Live, old life! play the part that looks back on the actor
     or actress!
Play the old role, the role that is great or small
     according as one makes it!
Consider, you who peruse me, whether I may not in
     unknown ways be looking upon you;
Be firm, rail over the river, to support those who lean
     idly, yet haste with the hasting current;
Fly on, sea-birds! fly sideways, or wheel in large circles
     high in the air;
Receive the summer sky, you water, and faithfully hold
     it till all downcast eyes have time to take it from
     you!
Diverge, fine spokes of light, from the shape of my
     head, or any one's head, in the sunlit water!
Come on, ships from the lower bay! pass up or down,
     white-sail'd schooners, sloops, lighters!
Flaunt away, flags of all nations! be duly lower'd at
     sunset!
Burn high your fires, foundry chimneys! cast black
     shadows at nightfall! cast red and yellow light over
     the tops of the houses!
Appearances, now or henceforth, indicate what you
     are,
You necessary film, continue to envelop the soul,
About my body for me, and your body for you, be
     hung our divinest aromas,
Thrive, cities – bring your freight, bring your shows,
     ample and sufficient rivers,
Expand, being than which none else is perhaps more
     spiritual,
Keep your places, objects than which none else is more
     lasting.

You have waited, you always wait, you dumb, beautiful
　　ministers,
We receive you with free sense at last, and are insatiate
　　hence-forward,
Not you any more shall be able to foil us, or withhold
　　yourselves from us,
We use you, and do not cast you aside – we plant you
　　permanently within us,
We fathom you not – we love you – there is perfection
　　in you also,
You furnish your parts toward eternity,
Great or small, you furnish your parts toward the soul.

OUT OF THE CRADLE ENDLESSLY
ROCKING.

Out of the cradle endlessly rocking,
Out of the mocking-bird's throat, the musical shuttle,
Out of the Ninth-month midnight,
Over the sterile sands and the fields beyond, where the
　　child leaving his bed wander'd alone, bareheaded,
　　barefoot,
Down from the shower'd halo,
Up from the mystic play of shadows twining and
　　twisting as if they were alive,
Out from the patches of briers and blackberries,
From the memories of the bird that chanted to me,
From your memories sad brother, from the fitful
　　risings and fallings I heard,
From under that yellow half-moon late-risen and
　　swollen as if with tears?
From those beginning notes of yearning and love there
　　in the mist,
From the thousand responses of my heart never to
　　cease,
From the myriad thence-arous'd words,
From the word stronger and more delicious than any,
From such as now they start the scene revisiting,
As a flock, twittering, rising, or overhead passing,
Borne hither, ere all eludes me, hurriedly,
A man yet by these tears a little boy again,
Throwing myself on the sand, confronting the waves,
I, chanter of pains and joys, uniter of here and
　　hereafter,
Taking all hints to use them, but swiftly leaping
　　beyond them,
A reminiscence sing.

Once Paumanok,
When the lilac-scent was in the air and Fifth-month
　　grass was growing,
Up this seashore in some briers,
Two feather'd guests from Alabama, two together,
And their nest, and four light-green eggs spotted with
　　brown,
And every day the he-bird to and fro near at hand,
And every day the she-bird crouch'd on her nest, silent,
　　with bright eyes,
And every day I, a curious boy, never too close, never
　　disturbing them,
Cautiously peering, absorbing, translating.

Shine! shine! shine!
Pour down your warmth, great sun!
While we bask, we two together.

Two together!
Winds blow south, or winds blow north,
Day come white, or night come black,
Home, or rivers and mountains from home,
Singing all time, minding no time,
While we two keep together.

Till of a sudden,
May-be kill'd, unknown to her mate,
One forenoon the she-bird crouch'd not on the nest,
Nor return'd that afternoon, nor the next,
Nor ever appear'd again.

And thenceforward all summer in the sound of the sea,
And at night under the full of the moon in calmer
　　weather,
Over the hoarse surging of the sea,
Or flitting from brier to brier by day,
I saw, I heard at intervals the remaining one, the he-
　　bird,
The solitary guest from Alabama.

Blow! blow! blow!
Blow up sea-winds along Paumanok's shore;
I wait and I wait till you blow my mate to me.

Yes, when the stars glisten'd,
All night long on the prong of a moss-scallop'd stake,
Down almost amid the slapping waves,
Sat the lone singer wonderful causing tears.

He call'd on his mate,
He pour'd forth the meanings which I of all men know.

Yes my brother I know,
The rest might not, but I have treasur'd every note,
For more than once dimly down to the beach gliding,
Silent, avoiding the moonbeams, blending myself with
  the shadows,
Recalling now the obscure shapes, the echoes, the
  sounds and sights after their sorts,
The white arms out in the breakers tirelessly tossing,
I, with bare feet, a child, the wind wafting my hair,
Listen'd long and long.

Listen'd to keep, to sing, now translating the notes,
Following you my brother.

Soothe! soothe! soothe!
Close on its wave soothes the wave behind,
And again another behind embracing and lapping, every one close,
But my love soothes not me, not me.

Low hangs the moon, it rose late,
It is lagging – O I think it is heavy with love, with love.

O madly the sea pushes upon the land,
With love, with love.

O night! do I not see my love fluttering out among the breakers?
What is that little black thing I see there in the white?

Loud! loud! loud!
Loud I call to you, my love!

High and clear I shoot my voice over the waves,
Surely you must know who is here, is here,
You must know who I am, my love.

Low-hanging moon!
What is that dusky spot in your brown yellow?
O it is the shape, the shape of my mate!
O moon do not keep her from me any longer.

Land! land! O land!
Whichever way I turn, O I think you could give me my mate back
  again if you only would,
For I am almost sure I see her dimly whichever way I look.

O rising stars!
Perhaps the one I want so much will rise, will rise with some of
  you.

O throat! O trembling throat!
Sound clearer through the atmosphere!

Pierce the woods, the earth,
Somewhere listening to catch you must be the one I want.

Shake out carols!
Solitary here, the night's carols!
Carols of lonesome love! death's carols!
Carols under that lagging, yellow, waning moon!
O under that moon where she droops almost down into the sea!
O reckless despairing carols.

But soft! sink low!
Soft! let me just murmur,
And do you wait a moment you husky-nois'd sea,
For somewhere I believe I heard my mate responding to me,
So faint, I must be still, be still to listen,
But not altogether still, for then she might not come immediately
  to me.

Hither my love!
Here I am! here!
With this just-sustain'd note I announce myself to you,
This gentle call is for you my love, for you.

Do not be decoy'd elsewhere,
That is the whistle of the wind, it is not my voice,

That is the fluttering, the fluttering of the spray,
Those are the shadows of leaves.

O darkness! O in vain!
O I am very sick and sorrowful.

O brown halo in the sky near the moon, drooping upon the sea!
O troubled reflection in the sea!
O throat! O throbbing heart!
And I singing uselessly, uselessly all the night.

O past! O happy life! O songs of joy!
In the air, in the woods, over fields,
Loved! loved! loved! loved! loved!
But my mate no more, no more with me!
We two together no more.

The aria sinking,
All else continuing, the stars shining,
The winds blowing, the notes of the bird continuous
  echoing,
With angry moans the fierce old mother incessantly
  moaning,
On the sands of Paumanok's shore gray and rustling,
The yellow half-moon enlarged, sagging down,

drooping, the face of the sea almost touching,
The boy ecstatic, with his bare feet the waves, with his
hair the atmosphere dallying,
The love in the heart long pent now loose, now at last
tumultuously bursting,
The aria's meaning, the ears, the soul, swiftly
depositing,
The strange tears down the cheeks coursing,
The colloquy there, the trio, each uttering,
The undertone, the savage old mother incessantly
crying,
To the boy's soul's questions sullenly timing, some
drown'd secret hissing,
To the outsetting bard.

Demon or bird! (said the boy's soul,)
Is it indeed toward your mate you sing? or is it really
to me?
For I, that was a child, my tongue's use sleeping, now I
have heard you,
Now in a moment I know what I am for, I awake,
And already a thousand singers, a thousand songs,
clearer, louder and more sorrowful than yours,
A thousand warbling echoes have started to life within
me, never to die.

O you singer solitary, singing by yourself, projecting
me,
O solitary me listening, never more shall I cease
perpetuating you,
Never more shall I escape, never more the
reverberations,
Never more the cries of unsatisfied love be absent from
me,
Never again leave me to be the peaceful child I was
before what there in the night,
By the sea under the yellow and sagging moon,
The messenger there arous'd, the fire, the sweet hell
within,
The unknown want, the destiny of me.

O give me the clew! (it lurks in the night here
somewhere,)
O if I am to have so much, let me have more!

A word then, (for I will conquer it,)
The word final, superior to all,
Subtle, sent up – what is it? – I listen;
Are you whispering it, and have been all the time, you
sea-waves?
Is that it from your liquid rims and wet sands?

Whereto answering, the sea,
Delaying not, hurrying not,
Whisper'd me through the night, and very plainly
before day-break,
Lisp'd to me the low and delicious word death
And again death, death, death, death,
Hissing melodious, neither like the bird nor like my
arous'd child's heart,
But edging near as privately for me rustling at my feet,
Creeping thence steadily up to my ears and laving me
softly all over,
Death, death, death, death, death.

Which I do not forget,
But fuse the song of my dusky demon and brother,
That he sang to me in the moonlight on Paumanok's
gray beach,
With the thousand responsive songs at random,
My own songs awaked from that hour,
And with them the key, the word up from the waves,
The word of the sweetest song and all songs,
That strong and delicious word which, creeping to my
feet,
(Or like some old crone rocking the cradle, swathed in
sweet garments, bending aside,)
The sea whisper'd me.

❦

AS I EBB'D WITH THE OCEAN OF LIFE

◄ 1 ►

As I ebb'd with the ocean of life,
As I wended the shores I know,
As I walk'd where the ripples continually wash you
Paumanok,
Where they rustle up hoarse and sibilant,
Where the fierce old mother endlessly cries for her
castaways,
I musing late in the autumn day, gazing off
southward,
Held by this electric self out of the pride of which I
utter poems,
Was seiz'd by the spirit that trails in the lines
underfoot,
The rim, the sediment that stands for all the water and
all the land of the globe.

Fascinated, my eyes reverting from the south, dropt, to
follow those slender windrows,

Chaff, straw, splinters of wood, weeds, and the sea-
    gluten,
Scum, scales from shining rocks, leaves of salt-lettuce,
    left by the tide,
Miles walking, the sound of breaking waves the other
    side of me,
Paumanok there and then as I thought the old
    thought of likenesses,
These you presented to me you fish-shaped island,
As I wended the shores I know,
As I walk'd with that electric self seeking types.

◄ 2 ►
As I wend to the shores I know not,
As I list to the dirge, the voices of men and women
    wreck'd,
As I inhale the impalpable breezes that set in upon me,
As the ocean so mysterious rolls toward me closer and
    closer,
I too but signify at the utmost a little wash'd-up drift,
A few sands and dead leaves to gather,
Gather, and merge myself as part of the sands and
    drift.

O baffled, balk'd, bent to the very earth,
Oppress'd with myself that I have dared to open my
    mouth,
Aware now that amid all that blab whose echoes recoil
    upon me I have not once had the least idea who or
    what I am,
But that before all my arrogant poems the real Me
    stands yet untouch'd, untold, altogether unreach'd,
Withdrawn far, mocking me with mock-congratulatory
    signs and bows,
With peals of distant ironical laughter at every word I
    have written,
Pointing in silence to these songs, and then to the
    sand beneath.

I perceive I have not really understood any thing, not a
    single object, and that no man ever can,
Nature here in sight of the sea taking advantage of me
    to dart upon me and sting me,
Because I have dared to open my mouth to sing at all.

◄ 3 ►
You oceans both, I close with you,
We murmur alike reproachfully rolling sands and drift,
    knowing not why,
These little shreds indeed standing for you and me and
    all.

You friable shore with trails of debris,
You fish-shaped island, I take what is underfoot,
What is yours is mine my father.

I too Paumanok,
I too have bubbled up, floated the measureless float,
    and been wash'd on your shores,
I too am but a trail of drift and debris,
I too leave little wrecks upon you, you fish-shaped
    island.

I throw myself upon your breast my father,
I cling to you so that you cannot unloose me,
I hold you so firm till you answer me something.

Kiss me my father,
Touch me with your lips as I touch those I love,
Breathe to me while I hold you close the secret of the
    murmuring I envy.

◄ 4 ►
Ebb, ocean of life, (the flow will return,)
Cease not your moaning you fierce old mother,
Endlessly cry for your castaways, but fear not, deny not
    me,
Rustle not up so hoarse and angry against my feet as I
    touch you or gather from you.

I mean tenderly by you and all,
I gather for myself and for this phantom looking down
    where we lead, and following me and mine.
Me and mine, loose windrows, little corpses,
Froth, snowy white, and bubbles,
(See, from my dead lips the ooze exuding at last,
See, the prismatic colors glistening and rolling,)
Tufts of straw, sands, fragments,
Buoy'd hither from many moods, one contradicting
    another,
From the storm, the long calm, the darkness, the
    swell,
Musing, pondering, a breath, a briny tear, a dab of
    liquid or soil,
Up just as much out of fathomless workings fermented
    and thrown,
A limp blossom or two, torn, just as much over waves
    floating, drifted at random,
Just as much for us that sobbing dirge of Nature,
Just as much whence we come that blare of the cloud-
    trumpets,
We, capricious, brought hither we know not whence,
    spread out before you,

You up there walking or sitting,
Whoever you are, we too lie in drifts at your feet.

VIGIL STRANGE I KEPT ON THE FIELD ONE NIGHT

Vigil strange I kept on the field one night;
When you my son and my comrade dropt at my side
    that day,
One look I but gave which your dear eyes return'd
    with a look I shall never forget,
One touch of your hand to mine O boy, reach'd up as
    you lay on the ground,
Then onward I sped in the battle, the even-contested
    battle,
Till late in the night reliev'd to the place at last again I
    made my way,
Found you in death so cold dear comrade, found your
    body son of responding kisses, (never again on earth
    responding,)
Bared your face in the starlight, curious the scene, cool
    blew the moderate night-wind,
Long there and then in vigil I stood, dimly around me
    the battle-field spreading,
Vigil wondrous and vigil sweet there in the fragrant
    silent night,
But not a tear fell, not even a long-drawn sigh, long,
    long I gazed,
Then on the earth partially reclining sat by your side
    leaning my chin in my hands,
Passing sweet hours, immortal and mystic hours with
    you dearest comrade – not a tear, not a word,
Vigil of silence, love and death, vigil for you my son
    and my soldier,
As onward silently stars aloft, eastward new ones
    upward stole,
Vigil final for you brave boy, (I could not save you,
    swift was your death,
I faithfully loved you and cared for you living, I think
    we shall surely meet again,)
Till at latest lingering of the night, indeed just as the
    dawn appear'd,
My comrade I wrapt in his blanket, envelop'd well his
    form,
Folded the blanket well, tucking it carefully over head
    and carefully under feet,
And there and then and bathed by the rising sun,

my son in his grave, in his rude-dug grave I
    deposited,
Ending my vigil strange with that, vigil of night and
    battle-field dim,
Vigil for boy of responding kisses, (never again on
    earth responding,)
Vigil for comrade swiftly slain, vigil I never forget, how
    as day brighten'd,
I rose from the chill ground and folded my soldier well
    in his blanket,
And buried him where he fell.

WHEN LILACS LAST IN THE DOORYARD BLOOM'D

◄ 1 ►

When lilacs last in the dooryard bloom'd,
And the great star early droop'd in the western sky in
    the night,
I mourn'd, and yet shall mourn with ever-returning
    spring.

Ever-returning spring, trinity sure to me you bring,
Lilac blooming perennial and drooping star in the west,
And thought of him I love.

◄ 2 ►

O powerful western fallen star!
O shades of night – O moody, tearful night!
O great star disappear'd – O the black murk that hides
    the star!
O cruel hands that hold me powerless – O helpless
    soul of me!
O harsh surrounding cloud that will not free my soul.

◄ 3 ►

In the dooryard fronting an old farm-house near the
    white-wash'd palings,
Stands the lilac-bush tall-growing with heart-shaped
    leaves of rich green,
With many a pointed blossom rising delicate, with the
    perfume strong I love,
With every leaf a miracle – and from this bush in the
    dooryard,
With delicate-color'd blossoms and heart-shaped leaves
    of rich green,
A sprig with its flower I break.

<4>

In the swamp in secluded recesses,
A shy and hidden bird is warbling a song.

Solitary the thrush,
The hermit withdrawn to himself, avoiding the
    settlements,
Sings by himself a song.

Song of the bleeding throat,
Death's outlet song of life, (for well dear brother I know,
If thou wast not granted to sing thou would'st surely
    die.)

<5>

Over the breast of the spring, the land, amid cities,
Amid lanes and through old woods, where lately the
    violets peep'd from the ground, spotting the gray
    debris,
Amid the grass in the fields each side of the lanes,
    passing the endless grass,
Passing the yellow-spear'd wheat, every grain from its
    shroud in the dark-brown fields uprisen,
Passing the apple-tree blows of white and pink in the
    orchards,
Carrying a corpse to where it shall rest in the grave,
Night and day journeys a coffin.

<6>

Coffin that passes through lanes and streets,
Through day and night with the great cloud darkening
    the land,
With the pomp of the inloop'd flags with the cities
    draped in black,
With the show of the States themselves as of crape-
    veil'd women standing,
With processions long and winding and the flambeaus
    of the night,
With the countless torches lit, with the silent sea of
    faces and the unbared heads,
With the waiting depot, the arriving coffin, and the
    sombre faces,
With dirges through the night, with the thousand
    voices rising strong and solemn,
With all the mournful voices of the dirges pour'd
    around the coffin,
The dim-lit churches and the shuddering organs –
    where amid these you journey,
With the toiling tolling bells' perpetual clang,
Here, coffin that slowly passes,
I give you my sprig of lilac.

<7>

(Nor for you, for one alone,
Blossoms and branches green to coffins all I bring,
For fresh as the morning, thus would I chant a song
    for you O sane and sacred death.

All over bouquets of roses,
O death, I cover you over with roses and early lilies,
But mostly and now the lilac that blooms the first,
Copious I break, I break the sprigs from the bushes,
With loaded arms I come, pouring for you,
For you and the coffins all of you O death.)

<8>

O western orb sailing the heaven,
Now I know what you must have meant as a month
    since I walk'd,
As I walk'd in silence the transparent shadowy night,
As I saw you had something to tell as you bent to me
    night after night,
As you droop'd from the sky low down as if to my side,
    (while the other stars all look'd on,)
As we wander'd together the solemn night, (for
    something I know not what kept me from sleep,)
As the night advanced, and I saw on the rim of the
    west how full you were of woe,
As I stood on the rising ground in the breeze in the
    cool transparent night,
As I watch'd where you pass'd and was lost in the
    netherward black of the night,
As my soul in its trouble dissatisfied sank, as where
    you sad orb,
Concluded, dropt in the night, and was gone.

<9>

Sing on there in the swamp,
O singer bashful and tender, I hear your notes, I hear
    your call,
I hear, I come presently, I understand you,
But a moment I linger, for the lustrous star has
    detain'd me,
The star my departing comrade holds and detains
    me.

<10>

O how shall I warble myself for the dead one there I
    loved?
And how shall I deck my song for the large sweet soul
    that has gone?
And what shall my perfume be for the grave of him I
    love?

Sea-winds blown from east and west,
Blown from the Eastern sea and blown from the
  Western sea, till there on the prairies meeting,
These and with these and the breath of my chant,
I'll perfume the grave of him I love.

◄ 11 ►

O what shall I hang on the chamber walls?
And what shall the pictures be that I hang on the
  walls,
To adorn the burial-house of him I love?

Pictures of growing spring and farms and homes,
With the Fourth-month eve at sundown, and the gray
  smoke lucid and bright,
With floods of the yellow gold of the gorgeous,
  indolent, sinking sun, burning, expanding the air,
With the fresh sweet herbage under foot, and the pale
  green leaves of the trees prolific,
In the distance the flowing glaze, the breast of the
  river, with a wind-dapple here and there,
With ranging hills on the banks, with many a line
  against the sky, and shadows,
And the city at hand with dwellings so dense, and
  stacks of chimneys,
And all the scenes of life and the workshops, and the
  workmen homeward returning.

◄ 12 ►

Lo, body and soul – this land,
My own Manhattan with spires, and the sparkling and
  hurrying tides, and the ships,
The varied and ample land, the South and the North
  in the light, Ohio's shores and flashing Missouri,
And ever the far-spreading prairies cover'd with grass
  and corn.

Lo, the most excellent sun so calm and haughty,
The violet and purple morn with just-felt breezes,
The gentle soft-born measureless light,
The miracle spreading bathing all, the fulfill'd noon,
The coming eve delicious, the welcome night and the
  stars,
Over my cities shining all, enveloping man and land.

◄ 13 ►

Sing on, sing on you gray-brown bird,
Sing from the swamps, the recesses, pour your chant
  from the bushes,
Limitless out of the dusk, out of the cedars and pines.

Sing on dearest brother, warble your reedy song,
Loud human song, with voice of uttermost woe.

O liquid and free and tender!
O wild and loose to my soul – O wondrous singer!
You only I hear – yet the star holds me, (but will soon
  depart,)
Yet the lilac with mastering odor holds me.

◄ 14 ►

Now while I sat in the day and look'd forth,
In the close of the day with its light and the fields of
  spring, and the farmers preparing their crops,
In the large unconscious scenery of my land with its
  lakes and forests,
In the heavenly aerial beauty, (after the perturb'd
  winds and the storms,)
Under the arching heavens of the afternoon swift
  passing, and the voices of children and women,
The many-moving sea-tides, and I saw the ships how
  they sail'd,
And the summer approaching with richness, and the
  fields all busy with labor,
And the infinite separate houses, how they all went on,
  each with its meals and minutia of daily usages,
And the streets how their throbbings throbb'd, and the
  cities pent – lo, then and there,
Falling upon them all and among them all, enveloping
  me with the rest,
Appear'd the cloud, appear'd the long black trail,
And I knew death, its thought, and the sacred
  knowledge of death.

Then with the knowledge of death as walking one side
  of me,
And the thought of death close-walking the other side
  of me,
And I in the middle as with companions, and as
  holding the hands of companions,
I fled forth to the hiding receiving night that talks
  not,
Down to the shores of the water, the path by the
  swamp in the dimness,
To the solemn shadowy cedars and ghostly pines so
  still.

And the singer so shy to the rest receiv'd me,
The gray-brown bird I know receiv'd us comrades
  three,
And he sang the carol of death, and a verse for him I
  love.

From deep secluded recesses,
From the fragrant cedars and the ghostly pines so still,
Came the carol of the bird.

And the charm of the carol rapt me,
As I held as if by their hands my comrades in the night,
And the voice of my spirit tallied the song of the bird.

Come lovely and soothing death,
Undulate round the world, serenely arriving, arriving,
In the day, in the night, to all, to each,
Sooner or later delicate death.

Prais'd be the fathomless universe,
For life and joy, and for objects and knowledge curious,
And for love, sweet love – but praise! praise! praise!
For the sure-enwinding arms of cool-enfolding death.

Dark mother always gliding near with soft feet,
Have none chanted for thee a chant of fullest welcome?
Then I chant it for thee, I glorify thee above all,
I bring thee a song that when thou must indeed come, come
*   unfalteringly.*

Approach strong deliveress,
When it is so, when thou hast taken them I joyously sing the dead,
Lost in the loving floating ocean of thee,
Laved in the flood of thy bliss O death.

From me to thee glad serenades,
Dances for thee I propose saluting thee, adornments and feastings
*   for thee,*
And the sights of the open landscape and the high-spread sky are
*   fitting,*
And life and the fields, and the huge and thoughtful night.

The night in silence under many a star,
The ocean shore and the husky whispering wave whose voice I know,
And the soul turning to thee O vast and well-veil'd death,
And the body gratefully nestling close to thee.

Over the tree-tops I float thee a song,
Over the rising and sinking waves, over the myriad fields and the
*   prairies wide,*
Over the dense-pack'd cities all and the teeming, wharves and ways,
I float this carol with joy, with joy to thee O death.

<15>
To the tally of my soul,
Loud and strong kept up the gray-brown bird,
With pure deliberate notes spreading filling the night.

Loud in the pines and cedars dim,
Clear in the freshness moist and the swamp-perfume,
And I with my comrades there in the night.

While my sight that was bound in my eyes unclosed,
As to long panoramas of visions.

And I saw askant the armies,
I saw as in noiseless dreams hundreds of battle-flags,
Borne through the smoke of the battles and pierc'd
    with missiles I saw them,
And carried hither and yon through the smoke, and
    torn and bloody,
And at last but a few shreds left on the staffs, (and all
    in silence,)
And the staffs all splinter'd and broken.

I saw battle-corpses, myriads of them,
And the white skeletons of young men, I saw them,
I saw the debris and debris of all the slain soldiers of
    the war,
But I saw they were not as was thought,
They themselves were fully at rest, they suffer'd not,
The living remain'd and suffer'd, the mother suffer'd,
And the wife and the child and the musing comrade
    suffer'd,
And the armies that remain'd suffer'd.

<16>
Passing the visions, passing the night,
Passing, unloosing the hold of my comrades' hands,
Passing the song of the hermit bird and the tallying
    song of my soul,
Victorious song, death's outlet song, yet varying ever-
    altering song,
As low and wailing, yet clear the notes, rising and
    falling, flooding the night,
Sadly sinking and fainting, as warning and warning,
    and yet again bursting with joy,
Covering the earth and filling the spread of the
    heaven,
As that powerful psalm in the night I heard from
    recesses,
Passing, I leave thee lilac with heart-shaped leaves,
I leave thee there in the door-yard, blooming,
    returning with spring.

I cease from my song for thee,
From my gaze on thee in the west, fronting the west,
    communing with thee,
O comrade lustrous with silver face in the night.

Yet each to keep and all, retrievements out of the
    night,
The song, the wondrous chant of the gray-brown bird,
And the tallying chant, the echo arous'd in my soul,
With the lustrous and drooping star with the
    countenance full of woe,
With the holders holding my hand nearing the call of
    the bird,
Comrades mine and I in the midst, and their memory
    ever to keep, for the dead I loved so well,
For the sweetest, wisest soul of all my days and lands –
    and this for his dear sake,
Lilac and star and bird twined with the chant of my
    soul,
There in the fragrant pines and the cedars dusk and
    dim.

Oscar Wilde (1854–1900) is at his worst in his verse. Although he dutifully counts syllables and fits his rhymes to a formula, this is where we see him at his most unguarded. Every poem contains at least one dead line; some have nothing but. The style is derivative. Yet this is the man whose mother read *Leaves of Grass* to him when he was thirteen and who kissed Whitman on the lips in 1882.

The early doggerel is enlivened only by its sense of doom. (Many critics read this stuff retrospectively, as if Wilde always knew he was going to end up doing hard labour to pay for his pleasures.) Contrary to those who believe he only started fancying his own sex after he met Robbie Ross in 1886, the student verse is packed with boys. But they are boys with names or roles from Greek myth, and most of them are dying or dead. The mood is both wistful and wasteful. The humour seems unintended.

Inside every sentimentalist there is a cynic waiting to come out. First Wilde found wit; then he found rage. Once his sentimentality became charged with anger, as it did in 'The Ballad of Reading Gaol', it acquired a valid purpose. Wilde was never the fluffy wit the English like to think him. And although he was not as decadent as he sometimes pretended – in his sexual life he was not so much feasting with panthers as scavenging with tomcats – his writing became all the better when sharpened by the astringency of paradox.

The poems in prose, biblical kitsch notwithstanding, are not merely picturesque: they address topics of the utmost seriousness. However, nothing Wilde wrote would ever be read with such intensity or taken so seriously as the stains on his bedsheets at the Savoy Hotel.

Wasted Days

*‹From a picture painted by Miss V[iolet]
T[roubridge] ›*

A fair slim boy not made for this world's pain,
    With hair of gold thick clustering round his ears,
    And longing eyes half veiled by foolish tears
Like bluest water seen through mists of rain;
Pale cheeks whereon no kiss hath left its stain,
    Red under-lip drawn in for fear of Love,
    And white throat whiter than the breast of dove –

Alas! Alas! If all should be in vain.
Corn-fields behind, and reapers all a-row
    In weariest labour, toiling wearily,
    To no sweet sound of laughter, or of lute;
And careless of the crimson sunset-glow,
    The boy still dreams; nor knows that night is nigh,
    And in the night-time no man gathers fruit.

In the Forest

Out in the mid-wood's twilight
    Into the meadow's dawn,
Ivory limbed and brown-eyed,
    Flashes my Faun!

He skips through the copses singing,
    And his shadow dances along,
And I know not which I should follow,
    Shadow or song!

O Hunter, snare me his shadow!
    O Nightingale, catch me his strain!
Else moonstruck with music and madness
    I track him in vain!

Remorse

I love your topaz-coloured eyes
    That light with blame these midnight streets,
I love your body when it lies
    Like amber on the silken sheets.

I love the honey-coloured hair
    That ripples to your ivory hips;
I love the languid listless air
    With which you kiss my boyish lips.

I love the bows that bend above
    Those eyelids of chalcedony:
But most of all, my love! I love
    Your beautiful fierce chastity!

The Ballad of Reading Gaol

(lines 1–60; 535–76)

He did not wear his scarlet coat,
    For blood and wine are red,
And blood and wine were on his hands
    When they found him with the dead,
The poor dead woman whom he loved,
    And murdered in her bed.

He walked amongst the Trial Men
    In a suit of shabby grey;
A cricket cap was on his head,
    And his step seemed light and gay;
But I never saw a man who looked
    So wistfully at the day.

I never saw a man who looked
    With such a wistful eye
Upon that little tent of blue
    Which prisoners call the sky,
And at every drifting cloud that went
    With sails of silver by.

I walked, with other souls in pain,
    Within another ring,
And was wondering if the man had done
    A great or little thing,
When a voice behind me whispered low,
    'That fellow's got to swing.'

Dear Christ! the very prison walls
    Suddenly seemed to reel,
And the sky above my head became
    Like a casque of scorching steel;
And, though I was a soul in pain,
    My pain I could not feel.

I only knew what hunted thought
   Quickened his step, and why
He looked upon the garish day
   With such a wistful eye;
The man had killed the thing he loved,
   And so he had to die.

Yet each man kills the thing he loves,
   By each let this be heard,
Some do it with a bitter look,
   Some with a flattering word.
The coward does it with a kiss,
   The brave man with a sword!

Some kill their love when they are young,
   And some when they are old;
Some strangle with the hands of Lust,
   Some with the hands of Gold:
The kindest use a knife, because
   The dead so soon grow cold.

Some love too little, some too long,
   Some sell, and others buy;
Some do the deed with many tears,
   And some without a sigh:
For each man kills the thing he loves,
   Yet each man does not die.

He does not die a death of shame
   On a day of dark disgrace,
Nor have a noose about his neck,
   Nor a cloth upon his face,
Nor drop feet foremost through the floor
   Into an empty space.

[. . .]

I know not whether Laws be right,
   Or whether Laws be wrong;
All that we know who lie in gaol
   Is that the wall is strong;
And that each day is like a year,
   A year whose days are long.

But this I know, that every Law
   That men hath made for Man,
Since first Man took his brother's life,
   And the sad world began,
But straws the wheat and saves the chaff
   With a most evil fan.

This too I know – and wise it were
   If each could know the same –
That every prison that men build
   Is built with bricks of shame,
And bound with bars lest Christ should see
   How men their brothers maim.

With bars they blur the gracious moon,
   And blind the goodly sun;
And they do well to hide their Hell,
   For in it things are done
That Son of God nor son of Man
   Ever should look upon!

The vilest deeds like poison weeds,
   Bloom well in prison-air;
It is only what is good in Man
   That wastes and withers there:
Pale Anguish keeps the heavy gate,
   And the Warder is Despair.

For they starve the little frightened child
   Till it weeps both night and day:
And they scourge the weak, and flog the fool,
   And gibe the old and grey,
And some grow mad, and all grow bad,
   And none a word may say.

Each narrow cell in which we dwell
   Is a foul and dark latrine,
And the fetid breath of living Death
   Chokes up each grated screen,
And all, but Lust, is turned to dust
   In Humanity's machine.

❧

POEMS IN PROSE:
THE ARTIST

One evening there came into his soul the desire to
fashion an image of *The Pleasure that abideth for a
Moment*. And he went forth into the world to look
for bronze. For he could only think in bronze.

But all the bronze of the whole world had
disappeared, nor anywhere in the whole world was
there any bronze to be found, save only the bronze
of the image of *The Sorrow that endureth for Ever*.

Now this image he had himself, and with his
own hands, fashioned, and had set it on the tomb of

the one thing he had loved in life. On the tomb of the dead thing he had most loved had he set this image of his own fashioning, that it might serve as a sign of the love of man that dieth not, and a symbol of the sorrow of man that endureth for ever. And in the whole world there was no other bronze save the bronze of this image.

And he took the image he had fashioned, and set it in a great furnace, and gave it to the fire.

And out of the bronze of the image of The Sorrow that endureth for Ever he fashioned an image of The Pleasure that abideth for a Moment.

THE MASTER

Now when the darkness came over the earth Joseph of Arimathea, having lighted a torch of pinewood, passed down from the hill into the valley. For he had business in his own home.

And kneeling on the flint stones of the Valley of Desolation he saw a young man who was naked and weeping. His hair was the colour of honey, and his body was as a white flower, but he had wounded his body with thorns and on his hair had he set ashes as a crown.

And he who had great possessions said to the young man who was naked and weeping, 'I do not wonder that your sorrow is so great, for surely He was a just man.'

And the young man answered, 'It is not for Him that I am weeping, but for myself. I too have changed water into wine, and I have healed the leper and given sight to the blind. I have walked upon the waters, and from the dwellers in the tombs I have cast out devils. I have fed the hungry in the desert where there was no food, and I have raised the dead from their narrow houses, and at my bidding, and before a great multitude of people, a barren fig-tree withered away. All things that this man has done I have done also. And yet they have not crucified me.'

On the assumption that there are no hackneyed poems but only hackneyed readers, it would be pardonable for an anthologist to present once more poems of Wordsworth (1770–1850) that are both acknowledged masterpieces and old favourites. One's thoughts turn at once to 'Tintern Abbey' which is unsurpassable, 'Resolution and Independence' and the dozen or so shorter poems we all know so well. But what of those less familiar pieces that by now should also be in readers' memories? 'When to the attractions of the busy world', for example, is not a title that produces instant recognition, yet it has always seemed to me a major poem. This is one of those works whose revision greatly improves on Wordsworth's earlier version. Such is not always the case. Thus the extracts from The Prelude here are from the text of 1805, rather than that of 1850. Determined to reveal some lesser known beauties, I cast lingering, regretful glances at 'Michael', the Lucy poems, 'Composed Upon Westminster Bridge' 'I wandered lonely as a Cloud'. But I had to remind myself that these are already widely known and easily come by (though I could not forego 'A slumber did my spirit seal'). I wanted also to print some of the poems which a modern reader might well still resist as Wordsworth's first readers did. People simply have not made up their minds about, or perhaps even read, poems like 'By their floating Mill', a rhythmic tour de force, brooded over by that unforgettable line, 'In the broad open eye of the solitary sky'. The poise of a poem like 'To A Butterfly' is, as F. R. Leavis has said of a Lucy poem, 'an extremely delicate one and our sense of its success is bound up with this feeling'. The texts I have used are often of earlier versions than anthologies tend to contain. (My texts follow the editing of Stephen Gill's Oxford Authors William Wordsworth and John O. Hayden's 2-volume Penguin William Wordsworth.) I have tried to represent not only Wordsworth the 'nature poet', but also the public Wordsworth who challenged the Poor Laws, wrote of the French Revolution and of Buonaparte, and rejected the plausible abstractions of revolutionaries and the men of power in favour of basic human affections.

WILLIAM WORDSWORTH

THE OLD CUMBERLAND BEGGAR

‹A Description›
(lines 1–21; 67–87)

The class of Beggars to which the old man here described belongs, will probably soon be extinct. It consisted of poor, and, mostly, old and infirm persons, who confined themselves to a stated round in their neighbourhood, and had certain fixed days, on which, at different houses, they regularly received charity; sometimes in money, but mostly in provisions.

I saw an aged Beggar in my walk,
And he was seated by the highway side
On a low structure of rude masonry
Built at the foot of a huge hill, that they
Who lead their horses down the steep rough road
May thence remount at ease. The aged man
Had placed his staff across the broad smooth stone
That overlays the pile, and from a bag
All white with flour the dole of village dames,
He drew his scraps and fragments, one by one,
And scanned them with a fixed and serious look
Of idle computation. In the sun,
Upon the second step of that small pile,
Surrounded by those wild unpeopled hills,
He sate, and eat his food in solitude;
And ever, scattered from his palsied hand,
That still attempting to prevent the waste,
Was baffled still, the crumbs in little showers
Fell on the ground, and the small mountain birds,
Not venturing yet to peck their destined meal,
Approached within the length of half his staff.

[. . .]

But deem not this man useless – Statesman! ye
Who are so restless in your wisdom, ye
Who have a broom still ready in your hands
To rid the world of nuisances; ye proud,
Heart-swoln, while in your pride ye contemplate
Your talents, power, and wisdom, deem him not
A burthen of the earth. 'Tis Nature's law
That none, the meanest of created things,
Of forms created the most vile and brute,
The dullest or most noxious, should exist
Divorced from good, a spirit and pulse of good,
A life and soul to every mode of being
Inseparably linked. While thus he creeps
From door to door, the Villagers in him
Behold a record which together binds
Past deeds and offices of charity
Else unremembered, and so keeps alive

The kindly mood in hearts which lapse of years,
And that half-wisdom half-experience gives
Make slow to feel, and by sure steps resign
To selfishness and cold oblivious cares.

'A WHIRL-BLAST FROM BEHIND THE HILL'

A whirl-blast from behind the hill
Rushed o'er the wood with startling sound:
Then all at once the air was still,
And showers of hail-stones pattered round.
Where leafless Oaks towered high above,
I sate within an undergrove
Of tallest hollies, tall and green,
A fairer bower was never seen.
From year to year the spacious floor
With withered leaves is covered o'er,
You could not lay a hair between:
And all the year the bower is green.
But see! where'er the hailstones drop
The withered leaves all skip and hop,
There's not a breeze – no breath of air –
Yet here, and there, and every where
Along the floor, beneath the shade
By those embowering hollies made,
The leaves in myriads jump and spring,
As if with pipes and music rare
Some Robin Good-fellow were there,
And all those leaves, that jump and spring,
Were each a joyous, living thing. . . .

'A SLUMBER DID MY SPIRIT SEAL'

A slumber did my spirit seal;
    I had no human fears:
She seemed a thing that could not feel
    The touch of earthly years.

No motion has she now, no force;
    She neither hears nor sees,
Rolled round in earth's diurnal course
    With rocks and stones and trees.

TO A BUTTERFLY

Stay near me – do not take thy flight!
A little longer stay in sight!
Much converse do I find in Thee,
Historian of my Infancy!
Float near me; do not yet depart!
Dead times revive in thee:
Thou bring'st, gay Creature as thou art!
A solemn image to my heart,
My Father's Family!

Oh! pleasant, pleasant were the days,
The time, when in our childish plays
My sister Emmeline and I
Together chaced the Butterfly!
A very hunter did I rush
Upon the prey: – with leaps and springs
I followed on from brake to bush;
But She, God love her! feared to brush
The dust from off its wings.

'AMONG ALL LOVELY THINGS MY LOVE HAD BEEN'

Among all lovely things my Love had been;
Had noted well the stars, all flowers that grew
About her home; but she had never seen
A Glow-worm, never one, and this I knew.

While riding near her home one stormy night
A single Glow-worm did I chance to espy;
I gave a fervent welcome to the sight,
And from my Horse I leapt; great joy had I.

Upon a leaf the Glow-worm did I lay,
To bear it with me through the stormy night:
And, as before, it shone without dismay;
Albeit putting forth a fainter light.

When to the Dwelling of my Love I came,
I went into the Orchard quietly;
And left the Glow-worm, blessing it by name,
Laid safely by itself, beneath a Tree.

The whole next day, I hoped, and hoped with fear;
At night the Glow-worm shone beneath the Tree:

I led my Lucy to the spot, 'Look here!'
Oh! joy it was for her, and joy for me!

WRITTEN IN MARCH

‹ While resting on the bridge at the foot of Brother's Water ›

The cock is crowing,
The stream is flowing,
The small birds twitter,
The lake doth glitter,
The green field sleeps in the sun;
The oldest and youngest
Are at work with the strongest;
The cattle are grazing,
Their heads never raising;
There are forty feeding like one!

Like an army defeated
The Snow hath retreated,
And now doth fare ill
On the top of the bare hill;
The Plough-boy is whooping – anon – anon:
There's joy in the mountains;
There's life in the fountains;
Small clouds are sailing,
Blue sky prevailing;
The rain is over and gone!

'I GRIEVED FOR BUONAPARTE'

I grieved for Buonaparte, with a vain
And an unthinking grief! the vital blood
Of that Man's mind what can it be? What food
Fed his first hopes? What knowledge could He gain?
'Tis not in battles that from youth we train
The Governor who must be wise and good,
And temper with the sternness of the brain
Thoughts motherly, and meek as womanhood.
Wisdom doth live with children round her knees:
Books, leisure, perfect freedom, and the talk
Man holds with week-day man in the hourly walk
Of the mind's business: these are the degrees

By which true Sway doth mount; this is the stalk
True Power doth grow on; and her rights are these.

❧

'She was a Phantom of delight'

She was a Phantom of delight
When first she gleamed upon my sight;
A lovely Apparition, sent
To be a moment's ornament;
Her eyes as stars of Twilight fair;
Like Twilight's, too, her dusky hair;
But all things else about her drawn
From May-time and the cheerful Dawn;
A dancing Shape, an Image gay,
To haunt, to startle, and way-lay.

I saw her upon nearer view,
A Spirit, yet a Woman too!
Her household motions light and free,
And steps of virgin liberty;
A countenance in which did meet
Sweet records, promises as sweet;
A Creature not too bright or good
For human nature's daily food;
For transient sorrows, simple wiles,
Praise, blame, love, kisses, tears, and smiles.

And now I see with eye serene
The very pulse of the machine;
A Being breathing thoughtful breath;
A Traveller betwixt life and death;
The reason firm, the temperate will,
Endurance, foresight, strength and skill;
A perfect Woman; nobly planned,
To warn, to comfort, and command;
And yet a Spirit still, and bright
With something of an angel light.

❧

'By their floating Mill'

' – Pleasure is spread through the earth
In stray gifts to be claimed by whoever shall find.'

By their floating Mill,
  Which lies dead and still,
Behold yon Prisoners three!
The Miller with two Dames, on the breast of the
    Thames;
The Platform is small, but there's room for them all;
And they're dancing merrily.

From the shore come the notes
  To their Mill where it floats,
To their House and their Mill tethered fast!
To the small wooden isle where their work to beguile
They from morning to even take whatever is given: –
And many a blithe day they have past.

In sight of the Spires
  All alive with the fires
Of the Sun going down to his rest,
In the broad open eye of the solitary sky,
They dance, – there are three, as jocund as free,
While they dance on the calm river's breast.

Man and Maidens wheel,
  They themselves make the Reel,
And their Music's a prey which they seize;
It plays not for them, – what matter! 'tis their's;
And if they had care it has scattered their cares,
While they dance, crying, 'Long as ye please!'

They dance not for me,
  Yet mine is their glee!
Thus pleasure is spread through the earth
In stray gifts to be claimed by whoever shall find;
Thus a rich loving-kindness, redundantly kind,
Moves all nature to gladness and mirth.

The Showers of the Spring
  Rouze the Birds and they sing;
If the Wind do but stir for his proper delight,
Each Leaf, that and this, his neighbour will kiss,
Each Wave, one and t'other, speeds after his Brother;
They are happy, for that is their right!

❧

'When, to the attractions of the busy world'

When, to the attractions of the busy world,
Preferring studious leisure, I had chosen
A habitation in this peaceful Vale,
Sharp season followed of continual storm
In deepest winter; and, from week to week,
Pathway, and lane, and public road, were clogged
With frequent showers of snow. Upon a hill
At a short distance from my cottage, stands
A stately Fir-grove, whither I was wont
To hasten, for I found, beneath the roof
Of that perennial shade, a cloistral place
Of refuge, with an unincumbered floor.
Here, in safe covert, on the shallow snow,
And, sometimes, on a speck of visible earth,
The redbreast near me hopped; nor was I loth
To sympathize with vulgar coppice birds
That, for protection from the nipping blast,
Hither repaired. – A single beech-tree grew
Within this grove of firs! and, on the fork
Of that one beech, appeared a thrush's nest;
A last year's nest, conspicuously built
At such small elevation from the ground
As gave sure sign that they, who in that house
Of nature and of love had made their home
Amid the fir-trees, all the summer long
Dwelt in a tranquil spot. And oftentimes
A few sheep, stragglers from some mountain-flock,
Would watch my motions with suspicious stare,
From the remotest outskirts of the grove, –
Some nook where they had made their final stand,
Huddling together from two fears – the fear
Of me and of the storm. Full many an hour
Here did I lose. But in this grove the trees
Had been so thickly planted, and had thriven
In such perplexed and intricate array,
That vainly did I seek, beneath their stems
A length of open space, where to and fro
My feet might move without concern or care;
And, baffled thus, though earth from day to day
Was fettered, and the air by storm disturbed,
I ceased the shelter to frequent, – and prized,
Less than I wished to prize, that calm recess.

The snows dissolved, and genial Spring returned
To clothe the fields with verdure. Other haunts
Meanwhile were mine; till, one bright April day,
By chance retiring from the glare of noon
To this forsaken covert, there I found

A hoary pathway traced between the trees,
And winding on with such an easy line
Along a natural opening, that I stood
Much wondering how I could have sought in vain
For what was now so obvious. To abide,
For an allotted interval of ease,
Under my cottage-roof, had gladly come
From the wild sea a cherished Visitant;
And with the sight of this same path – begun,
Begun and ended, in the shady grove,
Pleasant conviction flashed upon my mind
That, to this opportune recess allured,
He had surveyed it with a finer eye,
A heart more wakeful; and had worn the track
By pacing here, unwearied and alone,
In that habitual restlessness of foot
That haunts the Sailor measuring o'er and o'er
His short domain upon the vessel's deck,
While she pursues her course through the dreary sea.

When thou hadst quitted Esthwaite's pleasant
    shore,
And taken thy first leave of those green hills
And rocks that were the play-ground of thy youth,
Year followed year, my Brother! and we two,
Conversing not, knew little in what mould
Each other's mind was fashioned; and at length,
When once again we met in Grasmere Vale,
Between us there was little other bond
Than common feelings of fraternal love.
But thou, a School-boy, to the sea hadst carried
Undying recollections; Nature there
Was with thee; she, who loved us both, she still
Was with thee; and even so didst thou become
A *silent* Poet; from the solitude
Of the vast sea didst bring a watchful heart
Still couchant, an inevitable ear,
And an eye practised like a blind man's touch.
– Back to the joyless Ocean thou art gone;
Nor from this vestige of thy musing hours
Could I withhold thy honoured name, – and now
I love the fir-grove with a perfect love.
Thither do I withdraw when cloudless suns
Shine hot, or wind blows troublesome and strong;
And there I sit at evening, when the steep
Of Silver-how, and Grasmere's peaceful lake,
And one green island, gleam between the stems
Of the dark firs, a visionary scene!
And, while I gaze upon the spectacle
Of clouded splendour, on this dream-like sight
Of solemn loveliness, I think on thee,

My Brother, and on all which thou hast lost.
Nor seldom, if I rightly guess, while Thou,
Muttering the verses which I muttered first
Among the mountains, through the midnight watch
Art pacing thoughtfully the vessel's deck
In some far region, here, while o'er my head,
At every impulse of the moving breeze,
The fir-grove murmurs with a sea-like sound,
Alone I tread this path; – for aught I know,
Timing my steps to thine; and, with a store
Of undistinguishable sympathies,
Mingling most earnest wishes for the day
When we, and others whom we love, shall meet
A second time, in Grasmere's happy Vale.

THE EXCURSION: BOOK IX
(lines 433–51)

‹ 'The Snow-white ram' ›

   Forth we went,
And down the vale along the streamlet's edge
Pursued our way, a broken company,
Mute or conversing, single or in pairs.
Thus having reached a bridge, that overarched
The hasty rivulet where it lay becalmed
In a deep pool, by happy chance we saw
A twofold image; on a grassy bank
A snow-white ram, and in the crystal flood
Another and the same! Most beautiful,
On the green turf, with his imperial front
Shaggy and bold, and wreathd horns superb,
The breathing creature stood; as beautiful,
Beneath him, showed his shadowy counterpart.
Each had his glowing mountains, each his sky,
And each seemed centre of his own fair world:
Antipodes unconscious of each other,
Yet, in partition, with their several spheres,
Blended in perfect stillness, to our sight!

THE RIVER DUDDON

‹ Sonnet XXI ›

Whence that low voice? – A whisper from the heart,
That told of days long past, when here I roved
With friends and kindred tenderly beloved;

Some who had early mandates to depart,
Yet are allowed to steal my path athwart
By Duddon's side; once more do we unite,
Once more beneath the kind Earth's tranquil light;
And smothered joys into new being start.
From her unworthy seat, the cloudy stall
Of Time, breaks forth triumphant Memory;
Her glistening tresses bound, yet light and free
As golden locks of birch, that rise and fall
On gales that breathe too gently to recall
Aught of the fading year's inclemency!

THE PRELUDE

‹ Book I ›
(lines 372–427)

  One evening (surely I was led by her)
I went alone into a Shepherd's Boat,
A Skiff that to a Willow tree was tied
Within a rocky Cave, its usual home.
'Twas by the shores of Patterdale, a Vale
Wherein I was a Stranger, thither come
A School-boy Traveller, at the Holidays.
Forth rambled from the Village Inn alone,
No sooner had I sight of this small Skiff,
Discovered thus by unexpected chance,
Than I unloosed her tether and embarked.
The moon was up, the Lake was shining clear
Among the hoary mountains; from the Shore
I pushed, and struck the oars and struck again
In cadence, and my little Boat moved on
Even like a Man who walks with stately step
Though bent on speed. It was an act of stealth
And troubled pleasure; not without the voice
Of mountain-echoes did my Boat move on,
Leaving behind her still on either side
Small circles glittering idly in the moon,
Until they melted all into one track
Of sparkling light. A rocky Steep uprose
Above the Cavern of the Willow tree
And now, as suited one who proudly rowed
With his best skill, I fixed a steady view
Upon the top of that same craggy ridge,
The bound of the horizon, for behind
Was nothing but the stars and the grey sky.
She was an elfin Pinnace; lustily
I dipped my oars into the silent Lake,
And, as I rose upon the stroke, my Boat

Went heaving through the water, like a Swan;
When from behind that craggy Steep, till then
The bound of the horizon, a huge Cliff,
As if with voluntary power instinct,
Upreared its head. I struck, and struck again,
And, growing still in stature, the huge Cliff
Rose up between me and the stars, and still,
With measured motion, like a living thing,
Strode after me. With trembling hands I turned,
And through the silent water stole my way
Back to the Cavern of the Willow tree.
There, in her mooring-place, I left my Bark,
And, through the meadows homeward went, with
    grave
And serious thoughts; and after I had seen
That spectacle, for many days, my brain
Worked with a dim and undetermined sense
Of unknown modes of being; in my thoughts
There was a darkness, call it solitude,
Or blank desertion, no familiar shapes
Of hourly objects, images of trees,
Of sea or sky, no colours of green fields;
But huge and mighty Forms that do not live
Like living men moved slowly through my mind
By day and were the trouble of my dreams.

‹Book II›
(lines 237–80)

    Blessed the infant Babe,
(For with my best conjectures I would trace
The progress of our being) blest the Babe,
Nursed in his Mother's arms, the Babe who sleeps
Upon his Mother's breast, who, when his soul
Claims manifest kindred with an earthly soul,
Doth gather passion from his Mother's eye!
Such feelings pass into his torpid life
Like an awakening breeze, and hence his mind,
Even in the first trial of its powers,
Is prompt and watchful, eager to combine
In one appearance, all the elements
And parts of the same object, else detached
And loth to coalesce. Thus, day by day,
Subjected to the discipline of love,
His organs and recipient faculties
Are quickened, are more vigorous, his mind spreads,
Tenacious of the forms which it receives.
In one beloved presence, nay and more,
In that most apprehensive habitude
And those sensations which have been derived
From this beloved Presence, there exists

A virtue which irradiates and exalts
All objects through all intercourse of sense.
No outcast he, bewildered and depressed;
Along his infant veins are interfused
The gravitation and the filial bond
Of nature, that connect him with the world.
Emphatically such a Being lives,
An inmate of this *active* universe;
From nature largely he receives; nor so
Is satisfied, but largely gives again,
For feeling has to him imparted strength,
And powerful in all sentiments of grief,
Of exultation, fear, and joy, his mind,
Even as an agent of the one great mind,
Creates, creator and receiver both,
Working but in alliance with the works
Which it beholds. – Such, verily, is the first
Poetic spirit of our human life;
By uniform controul of after years
In most abated or suppressed, in some,
Through every change of growth or of decay,
Pre-eminent till death.

‹Book IV›
(lines 400–63)

    While thus I wandered, step by step led on,
It chanced a sudden turning of the road
Presented to my view an uncouth shape,
So near, that, slipping back into the shade
Of a thick hawthorn, I could mark him well,
Myself unseen. He was of stature tall,
A foot above man's common measure tall,
Stiff in his form, and upright, lank and lean;
A man more meagre, as it seemed to me,
Was never seen abroad by night or day.
His arms were long, and bare his hands; his mouth
Shewed ghastly in the moonlight; from behind
A milestone propped him, and his figure seemed
Half-sitting, and half-standing. I could mark
That he was clad in military garb,
Though faded, yet entire. He was alone,
Had no attendant, neither Dog, nor Staff,
Nor knapsack; in his very dress appeared
A desolation, a simplicity
That seemed akin to solitude. Long time
Did I peruse him with a mingled sense
Of fear and sorrow. From his lips, meanwhile,
There issued murmuring sounds, as if of pain
Or of uneasy thought; yet still his form
Kept the same steadiness, and at his feet

His shadow lay, and moved not. In a Glen
Hard by, a Village stood, whose roofs and doors
Were visible among the scattered trees,
Scarce distant from the spot an arrow's flight.
I wished to see him move, but he remained
Fixed to his place, and still from time to time
Sent forth a murmuring voice of dead complaint,
Groans scarcely audible. Without self-blame
I had not thus prolonged my watch; and now,
Subduing my heart's specious cowardice.
I left the shady nook where I had stood,
And hailed him. Slowly from his resting-place
He rose, and with a lean and wasted arm
In measured gesture lifted to his head,
Returned my salutation, then resumed
His station as before. And when, erelong,
I asked his history, he in reply
Was neither slow nor eager, but unmoved,
And with a quiet, uncomplaining voice,
A stately air of mild indifference,
He told, in simple words, a Soldier's tale.
That in the Tropic Islands he had served,
Whence he had landed scarcely ten days past,
That on his landing he had been dismissed,
And now was travelling to his native home.
At this, I turned and looked towards the Village
But all were gone to rest; the fires all out;
And every silent window to the Moon
Shone with a yellow glitter. 'No one there,'
Said I, 'is waking, we must measure back
The way which we have come: behind yon wood
A Labourer dwells, and, take it on my word
He will not murmur should we break his rest,
And with a ready heart will give you food
And lodging for the night.' At this he stooped,
And from the ground took up an oaken Staff,
By me yet unobserved, a Traveller's Staff,
Which, I suppose, from his slack hand had dropped,
And lain till now neglected in the grass.

‹Book V›

(lines 389–413)

There was a Boy, ye knew him well, ye Cliffs
And Islands of Winander! many a time
At evening, when the stars had just begun
To move along the edges of the hills,
Rising or setting, would he stand alone
Beneath the trees, or by the glimmering Lake,
And there, with fingers interwoven, both hands
Pressed closely, palm to palm, and to his mouth

Uplifted, he, as through an instrument,
Blew mimic hootings to the silent owls
That they might answer him. – And they would
     shout
Across the wat'ry Vale, and shout again,
Responsive to his call, with quivering peals,
And long halloos, and screams, and echoes loud
Redoubled and redoubled; concourse wild
Of mirth and jocund din! And when it chanced
That pauses of deep silence mocked his skill,
Then sometimes, in that silence, while he hung
Listening, a gentle shock of mild surprize
Has carried far into his heart the voice
Of mountain torrents; or the visible scene
Would enter unawares into his mind
With all its solemn imagery, its rocks,
Its woods, and that uncertain Heaven, received
Into the bosom of the steady Lake.

‹Book VI›

(lins 553–72)

     The brook and road
Were fellow-travellers in this gloomy Pass,
And with them did we journey several hours
At a slow step. The immeasurable height
Of woods decaying, never to be decayed,
The stationary blasts of water-falls,
And every where along the hollow rent
Winds thwarting winds, bewildered and forlorn,
The torrents shooting from the clear blue sky,
The rocks that muttered close upon our ears,
Black drizzling crags that spake by the way-side
As if a voice were in them, the sick sight
And giddy prospect of the raving stream,
The unfettered clouds and region of the heavens,
Tumult and peace, the darkness and the light
Were all like workings of one mind, the features
Of the same face, blossoms upon one tree,
Characters of the great Apocalypse,
The types and symbols of Eternity,
Of first and last, and midst, and without end.

‹Book X›

(lines 692–727; 805–29)

Bliss was it in that dawn to be alive,
But to be young was very heaven! O times,
In which the meagre, stale, forbidding ways
Of custom, law, and statute took at once
The attraction of a Country in Romance;
When Reason seemed the most to assert her rights

When most intent on making of herself
A prime Enchanter to assist the work
Which then was going forwards in her name.
Not favored spots alone, but the whole earth
The beauty wore of promise, that which sets,
To take an image which was felt, no doubt,
Among the bowers of paradise itself,
The budding rose above the rose full blown.
What temper at the prospect did not wake
To happiness unthought of? The inert
Were rouzed, and lively natures rapt away:
They who had fed their childhood upon dreams,
The Play-fellows of Fancy, who had made
All powers of swiftness, subtlety, and strength
Their ministers, used to stir in lordly wise
Among the grandest objects of the sense,
And deal with whatsoever they found there
As if they had within some lurking right
To wield it; they too, who, of gentle mood
Had watched all gentle motions, and to these
Had fitted their own thoughts, schemers more mild,
And in the region of their peaceful selves,
Did now find helpers to their hearts' desire,
And stuff at hand, plastic as they could wish,
Were called upon to exercise their skill
Not in Utopia, subterraneous Fields,
Or some secreted Island, Heaven knows where,
But in the very world which is the world
Of all of us, the place in which, in the end,
We find our happiness, or not at all.

[...]

This was the time when, all things tending fast
To depravation, the Philosophy
That promised to abstract the hopes of man
Out of his feelings, to be fixed thenceforth
For ever in a purer element
Found ready welcome. Tempting region that
For Zeal to enter and refresh herself,
Where passions had the privilege to work,
And never hear the sound of their own names;
But, speaking more in charity, the dream
Was flattering to the young ingenuous mind
Pleased with extremes, and not the least with that
Which makes the human Reason's naked self
The object of its fervour. What delight!
How glorious! in self-knowledge and self-rule,
To look through all the frailties of the world,
And, with a resolute mastery shaking off
The accidents of nature, time, and place,
That make up the weak being of the past,

Build social freedom on its only basis:
The freedom of the individual mind,
Which, to the blind restraint of general laws
Superior, magisterially adopts
One guide, the light of circumstances, flashed
Upon an independent intellect.

‹ Book XI ›

(lines 279–316)

At a time
When scarcely (I was then not six years old)
My hand could hold a bridle, with proud hopes
I mounted, and we rode towards the hills:
We were a pair of Horsemen; honest James
Was with me, my encourager and guide.
We had not travelled long ere some mischance
Disjoined me from my Comrade, and, through fear
Dismounting, down the rough and stony Moor
I led my Horse, and stumbling on, at length
Came to a bottom, where in former times
A Murderer had been hung in iron chains.
The Gibbet-mast was mouldered down, the bones
And iron case were gone, but on the turf,
Hard by, soon after that fell deed was wrought,
Some unknown hand had carved the Murderer's
    name.
The monumental writing was engraven
In times long past, and still from year to year
By superstition of the neighbourhood
The grass is cleared away; and to this hour
The letters are all fresh and visible.
Faltering, and ignorant where I was, at length
I chanced to espy those characters inscribed
On the green sod: forthwith I left the spot
And, reascending the bare Common, saw
A naked Pool that lay beneath the hills,
The Beacon on the summit, and more near,
A Girl who bore a Pitcher on her head
And seemed with difficult steps to force her way
Against the blowing wind. It was, in truth,
An ordinary sight; but I should need
Colours and words that are unknown to man
To paint the visionary dreariness
Which, while I looked all round for my lost guide,
Did at that time invest the naked Pool,
The Beacon on the lonely Eminence,
The Woman, and her garments vexed and tossed
By the strong wind.

‹Book XIII›

(lines 10–65)

It was a Summer's night, a close warm night,
Wan, dull and glaring, with a dripping mist
Low-hung and thick that covered all the sky,
Half threatening storm and rain; but on we went
Unchecked, being full of heart and having faith
In our tried Pilot. Little could we see,
Hemmed round on every side with fog and damp,
And, after ordinary travellers' chat
With our Conductor, silently we sank
Each into commerce with his private thoughts.
Thus did we breast the ascent, and by myself
Was nothing either seen or heard the while
Which took me from my musings, save that once
The Shepherd's Cur did to his own great joy
Unearth a hedgehog in the mountain crags
Round which he made a barking turbulent.
This small adventure, for even such it seemed
In that wild place and at the dead of night,
Being over and forgotten, on we wound
In silence as before. With forehead bent
Earthward, as if in opposition set
Against an enemy, I panted up
With eager pace, and no less eager thoughts.
Thus might we wear perhaps an hour away,
Ascending at loose distance each from each,
And I, as chanced, the foremost of the Band;
When at my feet the ground appeared to brighten,
And with a step or two seemed brighter still;
Nor had I time to ask the cause of this,
For instantly a Light upon the turf
Fell like a flash: I looked about, and lo!
The Moon stood naked in the Heavens, at height
Immense above my head, and on the shore
I found myself of a huge sea of mist,
Which, meek and silent, rested at my feet.
A hundred hills their dusky backs upheaved
All over this still Ocean, and beyond,
Far, far beyond, the vapours shot themselves,
In headlands, tongues, and promontory shapes,
Into the Sea, the real Sea, that seemed
To dwindle and give up its majesty,
Usurped upon as far as sight could reach.
Meanwhile, the Moon looked down upon this shew
In single glory, and we stood, the mist
Touching our very feet; and from the shore
At distance not the third part of a mile
Was a blue chasm; a fracture in the vapour,
A deep and gloomy breathing-place, through which

Mounted the roar of waters, torrents, streams
Innumerable, roaring with one voice.
The universal spectacle throughout
Was shaped for admiration and delight,
Grand in itself alone, but in that breach
Through which the homeless voice of waters rose,
That dark deep thoroughfare, had Nature lodged
The Soul, the Imagination of the whole.

Thomas Wyatt (1503–42) stares out of Holbein's portrait like a contemporary friend: handsome, bold, loyal, a little angry. And I continue to find a similar human resonance in his poetry, though he was writing at the very beginning of the English lyric; and even though his life as Tudor knight, courtier, and diplomat is so far removed from my own. What seduces me is the awkwardness of his measure, which catches so plangently the movement and tone of speech. His feelings seem genuine in a way the perfectly tuned rhythms of his younger contemporary, the Earl of Surrey, do not. Wyatt was the earliest English exponent of that tug between speech and melody on which a whole tradition of English lyric depends; he broke the iambic line four hundred years before Pound. Yet he could handle *terza rima* with ease, and introduced into England the sonnet that Shakespeare was to use after him. While Wyatt learnt from Petrarch, his complaint is much closer to the modern spirit; his hurt open, his imprisonment in the Tower literal. He has no interest in boasting of the beauty of his faithless love; it is an irrelevance compared with her neglect, ingratitude and unfairness. His famous lyric 'They flee from me that sometime did me seek' still moves me as much by his evocation of the pleasures of touch and nakedness as by the defiant loneliness of his spirit. His complaint is directed against the whole female sex, with whom he once found favour and who now have no time for him; yet it is one love in particular whose treachery he reproaches. And his irony in 'Blame not my lute' defends all poet-lovers from the wrath of those who see their own faces mirrored unkindly in verse.

'YOU THAT IN LOVE FIND LUCK ...'

You that in love find luck and abundance,
And live in lust and joyful jollity,
Arise, for shame, do away your sluggardy,
Arise, I say, do May some observance!
Let me in bed lie dreaming in mischance,
Let me remember the haps most unhappy
That me betide in May most commonly,
As one whom love list little to advance.
Sephame said true that my nativity
Mischanced was with the ruler of the May.
He guessed, I prove of that the verity,
In May my wealth and eke my life, I say,
Have stood so oft in such perplexity.
Rejoice! Let me dream of your felicity.

'I ABIDE ...'

I abide and abide and better abide,
And after the old proverb, the happy day,
And ever my lady to me doth say,
'Let me alone and I will provide.'
I abide and abide and tarry the tide,
And with abiding speed well ye may.
Thus do I abide, I wot, alway,
Neither obtaining nor yet denied.
Aye me, this long abiding
Seemeth to me, as who sayeth,
A prolonging of a dying death,
Or a refusing of a desired thing.
Much were it better for to be plain
Than to say 'abide', and yet shall not obtain.

'BLAME NOT MY LUTE ...'

Blame not my lute, for he must sound
Of this or that as liketh me;
For lack of wit the lute is bound
To give such tunes as pleaseth me.
Though my songs be somewhat strange
And speak such words as touch thy change,
    Blame not my lute.

My lute, alas, doth not offend,
Though that perforce he must agree
To sound such tunes as I intend,
To sing to them that heareth me.
Then though my songs be somewhat plain
And toucheth some that use to feign,
    Blame not my lute.

My lute and strings may not deny,
But as I strike they must obey.
Break not them then so wrongfully,
But wreak thyself some wiser way;
And though the songs which I indite
Do quit thy change with rightful spite,
    Blame not my lute.

Spite asketh spite, and changing change,
And falsèd faith must needs be known;
The faults so great, the case so strange,
Of right it must abroad be blown.
Then since that by thine own desert
My songs do tell how true thou art,
    Blame not my lute.

Blame but thyself that hast misdone,
And well deservèd to have blame;
Change thou thy way so evil begun,
And then my lute shall sound that same.
But if till then my fingers play
By thy desert their wonted way,
    Blame not my lute.

Farewell, unknown, for though thou break
My strings in spite with great disdain,
Yet have I found out, for thy sake,
Strings for to string my lute again.
And if perchance this foolish rhyme
Do make thee blush at any time,
    Blame not my lute.

❧

'THEY FLEE FROM ME . . .'

They flee from me that sometime did me seek
With naked foot stalking in my chamber.
I have seen them gentle, tame, and meek
That now are wild and do not remember
That sometime they put themself in danger

To take bread at my hand, and now they range
Busily seeking with a continual change.

Thanked be fortune it hath been otherwise
Twenty times better, but once in special,
In thin array after a pleasant guise,
When her loose gown from her shoulders did fall
And she caught me in her arms long and small,
Therewithal sweetly did me kiss,
And softly said, 'Dear heart, how like you this?'

It was no dream, I lay broad waking.
But all is turned thorough my gentleness
Into a strange fashion of forsaking;
And I have leave to go of her goodness,
And she also to use newfangleness.
But since that I so kindly am served,
I would fain know what she hath deserved.

❧

'IF THOU WILT MIGHTY BE . . .'

If thou wilt mighty be, flee from the rage
Of cruel will, and see thou keep thee free
From the foul yoke of sensual bondage.
For though thy empire stretch to Indian sea,
And for thy fear trembleth the farthest Thule,
If thy desire have over thee the power,
Subject then art thou, and no governor.

If to be noble and high thy mind be moved,
Consider well thy ground and thy beginning,
For he that hath each star in heaven fixed,
And gives the moon her horns and her eclipsing,
Alike hath made thee noble in his working,
So that wretched no way thou may be,
Except foul lust and vice do conquer thee.

All were it so thou had a flood of gold,
Unto thy thirst yet should it not suffice,
And though with Indian stones, a thousand fold
More precious than can thyself devise,
Ycharged were thy back, thy covetise
And busy biting yet should never let
Thy wretched life, nor do thy death profit.

❧

'Whoso list to hunt...'

Whoso list to hunt, I know where is an hind,
But as for me, alas, I may no more.
The vain travail hath wearied me so sore,
I am of them that farthest cometh behind,
Yet may I by no means my wearied mind
Draw from the deer, but as she fleeth afore
Fainting I follow. I leave off therefore
Since in a net I seek to hold the wind.
Who list her hunt, I put him out of doubt,
As well as I may spend his time in vain,
And graven with diamonds in letters plain
There is written her fair neck round about:
'Noli *me tangere* for Caesar's I am,
And wild for to hold though I seem tame.'

'Forget not yet...'

Forget not yet the tried intent
Of such a truth as I have meant,
My great travail so gladly spent,
    Forget not yet.

Forget not yet when first began
The weary life ye know since when,
The suit, the service none tell can,
    Forget not yet.

Forget not the great assays,
The cruel wrong, the scornful ways,
The painful patience in denays,
    Forget not yet.

Forget not yet, forget not this,
How long ago hath been and is
The mind that never meant amiss,
    Forget not yet.

Forget not then thine own approved,
The which so long hath thee so loved,
Whose steadfast faith yet never moved,
    Forget not this.

'Disdain me not...'

Disdain me not without desert,
Nor leave me not so suddenly,
Since well ye wot that in my heart
I mean it not but honestly,
    Refuse me not.

Refuse me not without cause why,
Nor think me not to be unjust,
Since that by lot of fantasy
The careful knot needs knit I must,
    Mistrust me not.

Mistrust me not, though some there be
That fain would spot my steadfastness;
Believe them not since well ye see
The proof is not as they express:
    Forsake me not.

Forsake me not till I deserve,
Nor hate me not till I offend,
Destroy me not till that I swerve:
Since ye well wot what I intend
    Disdain me not.

Disdain me not that am your own,
Refuse me not that am so true,
Mistrust me not till all be known,
Forsake me not now for no new:
    Disdain me not.

There is an excess of performance in the earliest poems of William Butler Yeats (1865–1939): a special narrative tone, with a dominant verbal melody. He quickly found a more direct poetic speech; always retaining the special tone, but giving sensual access to the facts and matching 'music' organically to content. The books before *Responsibilities* show the stages of this achievement.

It is not an orderly process. There are poems that found maturity early: in the opening and closing poems of *The Rose* (1893) – 'To the Rose upon the Rood of Time' and 'To Ireland in the Coming Times' – concerns and technique are already in harmony. There are setbacks, like the Victorian entertainment 'The Fiddler of Dooney' in *The Wind among the Reeds* (1899). 'Adam's Curse' from *In the Seven Woods* (1904), soon after, is a major poem in Yeats's mature poetic voice.

By *The Green Helmet* (1912) the achievement is complete, as in the epigrams on page 429; the poetry in *Responsibilities*, and later, is of a new kind.

Crossways (1889)
To an Isle in the Water; Down by the Salley Gardens

The Rose (1893)
To the Rose ...; A Faery Song; Who Goes with Fergus?; The Two Trees; To Ireland in the Coming Times

The Wind Among the Reeds (1899)
The Song of Wandering Aengus; The Secret Rose

In the Seven Woods (1904)
In the Seven Woods; Adam's Curse; Red Hanrahan's Song about Ireland

The Green Helmet (1912)
No Second Troy; Reconciliation; The Fascination of What's Difficult; A Drinking Song; The Coming of Wisdom with Time; On Hearing that the Students ...; To a Poet ...; Upon a House ...; All things can tempt me.

To an Isle in the Water

Shy one, shy one,
Shy one of my heart,
She moves in the firelight
Pensively apart.

She carries in the dishes,
And lays them in a row.
To an isle in the water
With her would I go.

She carries in the candles,
And lights the curtained room,
Shy in the doorway
And shy in the gloom;

And shy as a rabbit,
Helpful and shy.
To an isle in the water
With her would I fly.

Down by the Salley Gardens

Down by the salley gardens my love and I did meet;
She passed the salley gardens with little snow-white feet.
She bid me take love easy, as the leaves grow on the tree;
But I, being young and foolish, with her would not agree.

In a field by the river my love and I did stand,
And on my leaning shoulder she laid her snow-white hand.
She bid me take life easy, as the grass grows on the weirs;
But I was young and foolish, and now am full of tears.

To the Rose upon the Rood of Time

Red Rose, proud Rose, sad Rose of all my days!
Come near me, while I sing the ancient ways:
Cuchulain battling with the bitter tide;

The Druid, grey, wood-nurtured, quiet-eyed,
Who cast round Fergus dreams, and ruin untold;
And thine own sadness, whereof stars, grown old
In dancing silver-sandalled on the sea,
Sing in their high and lonely melody.
Come near, that no more blinded by man's fate,
I find under the boughs of love and hate,
In all poor foolish things that live a day,
Eternal beauty wandering on her way.

Come near, come near, come near – Ah, leave me still
A little space for the rose-breath to fill!
Lest I no more hear common things that crave;
The weak worm hiding down in its small cave,
The field-mouse running by me in the grass,
And heavy mortal hopes that toil and pass;
But seek alone to hear the strange things sad
By God to the bright hearts of those long dead,
And learn to chaunt a tongue men do not know.
Come near; I would, before my time to go,
Sing of old Eire and the ancient ways:
Red Rose, proud Rose, sad Rose of all my days.

A FAERY SONG

*‹ Sung by the people of Faery over Diarmuid and
Grania, in their bridal sleep under a Cromlech ›*

We who are old, old and gay,
O so old!
Thousands of years, thousands of years,
If all were told:

Give to these children, new from the world,
Silence and love;
And the long dew-dropplng hours of the night,
And the stars above:

Give to these children, new from the world,
Rest far from men.
Is anything better, anything better?
Tell us it then:

Us who are old, old and gay,
O so old!
Thousands of years, thousands of years,
If all were told.

WHO GOES WITH FERGUS?

Who will go drive with Fergus now,
And pierce the deep wood's woven shade,
And dance upon the level shore?
Young man, lift up your russet brow,
And lift your tender eyelids, maid,
And brood on hopes and fear no more.

And no more turn aside and brood
Upon love's bitter mystery;
For Fergus rules the brazen cars,
And rules the shadows of the wood,
And the white breast of the dim sea
And all dishevelled wandering stars.

THE TWO TREES

Beloved, gaze in thine own heart,
The holy tree is growing there;
From joy the holy branches start,
And all the trembling flowers they bear.
The changing colours of its fruit
Have dowered the stars with merry light;
The surety of its hidden root
Has planted quiet in the night;
The shaking of its leafy head
Has given the waves their melody,
And made my lips and music wed,
Murmuring a wizard song for thee.
There the Loves a circle go,
The flaming circle of our days,
Gyring, spiring to and fro
In those great ignorant leafy ways;
Remembering all that shaken hair
And how the wingèd sandals dart,
Thine eyes grow full of tender care:
Beloved, gaze in shine own heart.

Gaze no more in the bitter glass
The demons, with their subtle guile,
Lift up before us when they pass,
Or only gaze a little while;
For there a fatal image grows
That the stormy night receives,
Roots half hidden under snows,
Broken boughs and blackened leaves.
For all things turn to barrenness

In the dim glass the demons hold,
The glass of outer weariness,
Made when God slept in times of old.
There, through the broken branches, go
The ravens of unresting thought;
Flying, crying, to and fro,
Cruel claw and hungry throat,
Or else they stand and sniff the wind,
And shake their ragged wings; alas!
Thy tender eyes grow all unkind:
Gaze no more in the bitter glass.

To Ireland in the Coming Times

Know, that I would accounted be
True brother of a company
That sang, to sweeten Ireland's wrong,
Ballad and story, rann and song;
Nor be I any less of them,
Because the red-rose-bordered hem
Of her, whose history began
Before God made the angelic clan,
Trails all about the written page.
When Time began to rant and rage
The measure of her flying feet
Made Ireland's heart begin to beat;
And Time bade all his candles flare
To light a measure here and there;
And may the thoughts of Ireland brood
Upon a measured quietude.

Nor may I less be counted one
With Davis, Mangan, Ferguson,
Because, to him who ponders well,
My rhymes more than their rhyming tell
Of things discovered in the deep,
Where only body's laid asleep.
For the elemental creatures go
About my table to and fro,
That hurry from unmeasured mind
To rant and rage in flood and wind;
Yet he who treads in measured ways
May surely barter gaze for gaze.
Man ever journeys on with them
After the red-rose-bordered hem.
Ah, faeries, dancing under the moon,
A Druid land, a Druid tune!

While still I may, I write for you
The love I lived, the dream I knew.
From our birthday, until we die,
Is but the winking of an eye;
And we, our singing and our love,
What measurer Time has lit above,
And all benighted things that go
About my table to and fro,
Are passing on to where may be,
In truth's consuming ecstasy,
No place for love and dream at all;
For God goes by with white footfall.
I cast my heart into my rhymes,
That you, in the dim coming times,
May know how my heart went with them
After the red-rose-bordered hem.

The song of Wandering Aengus

I went out to the hazel wood,
Because a fire was in my head,
And cut and peeled a hazel wand,
And hooked a berry to a thread;
And when white moths were on the wing,
And moth-like stars were flickering out,
I dropped the berry in a stream
And caught a little silver trout.

When I had laid it on the floor
I went to blow the fire aflame,
But something rustled on the floor,
And some one called me by my name:
It had become a glimmering girl
With apple blossom in her hair
Who called me by my name and ran
And faded through the brightening air.

Though I am old with wandering
Through hollow lands and hilly lands,
I will find out where she has gone,
And kiss her lips and take her hands;
And walk among long dappled grass,
And pluck till time and times are done
The silver apples of the moon,
The golden apples of the sun.

THE SECRET ROSE

Far-off, most secret, and inviolate Rose,
Enfold me in my hour of hours; where those
Who sought thee in the Holy Sepulchre,
Or in the wine-vat, dwell beyond the stir
And tumult of defeated dreams; and deep
Among pale eyelids, heavy with the sleep
Men have named beauty. Thy great leaves enfold
The ancient beards, the helms of ruby and gold
Of the crowned Magi; and the king whose eyes
Saw the Pierced Hands and Rood of elder rise
In Druid vapour and make the torches dim;
Till vain frenzy awoke and he died; and him
Who met Fand walking among flaming dew
By a grey shore where the wind never blew,
And lost the world and Emer for a kiss;
And him who drove the gods out of their liss,
And till a hundred morns had flowered red
Feasted, and wept the barrows of his dead;
And the proud dreaming king who flung the crown
And sorrow away, and calling bard and clown
Dwelt among wine-stained wanderers in deep
    woods;
And him who sold tillage, and house, and goods,
And sought through lands and islands numberless
    years,
Until he found, with laughter and with tears,
A woman of so shining loveliness
That men threshed corn at midnight by a tress,
A little stolen tress. I, too, await
The hour of thy great wind of love and hate.
When shall the stars be blown about the sky,
Like the sparks blown out of a smithy, and die?
Surely thine hour has come, thy great wind blows,
Far-off, most secret, and inviolate Rose?

IN THE SEVEN WOODS

I have heard the pigeons of the Seven Woods
Make their faint thunder, and the garden bees
Hum in the lime-tree flowers; and put away
The unavailing outcries and the old bitterness
That empty the heart. I have forgot awhile
Tara uprooted, and new commonness
Upon the throne and crying about the streets
And hanging its paper flowers from post to post,
Because it is alone of all things happy.

I am contented, for I know that Quiet
Wanders laughing and eating her wild heart
Among pigeons and bees, while that Great Archer,
Who but awaits His hour to shoot, still hangs
A cloudy quiver over Pairc-na-lee.

ADAM'S CURSE

We sat together at one summer's end,
That beautiful mild woman, your close friend,
And you and I, and talked of poetry.
I said, 'A line will take us hours maybe;
Yet if it does not seem a moment's thought,
Our stitching and unstitching has been naught.
Better go down upon your marrow-bones
And scrub a kitchen pavement, or break stones
Like an old pauper in all kinds of weather;
For to articulate sweet sounds together
Is to work harder than all these, and yet
Be thought an idler by the noisy set
Of bankers, schoolmasters, and clergymen
The martyrs call the world.'

                And thereupon
That beautiful mild woman for whose sake
There's many a one shall find out all heartache
On finding that her voice is sweet and low
Replied, 'To be born woman is to know –
Although they do not talk of it at school –
That we must labour to be beautiful.'

I said, 'It's certain there is no fine thing
Since Adam's fall but needs much labouring.
There have been lovers who thought love should be
So much compounded of high courtesy
That they would sigh and quote with learned looks
Precedents out of beautiful old books;
Yet now it seems an idle trade enough.'

We sat grown quiet at the name of love;
We saw the last embers of daylight die,
And in the trembling blue-green of the sky
A moon, worn as if it had been a shell
Washed by time's waters as they rose and fell
About the stars and broke in days and years.

I had a thought for no one's but your ears:
That you were beautiful, and that I strove

To love you in the old high way of love;
That it had all seemed happy, and yet we'd grown
As weary-hearted as that hollow moon.

RED HANRAHAN'S SONG ABOUT IRELAND

The old brown thorn-trees break in two high over
    Cummen Strand,
Under a bitter black wind that blows from the left
    hand;
Our courage breaks like an old tree in a black wind
    and dies,
But we have hidden in our hearts the flame out of
    the eyes
Of Cathleen, the daughter of Houlihan.

The wind has bundled up the clouds high over
    Knocknarea,
And thrown the thunder on the stones for all that
    Maeve can say.
Angers that are like noisy clouds have set our hearts
    abeat;
But we have all bent low and low and kissed the
    quiet feet
Of Cathleen, the daughter of Houlihan.

The yellow pool has overflowed high up on Clooth-
    na-Bare,
For the wet winds are blowing out of the clinging
    air;
Like heavy flooded waters our bodies and our
    blood;
But purer than a tall candle before the Holy Rood
Is Cathleen, the daughter of Houlihan.

NO SECOND TROY

Why should I blame her that she filled my days
With misery, or that she would of late
Have taught to ignorant men most violent ways,
Or hurled the little streets upon the great,
Had they but courage equal to desire?
What could have made her peaceful with a mind
That nobleness made simple as a fire,

With beauty like a tightened bow, a kind
That is not natural in an age like this,
Being high and solitary and most stern?
Why, what could she have done, being what she is?
Was there another Troy for her to burn?

RECONCILIATION

Some may have blamed you that you took away
The verses that could move them on the day
When, the ears being deafened, the sight of the eyes
    blind
With lightning, you went from me, and I could
    find
Nothing to make a song about but kings,
Helmets, and swords, and half-forgotten things
That were like memories of you – but now
We'll out, for the world lives as long ago;
And while we're in our laughing, weeping fit,
Hurl helmets, crowns, and swords into the pit.
But, dear, cling close to me; since you were gone,
My barren thoughts have chilled me to the bone.

THE FASCINATION OF WHAT'S DIFFICULT

The fascination of what's difficult
Has dried the sap out of my veins, and rent
Spontaneous joy and natural content
Out of my heart. There's something ails our colt
That must, as if it had not holy blood
Nor on Olympus leaped from cloud to cloud,
Shiver under the lash, strain, sweat and jolt
As though it dragged road-metal. My curse on
    plays.
That have to be set up in fifty ways,
On the day's war with every knave and dolt,
Theatre business, management of men.
I swear before the dawn comes round again
I'll find the stable and pull out the bolt.

A Drinking Song

Wine comes in at the mouth
And love comes in at the eye;
That's all we shall know for truth
Before we grow old and die.
I lift the glass to my mouth,
I look at you, and I sigh.

The Coming of Wisdom with Time

Though leaves are many, the root is one;
Through all the lying days of my youth
I swayed my leaves and flowers in the sun;
Now I may wither into the truth.

On hearing that the students of our new University have joined the agitation against immoral literature

Where, where but here have Pride and Truth,
That long to give themselves for wage,
To shake their wicked sides at youth
Restraining reckless middle-age?

To a Poet, who would have me praise certain bad poets, imitators of his and mine

You say, as I have often given tongue
In praise of what another's said or sung,
'Twere politic to do the like by these;
But was there ever dog that praised his fleas?

Upon a House shaken by the Land Agitation

How should the world be luckier if this house,
Where passion and precision have been one
Time out of mind, became too ruinous
To breed the lidless eye that loves the sun?
And the sweet laughing eagle thoughts that grow
Where wings have memory of wings, and all
That comes of the best knit to the best? Although:
Mean roof-trees were the sturdier for its fall,
How should their luck run high enough to reach
The gifts that govern men, and after these
To gradual Time's last gift, a written speech
Wrought of high laughter, loveliness and ease?

All things can tempt me

All things can tempt me from this craft of verse:
One time it was a woman's face, or worse –
The seeming needs of my fool-driven land;
Now nothing but comes readier to the hand
Than this accustomed toil. When I was young,
I had not given a penny for a song
Did not the poet sing it with such airs
That one believed he had a sword upstairs;
Yet would be now, could I but have my wish,
Colder and dumber and deafer than a fish.

Few poets' reputations have altered as dramatically as that of Edward Young (1683–1765) who is included in neither the *Oxford Book of English Verse* nor the *New Oxford Book of English Verse*. Yet for more than a century after the publication in 1742 of *Night Thoughts*, it was one of the most praised and well-known poems in the English language.

'It is not possible for me to express my admiration of such gifts, such talents,' wrote Samuel Richardson when he first read *Night Thoughts*. Samuel Johnson described Young as 'a man of genius and a poet,' and Young's French translator claimed that the poem was 'la plus sublime élégie qui ait jamais été faite…'

The Complaint: or Night Thoughts was written after the death of Young's wife, and the deaths of his step-daughter and her husband soon after. Its 10,000 lines of blank verse divided into nine sections of moralising, melancholy reflections on death and immortality, express an orthodoxy of religious sentiment which is hard to read today. By the mid-19th century, the work was already viewed critically. In her essay, 'Worldliness and Other-Worldliness', published in 1857, George Eliot describes Young as 'a sort of cross between a sycophant and a psalmist'. 'His religion exhausts itself in ejaculations and rebukes, and knows no medium between the ecstatic and the sententious.' But she also acknowledges the passages of genuine poetry, and the following excerpts should give some indication of the range and feeling of Young's work.

THE COMPLAINT: OR NIGHT-THOUGHTS

◄ Book I ►

(lines 1–89; 220–9)

Tir'd nature's sweet restorer, balmy sleep!
He, like the world, his ready visit pays,
Where fortune smiles; the wretched he foresakes;
Swift on his downy pinion flies from woe,
And lights on lids unsully'd with a tear.
    From short, (as usual) and disturb'd repose,
I wake: how happy they who wake no more!
Yet that were vain, if dreams infest the grave.
I wake, emerging from a sea of dreams
Tumultuous; where my wreck'd, desponding
        thought
From wave to wave of fancied misery,
At random drove, her helm of reason lost;
Tho' now restored, 'tis only change of pain,
A bitter change; severer for severe:
The day short for my distress! and night
Even in the zenith of her dark domain,
Is sun-shine, to the colour of my fate.
    Night, sable goddess! from her ebon throne,
In rayless majesty, now stretches forth
Her leaden scepter o'er a slumbering world:
Silence, how dead? and darkness, how profound?
Nor eye, nor list'ning ear an object finds;
Creation sleeps. 'Tis, as the general pulse
Of life stood still, and nature made a pause;
An awful pause! prophetic of her end.
And let her prophesy be soon fulfil'd
Fate! drop the curtain; I can lose no more.
    Silence, and darkness! solemn sisters! twins
From antient night, who nurse the tender thought
To reason, and on reason build resolve,
(That column of true majesty in man!)
Assist me: I will thank you in the grave;
The grave, your kingdom: there this frame shall fall
A victim sacred to your dreary shrine:
But what are ye? Thou who didst put to flight
Primaeval silence, when the morning stars
Exulting, shouted o'er the rising ball;
Oh Thou! whose word from solid darkness struck
That spark, the sun; strike wisdom from my soul;
My soul which flies to thee, her trust, her treasure;
As misers to their gold, while others rest.
    Thro' this opaque of nature, and of soul,
This double night, transmit one pitying ray,
To lighten, and to cheer: O lead my mind,
(A mind that fain would wander from its woe,)
Lead it thro' various scenes of life and death,

And from each scene, the noblest truths inspire:
Not less inspire my conduct, than my song;
Teach my best reason, reason; my best will
Teach rectitude; and fix my firm resolve
Wisdom to wed, and pay her long arrear.
Nor let the vial of Thy vengeance pour'd
On this devoted head, be pour'd in vain.

    The bell strikes one: we take no note of time,
But from its loss. To give it then a tongue,
Is wise in man. As if an angel spoke,
I feel the solemn sound. If heard aright,
It is the knell of my departed hours;
Where are they? with the years beyond the flood:
It is the signal that demands dispatch;
How much is to be done? my hopes and fears
Start up alarm'd, and o'er life's narrow verge
Look down – on what? a fathomless abyss;
A dread eternity! how surely mine!
And can eternity belong to me,
Poor pensioner on the bounties of an hour?

    How poor? how rich? How abject? how august?
How complicat? how wonderful is man?
How passing wonder He, who made him such?
Who center'd in our make such strange extremes?
From different natures, marvelously mixt,
Connection exquisit of distant worlds!
Distinguisht link in being's endless chain!
Midway from nothing to the deity!
A beam etherial sully'd and absorpt!
Tho' surly'd, and dishonour'd, still divine!
Dim miniature of greatness absolute!
An heir of glory! a frail child of dust!
Helpless immortal! Insect infinite!
A worm! A god! I tremble at myself,
And in myself am lost! At home a stranger,
Thought wanders up and down, surpriz'd, aghast,
And wond'ring at her own: how reason reels?
O what a miracle to man is man,
Triumphantly distrest? What joy, what dread?
Alternately transported, and alarm'd!
What can preserve my life? or what destroy?
An angel's arm can't snatch me from the grave;
Legions of angels can't confine me there.

[. . .]

In every vary'd posture, place, and hour,
How widow'd every thought of every joy?
Thought, busy thought! too busy for my peace,
Thro' the dark postern of time long elapsed
Led softly, by the stillness of the night,
Led, like a murderer, (and such it proves!)

Strays, wretched, rover, o'er the pleasing past,
Inquest of wretchedness perversely strays;
And finds all desert now, and meets the ghosts
Of my departed joys.

‹ Book II ›
(lines 64–66)

Who wants amusement in the flame of battle?
Is it not treason, to the soul immortal,
Her foes in arms, eternity the prize?

‹ Book V ›
(lines 403–8)

In the same brook, none ever bathed him twice:
To the same life none ever twice awoke.
We call the brook the same – the same we think
Our life, though still more rapid in its flow;
Nor mark the much irrevocably lapsed
And mingled with the sea.

‹ Book VI ›
(lines 164–90)

    If inextinguishable thirst in man
To know; how rich, how full our banquet there?
There, not the moral world alone unfolds;
The world material lately seen in shades,
And in those shades, by fragments, only seen,
And seen those fragments by the labouring eye,
Unbroken, then, illustrious, and entire,
Its ample sphere, its universal frame,
In full dimensions, swells to the survey;
And enters, at one glance, the ravished sight.
From some superior point (where, who can tell?
Suffice it, 'tis a point where gods reside)
How shall the stranger man's illumin'd eye,
In the vast ocean of unbounded space,
Behold an infinite of floating worlds
Divide the crystal waves of ether pure,
In endless voyage, without port? The least
Of these disseminated orbs, how great?
Great as they are, what numbers these surpass
Huge, as Leviathan, to that small race,
Those twinkling multitudes of little life,
He swallows unperceiv'd? Stupendous these!
Yet what are these stupendous to the whole?
As particles, as atoms ill-perceived;
As circulating globules in our veins;
So vast the plan: fecundity divine!
Exuberant source!

'A moth ate words...' is one of the earliest and simplest riddles in the language and is from the Exeter Book, a tenth-century manuscript collection of Old English poetry. A more difficult riddle is the medieval 'Have A Young Sister' – or it would be if it did not answer itself within the song. It's a great survivor – I heard a version of it sung recently by a busker in Galway, Ireland.

'Tom o' Bedlam's Song' was collected by a friend of Thomas Campion called Giles Earle in 1615 and there have been various rewrites of the poem since. The manuscript can be found in the British Museum.

A few manuscript copies of 'Thomas Rymer' also exist, dating back to the mid-fifteenth century. Stories of humans being snatched away to Elfland have their counterpart now in stories of people being snatched by aliens and taken up into UFOs and were no doubt believed by the same proportion of people.

I wonder whatever happened to a manuscript Walter de la Mare claims inspired him? 'This Is the Key' is one of hundreds of nursery rhymes (or dandling rhymes as he called them) transcribed by Walter de la Mare as a child from a manuscript book of poems he tells us he found in the cluttered room of an isolated country house. On the manuscript's cover in faded handwriting was the title, *Theeothaworldie*, and the name of the compiler Nahum Tarune.

'The Grey Cock' as printed here is an anonymous American folk-song first collected in North Carolina in 1916, and is a version of a Scottish folk-song from the 16th century. The last verse in this American version seems to be a tagged-on moral. Earlier versions simply lament that the lovers separated before they needed to, the cock having crowed too soon.

OLD ENGLISH RIDDLE

A moth ate words; a marvellous event
I thought it when I heard about that wonder,
A worm had swallowed some man's lay, a thief
In darkness had consumed the mighty saying
With its foundation firm. The thief was not
One whit the wiser when he ate those words.

The 'answer' is bookworm.

I HAVE A YOUNG SISTER

I have a yong suster
    Fer beyonden sea,
Many be the keepsakes
    That she sente me.

She sente me the cherye
    Withouten any stone,
And so she did the dove
    Withouten any bone.

She sente me the briar
    Withouten any rind,
She bade me love my sweet-heart
    Withouten longing.

How shuld any cherye
    Be withouten stone?
And how shuld any dove
    Ben withouten bone?

How shuld any briar
    Be withouten rind?
How shuld I love myn sweet-heart
    Withouten longing?

When the cherye was a flowr
    Then hadde it non stone.
When the dove was an egg
    Then hadde it non bone.

When the briar was unbred
    Then hadde it non rind.
When the maiden hath that she loveth
    She is withoute longing.

TOM O' BEDLAM'S SONG

From the hagg and hungry goblin
That into rags would rend ye,
And the spirit that stands by the naked man
In the Book of Moons defend ye!
That of your five sound senses
You never be forsaken,
Nor wander from your selves with Tom
Abroad to beg your bacon.

> *While I do sing 'any food, any feeding,*
> *Feeding, drink or clothing,'*
> *Come dame or maid, be not afraid*
> *Poor Tom will injure nothing.*

Of thirty bare years have I
Twice twenty been enragèd
And of forty been three times fifteen
In durance soundly cagèd.
On the lordly lofts of Bedlam,
With stubble soft and dainty,
Brave bracelets strong, sweet whips ding-dong
With wholesome hunger plenty.

And now I sing 'any food. any feeding, . . .

With a thought I took for Maudline
And a cruse of cockle pottage,
With a thing thus tall, sky bless you all,
I befell into this dotage.
I slept not since the Conquest,
Till then I never wakèd.
Till the roguish boy of love where I lay
Me found and stripped me naked.

And now I sing 'any food, any feeding, . . .

When I short have shorn my sour face
And swigged my horny barrel.
In an oaken inn I pound my skin
As a suit of gilt apparel.
The moon's my constant Mistress
And the lowly owl my morrow.
The flaming Drake and the Nightcrow make
Me music to my sorrow.

While I do sing 'any food, any feeding, . . .

The palsy plagues my pulses
When I prigg your pigs or pullen,

Your culvers take, or matchless make
Your Chanticleare, or sullen.
When I want provant, with Humfry
I sup, and when benighted,
I repose in Paul's with waking souls
Yet never am affrighted.

But I do sing 'any food, any feeding, . . .

I know more than Apollo.
For oft, when he lies sleeping,
I see the stars at bloody wars
In the wounded welkin weeping;
The moon embrace her shepherd
And the queen of Love her warrior,
While the first doth horn the star of morn,
And the next the heavenly Farrier.

While I do sing 'any food, any feeding,. . .

The Gipsy Snap and Pedro
Are none of Tom's comrados.
The punk I scorn and the cut purse sworn
And the roaring boys bravado.
The meek, the white, the gentle,
Me handle touch and spare not,
But those that cross Tom Rynosseros
Do what the panther dare not.

Although I sing 'any food, any feeding, . . .

With an host of furious fancies,
Whereof I am commander,
With a burning spear and a horse of air,
To the wilderness I wander.
By a knight of ghosts and shadows
I summoned am to tourney
Ten leagues beyond the wide world's end.
Me think it is no journey.

Yet will I sing 'any food, any feeding, . . .

Glossary

HAGG: haggard; ENRAGÈD: mad; DURANCE: confinement; MAUDLINE;
Tom's 'lady'; CRUSE: pitcher; ROGUISH BOY OF LOVE; Cupid; PRIGG:
steal; PULLEN: chicken; CULVERS: wood pigeon

THOMAS RYMER

True Thomas lay oer yond grassy bank,
 And he beheld a ladie gay,
A ladie that was brisk and bold,
 Come riding oer the fernie brae.

Her skirt was of the grass-green silk,
 Her mantel of the velvet fine,
At ilka tett of her horse's mane
 Hung fifty silver bells and nine.

True Thomas he took off his hat,
 And bowed him low down till his knee:
'All hail, thou mighty Queen of Heaven!
 For your peer on earth I never did see.'

'O no, O no, True Thomas,' she says,
 'That name does not belong to me;
I am but the queen of fair Elfland,
 And I'm come here for to visit thee . . .

'But ye maun go wi me now, Thomas,
 True Thomas, ye maun go wi me,
For ye maun serve me seven years,
 Thro weel or wae as may chance to be.

'Then harp and carp, Thomas,' she said,
 'Then harp and carp, alang wi me:
But it will be seven years and a day
 Till ye win back to yere ain countrie.'

She turned about her milk-white steed,
 And took True Thomas up behind,
And aye wheneer her bridle rang,
 The steed flew swifter than the wind.

For forty days and forty nights
 He wade thro red blude to the knee,
And he saw neither sun nor moon,
 But heard the roaring of the sea.

O they rade on, and further on,
 Until they came to a garden green:
'Light down, light down, ye laddie free,
 Some of that fruit let me pull to thee.'

'O no, O no, True Thomas,' she says,
 'That fruit maun not be touched by thee,
For a' the plagues that are in hell
 Light on the fruit of this countrie.

'But I have a loaf here in my lap,
 Likewise a bottle of claret wine,
And now ere we go farther on,
 We'll rest a while, and ye may dine.'

When he had eaten and drunk his fi!l: –
 'Lay down your head upon my knee,'
The lady sayd, 'ere we climb yon hill
 And I will show you fairlies three.

'O see not ye yon narrow road,
 So thick beset wi thorns and briers?
That is the path of righteousness,
 Tho after it but few enquires.

'And see not ye that braid braid road,
 That lies across yon lillie leven?
That is the path of wickedness,
 Tho some call it the road to heaven.

'And see not ye that bonny road,
 Which winds about the fernie brae?
That is the road to fair Elfland,
 Where you and I this night maun gae.

'But Thomas, ye maun hold your tongue,
 Whatever you may hear or see,
For gin ae word you should chance to speak,
 You will neer get back to your ain countrie.'

He has gotten a coat of the even cloth,
 And a pair of shoes of velvet green:
And till seyen years were past and gone
 True Thomas on earth was never seen.

❧

THIS IS THE KEY

This is the Key of the Kingdom
In that Kingdom is a City;
In that city is a town;
In that town there is a street;
In that street there winds a lane;
In that lane there is a yard;
In that yard there is a house;
In that house there waits a room;
In that room an empty bed;
And on that bed a basket –

A Basket of Sweet Flowers:
> *Of Flowers, of Flowers;*
> *A Basket of Sweet Flowers.*

Flowers in a Basket;
Basket on the bed;
Bed in the chamber;
Chamber in the house;
House in the weedy yard;
Yard in the winding lane;
Lane in the broad street;
Street in the high town;
Town in the city;
City in the Kingdom –
This is the Key of the Kingdom.
> *Of the Kingdom this is the Key.*

ᕯ

THE GREY COCK

All on one summer's evening when the fever were a-
    dawning
I heard a fair maid make a moan.
She was a-weeping for her father and a-grieving for
    her mother,
and a-thinking of her true love John.
At last John came and he found the doors all shut,
and he dingled so low at the ring.
Then this maid she rose and hurried on some of her
    clothes
to make haste to let Johnny come in.

All around the waist he caught her and unto the
    bed he brought her,
and they lay there a-talking awhile.
She says, O you feathered fowls, you pretty feathered
    fowls,
don't you crow till it's almost day,
and your comb it shall be of the pure ivory
and your wings of the bright silver grey.
But him a-being young he crowed very soon,
he crowed two long hours before day;
and she sent her love away, for she thought 'twas
    almost day,
and 'twas all by the light of the moon.

It's, when will you be back? dear John,
when will you be back to see me?
When the seventh moon is done and passed

and shines on yonder lea,
and you know that will never be.
What a foolish girl I was when I thought he was as
    true
as the rocks that grow to the ground;
but since I do find he has altered his mind,
it's better to live single than bound.

From a modern point of view, many nineteenth-century American poets were afflicted with the fatal delusion of believing that the purpose of poetry is to generate wisdom. After the mysteriously archaic Anne Bradstreet, and the deft metaphysical pieties of Edward Taylor (1645–1729), much of the poetry of the period seems to wish passionately to say morally useful things, and it usually tries to do so by secreting generalizations in a formula of late Romantic nature observation.

We tend to forget, though, what a perplexing experience it was to be an artist in America just then, to be trying to create a national culture almost from scratch: that grand principles should have been sought for such an unlikely undertaking is hardly surprising. What *is* surprising, of course, is that when authentic American poetics were developed, it was the outsiders Whitman and Dickinson who created visions which still actively compel our own sensibilities.

But if there aren't any other poets whose bodies of work have such overwhelming originality and depth, there are certainly enough of considerable interest and energy. Frederick Tuckerman (1821–73) for one, deserves to be better known: he wrote deft and moving sonnets. Emerson (1803–82) and Thoreau (1817–62) who *were* wise men, left evidence of it in some of their poetic work, and Melville (1819–91), if not the enormous genius he was in prose, wrote verse informed by similar dark fires. For the rest, there are quite compelling individual poems: the famous meditation on Indian life by Freneau (1752–1832) and his harsh depiction of slavery; 'Thanatopsis' by Bryant (1794–1878) the very model of a young person's death rapture; the rural studies of Whittier (1807–92), which are surprisingly strong precursors of Frost's. The sonnets of Jones Very (1813–80) are competent reflections of his religious enthusiasm. Lanier (1842–81) was a deft metrical technician: Markham (1852–1940) and Stickney (1874–1904) and Crane (1871–1900) have moments of quirky originality, and the poem by Emma Lazarus (1849–87) has some of the most famous lines of American political rhetoric. With more space, I would have included some of the vital folk-songs and spirituals of the time.

Upon a Spider Catching a Fly

‹ Edward Taylor ›

Thou sorrow, venom Elf:
   Is this thy play,
To spin a web out of thyself
   To Catch a Fly?
     For why?

I saw a pettish wasp
   Fall foul therein:
Whom yet thy whorl pins did not hasp
   Lest he should fling
     His sting.

But as afraid, remote
   Didst stand hereat,
And with thy little fingers stroke
   And gently tap
     His back.

Thus gently him didst treat
   Lest he should pet,
And in a froppish, aspish heat
   Should greatly fret
     Thy net.

Whereas the silly Fly,
   Caught by its leg,
Thou by the throat took'st hastily,
   And 'hind the head
     Bite Dead.

This goes to pot, that not
   Nature doth call.
Strive not above what strength hath got,
   Lest in the brawl
     Thou fall.

This Fray seems thus to us:
   Hell's Spider gets
His intrails spun to whip Cords thus,
   And wove to nets,
     And sets.

To tangle Adam's race
   In's stratagems
To their Destructions, Spoil'd, made base
   By venom things,
     Damn'd sins.

But mighty, Gracious Lord,
   Communicate
Thy Grace to breake the Cord; afford
   Us Glory's Gate
     And State.

We'll Nightingale sing like,
   When pearcht on high
In Glories Cage, thy glory, bright:
   Yea, thankfully,
     For joy.

HUSWIFERY

‹ Edward Taylor ›

Make me, O Lord, thy Spinning Wheel compleat;
   Thy Holy Worde my Distaff make for me.
Make mine Affections thy Swift Flyers neat,
   And make my Soule thy holy Spool to be.
   My Conversation make to be thy Reel,
   And reel the yarn thereon spun of thy Wheel.

Make me thy Loom then, knit therein this Twine:
   And make thy Holy Spirit, Lord, wind quills:
Then weave the Web thyself. The yarn is fine.
   Thine Ordinances make my Fulling Mills.
   Then dye the same in Heavenly Colours Choice,
   All pinkt with Varnish't flowers of Paradise.

Then cloath therewith mine Understanding, Will,
   Affections, Judgment, Conscience, Memory;
My Words and Actions, that their shine may fill
   My ways with glory and thee glorify.
   Then mine apparell shall display before ye
   That I am Cloathd in Holy robes for glory.

MEDITATION

‹ Edward Taylor ›

What Love is this of shine, that Cannot be
   In shine Infinity, O Lord, Confined
Unless it in thy very Person see,
   Infinity, and Finity Conjoyn'd?
   What hath thy Godhead, as not satisfied
   Married our Manhood, making it its Bride?

Oh, Matchless Love! filling Heaven to the brim!
   O're running it: all running o're beside
This World! Nay Overflowing Hell; wherein
   For shine Elect, there rose a mighty Tide!
   That there our Veins might through thy Person
   bleed,
   To quench those flames, that else would on us
   feed.

Oh! that thy Love might overflow my Heart!
   To fire the same with Love: for Love I would.
But oh! my streight'ned Breast! my Lifeless Spark!
   My Fireless Flame! What Chilly Love, and Cold?
   In measure small! In Manner Chiliy! See.
   Lord blow the Coal: Thy Love Enflame in me.

TO SIR TOBY
*A Sugar Planter in the Interior Parts of Jamaica,
Near the City of San Jago de la Vega, (Spanish
Town) 1784*

‹ Philip Freneau ›

   *'The motions of his spirit are black as night,
   And his affections dark as Erebus.'*
                      – Shakespeare

If there exists a hell – the case is clear –
   Sir Toby's slaves enjoy that portion here:
Here are no blazing brimstone lakes – 'tis true;
But kindled rum too often burns as blue;
In which some fiend, whom nature must detest,
Steeps Toby's brand, and marks poor Cudjoe's breast.
   Here whips on whips excite perpetual fears,
And mingled howlings vibrate on my ears:
Here Nature's plagues abound, to fret and tease
Snakes, scorpions, despots, lizards, centipedes –
No art, no care escapes the busy lash;
All have their dues – and all are paid in cash –
The eternal driver keeps a steady eye
On a black herd, who would his vengeance fly,
But chained, imprisoned, on a burning soil,
For the mean avarice of a tyrant toil!
The lengthy cart-whip guards this monster's reign –
And cracks, like pistols, from the fields of cane.
   Ye powers! who formed these wretched tribes,
     relate,
What had they done, to merit such a fate!
Why were they brought from Eboe's sultry waste,
To see that plenty which they must not taste –

Food, which they cannot buy, and dare not steal;
Yams and potatoes – many a scanty meal! –

One, with a gibbet wakes his negro's fears,
One to the windmill nails him by the ears;
One keeps his slave in darkened dens, unfed,
One puts the wretch in pickle ere he's dead:
This, from a tree suspends him by the thumbs,
That, from his table grudges even the crumbs!

O'er yond' rough hills a tribe of females go,
Each with her gourd, her infant, and her hoe;
Scorched by a sun that has no mercy here,
Driven by a devil, whom men call overseer –
In chains, twelve wretches to their labors haste;
Twice twelve I saw, with iron collars graced! –

Are such the fruits that spring from vast domains?
Is wealth, thus got, Sir Toby, worth your pains! –
Who would your wealth on terms, like these, possess,
Where all we see is pregnant with distress –
Angola's natives scourged by ruffian hands,
And toil's hard product shipped to foreign lands.

Talk not of blossoms, and your endless spring;
What joy, what smile, can scenes of misery bring? –
Though Nature, here, has every blessing spread,
Poor is the laborer – and how meanly fed! –

Here Stygian paintings light and shade renew,
Pictures of hell, that Virgil's pencil drew:
Here, surly Charons make their annual trip,
And ghosts arrive in every Guinea ship,
To find what beasts these western isles afford,
Plutonian scourges, and despotic lords: –

Here, they, of stuff determined to be free,
Must climb the rude cliffs of the Liguanee;
Beyond the clouds, in sculking haste repair,
And hardly safe from brother traitors there. –

❧

THE INDIAN BURYING GROUND

‹Philip Freneau›

Inspite of all the learned have said,
    I still my old opinion keep;
The posture, that we give the dead,
    Points out the soul's eternal sleep.

Not so the ancients of these lands –
    The Indian, when from life released,
Again is seated with his friends,
    And shares again the joyous feast.

His imaged birds, and painted bowl,
    And venison, for a journey dressed,
Bespeak the nature of the soul,
    Activity, that knows no rest.

His bow, for action ready bent,
    And arrows, with a head of stone,
Can only mean that life is spent,
    And not the old ideas gone.

Thou, stranger, that shalt come this way,
    No fraud upon the dead commit –
Observe the swelling turf, and say
    They do not lie, but here they sit.

Here still a lofty rock remains,
    On which the curious eye may trace
(Now wasted, half, by wearing rains)
    The fancies of a ruder race.

Here still an aged elm aspires,
    Beneath whose far-projecting shade
(And which the shepherd still admires)
    The children of the forest played!

There oft a restless Indian queen
    (Pale Shebah, with her braided hair)
And many a barbarous form is seen
    To chide the man that lingers there.

By midnight moons, o'er moistening dews;
    In habit for the chase arrayed,
The hunter still the deer pursues,
    The hunter and the deer, a shade!

And long shall timorous fancy see
    The painted chief, and pointed spear,
And Reason's self shall bow the knee
    To shadows and delusions here.

❧

THANATOPSIS

‹William Cullen Bryant›

To him who in the love of Nature holds
Communion with her visible forms, she speaks
A various language; for his gayer hours
She has a voice of gladness, and a smile
And eloquence of beauty, and she glides

Into his darker musings, with a mild
And healing sympathy, that steals away
Their sharpness, ere he is aware. When thoughts
Of the last bitter hour come like a blight
Over thy spirit, and sad images
Of the stern agony, and shroud, and pall,
And breathless darkness, and the narrow house,
Make thee to shudder, and grow sick at heart; –
Go forth, under the open sky, and list
To Nature's teachings, while from all around –
Earth and her waters, and the depths of air –
Comes a still voice – Yet a few days, and thee
The all-beholding sun shall see no more
In all his course; nor yet in the cold ground,
Where thy pale form was laid, with many tears,
Nor in the embrace of ocean, shall exist
Thy image. Earth, that nourished thee, shall claim
Thy growth, to be resolved to earth again,
And, lost each human trace, surrendering up
Thine individual being, shalt thou go
To mix for ever with the elements,
To be a brother to the insensible rock
And to the sluggish clod, which the rude swain
Turns with his share, and treads upon. The oak
Shall send his roots abroad, and pierce thy mould.

Yet not to thine eternal resting-place
Shalt thou retire alone, nor couldst thou wish
Couch more magnificent. Thou shalt lie down
With patriarchs of the infant world – with kings,
The powerful of the earth – the wise, the good,
Fair forms, and hoary seers of ages past,
All in one mighty sepulchre. The hills
Rock-ribbed and ancient as the sun, – the vales
Stretching in pensive quietness between;
The venerable woods – rivers that move
In majesty, and the complaining brooks
That make the meadows green; and, poured round
all,
Old Ocean's gray and melancholy waste, –
Are but the solemn decorations all
Of the great tomb of man. The golden sun,
The planets, all the infinite host of heaven
Are shining on the sad abodes of death,
Through the still lapse of ages. All that tread
The globe are but a handful to the tribes
That slumber in its bosom. – Take the wings
Of morning, pierce the Barcan wilderness,
Or lose thyself in the continuous woods
Where rolls the Oregon, and hears no sound,
Save his own dashings – yet the dead are there:

And millions in those solitudes, since first
The flight of years began, have laid them down
In their last sleep – the dead reign there alone.
So shalt thou rest, and what if thou withdraw
In silence from the living, and no friend
Take note of thy departure? All that breathe
Will share thy destiny. The gay will laugh
When thou art gone, the solemn brood of care
Plod on, and each one as before will chase
His favourite phantom; yet all these shall leave
Their mirth and their employments, and shall come
And make their bed with thee. As the long train
Of ages glide away, the sons of men,
The youth in life's green spring, and he who goes
In the full strength of years, matron and maid,
The speechless babe, and the gray-headed man –
Shall one by one be gathered to thy side,
By those, who in their turn shall follow them.

So live, that when thy summons comes to join
The innumerable caravan, which moves
To that mysterious realm, where each shall take
His chamber in the silent halls of death,
Thou go not, like the quarry-slave at night,
Scourged to his dungeon, but, sustained and
soothed
By an unfaltering trust, approach thy grave,
Like one who wraps the drapery of his couch
About him, and lies down to pleasant dreams.

BRAHMA

‹ Ralph Waldo Emerson ›

If the red slayer think he slays,
    Or if the slain think he is slain,
They know not well the subtle ways
    I keep, and pass, and turn again.

Far or forgot to me is near;
    Shadow and sunlight are the same;
The vanished gods to me appear;
    And one to me are shame and fame.

They reckon ill who leave me out;
    When me they fly, I am the wings;
I am the doubter and the doubt,
    And I the hymn the Brahmin sings.

The strong gods pine for my abode,
  And pine in vain the sacred Seven;
But thou, meek lover of the good!
  Find me, and turn thy back on heaven.

DAYS

‹Ralph Waldo Emerson›

Daughters of Time, the hypocritic Days,
Muffled and dumb like barefoot dervishes,
And marching single in an endless file,
Bring diadems and fagots in their hands.
To each they offer gifts after his will,
Bread, kingdoms, stars, and sky that hold them all.
I, in my pleached garden, watched the pomp,
Forgot my morning wishes, hastily
Took a few herbs and apples, and the Day
Turned and departed silent. I, too late,
Under her solemn fillet saw the scorn.

HAMATREYA

‹Ralph Waldo Emerson›

Bulkeley, Hunt, Willard, Hosmer, Meriam, Flint,
Possessed the land which rendered to their toil
Hay, corn, roots, hemp, flax, apples, wool and wood.
Each of these landlords walked amidst his farm,
Saying, ''Tis mine, my children's and my name's.
How sweet the west wind sounds in my own trees!
How graceful climb those shadows on my hill!
I fancy these pure waters and the flags
Know me, as does my dog: we sympathise;
And, I affirm, my actions smack of the soil.'

Where are these men? Asleep beneath their grounds:
And strangers, fond as they, their furrows plough.
Earth laughs in flowers, to see her boastful boys
Earth-proud, proud of the earth which is not theirs;
Who steer the plough, but cannot steer their feet
Clear of the grave.
They added ridge to valley, brook to pond,
And sighed for all that bounded their domain;
'This suits me for a pasture; that's my park;

We must have clay, lime, gravel, granite-ledge,
And misty lowland, where to go for peat.

The land is well, – lies fairly to the south.
'Tis good, when you have crossed the sea and back,
To find the sitfast acres where you left them.'
Ah! the hot owner sees not Death, who adds
Him to his land, a lump of mould the more.
Hear what the Earth says: –

Earth-Song

'Mine and yours;
Mine, not yours,
Earth endures;
Stars abide –
Shine down in the old sea;
Old are the shores;
But where are old men?
I who have seen much,
Such have I never seen.

'The lawyer's deed
Ran sure,
In tail,
To them, and to their heirs
Who shall succeed,
Without fail,
Forevermore.

'Here is the land,
Shaggy with wood,
With its old valley,
Mound and flood.
But the heritors?
Fled like the flood's foam. –
The lawyer, and the laws,
And the kingdom,
Clean swept herefrom.

'They called me theirs,
Who so controlled me;
Yet every one
Wished to stay, and is gone,
How am I theirs,
If they cannot hold me,
But I hold them?'

When I heard the Earth-song
I was no longer brave;
My avarice cooled
Like lust in the chill of the grave.

TELLING THE BEES

◄ John Greenleaf Whittier ►

Here is the place; right over the hill
   Runs the path I took;
You can see the gap in the old wall still,
   And the stepping-stones in the shallow brook.

There is the house, with the gate red-barred,
   And the poplars tall;
And the barn's brown length, and the cattle-yard,
   And the white horns tossing above the wall,

There are the beehives ranged in the sun;
   And down by the brink
Of the brook are her poor flowers, weed-o'errun,
   Pansy and daffodil, rose and pink.

A year has gone, as the tortoise goes,
   Heavy and slow;
And the same rose blows, and the same sun glows,
   And the same brook sings of a year ago.

There's the same sweet clover-smell in the breeze;
   And the June sun warm
Tangles his wings of fire in the trees,
   Setting, as then, over Fernside farm.

I mind me how with a lover's care
   From my Sunday coat
I brushed off the burrs, and smoothed my hair,
   And cooled at the brookside my brow and throat.

Since we parted, a month had passed, –
   To love, a year;
Down through the beeches I looked at last
   On the little red gate and the well-sweep near.

I can see it all now, – the slantwise rain
   Of light through the leaves,
The sundown's blaze on her window-pane,
   The bloom of her roses under the eaves.

Just the same as a month before, –
   The house and the trees,
The barn's brown gable, the vine by the door, –
   Nothing changed but the hives of bees.

Before them, under the garden wall,
   Forward and back,

Went drearily singing the chore-girl small,
   Draping each hive with a shred of black.

Trembling, I listened: the summer sun
   Had the chill of snow;
For I knew she was telling the bees of one
   Gone on the journey we all must go!

Then I said to myself, 'My Mary weeps
   For the dead to-day:
Haply her blind old grandsire sleeps
   The fret and the pain of his age away.'

But her dog whined low; on the doorway sill,
   With his cane to his chin
The old man sat; and the chore-girl still
   Sung to the bees stealing out and in.

And the song she was singing ever since
   In my ear sounds on: –
'Stay at home, pretty bees, fly not hence!
   Mistress Mary is dead and gone!'

SNOW-BOUND

◄ John Greenleaf Whittier ►

(lines 1–70)

The sun that brief December day
Rose cheerless over hills of gray,
And, darkly circled, gave at noon
A sadder light than waning moon.
Slow tracing down the thickening sky
Its mute and ominous prophecy,
A portent seeming less than threat,
It sank from sight before it set.
A chill no coat, however stout,
Of homespun stuff could quite shut out,
A hard, dull bitterness of cold,
That checked, mid-vein, the circling race
Of life-blood in the sharpened face,
The coming of the snow-storm told.
The wind blew east; we heard the roar
Of Ocean on his wintry shore,
And felt the strong pulse throbbing there
Beat with low rhythm our inland air.

Meanwhile we did our nightly chores, –
Brought in the wood from out of doors,

Littered the stalls, and from the mows
Raked down the herd's-grass for the cows;
Heard the horse whinnying for his corn;
And, sharply clashing horn on horn,
Impatient down the stanchion rows
The cattle shake their walnut bows;
While, peering from his early perch
Upon the scaffold's pole of birch,
The cock his crested helmet bent
And down his querulous challenge sent.

Unwarmed by any sunset light
The gray day darkened into night,
A night made hoary with the swarm
And whirl-dance of the blinding storm,
As zigzag, wavering to and fro,
Crossed and recrossed the wingëd snow:
And ere the early bedtime came
The white drift piled the window-frame,
And through the glass the clothes-line posts
Looked in like tall and sheeted ghosts.
So all night long the storm roared on:
The morning broke without a sun;
In tiny spherule traced with lines
Of Nature's geometric signs,
In starry flake, and pellicle,
All day the hoary meteor fell;
And, when the second morning shone,
We looked upon a world unknown,
On nothing we could call our own.
Around the glistening wonder bent
The blue walls of the firmament,
No cloud above, no earth below, –
A universe of sky and snow!
The old familiar sights of ours
Took marvellous shapes; strange domes and towers
Rose up where sty or corn-crib stood,
Or garden-wall, or belt of wood;
A smooth white mound the brush-pile showed,
A fenceless drift what once was road;
The bridle-post an old man sat
With loose-flung coat and high cocked hat;
The well-curb had a Chinese roof,
And even the long sweep, high aloof,
In its slant splendor, seemed to tell
Of Pisa's leaning miracle.

A prompt, decisive man, no breath
Our father wasted: 'Boys, a path!'
Well pleased, (for when did farmer boy

Count such a summons less than joy?)
Our buskins on our feet we drew [. . .]

THE SPIRIT

‹Jones Very›

I would not breathe, when blows thy mighty wind
O'er desolate hill and winter-blasted plain,
But stand in waiting hope if I may find
Each flower recalled to newer life again;
That now unsightly hide themselves from Thee,
Amid the leaves or rustling grasses dry,
With ice-cased rock and snowy-mantled tree
Ashamed lest Thou their nakedness should spy;
But Thou shalt breathe and every rattling bough
Shall gather leaves; each rock with rivers flow;
And they that hide them from thy presence now
In new found robes along thy path shall glow,
And meadows at thy coming fall and rise,
Their green waves sprinkled with a thousand eyes.

THE ROBE

‹Jones Very›

Each naked branch, the yellow leaf or brown,
The rugged rock, and death-deformed plain
Lies white beneath the winter's feathery down,
Nor doth a spot unsightly now remain;
On sheltering roof, on man himself it falls;
But him no robe, not spotless snow makes clean;
For 'neath his corse-like spirit ever calls,
That on it too may fall the heavenly screen;
But all in vain, its guilt can never hide
From the quick spirit's heart-deep searching eye,
With all his faith still aid me in the strife,
Till I through blood like him the prize have
    bought;
And I shall hang upon the accursed tree,
Pierced through with many spears that all may see.

Sic Vita

‹ Henry David Thoreau ›

I am a parcel of vain strivings tied
   By a chance bond together,
Dangling this way and that, their links
    Were made so loose and wide,
      Methinks,
     For milder weather.

A bunch of violets without their roots,
   And sorrel intermixed,
Encircled by a wisp of straw
    Once coiled about their shoots,
      The law
     By which I'm fixed.

A nosegay which Time clutched from out
   Those fair Elysian fields,
With weeds and broken stems, in haste,
    Doth make the rabble rout
      That waste
     The day he yields.

And here I bloom for a short hour unseen,
   Drinking my juices up,
With no root in the land
    To keep my branches green,
      But stand
     In a bare cup.

Some tender buds were left upon my stem
   In mimicry of life,
But ah! the children will not know,
    Till time has withered them,
      The woe
     With which they're rife.

But now I see I was not plucked for naught,
   And after in life's vase
Of glass set while I might survive,
    But by a kind hand brought
      Alive
     To a strange place.

That stock thus thinned will soon redeem its hours,
   And by another year,
Such as God knows, with freer air,
    More fruits and fairer flowers
      Will bear,
     While I droop here.

'Light-winged Smoke, Icarian bird'

‹ Henry David Thoreau ›

Light-winged Smoke, Icarian bird,
Melting thy pinions in thy upward flight,
Lark without song, and messenger of dawn,
Circling above the hamlets as thy nest;
Or else, departing dream, and shadowy form
Of midnight vision, gathering up thy skirts;
By night star-veiling, and by day
Darkening the light and blotting out the sun;
Go thou my incense upward from this hearth,
And ask the gods to pardon this clear flame.

'Woof of the sun, ethereal gauze'

‹ Henry David Thoreau ›

Woof of the sun, ethereal gauze,
Woven of Nature's richest stuffs,
Visible heat, air-water, and dry sea,
Last conquest of the eye;
Toil of the day displayed, sun-dust,
Aerial surf upon the shores of earth,
Ethereal estuary, frith of light,
Breakers of air, billows of heat,
Fine summer spray on inland seas;
Bird of the sun, transparent-winged
Owlet of noon, soft-pinioned,
From heath or stubble rising without song;
Establish thy serenity o'er the fields.

The House-top
A Night Piece

‹ Herman Melville ›

No sleep. The sultriness pervades the air
And binds the brain – a dense oppression, such
As tawny tigers feel in matted shades,
Vexing their blood and making apt for ravage.

Beneath the stars the roofy desert spreads
Vacant as Libya. All is hushed near by.
Yet fitfully from far breaks a mixed surf
Of muffled sound, the Atheist roar of riot.
Yonder, where parching Sirius set in drought,
Balefully glares red Arson – there – and there.
The Town is taken by its rats – ship-rats
And rats of the wharves. All civil charms
And priestly spells which late held hearts in awe –
Fear-bound, subjected to a better sway
Than sway of self; these like a dream dissolve,
And man rebounds whole aeons back in nature
Hail to the low dull rumble, dull and dead,
And ponderous drag that shakes the wall.
Wise Draco comes, deep in the midnight roll
Of black artillery; he comes, though late;
In code corroborating Calvin's creed
And cynic tyrannies of honest kings;
He comes, nor parlies; and the Town, redeemed,
Gives thanks devout; nor, being thankful, heeds
The grimy slur on the Republic's faith implied,
Which holds that Man is naturally good,
And – more – is Nature's Roman, never to be
   scourged.

Note

This poem was written in response to the 'draft riots' during the American
Civil War, when a Negro orphanage and church were burned, and more
than a thousand casualties inflicted.

❧

35. PRELUSIVE
(*CLAREL*, PART II)

‹Herman Melville›

In Piranesi's rarer prints,
Interiors measurelessly strange,
Where the distrustful thought may range
Misgiving still – what mean the hints?
Stairs upon stairs which dim ascend
In series from plunged Bastiles drear –
Pit under pit; long tier on tier
Of shadowed galleries which impend
Over cloisters, cloisters without end;
The hight, the depth – the far, the near;
Ring-bolts to pillars in vaulted lanes,
And dragging Rhadamanthine chains;
These less of wizard influence lend

Than some allusive chambers closed.
   Those wards of hush are not disposed
In gibe of goblin fantasy –
Grimace – unclean diablery:
Thy wings, Imagination, span
Ideal truth in fable's seat:
The thing implied is one with man,
His penetralia of retreat –
The heart, with labyrinths replete:
In freaks of intimation see
Paul's 'mystery of iniquity:'
Involved indeed, a blur of dream;
As, awed by scruple and restricted
In first design, or interdicted
By fate and warnings as might seem;
The inventor miraged all the maze,
Obscured it with prudential haze;
Nor less, if subject unto question,
The egg left, egg of the suggestion.
   Dwell on those etchings in the night,
Those touches bitten in the steel
By aqua-fortis, till ye feel
The Pauline text in gray of light;
Turn hither then and read aright.

❧

THE BERG
A DREAM

‹Herman Melville›

I saw a ship of martial build
(Her standards set, her brave apparel on)
Directed as by madness mere
Against a stolid iceberg steer,
Nor budge it, though the infatuate ship went down.
The impact made huge ice-cubes fall
Sullen, in tons that crashed the deck;
But that one avalanche was all –
No other movement save the foundering wreck.

Along the spurs of ridges pale,
Not any slenderest shaft and frail,
A prism over glass-green gorges lone,
Toppled; nor lace of traceries fine,
Nor pendant drops in grot or mine
Were jarred, when the stunned ship went down.

Nor sole the gulls in cloud that wheeled
Circling one snow-flanked peak afar,

But nearer fowl the floes that skimmed
And crystal beaches, felt no jar.
No thrill transmitted stirred the lock
Of jack-straw needle-ice at base;
Towers undermined by waves – the block
Atilt impending – kept their place.
Seals, dozing sleek on sliddery ledges
Slipt never, when by loftier edges
Through very inertia overthrown,
The impetuous ship in bafflement went down.

Hard Berg (methought), so cold, so vast,
With mortal damps self-overcast;
Exhaling still thy dankish breath –
Adrift dissolving, bound for death;
Though lumpish thou, a lumbering one –
A lumbering lubbard loitering slow,
Impingers rue thee and go down,
Sounding thy precipice below,
Nor stir the slimy slug that sprawls
Along thy dead indifference of walls.

❧

THE MALDIVE SHARK

‹ Herman Melville ›

About the Shark, phlegmatical one,
Pale sot of the Maldive sea,
The sleek little pilot-fish, azure and slim,
How alert in attendance be.
From his saw-pit of mouth, from his charnel of
    maw
They have nothing of harm to dread,
But liquidly glide on his ghastly flank
Or before his Gorgonian head;
Or lurk in the port of serrated teeth
In white triple tiers of glittering gates,
And there find a haven when peril's abroad,
An asylum in jaws of the Fates!
They are friends; and friendly they guide him to
    prey,
Yet never partake of the treat –
Eyes and brains to the dotard lethargic and dull,
Pale ravener of horrible meat.

❧

SONNETS

‹ Frederick Goddard Tuckerman ›

‹ XIX ›

And faces, forms and phantoms, numbered not,
Gather and pass like mist upon the breeze,
Jading the eye with uncouth images:
Women with muskets, children dropping shot
By fields half harvested or left in fear
Of Indian inroad, or the Hessian near;
Disaster, poverty, and dire disease.
Or from the burning village, through the trees
I see the smoke in reddening volumes roll,
The Indian file in shadowy silence pass
While the last man sets up the trampled grass,
The Tory priest declaiming, fierce and fat,
The Shay's man with the green branch in his hat,
Or silent sagamore, Shaug or Wassahoale.

‹ IX ›

But into order falls our life at last,
Though in the retrospection jarred and blent.
Broken ambition, love misplaced or spent
Too soon, and slander busy with the past:
Sorrows too sweet to lose, or vexing joy.
But Time will bring oblivion of annoy,
And Silence bind the blows that words have lent;
And we will dwell, unheeding Love or Fame
Like him who has outlived a shining Name:
And Peace will come, as evening comes to him,
No leader now of men, no longer proud
But poor and private, watching the sun's rim;
Contented too, to fade as yonder cloud
Dim fades, and as the sun fades, fades alike, like dim.

‹ X ›

Hast thou seen reversed the prophet's miracle –
The worm that, touched, a twig-like semblance
    takes?
Or hast thou mused what giveth the craft that makes
The twirling spider at once invisible,
And the spermal odor to the barberry flower,
Or heard the singing sand by the cold coast foam,
Or late – in inland autumn groves afar –
Hast thou ever plucked the little chick-wintergreen
    star
And tasted the sour of its leaf? Then come
With me betimes, and I will show thee more
Than these, of nature's secrecies the least:
In the first morning, overcast and chill,

And in the day's young sunshine, seeking still
For earliest flowers and gathering to the east.

◄ XVI ►

Under the mountain, as when first I knew
Its low dark roof and chimney creeper-twined,
The red house stands; and yet my footsteps find,
Vague in the walks, waste balm and feverfew.
But they are gone: no soft-eyed sisters trip
Across the porch or lintels; where, behind,
The mother sat, sat knitting with pursed lip.
The house stands vacant in its green recess,
Absent of beauty as a broken heart.
The wild rain enters, and the sunset wind
Sighs in the chambers of their loveliness
Or shakes the pane – and in the silent noons
The glass falls from the window, part by part,
And ringeth faintly in the grassy stones.

◄ XVIII ►

And change with hurried hand has swept these
        scenes:
The woods have fallen, across the meadow-lot
The hunter's trail and trap-path is forgot,
And fire has drunk the swamps of evergreens;
Yet for a moment let my fancy plant
These autumn hills again: the wild dove's haunt,
The wild deer's walk. In golden umbrage shut,
The Indian river runs, Quonecktacut!
Here, but a lifetime back, where falls tonight
Behind the curtained pane a sheltered light
On buds of rose or vase of violet
Aloft upon the marble mantel set,
Here in the forest-heart, hung blackening
The wolfbait on the bush beside the spring.

◄ X ►

An upper chamber in a darkened house,
Where, ere his footsteps reached ripe manhood's
        brink,
Terror and anguish were his lot to drink;
I cannot rid the thought nor hold it close
But dimly dream upon that man alone:
Now though the autumn clouds most softly pass,
The cricket chides beneath the doorstep stone
And greener than the season grows the grass.
Nor can I drop my lids nor shade my brows,
But there he stands beside the lifted sash;
And with a swooning of the heart, I think
Where the black shingles slope to meet the boughs

And, shattered on the roof like smallest snows,
The tiny petals of the mountain ash.

The Marshes of Glynn
(lines 1–36)

◄ Sidney Lanier ►

Glooms of the live-oaks, beautiful-braided and woven
With intricate shades of the vines that myriad-cloven
    Clamber the forks of the multiform boughs, –
            Emerald twilights, –
            Virginal shy lights.
Wrought of the leaves to allure to the whisper of vows,
When lovers pace timidly down through the green
        colonnades
Of the dim sweet woods, of the dear dark woods,
    Of the heavenly woods and glades,
That run to the radiant marginal sand-beach within
        The wide sea-marshes of Glynn; –

Beautiful glooms, soft dusks in the noon-day fire, –
Wildwood privacies, closets of lone desire,
Chamber from chamber parted with wavering arras of
        leaves, –
Cells for the passionate pleasure of prayer to the soul
        that grieves,
Pure with a sense of the passing of saints through the
        wood,
Cool for the dutiful weighing of ill with good; –

O braided dusks of the oak and woven shades of the
        vine,
While the riotous noon-day sun of the June-day long
        did shine
Ye held me fast in your heart and I held you fast in
        mine;
But now when the noon is no more, and riot is rest,
And the sun is a-wait at the ponderous gate of the
        West,
And the slant yellow beam down the wood-aisle doth
        seem
Like a lane into heaven that leads from a dream, –
Ay, now, when my soul all day hath drunken the soul
        of the oak,
And my heart is at ease from men, and the wearisome
        sound of the stroke
    Of the scythe of time and the trowel of trade is low,

And belief overmasters doubt, and I know that I
  know,
And my spirit is grown to a lordly great compass
  within,
That the length and the breadth and the sweep of the
  marshes of Glynn
Will work me no fear like the fear they have wrought
  me of yore
When length was fatigue, and when breadth was but
  bitterness sore,
And when terror and shrinking and dreary unnamable
  pain
Drew over me out of the merciless miles of the plain, –

Oh, now, unafraid, I am fain to face
  The vast sweet visage of space.

THE NEW COLOSSUS

‹Emma Lazarus›

Not like the brazen giant of Greek fame,
With conquering limbs astride from land to land;
Here at our sea-washed, sunset gates shall stand
A mighty woman with a torch, whose flame
Is the imprisoned lightning, and her name
Mother of Exiles. From her beacon-hand
Glows world-wide welcome; her mild eyes command
The air-bridged harbor that twin cities frame.
'Keep, ancient lands, your storied pomp!' cries she
With silent lips. 'Give me your tired, your poor,
Your huddled masses yearning to breathe free,
The wretched refuse of your teeming shore.
Send these, the homeless, tempest-tost to me,
I lift my lamp beside the golden door!'

THE MAN WITH THE HOE
Written after seeing Millet's World-
Famous Painting

‹Edwin Markham›

  God made man in His own image,
    in the image of God made He him. – *Genesis.*

Bowed by the weight of centuries he leans
Upon his hoe and gazes on the ground,
The emptiness of ages in his face,
And on his back the burden of the world.

Who made him dead to rapture and despair,
A thing that grieves not and that never hopes,
Stolid and stunned, a brother to the ox?
Who loosened and let down this brutal jaw?
Whose was the hand that slanted back this brow?
Whose breath blew out the light within this brain?
Is this the Thing the Lord God made and gave
To have dominion over sea and land;
To trace the stars and search the heavens for power;
To feel the passion of Eternity?
Is this the Dream He dreamed who shaped the suns
And pillared the blue firmament with light?
Down all the stretch of Hell to its last gulf
There is no shape more terrible than this –
More tongued with censure of the world's blind
  greed –
More filled with signs and portents for the soul –
More fraught with menace to the universe.

What gulfs between him and the seraphim!
Slave of the wheel of labor, what to him
Are Plato and the swing of Pleiades?
What the long reaches of the peaks of song,
The rift of dawn, the reddening of the rose?

Through this dread shape the suffering ages look;
Time's tragedy is in that aching stoop;
Through this dread shape humanity betrayed,
Plundered, profaned and disinherited,
Cries protest to the Judges of the World,
A protest that is also prophecy.

O masters, lords and rulers in all lands,
Is this the handiwork you give to God,
This monstrous thing distorted and soul-quenched?
How will you ever straighten up this shape;
Touch it again with immortality;
Give back the upward looking and the light;
Rebuild in it the music and the dream;
Make right the immemorial infamies,
Perfidious wrongs, immedicable woes?

O masters, lords and rulers in all lands,
How will the Future reckon with this Man?
How answer his brute question in that hour
When whirlwinds of rebellion shake the world?
How will it be with kingdoms and with kings –
With those who shaped him to the thing he is –
When this dumb Terror shall reply to God,
After the silence of the centuries?

III 'IN THE DESERT'
(from *The Black Riders*)

‹Stephen Crane›

In the desert
I saw a creature, naked, bestial,
Who, squatting upon the ground,
Held his heart in his hands,
And ate of it.
I said, 'Is it good, friend?'
'It is bitter – bitter,' he answered;
'But I like it
Because it is bitter,
And because it is my heart.'

XII 'A NEWSPAPER IS A COLLECTION OF HALF-INJUSTICES'
(from *War is Kind*)

‹Stephen Crane›

A newspaper is a collection of half-injustices
Which, bawled by boys from mile to mile,
Spreads its curious opinion
To a million merciful and sneering men,
While families cuddle the joys of the fireside
When spurred by tale of dire lone agony.
A newspaper is a court
Where every one is kindly and unfairly tried
By a squalor of honest men.
A newspaper is a market
Where wisdom sells its freedom
And melons are crowned by the crowd.
A newspaper is a game
Where his error scores the player victory
While another's skill wins death.
A newspaper is a symbol;
It is feckless life's chronicle,
A collection of loud tales
Concentrating eternal stupidities,
That in remote ages lived unhaltered,
Roaming through a fenceless world.

QUIET AFTER THE RAIN OF MORNING

‹Trumbell Stickney›

Quiet after the rain of morning
Midday covers the dampened trees,
Sweet and fresh in the languid breeze
Still returning
Birds are twittering at ease.

And to me in the far and foreign
Land as further I go and come,
Sweetly over the wearisome
Endless barren
Flutter whisperings of home.

There between the two hillocks lightens
Straight and little a bluish bar:
I feel the strain of the mariner
Grows and tightens
After home and after her.

For tens of thousands of years, Australia was ruled by poetry; prose arrived with the First Fleet in 1788. In parts of the continent which European eyes might see as remote, the ritual song-poetry of the Aboriginal Law is still powerful. I was tempted to give examples, but translation of this material only began in the twentieth century, and in the nineteenth it had no influence on what was emerging as the country's mainstream literature.

Along with prose, many of the well-known British poetic forms also arrived in 1788: literary verse, broadsheet ballads, folk-song, as well as englynion and other Celtic verse-types. Towards the mid-century there followed vaudeville songs such as those which Essex-born Charles Thatcher made enormously popular on the Victorian gold-fields; as elsewhere in the former Empire, too, newspapers began printing lots of squibs and light verse, and this practice endured into the 1950s. Most of the upbeat material in this brief survey would have had its first airing in the popular prints, whose conventions tended to keep verse sprightly and not very profound, though it was allowed to be moving. A tradition of literary ballads derived from earlier folk balladry, such as the ex-miner's lament given here, arose late in the century and attained great popularity. Along with gen-uine folk-songs such as 'The Banks of the Condamine', the balladry of 'Banjo' Pater-son, Henry Lawson and many others feeds nowadays into the country music industry, the fastest growing musical genre in the nation.

Literary verse rarely saw print outside of the genteel magazines and the slim vol-umes which began to be self-published quite early in the century and moved on to regular, royalty-paying publication after the 1860s. The more rebellious bushranger ballads, derived from earlier convict-era models and often full of legalese – the only educated speech many poor folk ever heard – were often banned; they survived only precariously in the oral tradition until collected in this century. Here, we owe a considerable debt to Communist folklorists keen to uncover a popular culture. To two such men, John Meredith and Rex Whalan, we owe the retrieval of an important corpus of work by the convict Francis 'Frank the Poet' MacNamara. Poetry of a high order begins in Australia with the writing of Kenneth Slessor in the 1930s, or some might argue that it begins with the work of Lesbia Harford and John Shaw Neilson a

decade or two earlier, but arguably the first considerable poem to be written in English in Australia was MacNamara's Dantean satire, 'A Convict's Tour to Hell' (too lengthy to be included here), from the 1830s. MacNamara seems to have had a love of Robert Burns and a connection with the Irish-language MacNamara bards of Tipperary. Much of the rebel tradition in Australian folk-song derives from him, but here I have illustrated his links with the older, half-clandestine poetics of Ireland. His defiance of the dour Australian Agri-cultural Company with its Newcastle coal concession is unlikely to have succeeded, and may well have earned him a few score lashes.

FOR THE COMPANY UNDERGROUND

‹Francis MacNamara (b. 1812?)›

Francis MacNamara of Newcastle to J. Crosdale Esq. greeting

When Christ from Heaven comes down straightway,
All His Father's laws to expound,
MacNamara shall work that day
For the Company underground.

When the man in the moon to Moreton Bay
Is sent in shackles bound,
MacNamara shall work that day
For the Company underground.

When the Cape of Good Hope to Twofold Bay
Comes for the change of a pound,
MacNamara shall work that day
For the Company underground.

When cows in lieu of milk yield tea,
And all lost treasures are found,
MacNamara shall work that day
For the Company underground.

When the Australian Co.'s heaviest dray
Is drawn 80 miles by a hound,
MacNamara shall work that day
For the Company underground.

When a frog, a caterpillar and a flea
Shall travel the globe all round,
MacNamara shall work that day
For the Company underground.

When turkeycocks on Jews harps play
And mountains dance at the sound,
MacNamara shall work that day
For the Company underground.

When milestones go to church to pray
And whales are put in the Pound,
MacNamara shall work that day
For the Company underground.

When Christmas falls on the 1st of May
And O'Connell's King of England crown'd,
MacNamara shall work that day
For the Company underground.

When thieves ever robbing on the highway
For their sanctity are renowned,
MacNamara shall work that day
For the Company underground.

When the quick and the dead shall stand in array
Cited at the trumpet's sound,
Even then, damn me if I'd work a day
For the Company underground.

     Nor over ground.

Taking the Census

‹Charles R. Thatcher (1831–1882)›

A New Original Song, as written and sung by Thatcher, with
deafening applause, at the 'Shamrock'.

   (Air – 'Miser's Man')
When the census is taken, of course,
 All the elderly females are furious,
They don't like to tell their real age,
 For gov'ment they say is too curious:
I got hold of a chap that went round,
 For I wanted to twig their rum capers,
So I tipped him a crown on the sly
 To let me look over his papers.

There's that elderly dame, Mother Baggs,
 Has marked down her age twenty-seven,
Although she's possessed of five kids,
 The eldest of which is eleven;
Miss Fluffen says she's thirty-two,
 But to tell such a story is naughty,

She's a regular frumpish old maid,
 And if she's a year old she's forty.

There's another thing struck me as queer,
 As the papers I sat overhauling,
Beneath occupation, thinks I,
 I'll soon find out each person's calling;
But the first I looked at made me grin,
 My wash'woman, old Mother Archer,
Beneath occupation I found
 Had described herself as a clear starcher.

The chemist's assistant up here,
 When his paper I happened to see, sirs,
'Pon my honour had had the vile cheek
 To mark after his name M.D., sirs,
And Bolus, that wretched old quack,
 Whom folks here regard with suspicion,
When his paper I looked at, I found
 He'd put himself down a physician!

Here's a *barberous* custom you'll say,
 No less than three diff'rent hairdressers,
In the papers which they have filled up
 Have described themselves all as *professors*;
In Heidelberg district I find
 My bounceable friend, Harry Potter,
In the paper that he has sent in,
 Tries to make us believe he's a squatter.

My friend said he called on two girls,
 Who are noted for cutting rum capers,
They live in an elegant crib,
 And he knocked at the door for their papers;
They handed him what he required,
 He read, but exclaimed with vexation,
'The instructions you haven't fulfilled –
 'You've not put down your occupation.'

'Well, Poll, that's a good 'un,' says one,
 And both of them burst out a-laughing,
But the young man exclaimed precious quick
 'I can't stay all day while you're chaffing;'
'Occupation' says she, with a scream,
 (Her laughter was pretty near killing her),
'Poll, I'm blowed if I knows what you are,
 But, young man, shove me down as a milliner.'

THE BANKS OF THE CONDAMINE

‹Anonymous›

Oh, hark the dogs are barking, love,
I can no longer stay,
The men are all gone mustering
And it is nearly day.
And I must off by the morning light
Before the sun doth shine,
To meet the Sydney shearers
On the banks of the Condamine.

Oh Willie, dearest Willie,
I'll go along with you,
I'll cut off all my auburn fringe
And be a shearer, too,
I'll cook and count your tally, love,
While ringer-o you shine,
And I'll wash your greasy moleskins
On the banks of the Condamine.

Oh, Nancy, dearest Nancy,
With me you cannot go,
The squatters have given orders, love,
No woman should do so;
Your delicate constitution
Is not equal unto mine,
To stand the constant tigering
On the banks of the Condamine.

Oh Willie, dearest Willie,
Then stay back home with me,
We'll take up a selection
And a farmer's wife I'll be:
I'll help you husk the corn, love,
And cook your meals so fine
You'll forget the ram-stag mutton
On the banks of the Condamine.

Oh, Nancy, dearest Nancy,
Please do not hold me back,
Down there the boys are waiting,
And I must be on the track;
So here's a good-bye kiss, love,
Back home here I'll incline
When we've shore the last of the jumbucks
On the banks of the Condamine.

THE STRINGYBARK COCKATOO

‹Anonymous›

I'm a broken-hearted miner, who loves his cup to drain,
Which often times has caused me to lie in frost and rain.
Roaming about the country, looking for some work to
   do,
I got a job of reaping off a stringybark cockatoo.

Chorus Oh, the stringybark cockatoo,
      Oh, the stringybark cockatoo,
         I got a job of reaping off a stringybark cockatoo.

Ten bob an acre was his price – with promise of fairish
   board.
He said his crops were very light, 'twas all he could
   afford.
He drove me out in a bullock dray, and his piggery
   met my view.
Oh, the pigs and geese were in the wheat of the
   stringybark cockatoo.

The hut was made of the surface mud, the roof of a
   reedy thatch,
The doors and windows open flew without a bolt or
   latch.
The pigs and geese were in the hut, the hen on the
   table flew,
And she laid an egg in the old tin plate for the
   stringybark cockatoo.

For breakfast we had pollard, boys, it tasted like
   cobbler's paste,
To help it down we had to eat brown bread with
   vinegar taste.
The tea was made of the native hops which out on the
   ranges grew;
'Twas sweetened with honey bees and wax for the
   stringybark cockatoo.

For dinner we had goanna hash, we thought it mighty
   hard;
They wouldn't give us butter, so we forced down bread
   and lard.
Quondong duff, paddymelon pie, and wallaby Irish stew
We used to eat while reaping for the stringybark
   cockatoo.

When we started to cut, the rust and smut was just
   beginning to shed,

And all we had to sleep on was a dog and a sheepskin
    bed.
The bugs and fleas tormented me, they made me
    scratch and screw;
I lost my rest while reaping for the stringybark
    cockatoo.

At night when work was over I'd nurse the youngest
    child,
And when I'd say a joking word, the mother would
    laugh and smile.
The old cocky, he grew jealous, and he thumped me
    black and blue,
And he drove me off without a rap – the stringybark
    cockatoo.

❧

Fashion

‹Ada Cambridge (1844–1926)›

See those resplendent creatures, as they glide
    O'er scarlet carpet, between footmen tall,
    From sumptuous carriage to effulgent hall –
A dazzling vision in their pomp and pride!
See that choice supper – needless – cast aside –
    Though worth a thousand fortunes, counting all,
    To them for whom no crumb of it will fall –
The starved and homeless in the street outside.

Some day the little great god will decree
    That overmuch connotes the underbred,
    That pampered body means an empty head,
And wealth displayed the last vulgarity.
When selfish greed becomes a social sin
The world's regeneration may begin.

❧

The Wail of the Waiter
(A Tavern Catch)

‹Marcus Clarke (1846–1881)›

All day long, at Scott's or Menzies', I await the gorging
    crowd,
Panting, penned within a pantry, with the blowflies
    humming loud.
There at seven in the morning do I count my daily
    cash,

While the home-returning reveller calls for 'soda and a
    dash'.
And the weary hansom-cabbies set the blinking
    squatters down,
Who, all night, in savage freedom, have been 'knocking
    round the town'.
Soon the breakfast gong resounding bids the festive
    meal begin,
And, with appetites like demons, come the gentle
    public in.
'Toast and butter!' 'Eggs and coffee!' 'Waiter, mutton
    chops for four!'
'Flatheads!' 'Ham!' 'Beef!' 'Where's the mustard?' 'Steak
    and onions!' 'Shut the door!'
Here sits Bandicoot, the broker, eating in a desperate
    hurry,
Scowling at his left-hand neighbour, Cornstalk from
    the Upper Murray,
Who with brandy-nose empurpled, and with blue lips
    cracked and dry,
In incipient delirium shoves the eggspoon in his eye.
'Bloater paste!' 'Some *tender* steak, sir?' 'Here, *confound*
    you, where's my chop?'
'Waiter!' 'Yessir!' '*Waiter!*' 'Yessir!!' – running till I'm fit
    to drop.
Then at lunch time – fearful crisis! In by shoals the
    gorgers pour,
Gobbling, crunching, swilling, munching – ten times
    hungrier than before.
'Glass of porter!' '*Ale* for me, John!' 'Where's my stick?'
    'And where's my *hat*!'
'Oxtail soup!' 'I asked for curry!' 'Cold boiled beef, and
    cut it fat!'
'Irish stew!' 'Some pickled cabbage!' 'What, no *beans*?'
    'Bring *me* some pork!'
'Soup, sir?' 'Yes. You grinning idiot, can I eat it with a
    FORK?'
'Take care, waiter!' 'Beg your pardon.' 'Curse you, have
    you two left legs?'
'I asked for *bread* an hour ago, sir!' 'Now then, have you
    laid those eggs?'
'Sherry!' 'No, I called for *beer* – of all the fools I ever
    saw!'
'Waiter!' 'Yessir!' 'WAITER!!' 'Here, sir!' 'Damme, sir,
    this steak is RAW!'

Thus amid this hideous Babel do I live the livelong day,
While my memory is going, and my hair is turning grey.
All my soul is slowly melting, all my brain is softening
    fast,
And I know that I'll be taken to the Yarra Bend at last.

For at night from fitful slumbers I awaken with a start,
Mumuring of steak and onions, babbling of apple-tart.
While to me the Poet's cloudland a gigantic kitchen
    seems,
And those mislaid table-napkins haunt me even in my
    dreams
Is this right? – Ye sages tell me! – Does a man live but
    to eat?
Is there nothing worth enjoying but one's miserable
    meat?
Is the mightiest task of Genius but to swallow buttered
    beans,
And has Man but been created to demolish pork and
    greens?
Is there no *unfed* Hereafter, where the round of chewing
    stops?
Is the atmosphere of heaven clammy with perpetual
    chops?
Do the friends of Mr Naylor sup on spirit-reared cow-
    heel?
Can the great Alexis Soyer really say 'Soyez tranquille?'
Or must I bring spirit beefsteak grilled in spirit regions
    hotter
For the spirit delectation of some spiritual squatter?
Shall I in a spirit kitchen hear the spirit blowflies
    humming,
Calming spiritual stomachs with a spiritual 'Coming!'?
Shall – but this is idle chatter, I have got my work to do.
'WAITER!!' 'Yessir.' 'Wake up, stupid! Biled calves' feet
    for Number Two!'

❧

THE DOVE

‹ Victor Daley (1858–1905) ›

Within his office, smiling,
    Sat JOSEPH CHAMBERLAIN,
But all the screws of Birmingham
    Were working in his brain.

The heart within his bosom
    Was as a millstone hard;
His eye was cold and cruel,
    His face was frozen lard.

He had the map of Africa
    Upon his table spread:
He took a brush, and with the same
    He painted it blood-red.

He heard no moan of widows,
    But only the hurrah
Of charging lines and squadrons
    And 'Rule Britannia.'

A white dove to his window
    With branch of olive sped –
He took a ruler in his hand,
    And struck the white dove dead.

❧

THE DUKE OF BUCCLEUCH

‹ J. A. Phelp ›

There once was a bull named the Duke of Buccleuch
Whose hide it was shiny, whose blood it was blue,
He was shipped to Australia, stud-duty to do,
Was this highly-priced bovine, the Duke of Buccleuch.

And a lord-loving cableman sent out a line
To announce to Australia its visitor fine,
But if it was human, or if it was kine,
Was left quite in doubt – merely 'Duke of Buccleuch'.

And Sydney lickspittledom went off its head
As the news round the club-room like lightning did
    spread;
A jook, a live jook, and perhaps he ain't wed!
Let us hasten to welcome the Duke of Buccleuch!

When the steamer arrived, the crowd it was great,
And Circular Quay seemed to be quite en fête;
And the Gov. he was there in vice-regal state
To receive his old pal the Duke of Buccleuch.

And the Mayor was there too with a speech in his
    hand,
To read to the Duke as he stepped on the land
And spruce Dan O'Connor, a-smiling so bland
All ready to cheer for the Duke of Buccleuch.

And Railway-Commissioner Eddy was there,
All properly clobbered, with nicely-brushed hair
And he had in his pocket – oh, courtesy rare –
A gilt-edged free pass for the Duke of Buccleuch.

There was horror, confusion, a frightful to-do –
How the larrikins laughed – and the jeers from the
    crew!

And the maidens and matrons shamefacedly flew
When they learned 'twas a bull – the great Duke of
  Buccleuch!

THE LITTLE SHOES THAT DIED

‹Mary Gilmore (1863–1962)›

These are the little shoes that died.
  We could not keep her still,
But all day long her busy feet
  Danced to her eager will.

Leaving the body's loving warmth,
  The spirit ran outside;
Then from the shoes they slipped her feet,
  And the little shoes died.

A BAD BREAK!

‹W. T. Goodge (1862–1909)›

The preacher quoted, and the cranks
  Among his congregation smiled,
'How sharper than a serpent's thanks
  It is to have a toothless child.'

He saw he erred, his eye grew wild,
  He frowned upon the mirthful ranks:
'How toothless than a serpent's child
  It is to have a sharper's thanks!'

FEDERATION

‹W. T. Goodge›

  Let us sing of Federation
    ('T is the theme of every cult)
  And the joyful expectation
    Of its ultimate result.
  'T will confirm the jubilation
  Of protection's expectation,
  And the quick consolidation
  Of freetrade with every nation;
  And teetotal legislation

Will achieve its consummation
And increase our concentration
On the art of bibulation.
We shall drink to desperation,
And be quite the soberest nation
We'll be desperately loyal
Unto everything that's royal,
And be ultra-democratic
In a matter most emphatic.
We'll be prosperous and easeful,
And pre-eminently peaceful,
And we'll take our proper station
As a military nation!
We shall show the throne affection,
Also sever the connection,
And the bonds will get no fainter
And we'll also cut the painter.
We'll proclaim with lute and tabor
The millennium of labour,
And we'll bow before the gammon
Of plutocracy and Mammon.
We'll adopt all fads and fictions
And their mass of contradictions
If all hopes are consummated
When Australia's federated;
For the Federation speeches
This one solid moral teach us –
That a pile of paradoxes are expected to result!

THE TRAVELLING POST OFFICE

‹Andrew Barton Paterson (1864–1941)›

'The Banjo'

The roving breezes come and go, the reed beds sweep
  and sway,
The sleepy river murmurs low, and loiters on its way,
It is the land of lots o'time along the Castlereagh.
The old man's son had left the farm, he found it dull
  and slow,
He drifted to the great North-west where all the rovers
  go.
'He's gone so long,' the old man said, 'he's dropped
  right out of mind,
'But if you'd write a line to him I'd take it very kind;
'He's shearing here and fencing there, a kind of waif
  and stray,
'He's droving now with Conroy's sheep along the
  Castlereagh.

'The sheep are travelling for the grass, and travelling
    very slow;
'They may be at Mundooran now, or past the
    Overflow,
'Or tramping down the black soil flats across by
    Waddiwong,
'But all those little country towns would send the
    letter wrong,
'The mailman, if he's extra tired, would pass them in
    his sleep,
'It's safest to address the note to "Care of Conroy's
    sheep,"
'For five and twenty thousand head can scarcely go
    astray,
'You write to "Care of Conroy's sheep along the
    Castlereagh."'

By rock and ridge and riverside the western mail has
    gone,
Across the great Blue Mountain Range to take that
    letter on.
A moment on the topmost grade while open fire doors
    glare,
She pauses like a living thing to breathe the mountain
    air,
Then launches down the other side across the plains
    away
To bear that note to 'Conroy's sheep along the
    Castlereagh.'

And now by coach and mailman's bag it goes from
    town to town,
And Conroy's Gap and Conroy's Creek have marked it
    'further down.'
Beneath a sky of deepest blue where never cloud
    abides,
A speck upon the waste of plain the lonely mailman
    rides.
Where fierce hot winds have set the pine and myall
    boughs asweep
He hails the shearers passing by for news of Conroy's
    sheep.
By big lagoons where wildfowl play and crested
    pigeons flock
By camp fires where the drovers ride around their
    restless stock,
And past the teamster toiling down to fetch the wool
    away
My letter chases Conroy's sheep along the Castlereagh.

'Guinea Corn' was one of the work-songs recorded in the 1790s by J. B. Moreton (published in *West Indian Customs and Manners*, 1793) when he was gathering material for a guide to Jamaica. The 'Ballad' attributed to him shows an attempt to simulate the thought and language of a slave woman.

Emphasizing 'song' rather than 'work' was the *kaiso* (calypso) associated with Trinidad, but present in most East Caribbean islands after colonization, the French influence being maintained until well into the twentieth century. Lament and social commentary vied with female sexuality as the main themes. The tone is often upbeat and witty, as in the folk-song 'Quaco Sam', composed between c. 1812 and c. 1825.

I've had no room to include the 'newspaper poets' – Michael McTurk, Edward Cordle and James Martinez – whose efforts formed something of a bridge between oral and scribal work in the later nineteenth century; so the focus must be on Francis Williams (c. 1700–c. 1770) and Claude McKay (1889–1948) as our signposts to West Indian poetry.

Williams, a free-born Jamaican, was sent to school in England and to Cambridge as an 'experiment' by the Duke of Montagu. He wrote verses in Latin and English, the 'Ode' being the only surviving sample. It must be said, in his favour, that the contemporary literary mode was then the pastoral.

Claude McKay, a sometime policeman in Jamaica, later associated with the Harlem Renaissance, wrote in the vernacular and in standard idioms. He could be sentimental and, in his more public role, sententious. I've chosen not his hymn of defiance, 'If We Should Die', but another sonnet, 'America'. The wonderfully balanced irony here is not often achieved in much of the poet's work of the period, where he struggles with the twin daemons of race and exile.

After McKay, the names that keep us on track are: Una Marson (1905–65), A. J. Seymour (1914–89), George Campbell (b. 1916), Louise Bennett (b. 1919), Louis Simpson (b. 1923), Martin Carter (b. 1927) ... leading to Brathwaite and Walcott, and beyond.

GUINEA CORN

Guinea Corn, I long to see you
Guinea Corn, I long to plant you
Guinea Corn, I long to mould you
Guinea Corn, I long to weed you
Guinea Corn, I long to hoe you
Guinea Corn, I long to top you
Guinea Corn, I long to cut you
Guinea Corn, I long to dry you
Guinea Corn, I long to beat you
Guinea Corn, I long to trash you
Guinea Corn, I long to parch you
Guinea Corn, I long to grind you
Guinea Corn, I long to turn you
Guinea Corn, I long to eat you

EARLY *Kaiso* FROM TRINIDAD

◄(19th century)►

Belle ti beke epi dez ye sible
Belle ti Zindien epi de nat chevez
Belle ti Negresse epi bondai mate
P'is bondai mate ca fair dondon bave
Glo, Glo, Gloria, Glo Glo Gloria
Glo, Glo, Gloria, Gloria c'est pou ou
Gloria pas pou moen.

A beautiful white girl with two eyes of blue
A beautiful little Carib Indian with two plaits of
    hair
A beautiful Negress with well-developed posterior
Because she had a well developed posterior it made
    Dondon dribble.
Glo, Glo, Gloria, Glo Glo Gloria
Glo, Glo, Gloria, Gloria is for you
Gloria not for me.

KAISO

◄(19th century, originally from Martinique; popular in the 'English' islands)►

L'annee passer moen 'tait youn fille
Youn jeune 'ti fille caille mama moen
L'annee-ca la moen c'est youn famme

Moen ka debat pour la vie moen
Aie, Aie
Sucouer corps-ou moen kay ba-ou (repeat twice.)

Jalle-la
Sucouer corps-ou moen kay ba-ou
Moen kay ba-ou moen kay ba-ou
En gwo misiyi.

A year ago I was a girl
A young little girl in my mother's house
This year I am a woman
Fighting to make a living for myself
Aie, Aie
Shake your body and I will give you
Naughty girl
Shake your body and I will give you
I will give you, I will give you
A hefty mister.

BALLAD

◄J. B. Moreton►

(Air 'What care I for Mam or Dad')

Altho' a slave me is born and bred,
    My skin is black, not yellow:
I often sold my maidenhead
    To many a handsome fellow.

My massa keep me once, for true,
    And gave me clothes, wid busses:
Fine muslin coats, wid bitty, too,
    To gain my sweet embraces.

When pickinniny him come black,
    My massa starve and fum me,
He tear the coat from off my back,
    And naked him did strip me.

Him turn me out into the field,
    Wid hoe, the ground to clear-o,
Me take pickinniny on my back,
    And work him te-me weary.

Him, Obissha, him de come one night,
    And give me gown and busses,
Him get one pickinniny, white!
    Almost as white as missess.

Then missess fum me wid long switch,
   And say him da for massa,
My massa curse her, 'lying bitch!'
   And tell her, 'buss my rassa!'

Me fum'd when me no condescend,
   Me fum'd too if me do it,
Me no have no one for'tand my friend,
   So me am for'd to do it.

Me know no law, me know no sin,
   Me is just what ebba dem make me,
This is the way dem bring me in,
   So God nor devil take me!

❧

Quaco Sam

‹Anonymous›

Come, cousin Cuba, me yerry some news,
Me yerry say you buy one new pair a shoes,
Me yerry say you buy one dandy hat –
Come tell me, cousin Cuba, wha you pay fe dat?
   Wid me ring ding ding an me pam pam pam,
   Me nebber see a man like-a Quaco Sam.

Me yerry say one dance deh a Berry Hill:
Unco Jack fe play de fiddle, one hog deh fe kill;
Come tell me, cousin Cuba, how ebry ting 'tan,
Mek me ax sista Susan, mek me call sista Ann.
   Wid me ring ding ding etc.

Regen' gown me hab, me gingham coat;
Hankecha tie me head, tanky-massa be me troat –
An da warra mo me wanty? me hat, me junka fan,
Fe go da Berry Hill fe go see Quaco Sam.
   Wid me ring ding ding etc.

Oh Lard! how me wi dance when me yerry fiddle an
   drum!
Me no tink pon backra wuk, me no care fe fum-fum!
Me wi dance de shay-shay, me wi dance de 'cotch
   reel,
Me wi dance till ebry craps a me foot-battam peel.
   Wid me ring ding ding etc.

Monday marnin, Driber Harry, jus da cock da crow,
Tek him cudjo da him han, pop him whip da busha
   do'.

Wid me hoe da me shoulder, wid me bill da me
   back,
Me da mash putto-putto, me da tink pan Unco Jack.
   Wid me ring ding ding etc.

Me tek me road da cane-piece, weh de people-dem
   da run,
An all come behin' me, get de fum-fum.
Wid de centung da me back, chacolata da me pahn,
Me da wuk, me da laugh, me da tink pan Quaco
   Sam.
   Wid me ring ding ding etc.

❧

from An Ode to George Haldane, Governor of the Island of Jamaica

‹Francis Williams›

Hoe demum accipias, multa fuligine fusum
   Ore sonaturo, non cute, corde valet.
Pollenti stabilita manu, (Deus almus, candem
   Omnigenis animam, nil prohibente dedit)
Ipsa coloris egens virtus, prudentia, honesto
   Nullus inest animo, nullus in arte color.
Cur timeas, quamvis, dubitesve, nigerrima celsam
   Caesaris occidui, scandere Musa domum?
Vade salutatum, nee sit tibi causa pudoris,
   Candida quod nigra corpora pelle geris!
Integritas morum Maurum magis ornat, et ardor
   Ingenii, et docto dulcis in ore decor,
Hunc, mage cor sapiens, patriae virtutis amorque,
   Eximit e sociis, conspicuumque facit.
Insula me genuit, celebres aluere Britanni,
   Insula, te salvo non dolitura patre!
Hoc precor, o nullo vidant te fine, regentem
   Florentes populos, terra, Deique locus!

[Accept this, uttered with much soot from a mouth
that wishes to sing, not from the skin but from the
heart comes its strength. Established by a mighty
hand (God the creator gave the same soul to all his
creatures, without exception), virtue itself, like
wisdom, is devoid of colour. There is no colour in
an honourable mind, none in art. Why do you fear
so much, and hesitate, my Muse so black, to mount
to the lofty abode of the Caesar of the setting sun?
Go and greet him, nor let it be a source of shame to
you that a black skin covers your fair body! All the
more does moral integrity adorn an African, as does

ardour of intellect, and attractive eloquence in a
learned mouth. Rather, a wise heart, and love both
of country and of virtue, distinguish such a man
from his fellows, and make him outstanding. An
island gave me birth, the renowned Britons
nurtured me, this island which will have no cause
to grieve while you, its father, thrive! This I pray, O
may this land and place of God see you ruling
without end over a flourishing people.]

AMERICA

‹Claude McKay›

Although she feeds me bread of bitterness,
And sinks into my throat her tiger's tooth,
Stealing my breath of life, I will confess
I love this cultured hell that tests my youth!
Her vigor flows like tides into my blood,
Giving me strength erect against her hate,
Her bigness sweeps my being like a flood.
Yet as a rebel fronts a king in state,
I stand within her walls with not a shred
Of terror, malice, not a word of jeer,
Darkly I gaze into the days ahead,
And see her might and granite wonders there,
Beneath the touch of Time's unerring hand,
Like priceless treasures sinking in the sand.

There is not much pre-twentieth-century
Indian poetry written in English – in fact,
as Indians began writing poetry in English
not quite 180 years ago, one can imagine
how very little there is to choose from. And
if one happens to be an Indian poet writing
in English today, one can still feel, at times,
like a pioneer in the field.

I have selected work by the following
poets: Kasiprasad Ghosh, Gooroo Churn
Dutt (dates unknown, but published in
1839), Shoshee Chunder Dutt, Ram Sharma
(the pseudonym of Nobo Kissen Ghose),
and Toru Dutt – the last being the only
woman among them. They are all Indians,
in fact they all happen to be Bengalis –
which is another story! Although all of
these poems are highly derivative, they do
focus on Indian themes with a certain
amount of good faith and integrity – and
that of course led me to choose them over
the vague romantic/sentimental work so
popular at the time.

To a Young Hindu Widow

‹Kasiprasad Ghosh (1809–1873)›

Ah, fair one! lone as desert flower,
   Whose bloom and beauty are in vain;
How dark was that too fatal hour
   Which brought thee lasting grief and pain!
What is the world to thee forlorn!
   Thine every path is desolate;
From all enjoyments rudely torn,
   How drear and comfortless thy fate!
What pity, friendless, helpless, poor!
   That such should be thine early lot –
Doomed to remain for ever more
   As if thou in this world wert not.
And is there none – O! can it be?
   None warm or friendly in thy cause?
Has pitiless humanity
   Forgot its sacred ties and laws?
The rigours of a life austere,
   Followed by every fear and shame
Await thee as thy portion here:
   What is thy being but a name?
Thou may'st not, dar'st not, must not hope
   A joy upon the world beneath;
But thou must e'er with sorrows cope,
   Sorrows which only end in death.
And thou art doomed to be at strife
   For ever with thyself, to quell
The very elements of life
   And brighter thought repel.
       *   *   *   *
Is this the all, or should it be
   The all that here to thee is left?
And must the world remain to thee
   A scene of every charm bereft?

Introductory Lines

‹Gooroo Churn Dutt›

If then amongst thy sons a fallen race,
Alas! degraded low, (unhappy days!)
I a poor school boy with my scanty store,
Unlearned in thy mysterious shastras' lore,
On painted wings of fancy strive to soar,
And hail thee, India, from thy days of yore,
Then welcome to my breast, forever dear,
While on thy sad remains I drop a tear.

And tho' I'm born in this unlucky age,
Without the fire of any ancient sage,
Accept the tribute of a heart sincere.

India

‹Shoshee Chunder Dutt (1825–1886)›

And shall I to the future turn my gaze?
The future is a sealed book to man,
And none so high presumes his sight to raise;
God's mystic secrets who shall dare to scan?
But sure it is no mighty sin to dream;
I dreamt a dream of strange and wild delight,
Freedom's pure shrine once more illumed did seem,
The clouds had pass'd beneath the morning light;
On beauty's cheek I mark'd the tear-drops dry,
And sighs and groans for ever fled the land;
Science again aspired to the sky,
And patriot valour watch'd the smiling strand:
A dream! a dream! Why should a dream it be?
Land of my fathers! Canst thou ne'er be free?

Lines Addressed to James Skribblerus

‹Ram Sharma (1837–1918)›

Born in a garret, on low rations fed,
Exiled from home to find in Ind his bread,
See Skribblerus comes from beyond the main,
With empty pockets and still emptier brain,
Sustained by vanity and front of brass,
Tho' still a fool in wit, in sense an ass
       *   *   *
With fool's cap for helm and sword of lath,
The Grub Street Hero apes Pelides' wrath,
And dares like Phaeton drive Apollo's car,
With sense and taste and virtue still at war.
Once brave Cl-ke well nigh shook him into sense,
He blares again in raging impotence.
See him rush where his betters fear to tread
And pour, morn after morn, dull stream of lead.
He teaches, preaches and still as he maunders
Mistakes his cackles for Jove's awful thunders.
Bengala still his scorn, her sons his hate, –
All false to truth and servile to the great …
Unhappy land! that sees an errand boy

A printer's imp, – the good and wise annoy;
Unhappy land! condemned by ruthless fate
Still to endure his nauseous Billingsgate.
But, O grieve not for Britain's generous sons,
All, all detest the bore, the foul-mouthed dunce.
Let him jeer on and be a jackass still,
The brute may bray and vex, but do no ill.

❧

OUR CASUARINA TREE

‹Toru Dutt (1856–1877)›

Like a huge Python, winding round and round
    The rugged trunk, indented deep with scars
    Up to its very summit near the stars,
A creeper climbs, in whose embraces bound
    No other tree could live. But gallantly
The giant wears the scarf, and flowers are hung
In crimson clusters all the boughs among,
    Whereon all day are gathered bird and bee;
And oft at nights the garden overflows
With one sweet song that seems to have no close,
Sung darkling from our tree, while men repose.

When first my casement is wide open thrown
    At dawn, my eyes delighted on it rest;
    Sometimes, and most in winter, – on its crest
A gray baboon sits statue-like alone
    Watching the sunrise; while on lower boughs
His puny offspring leap about and play;
And far and near kokilas hail the day;
    And to their pastures wend our sleepy cows;
And in the shadow, on the broad tank cast
By that hoar tree, so beautiful and vast,
The water-lilies spring, like snow enmassed.

But not because of its magnificence
    Dear is the Casuarina to my soul:
    Beneath it we have played; though years may roll,
O sweet companions, loved with love intense,
    For your sakes shall the tree be ever dear!
Blent with your images, it shall arise
In memory, till the hot tears blind mine eyes!
What is that dirge-like murmur that I hear
Like the sea breaking on a shingle-beach?
It is the tree's lament, an eerie speech,
That haply to the unknown land may reach.

Unknown, yet well-known to the eye of faith!
    Ah, I have heard that wail far, far away
    In distant lands, by many a sheltered bay,
When slumbered in his cave the water-wraith
    And the waves gently kissed the classic shore
Of France or Italy, beneath the moon
When earth lay tranced in a dreamless swoon:
    And every time the music rose, – before
Mine inner vision rose a form sublime,
Thy form, O Tree, as in my happy prime
I saw thee, in my own loved native clime.

Therefore I fain would consecrate a lay
    Unto thy honour, Tree, beloved of those
    Who now in blessed sleep for aye repose,
Dearer than life to me, alas! were they!
    Mayst thou be numbered when my days are done
    With deathless trees – like those in Borrowdale,
Under whose awful branches lingered pale
    'Fear, trembling Hope, and Death, the skeleton,
And Time the shadow' and though weak the verse
That would thy beauty fain, oh fain rehearse,
May Love defend thee from Oblivion's curse.

❧

from BUTTOO

‹Toru Dutt›

What glorious trees! The sombre saul
On which the eye delights to rest,
The betel-nut, – a pillar tall,
With feathery branches for a crest,
The light-leaved tamarind spreading wide,
The pale faint-scented bitter neem,
The seemul, gorgeous as a bride,
With flowers that have the ruby's gleam,
That Indian fig's pavilion tent
In which whole armies might repose,
With here and there a little rent,
The sunset's beauty to disclose,
The bamboo boughs that sway and swing
'Neath bulbuls as the south wind blows,
The mangoe-tope, a close dark ring,
Home of the rooks and clamorous crows,

The champac, bok, and South-sea pine,
The nagessur with pendant flowers
Like ear-rings, – and the forest vine
That clinging over all, embowers,

The sirish famed in Sanscrit song
Which rural maidens love to wear,
The peepul giant-like and strong,
The bramble with its matted hair,

All these, and thousands, thousands more,
With helmet red, or golden crown,
Or green tiara, rose before
The youth in evening's shadows brown.
He passed into the forest, – there
New sights of wonder met his view,
A waving Pampas green and fair
All glistening with the evening dew.

The anonymous come-all-you 'David Lowston' (c. 1810–15) is one of the earliest known New Zealand compositions in English verse: the country's desolate southernmost coasts were the scene, at the dawn of the nineteenth century, of a wholesale slaughter of great herds of seals, by gangs 'set down' from American or Australian ships...

The lines by William Pember Reeves are by no means fanciful in their claim for 'architects of State': as Minister of Labour in the 1890s, he drew world attention to the remote colony by his radical social and industrial measures, including 'the most progressive labour code in the world'. A pity to see, a hundred years after, so much of his work undone by 'market forces' fanaticism...

Blanche Baughan would not have been unmindful of the irony in her title, 'The Old Place' – only fifteen years since her protagonist cleared his land, built his first house, drove 5,000 sheep down the coast! His flock shrunken to 1,150, disenchanted and a widower, making way for 'the incoming man'...

Arnold Wall, born in Ceylon, was educated in London and Cambridge; he migrated to New Zealand in 1898 to be professor of English language, literature, and history at the young university college of Canterbury; he was philologist, mountaineer and alpine botanist. The source for Wall's 'Pope Joan' may have been more copious than the thirty-five words devoted to the 'vulgar tale' in Brewer's *Dictionary of Phrase and Fable*. Gibbon (it seems) disposed of her in even fewer. Wall remains for me one of the very few who last century wrote verse of any distinction in this corner of the world. In the re-telling, he manages, somehow, to hold attention, possibly in some way that has more to do with the next century than the last? And perhaps not altogether auspiciously.

David Lowston

‹Anonymous›

My name is David Lowston, I did seal, I did seal,
My name is David Lowston, I did seal.
Though my men and I were lost,
Though our very lives 'twould cost,
We did seal, we did seal, we did seal.

'Twas in eighteen hundred and ten we set sail, we
    set sail,
'Twas in eighteen hundred and ten, we set sail.
We were left, we gallant men,
Never more to sail again,
For to seal, for to seal, for to seal.

We were set down in Open Bay, were set down, were
    set down,
We were set down in Open Bay, were set down.
Upon the sixteenth day,
Of Februar-aye-ay,
For to seal, for to seal, for to seal.

Our Captain, John Bedar, he set sail, he set sail,
Yes, for Port Jackson he set sail.
'I'll return, men, without fail,'
But she foundered in a gale,
And went down, and went down, and went down.

We cured ten thousand skins for the fur, for the fur,
Yes we cured ten thousand skins for the fur.
Brackish water, putrid seal,
We did all of us fall ill,
For to die, for to die, for to die.

Come all you lads who sail the sea, sail the sea,
Come all you jacks who sail upon the sea.
Though the schooner, *Governor Bligh*,
Took on some who did not die,
Never seal, never seal, never seal.

The Old Place

‹Blanche Baughan (1870–1958)›

So the last day's come at last, the close of my fifteen
    year –
The end of the hope, an' the struggles, an' messes
    I've put in here.

All of the shearings over, the final mustering
    done, –
Eleven hundred an' fifty for the incoming man, near
    on.
Over five thousand I drove 'em, mob by mob, down
    the coast;
Eleven-fifty in fifteen year ... it isn't much of a
    boast.

  Oh, it's a bad old place! Blown out o' your bed
    half the nights,
And in summer the grass burnt shiny an' bare as
    your hand, on the heights:
The creek dried up by November, and in May a
    thundering roar
That carries down toll o' your stock to salt 'em
    whole on the shore.
Clear'd I have, and I've clear'd an' clear'd, yet
    everywhere, slap in your face,
Briar, *tauhinu*, an' ruin! – God! it's a brute of a
    place.
... An' the house got burnt which I built, myself,
    with all that worry and pride;
Where the Missus was always homesick, and where
    she took fever, and died.

  Yes, well! I'm leaving the place. Apples look red
    on that bough.
I set the slips with my own hand. Well – they're the
    other man's now.
The breezy bluff: an' the clover that smells so over
    the land,
Drowning the reek o' the rubbish, that plucks the
    profit out o' your hand:
That bit o' Bush paddock I fall'd myself, an'
    watch'd, each year, come clean
(Don't it look fresh in the tawny? A scrap of Old-
    Country green):
This air, all healthy with sun an' salt, an' bright
    with purity:
An' the glossy *karakas* there, twinkling to the big
    blue twinkling sea:
Ay, the broad blue sea beyond, an' the gem-clear
    cove below,
Where the boat I'll never handle again, sits rocking
    to and fro:
There's the last look to it all! an' now for the last
    upon
This room, where Hetty was born, an' my Mary
    died, an' John ...

Well! I'm leaving the poor old place, and it cuts as
    keen as a knife;
The place that's broken my heart – the place where
    I've lived my life.

from A Colonist in his Garden

‹William Pember Reeves (1857–1932)›

'No art?' Who serve an art more great
Than we, rough architects of State
    With the old Earth at strife?
'No colour!' On the silent waste,
In pigments not to be effaced,
    We paint the hues of life.

'A land without a past?' Nay, nay.
I saw it, forty years this day.
    – Nor man, nor beast, nor tree:
Wide, empty plains where shadows pass
Blown by the wind o'er whispering grass
    Whose sigh crept after me.

Now when at midnight round my doors
The gale through sheltering branches roars,
    What is it to the might
Of the mad gorge-wind that o'erthrew
My camp – the first I pitched – and blew
    Our tents into the night?

Mine is the vista where the blue
And white-capped mountains close the view.
    Each tapering cypress there
At planting in these hands was borne,
Small, shivering seedlings and forlorn,
    When all the plain was bare!

Skies without music, mute through time,
Now hear the skylark's rippling climb
    Challenge their loftier dome.
And hark! A song of garden floats,
Rills, gushes clear, – the self-same notes
    Your thrushes flute at Home.

Psychical Research

‹Arnold Wall (1869–1966)›

Flutter no more, poor bird,
Flutter no more, nor dash
Thy tender breast
Against the cruel bars,
Seeking some paradise
Which thou imaginest
Before thy cheated eyes;
Flutter no more, nor gird,
Hasty and rash,
At unpropitious stars.
Dear bird, flutter no more,
Because thou canst descry
Through the half-open door
Fields and enthralling woods,
Sunshine and liberty
New and enchanting foods
Take the gods' gifts, nor heed
The wheedling of thy lust,
Flutter no more, but thrust
Thy beak into the seed.

from The Ballad of Pope Joan

‹Arnold Wall›

Alone, neglected, here I lie,
The time has come for me to die,
Now poor sinful erring Joan
Must die, neglected and alone.

With none to take me by the hand
Before my Maker I shall stand,
And with a contrite heart confess
All my dreadful wickedness.

[…]

When I was innocent and young,
Proud of my wit and nimble tongue,
My marble cheek, my raven hair,
The devil took me in his snare.

When I was young and innocent
To hear the Mass I often went,
And watched the brethren in their stalls,
Bishops, priests and cardinals.

Among the brethren old and wise
Brother Folda charmed my eyes,
So young so fair, so pure, so good,
The glory of the brotherhood.

Beneath the cassock and the cowl,
The unearthly ardours of his soul,
Beyond the beauty of his mind,
His comely body I divined.

So smooth his skin, so clear his eye,
His ivory brow so white and high,
His kissing lip so rosy red,
Ah, would I had him in my bed!

I fell from virtue, fell from grace,
Entranced I gazed upon his face,
My heart grew faint, my eyes were dim,
And I was sick for need of him.

[. . .]

The devil whispered me a plan,
I hid my sex, I dressed as man,
And with my master's artful aid
A holy brother I was made.

Within the Abbey's sacred bound
A model brother I was found,
I was beloved, and in the end,
Became poor Folda's dearest friend.

Upon the Fathers I would pore,
I mastered all the Church's lore,
My fame, the Abbey's joy and pride,
Through Christendom ran far and wide.

[. . .]

They held me in such great regard,
That swift success was my reward;
I was not long a simple friar,
But soon became their holy Prior.

Then one day, in a lonely field,
My sex, my passion, I revealed,
By swift assault broke his defence
And won him to concupiscence.

Together oft we'd fondly stray,
And in dark woods together lay,
I found the man, I killed the saint,
We loved and sinned and were content.

While the poor brothers, good as gold,
Their midnight services would hold,
We two, excused on specious pleas,
Sank deep in vile debaucheries.

[. . .]

To cloak my crime I had to learn,
I kept an aspect cold and stern,
All harmless merriment restrained,
An iron discipline maintained.

My master's maxims served me well,
Delivered in my midnight cell,
I found myself, at thirty-three,
Elected to the Holy See.

Alas, that honour sealed my doom,
By then the child was in my womb,
The devil watched, with sneering grin,
The sprouting of the seed of sin.

Bereft of sense, bereft of force,
I must pursue my destined course.
While inwardly I sighed and groaned,
Great crowds came on to see me throned.

I moved, I walked, as one in dream,
Borne on by some relentless stream,
All gorgeous in the vestments bright,
With censer, bell and acolyte.

Alas, my time was drawing near,
My heart and soul were numb with fear,
As through the nave I marched along,
Attended by the joyful throng.

My pains came on, the pains of hell,
Upon the chancel-steps I fell,
My secret, long in darkness nursed,
My secret from my body burst.

As I lay weeping on the ground,
The affrighted clergy gathered round,
Appalled, aghast, shaking and pale,
They heard my baby's puny wail.

No woman by, my state to ease,
Or stay me in my agonies,
Ah, there I lay upon the stone,
No pope, a mother, and alone.

The helpless clerics stood and stared,
They saw my female body bared,
They gazed in horror on the child,
My blood the holy robes defiled.

The blazoned saints, in windows high,
Shrank back to hear my bitter cry,
The eyes of Christ in agony
Looked down upon my babe and me.

Without a home, without a name,
Through the long years I've lived in shame,
In foul rags clad, on offal fed,
With hate and curses on my head.

[. . .]

They took my little babe away,
I've never seen him to this day –
This day, this day, when it is passed,
The devil has his own at last.

Alone, neglected, and disguised,
By all abhorred, by all despised,
Alone, neglected, here I lie,
The time has come for me to die.

Good Christians all, I beg you pray
For my poor soul, as well you may,
Pray for my soul, I do implore,
That burns in hell for evermore.

                          Amen.

The weight of the South African English language cannon on the shoulders of the South African poet has not been particularly heavy. Succeeding generation of poets have reinvented themselves, their reference points located in the grand traditions of the West, and/or Africa, and the African diaspora. Only since the 1970s perhaps, has South African writing become, in a significant way, *writing to write out of*, its 'traditions' existing not as patterns observable chiefly to the academic, but as felt realities. To state the obvious, English language poetry written in South Africa before 1914 was the literature of displaced Europeans, ideas of 'literariness' ultimately tied to the apron strings of Europe. Among those represented here, only Olive Schreiner was born in South Africa. Bain, Pringle (who arrived with the 1820 settlers) and Broderick all came from Europe as adults, Alder from Australia. What does this say about South African poetry? I think, in the end, nothing. Cultural nationalism in Africa has been a necessary reaction, but an unworkable reality. Nationalism in Africa, and certainly in South Africa, has always been ultimately territorial; and there is a sense in which aspects of these few poems – though excluding as they (necessarily) do the bulk of South African experience – suggest what the term 'South African literature' might come to mean. For the stuff of national community is our shared histories, privileged events, narratives and geographies, tokens the meaning of which may be debated, but in so being debated and recognised as common, constitute the language in which whatever can be expressed is expressed.

The Cape of Storms

‹Thomas Pringle (1789–1834)›

O Cape of Storms! although thy front be dark,
And bleak thy naked cliffs and cheerless vales,
And perilous thy fierce and faithless gales
To staunchest mariner and stoutest bark;
And though along thy coasts with grief I mark
The servile and the slave, and him who wails
An exile's lot – and blush to hear thy tales
Of sin and sorrow and oppression stark: –
Yet, spite of physical and moral ill,
And after all I've seen and suffeed here,
There are strong links that bind me to thee still,
And render even thy rocks and deserts dear;
Here dwell kind hearts which time nor place can
    chill –
Loved Kindred and congenial Friends sincere.

Kaatje Kekkelbek
or Life among the Hottentots

‹Andrew Geddes Bain (1797–1864)›

My name is Kaatje Kekkelbek,
    I come from Katrivier,
Daar is van water geen gebrek,
    But scarce of wine and beer.
Myn A B C at Ph'lipes school
    I learnt a kleine beetje,
But left it just as great a fool
    As gekke Tante Meitje.

But a b, ab and i n, ine,
    I dagt met uncle Plaatje,
Aint half so good as brandewyn,
    And vette karbonatje.
So off we set, een heele boel,
    Stole a fat cow and sack'd it,
Then to an Engels setlaars fool,
    We had ourselves contracted.

We next took to the Kowie Bush,
    Found sheep dat was not lost, aye
But a schelm boer het ons gavang,
    And brought us voor McCrosty.
Daar was Saartje Zeekoegat en ik,
    En ouw Dirk Donderwetter,

Klaas Klauterberg, en Diederick Dik,
    Al sent to the tronk together.

Drie months we daar got banjan kos
    For stealing os en hammel,
For which when I again got los;
    I thank'd for Capt. Campbell.
The Judge came around, his sentence such
    As he thought just and even.
'Six months hard work,' which means in Dutch
    'Zes maanden lekker leven.'

De tronk it is een lekker plek
    Of 'twas not juist so dry,
But soon as I got out again
    At (Todds) I wet mine eye,
At Vice's house in Market-Square
    I drown'd my melancholies;
And at Barrack hill found soldiers there
    To treat me well at Jolly's.

Next morn dy put me in blackhole,
    For one Rixdollar stealing,
And knocking down a vrouw dat had
    Met myn sweet heart some dealing.
But I'll go to the Gov'nor self
    And tell him in plain lingo,
I've as much right to steal and fight
    As kaffir has or Fingoe.

Oom Andries Stoffels in England told
    (Fine compliments he paid us,)
Dat Engels dame was juist de same
    As our sweet Hotnot ladies.
When drest up in my voersits pak
    What hearts will then be undone,
Should I but show my face or back
    Among the beaux of London.

Epitaph on a Diamond Digger

‹Albert Broderick (1830–1908)›

Here lies a digger, all his chips departed –
A splint of nature, bright, and ne'er down-hearted:
He worked in many claims, but now (though
    stumped)
He's got a claim above that can't be jumped.
May he turn out a pure and spotless 'wight,'

When the Great Judge shall sift the wrong from
   right,
And may his soul, released from this low Babel,
Be found a gem on God's great sorting table.

❧

THE CRY OF SOUTH AFRICA

‹Olive Schreiner (1855–1920)›

Give back my dead!
They who by kop and fountain
First saw the light upon my rocky breast!
Give back my dead,
The sons who played upon me
When childhood's dews still rested on their heads.
Give back my dead
Whom thou has riven from me
By arms of men loud called from earth's farthest
   bound
To wet my bosom with my children's blood!
Give back my dead,
The dead who grew up on me!

Wagenaar's Kraal,
   Three Sisters.
      May 9, 1900.

❧

THE STREET OF PEACOCKS

‹Alice Mabel Alder (b. 1879/89)›

Down the blue chasm of the street,
Where the tall sightless houses stood
With walls of ice, in solitude –
Its blue-green shadows, cold and sweet –
The vision of the peacocks came,
A murmuring river: in God's name
Some old lost bells remembered time:
And to the dreaming of that chime,
The stream of peacocks stepping slow,
Shadowed with gleaming blues and greens,
Clucking and rustling like a river,
And coroneted like old queens,
Flowed onward down the street for ever.

Far up the shadows of the street,
Between a rift of timbered walls,

A tender light of earthly sun
Bestowed a golden shaft of gleam,
And birds of snow, with unheard calls,
Passed on the ray, and, one by one,
Departed from the street of dream.

Then in the shadows of the street
A shadow rose and spoke to me –
Hands to my hands, with no words said,
Palms on my palms spoke silently
Among the houses of the dead,
Where, moving, rustling like a river,
The blue-green peacocks streamed for ever.

NOTES ON CONTRIBUTORS

FERGUS ALLEN
Born in London and grew up in Ireland. He has spent much of his career as a civil servant in England; his two poetry collections are *The Brown Parrots of Providencia* (1993) and *Who Goes There?* (1996).

SIMON ARMITAGE
Born in Huddersfield in 1963. His first collection, *Zoom*, was published in 1989; his most recent collections are *The Dead Sea Poems* (1995) and *Cloudcuckooland* (1997). He works as a freelance writer and broadcaster.

JOHN ASHBERY
Born in Rochester, New York, in 1927. He published his first volume of poetry in 1953; his latest are *Can You Hear, Bird* (1995/6) and *The Mooring of Starting Out* (1997). He is currently Professor of English at Bard College.

IAIN BAMFORTH
Born in 1959, grew up in Glasgow. A doctor and scientific translator, practising in Strasbourg, he has published two collections of poetry: *Sons and Pioneers* (1992) and *Open Workings* (1996).

PATRICIA BEER
Born in 1919 in Exmouth. She taught English Literature in Padua and London, leaving teaching in 1968 to become a full-time writer, and lives in Devon. Her *Collected Poems* (1988) were followed by *Friends of Heraclitus* (1993) and *Autumn* (1997).

SUJATA BHATT
Born in Ahmedabad, India in 1956. Educated in the USA, she now lives in Germany, working as a writer and as a translator from Gujarati. Her collections

include *The Stinking Rose* (1995) and *Point No Point* (1997).

EAVAN BOLAND
Born in Dublin in 1944, where she works as a lecturer and reviewer, also teaching regularly in America. Her *Collected Poems* were published in 1996, and her essays, *Object Lessons*, in 1995.

CHARLES BOYLE
Born in Leeds in 1951. He taught English in Sheffield and North Africa before the publication of *Affinities* in 1977; his fifth collection, *Paleface*, was published in 1996. He lives and works in London.

ALISON BRACKENBURY
Born in Lincolnshire in 1953. She lives in Cheltenham and has worked as a librarian, now works for an engineering firm. Her five collections include *Christmas Roses* (1988), *Selected Poems* (1991) and *1829* (1995).

ALAN BROWNJOHN
Born in Catford, south London in 1931. He has taught English in schools and colleges of further education, and worked extensively as an editor and critic. His *Collected Poems* appeared in 1983, and his latest volume, *In the Cruel Arcade*, in 1994.

JOHN BURNSIDE
Born in 1955 in Dunfermline. He now lives in Fife and is a freelance writer, having published six collections of poetry, of which the most recent is *A Normal Skin* (1997), and one novel, *The Dumb House* (1997).

GILLIAN CLARKE
Born in Cardiff in 1937. She has lived in South Wales for most of her life, and

has been a part-time teacher, and editor of the *Anglo-Welsh Review*. Her most recent volume is *The King of Britain's Daughter* (1993); her *Collected Poems* are due out in 1997.

ANNE CLUYSENAAR
Born in Brussels in 1936. She now runs a self-catering smallholding, and teaches creative writing at the University of Wales, Cardiff, as well as taking writing and painting workshops. *Timeslips: new and selected poems* was published in 1997.

DAVID CONSTANTINE
Born in Salford in 1944. He lives in Oxford, where he is Fellow in German at the Queen's College. His *Selected Poems* were published in 1991, and *Caspar Hauser* in 1994.

WENDY COPE
Born in Erith, Kent in 1945. She worked as a teacher and is now a freelance writer, living in London. Her books include two poetry collections: *Making Cocoa for Kingsley Amis* (1986) and *Serious Concerns* (1992).

ALLEN CURNOW
Born in Timaru, New Zealand in 1911. He taught English Literature at the University of Auckland, has published plays, poetry and criticism, and edited two anthologies of New Zealand verse. *Early Days Yet: New and Collected Poems 1941–1995* was published in 1997.

DICK DAVIS
Born in Portsmouth in 1945. Having lived in Iran for eight years, he now teaches Persian at Ohio State University. His new and selected poems, *Devices and*

Desires were published in 1989, and *Touchwood* in 1996.

MARK DOTY

Born in 1953 in Maryville, Tennessee. He teaches at the University of Iowa Writers' Workshop, and lives in Provincetown, Massachusetts. His books include two poetry collections: *My Alexandria* (1995) and *Atlantis* (1996).

MAUREEN DUFFY

Born in Worthing in 1933. She published her first novel in 1962, and has since written further novels, plays, poetry, and biographical studies of Aphra Behn and Purcell. She led the campaign for the Public Lending Right.

IAN DUHIG

Born in Hammersmith in 1954. He has worked in homelessness projects in London and Belfast, and now lives in Leeds. He has published two poetry collections: *The Bradford Count* (1991) and *The Mersey Goldfish* (1995).

ALISTAIR ELLIOT

Born in Liverpool in 1932. He has travelled the world and had a wide variety of jobs; now he lives in Newcastle upon Tyne. His *Collected Poems* (1989) has been followed by *Turning the Stones* (1993) and *Facing Things* (1997).

D. J. ENRIGHT

Born in Leamington in 1920. He has taught at universities both abroad and in Britain. Since his *Collected Poems* (1987) he has published several collections, most recently *Old Men and Comets* (1993); and he has edited several anthologies, including *The Oxford Book of Contemporary Verse* (1980).

RUTH FAINLIGHT

Born in New York in 1931. Educated in the USA and England, she published her first collection, *Cages*, in 1967. Her *Selected Poems* appeared in 1995.

U. A. FANTHORPE

Born in Kent in 1929. She lives in Gloucestershire and works as a freelance writer, having been a teacher and a hospital clerk. Her most recent poetry collections are *Neck-Verse* (1992) and *Safe as Houses* (1995).

VICKI FEAVER

Born in Nottingham in 1943. She teaches at the West Sussex Institute in Chichester, and has published two poetry collections: *Close Relatives* (1981) and *The Handless Maiden* (1994).

ELAINE FEINSTEIN

Born in Lancashire in 1930. She is a freelance writer, living in London; she has translated Russian poets, notably Marina Tsvetayeva, and published over thirty books, including her *Selected Poems* (1994) and *Daylight* (1997).

ROY FISHER

Born in Handsworth, Birmingham, in 1930. Formerly a university lecturer in American Literature, he is now a freelance writer and jazz musician, living in Derbyshire. *The Dow Low Drop: new and selected poems* was published in 1996.

MARK FORD

Born in Kenya in 1962. He has taught at universities in Britain and Japan, and now lectures at University College, London. His first collection, *Landless*, was published in 1992.

MATTHEW FRANCIS

Born in 1956. Having worked in the computer industry, he is now writing a thesis on W. S. Graham's poetry. His first novel, *Whom*, was published in 1989, and his first collection of poems, *Blizzard*, in 1996.

THOM GUNN

Born in Gravesend in 1929. His first book, *Fighting Terms*, was published while he was an undergraduate at Cambridge. He moved to California in 1954 and now lives in San Francisco, teaching at Berkeley. *The Man with Night Sweats* was published in 1992, followed by his *Collected Poems* (1993).

MICHAEL HAMBURGER

Born in Berlin in 1924. Now lives in Suffolk, translating German poetry and writing. Recent publications include *Collected Poems 1941-1994* (1995) and his translations of Goethe's *Roman Elegies* (1996).

SOPHIE HANNAH

Born in Manchester in 1971. She has been Writer in Residence at the Portico Library, Manchester, and has published two collections: *The Hero and the Girl Next Door* (1995) and *Hotels Like Houses* (1996).

JOHN HEATH-STUBBS

Born in 1918 and educated at Oxford. He is a critic, anthologist and translator, living in London. His *Collected Poems* were published in 1988, and the further collections *Sweetapple Earth* in 1993, *Galileo's Salad* in 1996.

MICHAEL HOFMANN

Born in Germany in 1957. He came to England in 1961 and has published three collections of poetry – most recently *Corona, Corona* (1993) – as well as a number of translations from the German.

ELIZABETH JENNINGS

Born in Boston, Lincolnshire, in 1926. She has lived in Oxford for most of her life, and drew upon seventeen collections of poetry for her *Collected Poems 1953-1985* (1986). Subsequent publications include *Times and Seasons* (1992) and *In the Meantime* (1996), and a reissue of her critical essays, *Every Changing Shape* (1961; 1996).

P. J. KAVANAGH

Born in Worthing, Sussex, in 1931. He lives in Gloucestershire and works as a freelance writer. His *Collected Poems* were published in 1992; his books include a volume of autobiography, *A Perfect Stranger* (reissued 1995), and of essays, *People and Places* (1988); he also edited Ivor Gurney's poems.

THOMAS KINSELLA

Born in Dublin in 1928. He has been a civil servant, lecturer and publisher, and lives in Co. Wicklow. His most recent books include the poetry collections *From Centre City* (1994) and *The Pen Shop* (1997), and *The Dual Tradition: an essay on poetry and politics in Ireland* (1995).

MIMI KHALVATI

Born in Tehran in 1944. She lives in London and has worked as a director and actor. Her poetry collections are: *In*

White Ink (1991), Mirrorwork (1995) and Entries on Light (1997).

KENNETH KOCH

Born in Cincinnati, Ohio in 1925. He teaches at Columbia University in New York and has published many collections of poetry, a representative selection from which was published in Great Britain in 1991, Selected Poems, followed by One Train (1994/1997).

FRANK KUPPNER

Born in Glasgow in 1951. He lives and writes in Glasgow, and has published five collections of poetry, of which the most recent are Everything is Strange (1994) and Second Best Moments in Chinese History (1997); also four novels, notably Something Very Like Murder (1995).

PETER LEVI

Born in Ruislip in 1931. He was a Jesuit priest until resigning orders in 1977, and Professor of Poetry at Oxford 1984–9. He has written biographies of Milton and Shakespeare, and since his Collected Poems 1955-1975 has published Rags of Time (1994) and Reed Music (1997).

GREVEL LINDOP

Born in Liverpool in 1948. He lives in Manchester and teaches English at the University. His books include a biography of Thomas de Quincey and the poetry collections Tourists (1987) and A Prismatic Toy (1991).

CHRISTOPHER LOGUE

Born in Portsmouth in 1926. He lives in Camberwell and has published three volumes of his version of Homer's Iliad, several collections of poetry and a pornographic novel. His Selected Poems were published in 1996.

ROGER MCGOUGH

Born in Liverpool in 1937. His work was famously anthologised in Penguin's The Mersey Sound (1967), and of his numerous poetry collections for adults and children, the most recent is Defying Gravity (1992).

LACHLAN MACKINNON

Born in Aberdeen in 1956. He works as a teacher, critic and reviewer, and published his first collection of poems,

Monterey Cypress, in 1988, followed by The Coast of Bohemia in 1991.

E. A. MARKHAM

Born in Montserrat in 1939. He has lived in many places, and is currently Professor of Creative Writing at Sheffield Hallam University. His most recent book of poems is Misapprehensions (1995) and his memoir A Papua New Guinea Sojourn: more pleasures of exile is due out in 1997.

CHRISTOPHER MIDDLETON

Born in Truro, Cornwall, in 1926. He was Professor of Germanic Languages at the University of Texas, Austin, where he lives, and has translated many German-language authors. His books include Selected Writings (1989) and Intimate Chronicles (poems, 1996).

EDWIN MORGAN

Born in Glasgow in 1920. He lectured in English and American Literature at the University of Glasgow, and has published many volumes of poetry and translations; his Collected Poems were followed by Sweeping Out the Dark (1994), Collected Translations (1996), and Virtual and Other Realities (1997).

ANDREW MOTION

Born in London in 1952. Now lives in London after a period of teaching in Hull. Biographer of Philip Larkin, the Lamberts and Keats, his most recent poetry collections are Natural Causes (1987) and Salt Water (1997).

LES MURRAY

Born in Bunyah, New South Wales, in 1938. He lives in Bunyah and has been a full-time writer since 1971; his books include his Collected Poems (1991), Subhuman Redneck Poems (1996), his verse novel The Boys Who Stole the Funeral and prose collection, The Paperbark Tree (1992).

JAMES NUNN

Born in Bradford in 1973. His poetry has been read on Radio 3 and appeared in a number of magazines. He lives in Manchester, where he works as a bookseller.

ROBERT NYE

Born in London in 1939. He is best known for novels such as Falstaff and

The Voyage of the Destiny, but has always written poetry; Poems (1995) collected work from the 1950s to the 1990s.

BERNARD O'DONOGHUE

Born in Cullen, Co. Cork, in 1945. He teaches medieval literature at Oxford University. His second poetry collection, Gunpowder, was published in 1995.

DOUGLAS OLIVER

Born in 1937. After working in England and France, and living in New York, he now teaches at the British Institute in Paris. Of his eight poetry volumes, the most recent are Selected Poems (NJ, 1996) and Penniless Politics (1994).

ALICE OSWALD

Born in 1966. She read Classics at Oxford then trained as a gardener. She lives in Devon and has published one collection, The Thing in the Gap-Stone Stile (1996).

DON PATERSON

Born in Dundee in 1963. He works as a musician and co-leads the jazz-folk ensemble Lammas. His two poetry collections are Nil Nil (1993) and God's Gift to Women (1997).

BRIAN PATTEN

Born in Liverpool in 1946. He was one of the poets in Penguin's famous Mersey Sound anthology (1967), and has published numerous volumes of poetry for adults and children, most recently Grinning Jack (1992) and Armada (1996).

KATHERINE PIERPOINT

Born in Northampton in 1961. She lives and works as a freelance writer, editor and translator based in Cambridge. Truffle Beds (1995) is her first poetry collection.

ROBERT PINSKY

Born in Long Branch, New Jersey, in 1940. He has taught at Berkeley and Wellesley, and now teaches in the graduate writing programme of Boston University. His most recent volumes are a translation of Dante's Inferno (1994) and The Figured Wheel: new and collected poems 1966-1996 (1996).

PETER PORTER

Born in Brisbane, Australia in 1929. He came to Britain in 1951 and has been a freelance writer and broadcaster for thirty years. His *Collected Poems* appeared in 1983, followed by other collections, most recently *Dragons in Their Pleasant Palaces* (1997).

NEIL POWELL

Born in 1948, grew up in Surrey and Kent. Now lives in Aldeburgh, working as a freelance writer, editor and lecturer. His recent books include a biography of Roy Fuller and *The Stones on Thorpeness Beach* (poems, 1994).

F. T. PRINCE

Born in South Africa in 1912. He lives in Southampton, where he was Professor of English at the University 1957–74. His first collection was published in 1938, and his *Collected Poems 1935–1992* appeared in 1993.

KATHLEEN RAINE

Born in Ilford, Essex, in 1908. She lives in London; as well as poetry and criticism, she has written three volumes of autobiography and was a founding editor of the review *Temenos*. Her *Collected Poems* were published in 1981.

NICK RENNISON

Born in Yorkshire in 1955. Since graduating from Cambridge he has worked in the book trade. He has edited *Waterstone's Guide to Poetry Books* (1996) and *Waterstone's Guide to History Books* (1997).

ANNE RIDLER

Born in 1912. She worked on the editorial staff of Faber and Faber, and besides poetry has written and translated opera libretti; she lives in Oxford. Her *Collected Poems* were published in 1994.

CHRISTOPHER REID

Born in Hong Kong in 1949. He is Poetry Editor at Faber and Faber. His poetry collections include *Katerina Brac* (1985) and *Expanded Universes* (1996).

LAWRENCE SAIL

Born in London in 1942. He now lives in Exeter and has been Chairman of the Arvon Foundation. His first collection,

---

Opposite Views was published in 1974 and his most recent, *Building into Air*, in 1995.

PETER SANSOM

Born in 1958 in Nottinghamshire. He is the author of two poetry collections, *Everything You've Heard Is True* (1990) and *January* (1994), director of Poetry Business in Huddersfield and editor of *The North*.

MICHAEL SCHMIDT

Born in Mexico in 1947. He is the Managing Director of Carcanet Press, of which he was co-founder, and lectures at Manchester University. Critic, novelist, broadcaster, anthologist and poet, his most recent collection is *The Love of Strangers* (1989). He also edits PN Review.

ADAM SCHWARTZMAN

Born in Johannesburg in 1973. He is currently studying in Oxford and intends returning to work in South Africa. His two collections are *The Good Life. The Dirty Life* (1995) and *Merrie Afrika!* (1997).

PETER SCUPHAM

Born in Liverpool in 1933. He has worked as a teacher, and founded the Mandeville Press. His *Selected Poems 1972–1990* were published in 1990, and among recent publications is *The Ark* (1994).

C. H. SISSON

Born in Bristol in 1914. He worked as a civil servant, retiring in 1974; his essays, translations and poems fill many volumes, the most recent being *Is there a Church of England?* (essays, 1993); *Collected Poems* (1984), *Antidotes* (1991), *What and Who* (1994); and *Collected Translations* (1996).

IAIN CRICHTON SMITH

Born on the island of Lewis in 1925. He was a teacher, resigning in 1977 to write full-time, in Gaelic and English. His *Collected Poems* (1992) were followed by *Ends and Beginnings* (1995) and *The Human Face* (1996); his *Selected Stories* (1990) are also available.

JON STALLWORTHY

Born in 1935. Having worked for Oxford University Press, he taught in the USA

---

then returned to Oxford, where he is now a Professor of English. Biographer of Wilfred Owen and Louis MacNeice, he has published seven collections of poetry, most recently *The Guest from the Future* (1995).

ANNE STEVENSON

Born in Cambridge to American parents in 1933. Now living in England and Wales, she is a biographer (of Sylvia Plath) and critic as well as a poet. Her *Collected Poems 1955–1995* (1996) gathers work from ten collections.

MARK STRAND

Born on Prince Edward Island, Canada, in 1934. He is currently a Professor in the Writing Seminars at the Johns Hopkins University, Maryland. Translator and art critic as well as poet, his nine books of poems have been the source for a *Selected Poems* published in 1995.

MATTHEW SWEENEY

Born in Co. Donegal in 1952. He moved to England in 1973 and works as a freelance writer and broadcaster. His recent collections include *Blue Shoes* (1989) and *Cacti* (1992).

ANTHONY THWAITE

Born in Chester in 1930. He has worked as a BBC producer, literary editor, and lecturer in the Middle East and Japan. His recent work includes *Poems 1953–1988* (1989), also editions of Philip Larkin's poems and letters.

CHARLES TOMLINSON

Born in Stoke-on-Trent in 1927. He taught at the University of Bristol, retiring as Professor of English Literature. His recent collections include *The Door in the Wall* (1992) and *Jubilation* (1995), and his *Translations* (1983) are from poets such as Vallejo, Paz and Ungaretti.

MICHAEL VINCE

Born near London in 1947. He has taught in England and on the Continent, and published his first collection, *The Orchard Well*, in 1978.

JEFFREY WAINWRIGHT

Born in Stoke-on-Trent in 1944. He currently teaches at Manchester Metropolitan University and is a theatre critic for the *Independent*. His *Selected Poems* were published in 1985, and *The Red-Headed Pupil* in 1994.

ANDREW WATERMAN

Born in south London in 1940. He teaches English at the University of Ulster, Coleraine. His books include *Selected Poems* (1986), *In the Planetarium* (1990) and *The End of the Pier Show* (1995).

ROBERT WELLS

Born in Oxford in 1947. He now lives in France and has translated Theocritus' *Idylls* (1988) and Virgil's *Georgics* (1982).

His *Selected Poems* were published in 1986.

RICHARD WILBUR

Born in New York City in 1921. Poet and translator, he published his first collection in 1947, and his *New and Collected Poems*, published in Britain in 1989, drew on six earlier volumes.

C. K. WILLIAMS

Born in New Jersey in 1936. He divides his time between Paris and America, where he teaches at Princeton University. His most recent books include *New and Selected Poems* (1995) and *The Vigil* (1997).

CLIVE WILMER

Born in 1945. He grew up in London and lives in Cambridge, where he works as a freelance writer and lecturer. As well as editing Ruskin, William Morris and D. G. Rossetti, he has published three volumes of poetry and his *Selected Poems* (1995).

GREGORY WOODS

Born in Cairo in 1953. He came to Britain in 1962 and has taught in Italy, London and Nottingham. *We Have the Melon*, his first poetry collection, was published in 1992.

INDEX OF FIRST LINES